# ANNUAL REVIEW OF
# INFORMATION
# SCIENCE AND
# TECHNOLOGY

VOLUME 35 2001

ISBN: 1-57387-115-X
ISSN: 0066-4200
CODEN: ARISBC
LC No. 66-25096

# ANNUAL REVIEW OF
# INFORMATION
# SCIENCE AND
# TECHNOLOGY

## Volume 35, 2001

Edited by

### Martha E. Williams
University of Illinois
Urbana, Illinois, USA

Published on behalf of the
American Society for Information Science and Technology
by Information Today, Inc.

 Information Today, Inc.
Medford, New Jersey

ISBN: 1-57387-115-X
ISSN: 0066-4200
CODEN: ARISBC
LC No. 66-25096

*Published and distributed by:*
Information Today, Inc.
143 Old Marlton Pike
Medford, NJ 08055-8750

*for the*

American Society for Information Science and Technology
1320 Fenwick Lane, Suite 510
Silver Spring, MD 20910, U.S.A.

Publisher: Thomas H. Hogan, Sr.
Editor-in-Chief: John B. Bryans
Managing Editor: Deborah R. Poulson
Production Manager: M. Heide Dengler

*ARIST Production staff, for ASIST:*
Charles & Linda Holder, Graphic Compositors
Cover design by Sandy Skalkowski
Printed in Canada.

# Contents

## I
## Planning Information Systems and Services     1

## II
## Basic Techniques and Technologies     247

# Preface

## EDITORIAL AND PUBLISHING HISTORY

This is the 35th volume of the *Annual Review of Information Science and Technology (ARIST)*. It is the 25th and final volume edited by Martha E. Williams. *ARIST* is produced for the American Society for Information Science and Technology (ASIST), formerly the American Society for Information Science (ASIS). ASIS initiated the annual review series in 1966 with the publication of Volume 1 under the editorship of Carlos A. Cuadra, who continued as Editor through Volume 10. Martha E. Williams assumed the responsibilities of Editor starting with Volume 11 in 1976. ASIST is the owner of *ARIST*, maintains the editorial control, and has the sole rights to the series in all forms.

Through the years several organizations have been responsible for publishing and marketing *ARIST*. Volumes 1 and 2 were published by Interscience Publishers, a division of John Wiley & Sons. Volumes 3 through 6 were published by Encyclopaedia Britannica, Inc. Volumes 7 through 11 were published by ASIS itself. Volumes 12 through 21 were published by Knowledge Industry Publications, Inc. Volumes 22 through 25 were published by Elsevier Science Publishers B.V., Amsterdam, The Netherlands. With Volume 26 Learned Information, Inc. assumed the role of publisher of *ARIST* for ASIS. In 1995 Learned changed its name to Information Today, Inc.

Each volume of the *Annual Review of Information Science and Technology* has a unique volume number and is intended for completion and publication in a specific year. The volume number and the year associated with it appear on the title page, half title page, in each chapter within the book, and on the book cover and spine. In all but a few cases the copyright year coincides with the intended publication year. As happens occasionally with other serial publications, such as journals and conference proceedings, a delay in publication may cause the copyright date to be later than the year associated with the volume. Volume 34 has a combined cover date of 1999-2000, and Volume 35 is dated 2001. When an author of a chapter cites another chapter in the same or an earlier volume of *ARIST*, the volume number and the year associated with the volume appear in the citation (not necessarily the copyright year).

## POLICY

*ARIST* is an annual publication that reviews numerous topics within the broad field of information science and technology. The contents vary from year to year; no single topic is treated on an annual basis. Inasmuch as the field is dynamic, the contents (chapters) of the various *ARIST* volumes must change to reflect this dynamism. *ARIST* chapters are scholarly reviews of specific topics as substantiated by the published literature. Some material may be included, even though not backed up by literature, if it is needed to provide a balanced and complete picture of the state of the art for the subject of the chapter. The time period covered varies from chapter to chapter, depending on whether the topic has been treated previously by *ARIST* and, if so, on the length of the interval from the last treatment to the current one. Thus, reviews may cover a one-year or a multiyear period. The reviews aim to be critical in that they provide the author's expert opinion regarding developments and activities within the chapter's subject area. The review guides the reader to or from specific publications. Chapters aim to be scholarly, thorough within the scope defined by the chapter author, up to date, well written, and readable by an audience that goes beyond the author's immediate peer group to researchers and practitioners in information science and technology, in general, and ASIS members, in particular.

## PURPOSE

The purpose of *ARIST* is to describe and to appraise activities and trends in the field of information science and technology. Material presented should be substantiated by references to the literature. *ARIST* provides an annual review of topics in the field. One volume is provided each year. A master plan for the series encompasses the entire field in all its aspects, and topics for each volume are selected from the plan on the basis of timeliness and an assessment of reader interest.

## REFERENCES CITED IN TEXT AND BIBLIOGRAPHY

The format for referring to bibliographic citations within the text involves use of the cited author's name instead of reference numbers. The cited author's surname is printed in upper case letters. The reader, wishing to find the bibliographic references, can readily locate the appropriate reference in the bibliography (alphabetically arranged by first author's last name). A single author appears as SMITH; co-authors as SMITH & JONES; and multiple authors as SMITH ET AL. If multiple papers by the same author are cited, the distinction is made by indicating the year of publication after the last name (e.g., SMITH, 1986), and if a further distinction is required for multiple papers within the same year, a lower case alpha character follows the year (e.g., SMITH, 1986a). Except for the fact that all authors in multi-authored papers are included in bibliographic references, the same basic conventions are used in the chapter bibliographies. Thus, the reader can easily locate in the bibliography any references discussed in the text.

Because of the emphasis placed on the requirement for chapter authors to discuss the key papers and significant developments reported in the literature, and because *ARIST* readers have expressed their liking for comprehensive bibliographies associated with the chapters, more references may be listed in the bibliographies than are discussed and/or cited in the text.

The format used for references in the bibliographies is based on the *American National Standard for Bibliographic References*, ANS Z39.29. We have followed the ANSI guidelines with respect to the sequence of bibliographic data elements and the punctuation used to separate the elements. Adoption of this convention should facilitate conversion of the references to machine-readable form as need arises. Journal article references follow the ANSI guide as closely as possible. Conference papers and microform publications follow an *ARIST* adaptation of the format.

As the information world becomes more networked and as publishing becomes increasingly electronic, more publications are appearing on the Internet with no complementary hard copy version. In such cases the only option for citing the publication is a cite to the uniform resource locator (URL). Unfortunately, most of these publications are not permanently archived, and many of the sites (e.g., World Wide Web (WWW) sites) are not maintained or updated, and they do not retain permanent addresses. Some move to other servers, and others die as sponsorship or funding wanes. The *ARIST* staff verifies all cited URLs during the course of editing chapters, but by the time this volume is published some URLs will undoubtedly no longer be valid. While *ARIST* has always required page numbers for quotations, electronic documents do not consistently have explicit pagination noted; thus some quotes from URLs are cited without page numbers.

## STRUCTURE OF THE VOLUME

In accordance with the *ARIST* master plan, this volume's nine chapters fit within a basic framework: I. Planning Information Systems and Services; II. Basic Techniques and Technologies; III. Applications; and IV. The Profession. Chapter titles are provided in the Table of Contents, and an Introduction to each section highlights the events, trends, and evaluations given by the chapter authors. An Index to the entire volume is provided to help the user locate material relevant to the subject content, authors, and organizations cited in the book. An explanation of the guidelines employed in the Index is provided in the Introduction to the Index. A Cumulative Keyword and Author Index of *ARIST* Titles to this and all prior volumes follows the Index.

## DATABASES AND ABSTRACTING AND INDEXING
## SERVICES COVERING *ARIST*

*ARIST* as a whole and/or individual chapters are included in a number of abstracting and indexing (A&I) journals both within the United States and internationally. Databases that both cover *ARIST* and are available through major online services in the United States are:

BIOSIS (Biological Abstracts)
Current Contents
ERIC (Educational Resources Information Center)
Information Science Abstracts
INSPEC (Computer and Control Abstracts)
Library Literature
LISA (Library and Information Science Abstracts)
Social SciSearch (Social Sciences Citation Index)

Publishers of other A&I journals and databases who would like to include *ARIST* in their coverage are encouraged to contact the publisher for a review copy and notify the editor who will add the database name(s) to this list when appropriate.

## APPRECIATION

At the completion of my 25th year as Editor of *ARIST* I want to thank not only the chapter authors and editorial staff for volume 35 but the hundreds of authors and dozens of staff members who have worked with me on *ARIST* over the past 25 years. First and foremost are the authors of the individual chapters who have generously contributed their time and efforts in searching, reviewing, and evaluating the large body of literature on which their chapters are based. The *ARIST* Advisory Committee Members and *ARIST* Reviewers provided valuable feedback and constructive criticism of the content. The Dialog Corporation plc generously provided the authors with online access to databases. I would also like to acknowledge the excellent work of the editorial staff who have contributed so much to making *ARIST* a quality and scholarly series with every attention to detail. My special thanks go to Linda C. Smith, Linda Schamber, Mary Rakow, Debora Shaw, Kate Ambrose, Laurence Lannom, Elaine Tisch, and the typesetter, Linda Holder, who has set all 25 volumes during my editorship. I could not have had a better, more cooperative and dedicated staff. My undying thanks to all of you.

Martha E. Williams
Editor, *Annual Review of Information Science and Technology*

# Acknowledgments

The American Society for Information Science and Technology and the Editor wish to acknowledge the contributions of the three principals on the editorial staff and the technical support staff.

**Linda Schamber,** Copy Editor

**Debora Shaw,** Index Editor

**Linda C. Smith,** Bibliographic Editor

---

# Technical Support Staff

**Mary W. Rakow,** Technical Advisor

**Sheila Carnder,** Assistant

**Linda Holder,** Compositor

# Advisory Committee for *ARIST*

# Contributors

James Blustein
DalTech/Dalhousie University
Faculty of Computer Science
6050 University Avenue
Halifax, Nova Scotia B3H 1W5
Canada

Harry Bruce
University of Washington
The Information School
Box 352840
Seattle, WA 98195-2930

Miranda R. Callahan
National Center for
    Supercomputing Applications
NCSA MC 476
605 E. Springfield
Champaign, IL 61820

Colleen Cool
Queens College, CUNY
GSLIS
BRL, Room 254
65-30 Kissena Blvd.
Flushing, NY 11367-1597

Philip Doty
University of Texas at Austin
GSLIS SZB 564
Austin, TX 78712-1276

Raya Fidel
University of Washington
The Information School
Box 352840
Seattle, WA 98195-2930

Birger Hjørland
Royal School of Library &
    Information Science
6 Birketinget
DK-2300
Copenhagen S
Denmark

Ingrid Hsieh-Yee
The Catholic University of
    America
Room 240 Marist Hall
620 Michigan Avenue, NE
Washington, DC 20064

Elisabeth Logan
Florida State University
Shores Building
Tallahassee, FL 32306-2100

Noreen Mac Morrow
Department of Information
    Studies
University of Technology,
    Sydney
P.O. Box 123 Broadway
NSW 2007, Australia

Lykke Kyllesbech Nielsen
Royal School of Library and
    Information Science
6 Birketinget
DK-2300
Copenhagen S
Denmark

Michael A. Padgett
National Center for
    Supercomputing Applica-
    tions
NCSA MC 476
605 E. Springfield
Champaign, IL 61820

Karen E. Pettigrew
University of Washington
The Information School
Box 352840
Seattle, WA 98195-2930

William M. Pottenger
Lehigh University
19 Memorial Drive West
Bethlehem, PA 18015

Mark S. Staveley
University of Toronto
Dept. of Mechanical and Industrial
    Engineering
Interactive Media Group
4 Taddle Creek Road
Toronto, Ontario
M5S 1A4
Canada

Elizabeth Yakel
University of Michigan
School of Information
550 E. University Avenue
301a West Hall
Ann Arbor, MI 48109-4092

# Chapter Reviewers

Marcia J. Bates

David Becker

Nicholas J. Belkin

Christine L. Borgman

Wesley T. Brandhorst

Michael K. Buckland

Blaise Cronin

Pauline A. Cochrane

Raya Fidel

Margaret T. Fischer

Glynn Harmon

Donald Hawkins

John Hearty

Kathryn Luther Henderson

William T Henderson

Peter Hernon

Donald W. King

Michael E. D. Koenig

Katherine W. McCain

Jessica L. Milstead

Ronald E. Rice

Tefko Saracevic

Sharon Siegler

Thomas Surprenant

Peter A. Vigil

Judith E. Weedman

# ASIST and Its Members

For over 50 years the leading professional society for information professionals, the American Society for Information Science and Technology is an association whose diverse membership continues to reflect the frontiers and horizons of the dynamic field of information science and technology. ASIST owes its stature to the cumulative contributions of its members, past and present.

ASIST counts among its membership some 4,000 information specialists from such fields as computer science, management, engineering, librarianship, chemistry, linguistics, and education. As was true when the Society was founded, ASIST membership continues to lead the information profession in the search for new and better theories, techniques, and technologies to improve access to information through storage and retrieval advances. And now, as then, ASIST and its members are called upon to help determine new directions and standards for the development of information policies and practices.

# I

# Planning Information Systems and Services

Section I includes four chapters, "The Concept of Situation in Information Science" by Colleen Cool of Queens College, CUNY, "Conceptual Frameworks in Information Behavior" by Karen E. Pettigrew, Raya Fidel, and Harry Bruce of the University of Washington, "Distributed Information Management" by William M. Pottenger of Lehigh University, and Miranda R. Callahan and Michael A. Padgett of the National Center for Supercomputing Applications at the University of Illinois, and "Digital Privacy: Toward a New Politics and Discursive Practice" by Philip Doty of the University of Texas at Austin.

Colleen Cool's chapter is the first *ARIST* review devoted to the concept of situation as it occurs in information science. She has covered both the theoretical and empirical literature on the topic and points out that the concept of situation differs from that of context. She warns the reader to be careful in reading about situation as it is still ill defined and inconsistently applied. Cool states that the concept of situation has been investigated with respect to information-seeking processes, information interaction, and information retrieval behaviors. She discusses the background to the problem of situation, including terminology, context and situation, and situation and interaction. Next she treats perspectives on the concept of situation, and here she covers six major treatments of situation that provide the basis for her review: (1) problematic situation; (2) social interaction theory and information science; (3) the situated action model; (4) situated awareness theory; (5) person-in-situation theory and information science; and (6) situation as information environment.

After reviewing the above six approaches Colleen Cool concludes her chapter by observing: that situation is useful for information science (IS) as a focus of analysis in its own right; that there is no theory of situation in IS nor is there a single definition of what it is; and that the development of situation as a central unit of analysis in IS depends on further specification of the constitutive elements of situation that play a role in information behavior.

1

Karen Pettigrew, Raya Fidel, and Harry Bruce trace major conceptual developments in information behavior since 1986. They observe that conceptual development research in information behavior is on the increase despite the fact that some consider "information behavior" a misnomer because people, not information, exhibit behavior. Regardless of the appropriateness of the term, it has come into general acceptance and is used in the titles of publications as well as in academic courses. The authors of this chapter define information behavior as "the study of how people need, seek, give, and use information in different contexts, including the workplace and everyday living." Pettigrew, Fidel, and Bruce question the theoretical basis for information science in general and for information behavior in particular. They cite statistics from several studies indicating the percentage of articles in the field that discuss theory. One of the larger studies, which was by Pettigrew and McKechnie, reported that 34.1% of 1,160 articles in six key journals between 1993 and 1998 discussed theory and that within that group were 95 papers on information behavior; 58.9% of the information behavior papers discussed theory.

Pettigrew, Fidel, and Bruce review new developments in three sections: cognitive approaches—those that deal with the individual as the driving force underlying information behavior; social approaches—those that examine frameworks focusing on the social context; and multifaceted approaches—those that deal with multiple types of contexts, such as cognitive, social, and organizational. These authors conclude that a quantum leap has occurred in information behavior and a unifying theoretical body is emerging, but the real challenge is to provide guidance for system design, and that will require collaboration and communication between information behavior theorists and information systems designers.

William M. Pottenger, Miranda R. Callahan, and Michael A. Padgett address the timely topic of managing distributed information. They note that information management is changing drastically because of the ubiquity of digitized information and of networking. Digitized information can be identified, accessed, and acquired from virtually anywhere in the world through networks. One needs to use technologies, cultural influences, and societal forces from the fields of information science, computer science, and library science to understand what is happening and what can happen in the development of distributed information systems.

The authors of this chapter indicate the scope and effects of distributed information management by discussing cultural and social influences, such as the library and Internet cultures, loosely coupled digital collections (what should be contained in a digital library) and tightly coupled digital collections. Problems relate to the facts that information

in distributed systems tends to be volatile and ephemeral, digital resources cannot be fixed, and links frequently change. Some efforts to
overcome such problems are persistent object identifiers: the Persistent
Uniform Resource Locator (PURL) of OCLC; Uniform Resource Names
(URNs); Robust Hyperlinks; Digital Object Identifiers (DOIs), the use of
metadata, and the CNRI Handle System.

Other topics covered include search and retrieval in a distributed
environment and preservation in a distributed environment. Within
search and retrieval in a distributed environment Pottenger and his co-
authors discuss distributed catalog systems, the Cooperative Online
Resource Catalog (CORC) being developed  under the auspices of
OCLC, the virtual union catalog, the Networked Computer Science
Technical Reference Library (NCSTRL), and Smart Object, Dumb Archive
(SODA), an approach to facilitating interoperability in distributed digital libraries. Preservation or archiving in a distributed digital environment is quite complex in a system like the Internet because the network
of information is continuously evolving and the boundaries of a
hyperlinked document are ill defined. Other problem areas relate to the
cultural aspects of distributed preservation. Published Web documents
do not have a common structure as books do, no conventions have been
developed for library materials on the Web, digital publishing is still
immature, and there is no peer review system that determines what can
be published.

Pottenger, Callahan, and Padgett conclude that a considerable number of research areas exist for the future: the development of indexing,
search, and retrieval for nontextual data; acceptance of scholarly publishing of digitized documents which would require a paradigm shift
by the academic community; and the development of more personal
digital libraries.

Philip Doty provides an extensive and thorough treatment of digital
privacy. While this is the third *ARIST* chapter devoted to the problem of
privacy, it is the first to be specifically concerned with digital privacy.
Doty examines selected important policy and legal initiatives related to
policy, but the major focus of his chapter is on the nature and concepts
of privacy and digital privacy rather than policies. Doty is careful to
point out the important themes and literatures that he does not cover
and then goes on to delineate major concepts in privacy discourse, to
define privacy and related terms, and to discuss some of the historical
and philosophical foundations of privacy.

This chapter on privacy covers important legal and policy concepts
of privacy, such as: privacy protection by legislation in the United
States (Doty identifies and explains a variety of laws that have been
enacted); important U.S. Supreme Court cases (identifying litigants and
outcomes); torts as a theory of privacy; other theories of privacy; major

European and other efforts. A major section concentrates on surveilling modern society and treats surveillance and social control as well as digital surveillance and privacy enhancement. In the section entitled The Digital Persona, Doty discusses the implications and problems associated with the digital persona one creates as he/she makes bank withdrawals, submits tax returns, applies for government benefits, uses email, places orders online, browses the Web, and carries out other electronic activities. Information entrepreneurialism and information capitalism also have positive and negative implications.

Major sections are devoted to: the public/private dichotomy; the concern that there may be too much privacy or an overemphasis on privacy and personal liberty at the expense of civic responsibility; gendered perspectives on privacy; privacy in public; and privacy as property (including the boundaries and weaknesses of property rights). Philip Doty concludes his chapter by rethinking privacy, scholarship, social critique, and policy making. He says "what remains is the work of inventing what we want society and digital communication to be [and] to help create the kind of society to which we aspire to belong."

# 1

# The Concept of Situation in Information Science

**COLLEEN COOL**
**Queens College, CUNY**

## INTRODUCTION

This chapter reviews the theoretical and empirical literature on the concept of situation in information science (IS). Over the past decade, increasing attention has been given to this concept, often in connection with the related concept of context, in the IS literature. A common theme in this work is that in order to better understand information-seeking behavior (ISB) and information retrieval (IR) interaction, greater attention needs to be directed to the information spaces within which these activities are embedded. Closely related to developments in the cognitive viewpoint on information (BELKIN, 1990; INGWERSEN, 1996), conceptualizations of situation have evolved from early analyses of the individual-level knowledge states that precipitate information-seeking behavior to, more recently, the sociocognitive frameworks that explain a broader range of information interaction phenomena (see INGWERSEN (1999) for a recent review of the cognitive view in IR and JACOB & SHAW for a review of sociognitive perspectives). However, despite the seemingly widespread and growing attention to the importance of situation in IS, the concept itself remains ill defined and inconsistently applied. Thus, a review of the literature in this area seems both timely and important.

This is the first *ARIST* chapter devoted to the concept of situation in IS, although the topic has been given some attention in several earlier *ARIST* reviews. These include, in particular, the chapter by SCHAMBER (1994) on relevance, two chapters on the cognitive view in IR by ALLEN (1991) and INGWERSEN (1999), the review of social informatics by BISHOP & STAR, and the early *ARIST* review on information needs and uses by PAISLEY. This chapter attempts to extend, without dupli-

*Annual Review of Information Science and Technology (ARIST)*, Volume 35, 2001
Martha E. Williams, Editor
Published for the American Society for Information Science and Technology (ASIST)
By Information Today, Inc., Medford, NJ

cating, the discussions of situation in these earlier reviews. The goals are:

- To review and to evaluate critically the various conceptualizations of situation that have been applied to phenomena of interest to IS, including conceptualizations from areas outside IS; and
- To review the empirical studies within IS that have made situation a central object of analysis and to evaluate the usefulness of these projects with respect to their application to IS.

## Scope

This chapter focuses explicitly on the analytic concept of situation and not more generally on that of context. Although these two concepts are often used interchangeably, an attempt is made to disambiguate them. The theoretical literature reviewed spans several disciplines, including sociology, psychology, anthropology, and communication. With respect to the time frame covered, most of the empirical investigations of situation reviewed here have taken place within the past decade; however, the theoretical writing on situation, across the disciplines covered, spans a wider time period.

Within the field of IS, the concept of situation has been investigated primarily in studies of information-seeking processes, information interaction, and IR behaviors. These general areas constitute the central focus here. Other areas in which the term situation is used, such as in situation semantics or situation logic (VAN RIJSBERGEN & LALMAS) to describe formal models of IR, are outside the scope of this chapter, as is the literature on social informatics (BISHOP & STAR).

## Organization of the Chapter

The concept of situation has been a central unit of analysis in several disciplines related to IS, appearing in both the theoretical and empirical literature. Some of these conceptualizations have been adapted and used within the IS community to varying degrees, while others have not. This chapter first discusses briefly why we should care about situation at all in IS. Next, six theoretical perspectives on the concept of situation that are especially relevant to IS are presented, along with empirical applications. Within each section, the relative usefulness of different conceptual treatments of situation for understanding important phenomena of interest to IS is discussed.

## BACKGROUND TO THE PROBLEM OF SITUATION

### Situation, Context, and Interaction with Information

*Terminology.*    Although the concept of situation appears with increasing frequency in the IS literature, the concept itself is neither new nor well defined. Scattered across the fields of sociology, communication, IS, and other areas are statements such as these:

- Every situation develops out of an environing matrix, a *situational field*. The major elements in this field . . . are people, culture, and physical nature (CARR, p. 45);
- *Situation* is a general term that refers to combinations of people, places, and events. For example, a stressful situation is one in which these factors combine to make participants feel uncomfortable. Similarly, an economic situation is one in which people, places, and events combine to create opportunities for profit and loss . . . . Using the same vocabulary, we can say that an *interviewing situation* is one in which people, places and events combine to create an opportunity for an interview to take place (SKOPEC, p. 10);
- Situation, in this research, means the moment in time-space as perceived by the respondent (HERT, 1997, p. 76); and
- Informational support is sought in situations when the actor does not have sufficient prior knowledge to accomplish his purposeful action (VAKKARI, 1999, p. 39).

It is clear from these varied conceptualizations of situation that there is no agreed-upon definition. Further, definitions vary across individual, social, and environment levels of analysis.

*Context and situation.*    Conceptual understanding about situation becomes fuzzier when we take into account the related concept of context. Within the IS literature, it is not uncommon to come across the expression "context or situation" in studies of human information behavior. However, the use of situation and context interchangeably dilutes the explanatory power of each. Further, the conceptual murkiness surrounding these concepts has made it difficult to pursue methodologically rigorous investigation of either one. DERVIN (1997) refers to context as an "unruly beast" and discusses the problems of gaining methodological control over it. Situation is no less slippery. As VAKKARI (1997) states in his summary of the papers presented at the first International Conference on Information Seeking in Context (ISIC), "One of the striking features in many studies was the use of the central concepts, like information, knowledge, information need, seeking, and use as primitive concepts, i.e., without definition. The terms situation and context were also most commonly used without taking much trouble in seeking their meaning" (p. 460).

Recently, attempts have been made in the IS literature to describe the conceptual differences between context and situation. SONNENWALD presents an evolving framework for understanding human information behavior, in which context and situation are treated as separate foundational concepts. In her framework, situations are characterized as being embedded within contexts. "A context is somehow larger than a situation and may consist of a variety of situations; different contexts may have different possible types of situations" (p. 180). Although this distinction is still a bit loose, we might extend it a bit to suggest that contexts are frameworks of meaning, and situations are the dynamic environments within which interpretive processes unfold, become ratified, change, and solidify. ALLEN & KIM take another stab at disambiguating context and situation: "The relationships between contexts, situations, and tasks are complex. We view contexts as the socially defined settings in which information users are found. One context might be a work setting such as an office or a factory . . . . Within each of these broad contexts, different situations occur. Or, to put it differently, individuals may be situated in different ways in the context" (ALLEN & KIM, p. 1).

*Situation and interaction.* There are several good reasons to care about making situation a central unit of analysis or, to use the terminology of VAKKARI (1999), unit variable. Over the past decade of theoretical and empirical development in the field, the concepts of context and situation have been brought into the foreground as IS has undergone putative paradigm shifts from system-oriented to user-centered and then to cognitive frameworks for understanding human information behavior (DERVIN & NILAN; INGWERSEN, 1996, 1999; SUGAR). (See PETTIGREW ET AL., this volume, for a review of this literature.) A further extension of the cognitive viewpoint in IS is the recent development of models that explicitly treat interaction with information as a central concern This can be seen in Belkin's episodic model of IR interaction (BELKIN, 1996), Saracevic's stratified model (SARACEVIC, 1996a), and Ingwersen's polyrepresentation model of cognitive IR interaction (INGWERSEN, 1996). With the development of interactive information systems and models of IR interaction behavior, focus has been directed to the situations within which these interactions take place. Indeed, the theoretical models presented by Belkin, Ingwersen, Saracevic, and others treat situation as one level of analysis. One way in which these concerns are being addressed is by focusing more attention on understanding the multiple situations within which information behaviors take place.

Within the cognitive and interactionist frameworks discussed above, the distinction between context and situation is meaningful. When people interact with information resources, an interaction situation is constructed, albeit within some context. To further the interactionist perspective in IS, we might quite usefully direct our attention to the constitutive elements of the interaction situation and the processes or dynamics through which human information behavior is regulated. These characteristics of situation cut across a variety of contexts and make situation a useful unit variable or central object of analysis in its own right. However, at this time IS does not have such a concept of situation that can help to advance the interactionist models in IR. Therefore, it seems appropriate to examine various conceptualizations of situation that might prove useful in this direction.

## PERSPECTIVES ON THE CONCEPT OF SITUATION

Situation as an analytic construct has been treated in various theoretical ways that are of interest to IS. Six major treatments of situation form the basis of this review:

- The concept of problematic situation as first articulated in the phenomenological writings of SCHUTZ & LUCKMANN and later developed by WERSIG and by BELKIN (1980). In this theoretical treatment, situation is looked at as an individual-level internal cognitive state.
- Social interaction theory and its treatment of the definition of the situation. This perspective on the concept of situation moves away from the purely individual cognitive framework of the phenomenologists to view situation from a sociocognitive perspective, which attempts to understand the social basis of mind and ways in which meanings are constituted through interaction. Developed largely within the field of cognitive sociology and more recently applied to studies in IS, this perspective is strongly grounded in writings of sociologist GOFFMAN (1964; 1974).
- The Situated Action model. Developed by anthropologist SUCHMAN, this model attempts to explain human action, in particular human–machine communication, as an interactive process that is responsive and adaptive to elements in the technology use environment in contrast to the planned action model developed in cogni-

tive science. In this framework, Suchman argues that
rather than strictly adhering to a predetermined plan, a
person uses cues or elements in the interaction environment to determine action.

- The theory of Situation Awareness (SA) (ENDSLEY, 1990;
  1995a; 1995b). Developed within the industrial psychology and engineering communities and related to human
  factors research, this theoretical perspective attempts to
  understand the cognitive processes, group dynamics,
  and communication behaviors through which individuals and team members develop and maintain correct
  and mutually ratified consensus about the state of affairs in complex, dynamic task environments involving
  interaction with information technology.

- Person-in-Situation model. As articulated by REID and
  discussed by SNOW and by PERVIN, this theory attempts to explain how human information processing
  and decision-making capabilities, along with other individual variables, interact with situational level variables
  on task performance.

- Situation as information environment. This is an ecological treatment of situation, focusing on the concrete
  environment of information use. Various types of situation ecologies may include: institutional, organizational,
  or work task settings; physical elements of the information resource environment; or situations of accessibility
  to information. The early work of TAYLOR (1991) represents an important starting point in the development
  of this perspective. A more recent example can be found
  in the work of ALGON (1997; 1999).

These six perspectives on situation can be further classified into three
major overlapping categories representing cognitive, interactionist, and
environmental or ecological perspectives.

## THE PROBLEMATIC SITUATION

### Schutz and Luckmann's Phenomenological
### Concept of Situation

In the phenomenology of SCHUTZ & LUCKMANN every person
possesses a stock of knowledge that is sometimes insufficient for handling unknown aspects of situations that arise in everyday life. In this
theoretical formulation, a distinction is made between routine and

problematic situations, the latter of which creates a cognitive state of uncertainty that may lead to information seeking to resolve the problematic state. In a problematic situation, people may experience events or information that are inconsistent with their common stock of knowledge, or they may find themselves lacking information necessary to attain some desired goal. When problematic situations are tied to goals, action tends to ensue. Characteristics of the particular goal state, or problematic situation, such as priority, timeliness, and attainability, influence information-seeking behavior.

SCHUTZ & LUCKMANN describe the various "provinces of meaning" within which an event can be framed. Some of these ideas are related to similar thinking by phenomenologically oriented sociologists, and the essays in LUCKMANN provide an early overview. The framing of experiences as a sociomental activity has been given explicit attention by BATESON, GOFFMAN (1974), and ZERUBAVEL.

## The Problematic Situation in Information Science

Within the IS literature, early conceptualizations of situation focused on understanding individual-level psychological or cognitive states that act as precursors to information-seeking behavior. In noninteractive IR, the concept of situation first appeared in a 1979 article by WERSIG titled "The Problematic Situation as a Basic Concept of Information Science in the Framework of Social Sciences: A Reply to N. Belkin." For Wersig the problematic situation referred to an internal psychological state in which an individual recognized that his or her internal model about some aspect of the world was insufficient to accomplish a desired action or goal. This conceptualization of situation closely resembles the "visceral need" as a level in the information-seeking process as described by TAYLOR (1968), and the anomalous state of knowledge (ASK) model developed by BELKIN (1980). Belkin postulated that information-seeking behavior becomes instantiated when a person's conceptual state of knowledge about a particular topic is recognized as being insufficient with respect to the accomplishment of a desired goal. The ASK model and the Schutzian concept of problematic situation are closely related. Also related to these conceptualizations of situation as an individual, internal psychological state is the situation-gap-use model put forth by DERVIN (1983) and the uncertainty model proposed by KUHLTHAU (1993a; 1993b).

A common focus in this literature is on understanding precursors to information-seeking behaviors and processes of problem resolution. Unproblematic situations are those in which routine expectations about events in the everyday world are met and active information seeking is not needed as one passively monitors the environment (SAVOLAINEN).

As VAKKARI (1999) states, "The lack of understanding generates information actions for solving the problematic situation in order to proceed
in the task. The major elements in the situation are actions to be supported by information, insufficient prior knowledge of the actor and
informational support mechanisms" (p. 39).

An early and important contribution of the work by WERSIG and by
BELKIN ET AL. (1983) and others was the understanding of people's
problematic situations in terms of problem treatment rather than problem solving. The work by Belkin et al. was somewhat ahead of its time
with respect to the recognition that a user's problem is not merely
topical but needs to be understood within a wider situation of tasks and
goals, which they felt were best elicited through interaction. In describing the problem treatment approach, they state: "the information provision mechanism interacts iteratively with the user, assisting him/her
toward appropriate treatment of the problem by providing information
which is appropriate in terms of the individual solution path and the
characteristics of the problem situation" (BELKIN ET AL., 1983, p. 155).
Another forward-thinking element of this research agenda was the use
of simulated problem situations in the analysis of information provision mechanisms. This approach was used recently by BØRLUND,
who investigated the validity of simulated task situations in the evaluation of interactive IR systems.

A common criticism of the early cognitive models of problematic
situations is that they focus on individual-level cognitive states. These
early cognitive perspectives on the concept of situation have received
extensive coverage in the literature, and the reader is directed to recent
*ARIST* chapters by JACOB & SHAW and by INGWERSEN (1999) for
further explication. The earliest conceptualizations of problematic situation did not generally encompass social interpretations into their frameworks. More recently, the phenomenological concept of problematic
situation has been discussed within the context of interactive IR systems and the cognitive viewpoint. VAKKARI (1999) discusses problematic situations in terms of different cognitive states, which vary over
phases or episodes. Each episode represents different situations of
certainty or uncertainty, and within each episode are corresponding
information-seeking behaviors or IR interactions along with different
relevance judgment behaviors. Such a view is consistent with the recent
model of multiple information-seeking episodes presented by LIN &
BELKIN and in the research of SPINK and SPINK ET AL. on successive
searching behavior and on partial relevance judgments. In the partial
relevance model, it has been found that different assignments of relevance judgments are associated with different phases in the information problem situation. We can conceptualize each successive search
state in the Spink et al. model as a different goal state, representing a

different type of problematic situation in the search process. WANG has also analyzed users' cognitive changes over time in the search process, or, in different stages of their problematic situations. In a similar vein, T. D. WILSON (1999) discusses his "uncertainty project" and, citing SCHUTZ & LUCKMANN, he states that "the basis for a model of describing successive searching processes is a problem and a problem is defined as a state of uncertainty" (p. 56).

While theoretically rich, the concept of the problematic situation and the phenomenological perspective of SCHUTZ & LUCKMANN in general have been given rather short attention in the IS literature. Few authors have explicitly invoked this phenomenological stance in their writings, even though the concept offers insights into the epistemic context within which information interactions take place. Perhaps one reason is the general perception that the definition of situation in this theoretical stance has historically referred to individual-level cognitive states, and, as noted by INGWERSEN (1999), the cognitive view has moved away from purely individual-level analyses to more holistic perspectives, taking into account social as well as individual explanations. However, the phenomenological perspective on situation does offer insight into social as well as individual-level phenomena when two other concepts discussed by Schutz and Luckmann are included in the analysis. These are typification and intersubjectivity. Typification, further discussed by BERGER & LUCKMANN, involves a process of sociomental classification, that is, a social shorthand method of mentally compartmentalizing persons, events, and things into socially agreed-upon categories. Intersubjectivity, discussed not only by Schutz and Luckmann but also by social interaction theorists discussed below, refers to a process of mutual understanding or common ground.

In an extensive analysis of the work of Schutz and Luckmann, NG ET AL. argue that taking these concepts together provides a framework of direct relevance to IS. The authors argue, somewhat incompletely, that the concepts of problematic situation, typification, and intersubjectivity can be used to bridge the gap between individual and social levels of analysis of information behavior in IS. The arguments are difficult to summarize in this brief space without presupposing a fairly thorough reading of the Schutz and Luckmann text on the part of the reader. However, those who are interested are directed to the manuscript by Ng et al.

In another recent attempt to apply phenomenological conceptualizations of situation to IS, LIN & BELKIN describe a theoretical model of information-seeking behavior, called multiple information-seeking episodes (MISE), which is solidly grounded in the phenomenological tradition of Schutz and Luckmann. In this framework, which closely resembles the successive searching model of SPINK, information seekers are understood typically to engage in more than one information-seeking episode, each one characterized as a different type of problem situation. Lin and Belkin outline three properties related to the definition of the information problem situation: (1) level of domain knowledge; (2) complexity of the situation; and (3) degree of focus.

*Relevance and problematic situation.* The concept of relevance has a long tradition in IS, and in recent years the idea of situational relevance has been given wide attention, especially within the literature on the cognitive viewpoint in IR. First articulated by P. WILSON and further developed by SCHAMBER ET AL., SCHAMBER (1991; 1994), BARRY (1994), and BARRY & SCHAMBER, this body of work draws attention to dynamic, situational aspects of relevance judgments in IR interaction. The central importance of this theoretical contribution to IS is that it brought the concept of users' situations and intentions as goal states into consideration as a factor in nontopical relevance judgments. Although not explicitly grounded within the phenomenological tradition described above, the situational relevance perspective turns the problematic situation into a dynamic process by focusing on the interaction between situation and action. Taxonomies of user criteria for judging relevance with respect to some problem situation have been reported by BARRY (1993; 1994) and SCHAMBER (1991). Some of the situational criteria include depth and scope, currency, accuracy, novelty, and other factors directly related to the situation that has brought, or is currently keeping, a person in the information-seeking process. Other important work on cognitive approaches to relevance (BRUCE; FROEHLICH; PARK) is reported in a special issue of the *Journal of the American Society for Information Science (JASIS)* in April 1994.

*Usefulness of the problematic situation perspective.* The problematic situation was a centrally important concept in the early development of the cognitive view in IS. Its limitations have stemmed from a purely individual-level application to the study of important cognitive processes in information interactions, in which the emphasis was on problem in a topical sense and less on situation. An exception was the early work on distributed expert problem treatment reported by Belkin and his colleagues (BELKIN ET AL., 1983). More recently, however, the problematic situation has been reexamined from not only individual but also social levels of analysis within a variety of dynamic frameworks. For future research, an interesting and important question concerns the different types of problematic situations that arise in new interaction spaces, such as in digital libraries and the World Wide Web (WWW). A particularly interesting problem concerns how to represent problematic situations in IR system environments that rely on queries as representations of the information problem, in contrast to earlier problem resolution spaces that relied on human intermediaries to help construct the situation. A particularly difficult problem for IR systems is that of how to understand and to represent the salient aspects of a person's problematic situation based on queries that are entered into the IR system. The simulated problem situation and simulated task situation reported by BELKIN ET AL. (1983) and more recently by BORLUND are useful approaches to this problem because they view problem situations as related to tasks and goals. An open question at this time is how to design IR mechanisms that will better support total problematic situation resolution.

## COGNITIVE SOCIOLOGY AND SOCIAL INTERACTION THEORY
### The Definition of the Situation

Somewhat related to the phenomenological conceptualization of the problematic situation is the social interaction perspective on the concept of situation that has long been a central unit of analysis among social interaction theorists, primarily those who can be described as cognitive sociologists. Cognitive sociologists are concerned with the social basis of mind or, as ZERUBAVEL describes it, the realm of the sociomental. Symbolic interactionism, in the tradition of MEAD, along with ethnomethodology as represented by the work of GARFINKEL, are central schools of thought here. An early overview of symbolic interactionism can be found in BLUMER. For this review, social interaction theory and symbolic interactionism are discussed together with respect to the ways in which situation has been conceptualized and investigated. According to this perspective, all human action, including interaction with inanimate objects, takes place within social situations. In every social situation there is a socially prescribed definition to which interactants are attuned and by which they are regulated. The constitutive elements of situation to which people are attuned are perceptions of self-competence, norms of interaction, communication conventions, and intersubjectivity between self and others.

The importance of investigating the interaction situation itself as a unit of analysis is stated nicely by sociologist GOFFMAN (1964), a seminal figure in social interaction theory, in a paper titled "The Neglected Situation": "Your social situation is not your country cousin. It can be argued that social situations, at least in our society, constitute a reality *sui generis* . . . and therefore need and warrant analysis in their own right, much like that accorded other basic forms of social organization. . . . So let us face what we have been offhand about: social situations. I would define a social situation as an environment of mutual monitoring possibilities" (pp. 134, 135). From the perspective of social interaction theory, and in particular its variant, symbolic interactionism, people act according to both their definition of the situation and their perception of how they are being perceived or defined by others. A definition of a situation is the frame around an event that guides the interactions within it (GOFFMAN, 1974). When people enter into new or unfamiliar interaction environments, one of the first things they try to resolve is the question of how they should understand the event or what the appropriate definition of the situation is. "Presumably, a 'definition of the situation' is almost always to be found, but those who are in the situation ordinarily do not *create* this definition, even though their society often can be said to do so; ordinarily, all they do is to assess correctly what the situation ought to be for them and then act accordingly" (GOFFMAN, 1974, pp. 1-2).

Social interaction among strangers as well as among acquaintances is generally orderly and not chaotic because people have shared understandings about the definition of situation currently in play and, therefore, about the appropriate rules of conduct. These norms of appropriate behavior depend on the participation status of the interactants (GOFFMAN, 1961) or their social roles, rights, and responsibilities.

## Social Interaction Theory and Information Science

Many of the questions raised in this literature are directly related to those now being asked in IS about the social vs. the purely individual environments within which information interactions take place (FROHMANN, 1994; HJØRLAND & ALBRECHSTEN; INGWERSEN, 1999). The concept of situation is centrally important in this literature; it is believed that within situations of social interaction, among humans as well as between people and IR systems, meanings are constituted and negotiated.

In recent work, AUDUNSON writes explicitly about the importance of attending to social norms in studies of information-seeking behavior. He writes, "Organizational action is to a large extent seen as symbolic and ceremonial" (p. 73), further observing that people in organizations act according to "codes of appropriateness." Audunson continues to explore the usefulness of social interaction theory when he stresses the importance of norms of information behavior as a variable in models of information-seeking processes. To cite one of his examples, in certain social situations, such as courtroom juries, there are clearly established norms about the sources one can trust as credible information. In other social situations, there are socially prescribed norms about whom one can ask for information and how.

From the perspective of social interaction theory we can suggest the following definition of situation: a situation is the set of regulative norms governing behaviors within broader contexts, made up of roles, and role sets, with prescribed norms. Situations are social constructions; they are typified in the sense in which BERGER & LUCKMANN use the concept. MANTOVANI & BOLZONI present a typology of social situations involving information technology; specifically they refer to vocational guidance systems.

Adopting a social situation view of information behavior provides researchers with multiple areas of investigation within IS and in a variety of information interaction environments. Directly applying Goffman's notion of the definition of the situation, MOKROS ET AL. studied interaction patterns between library users and intermediaries. They looked for interactional strategies that showed evidence that intermediaries had internalized a model of personhood with respect to the library patron and a model of professional identity with respect to their own role. Using a microanalytic technique involving the quantification of pronouns associated with power and inclusion that were uttered by the intermediary, they discovered that embedded within the interaction between user and intermediary one could find evidence of a definition of the situation that evolved from internalized models of professional practice and personhood. Using a similar analytic framework, COCKETT looked at the emergence of individual, group, and social identities among librarians as constituted through interaction during a work-group situation. In particular, she examined the utility of the concept of personhood for understanding the dynamics of group interaction in collaborative decision-making situations. Recalling social interaction theory, personhood refers to an individual's beliefs about self, other, and the social world. Her research adopts a constitutive theory of communication, in which the multifunctionality of language is recognized and in which realities (including identities) are thought to exist not prior to but in moments of communication. A case study of one decision-making meeting forms the basis of this work, which examines the personhood orientations from which the individuals approach the situation.

The work reported by Cockett is closely related to other social interactional analyses of user–intermediary interactions, a slightly different work situation but one in which the value of social interaction theory can well be appreciated. CHELTON uses this framework in her study of the interaction between a school library clerk and an adolescent patron. Drawing on the theoretical writing of Goffman, she discusses the interactional strategies through which institutional power and control are maintained in this situation.

Within IS, an important issue at this time is how to apply social interaction conceptualizations of situation to contexts of IR interaction—that is, within situations in which users interact directly with inanimate information objects and systems.

IIVONEN & SONNENWALD have investigated some of the communication aspects of IR interaction by analyzing the search term selection process of professional searchers. They invoke a model in which shared communication conventions, or what they term the "navigation of different discourses," is a key decision-making element in the selection of search terms. "The results of our research suggest that when searchers select search terms to describe a certain search topic, they may step through various discourses in which this topic may be discussed and conceptualized differently" (IIVONEN & SONNENWALD, p. 313). The six discourses that were traversed by the searchers in their study are: (1) controlled vocabulary, (2) document, (3) indexing practice, (4) clients' search request, (5) database, and (6) searcher's previous searching experience.

In another example of directly applying social interaction theory to the study of IR interaction, COOL (1997a; 1997b) developed a model of user–system interaction that she labels situation assessment. Situation assessment is described as an inferential process through which people make sense of various dimensions of the IR interaction as a social interaction situation. Earlier COOL (1993) argues that IR can be construed as symbolic interaction between users and authors of texts through the mechanisms of the IR system.

Five dimensions of situation assessment were investigated by COOL (1997a; 1997b): assessment of (1) self-competence, (2) communication conventions, (3) appropriate norms of user–system interaction, (4) intersubjectivity, and (5) document topical relevance. An experiment was conducted in which subjects conducted searches on the same task and were asked to think-aloud during the interaction session. Verbal protocols were coded for the presence of situation assessment expressions.

A major finding was that expressions related to social interaction dimensions of the IR session outnumbered those related to topical relevance. Further, the greater the frequency of situation assessment expressed by subjects, the less well they performed the task, which was to find and to save as many good documents on a specified topic as they could. COOL (1997a; 1997b) concludes that the social interaction framework is useful for further understanding of IR interaction and that future work needs to explore the relationship between situation assessment and IR performance. She also argues for further research into the processes through which intersubjectivity—or mutual understandings between user and IR systems—is created and maintained.

*Usefulness of the social interaction perspective.* These studies, along with the theoretical literature cited above, argue strongly for taking into account the social interaction perspective of information seeking and IR interaction situations. With the development of interaction-based models of IR, the concept of situation that emerges from social interaction theory seems to provide an especially rich perspective on the nature of the communication strategies and communication goals that people bring to the IR experience. Within any situation of social interaction, participants orient themselves to the prevailing definition of the situation, the participation status of others present, and the appropriate norms of interaction, including communication and language. Within the social interaction literature, especially symbolic interactionism, the central concept of intersubjectivity seems to hold strong potential for development in future studies of IR interaction. If we view IR interaction as a process of communication between authors of texts and people for whom those texts might be useful, then an important problem for the user interacting with systems that provide access to unknown collections of information objects, such as are found in digital libraries and on the WWW, is the problem of calibrating the degree of intersubjective alliance between oneself and the creators of information items. The task for future research in IS will be to investigate the problematic situations further (in terms of tasks and communication goals) that people bring with them to the IR situation and to find ways to support them in future system environments.

## THE CONCEPT OF SITUATED ACTION

The concept of situated action appears primarily in the human–computer interaction (HCI) literature, and focuses somewhat narrowly on behaviors within the information technology use environment. This framework was developed by SUCHMAN, an anthropologist, who locates her work within the ethnomethodological tradition, especially the earlier work of GARFINKEL. Describing situated action as closer to a program of research than an actual theory, Suchman defines the concept as follows: "That term underscores the view that every course of action depends in essential ways upon its material and social circumstances. Rather than attempting to abstract action away from its circumstances and represent it as a rational plan, the approach is to study how people use their circumstances to achieve intelligent action" (SUCHMAN, p. 50).

Viewing HCI as a process of communication, Suchman shares some of the theoretical perspectives of the social interactionists described above. The motivation behind the development of the situated action model is a challenge to the cognitivist planned-action approach, which views human action as rational, purposeful, and planned. While not denying the existence of plans in people's interactions with computers and other inanimate objects, Suchman argues that what appears to be planned action is in fact the result of cooperative action and shared meanings built up during the context of the interaction. The significance of Suchman's model for understanding IR interaction is that it provides a bottom-up approach to understanding situation from a process perspective.

The notion of situated action is related to the symbolic interactionist view that meanings are built up within situations of interaction. Suchman makes a connection between her model and the ethnomethodological approach articulated earlier by GARFINKEL with respect to how people infer meanings within their situations. Ethnomethodologist Garfinkel developed a notion of how people routinely understand the situations they are in, which he terms the documentary method of interpretation. According to Garfinkel, people typically build up and reformulate their understandings of the larger social situation, or context, by using multiple sources of evidence available to them in the environment. Using a part-whole method of analysis, people begin with some idea of the situation, then they use each new appearance of information as evidence for confirmation or modification of their belief. The documentary method described by Garfinkel seems to be close to what BATES describes as berry-picking during information-seeking episodes and is also consistent with Kuhlthau's characterization of information-seeking behavior as an unfolding process of seeking meaning and of uncertainty reduction (KUHLTHAU, 1993a; 1993b).

## Situated Action in Studies of IR Interaction

The concept of situated action has found greater acceptance in the field of computer-supported collaborative work (CSCW) than it has in IS directly, although there have been several applications of interest to IS. Within IR, the concept of situated action has been explicitly addressed by HERT (1995; 1996; 1997). In this program of research, Hert was interested in studying the nature of people's information-seeking goals within the context of their interactions with IR systems. She studied OPAC users, beginning with an analysis of the initial user goals that brought people to the library. Results of her in-depth qualitative analysis revealed that users' goals were relatively unchanging, but behaviors varied according to situational elements in the information environment that were related to the goal. Hert did not begin her investigation with the intention of using SUCHMAN's model of situated action, but as her results unfolded, she adopted the framework to explain changes in user behaviors. She states: "An OPAC interaction is a series of situated actions on the part of the user. By situatedness is meant that as a user moves through an interaction, his or her actions are not completely predetermined, instead elements of the situation are utilized to influence action" (HERT, 1996, p. 507). In other recent work in this area, XIE (1997; 1998; 2000) has investigated the issue of planned vs. situated aspects of IR behaviors. In an analysis of library users' goals and intentions over the course of searching episodes in the library, Xie discovered that the concept of goal is much more multidimensional than had previously been conceptualized. Users were found to have a hierarchy of goals. High-level goals brought them to the library in the first place, but over the course of interaction with information items, a variety of microlevel goals, which Xie calls interactive intentions were observed. A number of interactive shifts, representing changes in the microlevel interactive intentions, were observed as a result of interaction with information and other situational elements. Xie further discusses the information-seeking strategies associated with shifts in interactive intentions, and a major conclusion of her study is that the planned vs. situated action models presents a false debate. Both dynamics are present in interactive information environments.

*Usefulness of the situated action model.*    The situated action model addresses a number of important questions related to information interactions that are directly relevant to a better understanding of interactive IR. A weakness in this perspective on situation is that there is no specification of the ways in which interactions are situated, what the situating elements of different information interaction environments are, and the extent to which the situated action model offers concrete guidelines for the design of more supportive information interaction environments.

## THE THEORY OF SITUATION AWARENESS

Developed within the industrial engineering and human factors community, situation awareness (SA) is a theoretical model that attempts to explain the processes central to performance and decision making in dynamic and complex environments, such as military operations, aircraft navigation, surgical teamwork, and other environments where technological decision making occurs. Extensions of the concept have appeared recently in the IS literature (SONNENWALD & PIERCE).

The concept of SA was first developed to account for military performance, especially aircraft pilot navigation, and much of the early work focused on pilot errors that were traceable to inadequate awareness of or attention to elements in the cockpit environment that signal flight and operating conditions. While the earliest literature on SA appeared in the military context during the 1980s (see CASTELLAN for an overview), it has since been applied to other civilian environments, such as operating-room situations (GABA ET AL.) and fire-fighting situations (ARTMAN). Later developments in this literature have focused on group as well as individual-level situation awareness.

ENDSLEY (1990; 1995a; 1995b) has been instrumental in developing a coherent theory of SA, distinguishing it from ordinary human processing. Her definition has since been adopted and used extensively in the human factors community: "True SA, it will be shown, involves far more than mere being aware of numerous pieces of data. It also requires a much more advanced level of situation understanding and a projection of future systems states in light of the operator's pertinent goals. As such, SA presents a level of focus that goes beyond traditional information-processing approaches in attempting to explain human behavior in operating complex systems" (ENDSLEY, 1995b, p. 32). ENDSLEY (1995a) further discusses some of the factors that appear to influence the SA process. They include individual abilities, in terms of perceptual capabilities, along with system design and interface features. In her process model of SA, Endsley (1995a) further proposes three levels: level 1, which involves perception of the elements in the environment; level 2, which is the comprehension of the current situation; and level 3, which is a projection of future status.

## Dimensions of Situation Awareness

*Mental models of the situation.* ENDSLEY (1995b) discusses mental models, or schemata, to describe one element of SA. She invokes the related concept of situational model (p. 43), which she borrows from VAN DIJK & KINTSCH, to describe a mental representation of the current state of the system model, including the projected future state of affairs. The ability of people to process large amounts of information in complex decision-making environments depends on the prototypical situations or scenarios that are stored in memory. The ideas about shared situational models and the mental categorization of types of situations are somewhat related to earlier frameworks discussed above, most notably in the phenomenology of SCHUTZ & LUCKMANN and the symbolic interactionism of BERGER & LUCKMANN and MEAD. CANNON-BOWERS ET AL. recognize that ideas about the existence and the importance of shared mental models in cooperative activity go way back. "As early as 1934, Mead maintained that 'complex cooperative activity' is only possible if each team member can direct his or her behavior according to shared notions of task processes and activities" (CANNON-BOWERS ET AL., p. 228).

*Group situation awareness.* SA and situation assessment have been looked at in individual-level and group- or team-level activity. The importance of group SA and shared situational models in team decision making is discussed by CANNON-BOWERS ET AL. and by WELLENS. Cannon-Bowers et al. provide a good overview of the literature on mental models in general and then explicitly on shared mental models in collaborative activity. A shared mental model in this literature is one in which there is a common model of the situation or problem or multilevel group SA. Wellens highlights the problem of facilitating group SA in geographically distributed work teams. Further developments of the SA model have turned to an analysis of the group or work team as the unit of analysis and to the processes of maintaining intra- and intergroup awareness in collaborative decision-making environments (ARTMAN; ENDSLEY ET AL.; JENTSCH ET AL.; SALAS ET AL.; STOUT ET AL.). The investigation by JENTSCH ET AL. focuses on the increased complexity that accompanies team-level SA, and they cast their discussion within a communication framework. "Intrateam communication, for example, has been identified as one determinant of team SA" (p. 1).

The effect of distributed information architectures and communication patterns on SA and cooperation in dynamic decision-making environments has received attention from ARTMAN and SALAS ET AL. Artman's study explicitly addressed the question of the relative effectiveness of different conditions of information flow in a simulated fire-fighting task. Artman found that the more successful team engaged in more frequent message exchanges, particularly, more cross checking with respect to establishing mutually held understandings of the situation. With respect to specific channels of communication, the most successful teams had commanders who engaged in frequent verbal interaction rather than relying on email.

We see in Artman's study and also in work by CANNON-BOWERS ET AL., SALAS ET AL., and STOUT ET AL. the importance of situational models in the coordination of efforts among members of work teams, the evaluation of the difference between individually constructed and consensually shared models of the situation on task performance, the information needs of team members, and the communication strategies that might most effectively support it.

## Situation Awareness Theory and Information Science

Attention to SA as a theoretical concept has only recently begun to appear in the IS literature. In a recent study of communication and information behavior among military team members in command and control environments, SONNENWALD & PIERCE discuss the social situational requirements for effective performance in that particular dynamic task environment. A central variable in their discussion is shared team awareness, which they describe as a multileveled process of interwoven situational awareness, consisting of individual, intra-group, and intergroup shared understandings of the situation. This particular framework combines elements of group SA theory along with social interaction theory as discussed above. Some correspondence between the work in SA and IS can be seen in the work of BELKIN ET AL. (1983) and to a lesser extent, in the work of COOL (1997a; 1997b) on situation assessment.

*Usefulness of situation awareness.* Since being introduced, the concept of situation awareness has been expanded to include both individual cognitive processes and group or team awareness in collaborative environments. SARTER & WOODS (1991; 1995) have argued that the concept is so nebulous as to be almost meaningless. Despite this conceptual looseness, a consistent body of work has been developed, much of it relevant to IS. The literature on SA, while developed within industrial engineering and human factors, addresses many concerns of relevance to information interaction behavior, especially at the point of interaction between users and system interface features and functionalities. The attention to individual-level awareness of control mechanisms in dynamic interaction environments, such as aircraft cockpits, has some relevance to IS with respect to the design of usable, understandable interface features and functionalities, particularly those that use visualization techniques as modes of presentation.

SA theory also has some direct relevance to issues of navigation in IR systems. For some time now there has been a concern with understanding how users navigate through complex physical information interaction spaces (CANTER ET AL.). Problems of wayfinding in physical and other spaces (BUTLER ET AL.) is another related area in which the concept of SA might offer some insights. UTTING & YANKELOVICH, in an earlier piece, describe the problems of disorientation in hypermedia systems. Certainly the design of multifunctional interfaces to facilitate interactive IR, especially in new information environments, places cognitive burdens on users that may be framed within the concept of SA.

The importance of collaboration, cooperation, and shared mental models of the situation are discussed in the SA literature, along with ways in which these processes can be facilitated through interaction (ARTMAN; ENDSLEY ET AL.; JENTSCH ET AL.; SALAS ET AL.; STOUT ET AL.). All of these concerns are of interest to IS and information retrieval. The study mentioned earlier by Sonnenwald and Pierce is relevant to and contributes to this body of literature. The earlier work on distributed expert problem solving by Belkin et al. (1983) relates to similar problems, especially those of communication mode and control structure.

Future work in interactive IR might well benefit from a more thorough look at SA theory. Although the concept appears in literatures quite different from the social interactionist material discussed above, a central element of SA is the cognitive assessment activity of maintaining a definition of the situation, which suggests some shared concerns there as well. Perhaps the most useful contribution of this work is the integration of individual and social levels of cognitive orientation in interaction information use environments. The elements in the environment of which one might be more or less aware will differ by systems and contexts. For example, for aircraft pilots, altitude heading, airspeed, traffic, and meteorological conditions are relevant elements, but their relevance will vary over time. In other situations, such as in interactive IR, different elements will be relevant, and a task for IR researchers is to specify these elements.

An obvious weakness of the SA model is that lack of specificity with respect to the identification of relevant elements of the IR or information-seeking situation. In her model, ENDSLEY (1995b) stresses the importance of particular elements in the environment that need to be perceived and understood, and since these elements are unique to individual systems and contexts, they obviously can't be specified across all interaction environments by the SA model. As she notes, "Although the pilot and power plant operator each relies on SA, it simply is not realistic or appropriate to expect the same elements to be relevant to both" (p. 37).

## PERSON-IN-SITUATION MODEL

In contrast to the SA theory, the person-in-situation model is a human decision-making model that attempts to account for the relationship between individual traits and situational-level variables on a variety of performance measures in different contexts. The person-in-situation model was first developed to account for attributes of persons, such as personality variables, cognitive traits, and abilities, as well as tasks associated with some larger goal that initiated the information seeking episode(s), that influence or interact with other information behaviors. In an early statement of this theory, SNOW presents an overview of person–situation interaction theory with respect to intelligence. The basic framework of this model is concerned with accounting for the multidimensional nature of intelligence, reasoning, and problem solving under varying conditions. Snow reviews several arguments about the nature of intelligence, noting that it is multifaceted, multileveled, hierarchical, and not modular. He then advances four propositions of his own about the personal nature of intelligence and learning abilities. Two are of interest here. Snow suggests that intelligence and learning ability are "both pervasive and situated" (p. 13) and that "intelligence is personal" (p. 15). By situated he means that there are a wide variety of situations that can be characterized as relatively unstructured and complex and that there exist incomplete learning environments that nevertheless require high performance. Such situations require "flexible adaptation and agility in inferential evaluation" by the learner (p. 14). Intelligence is personal to the extent that each person has a unique learning history, or stock of knowledge, among other reasons.

Although SNOW casts learning and intelligence in individual cognitive frameworks, he stresses the relational aspects of these two variables, and this is the crux of the person-in-situation theory.

> But to say that intelligence is situated and personal is to claim much more than that it is specialized by types of situations and types of persons. It is to claim that intelligence is fundamentally a relational, relativistic construct; that is, it should be interpreted as existing in the person-situation interaction, not in the head of the person alone or in the structure of the situation alone, but in the "interface" between them. This means that defining the situations in which intelligence operates is part of defining intelligence. It also means that person-in-situation—the person-situation union—is the unit of analysis, not persons or situations or bits and pieces of persons and situations independently. (SNOW, p. 15)

In simpler language, Snow describes the person–interface in terms of the affordance theory of GIBSON. Each situation is a stimulus environment with its own set of affordances or things that it can offer the person. At the same time, a person must have the capability to accept the affordances that are available. "So a situation is an assembly of affordances with respect to some particular person or kind of person . . . . Particular affordances reflect particular actions" (p. 18). As noted here by Snow, the nature of individual differences makes it unlikely that situations will be uniformly effective in the suitability of the affordances they offer. Further, Snow states that it is difficult to identify specific elements of situations that influence task performance in certain contexts. He uses the example of academic task performance and says, "On the situation side, one can think of instructional treatments as composed of particular sequences of learning tasks and embedded in particular classroom or school contexts. Situation variables might then be defined within or across these three levels. But so far there are no models, hierarchical or otherwise, of such situation variables" (SNOW, p. 12).

For a review of the person-in-situation approach from this perspective of individual-level decision making and intelligence, see PERVIN or the collection of papers in STERNBERG & WAGNER. In other, psychologically oriented formulations of the model, attention has been given to personality traits of individuals that are associated with situationally constrained behaviors. For example, DOERNER looked at judgment and reasoning abilities in experimental situations in which subjects were given a simulated computer version of a hypothetical town and asked to rule the town by acting as mayor. Some of the decision-making tasks concerned taxation, education policies, transportation, and so on. Of interest to the authors were the personality characteristics of the "bad" subjects, those who made poor judgments within this situation. One of the findings was that lack of positive feedback was associated with poor performance. The authors suggest that low self-esteem associated with lack of positive feedback in the uncertain situation in which subjects were placed created a feeling of fear and loss of control, which led to failure at the task. In another psychologically oriented approach to person-in-situation theory, DIENER ET AL. examined the relationship between personality characteristics of individuals and the types of situations they prefer to be in. The underlying idea in this psychological thinking is that people who have different personality traits may not be comfortable in the same situations. Common examples given in this literature are that introverts may not want to go to loud bars and serious intellectuals might tend to spend time in serious, reserved situations. Diener et al. challenge this assumption, and the experiment they conducted to test it did show mixed results. Whether there might be some match between personality trait and choice of information-seeking situation is an interesting but open question.

## Person-in-Situation Theory and Information Science

The person-in-situation theory has been looked at within IS, where explicit attention has been directed to task situations and performance variables as units of analysis (ALLEN, 1996, 1997; ALLEN & KIM; REID). In an early formulation of this approach, ALLEN (1996; 1997) provides a framework for understanding the matrix of social and individual factors that come into play in explaining information needs and uses and information-seeking behavior. Allen accounts for the social nature of information behaviors by placing individuals within organizational, institutional, and other social membership categories. Clearly, information behaviors are embedded within these social memberships, and much of the literature on social interaction theory takes this into account. However, Allen points out that while individuals are located within multiple social arenas, they also have personal, individual-level characteristics or traits that influence information behaviors. Examples of some of these individual-level variables may be knowledge structures, cognitive and learning styles, and personality traits. To develop models of information needs and uses further, according to Allen, we need to reconcile these two competing explanations of information behavior and even look further into fresh perspectives as well. Allen proposes the adoption of a person-in-situation approach in which he argues for an interactionist perspective on the relationship between situational and individual determinants of behavior. His conceptual thinking is grounded in the person-in-situation models described above, which he reviews (ALLEN & KIM) extensively, concluding that the literature has demonstrated inconclusive results with respect to the relative importance of situational vs. individual factors on task performance.

In recent research, ALLEN & KIM further extend the theoretical model of person-in-situation, first articulated in the IS literature by ALLEN (1996), by conducting an experimental evaluation of person-situation interactionism. Allen and Kim tested the hypothesis that characteristics of the specific task assigned to subjects (the situational variable) would interact with individual traits, such as cognitive style and abilities to influence types of information behaviors. In different experimental conditions, Allen and Kim found significant relationships between personal variables, such as cognitive abilities and task performance, but no significant interaction effects between these individual and situational variables on information behaviors. They conclude that individual traits and situational variables, such as information task environments, operate independently on information-seeking behaviors.

*Significance of person-in-situation model for information science.* The person-in-situation approach is an important attempt to bring together individual-level and social- or situational-level variables in a unified model of information-seeking behavior. In some respects, this perspective follows in the footsteps of PAISLEY and T. D. WILSON (1981), who gave early attention to the social situational matrix within which information behaviors occur. In evaluating the significance of the person-in-situation model on its own, however, it seems as if a weakness of the approach stems from its ambiguous conceptualization of situation. The work of Allen and Kim represents an important first step toward understanding human information behaviors from an interactionist perspective that tries to account for the relationship between individual traits and situational factors that influence information behaviors. However, further development of the framework will require considerable conceptual clarification with respect to the central concepts of situation, context, and tasks.

## SITUATION ENVIRONMENTS

### Information Environments and Information Science

The final perspective to be considered here looks at situation from an environmental or ecological perspective. While not representing any particular theoretical position as such, there have been studies in a number of domains that have looked at the concept of situation from within this framework. As an example of environmental concepts of situation, we can consider various insitutional, organizational, or task environments within which information behaviors take place. The salient aspects of situation in this framework concern the situations of use. The writing of TAYLOR (1991) on the information use environment is an early example of this perspective.

The concept of a situation environment traverses individual, social, and organizational contexts. In 1981, T. D. WILSON (1981) made the observation, "Because the situations in which information is sought and used are social situations, however, purely cognitive conceptions of information need are probably inadequate for research purposes" (p. 9). However, for Wilson, the social aspects of information-seeking behavior were not entirely contained within social interaction: "The search for determining factors related to information seeking behavior and uses must include aspects of the environment within which the work-role is performed. The immediate work-environment and its climate has been mentioned above, but the socio-cultural environment, and the physical environment, will all have an impact in particular ways" (p. 10). The usefulness of this framework comes into play when we examine the relationship between types of situational environments and information behaviors, such as information-seeking behaviors, information-use behaviors, and evaluation of information items.

*Task environments.* A significant body of research has looked at a person's task environment as a relevant situation within which information behaviors take place. ALGON (1997; 1999) presents a taxonomy of tasks and their relationship to information behaviors. Based on her field analysis of individuals working on project teams in the pharmaceutical industry, she developed a classification of tasks within the work-group situations that were related to information-related behaviors. The task environment she studied is especially interesting, owing to its highly competitive nature during the drug development process. Her analysis, conducted over three years, led to a classification of tasks and information-related behaviors. She discovered three important facets related to information finding/seeking, information using, and information providing. Each behavior was related to both tasks and stages in the research development process.

In other recent research, MIWA explored the task environment as the external social and environmental situation in which people turn to human intermediaries for help in solving information problems. In this case she studied users of the AskERIC telereference service. A significant result of this research is the development of a taxonomy of tasks requested of intermediaries and a classification of six situational categories that users perceived to be salient in requesting help from the intermediaries: (1) types of information problem-solving processes, (2) information needs, (3) cognitive states, (4) affective states, (5) social contexts, and (6) environmental conditions. This work is especially interesting because it takes a total environmental perspective on the use of the information resource, including task, cognitive level, and situational factors.

Within the communication literature, CALDWELL ET AL. examined the relationship between the appropriateness of different communication media for information exchange across task and situational variables. The most significant situational variables that were found to be related to type of information and media were time, urgency of the message, and distance between communicators.

*Usefulness of information environments.*   As mentioned above, attention to information use environments as situations of information use dates back at least a decade to TAYLOR (1991). There is by now a large and rich literature on the various information environments within which information behaviors take place. Within this literature, the concepts of information environment, context, and situation are often used interchangeably. The concept of situation is not treated as an analytic unit in itself. For this reason, the environmental perspective on situation is less useful than other perspectives discussed above in terms of furthering the development of situation as a unit variable in IS.

## CONCLUSION

### The Multiplicity of Perspectives
### on the Concept of Situation

This chapter has reviewed six approaches to conceptualizing and empirically investigating the concept of situation. All of these perspectives have some potential relevance to IS, and, indeed each has been looked at to some extent within the IS literature. The chapter has attempted to discuss the strengths and weaknesses of each for explaining phenomena of interest to information science. Based on the literature reviewed, several conclusions can be drawn.

First, this review illustrates the usefulness to IS of situation as a focus of analysis in its own right. While the concept of situation has deep historical roots in IR theory, more recently there has been a return to the concept of situation in the IS literature as a way of understanding IR interaction and information behavior within a social and broader environmental matrix. Situation has the potential for being an important unit variable in further theoretical developments of information-seeking behavior and use and IR interaction. On a theoretical level, the concept of situation has the potential for bringing together both individual cognitive-level and social-level analyses of human information behavior. While the concepts of context and situation are often used interchangeably in IS as well as in many other disciplines, if we embrace an interactionist framework in IS, the concept of situation can usefully be disambiguated from context. Situation is the dynamic aspect of context. Situations with respect to IS are interaction spaces. A fuller exploration of the concept of situation as a central unit of analysis offers the possibility of developing both interactionist and cognitive viewpoints further in IS.

Second, it is clear that there is no theory of situation in IS, and in the current literature there is no single definition of what constitutes a situation. However, rather than ask "what *is* a situation," we might more productively ask "what conceptualization of situation addresses what sorts of questions of interest to information science?" The perspectives on situation surveyed here are multilayered, spanning individual, interactional, and social levels of analysis. As discussed, each perspective draws attention to specific research questions that can further our knowledge of information-seeking behavior, use, and IR interaction in a variety of information spaces.

Finally, the development of situation as a central unit of analysis in IS depends on further specification of the constitutive elements of situation that play a role in information behaviors, especially within a variety of IR interaction situations. With respect to IR systems, people are increasingly interacting with new information features and functionalities. Future research needs to identify the important elements of these new information interaction situations that play a role in IR interaction and that warrant an analysis in their own right.

## BIBLIOGRAPHY

ALGON, JACQUELINE. 1997. Classification of Tasks, Steps, and Information-Related Behaviors of Individuals on Project Teams. In: Vakkari, Pertti; Savolainen, Reijo; Dervin, Brenda, eds. Information Seeking in

Context: Proceedings of an International Conference on Research in Information Needs, Seeking and Use in Different Contexts; 1996 August 14-16; Tampere, Finland. London, UK: Taylor Graham; 1997. 205-221. ISBN: 0-947568-71-9.

ALGON, JACQUELINE. 1999. The Effect of Task on the Information-Related Behaviors of Individuals in a Work-Group Environment. New Brunswick, NJ: Rutgers University, School of Communication, Information and Library Studies; 1999. 293p. (Ph.D. dissertation). Available from: UMI, Ann Arbor, MI. (UMI order no. 99-18306).

ALLEN, BRYCE L. 1991. Cognitive Research in Information Science: Implications for Design. In: Williams, Martha E., ed. Annual Review of Information Science and Technology: Volume 26. Medford, NJ: Learned Information, Inc. for the American Society for Information Science; 1991. 3-37. ISSN: 0066-4200; ISBN: 0-938734-55-5; CODEN: ARISBC.

ALLEN, BRYCE L. 1996. Information Tasks: Toward a User-Centered Approach to Information Systems. San Diego, CA: Academic Press; 1996. 308p. ISBN: 0-12-051040-5.

ALLEN, BRYCE L. 1997. Information Needs: A Person-in-Situation Approach. In: Vakkari, Pertti; Savolainen, Reijo; Dervin, Brenda, eds. Information Seeking in Context: Proceedings of an International Conference on Research in Information Needs, Seeking and Use in Different Contexts; 1996 August 14-16; Tampere, Finland. London, UK: Taylor Graham; 1997. 111-122. ISBN: 0-947568-71-9.

ALLEN, BRYCE L.; KIM, KYUNG-SUN 2000. Person and Context in Information Seeking: Interactions between Cognitive and Task Variables. Paper presented at ISIC 2000: Information Seeking in Context: The 3rd International Conference on Information Needs, Seeking and Use in Different Contexts; 2000 August 16-18; Gothenburg, Sweden. Available from: the authors, School of Infomation Science and Learning Technologies, University of Missouri-Columbia.

ARTMAN, HENRIK. 1999. Situation Awareness and Co-operation within and between Hierarchical Units in Dynamic Decision Making. Ergonomics. 1999; 42(11): 1404-1417. ISSN: 0014-0139.

AUDUNSON, RAGNAR. 1999. Can Institutional Theory Contribute to Our Understanding of Information Seeking Behaviour? In: Wilson, Thomas D.; Allen, David K., eds. Exploring the Contexts of Information Behaviour: Proceedings of the 2nd International Conference on Research in Information Needs, Seeking and Use in Different Contexts; 1998 August 13-15; Sheffield, UK. London, UK: Taylor Graham; 1999. 67-81. ISBN: 0-947568-75-1.

BALL-ROKEACH, SANDRA J. 1973. From Pervasive Ambiguity to a Definition of the Situation. Sociometry. 1973; 36: 378-389. ISSN: 0147-829X.

BARRY, CAROL L. 1993. The Identification of User Criteria of Relevance and Document Characteristics: Beyond the Topical Approach to Information Retrieval. Syracuse, NY: Syracuse University; 1993. 255p. (Ph.D. dissertation). Available from: UMI, Ann Arbor, MI. (UMI order no. 9422230).

BARRY, CAROL L. 1994. User-Defined Relevance Criteria: An Exploratory Study. Journal of the American Society for Information Science. 1994; 45(3): 149-159. ISSN: 0002-8231; CODEN: AISJB6.

BARRY, CAROL L.; SCHAMBER, LINDA. 1998. Users' Criteria for Relevance Evaluation: A Cross-Situational Comparison. Information Processing & Management. 1998; 31(2/3): 219-236. ISSN: 0306-4573; CODEN: IPMADK.

BATES, MARCIA J. 1989. The Design of Browsing and Berrypicking Techniques for the Online Search Interface. Online Review. 1989; 13(5): 407-424. ISSN: 0309-314X.

BATESON, GREGORY. 1987. Steps to an Ecology of Mind: Collected Essays in Anthropology, Psychiatry, Evolution and Epistemology. Northvale, NJ: Aronson; 1987. 545p. ISBN: 0-87668-950-0.

BELKIN, NICHOLAS J. 1980. Anomalous States of Knowledge as a Basis for Information Retrieval. Canadian Journal of Information Science. 1980 May; 5: 133-143. ISSN: 0380-9218.

BELKIN, NICHOLAS J. 1984. Cognitive Models and Information Transfer. Social Science Information Studies. 1984 April/July; 4(2/3): 111-129. ISSN: 0143-6236; CODEN: SOSSD3.

BELKIN, NICHOLAS J. 1990. The Cognitive Viewpoint in Information Science. Journal of Information Science. 1990; 16(1): 11-15. ISSN: 0165-5515.

BELKIN, NICHOLAS J. 1996. Intelligent Information Retrieval: Whose Intelligence? In: ISI '96: Proceedings of the 5th Internationalen Symposiums für Informationswissenschaft; 1996 October 17-19; Berlin, Germany. Konstanz, Germany: Universitätsverlag Konstanz; 1996. 25-31. ISBN: 3-87940-586-7.

BELKIN, NICHOLAS J.; COOL, COLLEEN; STEIN, ADELHEIT; THIEL, ULRICH. 1995. Cases, Scripts, and Information Seeking Strategies: On the Design of Interactive Information Retrieval Systems. Expert Systems with Applications. 1995; 9(3): 379-395. ISSN: 0957-4174.

BELKIN, NICHOLAS J.; SEEGER, THOMAS; WERSIG, GERNOT. 1983. Distributed Expert Problem Treatment as a Model for Information Systems Analysis and Design. Journal of Information Science. 1983; 5: 153-167. ISSN: 0165-5515.

BERGER, PETER L.; LUCKMANN, THOMAS. 1967. The Social Construction of Reality. Garden City, NY: Anchor; 1967. 219p. ISBN: 0-385-05898-5.

BISHOP, ANN PETERSON; STAR, SUSAN LEIGH. 1996. Social Informatics of Digital Library Use and Infrastructure. In: Williams, Martha E., ed. Annual Review of Information Science and Technology: Volume 31. Medford, NJ: Information Today, Inc. for the American Society for Information Science; 1996. 301-401. ISSN: 0066-4200; ISBN: 1-57387-033-1; CODEN: ARISBC.

BLUMER, HERBERT. 1969. Symbolic Interactionism: Perspective and Method. Englewood Cliffs, NJ: Prentice-Hall; 1969. 208p. ISBN: 0-13-879924-5.

BORLUND, PIA. 2000. Experimental Components for the Evaluation of Interactive Information Retrieval Systems. Journal of Documentation. 2000; 56(1): 71-90. ISSN: 0022-0418; CODEN: JDOCAS.

BORLUND, PIA; INGWERSEN, PETER. 1997. The Development of a Method for the Evaluation of Interactive Information Retrieval Systems. Journal of Documentation. 1997; 53(3): 225-250. ISSN: 0022-0418; CODEN: JDOCAS.

BRUCE, HARRY W. 1994. A Cognitive View of the Situational Determinism of User-Centered Relevance Estimation. Journal of the American Society for Information Science. 1994; 45(3): 142-148. ISSN: 0002-8231; CODEN: AISJB6.

BUTLER, DARRELL L.; ACQUINO, APRIL L.; HISSONG, ALICIA A.; SCOTT, PAMALA A. 1993. Wayfinding by Newcomers in a Complex Building. Human Factors. 1993; 35(1): 159-173. ISSN: 0018-7208.

CALDWELL, BARRETT S.; UANG, SHIAW-TSYR; TAHA, LILAS H. 1995. Appropriateness of Communications Media Use in Organizations: Situation Requirements and Media Characteristics. Behaviour and Information Technology. 1995; 14(4): 199-207. ISSN: 0144-929X.

CANNON-BOWERS, JANIS A.; SALAS, EDUARDO; CONVERSE, SHAROLYN. 1993. Shared Mental Models in Expert Team Decision Making. In: Castellan, John N., Jr. Individual and Group Decision Making: Current Issues. Hillsdale, NJ: Lawrence Erlbaum Associates; 1993. 221-246. ISBN: 0-8058-1090-0.

CANTER, DAVID; RIVERS, ROD; STORRS, GRAHAM. 1985. Characterizing User Navigation through Complex Data Structures. Behaviour and Information Technology. 1985; 4(2): 93-102. ISSN: 0144-929X.

CARR, LOWELL J. 1948. Situational Analysis. New York, NY: Harper; 1948. 178p. OCLC: 564835.

CASTELLAN, JOHN N., JR. 1993. Individual and Group Decision Making: Current Issues. Hillsdale, NJ: Lawrence Erlbaum Associates; 1993. 315p. ISBN: 0-8058-1090-0.

CHELTON, MARY K. 1997. The "Overdue Kid": A Face-to-Face Library Service Encounter as Ritual Interaction. Library and Information Science Research. 1997; 19(4): 387-399. ISSN: 0740-8188.

COCKETT, LYNN. 2000. Self, Other, and Situation in Collaborative Contexts: A Study of Personhood in a Group Decision-Making Meeting. New Brunswick, NJ: Rutgers University, School of Communication, Information and Library Studies; 2000. 265p. (Ph.D. dissertation). Available from: UMI, Ann Arbor, MI. (UMI order no. 9973281).

COOL, COLLEEN. 1993. Information Retrieval as Symbolic Interaction: Examples from Humanities Scholars. In: Bonzi, Susan; Katzer, Jeffrey; Kwasnik, Barbara, eds. ASIS '93: Proceedings of the American Society for Information Science (ASIS) 56th Annual Meeting: Volume 30; 1993 October 24-28; Columbus, OH. Medford, NJ: Learned Information, Inc. for ASIS; 1993. 274-277. ISSN: 0044-7870; ISBN: 0-938734-73-3; CODEN: PAISDQ.

COOL, COLLEEN. 1997a. The Nature of Situation Assessment in New Information Retrieval Environments. In: Schwartz, Candy; Rorvig, Mark E., eds. ASIS '97: Proceedings of the American Society for Information Science (ASIS) 60th Annual Meeting: Volume 34; 1997 November 1-6; Washington, DC. Medford, NJ: Information Today, Inc. for ASIS; 1997. 135-146. ISSN: 0044-7870; ISBN: 1-57387-048-X; CODEN: PAISDQ.

COOL, COLLEEN. 1997b. Situation Assessment in Information Retrieval Interaction. New Brunswick, NJ: Rutgers University, School of Communication, Information and Library Studies; 1997. 167p. (Ph.D. dissertation). Available from: UMI, Ann Arbor, MI. (UMI order no. 98-00243).

COOL, COLLEEN; BELKIN, NICHOLAS J.; KANTOR, PAUL; FRIEDER, OPHIR. 1993. Characteristics of Texts Affecting Relevance Judgements.

In: Williams, Martha E., ed. Proceedings of the 14th National Online Meeting; 1993 May 4-6: New York, NY. Medford, NJ: Learned Information, Inc.; 1993. 77-84. ISBN: 0-938734-73-3.

COOL, COLLEEN; PARK, SOYEON; BELKIN, NICHOLAS J.; KOENEMANN, JÜRGEN; NG, KWONG BOR. 1996. Information Seeking Behavior in New Searching Environments. In: Ingwersen, Peter; Pors, Niels Ole, eds. CoLIS 2: Proceedings of the 2nd International Conference on Conceptions of Library and Information Science: Integration in Perspective; 1996 October 13-16; Copenhagen, Denmark. Copenhagen, Denmark: Royal School of Librarianship; 1996. 403-416. ISBN: 87-7415-260-2.

DERVIN, BRENDA. 1983. An Overview of Sense-Making Research: Concepts, Methods and Results to Date. Paper presented at the Annual Meeting of the International Communication Association; 1983 May; Dallas, TX. Available WWW: http://communication.sbs.ohio-state.edu/sense-making/art/artdervin83.html.

DERVIN, BRENDA. 1997. Given a Context by Any Other Name: Methodological Tools for Taming the Unruly Beast. In: Vakkari, Pertti; Savolainen, Reijo; Dervin, Brenda, eds. Information Seeking in Context: Proceedings of an International Conference on Research in Information Needs, Seeking and Use in Different Contexts; 1996 August 14-16; Tampere, Finland. London, UK: Taylor Graham; 1997. 13-38. ISBN: 0-947568-71-9.

DERVIN, BRENDA; NILAN, MICHAEL S. 1986. Information Needs and Uses. In: Williams, Martha E., ed. Annual Review of Information Science and Technology: Volume 21. White Plains, NY: Knowledge Industry Publications, Inc. for the American Society for Information Science; 1986. 3-33. ISSN: 0066-4200; ISBN: 0-86729-209-1; CODEN: ARISBC.

DIENER, ED; LARSEN, RANDY J.; EMMONS, ROBERT A. 1984. Person X Situation Interactions: Choice of Situations and Congruence Response Models. Journal of Personality and Social Psychology. 1984; 47(3): 580-592. ISSN: 0022-3514.

DOERNER, DIETRICH. 1980. On the Difficulties People Have in Dealing with Complexity. Simulation & Gaming. 1980; 11(1): 87-106. ISSN: 1046-8781.

ENDSLEY, MICA R. 1990. Situation Awareness in Dynamic Human Decision Making: Theory and Measurement. San Diego, CA: University of Southern California, Department of Industrial and Systems Engineering; 1990. 140p. (Ph.D. dissertation).

ENDSLEY, MICA R. 1995a. Measurement of Situation Awareness in Dynamic Systems. Human Factors. 1995 March; 37(1): 65-84. ISSN: 0018-7208.

ENDSLEY, MICA R. 1995b. Toward a Theory of Situation Awareness in Dynamic Systems. Human Factors. 1995 March; 37(1): 32-64. ISSN: 0018-7208.

ENDSLEY, MICA R.; HANSMAN, R. JOHN; FARLEY, TODD C. 1999. Shared Situation Awareness in the Flight Deck—ATC System. IEEE Aerospace and Electronic Systems Magazine. 1999 August; 14(8): 25-30. ISSN: 0885-8985.

FISK, ARTHUR D.; ROGERS, WENDY A. 1988. The Role of Situational Context in the Development of High-Performance Skills. Human Factors. 1988; 30(6): 703-712. ISSN: 0018-7208.

FROEHLICH, THOMAS J. 1994. Relevance Reconsidered: Towards an Agenda for the 21st Century. Journal of the American Society for Information Science. 1994; 45(3): 124-133. ISSN: 0002-8231; CODEN: AISJB6.

FROHMANN, BERND. 1992. The Power of Images: A Discourse Analysis of the Cognitive Viewpoint. Journal of Documentation. 1992; 48: 365-386. ISSN: 0022-0418.

FROHMANN, BERND. 1994. Discourse Analysis as a Research Method in Library and Information Science. Library and Information Science Research. 1994 Spring; 16(2): 119-138. ISSN: 0740-8188.

GABA, DAVID M.; HOWARD, STEVEN K.; SMALL, STEPHEN D. 1995. Situation Awareness in Anesthesiology. Human Factors. 1995; 37(1): 20-31. ISSN: 0018-7208.

GARFINKEL, HAROLD. 1967. Studies in Ethnomethodology. Englewood Cliffs, NJ: Prentice-Hall; 1967. 288p. OCLC: 356659.

GIBSON, JAMES JEROME. 1979. The Ecological Approach to Visual Perception. Boston, MA: Houghton Mifflin; 1979. 332p. ISBN: 0-395-27049-9.

GOFFMAN, ERVING. 1961. Encounters; Two Studies in the Sociology of Interaction. Indianapolis, IN: Bobbs-Merrill; 1961. 152p. OCLC: 710786.

GOFFMAN, ERVING. 1963. Behavior in Public Places: Notes on the Social Organization of Gatherings. New York, NY: Free Press of Glencoe; 1963. 248p. OCLC: 343351.

GOFFMAN, ERVING. 1964. The Neglected Situation. American Anthropologist. 1964 December; 66: 133-136. ISSN: 0002-7294.

GOFFMAN, ERVING. 1974. Frame Analysis: An Essay on the Organization of Experience. New York, NY: Harper Colophon; 1974. 586p. ISBN: 0-06-090372-4.

HERT, CAROL A. 1995. Exploring a New Model for the Understanding of Information Retrieval Interactions. Syracuse, NY: Syracuse University; 1995. 286p. (Ph.D. dissertation). Available from: UMI, Ann Arbor, MI. (UMI order no. 9619041).

HERT, CAROL A. 1996. User Goals on an Online Public Access Catalog. Journal of the American Society for Information Science. 1996 July; 47(7): 504-518. ISSN: 0002-8231; CODEN: AISJB6.

HERT, CAROL A. 1997. Understanding Information Retrieval Interactions: Theoretical and Practical Implications. Greenwich, CT: Ablex Publishing Corp.; 1997. 150p. ISBN: 1-56750-305-5.

HJØRLAND, BIRGER; ALBRECHTSEN, HANNE. 1995. Toward a New Horizon in Information Science: Domain Analysis. Journal of the American Society for Information Science. 1995; 46(6): 400-425. ISSN: 0002-8231; CODEN: AISJB6.

HUMAN FACTORS. 1995. Special Issue: Situation Awareness. Human Factors. 1995 March; 37(1): 216p. (Entire issue on title topic). ISSN: 0018-7208.

IIVONEN, MIRJA; SONNENWALD, DIANE H. 1998. From Translation to Navigation of Different Discourses: A Model of Search Term Selection during the Pre-Online Stage of the Search Process. Journal of the American Society for Information Science. 1998; 49: 312-326. ISSN:0002-8231; CODEN:AISJB6.

INGWERSEN, PETER. 1996. Cognitive Perspectives of Information Retrieval Interaction: Elements of a Cognitive IR Theory. Journal of Documentation. 1996 March; 52(1): 3-50. ISSN: 0022-0418; CODEN: JDOCAS.

INGWERSEN, PETER. 1999. Cognitive Information Retrieval. In: Williams, Martha E., ed. Annual Review of Information Science and Technology: Volume 34. Medford, NJ: Information Today, Inc. for the American Society for Information Science; 1999. 3-51. ISSN: 0066-4200; ISBN: 1-57387-093-5; CODEN: ARISBC.

JACOB, ELIN K.; SHAW, DEBORA. 1998. Sociocognitive Perspectives on Representation. In: Williams, Martha E., ed. Annual Review of Information Science and Technology: Volume 33. Medford, NJ: Information Today, Inc. for the American Society for Information Science; 1998. 131-185. ISSN: 0066-4200; ISBN: 1-57387-065-X; CODEN: ARISBC.

JENTSCH, FLORIAN; BARNETT, JOHN; BOWERS, CLINT A. 1999. Who Is Flying This Plane Anyway? What Mishaps Tell Us about Crew Member Role Assignment and Air Crew Situation Awareness. Human Factors. 1999; 41(1): 1-14. ISSN: 0018-7208.

KRUKS, SONIA. 1990. Situation and Human Existence: Freedom, Subjectivity, and Society. London, UK: Unwin Hyman; 1990. 215p. ISBN: 0-04-445456-2.

KUHLTHAU, CAROL C. 1993a. A Principle of Uncertainty for Information Seeking. Journal of Documentation. 1993; 49: 339-355. ISSN: 0022-0418.

KUHLTHAU, CAROL C. 1993b. Seeking Meaning: A Process Approach to Library and Information Services. Norwood, NJ: Ablex Publishing Corp.; 1993. 199p. ISBN: 0-89391-968-3.

LAVE, JEAN; WENGER, ETIENNE. 1991. Situated Learning: Legitimate Peripheral Participation. Cambridge, UK: Cambridge University Press; 1991. 138p. ISBN: 0-521-42374-0.

LIN, SHIN-JENG; BELKIN, NICHOLAS J. 2000. Modeling Multiple Information Seeking Episodes. In: Kraft, Donald H., ed. ASIS 2000: Proceedings of the American Society for Information Science (ASIS) 63rd Annual Meeting: Volume 37; 2000 November 12-16; Chicago, IL. Medford, NJ: Information Today, Inc. for ASIS; 2000. 133-147. ISSN: 0044-7870; ISBN: 1-57387-108-7; CODEN: PAISDQ.

LUCKMANN, THOMAS. 1978. Phenomenology and Sociology. New York, NY: Penguin Books; 1978. 390p. ISBN: 0-14-080814-0.

MANTOVANI, GIUSEPPE; BOLZONI, MIRCO. 1994. Analysing and Evaluating Multi-Actor Multi-Goal Systems in Use: Social Contexts and Participation in Three Vocational Guidance Systems (VGS). Behaviour and Information Technology. 1994 May-June; 13(3): 201-215. ISSN: 0144-929X.

MEAD, GEORGE HERBERT. 1934. Mind, Self and Society from the Standpoint of a Social Behaviorist. Chicago, IL: University of Chicago Press; 1934. 400p. ISBN: 0-226-51667-9.

MILLS, C. WRIGHT. 1940. Situated Actions and Vocabularies of Motive. American Sociological Review. 1940; 5: 904-913. ISSN: 0003-1224.

MIWA, MAKIKO. 2000. Use of Human Intermediation in Information Problem-Solving: A Users' Perspective. Syracuse, NY: Syracuse University;

2000. 458p. (Ph.D. dissertation). Available from: UMI, Ann Arbor, MI. (UMI order no. 9977391).

MOKROS, HARTMUT B.; MULLINS, LYNN S.; SARACEVIC, TEFKO. 1995. Practice and Personhood in Professional Interaction: Social Identities and Information Needs. Library and Information Science Research. 1995; 17: 237-257. ISSN: 0740-8188.

NG, KWONG BOR; NORDLIE, RAGNAR; PARIS, C. GREGORY; PARK, SOYEON; RIEH, SOO YOUNG; SAVAGE, PAMELA; BELKIN, NICHOLAS J. 1996. On the Relevance of "Structures of the Life-World" to Problems of Information Science. New Brunswick, NJ: School of Communication, Information and Library Studies Research Report; 1996. Available from: the authors.

PAISLEY, WILLIAM J. 1968. Information Needs and Uses. In: Cuadra, Carlos, ed. Annual Review of Information Science and Technology: Volume 3. Chicago, IL: Encyclopaedia Britannica, Inc. for the American Society for Information Science; 1968. 1-30. LC: 66-25096.

PARK, TAEMIN KIM. 1994. Toward a Theory of User-Based Relevance: A Call for a New Paradigm of Inquiry. Journal of the American Society for Information Science. 1994; 45(3): 135-141. ISSN: 0002-8231; CODEN: AISJB6.

PERVIN, LAWRENCE A. 1989. Person, Situation, Interactions: The History of a Controversy and a Discussion of Theoretical Models. Academy of Management Review. 1989; 14: 350-360. ISSN: 0363-7425.

PETTIGREW, KAREN E.; FIDEL, RAYA; BRUCE, HARRY. 2000. Conceptual Frameworks in Information Behavior. In: Williams, Martha E., ed. Annual Review of Information Science and Technology. Volume 35. Medford, NJ: Information Today, Inc. for the American Society for Information Science; 2000. 43-78. ISSN: 0066-4200; ISBN: 1-57387-115-X. CODEN: ARISBC.

REID, JANE. 1999. A New, Task-Oriented Paradigm for Information Retrieval: Implications for Evaluation of Information Retrieval Systems. In: Aparac, Tatjana; Saracevic, Tefko; Ingwersen, Peter; Vakkari, Pertti, eds. Digital Libraries: Interdisciplinary Concepts, Challenges and Opportunities: Proceedings of the 3rd International Conference on Conceptions of Library and Information Science; 1999 May 23-26; Dubrovnik, Croatia. Lokve, Croatia: Naklada Benja; 1999. 97-108. ISBN: 953-6003-37-6.

ROCHBERG-HALTON, EUGENE. 1982. Situation, Structure, and the Context of Meaning. Sociological Quarterly. 1982 Autumn; 23(4): 455-476. ISSN: 0038-0253.

SALAS, EDUARDO; PRINCE, CAROLYN; BAKER, DAVID P.; SHRESTHA, LISA. 1995. Situation Awareness in Team Performance: Implications for Measurement and Training. Human Factors. 1995 March; 37(1): 123-136. ISSN: 0018-7208.

SARACEVIC, TEFKO. 1996a. Modeling Interaction in Information Retrieval (IR): A Review and Proposal. In: Hardin, Steve, ed. ASIS '96: Proceedings of the American Society for Information Science (ASIS) 59th Annual Meeting: Volume 33; 1996 October 21-24; Baltimore, MD. Medford, NJ: Information Today, Inc. for ASIS; 1996. 3-9. ISSN: 0044-7870; ISBN: 1-57387-037-4; CODEN: PAISDQ.

SARACEVIC, TEFKO. 1996b. Relevance Reconsidered '96. In: Ingwersen, Peter; Pors, Niels Ole, eds. CoLIS 2: Proceedings of the 2nd International Conference on Conceptions of Library and Information Science: Integration in Perspective; 1996 October 13-16; Copenhagen, Denmark. Copenhagen, Denmark: Royal School of Librarianship; 1996. 201-218. ISBN: 87-7415-260-2.

SARTER, NADINE; WOODS, DAVID. 1991. Situation Awareness: A Critical But Ill-Defined Phenomenon. International Journal of Aviation Psychology. 1991; 1: 45-57. ISSN: 1050-8414.

SARTER, NADINE; WOODS, DAVID. 1995. How in the World Did We Ever Get Into That Mode? Mode Error and Awareness in Supervisory Control. Human Factors. 1995 March; 37(1): 5-19. ISSN: 0018-7208.

SAVOLAINEN, REIJO. 1995. Everyday Life Information Seeking: Approaching Information Seeking in the Context of "Way of Life." Library and Information Science Research. 1995; 17: 259-294. ISSN: 0740-8188.

SCHAMBER, LINDA. 1991. Users' Criteria for Evaluation in Multimedia Information Seeking and Use Situations. Syracuse, NY: Syracuse University; 1991. 341p. (Ph.D. dissertation). Available from: UMI, Ann Arbor, MI. (UMI order no. 9214390).

SCHAMBER, LINDA. 1994. Relevance and Information Behavior. In: Williams, Martha E., ed. Annual Review of Information Science and Technology: Volume 29. Medford, NJ: Learned Information, Inc. for the American Society for Information Science; 1994. 3-48. ISSN: 0066-4200; ISBN: 0-938734-91-1; CODEN: ARISBC.

SCHAMBER, LINDA; EISENBERG, MICHAEL B.; NILAN, MICHAEL S. 1990. A Re-Examination of Relevance: Toward a Dynamic, Situational Definition. Information Processing & Management. 1990; 26(6): 755-776. ISSN: 0306-4573.

SCHUTZ, ALFRED; LUCKMANN, THOMAS. 1973. The Structures of the Life-World. Evanston, IL: Northwestern University Press; 1973. 335p. OCLC: 22499349.

SKOPEC, ERIC WILLIAM. 1986. Situational Interviewing. New York, NY: Harper & Row; 1986. 172p. ISBN: 0-06-046245-0.

SMITH, KIP; HANCOCK, P.A. 1995. Situation Awareness Is Adaptive, Externally Directed Consciousness. Human Factors. 1995 March; 37(1): 137-148. ISSN: 0018-7208.

SNOW, RICHARD E. 1994. A Person-Situation Interaction Theory of Intelligence in Outline. In: Demetriou, Andreas; Efklides, Anastasia, eds. Intelligence, Mind, and Reasoning: Structure and Development. Amsterdam, The Netherlands: North-Holland; 1994. 11-28. ISBN: 0-444-89714-3.

SONNENWALD, DIANE H. 1999. Evolving Perspectives of Human Behaviour: Contexts, Situations, Social Networks and Information Horizons. In: Wilson, Thomas D.; Allen, David K., eds. Exploring the Contexts of Information Behaviour: Proceedings of the 2nd International Conference on Research in Information Needs, Seeking and Use in Different Contexts; 1998

August 13-15; Sheffield, UK. London, UK: Taylor Graham; 1999. 176-190. ISBN: 0-947568-75-1.

SONNENWALD, DIANE H.; PIERCE, LINDA G. 2000. Information Behavior in Dynamic Group Work Contexts: Interwoven Situational Awareness, Dense Social Networks and Contested Collaboration in Command and Control. Information Processing & Management. 2000; 36(3): 461-479. ISSN: 0306-4573; CODEN: IPMADK.

SPINK, AMANDA. 1996. A Multiple Search Session Model of End-User Behavior: An Exploratory Study. Journal of the American Society for Information Science. 1996; 46: 603-609. ISSN: 0002-8231; CODEN: AISJB6.

SPINK, AMANDA; GREISDORF, HOWARD; BATEMAN, JUDY. 1998. From Highly Relevant to Not Relevant: Examining Different Regions of Relevance. Information Processing & Management. 1998; 34(5): 599-621. ISSN: 0306-4573; CODEN: IPMADK.

STERNBERG, ROBERT J.; WAGNER, RICHARD K. 1994. Mind in Context: Interactionist Perspectives on Human Intelligence. Cambridge, UK: Cambridge University Press; 1994. 245p. ISBN: 0-521-41114-9.

STOUT, RENEE J.; CANNON-BOWERS, JANIS A.; SALAS, EDUARDO; MILANOVICH, DANA M. 1999. Planning, Shared Mental Models, and Coordinated Performance: An Empirical Link Is Established. Human Factors. 1999; 41(1): 61-71. ISSN: 0018-7208.

SUCHMAN, LUCY A. 1987. Plans and Situated Actions: The Problem of Human-Machine Communication. Cambridge, UK: Cambridge University Press; 1987. 203p. ISBN: 0-521-33739-9.

SUGAR, WILLIAM. 1995. User-Centered Perspective on Information Retrieval Research and Analysis Methods. In: Williams, Martha E., ed. Annual Review of Information Science and Technology: Volume 30. Medford, NJ: Information Today, Inc. for the American Society for Information Science; 1995. 77-109. ISSN: 0066-4200; ISBN: 1-57387-019-6; CODEN: ARISBC.

TAYLOR, ROBERT S. 1968. Question Negotiation and Information-Seeking in Libraries. College and Research Libraries. 1968; 29(3): 178-194. ISSN: 0010-0870.

TAYLOR, ROBERT S. 1991. Information Use Environments. In: Dervin, Brenda; Voigt, Melvin, J., eds. Progress in Communication Sciences: Volume 10. Norwood, NJ: Ablex; 1991. 217-255. ISBN: 0-89391-645-5.

UTTING, KENNETH; YANKELOVICH, NICOLE. 1989. Context and Orientation in Hypermedia Networks. ACM Transactions on Information Systems. 1989; 7(1): 58-84. ISSN: 0734-2047.

VAKKARI, PERTTI. 1997. Information Seeking in Context: A Challenging Metatheory. In: Vakkari, Pertti; Savolainen, Reijo; Dervin, Brenda, eds. Information Seeking in Context: Proceedings of an International Conference on Research in Information Needs, Seeking and Use in Different Contexts; 1996 August 14-16; Tampere, Finland. London, UK: Taylor Graham; 1997. 451-464. ISBN: 0-947568-71-9.

VAKKARI, PERTTI. 1999. Task Complexity, Information Types, Search Strategies and Relevance: Integrating Studies on Information Seeking and Retrieval. In: Wilson, Thomas D.; Allen, David K., eds. Exploring the Contexts of Information Behaviour: Proceedings of the 2nd International Conference on Research in Information Needs, Seeking and Use in Different Contexts; 1998 August 13-15; Sheffield, UK. London, UK: Taylor Graham; 1999. 35-54. ISBN: 0-947568-75-1.

VAN DIJK, TEUN A.; KINTSCH, WALTER. 1983. Strategies of Discourse Comprehension. New York, NY: Academic Press; 1983. 418p. ISBN: 0-12-712050-5.

VAN RIJSBERGEN, C. J.; LALMAS, M. 1996. Information Calculus for Information Retrieval. Journal of the American Society for Information Science. 1996; 47(5): 385-398. ISSN: 0002-8231; CODEN: AISJB6.

WANG, PEILING. 1997. User's Information Needs at Different Stages of a Research Project: A Cognitive View. In: Vakkari, Pertti; Savolainen, Reijo; Dervin, Brenda, eds. Information Seeking in Context: Proceedings of an International Conference on Research in Information Needs, Seeking and Use in Different Contexts; 1996 August 14-16; Tampere, Finland. London, UK: Taylor Graham; 1997. 307-318. ISBN: 0-947568-71-9.

WANG, PEILING; HAWK, WILLIAM B.; TENOPIR, CAROL. 2000. Users' Interaction with World Wide Web Resources: An Exploratory Study Using a Holistic Approach. Information Processing & Management. 2000; 36: 229-251. ISSN: 0306-4573; CODEN: IPMADK.

WELLENS, A. RODNEY. 1993. Group Situation Awareness and Distributed Decision Making: From Military to Civilian Applications. In: Castellan, John N., Jr. Individual and Group Decision Making: Current Issues. Hillsdale, NJ: Lawrence Erlbaum Associates; 1993. 267-291. ISBN: 0-8058-1090-0.

WERSIG, GERNOT. 1979. The Problematic Situation as a Basic Concept of Information Science in the Framework of Social Sciences: A Reply to N. Belkin. In: Theoretical Problems of Informatics: New Trends in Informatics and Its Terminology. Moscow, Russia: International Federation for Documentation; 1979. 48-57. OCLC: 7978306.

WILSON, PATRICK. 1973. Situational Relevance. Information Storage and Retrieval. 1973; 9: 457-471. ISSN: 0020-0271.

WILSON, THOMAS D. 1981. On User Studies and Information Needs. Journal of Documentation. 1981; 37: 3-15. ISSN: 0022-0418.

WILSON, THOMAS D. 1999. Exploring Models of Information Behaviour: The 'Uncertainty' Project. In: Wilson, Thomas D.; Allen, David K., eds. Exploring the Contexts of Information Behaviour: Proceedings of the 2nd International Conference on Research in Information Needs, Seeking and Use in Different Contexts; 1998 August 13-15; Sheffield, UK. London, UK: Taylor Graham; 1999. 55-66. ISBN: 0-947568-75-1.

XIE, HONG. 1997. Planned and Situated Aspects in Interactive IR: Patterns of User Interactive Intentions and Information Seeking Strategies. In: Schwartz, Candy; Rorvig, Mark E., eds. ASIS '97: Proceedings of the American Society for Information Science (ASIS) 60th Annual Meeting: Volume 34; 1997 November 1-6; Washington, DC. Medford, NJ: Information Today, Inc. for ASIS; 1997. 101-110. ISSN: 0044-7870; ISBN: 1-57387-048-X; CODEN: PAISDQ.

XIE, HONG. 1998. Planned and Situated Aspects in Interactive IR: Patterns of User Interactive Intentions and Information Seeking Strategies. New

Brunswick, NJ: Rutgers University, School of Communication, Information and Library Studies; 1998. 210p. (Ph.D. dissertation). Available from: UMI, Ann Arbor, MI. (UMI order no. 9915495).

XIE, HONG. 2000. Shifts of Interactive Intentions and Information-Seeking Strategies in Interactive Information Retrieval. Journal of the American Society for Information Science. 2000; 51(9): 841-857. ISSN: 0002-8231; CODEN: AISJB6.

ZERUBAVEL, EVIATAR. 1997. Social Mindscapes: An Invitation to Cognitive Sociology. Cambridge, MA: Harvard University Press; 1997. 164p. ISBN: 0-674-81391-X.

# 2  Conceptual Frameworks in Information Behavior

**KAREN E. PETTIGREW, RAYA FIDEL, and HARRY BRUCE**
University of Washington

## INTRODUCTION

This chapter traces major conceptual developments in the information behavior literature since the user-centered paradigm shift observed by DERVIN & NILAN in 1986. In their landmark *ARIST* review, Dervin and Nilan emphasized calls in the post-1978 literature for conceptual enrichment within the field. Acknowledging that research studies have not informed practice, they noted calls for borrowing theory from the social sciences, for developing theories and conceptual frameworks, for examining basic assumptions and definitions, and for improving the predictive value of theory. They followed their insightful observation of a paradigmatic shift from a system/resource approach to an alternative one, characterized by its focus on constructive, active users, subjective information, situationality, holistic views of experience, internal cognition, systematic individuality, and qualitative research with three examples of scholarship that represent promising roads—namely, the user-values or value-added approach of TAYLOR (1984; 1985) and MACMULLIN & TAYLOR, the Sense-Making approach of DERVIN (1999a), and the anomalous-states-of-knowledge (ASK) approach of BELKIN ET AL. (1982a; 1982b). Documenting the field's quantum and revolutionary conceptual leap and achievement of critical mass, they challenged researchers to continue inventing new ways of looking at users and linking systems to them (DERVIN & NILAN, p. 24).

As HEWINS confirmed in her 1990 *ARIST* review, there is little doubt that a user-centered approach to studying information behavior has pervaded the literature and has begun underscoring the design and management of information systems. She also remarked on the prevalence of the cognitive approach for framing information behavior prob-

*Annual Review of Information Science and Technology (ARIST)*, Volume 35, 2001
Martha E. Williams, Editor
Published for the American Society for Information Science and Technology (ASIST)
By Information Today, Inc., Medford, NJ

lems, but have we invented new approaches to understanding users and systems? What roads have we taken toward developing a theoretical core complete with common assumptions and definitions and improved predictive value? In this chapter we review advancements in the development of conceptual frameworks for studying information behavior.

Conceptual development and research interest in information behavior is undoubtedly increasing. Since 1996 three conferences in the series INFORMATION SEEKING IN CONTEXT were held in Europe (Tampere, Finland, 1996; Sheffield, United Kingdom, 1998; and Göteborg, Sweden, 2000), and a fourth is planned for Edinburgh in 2002. In addition to drawing researchers from throughout the world, the conference series emphasizes doctoral research and holds a preconference workshop where students gain critical feedback on their dissertations from established scholars. In 1999, the American Society for Information Science (ASIS) established a special interest group entitled "Information Needs, Seeking, and Use" (SIGUSE). In 1999 the journal *Information Processing & Management* published a special issue on "Information Seeking in Context," which was guest edited by KUHLTHAU & VAKKARI. A special issue on everyday-life information seeking, which is being edited by Charles Cole and Amanda Spink, is scheduled for 2001 in the journal *Library & Information Science Research*.

While WILSON (1997; 1999a; 1999b; 2000) recently published several seminal overviews of information behavior, debate lingers over whether "information behavior" is an appropriate term for describing a body of academic study. In December 1999 subscribers of the listserv JESSE debated whether one should use the term information behavior to refer to the study of information seeking and use. Arguments for using the term were based largely on observations that the field has broadened to include such concepts as information need and information giving, in addition to the basic concepts of information seeking and information use. Others argued that the term information behavior is inappropriate because people outside the field might associate it too closely with the behaviorist paradigm in psychology and thus not consider the broad range of contextual factors of interest to information behavior research. Others further asserted that the term information behavior is incorrect, grammatically speaking, because information does not behave; only people do. The term, however, seems to have received general acceptance as it is now widely used in the titles of journal articles and academic courses. While researchers use various definitions of information behavior, for our purposes we define it as the study of how people need, seek, give, and use information in different contexts, including the workplace and everyday living. This definition is consistent with Wilson, who defines information behavior as "the totality of human behavior in relation to sources and channels of information, including both active and passive information seeking, and information use" (WILSON, 2000, p. 49). According to Wilson, information-seeking behavior, information searching behavior, and information use behavior are subcategories of information behavior.

## WHERE'S THE THEORY?

While bibliometric studies largely suggest that information science (IS), in general, is atheoretical, with theory mentioned in only 10–21% of the journal literature (FEEHAN ET AL.; JÄRVELIN & VAKKARI, 1990; NOUR; PERITZ), interesting variations occur if one considers only the information behavior literature. JULIEN, for example, in her study of the 1990–1994 journal literature, reported that 28% of the 165 articles sampled were theoretically grounded, meaning they were "based on a coherent and explicit framework of assumptions, definitions, and propositions that, taken together, have some explanatory power" (JULIEN, p. 56). However, in a related study, JULIEN & DUGGAN reported that of the 300 research studies sampled from 1984–1989 and 1995–1998 only 18.3% were based on theory, which they considered very low. Yet, their results do suggest that theory use may be increasing, given the finding of JÄRVELIN & VAKKARI (1993) that only 6–8% of research articles on information seeking sampled for the years 1965, 1975, and 1985 employed a conceptual framework. Julien also reported significant relationships regarding author type and journal type where both researchers and scholarly journals (as opposed to practitioners and professional journals) were more likely to produce or contain theoretically grounded publications.

Most recently, evidence of an increase in the use of conceptual frameworks within information behavior research was discussed by other authors. With regard to IS overall, PETTIGREW & MCKECHNIE reported that theory was discussed in 34.1% of the 1,160 articles published between 1993 and 1998 in six key journals, which is a substantial increase from the 10–21% reported in past studies. Their examination of different subfields revealed that studies of information behavior ranked second, after those about information science in general, in the degree to which authors discussed theory. Of the 95 information behavior papers examined, 58.9% used theory with 1.99 theory incidents per article. When only those articles using theory were considered, the average theory occurrence within the information behavior subset rose to 3.37. In a related work, MCKECHNIE ET AL. reported that the vast majority of theories cited in information behavior research were from the social sciences (64.4%), followed by information science (28.7%), the natural sciences (5.9%), and the humanities (1.0%) (similar results were found for IS in general). The prevalent use of social science theory suggests that researchers embraced Dervin and Nilan's earlier suggestion. Of particular interest is that new information behavior theories were proposed by 15 authors. However, their citation analysis of the two most frequently cited information behavior theories—Kuhlthau's information search process and Dervin's Sense-Making approach—suggests that information behavior theories have not yet had much impact outside information science. They concluded that substantive theoretical work is being undertaken within information behavior and that a paradigmatic core is showing early signs of maturation (KUHLTHAU; DERVIN, 1999a).

This chapter reviews these new developments in three sections: 1) Cognitive Approaches covers those that examine the individual as the main driving force behind information behavior; 2) Social Approaches examines frameworks that focus on the social context; and 3) Multifaceted Approaches deals with those that consider multiple types of context, such as the cognitive, social, and organizational context.

## COGNITIVE APPROACHES

In 1986 when Dervin and Nilan published their review of the literature on "Information Needs and Uses," the authors noted a "call for focusing on cognitive behavior and developing cognitive approaches to assessing information needs and uses" (DERVIN & NILAN, p. 15). Since the mid 1980s numerous researchers have identified themselves with the cognitive viewpoint and in so doing, have provided a new focus for developments in theory and concept definition for the discipline of information science. Research has occurred in a number of fields within the discipline but an area fundamentally affected by this orientation over the past decade is information behavior.

Not all researchers share precisely the same definition of the cognitive viewpoint, but there is, as Belkin has suggested, a kernel of meaning that is common to most. The essence of the viewpoint and its importance to information research is that it ". . . explicitly considers that the states of knowledge, beliefs and so on of human beings (or information processing devices) mediate (or interact with) that which they receive/ perceive or produce" (BELKIN, pp. 11-12).

For the purposes of this *ARIST* review, therefore, the cognitive viewpoint is defined as an approach and set of constructs for understanding information behavior, which focuses fundamentally upon attributes of the individual. This view of information behavior endorses research that examines the cognitive and emotional motivations for information behavior that carry across contexts or are independent of context. The cognitive viewpoint does not study the context of information behavior and is in this way distinguished from the social cognitive (discussed later in this review) where context (particularly attributes of the social and organizational context) becomes the focus for understanding information behavior.

At the heart of the cognitive viewpoint rests the concept of knowledge structures. This concept has been borrowed from the cognitive sciences. Knowledge structures are the sets of concept relationships that comprise each individual's model of the world. It is this model of the world that is seen to mediate an individual's information behavior. Each person will apply the knowledge structures that are required to perceive, interpret, modify, or transfer information. Information behavior research from the cognitive viewpoint acknowledges the thesis that ". . . any processing of information—whether perceptual (such as perceiving an object) or symbolic (such as understanding a sentence)—is mediated by a system of categories or concepts, which for the information processor, constitutes a representation or a model of his world" (DE MEY, p. 4). Information behavior research that applies the cognitive viewpoint is therefore interested in studying how an individual will apply his or her model or view of the world to the processes of needing, seeking, giving, and using information.

Much credit for transforming our understanding of the trigger to information behavior (information need), from an abstract concept that can be clearly articulated by the information user and systematically interpreted by the information mechanism to an intrinsic and somewhat unspecifiable anomaly in the user's model of the world, has been attributed to TAYLOR (1968). His model, though not explicitly identified as such, can be seen as a cognitive approach inasmuch as it is concerned with notions of "incompleteness in [the user's] picture of the world" and an implied tendency on the part of the user toward "cognitive consistency or balance." It is therefore cited in the work of those who explicitly identify their orientation with the cognitive viewpoint. In information behavior research, the cognitive viewpoint focuses fundamentally upon the individual, on understanding the way each person thinks and behaves in response to information needs.

By the end of the 1980s where the focus of this review begins, numerous examples of information research focused on the user as an individual, cognitive being and on the behaviors associated with information processing. The theoretical framework, called the cognitive viewpoint, and the focus on the individual as a unique information user was well accepted and widely applied, leading Belkin to state that there was strong evidence to support the claim that ". . . taking the cognitive viewpoint of information science can lead to highly beneficial results, in a variety of areas. . . " (BELKIN, pp. 14-15). Belkin further speculated, ". . . the cognitive viewpoint might serve as a means for integrating and relating work in a variety of areas of information science to one another, and therefore provide the structure for a unified and effective information science" (BELKIN, pp. 14-15).

To some extent, Belkin's statements have proved prophetic. The 1990s application of the cognitive viewpoint in terms of information behavior research has been characterized by an increased awareness among information researchers that more explicit statements regarding the theoretical orientation of the work being undertaken will enhance research in the discipline. In this way, we see numerous studies in which researchers promote the cognitive approach to studying information behavior by explicating the scope of their study within this construct.

This research has focused on the information user as a unique individual but has also sought to identify patterns in information behavior that can be applied to the development of information retrieval systems. The work of ELLIS, appearing at the very end of the 1980s, is an example. Ellis examined the information-seeking behavior of academic social scientists working at the University of Sheffield and identified six characteristics that he claims can provide a basis for system design and evaluation. The six features of the model he called starting, chaining, browsing, differentiating, monitoring, and extracting. Starting is looking for information in a new area or on a new topic. Chaining is searching using the technique of following citation connections between materials. Differentiating is selecting information sources based on their orientation and the audience for whom the source was intended. Monitoring refers to the continuous surveying of the developments in a field of study. Extracting is the behavior of going through a particular source selectively to identify relevant material from that source. Ellis explained in detail how each of these six features of his model could be used in connection with the design and evaluation of information systems.

The importance of Ellis's work from a cognitive point of view is that it reinforces the individual way in which these features can interact for any person seeking information. These interactions will depend, in Ellis's view, on unique attributes of the individual seeking information at a particular point in time. Ellis based his model of information seeking on his observations of people engaged in literature searching. We now know that the 1990s became the era of Web searching. This led CHOO ET AL. to reexamine and to extend the Ellis model in light of any new attributes to individual searching of information that may have emerged. The researchers worked with Ellis's generic features (starting, chaining, browsing, differentiating, monitoring, and extracting) to elaborate what happened within each feature when an individual searched the Web. Each of these characteristics of information seeking on the

Web was then related to scanning modes or motivations (undirected viewing, conditioned viewing, informal search, and formal search) that had first been formulated by AGUILAR. Choo et al. gathered data from 34 participants from seven companies using a questionnaire survey, a Web tracker application, and a personal interview. They identified and categorized 61 information-seeking episodes, which were then analyzed according to where they might fit on the framework created by cross tabulating Ellis's generic information-seeking features with Aguilar's formulation of search modes. They found the framework effective as a tool for analyzing and elaborating the Web searching behavior of individuals. They also found that data from their sample of searchers indicated that searching modes are characterized by particular features: information seeking motivated by undirected viewing commonly applies differentiating and browsing; conditioned viewing results in differentiating, browsing, and monitoring; informal searches use differentiating and localized extracting; and formal searches apply thorough extracting.

A landmark study published at the beginning of the 1990s by KUHLTHAU also set the scene across the decade for researchers within the cognitive framework. Kuhlthau's work represented a culmination of earlier research with collaborators Turock and Belvin (KUHLTHAU ET AL.) on facilitating information seeking through cognitive models of the search process. The study incorporated the theories of Kelly (personal construct theory), Taylor (levels of need), and Belkin (ASK hypothesis, based on the cognitive view of information seeking) to formulate a model of the information search process. This model presented three realms of activity—physical, affective, and cognitive—and was based on five studies conducted by Kuhlthau. The first of these studies was small in scale and in a naturalistic setting. This study was followed by two longitudinal studies and two quantitative studies. The studies covered a range of users, including college students, secondary school students, and public library users.

Kuhlthau identified six stages in the information search process, incorporating the attributes of feelings, thoughts, and actions for the individual information searcher into each stage. The first stage of the information search process is initiation, where the individual is confronted with the task of recognizing his or her need for information. Then follows selection, where the task is to identify and to select the general topic to be investigated. The third stage of Kuhlthau's model is exploration, where the information searcher is attempting to extend his or her understanding by exploring information on the general topic of the search. The fourth stage is formulation. The task is to form a focus from the information that the searcher has thus far encountered in the searching process. The next stage is collection, when the searcher begins to gather information from the system being searched related to the focused topic. The information search process is completed by the stage of presentation. Here the findings or outcomes of the search are used. The importance of Kuhlthau's model to the cognitive approach to studying information behavior is its explication of the various attributes of the individual that correspond to each stage of the search process but are independent of context. The feelings of uncertainty, confusion, optimism, frustration, relief, and satisfaction cut across searching context. Each is also a fundamentally unique response by an individual, at a point in time, engaging in a particular information-seeking episode.

Kuhlthau's work was widely cited by information behavior researchers through the 1990s. Building on Kuhlthau's work on uncertainty, for example, YOON & NILAN advocated a cognitive-linguistic framework that utilizes Dervin's Sense-Making approach for understanding the exchange of meaning within information behavior. VAKKARI (2000) also validated and elaborated Kuhlthau's model through his investigation of the information behavior of students writing a research proposal for a master's thesis. He found that Kuhlthau's model predicted the information behavior of the students that he observed in his study. The students in his sample followed the stages in Kuhlthau's model of the search process.

Kuhlthau was attempting to capture the whole experience of the information seeker and so, too, was BROWN. She used an organizational and behavioral framework for her model and identified three dimensions of information-seeking behavior that she found in the literature: the conditions, the context, and the process. The model presented attempted to display the interaction among these dimensions. The conditions of information behavior were exposure and discrimination (evaluation). Exposure refers to individuals' constantly being subjected to stimuli that, depending on strength or pertinence, may achieve sensory registration. Not all information is processed. The individual brain needs a medium level of arousal for information reception to occur. Once this information (stimulus) has gained cognitive attention, it becomes thoughts that can be used immediately or held for later evaluation and use. The context of information-seeking behavior that Brown represented as the backbone of her model consists of attributes of the individual information seeker (the self, role, and environment). The context is the backdrop against which the researcher observes individual information behaviors. It is not the object of study. The central element of the context in Brown's model was the individual's self, that is, the individual physiological, affective, and cognitive needs of the user. For Brown, the beginning point in the process of information seeking is the cognitive state arising from the preconceived need. The individual then enters a process of need evaluation, whereby the need is recognized as satisfied, or a gap is realized. The decision to search for information involves identifying where to seek information and how to seek it (source preference, searching behaviors, and searching strategies). Brown also reviewed a range of barriers that the individual confronts when engaging in information behavior, such as organizational structure, the physical environment, organizational function, personality, and imposed search strategies.

Brown's model fits the cognitive framework for this review because it focuses on the individual and explains manifestations of information behavior according to individual attributes both cognitive and affective. It follows that these attributes develop and change as a person grows older. Brown, therefore, claimed that information seeking as a behavior develops and improves throughout an individual's life in response to the changes that occur in the attributes that affect an individual's information behavior. This view of information seeking as a learning process or development process for the user also appears in BRUCE. Bruce explored techniques for observing and measuring what individuals think as well as what they do when searching for the information that they need. One of the key criticisms of information behavior research that focuses on individuals is that this cannot be achieved systematically. The general category for this criticism in Dervin and Nilan's review referred to research on the individual as chaotic. Bruce attempted to formulate techniques that could address this criticism. His study applied the cognitive viewpoint in IS as a conceptual framework for exploring the dynamism of relevance estimation by individual users as they moved from needing information (the problem state) to finding and using information (problem resolution). Bruce introduced the technique of magnitude estimation to map data representing the knowledge structures that subjects used for relevance estimation at various points in the information-seeking process observed.

YERBURY & PARKER also attempted to tap into the cognitive structures of individuals as they search for information. In this case the researchers focused on the behavior of information searching by individuals who were novices or inexperienced. The construct of information searching that they proposed modeled information searching as interpersonal communication. The researchers viewed information searching as a communication between the individual searcher and the information services used and the resources evaluated. Therefore, they used a talk-through protocol to observe how individuals use "familiar structures" to facilitate their information searching. The familiar structures that were revealed were metaphors. Yerbury and Parker found that individuals used metaphor to help them deal with the unknown or unfamiliar through credible association. Other researchers have used credible association more as a mechanism for labeling or characterizing information-seeking behaviors. SANDSTROM, for example, proposed an optimal foraging approach to understanding information behavior that was based on evolutionary ecology. Her behaviorist approach advocated using both bibliometric and ethnographic methods for studying the decision-making processes of scholars. BATES (1989) also employed an ecological theme in her berrypicking model that characterizes how users search online and in other environments. Challenging the classic model of information retrieval, Bates argued that the search process is best characterized as evolving, that is, users search for information a "bit-at-a-time" using various techniques such as chaining and scanning. Bates's model has been widely cited in the literature, and she has offered many concrete suggestions for how it might be implemented to improve the design of information retrieval systems.

COLE was also interested in identifying patterns in the cognitive activity that occurs for individuals during the information-seeking process. His research built on the work of Kuhlthau, Belkin, and Dervin. The basic assumption of his study was that information is subjectively constructed by each individual, a piece at a time (rather like Bates's "bit-at-a-time"). He proposed a five-stage model of the information process based on data that he collected from 45 doctoral students: stage 1: opening of information process; stage 2: representational (cognitive) activity; stage 3: corroborating evidence sought and found; stage 4: closing of process; and stage 5: effect of process. Cole saw a progression of awareness or consciousness of "information" occurring for the individual information seeker as each stage of the information-seeking process is completed. The outcome of this process is that the individual's knowledge structure(s) are modified. Cole also introduced a notion of stage zero, an initiating condition that is preawareness. The notion of gap as a trigger to information behavior was discussed, but the data gathered from the sample used in this study also suggested that there may be a threshold or optimal size of gap that triggers sufficient level of awareness to warrant action by the individual searcher. This is supportive of one of the general conditions for information-seeking behavior identified in Brown's model and discussed earlier in this review—optimal arousal for information reception.

The research of VAKKARI (1999) also focused on the conditions that arouse information behavior—attributes of an individual's perception of the information problems to be resolved. He linked information behavior to task complexity and the structure of the problem an individual is attempting to deal with. Vakkari examined information actions in work environments but did not take into account actual features of the work environment. The keys for Vakkari were: task complexity, which was the degree of predeterminability of the task to be performed by the individual; problem structure, which related to how well the information requirements and desired outcomes were known; and prior knowledge. He also emphasized the importance of the integration of new observations or information with prior knowledge.

Many of the authors we cite in this section were attempting to provide a model of information behavior based on research observations of individuals but generalizable across contexts. At the end of the 1990s WILSON (1999b) consolidated a number of these models in an attempt to present his own revised model of information behavior, which is a nested model. Wilson identifies information behavior as a general field of investigation; information-seeking behavior is then seen as a subset of this field while information search behavior is seen as a subset of information-seeking behavior. Like others who apply the cognitive viewpoint, Wilson attempted to articulate those attributes of the individual that explain information behaviors independent of variations in context. Wilson also introduced three theoretical perspectives that may be useful for the modeling of information behavior: stress/coping theory, risk/reward theory, and social learning theory. He saw human communication behavior as the way to understanding the cognitive dimensions of information behavior.

In contrast, ERDELEZ focused on accidental information discovery rather than on directed information seeking. She coined the term information encountering to describe the distinctive type of information acquisition that can occur when an individual is browsing or scanning the information environment (undirected viewing). The researcher used an exploratory research design (qualitative data collection—survey and in-depth interviewing) to explore the characteristics of information encountering according to: (1) the individual who encountered information, (2) the environment in which information was encountered, (3) the information that was encountered, and (4) the information need addressed with information that was encountered. She studied the individual behavioral, cognitive, and affective elements of the information encountering experienced by an individual. Erdelez found that information encountering was an integral part of the browsing and information-seeking activities performed by her study respondents. She categorized her subjects as superencounterers, encounterers, occasional encounterers, and nonencounterers. The key characteristic of information encountering is, of course, that it is an entirely random and unpredictable information behavior.

The work of information behavior researchers identified with the cognitive approach has therefore focused on explaining variations in information behavior according to characteristics or attributes of the individual and of the processes in which the individual is involved. Over the past decade, this body of work has contributed to our understanding of information need and use. A number of researchers have attempted to generalize from observations of individuals or groups of individuals (researchers, students, scholars, library users). These attempts have resulted in models of the information-seeking process that are context-independent. Where the environment or situation is mentioned, the term categorizes aspects or attributes of the individual's self rather than the social, professional, or information-seeking setting. This body of research reveals that there is an individual readiness to engage in information-seeking behavior that depends on various preconditions associated with a person's level of information arousal. It describes and analyzes a range of cognitive conditions and emotional responses that arise when people engage in information behavior. It also confirms that information-seeking behavior is a process or set of processes or stages that an individual moves through in space and time and that there are reliable methods for mapping these processes and observing the variations and consistent patterns of behavior that emerge.

## SOCIAL APPROACHES

Approaches to studying information behavior that focus on social contexts emerged slowly during the early 1990s and are becoming increasingly prominent. With their focus on the meanings and values associated with social, sociocultural, and sociolinguistic aspects of information behavior, studies based on social frameworks tend to employ naturalistic approaches, which have gained popularity within information behavior in general (FIDEL; WESTBROOK). Unlike behaviorist frameworks, which tend to objectify context by evoking and describing it as distinct, factual entities that are separate from the object of study, social frameworks consider context interpretively and holistically and consider it a "carrier of meaning" (TALJA ET AL., p. 752). In this sense, social approaches were developed to address information behavior phenomena that lie outside the realm of cognitive frameworks.

At the forefront of this shift in focus from primarily cognitive factors to social, cultural, and affective ones is the work of CHATMAN (2001). She developed three frameworks for studying information behavior: (1) theory of information poverty, (2) theory of life in the round, and (3) theory of normative behavior.

Chatman's theory of information poverty arose from several ethnographic studies that she conducted during the late 1980s and early 1990s (CHATMAN, 1996; 2001). For these studies she borrowed several theories from the social sciences to study everyday information flow in different small-world settings: diffusion theory and opinion leadership to study the working poor (1985; 1987b); alienation theory and gratification theory to study female janitors at a large university (1987a; 1990; 1991b); and social network theory to study elderly women residing in a retirement complex (1991a; 1992). Four key concepts—deception, risk taking, secrecy, and situational relevance—emerged repeatedly in Chatman's research, which formed the basis of her theory of information poverty. According to Chatman, people live in an impoverished world when they choose to ignore information despite knowing that it might be helpful for dealing with daily concerns and problems. To maintain an impression of coping well within their life worlds, individuals engage in self-protective behaviors, which form the boundaries of their world of poverty. In this sense, the theory explains how individuals define and use their life experiences to survive in a world of great distrust. It reveals situations in which people know that important, relevant, and potentially useful information exists but high social and other costs prompt them to ignore it.

In her keynote address at the 2000 conference on Information Seeking in Context in Göteborg, Sweden, CHATMAN (2001) explained how two other concepts, social norms and self-protective behaviors, emerged from her early studies. Her analysis of the information behavior of female inmates in a maximum security prison—another small-world setting—revealed a third concept: worldview (in the sense of CRESSEY regarding the taxi-dance hall). Together these three concepts, social norms, self-protective behaviors, and worldview, form the basis of Chatman's theory of life in the round (1999; 2001). It describes a dynamic world based largely on approximation where "members move in and out of the round depending on their need for more systematic, precise and defined information."[1]

Although this world contains an enormous degree of imprecision, it is also characterized by "surprisingly, accepted levels of uncertainty." Chatman's theory of life in the round comprises six propositions, two of which state that people will not cross boundaries of their small worlds to seek information and that people will only cross information boundaries when information is perceived as critical, the information is collectively perceived to be relevant, and a perception exists that life in the round is no longer functioning (CHATMAN, 2001). In essence, life in the round adversely affects information seeking for day-to-day situations because people will not search for information if there is no need to do so. Small-world inhabitants will choose to ignore information if they perceive that their world is working without it, that is, they have enough certainty, comfort, and situation predictability that the need to seek information is negated.

In her latest framework, theory of normative behavior, CHATMAN (2001) focused on how the everyday reality of people sharing a similar cultural space is characterized by common or routine events. The theory

----

[1]Chatman, Elfreda A. Personal communication, 8 December 2000.

has four concepts: social norms, social types, worldview, and information behavior (defined as states in which one may or may not act on
received information). According to Chatman's thesis statement, normative behavior comprises that which is viewed by inhabitants of a
social world as most appropriate within a particular public context or
situation. Through social norms, normative behavior dictates a predict-
able, routine, and manageable approach to everyday reality. In this
sense, it contains the lessons that one must learn to cope successfully in
a particular social world. Of interest to information behavior research
are those aspects of normative behavior that embody social existence by
legitimizing and justifying social values. The theory's five propositional
statements are:

- Proposition 1. Social norms are standards with which
  members of a social world comply in order to exhibit
  desirable expressions of public behavior;
- Proposition 2. Members choose compliance because it
  allows for a way by which to affirm what is normative
  for this context at this time;
- Proposition 3. Worldview is shaped by the normative
  values that influence how members think about the
  ways of the world. It is a collective, taken-for-granted
  attitude that sensitizes members to be responsive to
  certain events and to ignore others;
- Proposition 4. Everyday reality contains a belief that
  members of a social world do retain attention or interest
  sufficient enough to influence behavior. The process of
  placing persons in ideal categories of lesser or greater
  quality can be thought of as a social typification;
- Proposition 5. Human information behavior is a construct in which to approach everyday reality and its
  effect on actions to gain or to avoid the possession of
  information. The decision on the appropriate course of
  action is driven by what members' beliefs are necessary
  to support a normative way of life.

Within this framework, individuals strive to represent a positive social
type that shares the collective worldview and respects the social norms
upheld by other members of the social world. One's efforts at creating
and maintaining this social type will affect whether and how one
engages in information seeking. If a situation requires information
behavior that is inconsistent with the established worldview or contra-
dicts the social type one has established, then the individual is likely

either to avoid or to disengage in information seeking or to move to another social world where he or she can engage in the behavior more freely.

Due to the recent publication of her frameworks, Chatman's conceptual contributions to the study of information behavior are only beginning to emerge. With their focus on the social aspects of everyday situations, it is expected that her frameworks will be tested widely in a variety of settings. Most recently, her theory of normative behavior was used as a framework by BURNETT ET AL. on small-world information behavior within virtual communities and of feminist booksellers.

Beyond Chatman, the influence of social science theory on the development of social frameworks for information behavior is also seen in the work of TUOMINEN & SAVOLAINEN. Using a social constructionist approach, they developed a framework for studying the concept of "information use" as a form of discursive action. Focusing on everyday settings, they followed HARRÉ's social constructionist tenet that "the primary human reality is persons in conversation" (TUOMINEN & SAVOLAINEN, p. 81). In essence, instead of viewing information as an entity with fixed boundaries or as a commodity that is transferred through communication, they defined information as "a communicative construct which is produced in a social context" (TUOMINEN & SAVOLAINEN, p. 89). As they further explain: "the contextual nature of information means that the way in which a version of information is constructed always depends on the interactive nature or argumentative context of talk, as well as on the pragmatic social purposes this version is designed to accomplish" (TUOMINEN & SAVOLAINEN, p. 89). In their framework, the study of information use cannot be considered in terms of an isolated individual or outside a specific context. Instead, it must focus on the social context, interaction, and discourse through which the sharing of information occurs. They criticized earlier definitions of information because they enabled researchers to address only such "use" questions as how frequently particular sources are consulted for information over specific time periods. Alternative forms of use, such as clarifying a situation or receiving comfort in knowing help is available, were not conceptualized in such restrictive definitions. Another tenet of social constructionism implicit in Tuominen and Savolainen's definition of information is that people "construct versions of reality between [them]selves and that knowledge is something people do together rather than [as] an individual possession" (TUOMINEN & SAVOLAINEN, p. 83). They asserted that this socially and dialogically oriented approach to studying information flow is also supported by HJØRLAND & ALBRECHTSEN, ROSENBAUM, TALJA and TAYLOR (1991), and in particular by DERVIN (1994) in her work on communitarianism. DEWDNEY & MICHELL and SOLOMON (1997a) also commended the use of sociolinguistic approaches for studying information behavior.

PETTIGREW (1999; 2000) used Tuominen and Savolainen's information use as social–discursive action framework to derive her notion of an information ground. Using an ethnographic approach, she studied the flow of human services information (HSI) among nurses and the elderly at community foot clinics. HSI was defined as "a communicative construct involving the nature or availability of local services and programs that is produced in a social community-based context" (PETTIGREW, 1999, p. 811). Implicit in this definition is that the communicative construct is dynamic in nature and occurs among and is built by two or more people and that the construct may be used by the individuals involved to obtain cognitive, social, affective, and instrumental benefits. Using this definition, Pettigrew concluded that the clinic environment could best be described as an information ground, that is, an "environment temporarily created by the behavior of people who have come together to perform a given task, but from which emerges a social atmosphere that fosters the spontaneous and serendipitous sharing of information" (PETTIGREW, 1999, p. 811). She explained that the foot clinic functioned as a rich information ground because information was shared in multiple directions (i.e., anyone at the clinic could give and obtain HSI) and because HSI was shared both purposefully and serendipitously. Pettigrew suggested that her information ground framework might be used to study informal information flow in other community settings, including hair salons, playgrounds where parents interact as their children play, meetings of special interest clubs, and other health clinics.

A prevalent approach that yielded rich fodder for studying social aspects of information behavior is social network theory. CHATMAN (1992), for example, used social network theory to study information flow among retired women and ultimately derived her theory of information poverty. WILLIAMSON used a social network approach, along with uses and gratification theory and ecological theory, to derive her model of incidental information acquisition. Derived from studying the everyday information behavior of 202 Australian seniors using a qualitative approach, her model describes how people obtain information, both accidentally and purposefully through their intimate personal networks (family, friends), wider personal networks (clubs, churches, voluntary organizations), and the mass media (newspapers, television, radio, magazines). Her model accounts for individuals' lifestyles, values, socioeconomic circumstances, physical environment, and personal characteristics. Sonnenwald's theory of information horizons, which is discussed in the next section, is also largely drawn from general social network theory and shows how one may use the positioning of social ties to map the use of different information sources (SONNENWALD).

The use of social network theory in information behavior research has revealed many insights that might inform future work. PETTIGREW (2000), in testing Granovetter's theory of the strength of weak ties among nurses and the elderly, found that in addition to functioning as weak ties (who provide access to otherwise unavailable information), the nurses also exhibited characteristics of strong ties (who serve a legitimizing role), which doubly increased the value of their role as information providers to the elderly (GRANOVETTER, 1973; 1982). She labeled this new social type as "strong–weak ties," meaning they exhibit aspects of dual tie strength. HAYTHORNTHWAITE & WELLMAN used social network theory to study information exchange and media use among members of a university research group. Their findings regarding tie strength and the nature of ties yield broad implications for studying interpersonal relationships in other settings that might be woven into a theory of information behavior. Social capital theory, which is related to social network theory, also suggests promising approaches for basing future information behavior frameworks. HERSBERGER ET AL. are using the social capital theory (regarding individuals) of LIN to study how the homeless build and use social capital within their personal social networks to facilitate access to everyday information. At the community level, PETTIGREW & DURRANCE are working with the theory of social capital of PUTNAM (1995; 2000) in developing a framework that might explain how digital information services promote information flow and community cohesiveness.

In focusing on social aspects of information behavior, scholars seek to understand the impact of interpersonal relationships and dynamics on information flow and on how information sharing is a part of human communication. Since the 1980s Chatman was the sole researcher focusing primarily on social factors. In recent years she has been joined by several others who have largely turned to social network theory for guidance. This interest in the social and affective aspects of information behavior continues to draw increased research attention and, as discussed in the next section, is being incorporated into multifaceted models of information behavior.

## MULTIFACETED APPROACHES

Recognizing the complexity in human information behavior, a growing number of researchers have pointed out that multiple viewpoints are required to capture this behavior. A model based on one viewpoint, whether cognitive or social, is not powerful enough to describe, analyze, explain, or predict this multifaceted phenomenon. ALLEN, for example, observed that there were four models for studying information behavior: cognitive, social, social–cognitive, and organizational. Using the rationalistic model of problem solving, he showed that each model addressed a particular situation and a particular type of need in each of the steps of problem solving, but none could address all situations. Therefore, he concluded, there is a need for a new model that takes into consideration all four models at the same time, one that is guided by a person-in-situation approach.

Allen's call for a multifaceted approach was not created in a vacuum. Indeed, researchers have been developing such models through a variety of means. Some have modified existing models by adding new facets to them, others have reexamined what was known about information behavior to create holistic models, and yet others have developed conceptual frameworks that were informed by multiple theories from a variety of disciplines.

The need to modify an existing model usually arises when researchers realize certain limitations in a model and, at the same time, they see additional elements that might address these limitations. At times, researchers empirically test the new model to find out if the modifications are valid and how to improve the model further. ROSENBAUM noticed that the explanatory power of the value-added approach developed by TAYLOR (1984; 1985; 1986) was limited because it was not grounded in theory of social action. Focusing on information behavior in organizations, he integrated this approach with the structuration theory of GIDDENS to create the "structurationally-informed value-added" approach. While he did not test the new model, Rosenbaum demonstrated how it could address some basic issues in information science.

Still within the organizational setting, JOHNSON ET AL. developed a causal model to explain information-seeking behavior. The model suggested that a set of antecedent factors—which included sets of variables such as demographics, experience, and beliefs—provided the motivating force for a person to take information-seeking actions. These actions, in turn, were shaped by the information carrier factors, which determined the intention to seek information from a particular source (carrier). These factors included variables such as credibility and intention of the source. Through a series of tests in various organizations, this comprehensive model of information seeking (CMIS) has been developed gradually to include variables in each set of factors. It is an expansion of Johnson's model of media exposure and appraisal, and the variables in each set were also drawn from a variety of theories and models such as uses and gratification and the health belief model. Testing the model through a questionnaire that was distributed to engineers and others who provided technical services, Johnson and his colleagues concluded that the model presented a general framework for information seeking but that it required the incorporation of additional contextual factors.

Another causal model was developed by BYSTRÖM & JÄRVELIN. They set out to show that the complexity of a task a person performed on the job affected information seeking and use. They derived this notion from organizational psychology and added another facet to their approach from the area of expert systems by defining three types of information: problem information, domain information, and problem-solving information. To test the new variable, they asked civil servants in a city government to fill in questionnaires and diaries. Results showed that task complexity indeed affected certain variables in information behavior. More specifically, an increase in task complexity brought an increase in the complexity of the information need, an increased need for domain and problem-solving information, an increase in the use of general-purpose sources (as opposed to fact-oriented ones), a decrease in the success of information seeking, a decrease in the use of internal channels, and an increase in the number of sources. Byström and Järvelin concluded that all holistic models of information behavior should include this variable.

Sonnenwald (SONNENWALD; SONNENWALD & PIERCE; SONNENWALD ET AL.) incorporated theories and frameworks from other disciplines as well. In developing her theory of information horizons, she drew upon the work of several information behavior theorists—most notably, Belkin, Dervin, Ingwersen, Kuhlthau, and Wilson—and upon social network theory and other frameworks from communications, sociology, and psychology. Her model, which is based on five propositions, was derived from empirical work on different groups, including high-tech workers, students, and military personnel. It focuses on the contexts and situations that create evolving information horizons that map the location of different information sources (both personal and media-oriented) within it. For Sonnenwald, information behavior is a collaborative process among individuals and information resources, and she proposed this information resource sociogram be used to explain how individuals subsequently engage in exploration, seeking, filtering, use, and dissemination of information.

An inductive approach to building a conceptual framework is to review the work that has been carried out in the field in order to identify patterns and to extract general constructs. Many user studies have been done in the past decades, and their analysis can point to general structures and factors that are relevant to information behavior. Reexamining studies about information-seeking behavior of engineers, health care professionals, and lawyers, LECKIE ET AL. created a new holistic model. They based the model on the assumptions that studies of the information seeking of professionals should: understand the broader working context, examine in depth the details of the individual's work, include all the roles a professional had, and incorporate some flexibility to allow for the complexity and unpredictability in the process of information seeking. The model itself included six components: (1) work roles had (2) associated tasks, which in turn determined the (3) characteristics of an information need. Three additional components affected information-seeking behavior: (4) awareness of information, (5) sources of information, and (6) outcomes. These components were the main classes in the model, and each one contained variables that had been discovered in user studies.

The important role that the task and the context play in the processes associated with information behavior and the complexity and unpredictability of these processes were central to some conceptual constructs that were developed to guide and to inform the study of information behavior. Unlike the models described previously in this chapter, these constructs proposed a method for study rather than variables or other predictors that affect information behavior. They were developed to guide and to inform studies about human information behavior.

Cognitive work analysis (VICENTE) is a work-centered conceptual framework developed by RASMUSSEN ET AL. It was constructed as a general approach to help information system designers analyze and understand the complex interaction between (1) the activities, organizational relationships, and constraints of work domains and (2) users' cognitive and social activities and their subjective preferences during task performance. The framework's theoretical roots are in adaptive control systems and Gibson's ecological psychology and it is the result of the generalization of experiences from field studies that led to the design of support systems for a variety of modern work domains, such as process plants, manufacturing, hospitals, and libraries. Like cognitive systems engineering, it is based on the assumption that system design for work in dynamic environments should be based on the analysis of the factors that shape behavior rather than on the description of the procedures followed (PEJTERSEN ET AL.).

This approach assumes that information interaction is determined by a number of dimensions:

- the environment within which the workplace is operating;
- the work domain;
- the organization in terms of division of work and social organization;

- the task in terms of work domain;
- the decision making that is required for the task;
- the mental strategies that can be used for the task; and
- user characteristics, resources, and values.

Cognitive work analysis examines each dimension according to four abstraction levels: goals and constraints, priorities, work process, and physical resources. It thus provides a framework to guide in-depth analysis of information behavior and its context. Suppose, for example, that researchers study the information behavior of housewives. The cognitive work analysis framework suggests the research questions that they should ask. With relation to the strategies housewives employ, for instance, some questions would be: How do housewives make decisions? What are they looking for? How do they look for information? Why do they do it in this way? Where do they look for information? Why in these places? Do they have any preference about where to look for information? Why these preferences? Do they have any preferences about how to look for information? Why these preferences? Other dimensions will generate other questions about the decisions housewives make and the work they do. Thus, instead of determining a priori what variables affect housewives' information behavior, data collected to answer these questions present these variables and their manifestations for the population studied. Depending on the methods used, the findings of the analysis may be applicable to the behavior of a particular group of housewives or to all housewives.

This framework can be also used as a basis for the evaluation of information systems and services. The framework for system evaluation, which is based on the same dimensions, answers questions such as: Does the system support cooperative work and coordination? Does the system support the task repertoire of a work situation? Does the system support the relevant decision task? Are all relevant strategies supported? Does presentation match sensory characteristics? Therefore, the framework is both descriptive and prescriptive in nature because its purpose is not only to understand the current work but also to go beyond the observed work practice. This process of evaluation results in design recommendations. For example, if it is found that browsing is a desirable strategy for finding information that is not supported by a certain system, one can recommend that future systems and services be designed to support this strategy.

The cognitive work analysis approach has already been applied to various studies in information behavior. For example, PEJTERSEN & AUSTIN (1983; 1984) studied user interactions with reference librarians during fiction retrieval and MOREHEAD ET AL. considered problem formulation and application of computer-aided seeking in the same

environment. FIDEL ET AL. (1999) used this approach to study information-seeking behavior of high school students when they searched
the Web to complete homework assignments. In addition, PEJTERSEN
ET AL. investigated information needs during the design process in
concurrent engineering, and FIDEL ET AL. (2001) examined collaborative information retrieval of a design team in the software industry.
DUNLOP explained and demonstrated the application of this framework to the evaluation of information systems in his reflections on
interactive evaluation in information retrieval.

Unlike the cognitive work analysis, most conceptual frameworks
and models of information behavior do not lead directly to design
recommendations and specifications. Even though some researchers
noted that their constructs could be used for system design, none
among those reviewed here showed how it could be done. Most researchers who study information behavior are not personally interested
in the design of systems and services, and they report their studies to
the benefit of other researchers of information behavior. This separation
between the "human" side and the "system" side of information behavior is not useful if we believe that information systems and services
should be designed to support information behavior and that the design of such systems be based on our understanding of this behavior.
Therefore, one of the special strengths of the cognitive work analysis
framework is in providing a direct link from the study of information
behavior to system design.

System designers, on the other hand, have been developing interest
in human information behavior, and both practitioners and researchers
in this area have looked for methods to study information behavior.
Most prominent is the area of human–computer interaction (HCI).
BEYER & HOLTZBLATT, for example, summarized their system-build-
ing experience in a guide for students and design practitioners. They
showed how to understand the information needs of customers and
how to design systems that fit such needs. Other researchers employed
various theories and approaches to understanding work and designing
systems. A sample of these appeared in a special issue of the *International Journal of Human-Computer Studies* (FIELDS & WRIGHT), which
focused on how to bridge the technology side and the human and social
side. It contained articles that reported on studies and design projects
that were guided by a range of theories—including ethnography, cognitive psychology, and cultural-historical activity theory—and used a
variety of methods.

Because the context is an important factor in multifaceted approaches,
it is customary to view "work" and "everyday life" as two distinct types
of context, even though the distinction is not always clear
(SAVOLAINEN, 1998). As can be seen from this review, most such

approaches addressed information behavior on the job. SAVOLAINEN (1995), however, focused on everyday life. Informed by the Sense-Making approach (DERVIN, 1994), he used the Habitus theory (BOURDIEU) to define "way of life" as the order of things that was created when people used their preferences to make choices in everyday life, and "mastery of life" as making sure that people actually adhered to their own preferences when they took on everyday activities. He explained that information-seeking habits were usually developed as part of the mastery of life and that social, cultural, economic, and psychological factors all together affected both way and mastery of life. To test and to improve his model, Savolainen conducted theme interviews with working-class and middle-class people to compare their information-seeking behaviors. Results were complex, requiring the consideration of the type of information source—whether paper or electronic—and the nature of the information need—whether a practical need to resolve a specific problem or an orienting need that did not result from any specific problem. He concluded that the mastery of life definition had to be developed further to include additional specific concepts for information seeking in everyday life.

One framework that clearly addresses all types of context is the Sense-Making approach. DERVIN (1999b) explained that Sense-Making is a metatheory that can inform and guide methods of studying information seeking. It is based on concepts relating to time, space, movement, and gap and "pictures the person as moving through time-space, bridging gaps and moving on" (DERVIN, 1999a, p. 45). Sense-Making has been developed constantly since Dervin and her colleagues initiated this approach in 1972. Throughout its journey, it has been informed by many theories and philosophical approaches, and in 1999 Dervin described it as a post-constructivist or postmodern modernist approach (DERVIN, 1999b, p. 730). While originally developed to study information need, seeking, and use communicatively, researchers in various areas, such as media studies, cultural studies, education and pedagogy, health communication, and telecommunication theory, have employed the approach.

Throughout its development and use, several themes became prominent. Among them (DERVIN, 1999b): humans are anchored in material conditions and at the same time have mind and spirit and can make abstractions, dream, feel, plan, have ambitions and fantasies, and tell stories; humans are involved in a constant journey in time and space of sense-making and of sense-unmaking; humans and their worlds are constantly evolving, and their description, therefore, requires verbing; human movement is affected by forces, and those should be always considered; ordinary human beings are theory makers; humans can articulate emotions, spiritual experiences, and embodied unconscious;

patterns and connectivities among human beings take many forms, including the causal, spontaneous, and collaborative; no a priori assumption about human patterning should be made; and there is a need for a researcher to be self-conscious and self-reflexive.

Given these themes, DERVIN (1999b) showed how Sense-Making challenged the assumptions that have usually been guiding research in human information behavior. Some of these challenges are: Sense-Making requires that the concept of information will not be considered a static absolute ontological category but as a structural term instead; it requires that information creating, seeking, and use will not be limited to the cognitive realm because they might involve a variety of experiences such as emotions, feelings, wishes, and dreams; finding information does not always result in a positive outcome, but in some situations it might be better to miss information; Sense-Making is looking at differences rather than commonalities, at the situational and specific rather than at the prototypical; information seeking and use do not always take place in an ordered world—they may require the creation of new orders; studies of information seeking and use should not look at these activities as habitual patterns but also as innovations; studies of information seeking and use should not be limited to the present but should include the past and the future; studies should not attempt to be limited to finding one central pattern or a group of patterns, but should find all useful patterns and explicitly look for exceptions and disruptions; and the researcher should recognize that she herself is an information seeker.

DERVIN (1999b) made clear that Sense-Making was developed to redesign communications procedures and systems. While this metatheory does not directly guide system design, DERVIN (1999a) presented a number of examples in which the approach has been used to design systems in settings such as the reference interview, relevance assessment, development and organization of a library's video collection, information presentation at a blood donation center, and in constructing a research community.

Both approaches, cognitive work analysis and Sense-Making, have guided and informed many studies in information behavior. To date, scores of researchers in various fields have selected Dervin's Sense-Making approach to guide their work. To name just a few, GLUCK examined a possible collaboration with semiotics to understand the active use of information and proposed a set of experiments that would help the two approaches to develop further. SOLOMON (1997b; 1997c; 1997d) investigated its applications to information behavior when he studied the annual work planning of a unit of a public agency over three annual iterations. Finally, SAVOLAINEN (1995) investigated information behavior in everyday life, as discussed earlier. On the practical side, MORRIS demonstrated how this approach could provide the basis for rethinking and potentially redesigning the library's mission, the provision and measurement of services, and the design of systems. Unlike the models described earlier, cognitive work analysis and Sense-Making can be applied to almost all situations of information behavior. In addition, as general frameworks, they facilitate comparisons of the information behavior of different groups of people or of the same group of people at different times and situations.

While both approaches have been evolving since the early 1970s, interest in multifaceted approaches began to spread only in the early 1990s and is growing rapidly. In addition, research in information behavior is no longer limited to library and information science but has extended to other areas such as computer science, communications, and management. The construction of holistic, comprehensive, and multi-faceted models and frameworks has just begun, and most such models and frameworks are still being tested and developed.

## CONCLUSION

Our review suggests that another quantum leap has occurred within information behavior. A distinct, unifying theoretical body is emerging that, beyond its strong, user-centered core, emphasizes the contextual interplay of cognitive, social, cultural, organizational, affective, and linguistic factors and asserts that information behavior phenomena are part of the human communicative process. This theoretical basis is largely derived from the collective results of extensive empirical investigation conducted over several decades and reflects the importation of frameworks from cognate fields, which is consistent with the view of BATES (1999) that information science itself is an orthogonal field that examines information phenomena across different settings using inter-disciplinary perspectives. Theorists of information behavior are building upon one another's work by incorporating connecting features into new models and by enhancing existing models. The communication and collaboration that underlie this work have been greatly facilitated by the establishment of a biannual European conference series and a new special interest group within the American Society for Information Science as well as the recent publication of information behavior theme issues in several key journals.

The plethora of models found in the literature can be considered along three distinct categories that account for varying aspects of information behavior. While several general approaches to conceptualizing information behavior (e.g., Sense-Making, cognitive work analysis) that were developed in the 1980s have been refined and reflect a mature understanding of the phenomenon in terms of cognitive, social, and other factors, the need for in-depth study of these individual factors remains. Only through focused study can rich insights be obtained regarding such novel concepts as third-party or proxy searching (e.g., ERDELEZ & RIOUX; GROSS, 1999; 2001), lay information giving (e.g., PETTIGREW, 2000), and the non-use of information or information blunting (e.g., BAKER, 1996; 1997), which are only beginning to be addressed. Despite giant strides in building a theoretical basis of information behavior that addresses such key concepts as information need and seeking, theorists must continue to enhance existing frameworks and derive new ones that account for emerging concepts. The uncovering of these related aspects is an additional sign of the field's maturation. Researchers are moving beyond established or recognized concepts to explore new ones that lie deep beneath and may undergird information behavior.

For the field of information behavior, the challenge remains to provide concrete guidance for system design. As noted, few frameworks offer suggestions for improving the design of information systems. The foci and attributes identified in the models reviewed suggest that information systems need to complement users' natural inclinations when communicating information needs and when seeking and using information in addition to considering the multiple roles of context and social, cultural, organizational, and affective factors. However, specific directions on how this might be accomplished remain scant. To create working systems that are truly user centered and that reflect the foundations of information behavior theory, greater dialogue and collaboration are sorely needed between theorists of information behavior and designers of information systems.

## BIBLIOGRAPHY

AGUILAR, FRANCIS J. 1967. Scanning the Business Environment. New York, NY: Macmillan; 1967. LC: 67-11688; OCLC: 166317.
ALLEN, BRYCE. 1997. Information Needs: A Person-in-Situation Approach. In: Vakkari, Pertti; Savolainen, Reijo; Dervin, Brenda, eds. Information Seeking in Context: Proceedings of an International Conference on Research in Information Needs, Seeking and Use in Different Contexts; 1996 August 14-16; Tampere, Finland. London, UK: Taylor Graham; 1997. 111-122. ISBN: 0-947568-71-9; OCLC: 37137193.
BAKER, LYNDA M. 1996. A Study of the Nature of Information Needed by Women with Multiple Sclerosis. Library & Information Science Research. 1996 Winter; 18(1): 67-81. ISSN: 0740-8188; OCLC: 9844287.
BAKER, LYNDA M. 1997. Preference for Physicians as Information Providers by Women with Multiple Sclerosis: A Potential Cause for Communication Problems? Journal of Documentation. 1997 June; 53(3): 251-262. ISSN: 0022-0418; OCLC: 1754538.

BATES, MARCIA J. 1989. The Design of Browsing and Berrypicking Techniques for the Online Search Interface. Online Review. 1989 October; 13(5): 407-424. ISSN: 0309-314X; OCLC: 2998180.

BATES, MARCIA J. 1999. The Invisible Substrate of Information Science. Journal of the American Society for Information Science. 1999 October; 50(12): 1043-1050. ISSN: 0002-8231; OCLC: 1798118.

BELKIN, NICHOLAS J. 1990. The Cognitive Viewpoint in Information Science. Journal of Information Science. 1990; 16(1): 11-15. ISSN: 0165-5515; OCLC: 5094715.

BELKIN, NICHOLAS J.; ODDY, ROBERT N.; BROOKS, HELEN M. 1982a. ASK for Information Retrieval: Part I. Background and Theory. Journal of Documentation. 1982 June; 38(2): 61-71. ISSN: 0022-0418; OCLC: 1754538.

BELKIN, NICHOLAS J.; ODDY, ROBERT N.; BROOKS, HELEN M. 1982b. ASK for Information Retrieval: Part II. Results of a Design Study. Journal of Documentation. 1982 September; 38(3): 145-164. ISSN: 0022-0418; OCLC: 1754538.

BELKIN, NICHOLAS J.; VICKERY, ALINA. 1985. Interaction in Information Systems. London, UK: British Library; 1985. 250p. ISBN: 0-7123-3050-X; OCLC: 17105265.

BEYER, HUGH; HOLTZBLATT, KAREN. 1998. Contextual Design: Defining Customer-Centered Systems. San Francisco, CA: Morgan Kaufmann; 1998. 472p. ISBN: 1-55860-411-1; OCLC: 37443490.

BOURDIEU, PIERRE. 1984. Distinction: A Social Critique of the Judgment of Taste. Cambridge, MA: Harvard University Press; 1984. 613p. ISBN: 0-674-21277-0; OCLC: 10323218.

BROWN, MARY E. 1991. A General Model of Information-Seeking Behavior. In: Griffiths, José-Marie, ed. ASIS '94: Proceedings of the American Society for Information Science (ASIS) 54th Annual Meeting: Volume 28; 1991 October 27-31; Washington, DC. Medford, NJ: Learned Information, Inc. for ASIS; 1991. 9-14. ISSN: 0044-7870; ISBN: 0-938734-56-3.

BRUCE, HARRY W. 1994. A Cognitive View of the Situational Dynamism of User-Centered Relevance Estimation. Journal of the American Society for Information Science. 1994 April; 45(3): 142-148. ISSN: 0002-8231; OCLC: 1798118.

BURNETT, GARY; BESANT, MICHELE; CHATMAN, ELFREDA A. 2001. Small Worlds: Normative Behavior in Virtual Communities and Feminist Bookselling. Journal of the American Society for Information Science and Technology. 2001 May; 52(7): 536-547. ISSN: 1532-2882; OCLC: 45266164.

BYSTRÖM, KATRIINA; JÄRVELIN, KALERVO. 1995. Task Complexity Affects Information Seeking and Use. Information Processing & Management. 1995 March-April; 31(2): 191-213. ISSN: 0306-4573; OCLC: 2243314.

CHATMAN, ELFREDA A. 1985. Information, Mass Media Use and the Working Poor. Library & Information Science Research. 1985 April-June; 7(2): 97-113. ISSN: 0740-8188; OCLC: 9844287.

CHATMAN, ELFREDA A. 1987a. The Information World of Low-Skilled Workers. Library & Information Science Research. 1987 October-December; 9(4): 265-283. ISSN: 0740-8188; OCLC: 9844287.

CHATMAN, ELFREDA A. 1987b. Opinion Leadership, Poverty and Informa-
tion Sharing. RQ. 1987 Spring; 26(3): 341-353. ISSN: 0033-7072; OCLC:
1852823.
CHATMAN, ELFREDA A. 1990. Alienation Theory: Application of a Concep-
tual Framework to a Study of Information among Janitors. RQ. 1990
Spring; 29(3): 355-368. ISSN: 0033-7072; OCLC: 1852823.
CHATMAN, ELFREDA A. 1991a. Channels to a Larger Social World: Older
Women Staying in Contact with the Great Society. Library & Information
Science Research. 1991 July-September; 13(3): 281-300. ISSN: 0740-8188;
OCLC: 9844287.
CHATMAN, ELFREDA A. 1991b. Life in a Small World: Applicability of
Gratification Theory to Information-Seeking Behavior. Journal of the Ameri-
can Society for Information Science. 1991 July; 42(6): 438-449. ISSN: 0002-
8231; OCLC: 1798118.
CHATMAN, ELFREDA A. 1992. The Information World of Retired Women.
New York, NY: Greenwood Press; 1992. 150p. ISBN: 0-313-25492-3; OCLC:
25629560.
CHATMAN, ELFREDA A. 1996. The Impoverished Life-World of Outsiders.
Journal of the American Society for Information Science. 1996 March;
47(3): 193-206. ISSN: 0002-8231; OCLC: 1798118.
CHATMAN, ELFREDA A. 1999. A Theory of Life in the Round. Journal of the
American Society for Information Science. 1999 March; 50(3): 207-217.
ISSN: 0002-8231; OCLC: 1798118.
CHATMAN, ELFREDA A. 2001. Framing Social Life in Theory and Research.
In: Höglund, L., ed. Information Seeking in Context: Proceedings of the
3rd International Conference on Research in Information Needs, Seeking
and Use in Different Contexts; 2000 August 16-18; Göteborg, Sweden.
London, UK: Taylor Graham. (In press).
CHOO, CHUN WEI; DETLOR, BRIAN; TURNBULL, DON. 2000. Information
Seeking on the Web: An Integrated Model of Browsing and Searching.
First Monday. 2000 February 7; 5(2). ISSN: 1396-0466. Available WWW:
http://www.firstmonday.dk/issues/issue5_2/choo/index.html.
COLE, CHARLES. 1999. Activity of Understanding a Problem during Interac-
tion with an "Enabling" Information Retrieval System: Modeling Informa-
tion Flow. Journal of the American Society for Information Science. 1999
May; 50(6): 544-552. ISSN: 0002-8231; OCLC: 1798118.
CRESSEY, PAUL GOALBY. 1932. The Taxi-Dance Hall: A Sociological Study in
Commercialized Recreation and City Life. Chicago, IL: University of
Chicago Press; 1932. 300p. OCLC: 916800.
DE MEY, MARC. 1982. The Cognitive Paradigm: Cognitive Science, A Newly
Explored Approach to the Study of Cognition Applied in an Analysis of
Science and Scientific Knowledge. Dordrecht, The Netherlands: Reidel;
1982. 314p. ISBN: 90-277-1382-0; OCLC: 8494628.
DERVIN, BRENDA. 1994. Information—Democracy: An Examination of Un-
derlying Assumptions. Journal of the American Society for Information
Science. 1994 July; 45(6): 369-385. ISSN: 0002-8231; OCLC: 1798118.
DERVIN, BRENDA. 1999a. Chaos, Order, and Sense-Making: A Proposed
Theory for Information Design. In: Jacobson, Robert E., ed. Information

Design. Cambridge, MA: MIT Press; 1999. 35-57. ISBN: 0-262-10069-X; OCLC: 40693279.

DERVIN, BRENDA. 1999b. On Studying Information Seeking Methodologically: The Implications of Connecting Metatheory to Method. Information Processing & Management. 1999 November; 35(6): 727-750. ISSN: 0306-4573; OCLC: 2243314.

DERVIN, BRENDA; NILAN, MICHAEL. 1986. Information Needs and Uses. In: Williams, Martha E., ed. Annual Review of Information Science and Technology: Volume 21. White Plains, NY: Knowledge Industry Publications, Inc. for the American Society for Information Science; 1986. 3-33. ISSN: 0066-4200; ISBN: 0-86729-209-1.

DEWDNEY, PATRICIA; MICHELL, GILLIAN. 1997. Asking "Why" Questions in the Reference Interview: A Theoretical Justification. Library Quarterly. 1997 January; 67(1): 50-71. ISSN: 0024-2519; OCLC: 1755858.

DUNLOP, MARK. 2000. Reflections on Mira: Interactive Evaluation in Information Retrieval. Journal of the American Society for Information Science. 2000 December; 51(14): 1269-1274. ISSN: 0002-8231; OCLC: 1798118.

ELLIS, DAVID. 1989. A Behavioral Approach to Information Retrieval System Design. Journal of Documentation. 1989 September; 45(3): 171-212. ISSN: 0022-0418; OCLC: 1754538.

ERDELEZ, SANDA. 1997. Information Encountering: A Conceptual Framework for Accidental Information Discovery. In: Vakkari, Pertti; Savolainen, Reijo; Dervin, Brenda, eds. Information Seeking in Context: Proceedings of an International Conference on Research in Information Needs, Seeking and Use in Different Contexts; 1996 August 14-16; Tampere, Finland. London, UK: Taylor Graham; 1997. 412-421. ISBN: 0-947568-71-9; OCLC: 37137193.

ERDELEZ, SANDA; RIOUX, KEVIN. 2001. Sharing Information Encountered for Others on the Web. In: Höglund, L., ed. Information Seeking in Context: Proceedings of the 3rd International Conference on Research in Information Needs, Seeking and Use in Different Contexts; 2000 August 16-18; Göteborg, Sweden. London, UK: Taylor Graham. (In press).

FEEHAN, PATRICIA E.; GRAGG, W. LEE, II; HAVENER, W. MICHAEL; KESTER, DIANE D. 1987. Library and Information Science Research: An Analysis of the 1984 Journal Literature. Library & Information Science Research. 1987; 9: 173-185. ISSN: 0740-8188; OCLC: 9844287.

FIDEL, RAYA. 1993. Qualitative Methods in Information Retrieval Research. Library & Information Science Research. 1993 Summer; 15(3): 219-247. ISSN: 0740-8188; OCLC: 9844287.

FIDEL, RAYA; BRUCE, HARRY; PEJTERSEN, ANNELISE MARK; DUMAIS, SUSAN; GRUDIN, JONATHAN; POLTROCK, STEVEN. 2001. Collaborative Information Retrieval (CIR). In: Höglund, L., ed. Information Seeking in Context: Proceedings of the 3rd International Conference on Information Needs, Seeking and Use in Different Contexts; 2000 August 16-18; Göteborg, Sweden. London, UK: Taylor Graham. (In press).

FIDEL, RAYA; DAVIES, RACHEL K.; DOUGLASS, MARY H.: HOLDER, JENNY K.; HOPKINS, CARLA J.; KUSHNER, ELISABETH J.; MIYAGISHIMA, BRYAN K.; TONEY, CHRISTINA D. 1999. A Visit to the Information Mall:

Web Searching Behavior of High School Students. Journal of the American Society for Information Science. 1999 January; 50(1): 24-37. ISSN: 0002-8231; OCLC: 1798118.

FIELDS, ROBERT E.; WRIGHT, PETER C., eds. 2000. Understanding Work and Designing Artefacts. International Journal of Human-Computer Studies. 2000 July; 53(1): 1-221. (Special issue). ISSN: 1071-5819.

GIDDENS, ANTHONY. 1984. The Constitution of Society: Outline of a Theory of Structuration. Berkeley, CA: University of California Press; 1984. 402p. ISBN: 0-520-05292-7.

GLUCK, MYKE. 1997. Making Sense of Semiotics: Privileging Respondents in Revealing Contextual Geographic Syntactic and Semantic Codes. In: Vakkari, Pertti; Savolainen, Reijo; Dervin, Brenda, eds. Information Seeking in Context: Proceedings of an International Conference on Research in Information Needs, Seeking and Use in Different Contexts; 1996 August 14-16; Tampere, Finland. London, UK: Taylor Graham; 1997. 53-66. ISBN: 0-947568-71-9; OCLC: 37137193.

GRANOVETTER, MARK S. 1973. The Strength of Weak Ties. American Journal of Sociology. 1973 May; 78: 1360-1380. ISSN: 0002-9602; OCLC: 1831931.

GRANOVETTER, MARK S. 1982. The Strength of Weak Ties: A Network Theory Revisited. In: Marsden, Peter V.; Lin, Nan, eds. Social Structure and Network Analysis. Beverly Hills, CA: Sage; 1982. 105-130. ISBN: 0-8039-1888-7; OCLC: 8667513.

GROSS, MELISSA. 1999. Imposed Versus Self-Generated Questions: Implications for Reference Practice. Reference & User Services Quarterly. 1999 Fall; 39(1): 53-61. ISSN: 1094-9054; OCLC: 37395409.

GROSS, MELISSA. 2001. Imposed Information Seeking in School Library Media Centers and Public Libraries: A Common Behaviour? In: Höglund, L., ed. Information Seeking in Context: Proceedings of the 3rd International Conference on Research in Information Needs, Seeking and Use in Different Contexts; 2000 August 16-18; Göteborg, Sweden. London, UK: Taylor Graham. (In press).

HARRÉ, ROM. 1983. Personal Being. Oxford, UK: Basil Blackwell; 1983. 299p. ISBN: 0-631-13318-6; OCLC: 10209198.

HAYTHORNTHWAITE, CAROLINE; WELLMAN, BARRY. 1998. Work, Friendship, and Media Use for Information Exchange in a Networked Environment. Journal of the American Society for Information Science. 1998 October; 49(12): 1101-1114. ISSN: 0002-8231; OCLC: 1798118.

HERSBERGER, JULIA A.; PETTIGREW, KAREN E.; JAMES, LESLIE C. 2000. Social Capital as Embedded in the Social Support Networks of Homeless Populations. Paper presented at: Sunbelt XX: International Sunbelt Social Network Conference; 2000 April 13-16; Vancouver, British Columbia.

HEWINS, ELIZABETH T. 1990. Information Need and Use Studies. In: Williams, Martha E., ed. Annual Review of Information Science and Technology: Volume 25. Amsterdam, The Netherlands: Elsevier Science Publishers for the American Society for Information Science; 1990. 145-172. ISSN: 0066-4200; ISBN: 0-444-88531-5.

HJØRLAND, BIRGER; ALBRECHTSEN, HANNE. 1995. Toward a New Horizon in Information Science: Domain Analysis. Journal of the American Society for Information Science. 1995 July; 46(6): 400-425. ISSN: 0002-8231; OCLC: 1798118.

INFORMATION SEEKING IN CONTEXT. Web site: http://www.hb.se/bhs/bibvet/isic/Index.htm.

JÄRVELIN, KALERVO; VAKKARI, PERTTI. 1990. Content Analysis of Research Articles in Library and Information Science. Library & Information Science Research. 1990 October-December; 12(4): 395-421. ISSN: 0740-8188; OCLC: 9844287.

JÄRVELIN, KALERVO; VAKKARI, PERTTI. 1993. The Evolution of Library and Information Science 1965-1985: A Content Analysis of Journal Articles. Information Processing & Management. 1993; 29(1): 129-144. ISSN: 0306-4573; OCLC: 2243314.

JESSE. 1999. Discussion of Information Behavior. Available WWW: http://listserv.utk.edu/cgi-bin/wa?A1=ind9912&L=jesse.

JOHNSON, J. DAVID; DONOHUE, WILLIAM A.; ATKIN, CHARLES K.; JOHNSON, SALLY. 1995. A Comprehensive Model of Information Seeking: Tests Focusing on a Technical Organization. Science Communication. 1995 March; 16(3): 274-303. ISSN: 1075-5470; OCLC: 30083948.

JULIEN, HEIDI. 1996. A Content Analysis of the Recent Information Needs and Uses Literature. Library & Information Science Research. 1996 Winter; 18(1): 53-65. ISSN: 0740-8188; OCLC: 9844287.

JULIEN, HEIDI; DUGGAN, LAWRENCE J. 2000. A Longitudinal Analysis of the Information Needs and Uses Literature. Library & Information Science Research. 2000; 22(3): 291-309. ISSN: 0740-8188; OCLC: 9844287.

KUHLTHAU, CAROL C. 1991. Inside the Search Process: Information Seeking from the User's Perspective. Journal of the American Society for Information Science. 1991 June; 42(5): 361-371. ISSN: 0002-8231; OCLC: 1798118.

KUHLTHAU, CAROL C.; TUROCK, BETTY J.; BELVIN, ROBERT J. 1988. Facilitating Information Seeking through Cognitive Models of the Search Process. In: Borgman, Christine L.; Pai, Edward Y. H., eds. ASIS '88: Proceedings of the American Society for Information Science (ASIS) 51st Annual Meeting: Volume 25; 1988 October 23-27; Atlanta, GA. Medford, NJ: Learned Information, Inc. for ASIS; 1988. 70-75. ISSN: 0044-7870; ISBN: 0-938734-29-6.

KUHLTHAU, CAROL C.; VAKKARI, PERTTI. 1999. Information Seeking in Context (ISIC). Information Processing & Management. 1999 November; 35(6): 723-725. ISSN: 0306-4573; OCLC: 2243314.

LECKIE, GLORIA J.; PETTIGREW, KAREN E.; SYLVAIN, CHRISTIAN. 1996. Modeling the Information Seeking of Professionals: A General Model Derived from Research on Engineers, Health Care Professionals, and Lawyers. Library Quarterly. 1996 April; 66(2): 161-193. ISSN: 0024-2519; OCLC: 1755858.

LIN, NAN. 2001. Social Capital: A Theory of Social Structure and Action. New York, NY: Cambridge University Press; 2001. 278p. ISBN: 0-521-47431-0.

74     KAREN E. PETTIGREW, RAYA FIDEL, AND HARRY BRUCE

MACMULLIN, SUSAN E.; TAYLOR, ROBERT S. 1984. Problem Dimensions
 and Information Traits. The Information Society. 1984; 3(1): 91-111. ISSN:
 0197-2243; OCLC: 5986609.
MCKECHNIE, LYNNE; PETTIGREW, KAREN E.; JOYCE, STEVEN. 2001. The
 Origins and Contextual Use of Theory in Human Information Behavior
 Research. In: Höglund, L., ed. Information Seeking in Context: Proceed-
 ings of the 3rd International Conference on Research in Information
 Needs, Seeking and Use in Different Contexts; 2000 August 16-18; Göteborg,
 Sweden. London, UK: Taylor Graham. (In press).
MOREHEAD, DAVID R.; ROUSE, WILLIAM B.; PEJTERSEN, ANNELISE
 MARK. 1984. The Value of Information and Computer-Aided Informa-
 tion Seeking: Problem Formulation and Application to Fiction Retrieval.
 Information Processing & Management. 1984; 20(5/6): 583-601. ISSN:
 0306-4573; OCLC: 2243314.
MORRIS, RUTH C. T. 1994. Toward a User-Centered Information Service.
 Journal of the American Society for Information Science. 1994 January;
 45(1): 20-30. ISSN: 0002-8231; OCLC: 1798118.
NOUR, MARTYVONNE M. 1985. A Quantitative Analysis of the Research
 Articles Published in Core Library Journals of 1980. Library & Information
 Science Research. 1985; 7: 261-273. ISSN: 0740-8188; OCLC: 9844287.
PEJTERSEN, ANNELISE MARK. 1984. Design of a Computer-Aided User-
 System Dialogue Based on an Analysis of Users' Search Behaviour. Social
 Science Information Studies. 1984; 4(2/3): 167-183. ISSN: 0143-6236; OCLC:
 7700464.
PEJTERSEN, ANNELISE MARK; AUSTIN, JUTTA. 1983. Fiction Retrieval:
 Experimental Design and Evaluation of a Search System Based on Users'
 Value Criteria. Part 1. Journal of Documentation. 1983 December; 39(4):
 230-246. ISSN: 0022-0418; OCLC: 1754538.
PEJTERSEN, ANNELISE MARK; AUSTIN, JUTTA. 1984. Fiction Retrieval:
 Experimental Design and Evaluation of a Search System Based on Users'
 Value Criteria. Part 2. Journal of Documentation. 1984 March; 40(1): 25-35.
 ISSN: 0022-0418; OCLC: 1754538.
PEJTERSEN, ANNELISE MARK; SONNENWALD, DIANE H.; BUUR, J.;
 GOVINDAREJ, T.; VICENTE, KIM J. 1995. Using Cognitive Engineering
 Theory to Support Knowledge Exploration in Design. In: Hubka, V., ed.
 Proceedings of ICED 95: 10th International Conference on Engineering
 Design; 1995 August 22-24; Prague, Czechoslovakia. Zurich, Switzerland:
 HEURISTA; 1995. 219-229. ISBN: 3-85693-028-0.
PERITZ, BLUMA C. 1980. The Methods of Library Science Research: Some
 Results from a Bibliometric Study. Library Research. 1980 Fall; 2(3): 251-
 268. ISSN: 0164-0763; OCLC: 4572306.
PETTIGREW, KAREN E. 1999. Waiting for Chiropody: Contextual Results
 from an Ethnographic Study of the Information Behavior among Attend-
 ees at Community Clinics. Information Processing & Management. 1999
 November; 35(6): 801-817. ISSN: 0306-4573; OCLC: 2243314.
PETTIGREW, KAREN E. 2000. Lay Information Provision in Community
 Settings: How Community Health Nurses Disseminate Human Services
 Information to the Elderly. Library Quarterly. 2000 January; 70(1): 47-85.
 ISSN: 0024-2519; OCLC: 1755858.

PETTIGREW, KAREN E.; DURRANCE, JOAN C. 2000. Community Building Using the 'Net: Perceptions of Organizers, Information Providers and Internet Users. Paper presented at Internet Research 1.0: The State of the Interdiscipline, 1st Annual Conference of the Association of Internet Researchers; 2000 September 14-17; Lawrence, KS. Available WWW: http://www.cddc.vt.edu/aoir/2000/index.html.

PETTIGREW, KAREN E.; MCKECHNIE, LYNNE. 2001. The Use of Theory in Information Science Research. Journal of the American Society for Information Science and Technology. 2001 January; 52(1): 62-73. ISSN:1532-2882; OCLC: 45266164.

PUTNAM, ROBERT D. 1995. Bowling Alone: America's Declining Social Capital. Journal of Democracy. 1995 January; 6(1): 65-78. ISSN: 1045-5736; OCLC: 20333981.

PUTNAM, ROBERT D. 2000. Bowling Alone : The Collapse and Revival of American Community. New York, NY: Simon & Schuster; 2000. 541p. ISBN: 0-684-83283-6; OCLC: 43599073.

RASMUSSEN, JENS; PEJTERSEN, ANNELISE MARK; GOODSTEIN, L.P. 1994. Cognitive Systems Engineering. New York, NY: Wiley; 1994. 378p. ISBN: 0-471-01198-3; OCLC: 29521798.

ROSENBAUM, HOWARD. 1993. Information Use Environments and Structuration: Towards an Integration of Taylor and Giddens. In: Bonzi, Susan, ed. ASIS '93: Proceedings of the American Society for Information Science (ASIS) 56th Annual Meeting: Volume 30; 1993 October 24-28; Columbus, OH. Medford, NJ: Learned Information, Inc. for ASIS; 1993. 235-245. ISSN: 0044-7870; ISBN: 0-938734-78-4.

SANDSTROM, PAMELA EFFREIN. 1994. An Optimal Foraging Approach to Information Seeking and Use. Library Quarterly. 1994 October; 64(4): 414-449. ISSN: 0024-2519; OCLC: 1755858.

SARACEVIC, TEFKO; KANTOR, PAUL; CHAMIS, ALICE Y.; TRIVISON, DONNA. 1988. A Study of Information Seeking and Retrieving. I. Background and Methodology. Journal of the American Society for Information Science. 1988 May; 39(3): 161-176. ISSN: 0002-8231; OCLC: 1798118.

SAVOLAINEN, REIJO. 1995. Everyday Life Information Seeking: Approaching Information Seeking in the Context of "Way of Life." Library & Information Science Research. 1995 Summer; 17(3): 259-294. ISSN: 0740-8188; OCLC: 9844287.

SAVOLAINEN, REIJO. 1998. Use Studies of Electronic Networks: A Review of Empirical Research Approaches and Challenges for their Development. Journal of Documentation. 1998 June; 54(3): 332-351. ISSN: 0022-0418; OCLC: 1754538.

SOLOMON, PAUL. 1997a. Conversation in Information Seeking Contexts: A Test of an Analytical Framework. Library & Information Science Research. 1997; 19(3): 217-248. ISSN: 0740-8188; OCLC: 9844287.

SOLOMON, PAUL. 1997b. Discovering Information Behavior in Sense Making. I. Time and Timing. Journal of the American Society for Information Science. 1997 December; 48(12): 1097-1108. ISSN: 0002-8231; OCLC: 1798118.

SOLOMON, PAUL. 1997c. Discovering Information Behavior in Sense Making. II. The Social. Journal of the American Society for Information Science. 1997 December; 48(12): 1109-1126. ISSN: 0002-8231; OCLC: 1798118.

SOLOMON, PAUL. 1997d. Discovering Information Behavior in Sense Making. III. The Person. Journal of the American Society for Information Science. 1997 December; 48(12): 1127-1138. ISSN: 0002-8231; OCLC: 1798118.

SONNENWALD, DIANE H. 1999. Evolving Perspectives of Human Information Behaviour: Contexts, Situations, Social Networks and Information Horizons. In: Wilson, Thomas D.; Allen, D. K., eds. Exploring the Contexts of Information Behaviour: Proceedings of the 2nd International Conference on Research in Information Needs, Seeking and Use in Different Contexts; 1998 August 13-15; Sheffield, UK. London, UK: Taylor Graham; 1999. 176-190. ISBN: 0-947568-75-1; OCLC: 42308021.

SONNENWALD, DIANE H.; PIERCE, LINDA G. 2000. Information Behavior in Dynamic Group Work Contexts: Interwoven Situational Awareness, Dense Social Networks and Contested Collaboration in Command and Control. Information Processing & Management. 2000 May; 36(3): 461-479. ISSN: 0306-4573; OCLC: 2243314.

SONNENWALD, DIANE H.; WILDEMUTH, BARBARA M.; BRASSELL, EMILY; KINDON, VICTORIA; HARMON, GARY. 2001. A Research Method to Investigate Information Seeking Using the Concept of Information Horizons: An Example from a Study of Lower Socio-economic Students' Information Seeking Behavior. In: Höglund, L., ed. Information Seeking in Context: Proceedings of the 3rd International Conference on Research in Information Needs, Seeking and Use in Different Contexts; 2000 August 16-18; Göteborg, Sweden. London, UK: Taylor Graham. (In press).

SUTCLIFFE, ALISTAIR; ENNIS, MARK. 1998. Towards a Cognitive Theory of Information Retrieval. Interacting with Computers. 1998 June; 10(3): 321-351. ISSN: 0953-5438; OCLC: 20745502.

TALJA, SANNA. 1997. Constituting "Information" and "User" as Research Objects: A Theory of Knowledge Formations as an Alternative to the Information Man-Theory. In: Vakkari, Pertti; Savolainen, Reijo; Dervin, Brenda, eds. Information Seeking in Context: Proceedings of an International Conference on Research in Information Needs, Seeking and Use in Different Contexts; 1996 August 14-16; Tampere, Finland. London, UK: Taylor Graham; 1997. 67-80. ISBN: 0-947568-71-9; OCLC: 37137193.

TALJA, SANNA; KESO, HEIDI; PIETILAINEN, TARJA. 1999. The Production of "Context" in Information Seeking Research: A Metatheoretical View. Information Processing & Management. 1999 November; 35(6): 751-763. ISSN: 0306-4573; OCLC: 2243314.

TAYLOR, ROBERT S. 1968. Question-Negotiation and Information Seeking in Libraries. College and Research Libraries. 1968 May; 29(3): 178-194. ISSN: 0010-0870; OCLC: 2354797.

TAYLOR, ROBERT S. 1984. Value-Added Processes in Document-Based Systems: Abstracting and Indexing Services. Information Services and Use. 1984 June; 4(3): 127-146. ISSN: 0167-5265.

TAYLOR, ROBERT S. 1985. Information Values in Decision Contexts. Information Management Review. 1985; 1(1): 47-55. ISSN: 8756-1557; OCLC: 11481854.

TAYLOR, ROBERT S. 1986. Value-Added Processes in Information Systems. Norwood, NJ: Ablex; 1986. 257p. ISBN: 0-89391-273-5; OCLC: 12420071.

TAYLOR, ROBERT S. 1991. Information Use Environments. In: Dervin, Brenda; Voigt, M. J., eds. Progress in Communication Sciences: Volume 10. Norwood, NJ: Ablex; 1991. 217-255. ISSN: 0163-5689; ISBN: 0-89391-645-5.

TUOMINEN, KIMMO; SAVOLAINEN, REIJO. 1997. A Social Constructionist Approach to the Study of Information Use as Discursive Action. In: Vakkari, Pertti; Savolainen, Reijo; Dervin, Brenda, eds. Information Seeking in Context: Proceedings of an International Conference on Research in Information Needs, Seeking and Use in Different Contexts; 1996 August 14-16; Tampere, Finland. London, UK: Taylor Graham; 1997. 81-96. ISBN: 0-947568-71-9; OCLC: 37137193.

VAKKARI, PERTTI. 1999. Task Complexity, Problem Structure and Information Actions. Integrating Studies on Information Seeking and Retrieval. Information Processing & Management. 1999 November; 35(6): 819-837. ISSN: 0306-4573; OCLC: 2243314.

VAKKARI, PERTTI. 2000. Cognition, Sources and Contributory Information of Documents in Writing a Research Proposal: A Longitudinal Case Study. In: Kraft, Donald H., ed. ASIS 2000: Proceedings of the American Society for Information Science (ASIS) 63rd Annual Meeting: Volume 37; 2000 November 16-20; Chicago, IL. Medford, NJ: Information Today, Inc. for ASIS; 2000. 352-362. ISSN: 0044-7870; ISBN: 1-57387-108-7.

VICENTE, KIM J. 1999. Cognitive Work Analysis: Towards Safe, Productive, and Healthy Computer-Based Work. Mahwah, NJ: Lawrence Erlbaum Associates; 1999. 392p. ISBN: 0-8058-2396-4; OCLC: 39985534.

WESTBROOK, LYNN. 1994. Qualitative Research Methods: A Review of Major Stages, Data Analysis Techniques, and Quality Controls. Library & Information Science Research. 1994 Summer; 16(3): 241-254. ISSN: 0740-8188; OCLC: 9844287.

WILLIAMSON, KIRSTY. 1998. Discovered by Chance: The Role of Incidental Information Acquisition in an Ecological Model of Information Use. Library & Information Science Research. 1998; 20(1): 23-40. ISSN: 0740-8188; OCLC: 9844287.

WILSON, THOMAS D. 1997. Information Behaviour: An Interdisciplinary Perspective. Information Processing & Management. 1997 July; 33(4): 551-572. ISSN: 0306-4573; OCLC: 2243314.

WILSON, THOMAS D. 1999a. Exploring Models of Information Behaviour: The "Uncertainty" Project. Information Processing & Management. 1999 November; 35(6): 839-849. ISSN: 0306-4573; OCLC: 2243314.

WILSON, THOMAS D. 1999b. Models in Information Behaviour Research. Journal of Documentation. 1999 June; 55(3): 249-270. ISSN: 0022-0418; OCLC: 1754538.

WILSON, THOMAS D. 2000. Human Information Behavior. Informing Science. 2000; 3(2): 49-56. ISSN: 1521-4672. Available WWW: http://inform.nu/Articles/Vol3/v3n2p49-56.pdf.

YERBURY, HILARY; PARKER, JOAN. 1998. Novice Searchers' Use of Familiar Structures in Searching Bibliographic Information Retrieval Systems. Journal of Information Science. 1998; 24(4): 207-214. ISSN: 0165-5515; OCLC: 5094715.

YOON, KYUNGHYE; NILAN, MICHAEL S.   1999.   Toward a Reconceptualization of Information Seeking Research: Focus on the Exchange of Meaning. Information Processing & Management. 1999 November; 35(6): 871-890. ISSN: 0306-4573; OCLC: 2243314.

# 3 Distributed Information Management

**WILLIAM M. POTTENGER**
**Lehigh University**

**MIRANDA R. CALLAHAN and**
**MICHAEL A. PADGETT**
**National Center for Supercomputing**
**Applications**

## INTRODUCTION

A review of this sort commonly begins with the observation that current developments in computer technology are radically changing the nature of library science and information management. Widespread digitization of information and the ubiquity of networking have created fundamentally new possibilities for collecting, distributing, and preserving information. Just as important, however, as the changing technological and organizational systems themselves are the repercussions these powerful world-scale information networks will have on the social and cultural structures they have been developed to serve. Similarly, the formation and development of these new technologies will, to no small extent, depend on the cultural forces that brought them into existence in the first place, as the shape of information technology and the institutions it serves are in many ways interdependent. To capture the complexity of the interwoven technological and societal forces that guide the growth of information management, then, we need to cast a wide net over the fields of information, computer, and library science to gather topics and themes in all those areas that are shaping and being shaped by the development of distributed information systems.

A picture of such a dynamic field, encompassing so many different areas of social and technological significance, must of necessity be broadly painted. This chapter delineates the scope and effects of distributed information management, touching on current developments, ex-

We gratefully acknowledge the assistance of the staff in the Emerging Technologies Group at the National Center for Supercomputing Applications at the University of Illinois. William M. Pottenger gratefully acknowledges the aid of his Lord and Savior Jesus Christ in completing this work.

*Annual Review of Information Science and Technology (ARIST)*, Volume 35, 2001
Martha E. Williams, Editor
Published for the American Society for Information Science and Technology (ASIST)
By Information Today, Inc., Medford, NJ

periments, and cultural implications of this rapidly changing area of research. As any user of the Internet might guess, the large number of distributed information management projects makes a truly comprehensive review of the field impossible. Here we attempt to cover at least the most important and influential work being done in the area.

Because the technologies of networking and computing are now in a state of intense, expansive growth, it is also difficult to single out any trend or thrust in the development of distributed information systems as being especially noteworthy or important—too much research is going on in too many different areas, and the capabilities of computers, distribution systems, and search engines are continually increasing. To restrict a survey of this field to any given subset of developments, then, might risk becoming excessively narrow, or even arbitrary. Instead, basing this chapter on a generous interpretation of distributed information and digital libraries, we review some of the ways in which technology, social systems, and inherited knowledge structures intermesh to form, and be formed by, technologies of distributed information management. Another gray area in this review is the problem of the definition of boundaries in a distributed information system. In their discussion of the boundary problem, ACKERMAN & FIELDING distinguish the "broadly-construed" from the "narrowly-construed" library system (pp. 3-5). Because of the interconnection of most networked systems, and the variety of projects developed to manage distributed information, it is often difficult to determine the difference between being inside and outside a system like a distributed digital library. This survey, therefore, deals with themes relating both to closely knit systems under organized control, based on traditional ideas of the library, and to more open systems, in which control is distributed—the most bottom-up of these being, of course, the Internet (HARTER; WALLACE).

Most difficult, perhaps, is the problem of defining exactly what constitutes a distributed information management system (often termed a digital library). Given the fast-growing, constantly changing nature of this field, the only sort of definition possible at this time is an open and informal one, such as that given by ARMS, who defines a digital library as "a managed collection of information, with associated services" (ARMS, p. 2), such that the material is digitized and accessible over a network; or even more succinctly by LESK, who states that a digital library is "a collection of information that is both digitized and organized" (LESK, p. 1). Following this definition, this chapter can be seen most generally as an exploration of the various ways in which people are approaching these double problems of digitization and organization, and how their solutions are gradually creating the new form of the digital library.

This chapter is divided into five general areas; first, an introductory section deals with the cultural and social aspects of digital libraries. The following sections treat technological issues: searching in a loosely coupled distributed system; organization of a distributed collection; indexing, search, and retrieval in tightly coupled libraries, with specific examples; and, finally, problems with archiving in a distributed environment. A concluding section discusses future work.

## CULTURAL AND SOCIAL INFLUENCES

The traditional provider of information in modern society has been, up to the advent of computerized information services, the library. The most general function of the library, in both its public and private incarnations, is as a gathering center for information which, until recently, has always been artifactual. The sheer concreteness of books, journals, and other collected materials has necessitated that the basic form of the library be centered on a repository. The implication of substituting (or even just adding) digitized distributed information in this system is that, at the very least, the shape of the library and its services will evolve—although as many authors note, the social and cultural changes wrought by this shift will be at least as dramatic as the structural ones.

### Library and Internet Culture

The joining of the traditional library with the distributed information network has prompted some writers to examine the merging of library and Internet values, which they see as combining dialectically to create the culture of the digital library. The traditional library, claim LEVY & MARSHALL, is culturally associated with "notions of fixity and permanence" (1994, p. 5) that have almost automatically been carried over into the conception of the digital library, which is then expected to also exhibit these qualities. Contemporary authors and philosophers, however, almost invariably characterize current postmodern culture as fragmented, fluid, and ephemeral; YOUNG even argues that the impact of this new culture is most pervasive in the fields of library and information science. Indeed, many of the current controversies in digital library development can be seen as manifestations of the clash between traditional librarianship and a new, free-flowing cyberculture, managed by technologists from a computer science background. The break made by computer-oriented managers with standard library practices is often radical enough to be the source of heated argument; see HENRY, who finds fault with the "new paradigm" of digital preservation, or CRAWFORD's (1999) polemic against the purely digital library, for example.

Digital material is naturally ephemeral and aspatial, and it is this tension between solidity and impermanence that is one of the core issues governing the development of the distributed digital library. How and to what extent should a digital collection emulate the virtuous solidity of a set of concrete objects?

It is not only the insubstantiality made possible by the distributed network that will influence the development of the library, however, but also the cultural ideas that have sprung up to accompany new technological capabilities. Not just the computer qua machine, but also the very idea of the computer as a "metaphor for personal identity" (YOUNG, p. 113) will profoundly affect the ways in which society—and the institution of the library—will develop. In this sense, it is notable that BUSH, in his seminal essay "As We May Think," describes a mechanized electronic library as "an enlarged intimate supplement" to memory, evoking already in 1945 a hint of cyborgian melding of reader and machine.

On the other hand, there are also points of similarity between what are traditionally seen as research library and Internet values (ANTELMAN & LANGENBERG). A major goal of the university library has always been the free exchange of knowledge and information; on an even wider level, this goal has also been shared by the American public library system since its inception. In the age of the Internet, this ideal seems to have been elevated by some to an almost religious, unquestioned belief (LEVY, p. 4); indeed, FOX & MARCHIONINI go so far as to describe information as "a basic human need" (p. 31). Furthermore, Internet and research library cultures, seeing information as a valuable good, are generally both opposed to censorship and commercialization, which could be seen as hindrances to the free flow of information. ANTELMAN & LANGENBERG attribute this similarity in values to the common development of both in the university community (p. 54), although these values have often been seen as shared for the most part by the entire public library community. ATKINSON goes so far as to root the library's moral strength (its "ability to uphold social ethics" (p. 247)) in its nonprofit status; equally vehement pleas against commercialization of the Internet on moral grounds are too numerous to count.

## Information and Knowledge

The cultural valuing of information as a good per se leads in the extreme to a purely quantitative valuation of library service, where more is always better, in and of itself. (See COFFMAN, for example, for an enthusiastic discussion of the possibility of creating the largest library on earth.) This drive to deliver the most information possible reveals an important consequence of distributed digital information for the organization and structure of the library: When vast quantities of information are readily available electronically, what does the library become? Before the advent of the Internet, libraries were financially and spatially limited in what they could collect; the librarian acted as selector and sifter of information, choosing the artifacts that would be collected and maintained. The implication of fully networked world-scale information communities, however, seems, paradoxically, to presage a reduced role for the library: If all the information in the world is suddenly available, and nothing need be excluded because of spatial or budgetary restraints, what is the institutional function of the library?

As early as 1979, BOORSTIN pointed out the disadvantages of the information glut, in his reformulation of Gresham's law: "Information tends to drive knowledge out of circulation" (p. 3). A main point of Boorstin's speech is that a vital part of libraries is their intentionality: they exist not just as repositories, but as collections thoughtfully developed by people for a specific purpose. The danger of enthusiastically embracing wide-scale digital distribution at the expense of traditional libraries is that systems that collect vast amounts of information just because it is available will displace systems of knowledge—institutions that have been developed to further or to advance some human intention. Along the same lines, CRAWFORD (1998) asserts that communities want libraries to be mainly not a source of information, but a source of books. Seen this way, the expansion promised by a distributed library could in one sense create a sort of diminishment of services provided.

## The Electronic Librarian

This problem of purpose, or creating knowledge out of information, relates to the distributed digital library on many levels, centering on the question of how a library can create a knowledge structure out of (or impose one on) an unstructured sea of information. Many authors (ARNOLD; HARTER; ODLYZKO; YOUNG) foresee a fundamental shift in the role of the librarian in a distributed digital environment. Instead of tending to physical collections as in the past, the librarian will become a "knowledge navigator," a mediator between the patron or researcher and the trackless network (perhaps corresponding to the "trailblazers" first described by BUSH fifty years ago). When the idea of the library is expanded to include distributed collections that have not been grown and cultivated by its own staff, the metaphor of librarianship changes from that of the gardener to that of the tracker: instead of carefully planning and developing in a controlled environment, the librarian must carve paths through the wilderness of a network not of his or her own making, becoming an explorer as well as a guide (see GRIFFITHS for an excellent in-depth discussion of this transformation; WARD and SCHWARZWALDER are also relevant).

Similarly, LANHAM sees a metamorphosis "from [a] curatorial to [an] interpretive" role, describing the librarian's new function as the constructor of "human attention-structures." This function is a response to what he sees as the need for an "economics of attention" to counter the problem of overabundance of information in a networked environment. ARNOLD addresses this change head-on in his "The Electronic Librarian Is a Verb" lecture, describing the cyberlibrarian as heroically "creating a syntax of digital knowledge" (p. 5) in a library that has become "more a state of mind than a location . . . a set of neural connectors" (p. 12).

In a more short-term sense, bringing distributed digital systems into a library's purview will create very tangible problems for the librarian. Budgeting, for example, will need to be adjusted, if shelf space and acquisition are to be replaced or supplemented by net-accessed information (ARNOLD, YOUNG). The process of acquisition itself will also be changed, as libraries begin to link to resources not physically present, instead of actually bringing objects into the library. Finally, ideas about archival management will change, if the contents of a library shift from primarily concrete objects to mainly items that are only virtually accessible.

## Social Aspects of the Library

Another aspect of the shift to distributed information systems is the change in the social dynamic of the library. If the library becomes purely (or even just mostly) distributed, disappearing as a concrete place, the social interaction facilitated therein will be lost, unless it is deliberately replaced in electronic form. One role played by the traditional public library is that of the community center, offering programs and gathering possibilities for groups of patrons. Furthermore, in a university setting, the library can promote serendipitous encounters between students and among faculty members, thus serving a truly social purpose.

More to the point, perhaps, social interaction can be an integral part of library work, as researchers exchange information while searching (ACKERMAN; LEVY & MARSHALL). LEVY also cites a case study of the behavior of information analysts to show the centrality of collaborative activity (marking of papers, discussion) to the enterprise of research.

Here, the structure of the digital library intersects with the field of computer supported cooperative work, which generates various projects to facilitate group communication over a network, both in real time and as the construction of a "collective memory" of annotations. We can go back to BUSH to find a first description of this idea of the collective memory, in the "Memex" used to create trails of linked information, which can then be shared with other researchers. Generally, common tools such as email, listservs, chat rooms, and remote conferencing can all be seen as electronically supported means for group communication. These projects, however, tend to be general-purpose, not specifically developed for digital library use, and there are simply too many of them to begin to describe in this chapter.

SIMMONS gives an interesting description of the ideal electronic collaborative tool, characterized by ease of use, support for all kinds of media, and freedom from the restrictive keyboard and chair. This tool, furthermore, would be outfitted with artificially intelligent computational agents available to each user, and provide a large display— perhaps even a virtual reality. Basically, Simmons wants to fully use the capabilities of networked communication to promote the freest, most spontaneous and complete exchange of ideas possible.

MARSHALL also discusses the role of annotation in digital collections, noting that the traditional library's age-old admonitions against marking in books can now happily be reversed in a digital setting, as readers' annotations "may become important adjuncts to the primary text" (p. 131). MARSHALL's study of student behavior with respect to annotations in university textbooks demonstrates the value even of informal, disorganized reader-to-reader communication. Distributed digital collections, she feels, can facilitate this sort of collaborative reading and discussion of a work in a more open, well-organized format by providing the reader with books specifically designed to be marked up and thus adding new value to the library collection. Indeed, digitally annotated books could be seen as even more valuable than their untouched nondistributed counterparts.

One project in development that will incorporate interactive user-to-user communication is the National Engineering Education Delivery System (NEEDS) (NATIONAL ENGINEERING EDUCATION DELIVERY SYSTEM), which is being specifically designed to not only provide distributed digital information for a specific educational purpose, but also to generate and nurture a community of learners. User-added reviews and discussion groups are currently part of the NEEDS system, but part of the plan for future work involves the addition of pedagogical metadata, allowing educators to tag digital objects with information about its educational applicability (MURAMATSU).

The advantages of the distributed research collection, then, extend beyond the wide and instantaneous dissemination of digitalized text, with advanced searching and visualization technology. Even as the digital library reduces research to a more solitary activity, with patrons no longer gathered together at a single location to access resources, it can also make possible a whole new level of collaborative work, as readers-cum-annotators are able to grow simple texts into discussions across time and space (ROBERTSON ET AL.).

## LOOSELY COUPLED DIGITAL COLLECTIONS

The question of what should be contained in a digital library can be answered in many ways. The strictest definition is perhaps that given in 1994 by MIKSA & DOTY, who insisted that the definition of a library presupposes the existence of a bounded collection. The freest definition is that of the "anarchic and individualistic" Internet (HARTER), which lacks control and organization.

LAGOZE & FIELDING, taking into account the possibilities of unlimited information access as well as the need for the imposition of some sort of organization on a collection, define a digital library from two perspectives, the logical and the operational. In the logical sense, they see a collection as definable by a "set of criteria for selecting resources from the broader information space." Operationally, membership in a digital collection can be defined "in terms of resource discovery": the digital library consists of all resources that can be found using the library's resource discovery tools (excluding objects found only in links from the directly discoverable set).

Often, the trade-off seems to be between the selection of a collection itself, and the power of the indexing machines that service it. If a collection is not well-indexed, or not easily searchable, it should be small, and works without value should be excluded, or it will become difficult to use successfully. If, on the other hand, one can build sophisticated search engines, and clever indexing algorithms, capable of teasing a value hierarchy out of the text contained in a large collection of information, it becomes less harmful to let as much information as possible flow into the system.

## A Single Distributed Library: The Control Zone

An interesting compromise solution to the problem of scope is ATKINSON's idea of a control zone within an anarchic networked system. To create a control zone, a group would carve an organized, systematized space out of the uncontrolled Internet. This space would be a "single, distributed digital library—created and managed by the academic library community" (ATKINSON, p. 239), with information only coming into the zone after a process of review and selection. This idea is a variation on the theme of the single universal library—an idea that seems to have always been around. As with many such schemes, the possibility of its realization would in the end be dependent on patient diplomacy and committee work to bring together the participants necessary to make the zone function on such a large scale.

In the structure of the zone, ATKINSON sees the librarian's function as adding value to information through his or her work. In this sense, librarians should distinguish one book from another by adding access value to books of high worth (putting them in the zone), and denying it to those of lower value. The librarian becomes an evaluator of worth in some context, taking over part of the filtering role that is, in a print environment, to a large part fulfilled by the publishing community.

ATKINSON expands the idea of the value signifier in the control zone beyond the mere Boolean function of inclusion/exclusion by proposing the addition of two new types of metadata to accompany work in the zone. The first, use level, would track the history of use of digital objects, determining which items have been accessed by students, scholars, experts, and so on. Information about the accessor's status would be used to weight the importance or relevance of a given work. An object referenced often by expert users in a certain discipline, for example, could be automatically marked as highly important; whereas another object accessed just as often, but by student users rather than scholars, could then be marked accordingly. The second type of metadata, work level, would differentiate by level of difficulty and specialization. Although setting a work level would seem to require careful human deliberation, automatic use tracking is already being done today.

## Use Tracking to Facilitate Searching

The World Wide Web search engine GOOGLE, for example, could be seen as implementing a basic kind of static use-level algorithm to aid searching. Although the algorithm for this engine does not explicitly track user behavior in the Web, it directly adds access value to pages depending on how many links on the net point to them: in other words, it tracks net publisher behavior. This means that the more Web page creators decide that a specific site is valuable enough to be linked to, the more likely it is that this site will be returned by a search in the Google engine.

A dynamic prototype for user tracking to establish research-aiding metadata can be seen in KANTOR's AntWorld project. Antworld is a collaborative system to facilitate Internet searching by allowing a networked group of users to augment pages in the Web with information about their value. An Internet user can join the AntWorld by downloading software from the Web site and running an Antscape browser. This browser allows the user to enter a textual description of a quest (a search goal), and then, as he or she searches, to annotate links found with information as to how relevant they were to that quest. This information is then used to help other users evaluate search results. The basis for the AntWorld approach is the biological model of insect communication through pheromones; hence, the AntWorld term for meta-information about a link's value is Digital Information Pheromone. (Kantor's project does not go so far as ATKINSON suggests in that it does not take the professional or academic status of the user into account when weighting their evaluations. Concern for user privacy is understandably a major issue in user tracking projects.)

Similar work is being done by a group in France (BOUTHORS & DEDIEU) who have developed Pharos, a collaborative information sharing tool that allows users to contribute to a set of databases of annotations on Web pages. These annotations are then accessible through a browser assistant, which tracks pages browsed and displays relevant information. Pharos uses weighting algorithms based, in part, on the similarity of recommendations made, to automatically detect correlations between users. Thus, a user is situated in a group of (theoretically) similarly minded annotators, and can benefit from their evaluations without being flooded by the less useful information of an overall average evaluation.

Work funded as part of the second phase of the Digital Library Initiative is currently being done at the Oregon Graduate Institute of Science and Technology to create a system that can capture the document selections of experts and use them to aid subsequent problem solvers. This system to "track footprints" seems to be very similar to that proposed by ATKINSON for setting use levels in his control zone: The documents chosen by expert problem solvers are preserved in a trace, describing the path he or she took through a given collection. Navigation tools will then exploit this knowledge to help future problem solvers in their searches. Development of this system is still in its early phases (GORMAN ET AL.).

The Walden's Paths system developed by SHIPMAN ET AL. can be seen in one sense as the most highly directed path-based searching aid. This system allows educators to directly create paths for student use, as opposed to merely facilitating the passive gathering of information about sites as a side effect of regular browsing. An intermediary Path Server between a student's browser and the Web can automatically provide information about paths when a student downloads an annotated page. Shipman et al. describe paths so created as metadocuments. Here in the digital library, then, the functions of librarian and author meet, as the path organizer with his or her work lays down a new knowledge structure over the existing mass of digital information. This process of situating knowledge in the context of a path to aid students involved in a specific task is at the most directed, organized end of the continuum of searching aids.

## Hierarchical Distributed Dynamic Indexing

A novel approach to organizing large quantities of loosely coupled material is a system, in development jointly at Lehigh University and at the National Center for Supercomputing Applications at the University of Illinois, that will automatically create hierarchical models in a distributed, dynamic environment (see BOUSKILA & POTTENGER; POTTENGER). The Hierarchical Distributed Dynamic Indexing (HDDI™) strategy is based on the algorithmic creation of subtopic regions of semantic locality in sets of distributed documents, which allows automatic discovery of similarities at a fine level of granularity amongst concepts within documents. In this way, hierarchical indexes (now created manually in many places on the Web, such as YAHOO!) are generated for topics in documents in a volatile, distributed environment, providing the information seeker with an always up-to-date map of information spaces. The ability to generate large hierarchical indexes on the fly allows for a realistic, useful mapping of cyberspace without the need for time-consuming human intervention. This technique is most valuable when applied to documents within some institutional zone—to map out, for instance, large sets of corporate documents. Here, subjective issues relating to importance or quality can be sidestepped, and the power of the HDDI™ strategy can be fully leveraged. An unstructured set of documents lacking any sort of metadata can be bound to a hierarchical knowledge structure generated automatically based on word frequencies.

## TIGHTLY COUPLED DISTRIBUTED COLLECTIONS

The addition of distributed digital information to a collection presents unique opportunities and problems for the maintaining staff. As mentioned above, information stored in distributed systems tends to be both volatile and ephemeral. The information stored in Internet accounts, for example, is at the mercy of the owners of the computers where these accounts are stored—providers who naturally tend to treat these accounts as short-term, nonpermanent space (POCKLEY). More important, perhaps, is that digital resources cannot be fixed (except in an artificial sense, as when a digital copy of a paper object is created); they are continually open and therefore often subject to change. Almost any digital medium is always a sort of slate, or palimpsest, capable of being erased and rewritten without much ado—highly unlike ink on paper in book form. For now, much that is published on the Web behaves as if it were indeed concretized in a certain form, and is not changed; this situation, however, could be a temporary part of the movement to digital media, in which the old modes of work are carried over until new ways, which take advantage of the new possibilities presented by a digital format, come into being. The problem of constant reorganization and changing location of documents, however, is very much present even now, and on a distributed system, where information is provided in a set of links, this continual evolution can wreak havoc with nondynamic organization systems.

The issue of changing links reveals another source of problems in a distributed environment: the tension between local and global needs for information access. The addition of a distributed system to an information collection introduces a new layer of dependency, as maintainers must now depend on other institutions for the upkeep of the nonlocal portion of their collection. Some data show, however, that currently fifty percent of URLs are not available after two years (PASKIN, 1999a). Proposed solutions to this problem deal with systems from the loosely to the tightly coupled; from systems in which the library provides access to unknown, uncataloged resources (such as the Internet), to federations of libraries working closely together to achieve a common goal of formal cataloging.

## Persistent Object Identifiers

Perhaps the highest-level approach to the problem of continually changing information networks is the development of permanent link systems, so that local reorganization of sites will not affect global access to resources moved from one location to another. HODGE mentions several of these. First, the PURL project (PERSISTENT UNIFORM RESOURCE LOCATOR TEAM), supported by the Online Computer Library Center's Office of Research, is creating Persistent Uniform Resource Locators: URLs that point to an intermediate resolving service that returns the actual location of the desired resource (The resolving URL itself must be unchanging.) The PURL creators themselves see this solution as only temporary, until Uniform Resource Names (URNs) have become standardized and widely supported (SHAFER, 1999; WEIBEL ET AL.).

URNs, if implemented, would be persistent (they should last "longer even than the Internet," states ARMS (p. 235)), globally unique non-location-dependent resource names (ARMS ET AL.; LYNCH, 1997; SOLLINS & MASINTER). Like PURLs, however, URNs would need to be resolved into URLs in order to be used over a network. The basic problem in developing persistent links is the need to reconcile a static global name system with a dynamic location system or, more to the point, the need to standardize and coordinate the adaptation of such a system across the Internet.

Another recent project to treat the problem of broken links is the Robust Hyperlink, proposed by PHELPS & WILENSKY. A Robust Hyperlink can be implemented using the semantics of a regular URL, augmented with a lexical signature computed from the reference document. In the example given, the signatures are created by taking the terms in the document with the highest term frequency-inverse document frequency (TF-IDF) values. This signature can appear as a query appended to the URL, or as part of the HTML markup, etc., where it can then be used as a query submitted to search engines to find the keyed document. The authors claim that only a very small signature (about five words) is sufficient to facilitate quick location of individual documents, even in a space as vast as the Web. The advantages of this scheme are that it is lightweight, simple, and can be immediately implemented. The authors describe it as an example of the Web bootstrapping new features based on those already developed. The disadvantages seem mainly to be the same as for most of the permanent link schemes: they are not yet in general, widespread use.

One important project, described as the "ISBN for the 21st century" (PASKIN, 1999a), is the Digital Object Identifier, which would (as the name suggests) be a unique identifier for digital content. DOIs were developed specifically to facilitate the "management of copyrightable materials in an electronic environment" (PASKIN, 1999b) by creating a system for managing permissions and facilitating transactions on digital objects. The DOI is an abstract specification of an identifier and the system to process such identifiers; a prototype has, however, been built, based on the Corporation for National Research Initiatives (CNRI) Handle System, an identifier system capable of working with URNs. The Handle System is used to translate DOI to URL format, giving a location to a non-location-specific identifier.

The CNRI Handle System is perhaps the most extensively developed implementation of a global naming service currently in use. Like the systems described above, the Handle System uses globally unique names, which are then mapped by an organizing authority into their physical locations. The system works by creating a confederation of name spaces; this has the advantage that individual name systems can join a handle system and still retain their local names. Resolution management is based on a hierarchical model, so that names can be resolved into locations either by a local handle service or by a global registry—or by both. This allows the resolution process to be replicated and distributed across a system. The development of this system, planned in part to provide a framework for digital library infrastructure (SUN & LANNOM, part 6), influenced to a large extent the evolution of the

Networked Computer Science Technical Reference Library (NCSTRL) project, to be described later. The best introduction to the architecture of a handle system can be found in KAHN & WILENSKY's 1995 paper; the system itself is thoroughly described at CORPORATION FOR NATIONAL RESEARCH INITIATIVES, where a Handle Resolver can be downloaded to process Handle links even now.

## Metadata

Metadata—cataloging or indexing information about an object—could easily take up a chapter of its own; here we touch only on the newest aspects of metadata relating to distributed system development. In the distributed library, it seems that metadata has become more important than ever before, because it can facilitate the organization and management of networked information. On the other hand, some see the possibility that metadata for searching will become less significant in the future, as search engines are able to manipulate large amounts of text more rapidly, and thus become less dependent on finding aids (HARTER, p. 6).

Currently, the biggest obstacle to sophisticated wide-scale use of metadata in distributed systems seems to be not technological insufficiency, but lack of common standards. Imposing a single metadata protocol is difficult enough in a centrally controlled digital library; in a confederated system, where each local node has its own user base and requirements, it can become extremely complex. The problem of integrating local and distributed cataloging information is known as the problem of establishing interoperability: of creating systems that can get information from one another in a useful fashion. One method of allowing for information exchange is to make sure that crosswalking (automatic translation) between metadata formats is possible.

There are many projects aimed at developing systems of interoperable metadata. One tendency is to use a leaner, more abbreviated format such as the Dublin Core, to store only the most essential information about a work. HODGE mentions that it is also hoped that using a compact format will mean that publishers can provide metadata directly, so that the need for independent cataloging falls away (p. 8).

## Resource Description Framework

An important project that is attempting to address the problem of incompatible metadata standards is the Resource Description Framework (RDF), developed by the World Wide Web Consortium, along with others. RDF is basically an extension of XML (eXtensible Markup Language), and can be used to describe any resource that is uniquely identifiable by a Uniform Resource Identifier (URI). RDF has a simple data model, in which resources are associated with property-types, which can in turn point to other resources, or simple values (such as strings).

Such a simple data model, combined with structural and semantic rules, can be used to encode information from widely varying metadata in a single format. This heterogeneous encoding is achieved by using the XML namespace mechanism at the beginning of a record to give a pointer to a resource that has all the information about the metadata fields used in the record itself. Once a list of references has been given, providing a format for each metadata scheme to be used in the record, the XML tags in the data model are set up to include both the name of the tag, and the metadata model to which this tag belongs. Basically, instead of forcing all records to fit into a common scheme, a Resource Description Framework augments each tag with information about the metadata scheme to which it belongs. (MILLER gives an excellent introduction to this technology.) Thus, the RDF infrastructure can be used for the exchange of metadata among widely varying information-gathering communities; this sort of mechanism is pivotal for the creation of federated digital libraries on a large scale.

## The Open Archives Initiative

Another interesting current project that is exploring metadata interoperability from another perspective is the Open Archives (formerly the Universal Preprint Service) initiative (OAi). The OAi makes an excellent case study for this chapter—not only because of its currency, but also because it relates to many of the issues of loosely coupled distributed systems, on several levels. First, the OAi is concerned with developing infrastructure to support interoperability between digital collections. Also important, however, is that the nodes in the distributed system are author self-archiving (also known as e-print) systems. This initiative, then, aims to transform scholarly communication (VAN DE SOMPEL & LAGOZE) by taking full advantage of the capabilities of thoroughly networked communication systems. In this new paradigm, scholars can themselves disseminate information and results quickly on a wide scale, avoid giving up the rights to their work, and bypass the rigidity of peer review and expensive journal costs (VAN DE SOMPEL & LAGOZE).

Author self-archiving systems have been in existence for at least ten years, and their use is growing. One of the major archives is arXiv.org, at Los Alamos, established in 1991 by Paul Ginsparg for physics papers, but now also including other technical areas. Another is the Networked Computer Science Technical Reference Library (NCSTRL) collection of computer science reports, which is itself based on a distributed model, with services for exchanging information using the Dienst protocol. There are countless others, too many to mention here.

The aim of OAi is to facilitate search and retrieval services that span these archives, in part by establishing protocols for interoperability. The OAi's Santa Fe Convention, a set of specifications created at an October meeting in Santa Fe, lays out "a technical and organizational framework designed to facilitate the discovery of content stored in distributed e-print archives" (OPEN ARCHIVES INITIATIVE, 2000). This convention dealt with interoperability in metadata harvesting: the gathering of information about documents stored in the archives. First, a core set of metadata elements, the Open Archives Metadata Set (OAMS), was established. This set contains only nine elements, for maximum interoperability (and searchability at a coarse level of granularity) between dissimilar archives. Second, the convention determined that XML would be used for representing the OAMS as well as local metadata sets. Again, XML is an excellent choice for advancing interoperability, as it is highly flexible, and growing in popularity—an important factor in a field that has not yet settled into a group of common standards. Finally, it was agreed to use the Open Archives Dienst Subset protocol to exchange information about OAMS, as well as archive-specific metadata (VAN DE SOMPEL & LAGOZE).

Following steps outlined at the Open Archives Web site, e-print providers can bring an archive into compliance with the Santa Fe convention and register it with the OAi, thus making the data available as a node in a distributed system of archives. Service providers can then establish search engines to run over the available archives, accessing all the information through the interoperating protocols. At Virginia Tech, for example, FOX and others have done extensive work building on the Open Archives system, including the development of an "OAi Repository Explorer," which allows browsing of OAi-compliant archives

## Digital Object Models

At a different level of abstraction from that of metadata interoperability, libraries must deal with the problem of the format in which the contents of the library itself can be stored and presented. All materials stored in digital libraries must obviously be digitized in some standard format. This means that an issue that must be resolved to enable large-scale distributed libraries is the construction and standardization of effective digital object models. At the highest level, digital objects stored in libraries should exhibit enough uniformity to be stored, accessed, and presented using the same protocols. On the other hand, a wide variety of formats (text, sound, video) should be available across the system, each with its own methods of use and display. The most influential abstract digital object model seems to be that proposed by KAHN & WILENSKY, in which a digital object is divided into three components: a handle (unique identifier), a metadata container, and a data container. Most current ideas and implementations of digital objects expand in some way on this pattern. One project based on these theories that delivers the multilevel functionality desired from digital objects is the Flexible and Extensible Digital Object and Repository Architecture (FEDORA), developed at Cornell University by LAGOZE ET AL.

## FEDORA

The basic FEDORA digital object model is that of interoperating components. Currently, documents are generally provided in a variety of formats (such as HTML, PDF, image files, etc.), each of which requires a specialized program for viewing or manipulation; a goal of FEDORA is to make this specialization transparent, so that the user can access heterogeneous media over a single interface system.

A FEDORA object has, at the lowest level, packages called DataStreams, which contain the content of the object itself in some form. (These DataStreams can be either physically associated with the object, or distributed themselves, appearing in the object only as a link.) Above these content packages are interface components called Disseminators, which provide functions that allow a user to actually access and use the content of the object's data streams. The power of the Disseminator concept is its flexibility: each Disseminator can be associated with a different sort of interface to the object: one can provide a text view, another can give metadata information, etc. By creating different Disseminator components for different access methods, the behavior of an object can be made context-dependent.

On top of the FEDORA object model is the repository model. In this scheme, a Repository component manages storage of and access to the digital objects, which are handled at a high level, as interchangeable black boxes. This encapsulation of various formats into a generically manipulable object type greatly simplifies collection maintenance. More importantly, perhaps, for a developing system, the model is designed to be easily extensible, and to facilitate the addition of rights management schemes. Pivotal to this extensibility is FEDORA's data packaging system, which wraps content and presentation in a standardized package for manipulation by storage programs, thus allowing new item and presentation types to be easily folded into a preexisting repository. DUSHAY & PAYETTE provide a good short overview of FEDORA; PAYETTE & LAGOZE give a more thorough description.

## Multivalent Document Model

Another digital object model, developed at Berkeley as part of the Digital Library Initiative project, is the "multivalent document model," designed specifically for openness and extensibility across a distributed system (WILENSKY & PHELPS). In this model, objects are separated into layers of content, outfitted with functional modules called behaviors: small reusable programs that can be loaded dynamically. An interesting behavior that has been added to this model is a distributed annotation scheme, which allows users to mark up the objects themselves. A feature of this system is that the markings appear directly on the documents, as if they were part of the object itself. A prototype of this model has been implemented in Java (UNIVERSITY OF CALIFORNIA, BERKELEY).

## SEARCH AND RETRIEVAL IN A DISTRIBUTED ENVIRONMENT

Distributed digital objects are maintained and outfitted as described above with an appropriate identification system (and perhaps metadata) to facilitate the main business of the library, search and retrieval. The creation of interoperable metadata and unique, global object identifiers gives a foundation upon which the superstructure of a search system must be constructed, to do the work that gives the collection value above and beyond that of a mere repository. Indeed, when the supply of knowledge objects grows limitless, as more and more repositories are linked through networks, search algorithms and procedures may become the definitive core of a digital library. Collections, in the sense of a set of items discoverable through a certain interface, can become specialized and individually configurable—dynamic and responsive organizational systems in and of themselves. Here, we briefly discuss the main issues involved, and give a case study of the globally distributed NCSTRL digital library of computer science papers.

## Distributed Catalog Systems

The most basic, straightforward approach to cataloging distributed digital objects for retrieval is probably the centralized union catalog, where information about all available resources is gathered and pulled into a single location. Searches are then run quickly on this single machine, and need not pull information down from a network with each request. Most Internet search engines, for example, currently use a single merged catalog. The University of California's online MELVYL catalog for the California Digital Library system, which pulls information from twenty-nine separate facilities into a single database, is an example of a digital library system that uses this approach (COYLE). The largest union catalog currently in existence is the OCLC Online Union Catalog, which includes 35 million bibliographic records.

## Cooperative Online Resource Catalog

One project currently under development that extends the idea of the large union catalog to material available on the Web is the Cooperative Online Resource Catalog (CORC). This project, under the auspices of OCLC, is constructing a cooperative Web catalog through the distributed efforts of member libraries. In a cooperative process reminiscent of ATKINSON's control zone, staff at individual institutions create records of Web-based information, which are then merged into a central database to be shared with the rest of the participating community. Although the work of adding resource records must still be done by hand, CORC's record-editing tools help speed data creation by automating much of the data-collection process, filling in fields with information that can be machine-harvested. The CORC project also provides libraries with resource access tools that can be dynamically added to local Web portal pages. In this way, library service can be melded with Web searching services to provide an integrated point of access for a vast body of networked information—much of which has been selected and screened for quality by library personnel. Indeed, the real value of the CORC project lies perhaps in the cataloging standards that will need to be developed for the system, because it is in the creation and maintenance of such standards that library staff will guard the quality of the material recorded in the catalog; the combined personal time and effort of selectors distributed across a wide system sets CORC apart from a purely automatic cataloging project. The CORC project, currently still in a developmental phase, is accessible on the Internet from ONLINE COMPUTER LIBRARY CENTER.

While a centralized union catalog ensures speedy search times, it has disadvantages in large-scale systems. First, there is the obvious redundancy involved; each record at a remote site must be copied and stored locally. Perhaps more importantly, metadata records need to be molded to fit into a unified pattern for the single catalog, without undue homogenization and loss of information. Melding all records into one catalog makes it difficult for individual collections to maintain formats and metadata specific to their community. Furthermore, the dynamic nature of networked information space presents a real problem for a master index approach, as new information is continually being added and updated across a large library federation: the catalog would have to be in a state of perpetual change to reflect the volatility of the system.

## The Virtual Union Catalog

One approach to these problems is the concept of the virtual union catalog, currently being tested in the University of California library system. In a virtual catalog, records need not be merged together and stored in a redundant collection; instead, the grouping is generated by searching through distributed catalogs in real time. COYLE's description of the testing done on this system reveals the sort of problems that plague distributed systems on every level: lack of common standards makes query formulation that will work on all systems next to impossible; system downtime at local nodes compromises overall searching comprehensiveness; and the sorting and merging of a large set of retrieved records is highly computation-intensive.

## NCSTRL and Dienst

Probably the largest distributed library system currently on the Internet is the Networked Computer Science Technical Reference Library (NCSTRL). NCSTRL provides access to over 30,000 documents from over 100 educational and research institutions around the world. Key to the NCSTRL approach to combining heterogeneous libraries is an open architecture system: that is, protocols are given to specify interfaces to a set of digital library services, but each local organization is free to implement these interfaces in any way it wants. In this way, libraries can choose technologies appropriate for local needs, while still satisfying the requirements for membership in a distributed confederation. Another benefit of the open architecture approach is its extensibility; the general system can be augmented with services as required—an important feature of a growing digital library where standards are not yet set in stone. This modularity also allows institutions to plug into the library system as mediators, offering nonstandard, customized services. (See LEINER for a more detailed description of NCSTRL's open architecture system.)

The technical infrastructure for this federation of libraries is provided by a distributed library protocol called Distributed Interactive Extensible Network Server for Techreports (Dienst), which was developed by Jim Davis of Xerox and Carl Lagoze at Cornell University. This protocol was created specifically to allow distributed searching of locally managed collections. The Dienst protocol provides for four areas of library service: user interfaces, indexes, collections, and repositories. A user interface provides a front end for people to access the library system; this interface then communicates with index servers, which maintain metadata about information stored in repositories. The repositories are separate servers that can then feed document content to the user interface itself.

When Dienst was first developed, each institution had its own index, and any query had to traverse the entire networked system, gathering information from every server so as not to miss the material from any collection. This naïve form of distributed searching, in which quick response time was bounded by the slowest server or connection, failed to work well for international-scale systems, so a new regionally based system was devised as NCSTRL expanded.

In the current version of Dienst, the network is broken up into several regions of well-connected servers, called connectivity regions. Each of these regions has a single collection server and several index servers, which maintain replicated metainformation about the entire NCSTRL collection. Thus, a query from one connectivity region is directed to its regional collection server, which need only send queries through its own area, avoiding long waits for data from slow or badly maintained interregional connections. A single central collection server maintains information about the regional servers and the index servers that feed into them. This central manager communicates with the regional managing servers, which in turn serve as local controllers for each region of connectivity, thus forming a hierarchy of distributed control.

## Smart Object, Dumb Archive

One new approach to facilitating interoperability in distributed digital libraries is to endow digital objects themselves with functionality, thus removing the whole need to deal with different object formats at the collection level. In this Smart Object, Dumb Archive (SODA) approach, the collecting mechanism becomes a simple tool for forming buckets of (gathering) and disseminating intelligent objects, which are themselves capable of enforcing their own terms and conditions, negotiating access, and displaying their contents" (MALY ET AL.). NELSON ET AL. (1999) point out that this extreme modularization of digital library services, archives, and objects will allow each of these areas to develop independently, without dependence on the other two. Another benefit of moving functionality into the object is that it breaks the strong connection between an archive and the objects it contains. In most digital libraries, the structure of a digital object depends on the archive in which it appears, but in a distributed, dynamic environment, where objects are accessible across varying systems, this tight coupling tends to be an annoying source of interoperability problems (MALY ET AL.). Finally, buckets are capable of aggregating many different data types into a single package, so that video, text, images, etc. can be presented in one unit, each format with its own display method.

The SODA model was specifically designed to improve on the NCSTRL/Dienst distributed library system. One objection the developers raise to Dienst (as well as other digital library frameworks) is that archive access protocols "have become unnecessarily complex" (MALY ET AL., p. 5). Indeed, one reason brought for the simplification of archives with regard to object interoperability is that this can free archives to become "smart" with regard to functions that don't just duplicate mechanisms that are better associated with digital objects—thus evolving into a future Smart Object, Smart Archive (SOSA) format. NELSON ET AL. (1999) note that another drawback to the Dienst system is that it must explicitly define the definition and structure of a document, so that information about all possible media formats in use must be effectively hard-wired into the protocol. It would be more logical and straightforward to decouple such information from the archival system, and let the object take care of its own format.

Old Dominion University and NASA Langley Research Center have developed a prototype testbed implementing this concept based on the existing NCSTRL system, called NCSTRL+. NCSTRL+ uses the Dienst protocol, simplified to no longer control the presentation of documents to the user, and modified to handle bucket objects. An idea for dividing collections into partitions, called "clustering," has also been introduced into the system, thus giving Dienst the ability to subdivide a collection along something other than an institutional boundary. NCSTRL+ provides clusters such as subject category, source language, and publishing institution. NELSON ET AL. (1998) give a detailed description of the early phases of the NCSTRL+ implementation.

## PRESERVATION IN A DISTRIBUTED
## DIGITAL ENVIRONMENT

If one important function of the library is storing and facilitating access to documents, another is preserving the documents in a collection for long-term storage. The problem of preservation is especially complex in a distributed information system like the Internet. If a network of information material is constantly evolving, at what point should one take a "snapshot" of the available material? And what about hyperlinks—what are the boundaries of a document that is tightly woven into an information network? Again, the basic tension arises from the attempt to force virtual objects to behave as if they were concrete—from the desire to archive part of a virtual system using methods derived from traditional practices of object storage. This insistence on forcing new technologies to adapt to an older paradigm seems to mean that there will necessarily be a certain amount of arbitrariness involved in any decision about what parts of a hypertext document should be archived. HODGE writes that some organizations preserving hypertext documents store only links, but not the information therein—which has obvious disadvantages in an evolving system. Others store link content only from certain trusted sites, which is better, but still leaves opportunity for information to be lost. (The idea of the permanent digital object identifier, described above, could be a partial solution to this problem.)

## Cultural Aspects of Distributed Preservation

Sociologically, too, the Web is currently seen as a basically superficial medium, through which one browses or surfs, in which no conventions have yet been established for typical library-related information, such as provenance (POCKLEY, p. 15). Furthermore, LYNCH (1999) points out that published web material lacks a common structure (such as that of the book, with its table of contents, bibliography, etc.), meaning that pages have an unsettled, informal look, and their content is harder to quickly grasp; it becomes difficult to formulate archival policies for material that seems to exist in such an anarchic context. LYMAN & KAHLE put it succinctly: "Like oral culture, digital information has been allowed to become a medium for the present, neither a record of the past nor a message to the future" (p. 2).

Other preservation problems arise from the impermanence of material in a distributed system. When objects have no real substance, and exist only to be distributed (like email), who is responsible for their preservation? The importance of informal communication in the study of history and culture is witnessed by the large number of books of correspondence that have been published and found useful through the centuries; LUKESH warns that our current neglect of electronic correspondence will result in significant historical losses for future scholars. Likewise, MARCUM asserts that, in some disciplines, the traditional print records do not adequately capture the intellectual development, which is preserved instead in "on-line databases, on-line exchanges of preprints, listservs, and the like" (p. 357).

Another obstacle in the path of developing distributed digital preservation practice is the current immaturity of digital publishing (in this sense, making material available on the Internet) itself, which is still—and perhaps will always be, to a certain extent—a basically informal, unstructured medium. When publishing has become easy enough that ten-year-old children regularly create publicly available Web pages, what should the policy for legal deposit be? One problem with Internet publishing, from this perspective, is that it removes the screening effect that necessarily takes place in a print environment, where an intermediary publishing organization must decide what texts are worthy of becoming books (NATIONAL LIBRARY OF CANADA).

## Technologies and Approaches

Traditional preservation approaches mainly deal with problems of material preservation: how to preserve paper, tapes, or photographs so the content they carry will be available to future scholars. In a digital context, content can now be separated from a particular physical manifestation; indeed, long-term preservation often necessitates the wholesale migration of data from one form (or format) to another, as software formats grow obsolete and are replaced by more advanced models. In the context of long-term archiving, distribution of information occurs not only geographically, across networked systems, but also temporally, across time spans in which technologies and the formats they support vary much more than they do across spatial distances.

One approach is to preserve digital information in its simplest possible format, to make it as software-independent as possible (HEDSTROM). Another format-oriented approach is that of LYNCH (1999), who proposes canonical formats for preservation, which are capable of maintaining object authenticity across migrations, and standard definitions as to what is important in a document form. As usual, the difficulties with such an approach are not mainly technological, but organizational.

ROTHENBERG takes a different tack. Instead of changing data so that it can be read by future machines (through standard formats or migration), he would provide for the specification of hardware emulators, so that current (and past) programs can be run in the future on virtual versions of obsolete machines. This approach seems to transfer something of traditional preservation practices to the digital realm; content becomes bound not to a physical object, but to a specific bitstream, the interpretation of which is now always assured, by encapsulating information about display mechanisms along with the data itself. Intellectual property issues relating to the copying of operating system and software technology must be solved before this approach can be viable on a wide basis.

## CONCLUSION

This chapter has presented some of the major issues affecting the development of digital libraries at the beginning of the 21st century. There is as yet little consensus about the best way to organize a distributed digital library—indeed, there is not even agreement on a single definition of a digital library. Networking and digitization are facilitating the creation of an entirely new paradigm of information management, and standards and practices are still in a state of disorderly development. The course of the future, it seems, could be set by practitioners and organizers—those who not only devise intelligent, workable standards, but who also can put together working implementations, and muster the cooperation between institutions needed to make any solution a true standard.

## Future Work

It is difficult to separate future work from current projects in the field of digital libraries and distributed information management. The vast majority of such projects in existence are themselves essentially works in progress; if they are in operation today, it is often only as one stage of a trajectory aimed at some future functionality which is even faster and more powerful.

One area of research in which no general, scalable solutions have been found is indexing and search and retrieval techniques for nontextual data. Among many others, the Computer Vision group at UC Berkeley is currently working on a system for content-based image retrieval; Blobworld, a system that separates images into coherent regions, is described in detail in UNIVERSITY OF CALIFORNIA, BERKELEY DIGITAL LIBRARY PROJECT. The SIMPLIcity system (Semantics-sensitive Integrated Matching for Picture LIbraries), developed at Stanford, is another project to automatically semantically classify images, based on recognition and categorization of regions in the image itself. For sound files, MELDEX, an audio-based system for indexing and retrieval of melodies, has been created for the New Zealand digital library. This system will retrieve melodies from a database of almost 10,000 folk songs based on a few notes sung into a microphone. A demonstration page on the Web, at New Zealand Digital Library (UNIVERSITY OF WAIKATO), allows browsers to try a prototype out for themselves.

Another area in which great changes are foreseeable in the future is the field of scholarly publishing. This is not so much a technological problem to be resolved as a (coming) paradigm shift whose implications will have to be absorbed by the academic community. As the boundaries between author and publisher blur or dissolve, and centrally controlled systems give way to distributed, nonmonolithic models, peer-review systems to protect quality will need to evolve, and the concept and uses of academic publishing will have to adapt. (See especially HARNAD for an impassioned defense of this new publishing model.) The Open Archives initiative, described above, is one foray into this new mode of information dissemination. The growing number of electronic journals (such as several quoted in this bibliography) also bear witness to the developing change in paradigm.

Technologically, a general trend seems to be toward more specialization and personalization of the searching process; indeed, one current project aims specifically to create Personalized Information Environments (PIEs), which brings the idea of the collection down to the level of the user, who is able with this concept to create his or her own personal digital library out of a vast distributed system (FRENCH & VILES). But as the developers of the PIE themselves suggest, it is Vannevar Bush's idea of the Memex, from 1945, which still drives much conceptual work in distributed information management. In a sense, much of what is being done now, at the beginning of the 21st century, can be seen as an attempt to fulfill Bush's seminal vision of fifty years ago.

## BIBLIOGRAPHY

ACKERMAN, MARK S. 1994. Providing Social Interaction in the Digital Library. In: Schnase, John L.; Leggett, John J.; Furuta, Richard K.; Metcalfe, Ted, eds. Proceedings of Digital Libraries '94: The 1st Annual Conference on the Theory and Practice of Digital Libraries; 1994 June 19-21; College Station, TX. Available WWW: http://www.ics.uci.edu/~ackerman/pub/94b11/dl94.final.html.

ACKERMAN, MARK S.; FIELDING, ROY T. 1995. Collection Maintenance in the Digital Library. In: Proceedings of Digital Libraries '95: The 2nd Annual Conference on the Theory and Practice of Digital Libraries; 1995 June 11-13; Austin, TX. Available WWW: http://www.csdl.tamu.edu/DL95/papers/ackerman/ackerman.html.

ANDERSON, MARTHA. 1999. A Tool for Building Digital Libraries. D-Lib Magazine. 1999 February; 5(2). ISSN: 1082-9873. Available WWW: http://www.dlib.org/dlib/february99/02journalreview.html.

ANTELMAN, KRISTIN; LANGENBERG, DAVID. 1993. Collection Development in the Electronic Library. In: Proceedings of the 21st ACM SIGUCCS Conference on User Services; 1993 November 7-10; San Diego, CA. New York, NY: Association for Computing Machinery (ACM); 1993. 50-56. ISBN: 0-89791-631-X. Also available WWW: http://www.acm.org/pubs/articles/proceedings/userservices/263814/p50-antelman/p50-antelman.pdf.

ARMS, WILLIAM Y. 2000. Digital Libraries. Cambridge, MA: The MIT Press; 2000. 287p. ISBN: 0-262-01880-8.

ARMS, WILLIAM Y.; BLANCHI, CHRISTOPHE; OVERLY, EDWARD A. 1997. An Architecture for Information in Digital Libraries. D-Lib Magazine. 1997 February; 3(2). ISSN: 1082-9873. Available WWW: http://www.dlib.org/dlib/february97/cnri/02arms1.html.

ARMS, WILLIAM Y.; DAIGLE, LESLIE; DANIEL, RON, JR.; LALIBERTE, DAN; MEALLING, MICHAEL; MOORE, KEITH; WEIBEL, STUART. 1996. Uniform Resource Names: A Progress Report. D-Lib Magazine. 1996 February; 2(2). ISSN: 1082-9873. Available WWW: http://www.dlib.org/dlib/february96/02arms.html.

ARNOLD, KENNETH. 1994. The Electronic Librarian Is a Verb / The Electronic Library Is Not a Sentence: A Lecture Delivered at the New York Public Library. The Gilbert A. Cam Memorial Lecture Series. 1994 October 14. Available WWW: http://www.press.umich.edu/jep/works/arnold.eleclib.html.

ATKINSON, ROSS. 1996. Library Functions, Scholarly Communication, and the Foundation of the Digital Library: Laying Claim to the Control Zone. Library Quarterly. 1996 July; 66(3): 239-265. ISSN: 0024-2519.

BACA, MURTHA, ed. 2000. Introduction to Metadata: Pathways to Digital Information. Los Angeles, CA: Getty Information Institute; 2000. Available WWW: http://www.getty.edu/research/institute/standards/intrometadata/index.html.

BEARMAN, DAVID. 1999. Reality and Chimeras in the Preservation of Electronic Records. D-Lib Magazine. 1999 April; 5(4). ISSN: 1082-9873. Available WWW: http://www.dlib.org/dlib/april99/bearman/04bearman.html.

BOORSTIN, DANIEL J. 1980. Gresham's Law: Knowledge or Information? Remarks at the White House Conference on Library and Information Services; 1979 November 19; Washington, DC. Washington, DC: Library of Congress; 1980. 6p. (Center for the Book: Viewpoint series; no. 3). ISBN: 0-8444-0346-6.

BOUSKILA, FABIEN D.; POTTENGER, WILLIAM M. 2000. The Role of Semantic Locality in Hierarchical Distributed Dynamic Indexing. In: Proceedings of the 2000 International Conference on Artificial Intelligence (IC-AI 2000); 2000 June; Las Vegas, NV. Available WWW: http://www.ncsa.uiuc.edu/ET/HDDI/pubs.html.

BOUTHORS, VINCENT; DEDIEU, OLIVIER. 1999. Pharos, a Collaborative Infrastructure for Web Knowledge Sharing. In: Proceedings of the 3rd European Conference on Research and Advanced Technology for Digital Libraries (ECDL) '99; 1999 September 22-24; Paris, France. New York, NY: Springer-Verlag; 1999. 215-233. (Lecture Notes in Computer Science, 1696). ISBN: 3-540-66558-7. Also available WWW: http://link.springer.de/link/service/series/0558/tocs/t1696.htm.

BUSH, VANNEVAR. 1945. As We May Think Atlantic Monthly. 1945 July; 176(1): 101-108. Also available WWW: http://www.theatlantic.com/unbound/flashbks/computer/bushf.htm.

COFFMAN, STEVE. 1999. Building Earth's Largest Library: Driving into the Future. Searcher. 1999 March; 7(3): 34-47. ISSN: 1070-4795.

CORNELL DIGITAL LIBRARY RESEARCH GROUP. 2000. Dienst: Overview and Introduction. Available WWW: http://www.cs.cornell.edu/cdlrg/dienst/DienstOverview.htm.

CORPORATION FOR NATIONAL RESEARCH INITIATIVES. Handle System. Available WWW: http://www.handle.net/.

COX, RICHARD J. 2000. Searching for Authority: Archivists and Electronic Records in the New World at the Fin-de-Siécle. First Monday. 2000 January; 5(1). Available WWW: http://www.firstmonday.dk/issues/issue5_1/cox/index.html.

COYLE, KAREN. 2000. The Virtual Union Catalog: A Comparative Study. D-Lib Magazine. 2000 March; 6(3). ISSN: 1082-9873. Available WWW: http://www.dlib.org/dlib/march00/coyle/03coyle.html.

CRAWFORD, WALT. 1998. Paper Persists: Why Physical Library Collections Still Matter. Online. 1998 January/February; 22(1): 42-44, 46-48. ISSN: 0146-5422. Also available WWW: http://www.onlineinc.com/onlinemag/OL1998/crawford1.html.

CRAWFORD, WALT. 1999. Being Analog: Creating Tomorrow's Libraries. Chicago, IL: American Library Association; 1999. 245p. ISBN: 0-8389-0754-7.

CRESPO, ARTURO; GARCIA-MOLINA, HECTOR. 1998. Archival Storage for Digital Libraries. In: Witten, Ian H.; Akscyn, Robert M.; Shipman, Frank M., III, eds. Proceedings of the 3rd ACM Conference on Digital Libraries; 1998 June 23-26; Pittsburgh, PA. New York, NY: Association for Computing Machinery; 1998. 69-78. ISBN: 0-89791-965-3.

DANIEL, RON, JR.; LAGOZE, CARL; PAYETTE, SANDRA D. 1998. A Metadata Architecture for Digital Libraries. In: Proceedings of the IEEE International Forum on Research and Technology Advances in Digital Libraries (IEEE ADL '98); 1998 April 22-24; Santa Barbara, CA. Los Alamitos, CA: IEEE Computer Society Press; 1998. 276-288. ISBN: 0-8186-8464-X. Also available WWW: http://www.cs.cornell.edu/lagoze/papers/ADL98/dar-adl.html.

DAVIS, JAMES R.; LAGOZE, CARL. 2000. NCSTRL: Design and Deployment of a Globally Distributed Digital Library. Journal of the American Society for Information Science. 2000; 51(3): 273-280. ISSN: 0002-8231.

DAY, MICHAEL. 1999. Metadata for Digital Preservation: An Update. Ariadne. 1999 December; (22). ISSN: 1361-3200. Available WWW: http://www.ariadne.ac.uk/issue22/metadata/.

DUSHAY, NAOMI; PAYETTE, SANDRA. 2000. Flexible and Extensible Digital Object and Repository Architecture (FEDORA). Available WWW: http://www.cs.cornell.edu/cdlrg/FEDORA.html.

EDMUNDS, JEFF; BRISSON, ROGER. 2000. Cataloging in CORC: A Work in Progress. Journal of Internet Cataloging. 2001; 4(1/2): 89-109. ISSN: 1091-1367.

FOX, EDWARD A. 2000. Digital Libraries and the Open Archives Initiative. Powerpoint slides presented at: Louisiana State University; 2000 June 30; Baton Rouge, LA. Available WWW: http://www.ndltd.org/talks.

FOX, EDWARD; MARCHIONINI, GARY. 1998. Toward a Worldwide Digital Library: Guest Editors' Introduction to Special Section on Digital Libraries: Global Scope, Unlimited Access. Communications of the ACM. 1998 April; 41(4): 28-32. ISSN: 0001-0782.

FRENCH, JAMES C.; VILES, CHARLES L. 1999. Personalized Information Environments: An Architecture for Customizable Access to Distributed Digital Libraries. D-Lib Magazine. 1999 June; 5(6). ISSN: 1082-9873. Available WWW: http://www.dlib.org/dlib/june99/french/06french.html.

GOOGLE. Web site: http://www.google.com/.

GORMAN, PAUL; MAIER, DAVID; DELCAMBRE, LOIS. 1998. Tracking Footprints through an Information Space: Leveraging the Document Selections of Expert Problem Solvers. 1998; Portland, OR. (Project Overview). Available WWW: http://www.cse.ogi.edu/dot/research/footprints/.

GRIFFITHS, JOSÉ-MARIE. 1998. The New Information Professional. Bulletin of the American Society for Information Science. 1998 February/March; 24(3): 8-12. ISSN: 0095-4403. Available WWW: http://www.asis.org/Bulletin/Feb-98/griffiths.html.

HÄKLI, ESKO; HAKALA, JUHA. 1998. URN Implementation in National Libraries. 1998 October 1. Available WWW: http://www.lib.helsinki.fi/urn/urnimp.html.

HARNAD, STEVAN. 1999. Free at Last: The Future of Peer-Reviewed Journals. D-Lib Magazine. 1999 December; 5(12). ISSN: 1082-9873. Available WWW: http://www.dlib.org/dlib/december99/12harnad.html.

HARTER, STEPHEN P. 1997. Scholarly Communication and the Digital Library: Problems and Issues. Journal of Digital Information. 1997 April; 1(1). ISSN: 1368-7506. Available WWW: http://jodi.ecs.soton.ac.uk/Articles/v01/i01/Harter.

HAYNES, DAVID; STREATFIELD, DAVID. 1998. A National Co-ordinating Body for Digital Archiving? Ariadne. 1998 May; (15). ISSN: 1361-3200. Available WWW: http://www.ariadne.ac.uk/issue15/digital/.

HEDMAN, ANDERS. 1999. Creating Digital Libraries Together—Collaboration, Multimodality, and Plurality. In: Manaris, Bill, ed. Proceedings of the 4th Annual SIGCSE/SIGCUE Conference on Innovation and Technology in Computer Science Education (ITiCSE); 1999 June 27-July 1; Krakow, Poland. New York, NY: Association for Computing Machinery; 1999. 147-150. ISBN: 1-58113-087-2. Available WWW: http://www.acm.org/pubs/contents/proceedings/cse/305786/.

HEDSTROM, MARGARET. 1999. Digital Preservation: A Time Bomb for Digital Libraries. Paper presented at: NSF Workshop on Data Archival and Information Preservation; 1999 March 26-27; Washington, DC. Available WWW: http://cecssrv1.cecs.missouri.edu/NSFWorkshop/hedstrompp.html.

HEDSTROM, MARGARET; WALLACE, DAVID. 1999. And the Last Shall Be First: Recordkeeping Policies and the NII. Journal of the American Society for Information Science. 1999; 50(4): 331-339. ISSN: 0002-8231.

HEERY, RACHEL. 1998. What is. . .RDF? Ariadne. 1998 March; (14). ISSN: 1361-3200. Available WWW: http://www.ariadne.ac.uk/issue14/what-is/.

HENRY, LINDA J. 1998. Schellenberg in Cyberspace. The American Archivist. 1998 Fall; 61: 309-327. ISSN: 0360-9081.

HICKEY, THOMAS B. 1998. CORC—Cooperative Online Resource Catalog. Annual Review of OCLC Research. 1998. ISSN: 0894-198X. Available WWW: http://www.oclc.org/research/publications/arr/1998/hickey/corc.htm.

HODGE, GAIL M. 2000. Best Practices for Digital Archiving: An Information Life Cycle Approach. D-Lib Magazine. 2000 January; 6(1). ISSN: 1082-9873. Available WWW: http://www.dlib.org/dlib/january00/01hodge.html.

KAHN, ROBERT; WILENSKY, ROBERT. 1995. A Framework for Distributed Digital Object Services. 1995 May. Available WWW: http://www.cnri.reston.va.us/home/cstr/arch/k-w.html.

KANTOR, PAUL B. 1999. How the AntWorld Works. 1999 September. Available WWW: http://aplab.rutgers.edu/ant/.

KANTOR, PAUL B.; BOROS, ENDRE; MELAMED, BEN; MEÑKOV, VLADIMIR. 1999. The Information Quest: A Dynamic Model of User's Information Needs. In: ASIS '99: Proceedings of the American Society for Information Science (ASIS) 62nd Annual Meeting: Volume 36; 1999 October 31-November 4; Washington, DC. Medford, NJ: Information Today, Inc. for ASIS; 1999. 536-545. ISBN: 1-57387-091-9.

LAGOZE, CARL. 2000. The Cornell Digital Library Research Group: Architectures and Policies for Distributed Research Libraries. Invited Paper for Digital Libraries Workshop 17, Tsukuba, Japan. 2000 February. Available WWW: http://www.cs.cornell.edu/lagoze/lagoze.html.

LAGOZE, CARL; FIELDING, DAVID. 1998. Defining Collections in Distributed Digital Libraries. D-Lib Magazine. 1998 November; 4(11). ISSN: 1082-9873. Available WWW: http://www.dlib.org/dlib/november98/lagoze/11lagoze.html.

LAGOZE, CARL; FIELDING, DAVID; PAYETTE, SANDRA. 1998. Making Global Digital Libraries Work: Collection Services, Connectivity Regions, and Collection Views. In: Witten, Ian H.; Akscyn, Robert M.; Shipman, Frank M., III, eds. Proceedings of the 3rd ACM Conference on Digital Libraries; 1998 June 23-26; Pittsburgh, PA. New York, NY: Association for Computing Machinery; 1998. 134-143. ISBN: 0-89791-965-3. Also available WWW: http://www.cs.cornell.edu/lagoze/lagoze.html.

LAGOZE, CARL; FUHR, NORBERT. 1998. Resource Discovery in a Globally-Distributed Digital Library Working Group Report: Digital Library Collaborative Working Groups; 1998 February 26-27; Washington, DC. Available WWW: http://www.iei.pi.cnr.it/DELOS/NSF/resourcediscovery.htm.

LAGOZE, CARL; LYNCH, CLIFFORD A.; DANIEL, RON, JR. 1996. The Warwick Framework: A Container Architecture for Aggregating Sets of Metadata. 1996 June. (Cornell University Computer Science Technical Report TR96-1593). Available WWW: http://ncstrl.cs.cornell.edu:80/Dienst/UI/1.0/Display/ncstrl.cornell/TR96-1593.

LANHAM, RICHARD. 1993. The Electronic Word: Democracy, Technology, and the Arts. Chicago, IL: University of Chicago Press; 1993. 285p. ISBN: 0-226-46883-6.

LASSILA, ORA. 1997. Introduction to RDF Metadata. 1997 November 13. (W3C NOTE 1997-11-13). Available WWW: http://www.w3.org/TR/NOTE-rdf-simple-intro.

LEINER, BARRY M. 1998. The NCSTRL Approach to Open Architecture for the Confederated Digital Library. D-Lib Magazine. 1998 December; 4(12). ISSN: 1082-9873. Available WWW: http://www.dlib.org/dlib/december98/leiner/12leiner.html.

LESK, MICHAEL. 1997. Practical Digital Libraries: Books, Bytes, and Bucks. San Francisco, CA: Morgan Kaufmann Publishers, Inc.; 1997. 297p. ISBN: 1-55860-459-6.

LEVY, DAVID M. 2000. Digital Libraries and the Problem of Purpose. D-Lib Magazine. 2000 January; 6(1). ISSN: 1082-9873. Available WWW: http://www.dlib.org/dlib/january00/01levy.html.

LEVY, DAVID M.; MARSHALL, CATHERINE C. 1994. What Color Was George Washington's White Horse? A Look at Assumptions Underlying Digital Libraries. In: Schnase, John L.; Leggett, John J.; Furuta, Richard K.; Metcalfe, Ted, eds. Proceedings of Digital Libraries '94: The 1st Annual Conference on the Theory and Practice of Digital Libraries; 1994 June 19-21; College Station, TX. Available WWW: http://www.csdl.tamu.edu/DL94/paper/levy.html.

LEVY, DAVID M.; MARSHALL, CATHERINE C. 1995. Going Digital: A Look at Assumptions Underlying Digital Libraries. Communications of the ACM. 1995 April; 38(4): 77-84. ISSN: 0001-0782.

LUKESH, SUSAN S.. 1999. E-mail and Potential Loss to Future Archives and Scholarship or the Dog That Didn't Bark. First Monday. 1999 September; 4(9). ISSN: 1396-0466. Available WWW: http://www.firstmonday.org/issues/issue4_9/lukesh/index.html.

LYMAN, PETER; KAHLE, BREWSTER. 1998. Archiving Digital Cultural Artifacts: Organizing an Agenda for Action. D-Lib Magazine. 1998 July/August; 4(7/8). ISSN: 1082-9873. Available WWW: http://www.dlib.org/dlib/july98/07lyman.html.

LYNCH, CLIFFORD A. 1997. Identifiers and Their Role in Networked Information Applications. A.R.L.: A Bimonthly Newsletter of Research Library Issues and Actions. 1997 October; (194). ISSN: 0066-9652. Available WWW: http://www.arl.org/newsltr/194/identifier.html.

LYNCH, CLIFFORD A. 1999. Canonicalization: A Fundamental Tool to Facilitate Preservation and Management of Digital Information. D-Lib Magazine. 1999 September; 5(9). ISSN: 1082-9873. Available WWW: http://www.dlib.org/dlib/september99/09lynch.html.

MALY, KURT; NELSON, MICHAEL L.; ZUBAIR, MOHAMMAD. 1999. Smart Objects, Dumb Archives: A User-Centric, Layered Digital Library Framework. D-Lib Magazine. 1999 March; 5(3). ISSN: 1082-9873. Available WWW: http://www.dlib.org/dlib/march99/maly/03maly.html.

MARCUM, DEANNA B. 1997. A Moral and Legal Obligation: Preservation in the Digital Age. International Information and Library Review. 1997; 29(3-4): 357-365. ISSN: 1057-2317.

MARSHALL, CATHERINE C. 1997. Annotation: From Paper Books to the Digital Library. In: Proceedings of the 2nd ACM International Conference on Digital Libraries; 1997 July 23-26; Philadelphia, PA. New York, NY: Association for Computing Machinery; 1997. 131-140. ISBN: 0-89791-868-1. Also available WWW: http://www.acm.org/pubs/articles/proceedings/dl/263690/p131-marshall/p131-marshall.pdf.

MCNAB, RODGER J.; SMITH, LLOYD A.; BAINBRIDGE, DAVID; WITTEN, IAN H. 1997. The New Zealand Digital Library MELody inDEX. D-Lib Magazine. 1997 May; 3(5). ISSN: 1082-9873. Available WWW: http://www.dlib.org/dlib/may97/meldex/05witten.html.

MIKSA, FRANCIS L.; DOTY, PHILIP. 1994. Intellectual Realities and the Digital Library. In: Schnase, John L.; Leggett, John J.; Furuta, Richard K.; Metcalfe, Ted, eds. Proceedings of Digital Libraries '94: The 1st Annual

Conference on the Theory and Practice of Digital Libraries; 1994 June 19-21; College Station, TX. Available WWW: http://www.csdl.tamu.edu/DL94/paper/miksa.html.

MILLER, ERIC. 1998. An Introduction to the Resource Description Framework. D-Lib Magazine. 1998 May; 4(5). ISSN: 1082-9873. Available WWW: http://www.dlib.org/dlib/may98/miller/05miller.html.

MOURA, ANA MARIA DE CARVALHO; CAMPOS, MARIA LUIZA MACHADO; BARRETO, CÁSSIA MARIA. 1999. A Metadata Architecture to Represent Electronic Documents on the Web. In: Proceedings of the 3rd IEEE Meta-Data Conference; 1999 April 6-7; Bethesda, MD. Available WWW: http://www.computer.org/proceedings/meta/1999/papers/15/amoura.html.

MURAMATSU, BRANDON. 2000. A Digital Learning Space for Science, Mathematics, Engineering and Technology Education. Paper presented at: Mathematics/Science Education and Technology 2000 (M/SET); 2000 February 5; San Diego, CA. Available WWW: http://www.smete.org/smete/info/papers/MSET-0200/muramatsu-mset2000.pdf.

MURAMATSU, BRANDON; AGOGINO, ALICE M. 1999. The National Engineering Education Delivery System: A Digital Library for Engineering Education. D-Lib Magazine. 1999 April; 5(4). ISSN: 1082-9873. Available WWW: http://www.dlib.org/dlib/april99/muramatsu/04muramatsu.html.

NATIONAL ENGINEERING EDUCATION DELIVERY SYSTEM. Web site: http://www.needs.org.

NATIONAL LIBRARY OF CANADA. ELECTRONIC COLLECTIONS COORDINATING GROUP. 1998. Networked Electronic Publications Policy and Guidelines. 1998 October. Available WWW: http://www.nlc-bnc.ca/9/8/index-e.html.

NELSON, MICHAEL L.; MALY, KURT; CROOM, DELWIN R., JR.; ROBBINS, STEVEN W. 1999. Metadata and Buckets in the Smart Object, Dumb Archive (SODA) Model. In: Proceedings of the 3rd IEEE Meta-Data Conference; 1999 April 6-7; Bethesda, MD. Available WWW: http://www.computer.org/proceedings/meta/1999/papers/53/mnelson.html.

NELSON, MICHAEL L.; MALY, KURT; SHEN, STEWART N.T.; ZUBAIR, MOHAMMAD. 1998. NCSTRL+: Adding Multi-Discipline and Multi-Genre Support to the Dienst Protocol Using Clusters and Buckets. In: Proceedings of the 5th IEEE International Forum on Research and Technology Advances in Digital Libraries (IEEE ADL '98); 1998 April 22-24; Santa Barbara, CA. Los Alamitos, CA: IEEE Computer Society Press; 1998. 128-136. ISBN: 0-8186-8464-X. Available WWW: http://techreports.larc.nasa.gov/ltrs/PDF/1998/mtg/NASA-98-ieeedl-mln.pdf.

ODLYZKO, ANDREW M. 1997. Silicon Dreams and Silicon Bricks: The Continuing Evolution of Libraries. Library Trends. 1997 Summer; 46(1): 152-167. ISSN: 0024-2594. Also available WWW: http://www.research.att.com/~amo/doc/complete.html.

ONLINE COMPUTER LIBRARY CENTER. Cooperative Online Resource Catalog (CORC). Available WWW: http://www.oclc.org/corc/.

OPEN ARCHIVES INITIATIVE. 1999. Proceedings of the 1st Meeting of the Open Archives Initiative; 1999 October 21-22; Santa Fe, NM. Available WWW: www.openarchives.org/ups1-press.htm.

OPEN ARCHIVES INITIATIVE. 2000. Santa Fe Convention. Available WWW: http://www.openarchives.org/sfc/sfc_entry.htm.

PASKIN, NORMAN. 1999a. The Digital Object Identifier. Summary of Seminar Given as Part of the Online Computer Library Center's Distinguished Seminar Series; 1999 February 23. Available WWW: http://www.oclc.org/research/publications/arr/1999/paskin/doi.htm.

PASKIN, NORMAN. 1999b. DOI: Current Status and Outlook. D-Lib Magazine. 1999 May; 5(5). ISSN: 1082-9873. Available WWW: http://www.dlib.org/dlib/may99/05paskin.html.

PAYETTE, SANDRA; BLANCHI, CHRISTOPHE; LAGOZE, CARL; OVERLY, EDWARD A. 1999. Interoperability for Digital Objects and Repositories: The Cornell/CNRI Experiments. D-Lib Magazine. 1999 May; 5(5). ISSN: 1082-9873. Available WWW: http://www.dlib.org/dlib/may99/payette/05payette.html.

PAYETTE, SANDRA; LAGOZE, CARL. 1998. Flexible and Extensible Digital Object and Repository Architecture (FEDORA). In: Proceedings of the 2nd European Conference on Research and Advanced Technology for Digital Libraries (ECDL) '98; 1998 September 21-23; Heraklion, Greece. New York, NY: Springer-Verlag; 1998. 41-59. (Lecture Notes in Computer Science, 1513). ISBN: 3-540-65101-2. Also available WWW: http://www.cs.cornell.edu/payette/papers/ECDL98/FEDORA.html.

PERSISTENT UNIFORM RESOURCE LOCATOR TEAM. Persistent URL home page. Available WWW: http://purl.oclc.org/.

PHELPS, THOMAS A.; WILENSKY, ROBERT. 2000. Robust s Cost Just Five Words Each. 2000 January 10. (UCB Computer Science Technical Report UCB//CSD-00-1091). Available WWW: http://www.cs.berkeley.edu/~wilensky/robust-s.html.

POCKLEY, SIMON. 1995. Killing the Duck to Keep the Quack: Using the World Wide Web for Digital Preservation. Available WWW: www.cinemedia.net/FOD/FOD0055.html.

POTTENGER, WILLIAM M. 2001. HDDI™: Hierarchical Distributed Dynamic Indexing. In: Grossman, Robert; Kamath, Chandrika; Kumar, Vipin; Namburu, Raju, eds. Data Mining for Scientific and Engineering Applications. New York, NY: Kluwer Academic Publishers; 2001. (Forthcoming).

ROBERTSON, SCOTT; JITAN, SHERIF; REESE, KATHY. 1997. Web-Based Collaborative Library Research. In: Proceedings of the 2nd ACM International Conference on Digital Libraries; 1997 July 23-26; Philadelphia, PA. New York, NY: Association for Computing Machinery; 1997. 152-160. ISBN: 0-89791-868-1. Also available WWW: http://www.acm.org/pubs/citations/proceedings/dl/263690/p152-robertson/.

ROTHENBERG, JEFF. 1999. Avoiding Technological Quicksand: Finding a Viable Technical Foundation for Digital Preservation. Washington, DC: Council on Library and Information Resources; 1999 January. 35p. ISBN: 1-887334-63-7. Available WWW: http://www.clir.org/pubs/reports/rothenberg/contents.html.

SCHATZ, BRUCE; CHEN, HSINCHUN. 1999. Digital Libraries: Technological Advances and Social Impacts. Computer. 1999 February; 32(2): 45-50. ISSN: 0018-9162.

SCHATZ, BRUCE; MISCHO, WILLIAM; COLE, TIMOTHY; BISHOP, ANN; HARUM, SUSAN; JOHNSON, ERIC; NEUMANN, LAURA; CHEN, HSINCHUN; NG, DORBIN. 1999. Federated Search of Scientific Literature. Computer. 1999 February; 32(2): 51-59. ISSN: 0018-9162.

SCHWARZWALDER, ROBERT. 1999. Librarians as Knowledge Management Agents. EContent. 1999 August/September; 22(4): 63-65. ISSN: 0162-4105.

SHAFER, KEITH E. 1998. Mantis Project: A Toolkit for Cataloging. In: Annual Review of OCLC Research 1998. ISSN: 0894-198X. Available WWW: http://www.oclc.org/research/publications/arr/1998/shafer/mantis.htm.

SHAFER, KEITH E. 1999. ARMs, OCLC Internet Services, and PURLs. In: Annual Review of OCLC Research 1999. ISSN: 0894-198X. Available WWW: http://www.oclc.org/research/publications/arr/1999/shafer/arms.htm.

SHEPARD, THOM. 1999. Notes Toward a Universal Preservation Format. Paper presented at: NSF Workshop on Data Archival and Information Preservation; 1999 March 26-27; Washington, DC. Available WWW: http://cecssrv1.cecs.missouri.edu/NSFWorkshop/upfpp.html.

SHIPMAN, FRANK M., III; FURUTA, RICHARD; BRENNER, DONALD; CHUNG, CHUNG-CHI; HSIEH, HAO-WEI. 2000. Guided Paths through Web-Based Collections: Design, Experiences, and Adaptations. Journal of the American Society for Information Science. 2000; 51(3): 260-272. ISSN: 0002-8231.

SIMMONS, L. M., JR. 1997. Collaboration Dreams: Guest Editorial. D-Lib Magazine. 1997 March; 3(3). ISSN: 1082-9873. Available WWW: http://www.dlib.org/dlib/march97/03editorial.html.

SMITH, ABBY. 1999. Preservation in the Digital Age: What Is to Be Done? American Libraries. 1999 March; 30(3): 36-39. ISSN: 0002-9769.

SOLLINS, K.; MASINTER, L. 1994. Functional Requirements for Uniform Resource Names. 1994 December. (Network Working Group RFC 1737). Available WWW: http://www.w3.org/Addressing/rfc1737.txt.

SUN, SAM X.; LANNOM, LARRY. 2000. Handle System Overview. 2000 February. (Network Working Group, INTERNET-DRAFT). Available WWW: http://www.ietf.org/internet-drafts/draft-sun-handle-system-04.txt.

THIBODEAU, KENNETH. 1999. Resolving the Inherent Tensions in Digital Preservation. Paper presented at: NSF Workshop on Data Archival and Information Preservation; 1999 March 26-27; Washington, DC. Available WWW: cecssrv1.cecs.missouri.edu/NSFWorkshop/thibpp.html.

THOMAS, SPENCER W.; ALEXANDER, KEN; GUTHRIE, KEVIN. 1999. Technology Choices for the JSTOR Online Archive. Computer. 1999 February; 32(2): 60-65. ISSN: 0018-9162.

UNIVERSITY OF CALIFORNIA, BERKELEY. Multivalent Document Home Page. Available WWW: http://http.cs.berkeley.edu/~wilensky/MVD.html.

UNIVERSITY OF CALIFORNIA, BERKELEY. DIGITAL LIBRARY PROJECT. Computer Vision Research. Available WWW: http://elib.cs.berkeley.edu/vision.html.

UNIVERSITY OF WAIKATO. New Zealand Digital Library. Available WWW: http://www.nzdl.org/cgi-bin/library.

VAN DE SOMPEL, HERBERT; KRICHEL, THOMAS; NELSON, MICHAEL L.; HOCHSTENBACH, PATRICK; LYAPUNOV, VICTOR M.; MALY, KURT; ZUBAIR, MOHAMMAD; KHOLIEF, MOHAMED; LIU, XIAOMING; O'CONNELL, HEATH. 2000. The UPS Prototype: An Experimental End-User Service across E-Print Archives. D-Lib Magazine. 2000 February; 6(2). ISSN: 1082-9873. Available WWW: http://www.dlib.org/dlib/february00/vandesompel-ups/02vandesompel-ups.html.

VAN DE SOMPEL, HERBERT; LAGOZE, CARL. 2000. The Santa Fe Convention of the Open Archives Initiative. D-Lib Magazine. 2000 February; 6(2). ISSN: 1082-9873. Available WWW: http://www.dlib.org/dlib/february00/vandesompel-oai/02vandesompel-oai.html.

WALLACE, JONATHAN. 1996. The Internet Is a Library. Sex, Laws, and Cyberspace Bulletin 1. Available WWW: http://www.spectacle.org/cda/lib.html.

WANG, JAMES ZE; LI, JIA; CHAN, DESMOND; WIEDERHOLD, GIO. 1999. Semantics-Sensitive Retrieval for Digital Picture Libraries. D-Lib Magazine. 1999 November; 5(11). ISSN: 1082-9873. Available WWW: http://www.dlib.org/dlib/november99/wang/11wang.html.

WARD, SANDRA. 1999. Information Professionals for the Next Millennium. Journal of Information Science. 1999; 25(4): 239-247. ISSN: 0165-5515.

WEIBEL, STUART; JUL, ERIK; SHAFER, KEITH E. 2000. PURLs: Persistent Uniform Resource Locators. Available WWW: http://purl.oclc.org/OCLC/PURL/SUMMARY.

WILENSKY, ROBERT. 2000. Digital Library Resources as a Basis for Collaborative Work. Journal of the American Society for Information Science. 2000; 51(3): 228-245. ISSN: 0002-8231.

WILENSKY, ROBERT; PHELPS, TOM. 1998. Multivalent Documents: From Presentation to Collaboration. 1998 January. (Powerpoint presentation). Available WWW: http://www.dli2.nsf.gov/dlione/berkeley/ucb-mvd/sld001.htm.

WITTEN, IAN H.; MCNAB, RODGER J.; JONES, STEVE; APPERLEY, MARK; BAINBRIDGE, DAVID; CUNNINGHAM, SALLY JO. 1999. Managing Complexity in a Distributed Digital Library. Computer. 1999 February; 32(2): 74-79. ISSN: 0018-9162.

YAHOO!. Web site: http://www.yahoo.com/.

YOUNG, PETER R. 1996. Librarianship: A Changing Profession. Daedalus. 1996 Fall; 125(4): 103-125. ISSN: 0011-5266.

# 4 Digital Privacy: Toward a New Politics and Discursive Practice

**PHILIP DOTY**
**University of Texas at Austin**

> If information exists anywhere, no matter how carefully guarded, it exists somewhere else, where virtually anyone can gain access to it.
>
> —LANE (p. 45)

## INTRODUCTION

This is the third *ARIST* chapter to address the specific topic of privacy. Other *ARIST* chapters have treated related topics: information policy (BRAMAN; HERNON & MCCLURE; HERNON & RELYEA; RATH & CLEMENT; ROSENBERG), information ethics (M. M. SMITH), and intellectual property, especially copyright (BEARD; KEPLINGER; LIPINSKI; WEIL). The titles of the two previous privacy chapters by CARLSON ("Privacy," 1977) and TURN ("Privacy Protection," 1985) suggested a comprehensive review of privacy-related material. The current chapter focuses on a relatively select group of works, most published since TURN's 1985 chapter. Like Turn, however, this chapter focuses on more than the governmental record-keeping systems that animated CARLSON's work and most earlier work on privacy. This broadening of focus parallels the evolution of privacy concerns from debates about governmental databases to information held in a web of cross-sectoral, large-scale, distributed organizations of all kinds.

This chapter aims to underscore weaknesses in many current conceptions of privacy, especially in digital environments, and to offer a wider, more inclusive, and more complex understanding of privacy

I wish to thank Philip Agre, Colin Bennett, Gary Marx, Helen Nissenbaum, and Marc Rotenberg.

*Annual Review of Information Science and Technology (ARIST)*, Volume 35, 2001
Martha E. Williams, Editor
Published for the American Society for Information Science and Technology (ASIST)
By Information Today, Inc., Medford, NJ

developing in a wide array of disciplines, sources, and organizations. As such, the chapter is unapologetically advocative. While the current chapter examines selected important policy and legal initiatives related to privacy, the major focus of the chapter is on more general understandings of privacy and digital privacy. Policy instruments and discussions implement and shape these understandings, but most of the literature examined in this chapter is more concerned with conceptions of privacy and digital privacy rather than with policy questions per se. Based on the literature reviewed, the chapter also argues that current parochial definitions of the concept of privacy, unexamined and narrow views of public and private spheres, and other limitations have serious negative real-world effects. The link between good theory and rich conceptualizations on the one hand and important public conflicts on the other hand provides essential underpinning to the chapter. BROWN notes that we can achieve new political understandings if we see history and the conflicts it describes not as coherent narratives but rather "in terms of converging and conflicting discourses and genealogies" (p. 116). As the aphorism says, there is nothing so useful as a good theory; this chapter aims to highlight a new, enriched theory of privacy that many commentators are building, particularly in the process of analyzing digital tools.

Further, as noted by KAPLAN (p. 53) and others, the conceptualization of a dilemma or conflict "already prefigures" its resolution. FRAZER & LACEY note that the way we speak and the discourses in which we take part create the social and political reality we seek to understand, and that practices and discourse are inextricably bound together. Thus, any understanding of the nature and complexity of privacy and digital information must be discourse-analytic and aware of how privacy is constituted in the micropractices of everyday life, including descriptions of that life and privacy's place in it.

Another basic orientation of the chapter is that the analysis of important public dissensus leads not to solutions but rather to increased understanding and reconceptualization of what may appear to be intractable social difficulties (LINDBLOM, 1959, 1988; SCHÖN, 1983, 1993). The utility of enriched and more clearly articulated theories of privacy and of privacy in digital environments lies in their ability to help develop creative potential alternatives for public policy, for personal understanding and political action, and for scholarly initiative.

Among the major changes in the field since 1985 that this review reflects are:

- The immense growth in popular as well as scholarly material about privacy since the last *ARIST* chapters were written, including thousands of print items of sufficient quality to be reviewed, with at least several hundred digital-only publications of value

- The broad interest in privacy by a variety of disciplines including information technology studies, cryptography, information policy, law, women's studies, rhetoric, cultural theory, sociology, political science and government, business, psychology and psychoanalysis, and ethics

- The rise of privacy advocacy groups, meetings, Web sites, and electronic fora, such as the Electronic Privacy Information Center (EPIC), the Electronic Frontier Foundation (EFF), the Online Privacy Alliance, and the Computers, Freedom, and Privacy meetings

- The proliferation of information technologies in personal, civic, and professional life, especially the convergence of computing and telecommunications in networks such as the Internet

- Increased concern with the collection, processing, combination, and sale of personally identifiable information by commercial enterprises of all kinds.

The growing commodification of personally identifiable information is especially significant because important privacy protections such as the U.S. Constitution limit the actions only of government. So-called third parties such as commercial actors in the United States are largely free from many strictures that apply to governments in their collection and disposition of personal information. This and other concerns have been paralleled by increased interest in national and international information policy issues in information studies generally. This chapter does not, however, include discussion of this general information policy literature.

The chapter does address privacy in terms of American and international concerns about the protection and disclosure of electronic information. While the emphasis is clearly on American conflicts, authors, and developments, some international policy instruments and literatures also shed light on the current state of privacy and digital information. It is in the comparison of American with other privacy regimes, in fact, that some important policy concerns and potential responses become more apparent. The drive toward international harmonization described by BENNETT (1997) is a major impetus for increased concern about privacy among actors of all kinds.

It is a particularly good time to consider the status of privacy of digital information. We live in a time when networked information is an increasingly common and important part of our social, financial,

political, and medical lives. At the same time, it is growing clearer that
the first generation of privacy initiatives of the 1960s and 1970s alone
cannot provide adequate protection of information that individuals
and groups consider private (AGRE & ROTENBERG; BENNETT &
GRANT, 1999b). This first generation of protections included initiatives
such as U.S. and other national privacy statutes, privacy protection
boards, self-regulation of commercial actors, and reliance on informal
codes such as Fair Information Practices. These and related efforts are
discussed, as are their limitations. There is still justifiable concern about
governmental intrusion into the affairs of groups and individuals. As is
widely recognized, the commercialization of information once considered private, in conjunction with networked technologies and growing
society-wide surveillance, poses an increasingly widely recognized threat
to privacy.

   This chapter focuses on the protection of digital information related
to individuals and groups, including personal demographic and psychographic characteristics, opinions, attitudes, behavior, and relationships with others. Most discussions about privacy emphasize a sharp
dichotomy between individual privacy and widespread scrutiny. The
focus in this chapter is on literature describing the need for a new and
richer conception of privacy as a characteristic of social life. Privacy is at
the intersection of individual and group self-definition, not simply in
contrast to what we colloquially regard as public.

   The chapter has a number of sections and subsections. These sections
identify important current conceptions of privacy, supplemented with
additional ideas that help define what digital privacy is and important
conflicts related to digital privacy:

- Important themes not addressed by this chapter
- Major concepts in privacy discourse
- Defining privacy, with subsections on terminology and
  foundations
- Legal and policy conceptions of privacy, with subsec-
  tions on protecting privacy in the United States through
  federal legislation, Supreme Court decisions, torts, and
  other means, with brief remarks on European Union
  and other privacy initiatives
- The panopticon
- The digital persona
- Information entrepreneurialism
- Habermas and the public/private dichotomy, with sub-
  sections on public and private spheres and critiques of
  Habermas

- Analysis of claims of too much privacy, with subsections on communitarian conceptions of privacy, critiques of "rights talk," and commercial free speech
- Gendered perspectives on privacy
- Privacy in public
- Privacy as property
- Rethinking privacy, scholarship, and policy making, with subsections on general concepts of privacy, concepts of digital privacy, and roles of the politically engaged scholar and practitioner.

First, however, it is useful to identify themes and literatures the chapter does not address and then to get a general appreciation of the landscape of privacy, identifying prominent themes and conflicts that surround privacy and digital privacy as concepts.

## IMPORTANT THEMES AND LITERATURES NOT EXPLORED

There are many important conflicts related to privacy and digital information; only some of them are discussed in this chapter. Certain privacy areas that are of particular importance to readers of *ARIST* cannot be reviewed in great depth here, although many are touched upon throughout the chapter. Chief among these are:

- Encryption and the related topic of anonymity and pseudonymity (BAASE; CHAUM; DAM & LIN; LANDAU ET AL.; LESSIG; PHILLIPS; SCHNEIER)
- Computer security (CAMP; CARROLL; U.S. CONGRESS, OFFICE OF TECHNOLOGY ASSESSMENT, 1994)
- The privacy of medical information, including genetic information (BUCKOVICH ET AL.; CARMAN; DAVIS ET AL.; ETZIONI; FRAWLEY; STETSON)
- Privacy in the increasingly electronic work place (J. P. ALLEN; GANDY, 1993; SHEPARD ET AL.), including monitoring generally and the monitoring of employees' email in particular (AMERICAN CIVIL LIBERTIES UNION; BAASE, especially pp. 275-281; BYRNE; LOCH ET AL.; SIPIOR ET AL.)
- Digital privacy and the practice of the information professions, especially corporate and professional associations' codes of ethics for information professionals (BRIEN; CLEEK & LEONARD; FARRELL & FARRELL; JOHNSON, 1997; KAPTEIN & WEMPE). FLOOD (1997a)

and FORESTER & MORRISON identify many conflicts related to privacy in the practice of the information professions, while more general approaches to legal and ethical concerns in the information professions are addressed by BAASE, OPPENHEIM & EISENSCHITZ (especially pp. 240-246 on privacy), RUBIN & FROEHLICH, and ZWASS.

The practice of the information professions involves a number of major subthemes related to privacy of digital information not reviewed here; two of the most important that deserve explicit mention are:

- The general confidentiality of digital records in information systems, especially circulation, use of and subscription to public information services, individual and group profiles for information collection and distribution, and other records of clients' behavior (BIELEFIELD & CHEESEMAN; CARLSON; LAUDON, 1995; MACNEIL; NASRI, 1987a; SMITH & HASNAS)
- Legal liability for protecting and/or revealing confidential information in resources in digital collections, including information in archives (HODSON; MACNEIL; NASRI, 1987b).

The interested reader will find these of value in identifying and addressing many of the privacy dilemmas that digital technologies present to the information professions. These and other sources underscore the fundamental influence that concepts of privacy have for the practice of privacy, the local and contingent nature of privacy practice in the information professions, and the close link between privacy related to information and privacy related to action.

## MAJOR CONCEPTS IN PRIVACY DISCOURSE

Before beginning the review of sources proper, it is helpful to identify some of the major themes and conflicts related to digital privacy. The first and perhaps most telling theme is the emphasis on the individual and concepts of privacy that emphasize personal information. Most concepts of privacy and most privacy statements, whether of commercial, governmental, or other organizations, are concerned only with individuals. As discussed elsewhere in this chapter, that emphasis ignores important shared aspects of privacy and allows important privacy concerns to be obscured.

Another primary theme, especially from a historical perspective, is the importance and conceptual hegemony of the Fair Information Practices (FIPs); CARLSON and his references to WESTIN (1967) and A. R. MILLER (1971) provide a rich introduction to the history of FIPs. These FIPs arose initially from a U.S. Department of Health, Education, and Welfare Advisory Committee on Automated Personal Data System report in 1973 and have been commonly accepted as the basis of the majority of governmental and other privacy initiatives around the world. These principles include (BENNETT, 1997; CARLSON; GELLMAN, 1996; JOHNSON, 1994):

1.  No secret record-keeping system will exist.
2.  People must be able to determine what information about them exists in records and how it is used.
3.  Information should be used only for its original purpose; use for other purposes should require the explicit permission of the person(s) to whom the information refers.
4.  People must be able to correct and amend records of identifiable information about themselves.
5.  All organizations that create, maintain, use, or disseminate records of identifiable personal information must ensure the reliability of the information for its intended uses; further, these organizations must ensure that the information is not used for other purposes or is not misused.

These principles have staunch defenders (CULNAN & BIES; FLAHERTY, 1997, 1999), to a large extent because of their relatively widespread use and conceptual influence on policy makers of all kinds. At the same time, FIPs have been resisted by governmental and commercial organizations that indicate that such principles and restrictions limit their ability to do business, provide customized services to existing clients, and identify potential clients.

More fundamentally, critics of FIPs cite a changing sociotechnical landscape that creates an environment different from that in place or envisioned when FIPs were promulgated. The papers in AGRE & ROTENBERG are illustrative of the best of these arguments, and they are reviewed below. In essence, these critics identify the explosive growth in distributed networked computing, many public and private sector organizations' identification of themselves as essentially information enterprises, the increased value of information about individuals and groups in the marketplace, and the rise of for-profit, private information services and products as the main contributors to the erosion of the robustness of Fair Information Practices.

Another major theme is that, for many privacy advocates, the Internet and the Web especially pose major threats to personal privacy because of:

- The increasing ubiquity of these technologies and the resultant inability to remain an active, engaged member of contemporary society without using them
- The illusion of anonymity and invisibility when using the technologies, especially when performing passive activities (GOLDMAN), because of the lack of transparency of how digital information is collected, shared, and used
- Cookies that track use of Web sites. Many users of the Web do not know about cookies, do not know how to find cookies on their hard drives, do not know that they can disable and remove cookies from their hard drives, do not know how to disable or remove cookies, and/or resent the extreme inconvenience of being denied services if they refuse cookies or are asked to accept cookies dozens of times in an online session. While such denial or inconvenience might be considered trivial by some, to others it represents unnecessary intrusion.
- New modes of information aggregation and retrieval that were previously impossible and are commonly invisible to users.

A further theme is the growing international dimensions of privacy along multiple axes:

- The net is global and therefore brings political, social, and cultural practices and assumptions into conflict in ways that previously were unclear (e.g., MILBERG ET AL.).
- The nature and extent of participation in online activities is a growing determinant of the success of trade and global influence.
- Questions are being raised about trade protectionism, political identity, cultural integrity, and practices that surround and define the self across national borders.

Another important theme relating to privacy generally, especially digital privacy, is the conflict about letting persons opt in or opt out of information collection and distribution. Put a bit simplistically, opt out is a presumption that the collector of information, and any parties to whom the information is given, leased, or sold, can use it in any legal way unless explicitly told not to by the person(s) to whom the information refers. This weaker form of protection contrasts with opt in, which presumes that no information can be collected or distributed without the explicit consent of the person(s) to whom the information refers (DARKO). This conflict in presumptions is fundamental. Strong privacy advocates usually favor opt in. Most commercial and governmental actors, if they support any ability of persons to take more initiative in protecting information about themselves, favor opt out. BURKERT aims a pointed critique at opt-in/opt-out debates. In his opinion, only strong privacy-enhancing technologies avoid the political and social conundra left by such debates.

Both FIPs and opt-in/opt-out conflicts touch upon a fundamental element of the social context of privacy—the asymmetry of power between individuals or groups of individuals on the one hand and powerful commercial and governmental entities on the other. In order to address some of that asymmetry, some privacy advocates have introduced another growing theme in privacy discourse: the assertion of personal property interests in information, including confidential information. Thus, every time one's name, address, shopping preferences, credit history, or other personally identifiable information is traded, leased, sold, or otherwise distributed by for-profit enterprises, one is paid fair market value for the information. Other privacy advocates, as well as for-profit enterprises, take exception to the assertion of property interests in information by individuals or groups of individuals.

Since the seminal work of WESTIN (1967) and others, opinion polls indicate a growing concern of Americans with privacy, and, since Westin, privacy advocates have used such polls to justify privacy investigations and privacy protection, especially by legislation. Prominent polls include those done by Harris, often in concert with Equifax and Westin himself. More recently, concerns about privacy reflected in American opinion polls have fueled concern that both privacy and the fulfillment of the promise of electronic commerce are being compromised. This apparent paradox demonstrates the complexity of privacy policy, the complexity of citizens' opinions about digital technologies, and the foolishness of an easy good-guy/bad-guy mentality.

Another major element of privacy generally, and digital privacy (privacy in digital environments) as well, is its weak constitutional basis. In the U. S. Constitution, as in those of some other nation states, privacy is not explicitly mentioned. These states have provided some privacy protections through a patchwork of approaches, policy instruments, and actors. As is demonstrated below, multiple methods of privacy definition and protection often lead to fundamental and often irreconcilable conflicts.

A further theme relates to children. In the current U.S. political climate, statements about threats to children and blunting threats to them draw volatile reactions. Subthemes include protection of children from objectionable material, from the actions of sexual predators, and from the actions of unethical commercial actors that collect and distribute information about children. One of the questions left largely unexplored by the literature and by this review is the valorization of parents' and local communities' ability to control what children see, read, and do online at the expense of children's autonomy and self-direction. While the literature on torts between parents and children, between siblings, and between spouses addresses some of these concerns, they are not explored in this chapter.

A final important theme is the conflict between advocates of omnibus government regulation of privacy, especially of the actions of for-profit corporations, and advocates of the current sectoral approach, relying on businesses to regulate themselves. While most industrialized countries have adopted the omnibus approach implemented by a privacy commission with power over public and private organizations, the United States has not. The U.S. continues to rely upon what some have called a fragmented sectoral approach, trusting professional associations to design and implement voluntary principles for enterprises to regulate themselves. This conflict is among the most heated in privacy policy, and how it will evolve with regard to digital information, especially in a global context, is far from certain.

## DEFINING PRIVACY

One of the few areas of nearly universal agreement with regard to privacy is the difficulty in defining it. What CARLSON said nearly twenty-five years ago still holds true: "there are more questions than there are answers on the matter of an individual's privacy and its socially acceptable protection from misuse" (pp. 279-280). While privacy, its social status, its complex relationship with information technologies, and policy approaches to its protection are better understood, current challenges to privacy protection and to its analysis are many.

Technology-focused discussions of privacy frequently begin and end their analyses with the codes of Fair Information Practices (FIPs) that have been in play since the 1970s. It would be a mistake to do so, however, for at least two important reasons. First, such codes and practices are based on a number of assumptions that make them untenable for the current state of networked information. While the shortcomings of FIPs are discussed more fully below, the second reason for avoiding FIPs as an analytic category is that codes and procedures based on these practices instantiate beliefs about what it is to be a human being, about technology, about social relations, and about information control that any analysis of privacy must examine. These beliefs cannot be naturalized nor elided over. It seems clear that A. L. ALLEN is correct in asserting that "well-being and happiness depend upon there being a degree of privacy in human life. It is an open question just how much privacy and what forms of privacy individuals need in given contexts" (p. 1).

## Terminology

One of the major reasons for the definitional uncertainty and, therefore, the political uncertainty, about privacy is the weight that the term must bear. Turn, echoing CARLSON and many others, notes that "[p]rivacy is a concept that relates to individuals in various ways and with diverse meanings" (TURN, p. 28). Privacy is a complex and multifaceted phenomenon, implicated by social practice as well as by legal and political theory, everyday rhetoric, and social commentary. As such, when persons in the United States and other industrialized nations evoke "privacy," the term may include:

1.  Protection of information related to individual attributes (e.g., name, age, financial status, medical and educational history, and taste in food, clothing, and entertainment)
2.  Protection of information about transactions (e.g., retail purchases and Web site browsing, especially purchases mediated by telephone or computer)
3.  Protection of information related to social and other relationships, especially intimate relationships (e.g., marital and parental status, group membership, religious and political affiliation, and identities of correspondents)
4.  Protection of physical isolation (i.e., limitation of physical intrusion and searches by government and its agents as well as searches by commercial actors)
5.  Prohibition of access to the physical self (e.g., unwanted touching and the forced giving of fingerprints, and of blood, tissue, or DNA samples)
6.  Prohibition of access to one's attention (i.e., limitation of intrusion into awareness such as the calls of telemarketers and targeted as well as broadly aimed advertisements)
7.  Protection of information related to physical location and activity
8.  Freedom to act (e.g., to be politically active and to live an erotic life and make reproductive decisions largely free from social and governmental scrutiny).

These categories are not mutually exclusive, rather they are mutually constitutive and are separated here only for ease of analysis. As A. L.

ALLEN (p. 5) points out, the lack of a universally agreed-upon definition of privacy is not surprising, given that there are no universally
accepted accounts of concepts such as liberty, justice, or freedom despite some legal theorists' and philosophers' intimations to the contrary
(see also POSNER, 1984, 1995; PROSSER; THOMSON, 1984, 1990).

Most approaches to privacy, especially in fields of interest to many
*ARIST* readers and American Society for Information Science (ASIS)
members, emphasize what is loosely termed information(al) privacy,
that is, privacy especially related to individual attributes (WESTIN,
1985). This limitation, however, is misleading because informational
privacy, action, and the inviolability of the physical self cannot be
artificially separated. The proliferation of digital information about
individuals and their demographic and psychographic characteristics,
the trading and selling of that information, and the integration of
previously separated databases and spheres of activity make such easy
distinctions untenable (AGRE & ROTENBERG; KLING, 1996a). This
point is discussed further below.

Privacy obviously covers a large conceptual area, and, whether as
analysts or ordinary citizens, we need to be clear about which area(s)
are meant when discussing privacy. There is another major terminological problem in privacy analyses, however, that is clearly negative in
its conceptual and political consequences. The phrase "individual data
subject" is commonly used to refer to a person to whom information in
databases, particularly corporate and governmental databases, refers.
The three component words are all problematic. "Individual" obscures
the social nature of privacy, both in its development and definition as
discussed further below. "Data" implies large, often governmental,
record-keeping systems, largely separated and not integrated. The distributed, interoperable databases common in the corporate world, in
government, and in concert between corporate and governmental partners belie the apparently innocent term "data." Finally, the use of the
term "subject" renders the person powerless, de-individuated yet individually vulnerable and scrutinized (FOUCAULT), classified, and not-
a-person, unable to resist or define what happens to him or her. The
behavioral science methods literature is largely liberating itself from
the term "subject" for identifying persons (AMERICAN PSYCHOLOGI-
CAL ASSOCIATION, pp. 49-50), and methodological rigor in examining privacy demands similar care.

## Foundations

The primary belief on which most conceptions of privacy rely is the
self, an entity who is autonomous, free to enter into relations with
others, and the product of a series of rational, calculated decisions
about surrendering information to collectors of all types. This classi-

cally liberal ideology results in an atomistic view of the self, ignoring the constitutive nature of relationships, both in the individual maturation process and in the life of the adult. This kind of atomism fails to reflect the phenomenological reality that people experience as human beings and has a number of negative effects on our ability to conceptualize privacy, especially in digital environments (e.g., BROWN; BYRNE). In addition, conceptions of the individual "person as pre-social and transcendent" (FRAZER & LACEY, p. 46) leads to the conceptual dead end, described more fully below, of the valorization of individual rights and liberty as *freedom from* rather than *freedom to*.

Privacy is mistakenly assumed to accrue first and foremost to individuals. While there is often some mention of the need to conceive of privacy as a broader category, far too many privacy discussions limit their definition of privacy to individual concerns. It is clear from the literature about self-development that the self is, to a significant extent, a product of relations with others; thus, privacy must be conceived as a characteristic of relationships, not of individuals (SCHOEMAN, 1992). Some discussions of privacy give the impression that people release information in a kind of series of ever-widening concentric circles, from the "essential self," to their intimates (immediate family members and closest friends), to less immediate intimates (colleagues, classmates, members of face-to-face organizations), to fellow citizens, and to the state and other large, especially commercial, institutions. This kind of thinking is wrong-headed for its psychological essentialism and its simplification of a series of very complex social relationships. The concentric-circle image fails to recognize the dramaturgical nature of what it is to live in society with others (BERGER & LUCKMANN; GOFFMAN) and, more importantly, fails to recognize that relationships with others help define individuals—that relationships are not simply added to what already exists. POSNER (1995, pp. 531ff) offers a market-based view of one's multiple constructed selves. As TEDESCHI notes, we must resist any theory that posits a "homunculus inside the actor" (p. 17).

St. Augustine might be considered a primary source in the Western world of the concept of this inner "authentic self," capable of reflection and self-knowledge (MODELL). More recent conceptions, however, such as those of George Herbert Mead and GOFFMAN, emphasize the mutual, cooperative construction of the person by the self and others. In fact, there are multiple selves, each tied to the needs, history, and expectations of context. In particular, people distinguish between intimate and nonintimate relationships whereby their intimates are allowed to observe them in situations and get access to information of all types that they do not often give freely to strangers or acquaintances (TEDESCHI).

Intimacy is, however, a kind of chicken-or-egg phenomenon (DERLEGA ET AL.). Self-revelation precedes intimacy—one must reveal oneself to establish the trust necessary for intimacy with others. At the same time, however, self-revelation is a result of intimacy—self-disclosure follows from faith that another has "earned" intimacy. Derlega and co-authors offer a useful distinction between open and closed relationships. Relationships are closed if people expect that information shared in confidence will not be disclosed to another, whereas open relationships make no such assumption. The open/closed distinction is markedly similar to the concept of contextual integrity described in SCHOEMAN (1994) and NISSENBAUM (1997; 1998), discussed below. People willingly share information with others in circumstances they regard as contextually appropriate, and, therefore, object to the recording and distribution of that information in ways they consider contextually inappropriate. Modell cites the work of Mikhail Bakhtin on public and private selves: "I become myself only by revealing myself to another, through another and with another's help" (MODELL, p. 87, quoting Bakhtin).

Privacy is an extremely complex phenomenon—dynamic, contextual, and embedded in individuals' everyday practices of identity and in their ideas of themselves and of the social world in which they live. The false choices that are so often presented between secrecy, on the one hand, and revelation to all, on the other, are simply not true to their phenomenological sense of what it means to be a human being. Privacy can be understood as being at the very crux of personhood. Privacy is the ability to determine what kinds of relationships people have, with whom they have them, and what kinds of information about each other they share. The relationship(s) and privacy are coterminous and mutually defining—one does not precede the other; rather each determines the other.

## IMPORTANT LEGAL AND POLICY CONCEPTIONS OF PRIVACY

This chapter is neither a review of the policy literature related to privacy nor a privacy policy analysis. At the same time, however, several policy instruments and conflicts are important to considerations of digital privacy in significant ways. First, policy instruments are essential components of the ordinary, social understanding of privacy and digital privacy. In the United States, among the most important of these components are Fourth Amendment protections against unreasonable searches and seizures, Privacy Act protections of information held by federal executive agencies, and Supreme Court decisions related to abortion, wiretapping, and privacy. These general privacy themes are not peripheral to considering digital privacy. Quite the contrary; such conceptions are constitutive of evolving ideas of digital privacy and of threats to digital privacy, as much of the literature reviewed here makes clear. Thus, laying out some of the important policy and legal framings of privacy is required. These framings are important narratives, significant tellings, of how we imagine ourselves as members of society (BRUNER; GEERTZ; WHITE). Second, one of the important conflicts related to privacy of all kinds is whether there are too many or too few governmental protections of privacy, especially in digital environments. Third, looking closely at the weaknesses of influential policy and legal conceptions of privacy makes it clear that such conceptions, while important, cannot be the first nor the last word about what digital privacy is and what it should be.

As should be clear, there is no unitary, universally held definition of what privacy is. That situation both results from and helps to contribute to the wide array of privacy definitions, protections, and conceptions in the policy and legal worlds. While the literatures related to these topics are quite large, the review of material here is intended to highlight the themes, actors, and arguments of special interest in the context of developing new conceptions of privacy and exploring the relationship between privacy and digital information. Perhaps the most prominent theme in these pieces is the primacy of individual interests in privacy; group interests, if they are considered at all, are plainly of secondary interest.

Both BENNETT (1995) and WARWICK provide useful overviews of some of the more important policy conceptions of privacy. MAJONE & WILDAVSKY provide insight into the important, constitutive nature of policy as "disposition": "Implementation begins neither with words nor deeds, but with multiple dispositions to act or to treat certain situations in certain ways" (p. 144). CAVOUKIAN & TAPSCOTT also provide a useful overview of privacy laws (pp. 35-47). From a policy perspective, one of the major difficulties with privacy is that it is, in the phrase of LIGHT, "constituentless" (p. 236), that is, it has many supporters but a large number of potential and actual opponents (REGAN, 1995). As is clarified below, however, the practices of privacy are not always policy-centric and policy-determined.

## Protecting Privacy by Legislation in the United States

WARREN & BRANDEIS' pivotal paper in 1890 is commonly recognized as the catalyst that put privacy in play in modern American jurisprudence, especially in terms of torts, and in public policy generally. There have been hundreds of analyses of the paper, but this brief discussion is intended to underscore the parts of the paper that are of greatest interest to this chapter's approach to understanding privacy.

WARREN & BRANDEIS have several major themes that have had enormous influence on the development of privacy as a social concept. These themes continue to characterize many elements of privacy discourse:

- The first and most prominent is their adaptation of Judge Cooley's precept that privacy is "the right to be let alone." A growing number of critics have pointed out the weaknesses of this conception, especially that it means only freedom from rather than freedom to. Specifically, the criticism is that a negative conception of privacy such as the right to be let alone does little to conceptualize or theorize the strong link between informational privacy and decision privacy (A. L. ALLEN; ETZIONI; MACKINNON). Such criticism, however, has made little headway against the right to be let alone that animates virtually all of American statutory, case, and administrative law on privacy.
- Another major theme is their consistent denial that privacy rights are merely another form of property rights. Instead, they stress a right to an "inviolate personality." While this concept sounds deep chords in the American mythos of the self-determined individualist and the "sacredness" of the home, there are a growing number of commentators who seek to claim property rights in privacy (BRANSCOMB; LAUDON, 1996), especially among those who seek to protect privacy more vigorously. Both these themes are discussed more fully below. On a related note, the evocation of an inviolate personality recalls the Continental tradition of the moral rights of creators as a path parallel to intellectual property protection of creators' interests. This concern with personality and moral rights helped to create the context of the European Union Directive on privacy protection and other European initiatives discussed below.
- The concept of the inviolate personality naturally leads to an understanding of privacy as primarily an attribute and concern of individuals. Although Warren & Brandeis mention relationships, especially those within the family home, the nature and implication of these relationships for the right to be let alone are left unexplored (COOMBS).
- Finally, there is an assumption in the paper that there is a fundamental "bright line" dichotomy between the

rough-and-tumble exposed world of the public arena
and the protected domestic home. As will be made clearer
below, especially in the critiques of HABERMAS' theory
of the public sphere and in the section on gendered
analyses of privacy, this idea still animates privacy discourse despite the strong reservations of many commentators.

Warren & Brandeis is important for its constitutive influence on privacy, both in the law and in the imagination of ordinary citizens. This
influence is everywhere apparent in the development of major U.S.
legislation and other initiatives to protect privacy.

While the U.S. Privacy Act of 1974 (PL 93-579) and its amendments
were among the first and most influential laws protecting privacy, it
has been examined quite closely in previous work and is not reviewed
here. An exception is a very brief review by REGAN (1995), who
provides a rich and detailed look at privacy in a larger social and
political context. The CENTER FOR PUBLIC INTEGRITY also provides
a comprehensive and pointed discussion of the politics of privacy.

REGAN (1995) provides an extremely useful source for exploring
relations among privacy, tort, and public policy (Chapter 1); philosophical and legal concepts of privacy (Chapter 2); the role of privacy
generally in the United States (Chapter 3); and informational, communication, and psychological privacy (Chapters 4, 5, and 6). She lucidly
and carefully examines significant sources, describes important policy
conflicts, and analyzes any resultant policy instruments, whether in
statutory, regulatory, or other form. The engaged reader develops an
almost visceral understanding of the important players, historical developments, and tenor of the times.

One of Regan's most telling observations is in Chapter 7, where she
asks why it took Congress decades to respond to concerns about privacy. She names, among other causes, diffused public interest, extended interest group opposition to privacy legislation, lack of a cohe-
sive policy community with technical and policy analytic expertise as
well as with political influence, and the emphasis on individual interests in privacy. These causes still characterize the privacy environment
we currently face. The public interest in privacy, while widespread,
seems less than deep. There are many and strong opponents, particularly in large public and private organizations, to privacy legislation,
especially if that legislation is omnibus in focus and relies on opt-in
alternatives. We continue to emphasize individual interest in privacy,
with little understanding or consideration of shared privacy interests.
The one major change in Regan's description of the pre-Privacy Act
landscape is the large, sophisticated, and growing network of policy

experts in privacy (AGRE & ROTENBERG). These groups are often termed issue networks in the policy analysis literature. REGAN (1995) provides a firm grounding for understanding American policy directions and discourse related to privacy; see also BENNETT (1992; 1997), BENNETT & GRANT (1999b), CENTER FOR PUBLIC INTEGRITY, and GELLMAN (1996; 1997a; 1997b; 1999).

In addition to the main stream of privacy legislation, relatively few U.S. laws specifically protect privacy, and these few federal laws are highly limited exceptions. The list below focuses on legislation at the federal level, although there are a growing number of state statutes of interest, especially those dealing with drivers' licenses. Some of the more important privacy protection legislation in the United States, with a special emphasis on the privacy of information held by or for government is listed below (see BENNETT, 1992, 1995; GELLMAN, 1995, 1996; JOHNSON, 1994; KLING ET AL.; REGAN, 1995):

- Omnibus Crime Control and Safe Streets Act of 1968 (PL 90-351) is aimed at decreasing if not eliminating abuses of telephone wiretapping surveillance by federal executive agencies, especially the FBI. Restrictions include requiring an "intercept order," demonstrating that other methods of evidence gathering have proven inadequate, and limitations of the use of wiretapping to evidence connected to a limited number of felonies (e.g., murder, kidnapping, and narcotics trafficking). These limitations are often referred to by the section of the statute that outlines them, Title III. The Electronic Communications Privacy Act of 1986, described below, is intended to update these 1968 protections.
- Fair Credit Reporting Act of 1970 (PL 91-508) makes credit reporting and investigating agencies provide individuals with access to records about them, with the ability to amend those records, and with protection of release of those records only to "appropriate" customers. GELLMAN (1997a) calls this the "first modern American privacy law" (p. 258).
- Family Educational Rights and Privacy Act of 1974 (PL 93-380) protects educational information against disclosure to unauthorized third parties and gives students and their parents access to that information.
- Privacy Act of 1974 (PL 93-579) and its subsequent amendments require federal (Executive branch) agencies to adhere to guidelines for collecting, using, and disclosing personally identifiable information and al-

low individuals access to records about themselves. There are nine important exceptions to the Act.

- Right to Financial Privacy Act of 1978 (PL 95-630) provides some protection to bank customers about their financial records, while allowing federal access to them in specified conditions.
- Cable Communications Policy Act of 1984 (PL 98-549) requires cable TV providers to inform customers of information being collected about their viewing habits, how such information is used and revealed, and how customers may review that information. The law also constrains disclosure of the information to unauthorized third parties.
- Electronic Communications Privacy Act (ECPA) of 1986 (PL 99-508) provides some level of protection to pagers, cordless and cellular telephones, and digital networks, extending privacy protections against wiretapping to electronic communications including email. It also demands that providers of such services notify their customers if such communications can be or are intercepted in the ordinary course of business (e.g., if email is not afforded the same kind of protection given to paper mail). The two major exceptions to the ECPA have important implications for privacy, especially in the workplace: (1) employers' ability to invoke ordinary business use for electronic devices gives them a substantial presumption for monitoring the electronic communications of employees, and (2) employers may monitor employees' electronic communications if they provide prior notification that they might do so. Employees' consent can be either implicit or explicit.
- Computer Matching Privacy Act of 1988 (PL 100-503) prohibits, with some important exceptions, what some have called "fishing expeditions" in federal databases that seek to match a person in one database with a record in another (e.g., IRS records with voter registration records). The primary rationale is that the presumed guilt of all persons in the database cannot be supported and that any subsequent denial of benefits must be preceded by notification and opportunity to defend oneself.
- Video Privacy Protection Act of 1988 (PL 95-630) limits the disclosure of information about customers' renting or purchase of videotapes. Judge Robert Bork's nomina-

tion to the U.S. Supreme Court and the subsequent media frenzy about his nomination prompted this protection when his videotape rental records were retrieved by a reporter.

- Drivers Privacy Protection Act of 1994 (PL 103-322) prohibits states, the holders of drivers' license information, from releasing this kind of information as well as information about the registration of motor vehicles without a system that gives individuals the opportunity to opt out of third-party releases. Subsequent amendments to demand opt in (active agreement) rather than opt out (passive lack of disagreement) have been introduced in the Congress but have failed.

- Communications Assistance for Law Enforcement Act (CALEA) of 1994 (PL 103-414) aims to put restrictions on the electronic surveillance of citizens by police agencies, especially the FBI. At the same time, however, the main thrust of the Act is to require telecommunications carriers of all kinds to make all modifications to their equipment to ensure that "authorized electronic surveillance" can be carried out.

- Children's Online Privacy Protection Act of 1998 (PL 105-277) requires the Federal Trade Commission (FTC) to prescribe regulations to protect the privacy of information collected from and about children under 13 on the Internet. The law also aims to give parents greater control over the collection and use of such information and sprang partially from reactions to the first of three influential FTC reports that describe the lack of privacy online, *Online Privacy: A Report to Congress.*

Besides these laws, there are also important confidentiality protections in the Census Act, the Social Security Act, and other major federal legislation.

Such a list tends to generate increased confidence that there is a considerable amount of privacy protection, especially at the federal level. That impression, however, is mistaken: U.S. privacy protection is fragmented, largely unenforceable, and often contradictory; further, U.S. initiatives are not well integrated with the privacy protections of the international community (BENNETT, 1997; REGAN, 1999; REIDENBERG). Digital communications, especially using the Web, only underscore these difficulties. Additionally, governmental surveillance initiatives such as the FBI's Carnivore and the Clinton administration's Clipper Chip, important exceptions to surveillance restrictions by the federal government, and the lack of an integrated approach to privacy protection make confidence in privacy protection highly questionable.

## Selected Important U.S. Supreme Court Cases

Much of the privacy protection in the United States is provided by rulings of the U.S. Supreme Court. At the same time, as discussed elsewhere in this chapter, many of the sharp limits on privacy spring from these same cases. See the section in the chapter on gendered analysis for a more analytic and more comprehensive look at some of these and other cases (A. L. ALLEN; BOLING; MACKINNON). The profound influence that U.S. Supreme Court cases have had on theories, protections, and understandings of privacy throughout U.S. society has had a number of other negative effects, such as an emphasis on legalistic thinking, a concern with individual interests at the expense of groups, and a virtual fetishization of the letter of the law, especially related to search and seizure. This section of the chapter describes some of the major U.S. Supreme Court cases related to privacy.

Perhaps one of the most important and foundational cases is the 1886 decision in *SANTA CLARA COUNTY v. SOUTHERN PACIFIC RAILROAD COMPANY*. This case established corporations as persons within the meaning of the Fourteenth Amendment to the U.S. Constitution, which forbids states to deny any person equal protection of law. Assertion of the "personality" of businesses was common in American jurisprudence and statutes for decades before this decision, as the Congress, under the commerce clause, and other federal governmental entities enthusiastically supported the national growth catalyzed by the legal process of incorporation, westward expansion, and robust interstate trade. *Santa Clara*, however, gave corporate persons equal standing with natural persons before the law, guaranteeing due process and equal protection. The Court was "apparently so sure of its ground that it wrote no opinion on the point" (SCHWARTZ, p. 170). The implication for privacy has been that the privacy of corporations is guaranteed the same protection as that of natural persons. At times, that equal standing has resulted in severe harm to the privacy interests of individuals and groups because corporations have both privacy as persons and additional protections granted to businesses per se. Coupled with deeper pockets, aggressive legal representation, and significant political contributions, these advantages make relationships between ordinary citizens and corporations even more asymmetric. FREEDMAN (pp. 91-92) and POSNER (1984) provide more on the corporate right to privacy.

*OLMSTEAD v. UNITED STATES* in 1928 centered on telephone taps to deter illegal liquor distribution. Government agents tapped suspects' private telephones without trespassing on the property of the persons being investigated; these taps were found to be legal. Included in the Court's reasoning was that privacy is not a separate Constitutional right. Instead the Court found that privacy was embedded in property rights and, thus, had protection granted to the various forms of property.

Olmstead was overturned by KATZ v. UNITED STATES in 1967. The case involved using a recording device outside a public telephone booth to intercept illegal gambling calls. The plaintiff won the case, with the Court defending privacy as a characteristic of the person, not the place. Previously, privacy protections most often centered on the home and (private) work place. Katz extended the boundaries of privacy protection to what a "reasonable expectation" of privacy might be. While many privacy advocates celebrate Katz, other privacy advocates are less than enthusiastic about it. Gandy (1993) cites Laurence Benner that Katz eviscerated the Fourth Amendment by asserting that, if no reasonable citizen would have expected privacy to "survive inspection" in a particular situation (GANDY, 1993, p. 202), then no search actually took place. If no search took place, then there is no standing for a claim to protection under the Fourth Amendment. Judges can determine the reasonableness of expectations while defendants must convince them otherwise; thus, Benner claims, Fourth Amendment protections disappear. Goldman also says that Katz has, in fact, undermined privacy by allowing jurists to determine what a "reasonable" expectation of privacy is, when it exists, and to what extent it can deter state conduct (GOLDMAN, pp. 104-106).

GRISWOLD v. CONNECTICUT in 1965 is considered among the foundational privacy cases of the Court. The Court held that the state statute forbidding the sale of contraceptives and the counseling of married persons about contraception was an unconstitutional intrusion into the marital relationship. In his concurrence, Justice Goldberg asserts that: "To hold that a right so basic and fundamental and so deep-rooted in our society as the right of privacy in marriage may be infringed because the right is not guaranteed in so many words by the first eight amendments to the Constitution is to ignore the Ninth Amendment and to give it no effect whatsoever" (quoted in SCHWARTZ, p. 357). Judge Harlan, considered by some to be an archetypal conservative judge, in a 1961 dissent said that it is not the specific enumeration of rights alone that deserves Constitutional protection: "On the contrary, 'the character of Constitutional provisions . . . must be discerned from a particular provision's larger context. And . . . this context is one not of words, but of history and purposes'" (quoted in SCHWARTZ, p. 360). Literalists on the Court and elsewhere strongly disagree with Griswold, Goldberg's concurrence, and Harlan's dissent.

As is well known, Griswold was the catalyst for ROE v. WADE in 1973. While reproductive liberty and privacy advocates have tended to apotheosize *Roe* because it grants wider access to abortion in certain circumstances, it has been severely criticized by commentators of all stripes in ways important to privacy analysis. From the strict constructionist point of view, *Roe* unjustifiably creates a fiction of penumbras, going well beyond the framers' intentions in scope and in creating a virtually limitless and ill-defined right of privacy. The argument continues that this case is an example of judicial activism at its worst: jurisprudence that, in fact, legislates.

THOMSON (1990), writing about what she calls cluster-rights, furthers this argument. She asserts that there are fundamental rights that are cluster-rights, including the fundamental *troika* of life, liberty, and property. They are cluster-rights in that they contain or subsume other rights. For example, the right to liberty "presumably contains rights such as the liberty to do this or that, which themselves contain rights" (pp. 54-55). According to Thomson, cluster-rights have considerable overlap. She identifies privacy as a cluster-right that, in reality, "is entirely overlapped by other cluster-rights" (pp. 285-286). Thus, privacy is subsumable into other rights, and arguments that evoke privacy rights tend to obfuscate rather than illuminate. Rhetorically, Thomson's use of cluster-rights to eviscerate privacy is the mirror image of Justice Douglas' argument of penumbras to establish privacy.

GLENDON takes a quite different approach in criticizing *Roe*, in an argument that illustrates critiques of the case and subsequent decisions based on gendered analyses of privacy. Glendon says that *Roe* guaranteed nothing but the right to act alone, whether to get an abortion or to raise a child by oneself. The decision ignored the fact that American society provides few, and contested, social services for pregnant women and mothers, including services for birth control and prevention of pregnancy.

*HARRIS v. MCRAE* in 1980 upheld the right of the federal government to deny funds to indigent women seeking abortions. BROWN and similarly minded analysts argue that this and like decisions erode whatever choice there might be with regard to birth, partially because it exposes reproduction decisions and information to government and third parties other than medical specialists.

*EISENSTADT v. BAIRD* in 1972 made the privacy of birth control an individual right, not a marital or family right alone. Glendon, citing the work of Michael Sandel, notes that *Eisenstadt* marked movement from privacy as "'freedom from surveillance or disclosure of intimate affairs'" to a conception of privacy as "'the freedom to engage in certain activities'" and to "make certain sorts of choices without governmental interference'" (GLENDON, p. 57, quoting Sandel). As discussed elsewhere in this chapter, this conjunction of right of freedom from surveillance (so-called informational privacy) and freedom to act (so-called decisional privacy) is the strongest conceptual base for privacy in a digitized, networked world.

*UNITED STATES v. MILLER* in 1976 focused on the status of bank records. The court found that, other than some long-established concerns with confidentiality, individuals do not own or have standing to contest the disposition of records of their banking transactions. This decision, discussed further in the section of the chapter on information entrepreneurialism, is seen as one of the major roadblocks to the protection of the privacy of digital information. Granting banks property rights to information about their customers' transactions makes banks' use of these records and information beyond the reach of virtually any control. Banks, with rare exception, can do what they want with such records, including sell, lease, rent, aggregate, disaggregate, or otherwise use them.

Thus, the history of privacy, both informational and decisional, in the United States Supreme Court is mixed. This fact displays and contributes to the ambivalence that characterizes attitudes toward privacy generally.

## Torts as a Theory of Privacy

Generally speaking, torts, a complex concept in the common law, identify the fact of and responsibility for a loss sustained because of the positive act or failure to act by another. Tort law is uncodified, so it develops on a case-by-case basis. Among the chief questions of law to be determined by the court is whether the plaintiff has some form of formally recognized and legally protected right invaded by the tortfeasor (non-contractual wrong). There is special liability for torts, if one of the states denies certain Constitutionally guaranteed rights, including several implicated under privacy: illegal search and seizure, freedom of association, police harassment, and invasions of one's body.

According to PROSSER & KEETON, based on Prosser's original 1960 argument, privacy torts cover four distinct kinds of wrongs or harms: appropriation of the plaintiff's name or image, intrusion on the plaintiff's privacy or private affairs, public disclosure of private facts about the plaintiff, and placing the plaintiff in a false light to others (see FREEDMAN, pp. 33-73, for an expanded list). The tort for unreasonable intrusion is especially important because the tort is complete when the invasion occurs: there is no need for publicity, subsequent harm, or any other wrong to occur. In a similar vein, GANDY (1993), noting the work of BLOUSTEIN, describes the analogy between battery and the privacy tort of intrusion: just as the unwanted touch is the harm, irrespective of any subsequent injury, so the intrusion is the harm, despite whatever may occur or not occur subsequently. Prosser's classic identification in 1960 of these four areas of privacy torts and his more comprehensive assertion that existing tort law adequately addresses all aspects of privacy has been formally endorsed by the American Law Institute and has had widespread influence on conceptions of privacy and the law (see BYRNE; FREEDMAN; GELLMAN, 1997b).

Because legislation is not the basis for tort, community norms and expectations are of primary importance in gauging losses and harm and in assigning responsibility for them. Invasion of privacy as a tort historically grew out of WARREN & BRANDEIS. Tort law maintains that it is possible to measure wrongs and harms in terms of financial compensation, in order to compensate those harmed, to punish those responsible, and to discourage future torts.

GLENDON notes that privacy did not become a general unified right in tort law; rather, it became a kind of catchword for a variety of protections of individuals against intrusion by others. Instead of intrusion, THOMSON (1990, p. 205) uses the term "trespass," a "claim-infringing bodily intrusion or invasion" Thomson's view echoes that of PROSSER & KEETON. While it is clear that Thomson, Prosser, and others do not recognize privacy as a basis for legal or moral claims in and of itself, others do. Part of that recognition is the insufficiency of torts to exhaust the meaning of privacy.

For example, GELLMAN (1997b) recounts how torts cannot meet the larger goals of the Fair Information Practices and cannot address the concerns generated by networked information technologies, for example, the hidden nature of intrusion and collection of information and the lack of fully public disclosure of information collected. A further weakness of torts as privacy protection is their failure to recognize privacy as something different from commodities and to recognize that privacy contributes to the moral status of the person (DAVIES; FREEDMAN), particularly in torts' emphasis on monetary damages for infringement. If we rely on torts for a major part of the rationale and mechanisms for privacy protection, there are few incentives for actors, especially large private-sector enterprises, to protect privacy and few disincentives for them to compromise it. Further, some states provide immunity for privacy invasions by spouses and parents that would, if done by others, be deemed tortious. Thus, while the use of torts for privacy protection has some benefit, especially in the tort for unreasonable intrusion that identifies the intrusion itself as the harm, torts are not sufficient to define, implement, or otherwise protect privacy.

## Other Theories of Privacy

POSNER (1995) provides insight into other theories of privacy. He identifies three keys to legal theory: economics (explored in POSNER, 1984); philosophical pragmatism, "shorn however of postmodernist excesses"; and classical liberalism. He uses these, among other things, to substantiate what he calls "problems often obscured by sonorous talk of 'privacy'" (1995, p. 531), a concept he feels has been insufficiently questioned. He recounts that the Fourth Amendment was intended, understood, and enforced to protect property, not what is now deemed privacy. Recalling his earlier rhetoric (POSNER, 1984), he discusses how people sell the various selves they create in various markets. He erodes privacy's claim to moral status and, thus, to being a boon to the policy: "Crime, subversion, and fraud are all facilitated by privacy, so it is natural and not reprehensible that society has fought the trend toward greater privacy with such devices as wiretapping and computerized databases of personal information" (1995, p. 536). Thus, society has a presumptive right to compromise privacy. Further, privacy can be compromised when one is victimized by a crime, subject to a natural disaster, or an object of legitimate public interest or curiosity (see also WARREN & BRANDEIS on this point).

What some would call the extremity of Posner's position leads him to assert that the fact of a family member's rape is "not the kind of intimate personal fact that most people would wish to conceal" (1995, p. 542). He explains this position by noting that family members often use the publicity about such a heinous crime to find the perpetrator, to help effect political change, and to offer solidarity to other families who have been similarly hurt. What this position fails to recognize, of course, is that another common perspective on the question is that protection of the family from further, attention-induced suffering is a legitimate reason not to publicize such a crime. This weakness of his position parallels oft-cited weaknesses of econometric bases of public policy. While this theory is certainly worth attention, its sometimes smug dismissal of dissenting viewpoints betrays its intolerance and its claim to being unassailable.

## Major European and Other Efforts

There have been a number of important European efforts at protecting privacy, with an emphasis on harmonizing or regularizing different national traditions (BENNETT, 1992, 1997; FORESTER & MORRISON; GAUTHRONET & NATHAN; GELLMAN, 1997a; RAAB ET AL.; REGAN, 1999; STEFIK; SWIRE & LITAN). The three most important of these initiatives have been:

1. The 1980 Recommendations of Council Guidelines on the Protection of Privacy and Transborder Flows of Personal Data by the Organisation for Economic Co-Operation and Development (OECD) (1981 I.L.M. 422, O.E.C.D. Doc. No. C(80)58 final).

2. The 1981 Council of Europe Convention for the Protection of Individuals with Regard to Automatic Processing of Personal Data (1981 I.L.M. 377, Euro. T.S. No. 108).
3. The 1995 European Union (EU) Directive on the Protection of Personal Data and on the Free Movement of Such Data (OJ No. L281, 1995), which took effect in October 1998.

While there are important similarities between the OECD Guidelines and the Council of Europe Convention, especially their reliance on the principles that underlie the Fair Information Practices, there are important differences as well. GELLMAN (1997a) notes that the Council Convention (1) applies only to the computerized processing of personally identifiable data and (2) is legally binding for the signatory countries. The OECD Guidelines, on the other hand, (1) apply to all forms of data processing, automated or otherwise and (2) are voluntary. Both initiatives have rather vague provisions for enforcement, and neither gives member states specific guidance on how to apply these principles in a practical and consistent way.

BENNETT (1997) provides a useful retrospective and prospective view of the three major European efforts. Reviewing his earlier work in BENNETT (1992), he says that he had predicted the increased pressure for policy convergence, both in Europe and globally. REIDENBERG predicts similar convergence as the European Union Directive went into effect in late 1998. Bennett (1997) refers to the major divergences evident in the late 1980s among privacy policy regimes:

- While Europe applied its privacy protections to both the private and public sectors (taking an omnibus approach), the United States, Canada, Australia, and Japan maintained a sectoral approach that (1) relied on voluntarily self-imposed codes and (2) largely exempted private-sector organizations from governmental scrutiny of their privacy practices.
- Most European countries applied their privacy laws to both automated and manual record-keeping and -manipulation systems; Austria, Sweden, and the United Kingdom did not.
- The choice of policy instruments to enforce the privacy protections ranged from formal registration and licensing to the somewhat looser and less restrictive use of data commissions.

Bennett then extends his discussion of forces for policy convergence and policy divergence through the 1990s and later.

His analysis begins with identification of four major forces for policy convergence. The first is technological change, emphasizing two characteristics of this change: its pervasiveness and the proliferation of decentralized access to distributed databases. The second major force for policy convergence is the policy harmonization of the Council of Europe, OECD, and EU initiatives mentioned above, while the third is the effect of the 1995/1998 EU Directive on countries external to the EU. This force demands that countries outside the EU provide an "adequate level of protection" to personally identifiable information. The fourth force for convergence, according to Bennett, is the desire by some countries to demonstrate their status as developed democratic states by imitating the more stringent privacy protections of other countries.

Bennett describes three strong forces that are likely to lead to policy divergence rather than convergence. The first is what is commonly recognized as American exceptionalism, with its emphasis on a fragmented, sectoral approach that is reactive and relies on incrementalism. The current antiregulatory climate in the United States, combined with fiscal conservatism and antipathy toward government, makes it unlikely that the U.S. will, any time soon, join Europe and other countries providing omnibus privacy protection with genuine national oversight. Discussions of the U.S. and other noncomplying countries as data havens or safe harbors continue as speculation about the effects of the EU Directive proliferate.

The second major impetus for policy divergence is the drive toward self-regulation using privacy codes and even standards-setting in the private sector to implement policy principles. While such codes and standards are often steps forward in embedding privacy protection in everyday business practices, Bennett warns that such codes "institutionalize a certain divergence in policy implementation" (1997, p. 115). Private-sector privacy codes in the United States and Canada have been developing since the early 1980s, especially to conform to the OECD guidelines and to implement the general tenets of Fair Information Practices. Such initiatives, however, have been largely cosmetic and ineffectual, despite federal support by way of statements of policy principles (U.S. NATIONAL INFORMATION INFRASTRUCTURE TASK FORCE, 1995, 1997). GELLMAN (1997a) relates how American presidents from Reagan to Clinton have supported the OECD Guidelines and their adoption by American companies while failing to change the privacy practices of these companies.

The third and final force for privacy policy divergence that Bennett mentions is the proliferation of privacy-enhancing technology (PET) (AGRE, 1997a; BURKERT; CHAUM). Technologies such as strong encryption, anonymizers, and similar PETs have promise for protecting privacy, but Bennett expresses concern that these technologies do not obviate the need for public policy, especially in national and international contexts. PETs focus on individual protection and organizational policies, thereby tending to undermine concern for and efforts to achieve national privacy policies, much less national privacy policies that adhere to evolving international standards.

GELLMAN (1997a) provides three important insights about privacy regulation. First is the extent of conflict among differing regimes, especially with regard to jurisdictional questions. One source of such conflict is U.S. federalism, which guarantees conflicts among the states and their privacy regimes as well as conflict between the states and federal initiatives. Conflict also arises among private regulators as codes, standards, and practices proliferate. Another source of such conflict is differences between various countries' policy principles and enforcement mechanisms and, especially, those between EU and non-EU nations. These conflicts make adherence to privacy standards difficult to achieve and, more importantly, make enforcement, whether to gain injunctive relief or to recover damages, even more difficult.

The second major contribution of this paper is his discussion of the term "self-regulation." He notes that private sector self-regulation is intended to "implement or extend" privacy statutes. Instead, we tend to use the term much less precisely. There is a distinction to be made, less important in privacy than in other contexts, between (1) self-regulation that results from delegation of governmental authority and (2) voluntary standards that are developed by private organizations without any formal delegation of governmental regulatory authority to the organizations (GELLMAN, 1997a, p. 279, note 18).

The third useful element of Gellman's analysis is his reminder, per Bennett, that self-regulation, like PETs and statements of policy principles, tends to seduce us into thinking that privacy is being adequately protected by private- and public-sector organizations. Instead, we must remember that "[c]ooperative privacy codes are not a panacea," and, further, that "the presence and needs of government cannot be completely ignored" (GELLMAN, 1997a, p. 277). Nongovernmental relationships and "solutions" to privacy problems do not adequately account for the public interest in protecting privacy, the multiplicity of relationships each person has (especially in a networked world), the structural threats to privacy inherent in modern capitalism, and the threats of government control with regard to privacy. In a way similar to the conclusion of BENNETT & GRANT (1999a), Gellman says privacy protection efforts must focus on the local, the national, the international, the commercial, the governmental, PETs, and statements of policy principles, all in concert—if privacy has any chance of survival.

Another theme that Gellman, Bennett, and other commentators on the European initiatives to protect privacy share relates to real-world effects of policy statutes, statements, and principles. Just as the Fair Information Practices have proven insufficient to protect privacy both before and after the introduction of digital networks, so it is with other, similar initiatives. Without clear implementation guidelines and enforcement mechanisms, especially across jurisdictional borders, the EU Directive, the Council of Europe convention, the OECD Guidelines, U.S. National Information Infrastructure Task Force pronouncements, and similar efforts matter little to the practice of privacy and to citizens. SALVAGGIO states that privacy invasions, however defined, are very easy to rationalize by evoking the importance of the public interest, especially to prohibit crime, and the demands of organizational interests such as efficiency, competitiveness, and "being modern." Against such compelling counterweights, privacy codes without specific provisions for enforcement, implementation, and cooperation are of very limited usefulness.

A telling example is given by LAPERRIÈRE on the so-called Quebec Model. Quebec became the first North American jurisdiction to apply privacy protections common in governmental organizations to private-sector enterprises in 1993. This law, an Act Respecting the Protection of Personal Information in the Private Sector, is commonly seen as ground breaking because of its unique status in North America and its similarity to European policies. Laperrière explains why the distinction between public- and private-sector information systems and initiatives often cannot withstand scrutiny. The distinction, while useful in some contexts, is undermined by public/private contracts, cooperative agreements, grants, partnerships, subcontracts, and privatization efforts. What is especially useful, however, is his informed analysis of the failures of the Quebec law to achieve its goals (see GELLMAN, 1997b, on failures of privacy law generally). Its most important shortcoming is its failure to address the society-wide surveillance that characterizes modern polities. This failing springs from three primary sources: the lack of operational criteria for identifying what most regard as legitimate databases and information systems, the large and fundamental exceptions and exemptions to privacy protection statutes generally, and the discriminatory use of information technologies to surveil "the most vulnerable populations" (e.g., welfare recipients) (LAPERRIÈRE, pp. 190-191; see also FOUCAULT; GANDY, 1993; WHITAKER).

Laperrière specifies further weaknesses of the Quebec law. Information can still be exchanged among organizations of all kinds, including across the public/private divide, for the vague purposes of "verification." Private organizations, further, do not have to identify themselves when collecting information, do not have to reveal what rights respondents to such requests have, and do not have to appoint persons to implement privacy principles and respond to complaints. Recalling CULNAN & BIES and others, businesses can evoke "legitimate business" interests or purposes and thereby effectively escape limitations on the collection, use, and distribution of information about citizens in Quebec. The Act did not give increased financial resources to the governmental body responsible for enforcing and overseeing the implementation of the law. Most important to Laperrière, the law did not institutionalize the involvement of particular industry segments in the development of adequate and appropriate privacy guidelines for their respective segments. The method of regulatory oversight is too broad and generalized to realize the privacy protections that the proponents of the law and the Quebec Model in general hoped for and continue to hope for.

Laperrière offers an important insight: "to cut surveillance appetites, we must intervene before the meal is served: at the stage of the conception of the systems and well before their implementation" (p. 190). This insight, combined with the ongoing experiences of European and other countries, can offer models for the United States to emulate and to avoid in its own ongoing process of defining and implementing privacy.

## A Barbed *Apologia*

This section of the chapter has revealed a number of important legal and policy conceptions of privacy, both generally and in digital contexts. Among the major themes are: the growing evocation of self-regulation for American businesses, the increased interpenetration of private- and public-sector information systems, the growing importance of international initiatives in privacy invasion and protection, the proliferation of privacy standards and principles, and the limited usefulness of such standards and principles without "common procedures and effective enforcement" (GELLMAN, 1997a, p. 275). What is the meaning of these approaches to privacy?

While the current author makes no claims to being a philosopher, legal theorist, or expert in political history, that fact is not necessarily a major handicap. It is essential that we integrate legal and policy concepts of privacy, skeptically and in an informed way, into broader contexts for determining what privacy is, how it is embedded in the micropractices of life, and how best to protect it in digital environments. In one way, legal and philosophical thinking about rights may help protect privacy. Although she would object to her argument being so used, THOMSON (1990) says that rights, a priori, are based on some moral status of personhood in common use. Rights, a posteriori, then confer further moral status on persons and provide means for enforcement and remedies related to that status and the rights(s) based on and protecting it.

One of the weaknesses of legalistic reasoning, however, is how its vocabulary and deterministic rhetoric have tended to obscure rather than illuminate public problems. GLENDON argues that a particular form of legalistic reasoning, rights rhetoric, tends to foster absolute argument and to instill a sense of individual atomism that hurts everyone. GELLMAN (1997b) only somewhat facetiously notes that "Because a good deal of the development and nurturing of the legal right to privacy has taken place in law journals, the confusion and lack of agreement about the concept may be entirely reasonable" (p. 193). BYRNE argues that the proceduralization of privacy takes intimacy and those elements of personhood that privacy helps to create and reduces them to a minor consideration of large-scale organizations, especially government.

In discussing the nature of the law and its contributions to our understanding of individuals and of society, WHITE says that: "[L]aw is most usefully seen not, as it normally is by academicians and philosophers, as a system of rules, but as a branch of rhetoric; and that rhetoric, of which law is a species, is most usefully seen not, as it normally is, either as a failed science or as the art of persuasion, but as the central art by which community and culture are established, maintained, and transformed" (p. 298). As we grapple with the fundamental questions that legal and policy conceptions of privacy create and address, we are left with what White identifies as the first and hardest questions about law and policy more inclusively—what kind of community are we trying to build, what kind of culture are we trying to make, and what kind of meaning will they have? Georges Clemenceau famously said that war is too serious to leave to the generals. So, too, privacy is too important to be left to only the lawyers, jurists, policymakers, and even the philosophers.

## THE PANOPTICON: SURVEILLING MODERN SOCIETY

This section discusses theories of surveillance and social control in U.S. society generally, then focuses more specifically on digital surveillance and its effects on privacy, such as the privacy of transaction-generated information (TGI). While concerns about privacy of Web-based transactions, especially commercial transactions, are often the center of attention in discussions of digital privacy, such concerns are contextualized and better understood with a wider sensitivity to the use of electronic devices to track behavior, determine location, and other purposes.

## Surveillance and Social Control

One of the most powerful descriptions and images of social control in contemporary society is by FOUCAULT. He resurrects Jeremy Bentham's concept of the panopticon in order to characterize the means by which modern societies control and surveil their members. Foucault identifies Bentham's panopticon as the architectural expression of the modern desire to observe, control, discipline, and rank. Through a complex series of windows, hallways, and other apparatus, the jailer can see all the isolated inmates but can never be seen in return; and inmates cannot see each other. The inmates are not under surveillance at all times, but they can never tell when and if they are, thus reducing them to consciousness of their permanent visibility. The observed "subjects," through the internalization of the unpredictability but relentlessness of observation, assume the responsibility for self-surveillance and allow the surveillance to be increasingly disembodied and not corporal.

The goal of the panopticon is not sovereignty or the supremacy of the state but rather the canonization of discipline and its proliferation throughout society. Thus, the panopticon is a generalizable model, a political technology, "a new 'political anatomy,'" a "physics of power" that defines power relations beyond the specifics of any particular application. Bentham and his acolytes aimed for a social structure everywhere characterized by discipline as exemplified by the panopticon, a subtle but more effective means of social control. This form of social control aims to give individuals more utility to the society and pay greater dividends to the socially powerful.

Foucault evokes the panopticon in the context of his historical review of how power and relationships are formed and how power is applied in implicit, structurally un-obvious, but still substantive ways. This power is "everywhere and always alert, since by its very principle it leaves no zone of shade and constantly supervises . . . [It is] absolutely 'discreet,' for it functions permanently and in silence" (FOUCAULT, p. 177). Words such as "surveillance," "social control," "power," and "public discipline" evoke images of governmental control of individuals and political repression by the state. While such images are not mistaken, any conclusion that these terms apply only to the state is mistaken. Foucault and others clearly demonstrate that the state is only one of many institutions that use power. Foucault's book, while emphasizing the prison, the work place, the school, and the military barracks, implicates other large-scale organizations, especially those that practice information capitalism (CASTELLS, 1996, 1998; KLING, 1996b; KLING ET AL.) and control (AGRE, 1994a).

Classical liberalism has developed a largely positive narrative about the beginning of modernity, emphasizing increased democratization, respect of individual rights, the overthrow of social status and rank, and increased self-determination and autonomy. For that, Foucault substitutes a narrative that, while recognizing the changes in society stemming from the birth of Western modernism in the last 500 years, instead emphasizes constant examination, ubiquitous surveillance, normalization of behavior and beliefs, and incessant rankings and classification.

This new kind of power is invisible, objectifying, and assiduously archived. Institutions now depend implicitly on documentation of all kinds, translating complex behaviors and beliefs into codes that can be recorded, accumulated, and evaluated in dossiers about all members of society. Although government was once the major focus of fears about these kinds of activities, recent developments in social institutions and in information technologies make all organizations increasingly capable of this kind of suffocating social control. Permanent, constant, and unrelenting registration is intended to capture and forever fix the objects of its control, based on making the smallest details of everyday life consistently available for gathering and evaluation. Thus, writing and documentation (1) are the means by which institutions can individuate previously mass methods of identification and objectification, treating individuals as specific "cases," and (2) make possible the characterization of groups of individuals in increasingly specific ways.

Disciplinary apparatus and functions have, therefore, assumed a central position in the social world, freed from the prison, hospital, army barracks, and schools where they were born. We must remember, however, that discipline is not an apparatus and is not institutionally based. It is instead a type of power and the means to exercise it, "comprising a whole set of instruments, techniques, procedures, levels of applications, targets; it is . . . a technology. . . . the ensemble of minute technical inventions that made it possible to increase the useful size of multiplicities by decreasing the inconveniences of the power which, in order to make them useful, must control them" (FOUCAULT, pp. 215 and 220).

Citing the work of N. H. Julius, Foucault notes the change from a society of spectacle, where the many observed the few, to a society of surveillance or panopticism, where the few observe the many. It is in this social order that the individual is fabricated and from this social order that the individual emerges, appropriately objectified, categorized, cataloged, and docile. Such classification is especially important in large societies with increasingly mobile and heterogeneous populations; where disciplinary techniques aim to identify and "fix" nonconforming individuals. For Foucault, discipline aims to reduce the body as a political entity as cheaply as possible while maximizing individuals' utility. Thus, political systems that legally and at first glance seem egalitarian and liberating are based on practices of subjection. These practices are grounded in asymmetric power relations using character-ization and classification to rank individuals and to exclude those who cannot measure up. Those who do not match the norm are identified by and through the panopticon, "the infinitely minute web of panoptic techniques," and are disqualified the same way.

GANDY (1993) provides a lengthy and considered application of Foucault's and related ideas of social control like the panopticon to personal information from a critical or social-change point of view. His aim is to examine what he calls the political economy of personal information using a variety of social science perspectives. For him the panoptic sort is a kind of "high-tech, cybernetic triage" that depends on digital technologies and technical rationalization to collect, evaluate, store, and retrieve personal information and to control behavior. He describes it further as a "discriminatory process that sorts individuals on the basis of their estimated value or worth . . . [and] reaches into every aspect of individuals['] lives in their roles as citizens, employees, and consumers" (p. 1). As a result, individuals are isolated from each other, and communities are harder to form and maintain. While noting that Foucault's description of the panopticon is limited by its locational, visual roots, Gandy notes that distributed, powerful, and interoperable computer networks have proliferated disciplinary surveillance through-out society and organizations of all kinds.

Gandy specifically uses Karl Marx's concepts of exploitation and surplus value to differentiate his approach from what he refers to as the orthodoxy of mainstream neoclassical economics. He also relies on the work of Jacques Ellul on the weaknesses of the technicist approach, Max Weber on the weaknesses of rationalization and bureaucratization, Foucault on the panopticon, and Anthony Giddens on the mutual influence of individuals and other actors and institutions in ways that either reproduce or reconstitute the actors involved and the relations between them. These intellectual forebears give Gandy the tools to explore the relations between information and power, especially how the panoptic sort as a system of power relies on the processes of identi-fication, classification, and assessment to avoid risk. Thus, the panoptic sort is particularly subject to the limitations of inaccurate and invalid information and relies on the decontextualization of information. This decontextualization is a major means by which the panopticon rational-izes the complex, "messy" world of real social life and establishes and reinforces asymmetric relations of power between individuals and the sorting bureaucratic organizations (see AGRE, 1997a).

Gandy examines the gathering and analysis of information by gov-ernments and concludes that the facile distinction ordinarily made between public and private information activities cannot be defended. The growth of the number and kind of information files, the triumph of rational and bureaucratic approaches to the organization, and the trading of information between governmental and between governmental and private entities increasingly erode such a distinction. At the same time, there are some important characteristics that differentiate private from public organizations.

Corporate information-gathering activities are especially characterized by the monitoring of employees. Gandy reminds us about the unreliability of the surveillance of employees' performance: reductions of complex and unpredictable workplace behaviors to auditable and quantifiable metrics are notoriously reductionist, such information is prone to serious misinterpretation by managers, and workers often seriously modify their performance to "fool" the monitoring system (see J. P. ALLEN; ZUBOFF). Similarly, private organizations have been in the forefront in gathering and analyzing information about current and potential customers. It is the process of applying for the benefits of private and governmental products and services that most clearly contributes to the panoptic sort.

GANDY (1993) identifies eleven kinds of information (the labels and examples are his) that undergird the panoptic sort, especially as this information is combined, evaluated, retrieved, shared, and otherwise manipulated electronically:

1. Personal information for identification and qualification. Sources include birth certificates, passports, drivers' licenses, school and professional certification records, and voter registration.
2. Financial information such as that from bank records, ATM cards, credit cards, credit reports, tax returns, statements from stock transactions, and traveler's checks.
3. Insurance information about health, home, car, business, liability, and group and individual coverage.
4. Social-service information about health care, disability, social security, pensions, food stamps, welfare benefits, veterans' benefits, and employment benefits.
5. Utility services information about telephone, electricity, natural gas, cable television, sanitation, security, and deliveries.
6. Real-estate information related to purchase, sale, rental, and lease.
7. Entertainment and leisure information such as recreational profiles, travel itineraries, lodging reservations, entertainment reservations, newspaper and periodical subscriptions, and travel reservations.
8. Consumer information from such sources as store credit

cards, accounts (including what we now call preferred customer plans), and layaways; purchases and inquiries about purchases; and shoe and other clothing sizes.

9. Employment information about applications, medical examinations, references, awards and sanctions, performance assessments and rankings.

10. Educational information from sources such as school applications, references, academic records, extracurricular activities and memberships, awards and sanctions, and rankings.

11. Legal information including court records, attorney's records, newspaper reports, and indexing and abstracting services. (GANDY, p. 63, Table 3.1)

Since the 1993 publication of Gandy's book, of course, additional sources of information have grown such as online chat rooms, Internet mailing lists, online purchases, inquiries about and use of digital files, and other individually identifiable transactions. This information is often included under the rubric of transaction-generated information (TGI).

Gandy does discuss telephone transaction-generated information (TTGI), citing the work of Thomas McManus. There are several kinds of TTGI: white pages information, including listings by name or address of telephone service subscribers; new service ordering information, including former number and address; calling records, such as information about the date, time, and duration of calls to a specific number; billing and credit records, including information about history of payment and variety of specialized services; and calling number identification, often erroneously called Caller ID.

In discussing the specific ways that the panoptic sort works, Gandy reduces computer matching and its ill effects handily: "Increasingly, individuals are barred from enjoying one class of benefits or services because they have not met some requirement or obligation in some other area" (1993, p. 75). The panoptic sort as deselective and exclusionary clearly is in effect here. He also notes, citing Troy Duster, that routine genetic screening of newborns not only skews adults' self-images, but it also implicates children as possibly "defective" and as categorically guilty until proved innocent. Gandy follows the thread of classification and uses the work of Leigh Star and Mary Douglas to assert that classification does not emerge naturally from some intrinsic characteristic(s) of persons or things but rather from culturally and historically defined perspectives that often assert economic and political power (see also FOUCAULT and the sections in this chapter on the digital persona and information entrepreneurialism). Classification using geographic information systems (GIS) according to census tract, zip code, and other geographically referenced means is one of the growing and most invisible ways used to identify financial risk, potential customers, and possibilities of crime. After doing a deeply analytic examination of different sorts of organizations and how they collect and use information of many kinds, Gandy concludes that, despite the growing adoption of panoptic technologies by all sorts of organizations, there are some important differences among these organizations.

Much of what the book describes is empirical research on individuals' perceptions, attitudes, and beliefs related to privacy and panoptic technologies. Group interviews done in the late 1980s provided some insight into the weaknesses of polls for understanding privacy. Primary among these weaknesses is that, given the lack of a universally understood and accepted definition of privacy and without the ability to probe in depth, one can never be certain which aspect(s) of privacy respondents are invoking when responding to questions about their concerns with privacy (see POSCH, 1993). One of the most telling of the findings is that, while the research participants found the sharing of subscriber lists invasive, they objected most to the subsequent receipt of unwanted solicitations. This lack of concern with the seriousness of perceived moral transgressions "points to the underlying sense of faith that people have in the operation of the marketing system" (GANDY, 1993, p. 142).

This faith is reminiscent of WHITAKER's concept of the participatory panopticon, in which people are complicit in the surveillance activity. This should not, however, dismiss this widespread attitude as an example of either naiveté or false consciousness. Gandy also notes that the mass media, particularly television, reinforce "compliance with the dominant values that legitimate the operation of the panoptic sort" (1993, p. 175). He warns throughout his study that, while such a critique is easily defensible, it, too, must be resisted if it leads to any belief that the commentator occupies a privileged position.

HAYWOOD, too, underscores the relatively superficial commitment that many individuals and institutions have to privacy, largely because the threats to privacy are so invisible (see also GOLDMAN). Haywood notes that: "A single incident may arouse concern but it is soon swept away by the day-to-day need to collude with a technology that most of us believe that we cannot now live without" (p. 30). He points out that interaction with the most intrusive parts of Gandy's panoptic sort often occurs at very delicate moments, such as when seeking credit, a job, admittance to an educational institution, adopting a child, or obtaining a state-issued license. At these times, people are unlikely to either express their reservations about the intrusive elements of the system or to draw more attention to themselves through such complaints. At such times, as Gandy notes, they have few if any alternatives to cooperation with the panoptic sort. CLARKE (1994) also discusses how one becomes the center of unwanted attention when seeking to avoid surveillance.

In discussing the social origins of privacy, Gandy notes WACKS' (1989) differentiation between two kinds of information in terms of sensitivity: (1) the personal in contrast to the more public aspects of life and (2) the consequential, which involves the potential of significant harms beyond the moral. While such a distinction has some value in, for example, situations where confidential health-related information has been inappropriately accessed or used to deny employment, education, or other benefits, this distinction fails to recognize the fact that the privacy tort of intrusion makes it plain that privacy invasion is injurious in and of itself beyond any subsequent harm that may result. Gandy says that, despite Wacks' distinction, individuals evoke such distinctions in ways that are unpredictable and highly dependent on context. Further, the panoptic sort can find indexes or analogues that serve precisely the same function that supposedly sensitive information does, such as using zip code as a surrogate for ethnicity, economic status, and financial stability.

At the same time, however, Gandy often invokes the traditional distinction between informational and action-related or decisional privacy. As discussed elsewhere in the chapter (particularly in the section on gendered discussions of privacy), this distinction, especially with regard to digital technologies, has serious and negative limitations. Citing SIMITIS, he emphasizes that freedoms such as freedom of association and freedom of speech depend on citizens' knowledge of whether, when, how, and what information is gathered and analyzed. GOLDMAN further elucidates this point with regard to digital privacy: "The lack of accurate information about the collection, use, and disclosure practices of entities on the Internet may chill speech and political activity. Individuals may hesitate and pull back from participating in desirable activities such as signing online petitions to Congress. They may withdraw from participating in online discussions or visiting [W]eb sites that contain information on sensitive topics, such as sex and health" (p. 111).

Gandy continues by stating that, for state and private organizations, "all information becomes relevant" (1993, p. 189), especially as private and public organizations lay claim to comprehensive interests and responsibilities and as the predictive value of all kinds of information, especially for reducing risk, is accepted as an article of faith. The overwhelming incentive for enterprises is to gather more information under more circumstances. Given that individuals are patently disadvantaged with regard to the social power of institutions, contracts are not good candidates for privacy protection; this point is further explored in the section in this chapter on privacy as property.

In his discussion of public policy and the panoptic sort, Gandy takes exception to assertions by privacy advocates that small victories or strategic retreats (e.g., dealing with direct marketing), are positive signs of the health of privacy. Instead, he pointedly says that "instead of victory, these measured retreats actually have served to reify and legitimate practices that were previously carried on behind a screen of uncertainty" (1993, p. 209). This stance is entirely in keeping with Gandy's self-identification as a critical scholar interested in peeling back the skin of social practice and in questioning the assumptions that animate it. In seeking to address this extinction by erosion, Gandy suggests that both private and public organizations should adopt the twelve principles suggested by FLAHERTY (1989) for publicly controlled information systems. The principles are plainly in a straight line of descent from the Fair Information Practices that Flaherty enthusiastically embraces based on his research, writing, and five years' experience as the privacy commissioner of the province of British Columbia in Canada. The twelve principles are: openness, necessity, minimization, finality, identification of responsible parties, control of linkages, informed consent, accuracy and completeness, establishment of special rules for controlling access, establishment of special rules for controlling use, rights of individual access, and the right to be forgotten. While generally supporting them, Gandy sharply criticizes the principles, emphasizing their logical and political weaknesses.

Generally, Gandy asserts that "the bureaucracies of the modern state, both public and private, find that privacy, however defined, represents an obstacle to the pursuit of their organizational missions" (1993, p. 195). Given this state of affairs, which Gandy regards as constitutive of the modern American state, he concludes that the panoptic sort is antidemocratic by its nature and that it cannot be transformed or rehabilitated. So he asks: "what is to be done?" He is left as the critical scholar, asking questions, raising doubts, and documenting the dysfunctionality and mistrust that characterize society. He leaves it to his readers to choose what happens next.

## Digital Surveillance and Privacy Enhancement

Gary Marx has produced a large and influential body of work about surveillance and privacy that merits review here. MARX's 1985 article, "I'll Be Watching You: Reflections on the New Surveillance" (a trope on the popular song by the group Police), defines how computer technologies of the past 100 years feeding the culture of social control have, in his words, "crossed a critical threshold as a result of broad changes in technology and social organization" (MARX, 1985, p. 26). New methods of surveillance can examine records and transactions identifiable by person and group, such as phone calls and bank deposits. Computer matching of diverse databases, use of body cues (such as polygraphs, blood and urine analyses, and voice stress analysis), and passive telemetric devices such as ankle bracelets for in-house arrest were of special interest at this time because of Orwell's *1984*, and Marx spends some time examining the weaknesses of and threats to privacy inherent in these initiatives. These activities have also been accompanied by efforts at deinstitutionalization that, in his words, "diffuse the surveillance of the prison into the community" (p. 28).

Marx identifies nine characteristics of newer surveillance technologies that mark them as different from more traditional, coercive, penal surveillance technologies (pp. 30-31):

1.  They can overcome distance, lack of light, and other physical barriers.
2.  They can transcend time.
3.  They are capital- rather than labor-intensive.
4.  They focus on all possible wrongdoers, not on particular suspects; Marx calls this a change from specific to categorical suspicion.
5.  They focus on the prevention of violations rather than simply punishing violations.
6.  They are decentralized and thereby encourage self-policing and inhibition.
7.  They are actually or nearly invisible.
8.  They attempt to delve into personality and self, not simply the body.
9.  They deepen and widen surveillance to new areas.

While such technologies have benefits (e.g., safer policing, health monitoring, and financial savings), it is possible to "miss the time bombs that may be embedded therein" (p. 32). Significantly, the new surveillance invades privacy by eliminating rather than simply crossing barriers as older surveillance technologies did.

Marx lists further limitations of the new surveillance technologies and emphasizes how they tend to undermine an essential feature of social life and individual well-being: trust. They undermine trust to the extent that, he says, the system may not be reformable; rather, it should be delegitimized.

MARX's 1990 article is one of the *Harvard Business Review's* case studies. He describes a mythical company based on characteristics of actual companies and their employees; the article is an extended "quotation" from the supposed employee handbook. The rationale for what is, in fact, stifling and invasive surveillance of virtually all aspects of employees' home and work lives (from diet to genetic predispositions) is one that can be easily defended: ensuring employees' safety and well-being, keeping the company competitive, and ensuring the appropriate use of all company resources. The second part of the paper is the analysis of the case by four experts in technology and "human resource management." Shoshana Zuboff says the description evokes the managerial dream of the perfectly controlled, orderly world that has endured for almost 200 years (see also ZUBOFF). Karen Nussbaum remarks, "There are real problems facing employers, but substituting control and fear for supervision and training is not the answer. . . . To get there [professionalization and commitment in the workplace], we need education, training, and respect" (quoted in MARX, p. 30). This last point is key: essential elements of community are trust, reciprocity, and mutual respect. As GANDY (1993) and others state, surveillance technologies, no matter how effective, undermine the emotional and psychological commitment necessary for organizational cohesion and success.

All of the papers in AGRE & ROTENBERG are valuable to this discussion, but this review examines only a few. In their preface, they issue a warning worth reiterating: "Although the danger of surveillance technologies continues to grow and even accelerate, other innovations have invalidated the automatic identification between technology and [social and political] control" (p. vii). These innovations include privacy-enhancing technologies and new opportunities to debate and act on privacy provided by networked technologies.

AGRE (1997b) provides a comprehensive list of major changes in the socio-technical environment that, compared to the 1970s and 1980s, are more dangerous, more heterogeneous, and less controllable by Fair Information Practices. These include:

- The emergence of global digital communication networks
- Emerging technologies to protect identity and communication
- New digital media that facilitate new social relationships and new kinds of social relationships
- A new generation of privacy activists who are politically and technically sophisticated and active
- A substantial body of empirical and global experience with data protection laws, most based on the Fair Information Practices
- The very rapid globalization of material production, cultural production, and policy making
- The intimate ways in which users have woven digital technologies into their lives to the extent that any possible harm is largely invisible

- The spread of sectoral regulation
- Increased policy and technological pressures for what is termed "international harmonization" (BENNETT, 1992, 1997, 1998)
- Increasing erosion of what we usually regard as the distinction between the public and the private, especially, per BELOTTI, by joining together spaces that were once disparate (AGRE, 1997b, pp. 11-12)
- The somewhat paradoxical mismatch between the relatively high level of abstract and/or moral concern with privacy and the low level of political mobilization by ordinary citizens (GANDY, 1993).

Agre describes the 1980s as a time when the Fair Information Practices' emphasis was on centralized data collection, with a specified place and time of collection, by a particular and known organization or individual. FIPs are no longer useful as they were for the technological, social, and political climate of the 1970s and 1980s. Agre's analysis builds on an understanding of privacy as "the mechanisms through which people define themselves and conduct their relationships with one another" (AGRE, 1997b, p. 12). The paper continues with in-depth and crucial analyses of system architectures, standardization, data models, policy instruments to protect privacy, and the difficulty of protecting privacy in various settings and in various circumstances.

AGRE (1997a) provides a remarkable analysis of representation and modeling in computer science (see also AGRE, 1999). Granting computers status as immutable, ahistorical objects has blinded us to the mutability and contingency of computing and the assumptions about people and the world that it instantiates. Perhaps the most striking of his conclusions is the ill effects, both conceptual and otherwise, of the conflation of representations with the things they are intended to represent. Records and things, in his words, are blurred, leading to the "natural" use of identifiers such as names, dates of birth, and social security numbers as primary keys in relational databases. Along with CHAUM and others, he wonders why we do not insist on the use of arbitrarily assigned surrogate identifiers to protect privacy. While some commentators find solace in privacy-enhancing technologies (PETs), Agre says such technologies are not likely to be adopted because of the cognitive and work practices of system designers and implementers. He ends by reiterating that granting information epistemic status as a thing and the resultant coupling of records with identity pose serious problems for privacy protection that are not easily overcome.

BURKERT picks up the discussion of privacy-enhancing technologies, defined as "technical and organizational concepts that aim at protecting personal identity," usually involving encryption (p. 125). There are two important weaknesses in this conception of PETs: (1) its emphasis on individual identity, when we know that we often have important shared interests in privacy and (2) its reliance on cryptography that can protect the substance of a message from prying eyes but cannot protect the fact that communication took place or with whom it took place. Burkert provides a typology for PET concepts: subject-oriented that aim to reduce or eliminate entirely the ability to identify individual transactions, often relying on surrogates for identity; object-oriented that aim to reduce the traceability of items for exchange (e.g., digital cash or bartered goods); and transaction-oriented that aim to destroy records automatically.

PETs have serious limitations, which Burkert identifies according to two main categories: internal and external. The four internal limitations are:

- Unidirectional protection that depends on the organization to make a normative decision to protect privacy
- Anonymity, which may be compromised by indirect or surrogate identification
- Reliance of PETs on a system-centric view of the world whereby interconnections among systems are easily and dangerously ignored
- Assumptions about the strength of strong encryption that are subject to radical redefinition in unpredictable but expected ways and time periods.

The three major external limitations are:

- Long-term habits and economic structures of surrendering information for benefits (see FOUCAULT; GANDY, 1993; WHITAKER)
- Mobility and the resulting isolation and ongoing novelty of social relationships
- The inability of the normal view of privacy to cover what he terms "political privacy" that includes and, indeed, demands political action (see the discussion elsewhere in this chapter about so-called aesthetic and instrumental privacy) (BURKERT, pp. 130-135).

Burkert concludes by emphasizing the need for trust and interaction in spite of risk, not because of the supposed absence of risk. This normative position is at the heart of community and may, in fact, be one of the only ways out of the privacy conundrum.

LAUDON (1996) provides a further perspective on privacy-enhancing technologies by stating that both privacy problems and potential solutions are discursive constructions. What experts regard as (appropriate and acceptable) PETs may alienate or frustrate users. Also see CAVOUKIAN for the application of PETs to health information systems.

The December 1995 issue of the *Communications of the ACM* devotes several papers to discussions of email and privacy. WEISBAND & REINIG underscore the fact that any belief in the privacy of email is ill-founded and that users have immensely unrealistic expectations that email communications are and will be kept confidential. They identify three possible reasons for users' naive belief in the privacy of email:

- Password protections and interface design may seduce the user into thinking that no one can or will read email except the intended recipient(s).
- Lack of an email policy may lead users to believe that any and all communications are acceptable; policies help users to understand that their communications can and often will be monitored.
- Lack of the usual social cues may lead email users to forget the vulnerability of their communication to interception, examination, and retransmission.

Weisband & Reinig then discuss why users seem so likely to self-disclose online, concluding that it is easier to do so when they suspect that no one is looking. Their paper finishes with an examination of what factors should be considered when establishing policies related to email (citing Johnson and Podesta's *Privacy Toolkit*): stakeholders in establishing the policy, ethical and legal constraints on the policy, evaluation criteria for the policy, and whether the policy has been disclosed in advance. All four factors should help establish and further build an atmosphere of intra-organizational trust while allowing the enterprise to fulfill its obligations and protect its interests.

SIPIOR & WARD discuss privacy of employees' email and how it fits into a more general atmosphere of surveillance in the modern workplace. Their paper focuses on the differing expectations of employees and employers regarding the nature, extent, and ethical and legal status of privacy intrusions into email. They present a four-celled matrix for classifying invasions of employees' email, with internal/external interception as the rows and authorized/unauthorized invasion as the columns. In the cells are: (1) monitoring employees' performance (authorized internal); (2) eavesdropping on employees (unauthorized internal); (3) formal law enforcement investigations (authorized external); and (4) hacker activities (unauthorized external).

Generally Sipior & Ward say that employers seem eager to assert their interest in all uses of work-place communication technologies including email, especially to prevent abuse of corporate resources, to prevent or investigate theft or industrial espionage, to manage complex technical networks, and to achieve other goals. There is a growing body of case law supporting employers' claims in this regard, but "[b]ecause email is a relatively new form of commercial communication, it lacks extensive legal precedents to define the parameters [*sic*] of privacy associated with its use" (p. 51). The authors then discuss how the U.S. Constitution, state constitutions, federal and state statutes, and state common law protect privacy in various ways, for various purposes, and in various circumstances. This patchwork of protection makes internal organizational policies imperative for ensuring that employees' and employers' expectations for the privacy of email coincide and that the use of email systems is both ethical and legal.

CULNAN, alone and in collaboration with others, has accumulated a significant body of work related to privacy online. In 1993 she explores aspects of secondary information use, that is, the use of personally identifiable information for purposes other than that of the initial collection of the information, and consumers' attitudes toward secondary information use. While such use is often well within the law and seems ethical to many consumers and commercial enterprises, secondary information use may often be regarded with suspicion and as invasive, especially if such use is without the consent of the person(s) to whom the information refers.

Culnan's review of related literatures is notable for its depth and comprehensiveness, especially its description of historical developments in technology, privacy analysis, and related topics. Her Table 1 on characteristics of secondary information use is useful, if contestable, while her Figure 1 on dimensions of secondary information use is also of some value. What emerges, however, is the clear message that there is "no general theory of secondary information use that links the specific attributes or characteristics of an information practice with the perception by a majority of individuals that the practice is either beneficial or privacy-invasive" (1993, p. 345). To address this lacuna in the literature and conceptual basis of privacy studies, Culnan sought to profile consumers according to their attitudes toward direct marketing and reservations about privacy invasions based on their attitudes toward the secondary use of information. She used a self-administered anonymous written survey of 126 undergraduate students. Demographic information, concern for privacy, and attitudes toward direct-mail marketing were measured using multiple methods and items, and these data were supplemented by two open-ended questions.

Using discriminant analysis, Culnan determined there were few statistically significant differences between the students who had experienced privacy invasions and those who had not, based on their scores on an intermediate measure. Using these comparisons and the analysis of the open-ended questions, she concludes that the primary concern is control, that is, consumers well-disposed to direct-mail marketing and commerce also have lower concerns with privacy, and they have a more developed ability to cope with unsolicited mail. She also recommends that organizations would be well-served by clients and potential clients if the organizations voluntarily implemented the fair information practices and did so seriously, predictably, and publicly.

FORESTER & MORRISON note that most governmental initiatives for collecting and aggregating information have reasonable goals, for example, to save money, provide better health care, and increase the availability of social services. These "noble" goals, reminiscent of the rhetoric of "legitimate business interests" in the private sector, give rise to serious conflicts about the collection and review of information, especially in Europe. Thus they say, "In the absence of a consensus [about what constitutes necessary data collection and use], we are left with technological capabilities coupled with simple, instrumental ends" (p. 155). Later in their discussion they identify "this tireless idiot savant ability" of computers to perform routine functions endlessly without complaint as the means by which "the instrumentalism of efficiency" threatens to degrade the quality of life (p 159). The exercise of discriminating judgment by people controlling and contextualizing these computational machines seems incompatible with "the routinized, standardized repetition digital processing makes possible" (p. 159) and, one might add, almost inevitable (see KLING ET AL. and others on information entrepreneurialism).

The late 1990s saw a growing concern by users of the Web that commercial enterprises were unfairly collecting, collating, searching, and sharing information about them. A number of important hearings, reports, and initiatives sprang from these concerns, as illustrated by CULNAN (1999a; 1999b), CULNAN & MILBERG, and U.S. DEPARTMENT OF COMMERCE. Since this chapter is not limited to policy considerations, these and related documents are not closely analyzed here. What these documents do, however, is indicate the growing sense in the polity that citizens, businesses, government both in the United States and globally, as well as policy analysts, need to create a new and unpredictable set of alliances in order to address the policy conflicts generated by the Internet and Web.

## THE DIGITAL PERSONA

Computer networks and the integration of digital technologies and information into many phases of contemporary activity have given rise to a new version of a long-time concept in privacy studies. Commentators in times past (c. 1980-1995) would speak of the "information mosaic" (FORESTER & MORRISON, pp. 138-142) built by aggregating information about someone from originally disparate information sources. Such information could come from government records, retail transaction logs, insurance forms, and the like. Originally, this concept referred to a profile built of an individual that combined both print and electronic information.

Now, however, the concept of the information mosaic has been supplanted by the idea of what some call a digital persona, digital shadow, or digital individual. This change reflects the fact that people use digital technologies to perform such ordinary acts as withdraw money from banks, submit income tax returns, apply for governmental benefits, and interact with institutions all over the world. More importantly, however, the concept of the digital persona underscores the fact that they ineluctably are building digital representations of themselves when they use email, browse the Web, order books online, submit manufacturers' warranty cards, etc.

While the information mosaic has been widely regarded as a threat to individual and group privacy, the digital persona is much more complex. A full issue of *The Information Society* in 1994 is dedicated to exploring that complexity. AGRE (1994b), in the issue editor's introduction, says digital personae focus on the complex relationships between human beings and the digital representations of themselves that they and others produce. Such personae are not merely figments of theorists' imaginations or of privacy advocates' nightmares—rather, they are increasingly important elements of life in industrialized societies and "have material consequences for human well-being" (p. 74). The journal issue as a whole delimits ways in which the concept of the digital individual serves as a means to explore how cultural practice, political activism, system design, cultural theory, and governmental and institutional policy interact in the context of people, digital systems, and society.

CLARKE (1994) begins the discussion by defining the digital persona as a multifaceted construct: "a model of an individual's public personality based on data and maintained by transactions, and intended for use as a proxy for the individual" (p. 78). Clarke's persona can either be projected, and therefore subject to some control by the person to whom it is attached, or imposed by others. Similarly, the persona may be informal, based on others' (usually) individual perceptions, or formal, based on the aggregation, comparison, and distribution of structured information often contributed and verified by the individual. Clarke differentiates personae along another dimension, their level of activity. A persona may be passive, active, or autonomous. All of these alternatives can be combined in complex ways, and an individual may be represented by many digital personae. For example, a consumer is, according to the typology, ordinarily represented by a passive digital persona imposed by others. The same individual may have an active, projected digital persona when searching the digital realm for theater tickets.

Clarke is careful to demonstrate that the digital persona offers benefits as well as costs. The bulk of his analysis, however, discusses the threats to social and individual liberty and autonomy posed by digital personae. Clarke links this discussion to "dataveillance" (data + surveillance), "the systematic use of personal data systems in the investigation or monitoring of the actions or communications of one or more persons" (1994, p. 83; see also CLARKE, 1988). Dataveillance can be personal or mass, but can be differentiated from electronic and physical surveillance, according to Clarke, because it monitors data, not physical activity or location. This distinction, however, is increasingly fragile as all surveillance systems become digital and combine, process, and match data in real time. The threats to individuals and society as a whole come from (1) the fact that the digital persona is necessarily a reductionist model of the person, (2) computer matching, (3) the misbalance of power between large organizations, especially for-profit corporations, and individual actors, and (4) profiling and categorization. These threats are exacerbated by the weaknesses inherent in the digital persona used for matching and profiling. These involve everything from the limited nature of data sources to poor data quality to conflicting data definitions to "oppressive use of the results" of computer matching and profiling (1994, p. 87). As Clarke warns, echoing FOUCAULT's warnings about normalizing and power: "atypical, idiosyncratic, and eccentric people, and extenuating circumstances, tend not to be provided for. Inferences are readily drawn that with careful review may be quite unreasonable" (1994, p. 88).

Clarke describes even deeper threats to autonomy and freedom in highlighting the links between people's behavior and attributes on the one hand and the digital sources they consult, the individuals and organizations they contact, the online purchases they make, and the words and images they use in messages on the other hand. Not only can behavior and attitudes be tracked and inferred, however imperfectly, but attempts to thwart monitoring through the use of anonymizers, encryption, and use of multiple (sometimes spoofing) personae also bring further attention. Such attention can come from insurance companies, employers, retailers, creditors, the police, and other governmental agencies, as well as, more threateningly, from extortionists, kidnappers, ex-spouses, assassins, and private detectives.

Clarke mentions problems with erroneously attaching particular actions to particular digital personae. Extending his argument, there are at least four, non-mutually exclusive ways for actions to be mislabeled: (1) person A performs an act but is not given the appropriate credit or blame; (2) A performs an act, but it is misattributed to or misappropriated by person B; (3) A does not perform an act, but it is misattributed to A; and (4) A does not perform an act, but, after it is misattributed to A, A is thereby linked to other such acts and the people who commit them. All of these mistakes are becoming more common and have serious, real-world consequences that are rarely addressed or ameliorated. Clarke concludes that "Dataveillance is an inevitable outcome of the data intensity of contemporary administrative practice" (1994, p. 90). Focused research, lobbying, and governmental action might lessen the ill effects of dataveillance, but such an outcome is by no means assured.

The second article is by KILGER, who addresses how individuals construct themselves and form images of these constructions. Like CLARKE (1994), Kilger focuses on the individual and threats to individual privacy. Kilger identifies a form of social being he calls the "virtual self." This socially recognized and used entity is a "composite of multiple digital information sources" (p. 95). Like Clarke, Kilger enumerates several costs and advantages of the existence and use of virtual selves. Although the discussion of artificial life and the "reality" of virtual beings is a bit forced, the examples given of the digitally homeless (those with limited or no access to networked information), the digital morph (a specific electronic role), and the digitally insane (those with digital profiles suggesting "mental illness") are evocative. Kilger warns that the ubiquity and multidimensionality of the virtual self poses greater threats for computer matching and computer profiling than any so-called universal identifier such as social security number and driver's license number.

The third and most complex article is by AGRE (1994a). As in AGRE (1997a), the analysis here centers on the linguistic and cultural practices of information technologists and successfully links these practices to wider concerns of privacy and the social status of information technologies. The 1994a paper begins with a specific, extended description of methods of tracking employees, packages, commercial vehicles, prisoners, body parts, retail outlets' characteristics (e.g., sales statistics and customer traffic), hazardous materials, capital resources, identification cards, complex designs, and job applications. The characterization of these systems merits extended quotation: "Despite all of these variations, the various tracking systems have a great deal in common. In each case, some entity changes state, a computer internally represents those states, and certain technical and social means are provided for (intendedly at least) maintaining the correspondence between the representation and the reality. The computer may maintain a centralized database . . . or it may be more widely distributed. Each entity has a definite identity that remains stable over time, and if several entities are being tracked then the tracking system has some means of consistently 'attaching' a given entity to its corresponding representation" (AGRE, 1994a, pp. 104-105).

Agre's two major emphases are that (1) social choices and arrangements determine the nature of these systems and the uses to which they are put and (2) such systems are distributed, increasingly ubiquitous, and transparent. The discussion of tracking leads to the heart of his argument: the contrast between surveillance and capture models of privacy using five constituent elements:

1. Capture depends on linguistic metaphors that represent and subsume human activity and physical phenomena, while surveillance depends on visual metaphors like that of Big Brother.
2. Capture depends on intervention in and redefinition of human activity, while surveillance assumes that its watching generally goes unnoticed.
3. Capture emphasizes structural metaphors for constructing the captured activity from its constituent parts, while surveillance emphasizes territoriality, such as the distinction between private and public spheres.
4. Capture is distributed and decentralized, while surveillance uses and generates centralized dossiers and files.
5. Capture adheres to a formal ideal of mathematical formalism, while surveillance implicates a conspiratorial, repressive state.

Agre notes that the knot of cultural concepts about surveillance is very common in the literature of privacy and leads to a particular conception of privacy as freedom from scrutiny, especially by the state, in certain areas of activity, particularly domestic life. The capture model, in contrast, relies on building systematic models of activities, using what Agre describes as grammars of action.

These grammars, used to express the action in capturable terms, are imposed on human action through five stages: (1) analysis into components and relationships among them; (2) articulation in sensible combinations; (3) imposition of the grammar using normative power; (4) instrumentation to measure the activity, especially as actors adjust their activities to the imposed grammar and capture; and (5) elaboration of the records of the captured activity through, for example, storage, combination, processing, error detection, and quality control (AGRE, 1994a, pp. 109-110).

Agre enumerates eight ways in which the imposition and instrumentation phases reorganize and redefine an activity, from the introduction of new technologies, and self-adjustment of actors to meet the expectations of capture, to new intra-organizational relationships, and rearrangement of activity. Appreciation of these and other elements of capture are, in Agre's opinion, essential to a realistic, more satisfying and nuanced view of privacy and the cultural and social meaning of information technology. More importantly, system design can be made more responsive to important democratic political goals. A further strength of the article is its placing of concerns about privacy in the context of concerns about organizational change, job redefinition, and command and control efforts by organizations of all kinds. Agre's work complements that of Harold Innis on the extensions of communication in the British Empire, James Beniger on the "control revolution," Alfred Chandler on the managerial revolution in American private enterprise couched in the image of the "visible hand," and KLING ET AL. on the managerial mind-set that underlies information entrepreneurialism.

J. P. ALLEN, concentrating on the work place and what he calls mutual control, offers the fourth paper in *The Information Society* special issue on the digital persona. This paper goes beyond the usual, if justified, concern with universal, detailed electronic monitoring of individual employees. Allen does a deeper analysis of how distributed digital information in the work place makes workers more aware of and demanding of each other, recalling WENGER's mutual accountability in a joint enterprise (p. 81 and *passim*). The demands come from the continued integration and interdependence of workers across departments and across organizations. This development in the contemporary work place recalls the concept of the participatory panopticon (GANDY, 1993; WHITAKER). Mutual control in the work place is based on the interdependence of workers whose tasks are broken into discrete components and rigidly routinized. Then information about these parts of tasks is digitally recorded and shared with other workers both internal and external to the organization. In manufacturing, clerical work, and elsewhere, such systems include just-in-time delivery of matériel, real-time inventory tracking, worker-location systems, interdependent activity scheduling, behavioral tracking, and integrated work-flow automation.

The ideological and economic basis of mutual control is the El Dorado of information system design: (1) the seamless integration of all kinds of information and all kinds of information systems and (2) the fantasy of omniscience (BERNSTEIN; LYON; ZUBOFF). To counteract the serious political and organizational effects of mutual control, J. P. ALLEN says systems designers must appreciate how "specific representations of detailed activities are likely to be used, or not used, in specific organizational situations" (p. 136) and question the implications of integrated system design. Without such an appreciation, the ill effects of real-time contextualized work information used in mutual control are likely to increase.

In the fifth article, HILL & HOLLAN describe history-enriched digital objects, digital files that have histories of interactions and use embedded within them. The concept of such objects complements J. P. ALLEN, by providing a specific example of new work-place functionalities that increase mutual monitoring, knowledge, and interdependence of workers. The goal of embedding use histories in digital files is to imitate the wear inherent in the use of physical objects that identifies the most used and (supposedly) the most important components of these objects. Hill & Hollan describe a number of currently available computational devices in prototype that can generate history-embedded digital objects: programs that count editing changes per line per actor (edit wear), determine the number of times each line is viewed (read wear), record email characteristics such as message header and number of times viewed (email wear), count number of additions and deletions in source code (source-code wear), and color-coded spreadsheet cells to indicate number of recalculations (spreadsheet wear).

These facilities make important changes in how we think of computing and its relations to human activity:

- Reading and editing become more public.
- New kinds of conversations among coworkers occur because of the existence of such histories.
- Workers and others, for good and for ill, are made more aware of how work time is allocated.

Embedding history in digital files also incurs new costs such as those associated with increased storage, increased programming efforts, and difficulties in interface design and use. Important questions also arise about the nature and control of shared file history. The potential for eroding workers' self-determination and autonomy is highlighted by the uncertainty about relationships that these new history-encoding technologies foster.

In the conclusion of his editor's introduction to the special *Information Society* issue, AGRE (1994b) briefly alludes to the relationship between Donna Haraway's cyborgs/monsters and digital individuals. He ends his piece by noting that we need to recognize the human choices inherent in technological development and deployment, "throwing such light upon the monsters that we can recognize them as ourselves" (1994b, p. 76).

## INFORMATION ENTREPRENEURIALISM

KLING (1996b) offers an introduction to a section on privacy in his edited volume (see also GANDY, 1993, pp. 95-122, on corporate perspectives). Kling places privacy in the contemporary United States in the context of (1) individuals' geographic and social mobility and (2) relations between such mobile individuals and large-scale, national business and governmental organizations. These large organizations support "unregulated computerization" and, in that cause, have relied on their wealth, organization, and alliance with the antiregulatory sentiments current in U.S. federal politics since the early 1980s. He further contextualizes conflicts about privacy by describing five major value orientations that can help elucidate such conflicts. These orientations emphasize, respectively, (1) the profitability of private firms (the private enterprise model); (2) the strength of government institutions (statist model); (3) civil liberties (libertarian model); (4) the clarity and responsiveness of public and private enterprises (neo-populist model); and (5) the efficient, reliable organization of financial systems (systems model). All except the systems model have a history of significant support in the United States.

Kling notes that "During the last thirty years, people have lost control over their records" (1996b, p. 625). This situation has been intensified by court rulings that have made records about individuals the property of organizations holding such records. Especially important in this regard is the 1886 Supreme Court case *SANTA CLARA COUNTY v. SOUTHERN PACIFIC RAILROAD COMPANY* that gave corporations protection under the law (specifically the Fourteenth Amendment to the U.S. Constitution) equal to that accorded natural persons, including protection of privacy. *UNITED STATES v. MILLER* in 1976 is also significant in this context because it declared that individuals' bank records are the property of the banks holding them, denying individuals' interests in those records except for confidentiality of the weakest sort. Thus control over distribution of information in the records, correction of errors, and protection from ill effects are impossible to achieve, and these limitations can result in grievous harm to groups and individuals. BYRNE remarks, "Even dominant institutions and those who use them are likely to claim a right to privacy if by so doing they can exclude outsiders more effectively" (p. 658). This language is reminiscent of FOUCAULT, GANDY (1993), and WHITAKER on the panopticon. Most privacy legislation introduced in state and federal legislatures and designed to protect the privacy interests of ordinary citizens has been defeated through the concerted efforts of for-profits and executive branch agencies whose behavior such laws would have constrained (see the discussion by REGAN (1995) elsewhere in this chapter).

The bookend piece to this introduction is the final paper in the privacy section of Kling's edited volume. Here, KLING ET AL. identify what they see as the formidable dangers in a society dominated by centralized surveillance and widespread sharing of medical, financial, insurance, vehicle, property, legal, location, retail, and other information: "What is at stake is the extent to which the resulting social order enables people to live dignified lives; that they can participate in diverse social and economic relationships that they can adequately comprehend and control; and that people are not thrust into crises because of errors or sublime idiosyncrasies of personal record systems" (p. 728). The paper examines the institutional arrangements that encourage organizations to develop information services, products, and work patterns that use information technology to threaten privacy.

The focus of their chapter is what they and others term "information entrepreneurialism" and how this set of social practices undermines privacy. Foremost among the foundations of information entrepreneurialism is the growth of nationwide organizations dominated by a management ethos that valorizes data gathering, manipulation, and analysis (also see RULE ET AL.). These information techniques are essential to information capitalism, "the overarching economic system in which organizations are expected to profit from the use or sale of information" (KLING ET AL., p. 731), emphasizing innovation in financial management, market analysis, customer relations, and other information-based services and products. The widespread geographic reach of large organizations, mobility of the post-World War II American population, and the tenets of information entrepreneurialism and information capitalism all feed into the culture of control and rationalization of indirect social relationships that characterize the large organizations of modern societies (FOUCAULT; GANDY, 1993; LYON; ZUBOFF). The resulting surveillance is made up of a cult of risk-averse information systems full of highly detailed records of groups' and individuals' actions, characteristics, preferences, and beliefs. This surveillance is applied in a Taylorist and Fordist way to clients, employees, and citizens.

The drive to reduce business risk has fueled increasingly sophisticated analysis and integration of personally identifiable information. Managers seek to know more about current and potential customers and clients as well as current and potential employees and partners. These are the "micropractices" of information capitalism, despite any social ill effects of having, collecting, or otherwise using such knowledge. Governmental action to counteract these tendencies in contemporary America, with rare exceptions, has been fragmented, unenforced, and of limited influence, partly because the social and business interests that support unregulated computerization in enterprises of all kinds have been wealthy and politically influential. KLING ET AL. describe the lack of public policy emphasis on privacy with regard to individuals' relations with large organizations (see also REGAN, 1995).

The authors conclude that "broad systematic changes in United States information policies seem politically infeasible today" (p. 741).

While his emphasis is on financial instruments, BERNSTEIN's work is useful for analysis especially for the insight provided into the limits of risk management and the culture of management generally. He illustrates the dangerous extremes to which we have put the quantification of risk and of the tradeoff between risk and reward. He equates these extremes with excesses of religious belief, intolerance, and zealotry: they exhibit almost cult-like complexity and arcana. Risk management is built upon probability theory, but its enthusiasts often forget that probabilistic thinking is only that—it can issue no guarantees, only indicate likelihood. GANDY (1993, pp. 84-87) discusses risk assessment in the context of corporate liability for catastrophic events.

BERNSTEIN identifies three major threats from our sometimes excessive belief in risk management and probability theory:

1.  Exposure to discontinuity: we cannot account for the totally new and unexpected. Discontinuity is normal, but unpredictable in its nature, time of appearance, and effects.
2.  Arrogance of quantification: we assume that virtually everything can be quantified, such as people's reactions to a politician or the form that a fashion in financial behavior (like takeovers or mergers) might take.
3.  Threat of increasing risk: the tools of risk management encourage us to take risks we might not take otherwise. Instead, we are left with machines that reinforce our own conceptual errors, leaving our assumptions unexamined.

He finishes his argument by noting that:

> Those who live by the numbers may find that the mathematically inspired techniques of modernism have sown the seeds of a destructive technology in which computers have become mere replacements for the snake dances, the bloodlettings, the genuflections, and the visits to the oracles and witches that characterized risk management and decision making in days of yore (BERNSTEIN, p. 51).

Thus, Bernstein offers reason to question the religious fervor with which risk management and reduction are done, especially when done with advanced and computationally intensive techniques. RULE ET AL. assert that the only antidote to such techniques lies in reducing the levels of discrimination demanded by large organizations.

Information capitalism and informationalism are CASTELLS' (1996; 1998) terms for the knot of concepts that KLING ET AL. capture partially in information entrepreneurialism. The increased commodity value of information and information processes, according to Castells, characterizes contemporary advanced societies. There is a "new informational mode of development [where] the source of productivity lies in the technology of knowledge generation, information processing, and symbol communication" (1996, p. 17), a mode he further describes as "the qualitative capacity to optimize the combination and use of factors of production on the basis of knowledge and information" (1998, p. 7). Modes of development are important because Castells sees them as constitutive of culture, social interaction, and social control. Informationalism is oriented toward the generation and accumulation of knowledge and increased complexity and sophistication in information processing. Although he makes much of his admittedly arbitrary distinction between knowledge and information, that distinction need not concern us here.

Castells calls this new form of techno-economic system information capitalism, wherein the rationale, assumptions, and methods of capitalism are adapted to and changed by informationalism. These changes affect economic production, military, and political processes and structures, and media and knowledge industries. While citing Weber's *The Protestant Ethic and the Spirit of Capitalism*, Castells identifies important constituent elements of this form of capitalism: business networks, technological tools, competition on a global scale, and the state. This environment has given rise to the *"emergence and consolidation of the network enterprise"* (CASTELLS, 1996, p. 196), taking advantage of what he calls the parallel movements of the deregulation of markets, the privatization of public companies (especially in key areas such as communications, finance, and media production and distribution), and the concomitant globalization of capital.

One of the great strengths of CASTELLS' (1998) work is its vivid, empirically grounded description of the dark side of information capitalism. The most serious and repulsive aspect of this form of capitalism is a wide and unrelenting social exclusion of hundreds of millions of human beings from adequate food, clothing, education, shelter, health care, employment, and other necessities that informationalism supposedly gives to everyone. This Fourth World is characterized by social polarization, poverty, and inequity. This exclusion is not just a condition, rather it is a process (p. 73), "there is a systemic link between the *current*, unchecked characteristics of informational capitalism, and the destruction of lives in a large segment of the world's children" (p. 159). An apotheosized market logic, enhanced technologies and control mechanisms, and obsession with consumption and the present are the essential elements of this destruction.

Castells' (1996) work also has some serious weaknesses. Sometimes he betrays an attitude of technological determinism that is hard to defend, a determinism insufficiently analytic about claims of "revolution" being "caused" by information technologies. Similarly, he attributes agency to technology that is simply misplaced. He adopts the language of post-industrialism (despite his intentions to replace the rhetoric of post-industrialism with that of informationalism) and the supposed information society too easily, thereby laying bare some economic and econometric assumptions that lie unexamined. With those things said, however, his work is magisterial in its sweep, globally and in historical terms, and thoroughly engaging in its analysis.

SCHEMENT & CURTIS also ground current information practices in an analysis of information capitalism, emphasizing how the development of information as a cultural category has led to the current status of information in U. S. society. They begin with a description of how we have come to regard information as property, ranging from early institutionalization of the scientific paper, the invention of encyclopedias and dictionaries, and the contribution of knowledge to the formation and maintenance of industrial organizations. Especially important in this commoditization has been the integration of manufacturing and other production activities with "managerial hierarchies," the combination of information gathering, classification, and distribution strategies in industrial organizations. Schement & Curtis rely a great deal on A.D. Chandler's *The Visible Hand* and J.R. Beniger's *The Control Revolution* in describing this combination of information activities. Other works important to this conception of using communication to create and maintain geographically dispersed organizations are Harold Innis' *Empire and Communications* and *The Fur Trade in Canada* (see CAREY, especially pp. 142-172).

Schement & Curtis encapsulate this important social and organizational change: "Information replaced intuition and tradition [and empirical experience] as the currency for making decisions, first within the corporation and later beyond it" (p. 35). The intra-organizational canonization of information was matched by its increased commoditization and sale. These developments were paralleled, as CASTELLS (1996) also describes in great detail, by the inter-organizational exchange of information among commercial partners and by the increased gathering of information from retail customers and retail outlets. Information was weaned from its home in nonprofit organizations to being subject, in most analyses, to the "laws" of the market and the economy more generally. An important contribution that Schement & Curtis make to understanding information capitalism and to the implications of information capitalism for privacy is their assertion that information technologies are the result of long-term struggles "to sharpen vision, improve hearing, communicate over distances, record time, expand memory, speed up calculations, and expand knowledge" (p. 252). Surveillance, capture, and digital privacy are all implicated by this struggle.

The institutionalization of private property and the pursuit of profit are described as the driving forces behind the commoditization of information. These and other elements of their analysis lead Schement & Curtis, as they do others, to conclude that the so-called "Information Society" is much more likely an advanced form of (industrial) capitalism exhibiting continuity and change rather than an unprecedented revolutionary development.

POSTER helps clarify how information became the privileged term and category that it is today. His title, "The Mode of Information: Postmodernism and Social Context," plays with Karl Marx's image of the mode of production as the means by which to organize history into periods. Poster says, "By mode of information I similarly suggest that history may be periodized by variations in the structure in this case of symbolic exchange, but also that the current culture gives a certain fetishistic importance to 'information'" (pp. 4-5). He discusses how James Rule's earlier work indicates that the databases maintained by credit companies, health insurance companies, municipal police, state motor vehicle agencies, federal agencies, banks, utilities, and so on allow the reconstruction of most of the daily activities of individuals. Such knowledge lends itself, in his estimation, to an almost inexorable push toward commodifying the most intimate and confidential information.

Poster identifies the discursive nature of databases and their modes of representation (see AGRE, 1997a). He especially criticizes the way binary representation and the rigid categorization it supports and "demands" eliminate the ambiguity that constitutes ordinary experience. Digital reductionism also tends to create spurious relationships and conclusions: "The structure or grammar of the database *creates* relationships among pieces of information that do not exist in those relationships outside of the database" (POSTER, p. 96). Thus, the database as discursive practice reduces and extrapolates at the same time.

These writers on information capitalism indicate how information entrepreneurialism and information capitalism have contributed to a psychology, both in culture generally and in organizations that consider themselves on the cutting edge, that information and information technology are the keys to success. That these technologies, deployed and justified by managerial and cybernetic perspectives, must be networked and integrated is a matter of faith, believed so obvious by Taylorists and Fordists that it is beyond analysis or question. It is also increasingly an article of faith that organizations must use the converged technologies of computing and telecommunication to get more information from more sources, especially their clients, employees, and competing organizations; to aggregate that information according to complex algorithms and criteria; to massage it in any number of sophisticated ways (see AGRE, 1997a, on the inadequacy of the processing metaphor for information); to use such information to identify persons and groups that are safe risks and those that are not; and to use it as a resource to be bought, sold, and traded. WEBER warns that "[t]he reduction of modern office management to rules is deeply embedded in its very nature" (p. 261). Against such a techno-social-rhetorical juggernaut, claims of personal dignity and autonomy, especially based on a mistakenly atomistic privacy, have little chance for discussion, much less survival.

## HABERMAS AND THE PUBLIC/PRIVATE DICHOTOMY

The fundamental dichotomy of public and private on which most analyses of privacy depend is the product of Jürgen Habermas and the bourgeois/classical liberal ideas of the autonomous individual. This section of the chapter highlights Habermas' work and some fundamental critiques of that work.

### The Public and Private Spheres

In *The Structural Transformation of the Public Sphere: An Inquiry into a Category of Bourgeois Society,* HABERMAS provides the seminal, critical work on the growth and subsequent decline, as he sees it, of the public sphere. The argument begins by contrasting exclusive events, those available to only some, and public events, those open to all. The historical review that is the essence of the book finds the distinction between public and private in ancient Greek socio-political life that clearly demarcated the realm of the public/*polis* from the realm of households. At the same time, however, participation in the *polis* depended on one's status as the male head of a household. This deterministically gendered concept of citizenship strikes chords heard again in the section of the chapter about gendered conceptions of privacy.

Habermas provides a commonly cited definition of the public sphere: "The bourgeois public sphere may be conceived above all as the sphere of private people come together as a public . . . to engage themselves in a debate over the general rules governing relations in the basically privatized but publicly relevant sphere of commodity exchange and social labor" (p. 27). Ownership of property is also an essential part of this concept and is intimately related to the development of what we now recognize as the nuclear family in the early modern period. Habermas clearly traces the emancipation of commodity exchange and social labor, especially in and defined by the relationships of the family, from the scrutiny and influence of government. As he notes: "[I]n proportion to the increasing prevalence of the capitalist mode of production, social relationships assumed the form of exchange relationships. With the expansion and liberation of this sphere of the market, commodity owners gained private autonomy; the positive meaning of 'private' emerged precisely in reference to the concept of free power of control over property that functioned in capitalist fashion" (p. 74).

At the same time, however, Habermas levels a radical critique at contract and other forms of commercial freedom that are touted as characteristic of contemporary society and as based in the growth of early modernism. Specifically, he clarifies how freedom of contract and other commercial relations fail to take into account (1) the limitations on individual freedom based in expectations and narrowness of occupational status; (2) the immense advantage in "negotiation" that large for-profit enterprises have over individual and small groups; (3) family law (e.g., inheritance and domestic relations); and (4) social power of all kinds (also see ORREN on feudal remnants in American labor and family law).

The primary thesis of Habermas' work is the growth of a consensual, mercantile-based public sphere characteristic of a capitalizing, modernizing bourgeois society in contrast to the private sphere of intimate domestic relations. The secondary thesis is that the public sphere devolved in the 19th century into institutionalized compromise among competing private interests. These private interests were inimical to the development and cultivation of a public sphere because public concerns were seen as starkly contrasted to the concerns of private parties, whether individual or (interest) groups. There was also a subsequent growth in secrecy in areas formerly considered public, for example, the workings of government. This growth of private interests and wasting away of the public, in Habermas' opinion, were mutually constituted by the growth of the market economy and the growth of administrative procedures.

The market economy, from Habermas' critical perspective, has characteristics that make it structurally opposed to the development of equality and opportunity that are demanded in the creation and maintenance of a vital public sphere. Related effects of the degeneration of the public sphere have been the reduction of the private sphere to the family and the privileging of consumerism: "Private autonomy was maintained not so much in functions of control as in functions of consumption . . . . As a result there arose the illusion of an intensified privacy in an interior domain whose scope had shrunk to comprise the conjugal family only insofar as it constituted a society of consumers" (p. 156). This sort of critique, of course, has been echoed by countless other commentators on public life in industrialized countries, although such critiques have often been dismissed as "merely" the ideological griping of left-wing intellectuals. Habermas subsequently expanded upon and enriched his discussion, particularly the gendered nature, of the public/private dichotomy, but *The Structural Transformation* remains its classic expression.

## Critiques of Habermas

It is against the classic expression of HABERMAS and subsequent iterations of his work that the works of BENHABIB, ELEY, and FRASER gain significance and meaning. BENHABIB's chapter in CALHOUN (1992) is a consideration of the relationships between the work of Hannah Arendt and Habermas, and the role of the classical liberal tradition in both. The chapter begins by contrasting Arendt's idealized view of the Greek and Roman states with the concept of a modern public extended to include the formerly excluded and invisible: workers, women, people of color, and ethnic, linguistic, or religious minority groups. It is the expansion of the concept of the public sphere that erodes the classical and neo-liberal models of public dialogue and interaction. These eroded models rely on an assumed differentiation of the public and the private that has resulted in the silencing of persons traditionally excluded.

Specifically, foregrounding questions about power relations and justice become a matter of public dispute, based on the elimination of claims for dialogic neutrality and separation of concerns about "the good life" from concerns about justice and equity. BENHABIB notes that: "Democratic politics challenges, redefines, and renegotiates the divisions between the good and the just, the moral and the legal, the private and the public" (p. 83). More fundamentally, she hopes to question many social relations and concepts that have not been sufficiently analyzed, such as property, contract, family relations, gender, and privacy. Thus, according to her, we need to understand public space in order to conceptualize privacy. That public space is not like that of the Greek aristocracy and the landed; rather it is: "[N]ot understood *agonistically* as a space of competition for acclaim and immortality among a political elite; it is viewed democratically as the creation of procedures whereby those affected by general social norms and collective political decisions can have a say in their formulation, stipulation, and adoption" (p. 87).

Benhabib identifies at least three dimensions of the private, attempting to separate the heretofore conflated concepts of privacy, privacy rights, and the private sphere. The first is the sphere of moral and religious conscience and belief. The second relates to commodity relations and economic liberty, especially the protection of commodity relations from interference from the state. The third relates to the domain of relations and status of the intimate domestic household. Formerly, questions of justice were limited to the public sphere, while the private was thought of as outside the realm of justice by definition. Thus, relations of power, inequity, and domination in the domestic sphere were treated as non-existent and remained free of political and theoretical scrutiny. Benhabib concludes that one of the major difficulties in articulating what privacy is and why it is important is that "we have lacked a *critical mode of public space and public discourse*" (p. 94).

FRASER picks up the rhetorical gauntlet thrown down by both HABERMAS and BENHABIB. She begins by identifying three elements in the public sphere: the state, the officially sanctioned economy of paid work, and the locus of public discourse. It is this final element, Fraser asserts, that Habermas emphasizes—the public sphere as theater where talk, deliberation, discourse, and discursive interaction matter—at the expense of discussing the public arena as the site for market relations. This emphasis on discursive relations led Habermas to assert that the public sphere successfully bracketed and neutralized unequal power relations. This position is consonant with traditional classical liberal assumptions that political processes can be isolated from the supposedly prepolitical (e.g., culture, informal social relations, and the economy), a position that Fraser regards as indefensible.

Instead, she posits that there is not one public sphere; rather, there are other, alternative publics where women and others excluded from the supposed unitary public sphere are constitutive. These alternative publics are "arenas for the formation and enactment of social identities" (FRASER, p. 125). Fraser further theorizes how Habermas' concept of the bourgeois public sphere where private persons deliberate about public concerns conflates four elements of public relying on two elements of the private. Public means (1) state-related, (2) accessible to everyone, (3) of concern to everyone, and (4) pertaining to the common good or interest. Private pertains to (1) private property and (2) intimate domestic and/or personal life, especially sexual behavior. Using the example of how domestic violence has evolved from a formerly "private" domestic matter into a matter for public concern and policy, she emphasizes that there are no a priori, "natural" boundaries between what is private and what is public; rather, the terms are "cultural classifications and rhetorical labels" (p. 131).

Fraser further argues that the insistence on naturalizing the distinctions between the public and the private has led to the political dead end of liberal individualism. In its stead, she offers civic-republicanism (critiques of which are offered by FRAZER & LACEY below), which aims to transcend the fragmented interests of private individuals through public deliberation and consensus. Civic-republicanism, in her estimation, recognizes that "preferences, interests, and identities are as much outcomes as antecedents of public deliberation; indeed, they are discursively constituted in and through it" (FRASER, p. 130). Leaving questions of economic equity, power relations, and other unequal social relations as matters that are apolitical is a major obstacle to the participatory democratic project that a rich public sphere demands. This sphere, characterized by antagonism, conflict among differing perspectives, and difference, is in stark contrast to what Fraser identifies as community, characterized by boundedness, homogeneity, and consensus. Thus, the public sphere is expanded to allow for certain kinds of discursive relations, *not* for addressing certain kinds of topics or problems, that is, those considered to be related to the four elements of the public listed above. Privacy debates, according to Fraser, have often served to limit our understanding of power relations, especially those pertaining to domestic life, and our understanding of the exclusionary effects of unexamined acceptance of the public/private dichotomy. Fraser does not conclude that the public/private distinction is useless. Instead, that distinction can open opportunities for freedom of expression and can serve to foreground private inequality in public.

ELEY puts Habermas' view into the context of a deepened understanding of 19th-century politics and history. That understanding recognizes that the coffeehouses, literary clubs, voluntary associations related to science and education, political activity, and cultural groups identified by Habermas as the soil in which the public sphere grew up "all involved questions of *interests, prestige,* and *power,* as well as those of rational communication" (p. 307). Like FRASER, Eley discusses the effects of the silencing of public women and of the bourgeois society's dependence on women's domestic work, but he traces it to the development of new concepts of and relations between men and women. This conception idealized the universal public man, who was defined, in part, by the contrast with the feminine and feminized counterexample of nature, localism, and work.

Explicitly citing much of the work of Fraser beyond her work in this collection, Eley explores how the political left has endeavored to bring the economic, sexual, and intimate spheres, formerly considered outside of or prior to analysis, under public political scrutiny. He says that the left has taken four fundamental approaches:

- The "purely democratic" that seeks to guarantee strong autonomy and civil freedoms, based on a strong and radical separation of the public and private
- The classical socialist that emphasizes a nationalized economy and what has come to be known as the welfare state

- The utopian wherein all social relations are democratized and communalized including significant areas of domestic life and child raising (this is often considered a kind of communitarianism)
- Since 1968, the feminist that seeks to bring democracy to the center of all kinds of social and other relations. In doing so, this approach has given rise to new concepts related to the self, the forms and effects of subjectivity, motherhood, domestic labor, and other phenomena heretofore considered to be outside the realm of political consideration.

This last, feminist, or, more generally, gendered, approach aims to make explicit the gendered nature of the public/private distinction that society, per Habermas, has naturalized and privileged. This point is further explored later in this chapter on the contributions to conceptions of privacy and its role in the polity and domestic life made by gendered analysis.

## TOO MUCH PRIVACY?

While there is widespread agreement that digital technologies pose serious threats to privacy, there is also a growing body of work that concludes that, for a number of reasons, industrialized, networked societies overemphasize privacy or at least underappreciate the weaknesses of the public/private dichotomy. We can categorize these streams of thought into roughly four categories: communitarian thought that attacks what it regards as excessive individuation at the expense of social responsibility, critiques of what has come to be called "rights talk," work that emphasizes the conflict between privacy and freedom of (commercial) speech, and gendered analyses of the public/private distinction. The first three categories are discussed in this section of the chapter, while what can be roughly termed gendered, feminist thought is complex and rich enough to be discussed in a separate section.

### Communitarian Concepts of Privacy

This critique of privacy as commonly construed is perhaps best exemplified by ETZIONI. He identifies privacy quite clearly as a concept with two essential components: (1) privacy applies to the individual, and (2) privacy is precisely the Cooley/Warren/Brandeis individual "right to be let alone." He intended his book, *The Limits of Privacy*, to move the pendulum that has "swung too far to the individual side" (p. 1). To do so, he examines privacy in the context of five topical areas, the first four of which are: HIV testing of newborns, notification of residents if a convicted sex offender is moving to an area, encryption of digital messages, and ID cards and biometric identifiers. He concludes that the individual's interest in protecting the confidentiality of these kinds of information is far outweighed by compelling public interests in, respectively, public health, public safety, public order (prevention and tracking of crime), and public confidence (that persons are who they claim to be). Etzioni examines a fifth category of information, medical records generally, and concludes that the privacy of these records demands a much higher level of protection than that currently granted.

While there is much of value in Etzioni's analysis, as noted further below, his critique too often sounds like that of a frustrated scold. Phrases such as "radical individualists" and a naive belief that he is the first to recognize that for-profit information sellers and traders pose a threat to privacy perhaps more serious than that posed by government betray a demonization of ideological opponents and an unwillingness to recognize the weaknesses and ideological origins of his own argument. In particular, the utilitarian and econometric bases of his work are quite clear, if unexamined. He further asserts that privacy advocates hold a "belief that our emphasis on maintaining privacy has no negative consequences" (p. 7). As demonstrated elsewhere in this review, this assertion is inaccurate. He also assumes that all persons should not object to identifying themselves to "public authorities," brushing aside the skewed application of such requests (the fact that poor and ethnic/linguistic minority members are asked to do so much more often than members of other groups) and the desire for ordinary citizens of all kinds to be free of such requests except in the most unusual circumstances.

Despite these fundamental flaws, Etzioni's work is relevant for a number of reasons. He recognizes that private-sector threats to privacy are barely addressed by culture, concepts, legal doctrines, or governmental policies, and he thoughtfully critiques the conflation of exception from scrutiny (described elsewhere as informational privacy) and the right to control one's acts (decisional privacy). Unfortunately, he fails to see their interconnection and importance to the self and to groups. Etzioni does state that the concentration of information, given freely or under duress, in the hands of the U.S. Internal Revenue Service, the Immigration and Naturalization Service, the Federal Bureau of Investigation, and the Social Security Administration makes the possibility of totalitarianism much more likely if circumstances led the U.S. toward that possibility.

He concludes his book by arguing for a third realm, called communitarianism, between individual choice and the state or market, ignoring the importance of what we may call the social self and also ignoring the importance of mediating institutions such as churches, neighborhood associations, and civic groups. Etzioni approvingly cites William Donahue to the effect that "'The ACLU is driven by an atomistic vision of liberty'" (p. 214). Despite some references to the privacy of groups and to Regan's work, Etzioni, unfortunately, takes a radically atomistic view of privacy himself.

BELLAH ET AL. also take a communitarian view of contemporary U.S. society, but they do not share Etzioni's emphasis on privacy. Like Etzioni, they emphasize the common good element they believe is missing from much of contemporary American life and accept the traditional public/private dichotomy. Unlike Etzioni, however, they also emphasize how individual citizens band into small, highly localized groups that strive to overcome the supposedly radical split between the private world of loving domestic relations and the public world of agonistic financial, professional, and political struggle.

Relying on large-scale surveys, interviews, and other methods, Bellah et al. provide a rich and varied look at how Americans think about the relation between what are commonly construed as public and private provinces. This concern leads to an extended consideration of social capital, a concept whose currency is largely attributable to PUTNAM, discussed more fully below. At the heart of Bellah et al.'s discussion of social capital is how mediating organizations such as churches, public town meetings, local political party groups, libraries, clinics, Parent-Teacher Associations, the League of Women Voters, neighborhood associations, fraternal organizations, fire and police stations, and unions are important expressions of social capital as well as important, constituent causes of the creation of social capital. These kinds of organizations are fundamentally different from paper membership groups (the phrase is Robert Wuthnow's) that rely on shared interests but little interaction. A good example of a paper organization is the American Association of Retired Persons—a highly active, powerful political lobbying group that has little or no personal interaction among its millions of members. Paper membership groups and the decrease in public political participation are important indicators of a gradual loss of social self in America.

It is the renewal of common commitment, solidarity, and public discussion of moral questions that implicates privacy. Bellah et al. explicitly claim that hyper-individualism leads to insupportable divergence between public and private lives. Instead, they claim that: "A minimum of public decency and civility is a precondition for a fulfilling private life. . . . . A rewarding private life is one of the preconditions for a healthy public life" (p. 163). They maintain that a sense of privacy that focuses on only individual "rights" and not on how privacy is a constituent part of social life leads to hyper-individualism, alienation from one's fellow citizens, and self-alienation. Bellah et al. describe the symptoms of and some of the cures for a society that tears itself asunder. A new conception of privacy, a conception based on mutual respect and trust, would help weave the social fabric closer together.

PUTNAM caught the fancy of intellectuals, media commentators, politicians, and ordinary citizens with his trope in "Bowling Alone: America's Declining Social Capital." Here he argues that one of the widely recognized strengths of U.S. life, a commonplace since Alexis de Tocqueville's *Democracy in America*, is civic engagement, or involvement in the affairs of the community, that belies simple assumptions about American individualism. Much of the complexity and richness of Putnam's piece lies in its contextualization in political scientists' discussion of democracy, civic life, state-building, and society, and in his decades-long research into political life in Italy culminating in 1993 in *Making Democracy Work: Civic Traditions in Modern Italy*. The implications of "Bowling Alone" for this larger discussion are not addressed here.

The central concept in Putnam's "Bowling Alone" is social capital, "social organizations such as networks, norms, and social trust that facilitate coordination and cooperation for mutual benefit" (p. 67). He goes to great lengths to examine a wide variety of empirical data that show that Americans have increasingly withdrawn from civic engagement in the last two decades, thereby seriously degrading social capital and the civic life that depends on social capital. From the widely recognized fall of participation in national elections, to less participation in church-related, school-service, veterans', labor, sports, fraternal, and service groups, the evidence is strong that Americans are more likely not to engage in traditional expressions of civic life. Putnam provides some potential countertrends, such as the growth of environmental, feminist, support, age-specific, and nonprofit organizations, but asserts that these and similar organizations are paper organizations. There is little face-to-face, personal contact among members of such organizations, with participation often reduced to the writing of an annual membership check.

Putnam considers four potential causal factors of the decrease of participation in civic life (increased number of women in the labor force, increased geographic mobility, other demographic changes, and the "technological transformation of leisure"), while emphasizing the need not to romanticize or idealize stereotypes of 1950s middle America. The final part of his essay raises some important questions about social life and electronic technologies of specific interest to concerns about privacy. He asserts that Americans appear to be less trusting of each other compared to attitudes apparent in data from the 1960s and 1970s and, therefore, less likely to engage each other. He wonders what effects electronic networks have on social capital, indicating their limited opportunities for real engagement, and discusses how public policy can destroy or help create social capital. Putnam concludes with the usual call for more research into what he identifies as the erosion of American social capital.

While much of Putnam's argument is convincing, some of it is less so. TARROW questions what he sees as a simplistic causal link between civic society and the practice of democracy that underlies Putnam's work. Tarrow goes further and says that Putnam's diagnosis of the lack of social capital as the cause of such ills as impoverished civic life, urban decay, and weak support for democracy in developing countries is wrong. Instead, Tarrow asserts that "the absence of civic capacity is the by-product of politics, state building, and social structure" (p. 396), that is, the result of structural problems like the flight of capital (recalling BELLAH ET AL.) and exploitive social and governmental relationships. Tarrow says that Putnam mistakes symptoms (weakened civic life) for causes (structural and political relationships and institutions). Generally, communitarians and those whose work is often linked with theirs suffer from the kind of analytic narrowness that Tarrow finds in Putnam. Structural elements of social life are regarded by communitarians as prepolitical, not subject to critical and reflective examination. This point jibes well with the analysis of Habermas by ELEY and by FRASER above and is further discussed in the section on gendered analyses of privacy, particularly by FRAZER & LACEY.

BRINKLEY (1997a) is a strong supporter of civic culture, but he reminds us that, *contra* the communitarians, complaints about the decline of community have been common in America since the 17th century. He goes further in identifying three major weaknesses of communitarianism: (1) civic life may not have eroded to the extent that some communitarians claim, (2) the communitarian accusation that rights cannot go hand-in-hand with concerns about the good life and the moral society ignores much of the political discourse of the past several decades, and (3) the concept of community must be defined beyond mere localism and the homogeneous communities that communitarians extol. For example, Brinkley taps into a long-held American conviction that only a strong national community can preserve local communities and their vitality.

BRINKLEY (1997b) specifically addresses the erosion of public fora and their "replacement" by private, specifically electronic, communities. The primary limitation of these communities and the technologies that support them, according to Brinkley, is that they encourage people to speak alone, that is, communication among persons using digital media (specifically the Internet, and email, chat rooms, mailing lists, and the like) is often harsh and dogmatic. While many persons feel empowered to speak in digital fora, many use that power to make absolute assertions, intolerant of conflicting opinions and the concept of compromise and accommodation. He offers a reminder that: "Citizens of a democracy need to be heard. They also need to listen. And they need to be able to do both in public settings, where the search for agreement is at least as highly valued as the need to listen" (1997b, p. 150). Brinkley's strong support of civic culture, engagement, and accommodation is combined with an empirically grounded appreciation of the rhetorical and social limitations of communitarianism. This complex attitude illustrates the growing body of work that does not occupy the "middle ground" between the supposed dichotomies that he identifies but rather claims "other ground."

## Critiquing "Rights Talk"

Another line of argument picks up the communitarian standard in describing what is commonly called, in a pejorative way, "rights talk." GLENDON's legal analysis of "the impoverishment of political discourse" in her book has led to her wide recognition as the chief champion of this point of view. She explicitly acknowledges the contributions of Etzioni on communitarianism. She uses words such as "strident," "intemperate," "inadequate," and "trivializing" to characterize what she identifies as the American fetishization of rights that emphasizes personal liberty at the expense of civic responsibility. She notes that other liberal democracies do not share the limitations of American discourse about rights. The American rhetoric, in Glendon's estimation, is simplistic, prodigal in assigning rights, legalistic, absolute, obsessively individualized, dismissive of intermediate or mediating institutions between citizens and society at large, ahistorical, short-term, provincial, and insensitive to responsibilities. These characteristics make American rights talk a parody of American culture and incapable of addressing social dilemmas and catalyzing public discussion (the essence of Habermas' bourgeois public sphere), reducing political and social differences to uncompromising, all-or-nothing conflicts. She regards privacy as the archetypal example.

Her analysis recognizes the unusually strong hold that legal language, legal concepts, and legal institutions have on American culture. Glendon makes a convincing argument that this legalistic emphasis, remarked upon by de Tocqueville, is partially explained by and is reinforced by Americans' reliance on the law to hold a heterogeneous society together and by American political culture's dedication to the rule of law. Further, legitimacy has often been determined by legality— if an act is legal, it is, therefore, desirable and legitimate. As a legal historian and scholar, Glendon is strong on the Constitutional history that is one of the primary wellsprings of rights talk, including the legal and social environment of the past several decades that have seen remarkable strides in the social status of racial, ethnic, and other minority groups in the United States.

Glendon's third chapter on "The Lone Rights-Bearer" includes a significant section on privacy and takes advantage of Karl Marx's insight that the 18th-century rhetoric of rights of life, property, liberty, and other areas depends upon an assumption of human beings as separated, atomistic individuals. Privacy, in particular, emphasizes the autonomy of individuals and sheds light on "yet another distinctive feature of the American rights dialect—an extraordinary homage to independence and self-sufficiency . . . [with] the rights-bearer . . . connected to others only by choice" (GLENDON, p. 48).

While briefly referring to the place of privacy in tort law (noncontractual, noncriminal wrongs discussed in the section of this chapter on legal and policy conceptions of privacy), Glendon notes that it was only when privacy evolved from a tort to a constitutional law concern that the concept of privacy began to grow to its current expansiveness. It is important to note her examination of other nations' expression of the rights-bearer as a situated, socially defined individual with strong connections to other individuals and groups. She uses the rights of personality, especially in Germany, to highlight how such an individual right is always examined for its implications for other interests, both group and individual. Abortion, in particular, exemplifies how other nations' approaches to rights differ from the U. S. tradition. The (West) German major court ruling on abortion had three major differences from similar American cases: lack of rigidity in language and intent, consideration of important constitutional and legal elements beyond individual interest (e.g., birth control and significant social services for pregnant women and mothers), and recognition of the importance of legislative and other political processes in resolving rights conflicts. In a similar vein, Glendon recognizes the pro-activity of (West) German government in protecting citizens from the proliferation of digital information technologies, especially noting the delay of the federal census for four years because of concerns about privacy.

Glendon's chapter on "Rights Insularity" has an extended comparative analysis of court cases in the U.S. and elsewhere related to privacy claims for consensual, nonpublic homosexual behavior between adults. This comparison underscores the advantages of her comparative method, clearly illustrating the insularity, absoluteness, and provincialism of American jurisprudence in ignoring other legal traditions' approaches to conflicts that parallel those in America. This chapter also emphasizes other weaknesses of American attitudes about privacy discussed earlier: its *agonistic*, all-or-nothing, legalistic approach to social conflict and a concomitant unwillingness to recognize competing values, especially in ordinary discourse. The European tradition, in contrast to what is commonly construed as the American, tries very hard, even in the most highly charged atmosphere of the highest court's deliberations and decisions, not to alienate losers or allow winners to gloat (p. 155).

Unlike the argument of those who explicitly identify themselves as communitarians, however, Glendon's work does not fall into romanticizing about times and social arrangements where sexism and racism flourished. What she shares with the communitarians, however, is a fundamental assumption that rights of the individual make little sense without concomitant recognition of responsibilities and group interests beyond individual concerns. Thus, she evokes the Continental tradition, infused with Romano-Germanic elements, that sees rights in the context of social relations of all kinds. Glendon concludes that documents such as the European Social Charter have a more realistic, complex, and phenomenologically grounded understanding of human beings constituted by society even as they make society.

## Free (Commercial) Speech and Privacy

A number of commentaries defend the interests of organizations that collect, aggregate, analyze, and sell or lease information of all kinds about people. Only a few are described here. The interested reader will find the bibliographies in ETZIONI and KLING (1996a) especially helpful.

HATCH, seeking to assert the interests of direct marketers and their use of personally identifiable information, hopes to defend direct marketing from the negative effects of consumers' uneasiness about it. This concern leads him to insist that direct marketers should use self-regulation, with some real enforcement mechanisms and a record of accountability and public responsiveness, to address consumers' concerns. He cites the apparently reliable results of several privacy polls that indicate that only 6% to 7% of consumers ordinarily opt out of the use of information about them. This conclusion, however, is flawed in several ways. He does not mention opt-in alternatives at all; nor does he mention that an even smaller percentage of consumers opt in as a matter of course. His paper discusses concerns about privacy as a virtual conspiracy of "forces arrayed against us—the media, government, liberal do-gooders, as well as those in our own industry whose zeal for profits overwhelms their common sense and decency" (p. 676). The paper was originally published in *Targeted Marketing*, thus, the vehemence of this language is understandable if not particularly analytic. His point about media resistance is made up of three elements: (1) horror stories about privacy and supposedly wronged individuals make good reading; (2) newspapers rail about privacy only because they are in competition for advertising dollars with direct marketers; and (3) major media outlets (e.g., *The New York Times* and Public Broadcasting System) themselves use direct marketing techniques of all kinds.

Another piece in the Kling collection that takes a related but slightly different and less vitriolic approach is by POSCH (1996). This piece, like Hatch's, was originally written for *Direct Marketing*, where Posch regularly wrote a column. GANDY (1993) identifies Posch, vice president of legal affairs for Doubleday Book & Music Clubs, as a leader of corporate opinion (pp. 106ff.). The emphasis in Posch's 1996 paper is on self-regulation and a self-developed and self-enforced code of conduct. He also asserts that newspapers are jealous of the success of direct marketing's efforts and have seized the initiative to define the contemporary privacy debate. He does, however, use words like "scam," "prejudice," and similar terms to undermine all media's claims to discuss privacy and its status as a concern of public policy. More specifically, Posch defends the status of targeted mail in terms of protected speech, that is, speech that falls within the purview of the First Amendment to the U.S. Constitution. He further paints direct marketers as political underdogs, champions of the "little people" unable to speak for and defend themselves. This kind of sanctimonious "argument," again, is to be expected in a marketing business organ such as *Direct Marketing*.

POSCH (1993) takes on one of the fundamental bases of American concerns with privacy policy: the consistent polling data that indicate ordinary Americans' growing concern with privacy, including digital privacy. This piece is full of vitriol, wit, and the kind of behind-closed-doors candor unusual in discussions of privacy. While his tone is bracing and some of his points seriously engaging, we should have serious reservations about much of his discussion. His most important assertion is that privacy polls that indicate the large and growing concern of Americans about privacy fail to put such questions into what he calls real-world contexts. These are contexts where privacy is traded off for innovation, leadership in the information economy, achievement in the free market, and unfettered speech protected by the First Amendment. Among the most repugnant of his terms are the dismissive ones for privacy advocates: "chatter class," "immoral," eager to "confirm an agenda," "trying to impose their prejudice and phobias on society at large," and purveyors of an "anti-technology, anti-creativity, and anti-business ideology." These accusations are grossly inaccurate and would be dismissed except for the more substantial part of his argument: the need of contextualization for polling; the questionable research validity of poll responses (GANDY, 1993); the complex relationship among privacy, communication, and technological innovation; the increased difficulty in separating commercial and political/cultural acts; and the global competitiveness concerns raised by the European Directive on data privacy. GANDY (1993, pp. 193-194) provides an alternative view by citing the work of C. Edwin Baker that underscores the weaknesses of commercial speech in the context of the First Amendment.

SINGLETON (1998) views privacy as censorship. While some of the tenor of her paper results from being the director of information studies at the strongly rightist Cato Institute, much of her argument is engaging and must be seriously considered. The argument is grounded in arguments about the free speech of businesses and their need to communicate with each other as well as the important economic and social purposes that business-to-business communication serves. She says, "A country that takes the freedom of information seriously cannot properly prohibit one business from communicating information about real events and real people to other businesses" (1998, p. 7). Included in such categories are people's names, addresses, and buying habits.

Singleton identifies sale of goods as the primary reason that most businesses collect information about customers, "hardly . . . a sinister motive." What she offers instead is the threat of Big Brother who controls the army, courts, and police, not the coterie of dozens or hundreds of Little Brothers. While those fears are well-founded, the cavalier dismissal of concerns about private databases is some thirty years too late. Singleton identifies "pernicious economic effects" that the creation of what she calls "new privacy rights such as mandatory opt-in" will create. Among the ill effects are the near elimination of direct marketing, and the disappearance or severe limitations of customer and mailing lists. The results, she says, would hurt new businesses and nonprofits, and customers who shop at home, including the elderly, disabled, rural residents, and customers who do not own cars. Singleton says that "mandatory opt-in, enforced by direct or indirect regulatory pressure, makes no moral sense and would do real economic harm" (1998, p. 7).

While she is willing to admit that not all concerns about privacy are easily dismissed, she limits important concerns to governmental databases and to confidential information shared with doctors and lawyers. Like many commentators, including several justices of the U.S. Supreme Court, Singleton bases her critique of privacy in what she calls its "dubious origins." Like POSNER (1995), PROSSER, THOMSON (1990), and others, Singleton holds that property protections are sufficient to protect what we commonly include in privacy. She also expresses concern that governmental actors looking too closely at self-regulating industries are too intrusive and are, in fact, acting as regulators. She has major concerns with what she terms the creation of a new legal regime, although the assertion that strong privacy protections would constitute a new legal regime is contestable.

Singleton says that information in private databases is no more harmful than gossip, or unregulated private conversation, that serves useful social and economic functions (see POSNER, 1984; SCHOEMAN, 1994; THOMSON, 1984). She further believes that error rates in databases are quite low, especially credit reports. Singleton says that: "Databases are a natural entrepreneurial adaptation to a more urban world, freed of small-town gossip" (1998, p. 12). She further asserts that people cannot defensibly argue that they own information about themselves, although her argument conflates information collection with sharing and use. She says that, because list makers add value and cannot stop others from making lists, information about any transaction "belongs to" the person providing the product as well as to the person buying.

Singleton continues with the assertion that annoyance with free speech (i.e., buying and selling of customer information), does not justify stifling the speech. Similarly, concerns with direct marketing are "too trivial and too subjective [sic] to supply a moral foundation for the creation of new privacy rights" (1998, p. 17). She adds that claims of protecting children from offensive or intrusive speech is not sufficient grounds either, because many kinds of speech acts influence children. In particular, she sees mandatory opt-in rules as classic examples of prior restraint of speech and, therefore, unconstitutional.

Singleton does grant that concerns with private databases may be serious and she recommends a method of protection: do not get credit cards, do not order from catalogs, and inhibit online behavior. Like many other commentators, both privacy advocates and free commercial speech advocates, she warns that we cannot do the same with government (e.g., with the Internal Revenue Service). Unfortunately, her stance ignores the extreme difficulty in keeping information out of commercial databases while remaining an active, involved member of society. She further ignores the growing number and kinds of public/private partnerships that involve selling public databases.

SINGLETON (1999) presents a coherent argument with regard to "Know Your Customer," a policy proposed for all FDIC-insured banks. She dismisses this as bad policy because it takes choice out of the hands of citizens, ignores important Federal Trade Commission and other executive branch principles on privacy, and treats persons as suspects instead of as citizens. She also makes the important point that the complexity of individuals' financial lives is one way to keep authoritarianism at bay in financial and other venues.

COURT & ATKINSON assert the need to limit federal initiatives in the privacy arena by relying on businesses to self-regulate. They provide a number of reasons for government not to interfere in electronic commerce (ecommerce): (1) some market practices implicated by privacy advocates have not been clearly demonstrated to constitute "actual harms" to consumers; (2) government action may stultify online innovation; (3) we must avoid "a kind of EU-style regulatory regime" for want of a compelling case; (4) we must avoid having to choose between the bureaucracy of an EU-style approach and the predatory laissez-faire approach by instituting a third way—self-regulation. Such self-regulation should have a significant trial period, allowing customers to opt out and choose other privacy alternatives.

The key distinction in their argument is between sensitive information (e.g., medical information, financial information, and personal information about minors) on the one hand, and nonsensitive information (e.g., demographic data) on the other. They maintain that sensitive data should be closely guarded, while demographic data and other information commonly used in marketing should not be. This assertion, however, begs the question of why such a distinction should be made, especially in light of the everyday understanding and the empirical findings that context does matter in determining privacy concerns, not some inherent property of the information in question (see HINE & EVE; NISSENBAUM, 1997, 1998; SCHOEMAN, 1994). Court & Atkinson argue that the costs of opt out for what they term nonsensitive information would be stifling to innovation and might easily outweigh the benefits of increased privacy (POSNER, 1984). They identify such costs as information audits, lack of ability to identify and take advantage of market opportunities, and use of older-generation computers, especially for new and medium-sized businesses. They note that relying strictly on industry initiatives, however, means that nonparticipants in self-regulation will not suffer the ill effects of enforcement and strong remedies. Unfortunately, they somewhat naively refer to actions such as "simply . . . gathering data that other businesses might want to buy" (p. 5) as totally unproblematic and prerogative. This is a remarkably *faux naif* assertion that ignores that such an action is far from simple and far from commonly accepted by citizens as appropriate or desirable.

More seriously, however, the point about "actual harms" ignores the tort of unreasonable intrusion, where the intrusion itself is the harm. Similarly, Court & Atkinson dismiss cookies as simple devices for Web efficiency. They attribute users' reservations about cookies to ignorance, confusion, a shallow understanding of online environments, and paranoia rather than to justifiable reservations about forced revelation of information about themselves and their preferences and behaviors. The authors devote several pages to a discussion of the EU Directive as the ultimate regulatory, top-down approach, supposedly foreign to American concepts of freedom and privacy. In discussing Free-PC.com's offer of a free computer for two years in exchange for detailed information about the user and the user's household, they refer to the transaction as simply offering consumers the opportunity to trade "something of value (their personal information and preferences) for something else of value (a computer)" (p. 8). This terminology treats privacy only as another commodity, another kind of property, belying their earlier concern with sensitive information (see also RACHELS).

According to Court & Atkinson, privacy protection should encourage ecommerce and the ubiquitous adoption of the Internet and the digital economy (p. 9). Their conclusions are a set of recommendations for public policy designed to support economic progress (pp. 9-10). Space limitations dictate little further discussion of these assertions:

- Encourage the private sector to lead in providing privacy protections.
- Allow regulatory flexibility.
- If the choice is between no regulation and bad regulation, choose no regulation.
- Distinguish between sensitive and nonsensitive information.
- Favor no specific technologies over others.
- Favor no specific media over others.
- Catalog "actual harms" to consumers and weigh these against potential costs.
- Pass legislation empowering the Federal Trade Commission (FTC) to protect consumers' privacy, if and only if (1) there has been a significant period of self-regulation, (2) such self-regulation is not adopted by a large number of ecommerce Web sites, (3) consumers' concerns with privacy on the Internet do not diminish, and (4) a "record of significant abuses emerges."
- Make governmental agencies inform citizens and solicit consent before making public databases available for sale.
- Avoid any but national and international standards for privacy protection.
- Give the FTC power to monitor business' performance and adherence to their own privacy policies.

For Court & Atkinson, the underlying act of faith is that "industry will be better able than government to develop and implement best practices that will serve consumers' interests while also allowing innovation to thrive" (p. 13). That assumption, of course, can and must be questioned, as must its converse, that government is better able to protect privacy. It should be noted that GANDY (1993) provides a bracing retort to belief in the ability of private enterprises to regulate themselves by pointing out that the exceptions to the Privacy Act show the inherent weaknesses of self-regulation.

While privacy advocates can be accused of dark scenarios, so can the privacy deniers. The deniers' nightmares include fears of recession from inventory gluts resulting from lack of customers' preferences, stifling of online innovation, inability to offer customized products and services to individual customers, and inordinate bureaucratic regulation and red tape.

## GENDERED PERSPECTIVES ON PRIVACY

As stated earlier, one of the goals of this chapter is to contribute to the reconceptualization of privacy in general and to use that reconception to provide insight into the privacy of digital information. The gendered analysis of privacy has the ability to make plain the ill effects of naturalizing the supposed distinction between the public and private spheres and ways to overcome this commonly accepted distinction. Largely based on politically active feminism, gendered examination of privacy as a cultural practice aims to achieve at least four goals: (1) clarification of how the public/private distinction, based on some mistaken "gender-neutral" politics, is a social practice that has led to serious suffering by women and children; (2) clarification of how formerly "private" behaviors such as domestic physical assault and sexual abuse became matters of public concern; (3) erosion of the information/action dichotomy common in privacy studies; and (4) achievement of a more equitable society.

It is important to remember that "it would be absurd to unite the diversity of women's movements and feminist thought past and present in any very particular definition" (FRAZER & LACEY, p. 7). While this assertion is true for gendered thought generally, it is also true for gendered analyses of privacy. Similarly, it would be a serious conceptual and political mistake to dismiss gendered analyses of privacy as of interest to only women or to the political left. Instead, feminist and other gendered conceptions of privacy offer important conceptual tools and alternatives for better understanding what privacy and privacy protection mean for everyone.

FRAZER & LACEY explore the conflict between liberal theory and other conceptualizations of politics by focusing on what they call the debate between classical liberals and communitarians. A fundamental part of their discussion is their description of a relational self based on the assertion that practice, "human action which is socially based and organised, underpinned by formal or informal institutions" (p. 17), binds people together into communities that transcend the atomistic individual posited by liberal theory.

Frazer & Lacey say the liberal concept of government leads to the fundamental idea of freedom as largely negative, freedom as "the absence of constraint" (p. 60) or concerned largely with abstract decontextualized questions of form rather than substance such as what rights are, who holds them, and what being a citizen means (p. 99). This "absence of constraint" recalls the classic WARREN & BRANDEIS formulation of privacy as "the right to be let alone." Frazer & Lacey, echoing the feminist critiques of liberal individualism, call for a more positive idea of freedom, one that emphasizes freedom as the ability for self-fulfillment and for forming meaningful relations with others. According to this view, the best, real hope of a transformative and liberating politics is the transformation of consciousness. They describe feminism's emphasis on the collective or shared nature of social life, where "the community (although loosely and problematically defined) is the proper locus of politics" (p. 120).

Frazer & Lacey further contribute to an enriched conception of privacy through their discussion of an expanded idea of equality, one that moves beyond the ubiquitous negative frame (freedom from constraint and affirmation of autonomy) to a more positive expression (opportunity for fulfillment and formation of social relationships). They conclude by calling for a linguistic and conceptual revolution from the politics of today to a more liberatory and engaged politics. Dialogic communitarianism is the means they suggest—dialogic in that it recognizes the constitutive nature of dialogue and negotiation in the formation of self and society, and communitarian in that it emphasizes questions of the public good and politics in the context of mutual recognition and acceptance.

MACKINNON (1987a) offers a good example of one major thread of gendered or feminist thought about an essential aspect of privacy in the United States: reproductive behavior and abortion. For many ordinary persons, evocation of privacy in any discussion invariably leads to (often contentious) discussion of U.S. Supreme Court cases, especially ROE v. WADE. While it may appear that there is little if any connection between concerns about reproduction and the privacy of digital information, that appearance is misleading. Some of the more obvious links involve the record keeping and reporting requirements of information related to reproductive behavior, the increased distribution of digital medical information (particularly to third parties such as insurance companies), and, as discussed further below in work by A. L. ALLEN, the connection between information and behavior in an increasingly digital world.

In the introduction to her collection, MacKinnon asserts that abortion has mistakenly been framed within the concept of privacy "rather than a right to sex equality" (1987a, p. 1). She picks up the argument in her chapter on "Privacy v. Equality: Beyond *Roe v. Wade*" (MACKINNON, 1987b). She argues that privacy doctrine, intentionally or otherwise, reinforces the public/private dichotomy that, in turn, supports the oppression of women and children in the home and elsewhere. Further, she identifies an unquestioned assumption shared by both abortion's opponents and proponents: that women have substantial control over when, how, and in what circumstances they have sex; thus abortion becomes a matter of private preference, not public policy. While *Roe* used privacy doctrine to protect the decision to have an abortion, the Supreme Court decision in *HARRIS v. MCRAE* refused federal funds to indigent women seeking abortions. This decision further reinforces the identity of abortion as a matter of private choice.

BOLING takes on what she calls the "new conventional wisdom" that the feminist critique of the public/private distinction has become. She particularly defies the assertion that the personal must always and in all circumstances be political, while accepting the general utility of such an assertion—privacy must be, from her perspective, a "double-edged sword." She asserts that certain information (e.g., sexual preference and history), are largely no one else's business but also attempts a nuanced and complex exploration of privacy that attempts to connect the private and public without conflating the two concepts. Trying to understand and address the highly contested nature of privacy and its relation to what is known by others is chief among Boling's goals for her book. Another is trying to recognize and critique the skeptical feminist critique of privacy (including the private/public distinction) while recognizing and critiquing the liberal-legal defense of privacy (and the private/public distinction).

For Boling, in addition to the assertion that private domestic abuse of all kinds is a matter for public concern, one of the primary insights of the feminist critique of privacy is its recognition of how "private inequalities [especially related to violence against women, child care, housekeeping, sexual and reproductive decisions, and inequitable career sacrifices] may affect women's ability to participate equally in public life" (p. 6). Privacy, according to what Boling recognizes as well-founded feminist critiques, does not benefit women and men equally; for example, it exposes women to domestic violence outside of public scrutiny.

Boling also explores in depth how the United States Supreme Court has supported a conception of privacy that is politically and theoretically limited. She examines the major cases, especially *GRISWOLD v. CONNECTICUT* in 1965, *EISENSTADT v. BAIRD* in 1972, *ROE v. WADE* in 1973, and *CAREY v. POPULATION SERVICES INTERNATIONAL* in 1977. While privacy as a general concept is the thread binding these decisions together, there is a major difference between *Griswold* and the other cases. *Griswold* defends contraception in the context of the intimate relationship of marriage and the "outrageousness" of allowing searches in marital bedrooms for contraceptive use. The other three cases, however, articulate a sense of privacy in reproductive decisions that evokes language of personhood, autonomy, and self-direction, especially in the formation of relationships.

While such an expansion of the concept of privacy may seem promising to privacy advocates, Boling identifies at least three significant difficulties with this shift. First is a general lack of recognition that such a shift has occurred, leaving the rationale for it unspoken and undefended. Second, all three 1970s decisions fail to clarify what makes reproductive choices private. Third, this kind of *sub rosa* change hides what makes abortion and other reproductive choices a matter of public concern as opposed to being purely individual matters. Instead, the important public interest in child bearing, child rearing, sexual status, work-place arrangements, and child care are enveloped in a rhetoric of individual private choice.

Paradoxically, however, the privacy argument in *Roe* is constructed in such a way that, Boling says, "there is a clear recognition that a woman's right to abort does not deserve the same protection as privacy interests recognized in earlier decisions" (p. 90), such as those respecting parents' rights to control their children's education and defending marriage partners' use of contraceptives. Instead, she identifies four major themes of subsequent Supreme Court decisions that severely circumscribe privacy as personal autonomy:

- Cases limiting adults' access to abortion, especially funding for abortion
- Cases invoking parental notification and/or consent for abortions performed on minors
- Cases related to legally required public interventions in pregnancy because of the use of alcohol or other drugs by the mother, combining police and health-protection demands of government
- Cases explicitly refusing to extend privacy protections of heterosexual relationships to homosexual relationships and behavior.

As a whole, these cases underscore the continued advantage that the socially and financially privileged have in defending privacy; the danger of reducing privacy to a purely private (i.e., nonpublic) concern;

and the blindness inherent in ignoring compelling public concerns related to pregnancy such as fathers' interests, universality of health care, children born and raised in poverty, and reasons for drug addiction.

BROWN, through Karl Marx, highlights how the ambiguous nature of privacy interests can clearly result in a society of alienated individuals who can conceive of privacy only as an individual self-interest, a "right" to be zealously guarded but still alienable if the price is right. Social problems are reduced to matters of individual interest, thereby undermining the social reality of privacy and naturalizing inequity. Brown later discusses Patricia Williams' identification of "the private" as a major source of tyranny by its encouraging of commodification, as a source of potential "'life-crushing disenfranchisement of an entirely owned world'" (BROWN, p. 122 quoting Patricia Williams). Instead, Williams asks that privacy be reconstrued as a means by which people recognize the personhood and autonomy of others. Brown, like Marx and Williams, is very careful not to dismiss the struggle for rights, on the basis that rights help to define a political "subject" and confer that subject with protection and respect not attainable in other ways. Like Marx and Williams, however, Brown wants to alert us to the ambiguous nature of rights and the social relationships that rights support.

The final source to be discussed here deserves extended attention. A. L. ALLEN begins her analysis by reminding the reader that, although decisional privacy related to abortion is considered by some to be *the* privacy issue for women, "women have a great many other privacy interests and concerns" (A. L. ALLEN, p. x). In her first chapter, "Defining Privacy," the most essential parts of her argument are that:

- Privacy is of special interest to women.
- Privacy has considerable value beyond the purely personal, especially insofar as it creates and reinforces bonds of affection, intimacy, wider social connections, and common interests.
- At the same time, however, privacy poses threats to individuals and society through an unfettered emphasis on individual interest, domestic violence, and degradation of others.

Most importantly, Allen's identification of privacy plainly puts her in the "restricted-access camp," that is, she defines privacy as restrictions on access to persons, to information about them (especially their habits and past behavior), and to their physical and mental conditions. For her, the important kinds of privacy, then, are seclusion and solitude, anonymity and limited attention, and what she identifies as nondisclosure, confidentiality, and secrecy.

Allen's second chapter picks up the task of exploring the value of privacy. Much of her analysis reviews three approaches to privacy: (1) intrinsic value, that is, privacy as constitutive of personhood; (2) reductionist, or privacy as superfluous and reducible to other interests, such as property and torts; and (3) functionalist, that is, privacy as instrumental to the ends of liberal democracy as per WESTIN (1985) and other liberal theorists (POSNER, 1984; PROSSER; THOMSON, 1984, 1990). After examining several other aspects of arguments about the value of privacy, Allen concludes with the assertion that privacy's value is highly contingent on the form of privacy under discussion and on whether one is considering instrumental or moral value of privacy. At the same time, she adds that privacy has many (moral and immoral) practical uses and is an important component of moral personhood, with significant personal and communal benefits.

For Allen, reproductive liberty is a fundamental component of ensuring greater privacy for women (and others) at home. She reviews the major U.S. Supreme Court and other cases, as well as related literatures, dealing with contraception and abortion and places them in a context framed by religion, ethnicity, and character. This part of her argument is especially valuable, and her discussion is closely and clearly documented; it is also contrasted with that of BOLING outlined above.

Specifically, Allen explores the "distinct implications" decisional privacy has for women and women's ability to guarantee important forms of privacy. Allen notes that what is called decisional privacy as specified in free choice related to contraception and abortion does *not* fit easily with her preferred conception of privacy as restriction of access and is probably an artifact of the public/private distinction. She asserts, however, that the recognition of decisional privacy related to reproductive behavior allows women to achieve what she calls the paradigmatic form(s) of privacy. Thus, despite the attempts of many commentators to separate privacy and reproductive concerns, Allen and others insist that women's private choices related to reproduction are meaningless unless women can act on those choices. She bases her argument essentially on free choice as a requirement of moral personhood and as a guarantor of "the quality of individual and group life" (p. 122).

Allen has a long and quite detailed list of individual states' attempts to regulate abortion since *Roe v. Wade*. Among these have been:

1. Restrictions on the advertisement of reproductive services, especially abortions
2. Zoning restrictions on the placement of abortion facilities
3. Record-keeping and reporting regulations
4. Parental and spousal notification/consent
5. Mandated pre-abortion counseling by a physician

6. Mandated waiting periods
7. Required presence of a second physician during abortions
8. Requirements that insurance companies offer a discount for health insurance without coverage of elective abortions (A. L. ALLEN, pp. 106-107).

Many of these and related efforts have been deemed unconstitutional; the interested reader is encouraged to see A.L. ALLEN and BOLING, especially their notes. The current landscape is still largely the same as what Allen describes in 1988.

Generally, decisional privacy has special importance for questions related to privacy and digital information; as Allen notes, "[l]ack of informational privacy can eviscerate decisional privacy altogether" (p. 110). It has been a contention of this chapter that decisional privacy and so-called informational privacy cannot be completely separated. The larger argument lies on several bases. First, the ability to act in and move about society depends on interaction with large and increasingly integrated digital information systems. Second, digital information systems are controlled by large, powerful organizations such as government and private corporate interests; ordinary citizens are clearly disadvantaged in negotiations with such organizations. Such asymmetric relationships mean that decisions about what kinds of information to share and what information to withhold, especially about current and past behavior, are constituted by an understanding of this asymmetry. Third, enhanced control and capture, database searching, and retrieval technologies make it increasingly disingenuous to claim that one can assert meaningful decisional privacy without serious limitations created by information recording and reporting requirements, whether such requirements are the results of private or public policies.

## PRIVACY IN PUBLIC

One of the major theoretical and, thus, practical weaknesses of privacy as currently conceived involves what legal scholar A. L. ALLEN and philosopher and ethicist NISSENBAUM (1997; 1998) call privacy in public. The primary argument is that theories of privacy that consider only intimate information and relationships are useful but incomplete. More precisely, information and activities already public are not free of privacy restrictions imposed by strong norms and mores that surround them.

The 1988 book by A. L. ALLEN has a chapter titled "Privacy in Public." She begins by making it clear that the "concept of privacy in public is no contradiction" (p. 123). Instead, we have mores that clearly protect against intrusion and unwanted observation in public places such as museums, parks, airports, city streets, swimming pools, and the like. These mores, and the judicial tradition recognizing them, rely on the principles of physical distance, anonymity, and limited public attention. According to her analysis, public places can serve their public purposes if and only if they protect privacy.

At the same time, however, Allen recognizes that there are a number of unwanted intrusions and other compromises of privacy mores in public against which people often feel powerless. Allen analyzes sexual harassment, the public display of pornography, roles and relationships in the public sphere, and exclusion and group privacy as loci of important conflicts about privacy in public. While some of these concerns are addressed elsewhere in this chapter, one part of her analysis of roles and relationships merits specific attention here. In identifying where women may be especially vulnerable to compromises of privacy, Allen notes four causal factors, among them that "women are deemed safe targets because there are ineffective moral, institutional, or legal sanctions to serve as deterrents" (p. 141). This vulnerability extends, of course, beyond women to most members of society in circumstances where relationships between these persons and large, powerful institutions such as government and commercial organizations are fundamentally asymmetrical.

Nissenbaum's analysis of privacy in public helps make this point clearer. NISSENBAUM (1997; 1998) takes a related, but different, tack in identifying what privacy in public means. She relates the concept to what she calls publicly available information. This includes information shared with others in credit, medical, and other financial transactions; information about behavior in public places; and information in the hands of public agencies, such as drivers' license numbers, real estate holdings, and court records. Etzioni says that shopping in a supermarket is "a private act, but one that cannot be said to implicate privacy because its commission is quite visible to the public" (ETZIONI, p.211). He also asserts that a category of acts that are both public and private cannot make sense. On the contrary, the concept of privacy in public pertains to the fact that people act in public and usually do not mind that they are observed; at the same time, however, they would object strenuously to others' recording, distributing, or otherwise using information about their shopping. This concept echoes what Nissenbaum describes below as the importance of context.

NISSENBAUM (1997) criticizes two assumptions identified as major obstacles to a theory of privacy inclusive enough to address privacy in public. The first such misguided assumption is that there is some area of public information about people to which we do not apply norms of privacy. This information is considered not private because it does not involve personal or sensitive information, nor does it involve information gathered through eavesdropping or other ethically forbidden means. Nissenbaum erodes this assumption by clearly demonstrating that there are, in fact, quite strong norms about how publicly available information is to be used. For reasons ranging from inappropriateness to freedom from harassment and from physical attack, people do not expect their video rentals or drivers' license information to be publicized. In this context, Nissenbaum fails to include other kinds of information offered similar kinds of protection (e.g., library circulation records), that further undermine Etzioni's and others' simple dismissals of the concept of privacy in public. She does give examples of civil inattention (a concept in SCHOEMAN, 1994) and contextual integrity. People adjust their behavior in public places to recognize that they are on display (BELOTTI; GOFFMAN), as in nightclubs or supermarkets, and do not object to being observed there. They would, however, feel violated and object strongly if their actions in these public places were recorded and reported outside of these contexts, whether such reporting were to their intimates, governmental entities, or commercial firms. This reporting violates what Nissenbaum calls contextual integrity: the sharing of information in contextually appropriate circumstances.

The second erroneous assumption that Nissenbaum describes is the belief that it is noninvasive to aggregate information regarded as noninvasive in its parts. For a further counterargument to this assertion, see the discussion of the digital persona elsewhere in this chapter. As with the nightclub and other examples above, people do not object to other people and institutions having information about them in appropriate contexts, but privacy violations abound in the construction of a digital record of a person's characteristics, relationships, opinions, and actions. Without a wider conception of privacy that protects use, distribution, and aggregation of publicly available information, they are made unacceptably vulnerable to the scrutiny of others: "omnipresent record-taking opens one to unbearable exposure" (1997, p. 217). We have seen the proliferation of digital technologies, especially complex database tools, computer processing speeds and memory capacity, and information retrieval mechanisms. These technologies pose fundamental threats to privacy we have not had to address previously. These functionalities also underscore the dislocation between philosophical and legal theories of privacy on the one hand and moral norms about publicly held information on the other.

NISSENBAUM (1998) identifies four ways in which digital technologies threaten privacy in public: (1) they support and record transactions, (2) they are repositories for records of these and other transactions, (3) they facilitate secondary uses of transaction information, especially those of credit bureaus, medical insurance bureaus, and mailing list sellers, and (4) they facilitate and provide an economic rationale for government's sale of publicly held information to private-sector firms. These activities are major contributors to the current culture of surveillance.

As with her earlier paper, Nissenbaum describes the public outcry against Lotus and Equifax's 1990 initiative to develop and market "Lotus Marketplace: Households" (see also CULNAN & SMITH). This CD-ROM, intended for marketers and others, would have included verified and inferred information about 120 million Americans, such as name, address, gender, age, marital status, parental status, household income, lifestyle, and retail purchase habits and inclinations (NISSENBAUM, 1998, pp. 563-564). In January 1991, however, the CD-ROM was scrapped, although Nissenbaum says, "in hindsight the victory appears thin" (1997, p. 212) and the "legacy of Lotus Marketplace[:] Households for the course of data gathering has been negligible" (1998, p. 566). She makes this claim because (1) executives planning the product withdrew it only because they asserted that the public misunderstood the goals and possible effects of the CD-ROM not because, in their opinion, it would have violated privacy, (2) there were (and are) no clear, unequivocal articulations of the norms related to publicly held information, (3) there was no clear consensus among all of the players involved that this product would have violated such norms, and (4) there was no clear identification of how such a product would have violated such norms. While a growing number of similar products threaten the privacy of publicly held information, Nissenbaum says, "With no underlying thread to tie one effort to another, each must be fought on its own terms" (1998, p. 566).

Privacy in public has been dismissed, if considered at all, for several reasons. First and foremost are conceptual blind spots—we largely adhere to a rather simplistic dichotomy between public and private spheres. As noted earlier, there is a mistaken but very common assumption that privacy in public is an oxymoron. A second problem is how limited our normative arguments have been—we tend to devolve quickly from discussions of privacy to the need for balance between privacy and other interests regarded as equally compelling. Too often, these countervailing claims quickly outweigh concerns with privacy (see also REGAN, 1995) because publicly held information is thought to be unthreatening. In addition, restricting the collection, aggregation, and distribution of information about acts in public and other publicly held information is commonly construed to unfairly limit the freedom of others, especially commercial actors.

A final explanation for theorists' ignoring privacy in public is what Nissenbaum calls empirical; that is, virtual anonymity in public was heretofore assured by the sheer number of people and the impossibility of noticing them all. Plainly put, the major normative argument about privacy in public is that people expect to be seen but not noticed or scrutinized. This public anonymity, relying on SCHOEMAN's 1994 idea of civil inattention mentioned earlier, has been changed by the unprecedented power of information technologies to match, track, aggregate, infer, store, store forever, and retrieve information.

Nissenbaum concludes by noting that concerns about contextual integrity and distaste for aggregation apply to publicly held information: "the activities integral to public surveillance practices known as profiling, data aggregation, and data mining, which provide the means to reach, target, and possibly manipulate their subjects" are morally objectionable to ordinary men and women (1998, p. 590). At the same time, real-world protections of privacy in public will be long in coming. As individuals and a society, we need to overcome the conceptual and rhetorical limitations she identifies, as must commercial entities, the courts, and other governmental groups.

Further light on privacy in public is shed by SCHOEMAN (1994), the source of Nissenbaum's concept of civil inattention. Schoeman puts civil inattention into a contrast between dissemination and publication. For him, publication is "dissemination plus the conversion of a matter that is personal into a matter that is 'open' or acknowledged as a 'public fact'": "Just because something happens in public does not mean it becomes a public fact" (p. 81). He asserts that people do not object to others' knowledge of what they do in public (what he calls dissemination in this context) as long as information they regard as properly limited in public attention (e.g., the identity of victims of sexual assault, financial status, sexual behavior, and parental behavior), is indeed excluded from public discussion, recognition, and attribution. It is the protection of people's dignity and public persona, deference to the idea of "saving face," that leads them *not* to acknowledge publicly "what is apparent to all." This kind of civil inattention involves the idea of the integrity of context identified by GANDY (1993), HINE & EVE, and NISSENBAUM (1997; 1998). A further element of civil attention that Schoeman does not explore is that the number of individuals, groups, and behaviors ordinarily overwhelms most people's ability to know and notice them. Thus, individuals are afforded some modicum of protection to privacy in public by the simple fact of others' inability to notice everything. To many of the authors reviewed in this chapter, the power, ubiquity, and sophistication of digital technologies seriously undermine the *de facto* protections of privacy that this kind of civil attention provides.

SCHOEMAN (1994) makes an interesting contribution in his general discussion of privacy by demonstrating that gossip, in fact, recognizes privacy norms and thereby protects people from inappropriate social control (see also POSNER, 1984; SINGLETON, 1998; THOMSON, 1984). Schoeman's analysis explains how privacy supports social life rather than interfering with it. He asserts that protection of certain kinds of information, relationships, and behaviors from public knowledge and acknowledgement make deeper and more committed social relationships possible and more fruitful.

DE SOUSA defends gossip as an activity by identifying it as free speech in the private arena, as opposed to what is ordinarily regarded as free speech in public. The conceptual basis of this defense is the conviction that animates the entire chapter: "it seems likely that a world in which all information were universally available would be preferable to a world where immense power resides in the control of secrets" (p. 32; see also BRIN). THOMAS makes a distinction between malicious and admiring (nonmalicious) gossip and explores how the public status of information does not prevent the proliferation of malicious gossip about the persons involved. He also notes that "just about any conversation" combines gossip and nongossip, including conversations that are limited only to statements of admiration. POST (1994) evokes GOFFMAN's dramaturgical analysis of social life and reiterates Goffman's distinction between "front-stage" and "back-stage." Thus, gossip, to some extent, means revealing what is ordinarily kept backstage, and gossip in the mass media reveals the backstage faces of celebrities and others caught in the media gaze. Gossip, according to COLLINS, must be rehabilitated and recognized as a positive force in the formation of community, and the development of a sophisticated and concrete moral sense.

## PRIVACY AS PROPERTY

A number of voices with a wide variety of opinions about privacy assert that a desirable conceptual and policy outcome is the granting of formal, enforceable property rights in information. At the same time, other commentators insist that recognizing privacy as property would be a serious political and moral mistake. The aim of this section of the chapter is to describe these various claims and counterclaims, with a focus on consumer information and consumers' claims to property rights in transaction-generated information (TGI).

### Boundaries of Property Rights

The three most important bases for considering privacy as property are the recognition of information as an asset, the related growing commodity value of information, and a growing recognition that granting and protecting such property rights may be the best way to protect privacy interests in digital communication. This last basis is recognized by those who want to encourage ecommerce and thereby support industry self-regulation as well as those who are most concerned about privacy protection. In addition, these points of view generally regard privacy as a "possession" of individuals, not individuals and groups, and, thus, the most common rationales for privacy protection for individuals are evoked in discussions of privacy as (individual) property.

The work of THOMSON (1984), analyzed in many places and from many perspectives, is a good place to start in considering more recent expressions about privacy, ownership, and concepts of property. This work was perhaps the most influential with regard to privacy as property until LAUDON (1996) and BRANSCOMB.

In 1984 Thomson takes a radical, that is, fundamental, look at the right of privacy, one she describes as unclear especially with regard to what it entails and what its boundaries are. The important elements of her argument for this chapter are:

- The presumption that every right entails a negative right, for example, the right to liberty entails the right to enjoin others from taking that right.
- The simplifying hypothesis that privacy is a cluster-right (see the section in this chapter on legal and policy conceptions of privacy) that intersects with other rights, particularly the rights that consist in being a person, the right to be free from annoyance, and the right to property.
- The so-called right to privacy includes the rights not to be looked at and not to be listened to.

Thomson offers a point of view quite different from that of most commentators cited here and one that recalls the arguments about free commercial speech and privacy "[T]here is no such thing as violating a man's right to privacy by simply knowing something about him. . . . The question arises . . . Whether or not there are *any* rights in the right to privacy cluster which aren't also in some other right cluster. I suspect there aren't any, and that the right to privacy is everywhere overlapped by other rights" (1984, pp. 282, 284). Instead, she recognizes, among other things, a right to confidentiality which she presumes to cover personal or impersonal information. She enthusiastically criticizes *GRISWOLD v. CONNECTICUT* and *ROE v. WADE*, saying that there is no violation of privacy simply by implementing any state statute making it illegal to use contraceptives. She concludes by noting that the uncertainty about privacy as a right is so dark that simplicity, not the proliferation of rights, is called for.

THOMSON (1990), while addressing rights generally, discusses three meanings of the term "inalienable right" that are useful for this analysis of privacy and property: (1) others cannot take it away, (2) one cannot make him/herself cease to have the right by sale or other commercial transaction, and (3) one cannot make him/herself cease to have it by force or any other means. Inalienable rights, which are to her the traditional troika of life, liberty, and property, are inalienable only in the first sense of inalienable. While Thomson believes that privacy is subsumed under other rights (see the section of the chapter on legal and policy conceptions of privacy), she believes that privacy can be sold. This position is not as radical as it may appear at first glance, because Thomson also believes that one can sell oneself into slavery—she simply sees no good reason for or against that kind of conduct. Thus, to her way of thinking, any right can be sold.

POSNER's 1984 paper is also considered important in the historical development of the theory of privacy as property, largely because of his meticulous historical research into the economics of information and how, in his estimation, presumptions about economics have informed the common law. His approach in the paper is to assume that privacy and intrusion are instrumental rather than ends in themselves. He leaves it to the reader to determine whether that approach is useful and evocative. While this reader finds it less than convincing, Posner's care in building his argument demands careful attention. Like apologists for commercial free speech who deny any standing for the privacy of almost all information about persons, Posner's argument is a type indicative of many others.

One of the primary points of the paper, and among its most influential tenets, is that privacy often stands in the way of persons, businesses, and other organizations being able to establish reliable relationships with trustworthy persons. Posner, building on the work of psychology and sociology, believes that all people manipulate others' reactions to them to the point of deliberate deception, making what he terms "self-serving claims" (1984, p. 338). Such deception, according to this econometric analysis, leads to less-than-optimal relationships and increases the likelihood of significant economic and social penalties, such as financial loss through fraud, theft, and trusting the untrustworthy. This foundation leads to his high valuation of gossip that serves to identify important dangers and opportunities and what he says is misidentified as idle curiosity. As is well known, the economics of information is full of logical and other traps, and Posner falls into one when he says that "the economist does not believe . . . that supply creates demand" (1984, p. 335). Say's Law (see PALMER; SOWELL) asserts precisely that, and, as is so often the case with information products and services, demand simply does not exist until a product or service is offered and a market aggregated. The Internet is a prime example of such a phenomenon, as are many public libraries and other public information services. Despite its many faulty assumptions, Say's Law is useful here.

A critical part of Posner's 1984 argument is that transactional data rightly become the property of the organization rather than the person(s) to whom the information pertains because the enterprise is more likely to put the information to its most valuable use, that is, to create further value and use secrecy to innovate. Further, he concludes that the value realized in information such as subscription and customer lists far exceeds the individual's loss in having such information shared. This point, obviously, has been and remains highly contentious. What is less contentious is his condemnation of eavesdropping and other forms of intrusive surveillance which, naturally enough, he defends in terms of the (economic) justification that fear of surveillance would unnecessarily inhibit communication to the detriment of the production of wealth and other financial and social benefits. After decrying the un-economic basis of the Buckley Amendment protecting the confidentiality of students' educational records, he concludes with a broad condemnation of legislation, regulation, and other efforts to limit the information available to potential employers and creditors while increasing the privacy of persons with things to hide.

LAUDON (1996) is considered by many as foundational to the consideration of privacy as property. Some of his discussion is included in the section in this chapter about legal and policy conceptions of privacy. He urges consideration of market-based means, which he identifies as a National Information Market (NIM), for protecting privacy in the context of current information technologies and to do so in a way that encourages consistent innovation in technologies. He considers a number of related questions:

- Who should own and control the personal information available on information networks?
- Given the recognition of information as a personal asset, how should owners be compensated for the use of private information?
- How can we develop other mechanisms to complement legal foundations of privacy protection?
- Since the current use of personal information is wasteful and inefficient, how can we develop ways to make the protection of personal privacy less expensive?

One of Laudon's major points is that traditional laws, regulations, and concepts are incapable of giving privacy adequate protection. These traditional sources of protection, he says, are characterized by a scattershot approach that emphasizes records and is largely unenforceable, especially in the private sector. The Fair Information Practices (FIPs) that animated much of the first generation of privacy protection are inadequate for current technologies, social interactions, and mores (see, e.g., AGRE, 1997b).

Laudon argues that we should extend to all citizens the protection offered to celebrities protecting them from misappropriation of their images, voices, and names (see also PROSSER & KEETON). This conclusion is a natural extension, according to Laudon, of the fact that there is a large and very lucrative market in personal information but little protection of that information. It is in addressing this misbalance that the best hope for privacy protection, especially from private-sector organizations, lies. GANDY (1993, pp. 186-187) notes that such a solution may not be workable because the misappropriation of an ordinary person's image has little monetary value; such citizens are, therefore, not likely to succeed at protecting their images, whether under tort law or other protections.

The latter part of Laudon's paper is a discussion of how to achieve a market in personal information, recognizing that it would take political, social, and moral consensus to make it happen. The National Information Market (NIM) would rely on market prices to help ensure a situation where the demand for personal information would match the supply. The NIM is intended to imitate (1) the movement of financial assets in depository institutions that connect retailers, creditors, banks, and consumers and (2) the centralized mortgage market that pools many thousands of mortgages (1996, pp. 99-100). Individuals would deposit their information assets in local institutions in order to make these assets available to buyers for a defined period of time. A National Information Accounts Clearinghouse (NIAC) would ensure payment, perform auditing tasks, and report on that auditing. The NIM would serve as the only legal means for the use of individually identifiable information for purposes beyond those for which the information was originally obtained. Only secondary uses explicitly authorized by the individual would be allowed.

Laudon takes on several possible objections to his suggestion of an NIM, including concerns about selling a basic right, inequities in property regimes, concerns about need for new kinds of property law and increased regulation, increased transaction costs, the expense of operating the NIM, and concerns about too much privacy (especially from an economic perspective). He discusses and dismisses each of these categories of objections, based on his faith in markets, economic incentives, and privacy as an attribute of individuals as unquestioned assumptions. (As is made clearer at the conclusion of this section, the current author does not share his faith.)

Laudon concludes by saying that corporations waste billions of dollars in invading privacy, while incurring additional costs when individuals refuse to provide valuable information. He underscores his assertion that the glut of information we now have is wasteful and unnecessary, and, for him, only market solutions can begin to protect privacy and enhance the efficiency of the use of personal information.

BRANSCOMB provides a valuable review of a number of questions of interest to this chapter. She focuses on the importance and wide effects of the relationship between ownership of information, especially through intellectual property, and privacy. One of the aims of her book, in fact, is "to urge individuals who gripe about invasions of privacy by information entrepreneurs to stop complaining and bring their concerns to their elected representatives so that a more humane and comprehensive law governing information assets can be devised" (p. 8).

One of the foundations of Branscomb's argument is the identification of information as an asset in and of itself. It has, as per the information entrepreneurs discussed elsewhere in this chapter, ceased being of only instrumental value and has passed from being a signal and method of guaranteeing personal liberty to being a valuable social good. The results have included serious abuses of privacy, especially through the construction of information mosaics (see also AGRE, 1994b; CLARKE, 1994), and other values, including the idea of law as reflecting social consensus. She recommends that individuals claim personal, individual rights in information about themselves in order to protect themselves from these moral, political, and financial predations, from actors in both private and public organizations.

The main body of the book asks questions about ownership of names and addresses, telephone numbers, medical histories, images, electronic messages, choices in video entertainment, religious affiliations, computer software, and government information. Branscomb identifies thirteen legal principles, echoing the Fair Information Practices but also going beyond them: secrecy, privacy, confidentiality, publicity, commerciality, accessibility, reciprocity, integrity, interoperability, responsibility, liability, commonality, and equity (p. 181). Branscomb's clear and well-documented argument shows that mores, technology, and the law—the three traditional ways that we have protected property—can no longer achieve their goals in a networked world where information is often just another commodity. While she recognizes the ill effects of claiming property rights in information, she believes that such rights are the only realistic way to protect privacy and other social goods.

HAGEL & RAYPORT assert bluntly that customers will use property rights to claim ownership of personal information and will demand explicit and measurable value(s) whenever that information is collected, used, re-used, or otherwise made valuable to another party.

Repeating the usual claims of collectors of information examined more critically in the sections of this chapter on information entrepreneurialism and on claims of too much privacy, Hagel & Rayport identify four "legitimate" goals of collecting customer information: targeting particularly likely prospects, customization of products and services, improvement of customers' satisfaction and willingness to remain customers, and identification of new or existing market niches. Hagel & Rayport say that customers can use personal financial management software, smart cards, Web browsers, and similar technologies to alleviate privacy problems in three steps: (1) the technologies allow customers to create digital personae or portraits of themselves that no single company can, (2) this valuable product can then either be guarded zealously or (3) it can be sold for value, relying largely on contracts. Displaying a mindset similar to that of LAUDON (1996) and appropriate for readers of the *Harvard Business Review*, they go on to argue that commercial ownership of customer information as valuable information assets is only one element of concern; rather, using some of the rationale of the knowledge management literature, the authors criticize companies that do not sufficiently organize nor use the information they collect. Thus, delivering value to the customers who surrender such information is even more difficult and unlikely.

Echoing some of the argument of Laudon above (see also POSCH, 1993), they suggest an economic rationale and mechanism for privacy— that consumers, despite the strong indications of opinion polls for decades, are not "really" concerned about privacy at all. "We are witnessing the growth of a 'privacy backlash' among consumers, which we believe has less to do with the desire to keep information about themselves confidential and more to do with the pragmatic assessment that the returns for the information they divulge are, simply put, unsatisfactory." (HAGEL & RAYPORT, p. 65)

Hagel & Rayport grant that, while relatively few persons regard privacy as absolute, most consumers will eagerly surrender information if the potential benefits seem to outweigh the potentially compromising effects of the disclosure (see also GANDY, 1993; WHITAKER). They go so far as to say that, since people often make information available for some tangible value, "they can hardly be concerned about their privacy" (HAGEL & RAYPORT, p. 74). Like LAUDON (1996), they conclude by suggesting that some information intermediaries can act as brokers and customers' representatives, including elite service companies and upscale retailers, to respect this economic definition of privacy. This mechanism, in their opinion, would help protect commercial enterprises from the property-based claims of customers.

HINE & EVE rely on an empirical study of individuals' conceptions of privacy and the collection and use of personally attributable information in common circumstances in the United Kingdom. While there was a relatively small number of respondents (26), the research protocol involved in-depth interviews and scenario discussion that generated a rich description of the respondents' attitudes and beliefs. For the participants and the researchers, privacy is situation-dependent. Further, its infringement is largely constructed through talk, that is, understandings of privacy and how it is compromised develop from interactions among the technologies used by organizations in collecting and using information, representations of the organizations, and representations of the self. In order to elicit and understand such talk, the researchers had the respondents focus on shopping rather than on privacy as such. Their research project was inspired by a dissatisfaction with (1) the lack of qualitatively rich, empirical research about the complexities of privacy, (2) the emphasis on American concerns in the privacy literature, and (3) the legalistic basis of many privacy discussions. The literatures they cite on identity, consumption, trust, risk, and other concepts may also be of interest to readers of this review.

Some of their most important findings echo those of other researchers (GANDY, 1993; NISSENBAUM, 1997, 1998; SCHOEMAN, 1994): the study respondents did not regard any particular type of information as personal per se, and they regarded different types of information as personal depending upon the particular scenario and context presented. Hine & Eve identified five factors that influenced the formation of a description of an event that was regarded by the informants as intrusive:

1. The visibility of the meditating technology: Respondents regarded supermarket loyalty cards that allow them to accrue points for discounts or free goods as benefits; therefore, they were not at all concerned with the ability of merchants to track, aggregate, and analyze the customers' purchasing habits. Exceptions to this lack of worry were respondents with work or technical experience with such systems.

2. The perceived legitimacy of the reasons for information requests: Respondents regarded requests that they considered motiveless or as useful for only the requesting organization as inappropriate. Just as they constructed descriptions of the technology, they constructed narratives of the actions and motives of the organizations requesting and using information.

3. Disruption of respondents' ordinary activity, or intrusion: While respondents saw direct mail as a minor annoyance, they condemned personal visits or telephone calls by commercial actors, especially if these contacts

targeted particularly vulnerable groups such as the elderly and home-confined. Intrusiveness was defined by
the medium used, the timing of the communication, and
the source of the communication, not the particular information solicited.

4.  Asymmetry of power and control: Respondents felt in-
    vaded when commercial representatives in transactions
    indicated that the respondents were known but the in-
    formation gatherer/user was not, especially if the
    interviewees thought they could not terminate or other-
    wise control the interaction.

5.  Social context: Hine & Eve note that "accounts of pri-
    vacy infringement are reflexive . . . often positioned in
    contrast to a portrayal of what would be socially appro-
    priate or what is generally the case" (HINE & EVE, p.
    259). This construction of privacy and privacy infringe-
    ment is in contrast with what is expected and is in the
    context of particular relationships, not in contrast with
    privacy as an abstract concept. As noted above, this
    point echoes NISSENBAUM (1997; 1998) and
    SCHOEMAN (1994) on contextually appropriate use of
    publicly available information.

Hine & Eve conclude that, although concerns about privacy and technology are widespread, no single set of criteria or kind(s) of information
were used by their respondents to identify privacy infringements. Further, they warn that so-called technical fixes to perceived privacy problems may not be identified as positive by consumers (see also BURKERT;
LAUDON, 1996).

BENNETT & GRANT (1999b) offer several papers of value to this
chapter, with several of particular interest to discussions of privacy as
property. Part III of their collection addresses "Market Choices" and
focuses on privacy in the private sector. The first paper in that section is
by CULNAN & BIES, who begin their discussion of privacy in the
context of interaction between customers and commercial firms by
making two assertions: (1) such interaction must be shared across functions in the enterprise to enhance the value created in the organization,
especially to allow the appearance of a "personal relationship" between
a customer and 800-number operators or online interfaces and (2) firms
"have the right" to record and use transaction-generated data for "legitimate business purposes." As discussed below, the definition, extent,
and immutability of such "legitimate" purposes is very much at issue
and cannot be granted a priori. One of the particular values of this
paper, however, is its thoughtful contrast, not between individuals and

criminal behavior, but rather between personal privacy and legitimate business interests.

Culnan & Bies are strong supporters of Fair Information Practices (FIPs), citing them as the foundation of ethical and strong privacy protection of individuals. They say that "[f]or privacy, fair information practices operationalized procedural fairness . . . [that] communicates information about the firm's integrity and motivation to act in a trust-worthy manner" (pp. 155, 156), serving the social contract that helps individuals decide whether to reveal information about themselves. Their figure providing "An Organizational Perspective on Fairness and Privacy" is extremely useful in conceptualizing and then operationalizing a commitment to privacy in commercial practice (Figure 7.1, p. 158). The key is embedding FIPs in employees' work practices, leading to a "culture of privacy" created by a firm's policies, internal privacy cham-pions, and procedures for punishing behavior that erodes the FIPs. This culture, and earning the overall trust of customers, can establish en-hanced relationships with customers, leading to competitive advantage and increased sharing of information by customers. For Culnan & Bies, the current reliance on self-regulation lacks sufficient accountability to be effective, either in protecting privacy or in convincing customers that their privacy will be respected. They assert that international law and regulations may be the best hope for privacy in a global business environment, and they conclude on an almost plaintive note that their concern for human dignity as an essential part of management practice and theory puts them clearly at the periphery of management as a discipline.

The second paper in Bennett & Grant's Part III is by RULE & HUNTER. They echo LAUDON (1996) in asserting that: (1) privacy is currently ill-protected; (2) the primary cause is the unparalleled growth in the commercialization of data, especially transaction-based information; (3) formal policy approaches to privacy have been unsuccessful; and (4) creating a property right in commercial use of personal information is the best approach to protecting privacy. They, too, evoke the need for data rights agencies and assert that, without clearly expressed inten-tions to the contrary, information would not be released, that is, would rely on opt-in conditions. Then individual citizens would be able to negotiate with organizations, with the data rights agencies acting as intermediaries, presumably in the commercial interests of their citizen clients. Citizens could always stop the flow of information completely, depending on whether they like the price/benefits offered in return for information and/or the conditions set for its use and reuse. If they do so, however, they would then suffer the consequences as organizations "draw their own conclusions about the reasons for the missing data and guide their dealings with the subject . . . accordingly" (RULE & HUNTER, p. 179).

There is a great deal of merit in their response to anticipated objections to their suggestions and in their critique of what REGAN (1999), RAAB (1999), and others call the "balancing argument." The difficulty of relying on balancing arguments, especially the uncertainty of which criteria to evoke and how to calculate their interaction, is primarily two-fold. First, Rule & Hunter say that "As this on-the-one-hand-and-on-the-other discussion continues, the unrestricted appropriation of personal data grows apace" (p. 169). Second, the dichotomous thinking at the basis of this balancing approach to privacy is misleading (see the section in this chapter about gendered approaches to privacy).

Unfortunately, the approach of Rule & Hunter exhibits many of the same weaknesses as others:

- They rely on the atomistic individual as the conceptual and political bedrock of privacy; they also use the phrase "individual data subject" criticized earlier.
- They consistently underestimate the coercive effects of the asymmetric relationships between citizens and large, especially commercial, enterprises. It is an article of untested faith that their proposed data rights agencies would serve individual clients rather than the large, financially able, and socially powerful organizations that gather and use data.
- The kinds of contractual periods they recommend, while seemingly useful and "common sensical," ignore the merging of financial services organizations, the conglomeration of varied and horizontally integrated firms, and the fact that once information is in the system, it is there forever.

Rule & Hunter conclude with a reasonable assertion that they are not looking for the proverbial silver bullet to solve privacy concerns but rather for another way to protect privacy in concert with laws, regulations, social norms, and organizational and other practices. For them, having citizens own information about themselves is a key component to such protection.

## Weaknesses of Property Rights

There are a number of weaknesses as well as strengths in the conceptualization of privacy as property. One such weakness is an implicit belief in what some term a "privacy calculus" (CULNAN & BIES, p. 154). Individuals are presumed to be able to weigh potential benefits of sharing information with the potential costs of all kinds. Such a belief begs the question of whether people consciously make such choices or make them out of habit, make them out of unawareness of the potential negative effects of such choices, and/or are coerced into doing so (FOUCAULT; GANDY, 1993; HINE & EVE; WHITAKER). The more econometric approach to privacy analysis depends on this meta-rational ability to know and maximize self-interest. Serious questions remain about whether and how individuals and groups can calculate the risks of revealing information, especially in the long term. Assertion of the privacy calculus, of course, depends on the assumptions of the classically liberal individual, the epistemological and social assumptions of economics, and the tenets of utilitarianism. These are not further examined here, but their weaknesses have been widely recognized.

A second difficulty with privacy as property is the consistent evocation in many privacy analyses of "legitimate business interests." This critique is not to deny that there are such interests, but, as should be clear by now, it is highly contentious to identify what these interests are, how they can be realistically considered in the context of privacy, and when, if ever, they should trump privacy interests (LAPERRIÈRE). It is also essential to determine how long such interests should extend across organizations and across time, and how immutable such claims and interests are. Claims of legitimate business interests ignore the proliferation of large companies that merge, for example, financial firms, retailing, business-to-business information services, and the like. They also ignore the growing number of public/private partnerships that often obviate such distinctions and the general lack of knowledge about data use.

A further problem is the unexplored connections between privacy as property and some increasingly questionable bases of the Fair Information Practices (FIPs). More specifically, privacy as property seems to rely on some of the outdated assumptions about information that underlie FIPs, such as, centralization, discrete use, and one-time use.

Another considerable difficulty involves the ownability of information. While this point is one of the classic difficulties in and with the economics of information, SAMUELSON further questions the concept of the ownability of information, citing some case law of interest (e.g., *United States v. Neidorf* in the Chicago District Court (see DENNING) and *CARPENTER v. UNITED STATES* in the U.S. Supreme Court) and how those cases show some of the problems that develop when we try to subsume information into property. The nonconsumability of information is one of the prime causes of such problems, especially the difficulty of determining when information should be treated as property and when it should not. HUNTER further asks what it means to own information, especially in situations where more than one person can own it, as with transaction-generated information or shared privacy interests.

The concern with the ownability of information is extended by questions about propertizing information more generally. LESSIG and BOYLE discuss the values brought into risk because of the apparently inexorable drive to make all information into property, what Boyle calls "an intellectual land-grab" (p. 94). BROWN, discussed in the chapter section on gendered analyses of privacy, examines Patricia Williams' identification of the private as a major source of tyranny by its encouraging of commodification, in an entirely owned world. Lessig also cites the work of HALBERT on the propertization of information and of RADIN (1993; 1996a; 1996b) on evolving theories of property in the law.

A further weakness of privacy as property is underscored by RACHELS. In answer to THOMSON's (1984) "simplifying hypothesis," Rachels notes that it is not a property right that people invoke when they assert rights to privacy, for example, when they experience distress at being seen naked. Rather, privacy is related to the belief that such physical intimacy is reserved for special relationships.

This leads to the final and perhaps greatest weakness of the assertion of property rights in privacy, which involves questions about personhood. A. L. ALLEN refers to the work of Sara Ann Ketchum on "The Moral Status of the Bodies of Persons," stressing that "[H]uman beings surely do not own their bodies, but are their bodies. Our claims to exclusive access to our bodies can be based directly on our being persons in the moral sense whose bodies should not be reduced to involuntary instruments of service for others' needs. Hence, the concept of self-ownership is as superfluous as it is misleading" (A. L. ALLEN, p. 101). The evocation of property rights in one's body parallels the evocation of property rights in privacy, not least of all because many privacy cases center on topics such as blood and tissue tests and the integrity of the body.

More importantly, however, just as the assertion of *OLMSTEAD v. UNITED STATES* in 1928 that privacy is in property and places was superseded by the assertion of *KATZ v. UNITED STATES* in 1967 that privacy accrues to the person, we must go beyond thinking of privacy only as property. While we can all recognize the suitability of property as a category for some types of information, claiming property rights in privacy does not seem suitable for such a claim. It is not easy to reach this conclusion given some important political realities. First, it is clear that information has increasing financial value. Second, our information technology-intensive and networked culture, with its entrepreneurial elements, seriously threatens privacy, especially online. Third, given how property rights have consistently been valorized and thought unassailable in U.S. law and culture, evoking property rights in privacy might be considered the best hope of protecting privacy. Such a stance, however beneficial it may appear in the short term, is likely to result in long-term damage to the concept of privacy. Thinking of privacy as a commodity makes it *less likely*, not more likely, that we can build a social and policy consensus that recognizes privacy in meaningful and substantial ways. Privacy as a commodity ignores the moral status of persons, shared interests in privacy, and the constitutive role of privacy in individual self-definition. Privacy as property tends to morph privacy into nothing more than one more form of consumerism (DAVIES; GANDY, 1993; RAAB, 1999). The moral status of human beings leaves no choice but to follow another path.

## RETHINKING PRIVACY: SCHOLARSHIP, SOCIAL CRITIQUE, AND MAKING POLICY

Despite some claims that privacy is too zealously protected (ETZIONI) or that privacy protection should be eliminated (BRIN), there is widespread consensus that the first generation of U.S. privacy initiatives that relied primarily on data protection laws and principles are no longer adequate for the protection of privacy in distributed, networked systems (AGRE & ROTENBERG; BENNETT & GRANT, 1999b). That does not mean, however, that law as a tool, used in concert with other strategies, is not useful for the protection of privacy of digital information. The law is a rhetorical device, a clear indication of what is expected in relations among persons and groups. Mores, norms, and everyday practices are made explicit and codified so that, no matter what their inadequacies, laws can communicate how various entities should treat one another (GANDY, 1993; WHITE). Further, the law is the primary tool in securing the public space where strictly individual matters, the creeping surveillance characteristic of contemporary digitized societies, and the market are kept at bay (D. S. ALLEN; LAPERRIÈRE). D. S. ALLEN, quoting the work of James Boyd White, says that law is a "method of constructing a world, a self, a life" (p. 103). GANDY (1993), however, also says that while law is a useful and catalyzing ideal, as a system it embodies and perpetuates inequities of all kinds.

It is clear that concerns with the protection of transaction-generated information, the privacy of medical information, work-place privacy, the commercialization of individually identifiable information, and other problems are not imaginary, nor are they evanescent. In some quarters, there is a largely optimistic view of the protection of personal and group privacy. The current author cannot share that optimism, although promising privacy-enhancing technologies may serve as the means for groups and individuals to protect themselves from asymmetric information power relations with corporations and governments (see BURKERT; CAVOUKIAN). Many commentators see hope for privacy protection in the assertion of property rights in information by the person(s) with whom the information is linked. The current author and others, however, question the efficacy and wisdom of this privacy-as-property approach. At the same time, the use of digital technologies to mobilize privacy advocates, to influence policy makers at all levels of government, and to keep a large number of persons apprised of major initiatives in the protection and erosion of digital privacy offer some measure of hope for the future.

That promise will be fulfilled if and only if American actors are willing to adopt the intervention of government into relationships Americans ordinarily consider "private"—those that involve commerce and property. While the Federal Trade Commission, the Better Business Bureau, and the ratings system of films by the Motion Picture Association of America all offer models of varying degrees of public and private intrusion into commercial relationships, the current political climate in the United States seems unlikely to support omnibus efforts to protect privacy by government.

There have been a number of very positive changes in the way that we conceptualize and seek to protect privacy in digital environments. For example, the U.S. executive and legislative branches of government have greatly loosened restrictions on the export of encryption technologies and, further, encouraged American citizens to use encryption more in their digital communications. Similarly, additional statutory and regulatory protections have been provided for telephone communication, including the numbers called, the time and length of calls, and the amount of money spent on telephone services. These initiatives are accompanied by a growing number of bills to protect privacy introduced in the U.S. Congress, many with little chance of passage or enforcement, but some with promise. The interest of the Federal Trade Commission, the development of the WORLD WIDE WEB CONSORTIUM's P3P scheme (despite its severe limitations, especially with regard to policy concerns), and initiatives to protect client lists from failed dot-coms all display an increased awareness in the U.S. polity of the need to protect digital privacy. Such initiatives cannot, however, seduce us into thinking that threats to digital privacy, however construed, from governmental and corporate sources are not real, ever-changing, and never-ending.

GLENDON sees hope for addressing important social conflicts if, especially in the United States, we can overcome our "disdain for politics" and "tap the reserves of wisdom, virtue, and imagination" that we exercise in our local communities (p. xii). While admitting that the prospects for this kind of effort are rather dim, Glendon asserts that recent global events, such as the development of politically and socially open societies around the world, offer some hope. While the concept of rights cannot fully describe nor support privacy protection, thinking in terms of the abstractions of liberal rights talk helps to prefigure a world where political egalitarianism and respect for the socially marginalized could come into being.

CARLSON concludes with a discussion of trends: more self-regulation in the private sector in fear of public intervention, increased concern with the protection of health and employee records, concern with electronic transfer of funds, and the like. He asserts that: "The most critical aspect of the 'intervention decade' will be the world-wide effort to establish administrative procedures for the handling of personal information that will balance the individual's right to privacy with the public's need to have information necessary to the preservation of democratic institutions" (p. 294).

What does it take to achieve a social fabric where digital privacy is protected, while institutions that need digital information to achieve socially recognized goals have access to it? BYRNE says that "privacy talk assumes a zone of inaccessibility, the . . . [limits] of which are determined collectively" (p. 650). If we accept that assertion, what are the implications? While the answers to these questions are uncertain, we can revisit one of the primary goals of this chapter: the examination of a variety of sources that are helping to develop both a new discursive practice and a new politics of privacy. There are several elements of this new practice and politics.

## General Concepts of Privacy

First, concepts of privacy must move beyond the simple public/ private dichotomy. Privacy builds and results from relationships, not a simple atomistic individualism, and involves important group interests. Privacy can never be understood if we think of it simply in terms of an individual's alienation from others, of property, of an essentialized self, of an a priori right, of technological imperatives, or of a commodity. It is only in bringing understanding of the complex roles of privacy in the lives of individuals and communities that we can begin to decide what is necessary to protect privacy from intrusion while encouraging the revelation and trust that make communities live.

Further, privacy and being in public are not incompatible, as demonstrated in the work about privacy in public. We must eliminate an understanding of privacy as complete secrecy; without such a move, we are left with a false choice between secrecy and what amounts to global dissemination. Such a false choice denies experience. This move also helps avoid the conceptual dead end of simple dichotomies (public/ private, regulated/unregulated) that rely on an assumption of balance between constituencies.

Second, we must clarify and specify the links between information privacy and privacy to act, sometimes phrased as freedom from and freedom to (A. L. ALLEN; ETZIONI; MACKINNON, 1987a; THOMSON, 1990). These concepts are also sometimes termed aesthetic and instrumental privacy, in the words of RULE ET AL. For example, ETZIONI's critique of the conflation of freedom from surveillance with freedom of self-determination results from both his atomistic view of privacy and his dismissal of the important contributions of gendered analyses of privacy to an understanding of it. Somewhat paradoxically, MACKINNON (1987a) shares Etzioni's sense that informational and act privacy are in fundamental tension and not merely two aspects of the same right. The increased ubiquity and power of networked technologies make these forms of privacy even more inextricably intertwined than ever. Because networked activities are increasingly constitutive of the modern individual, decisional and informational privacy are no longer so easily distinguished. PROSSER's concept of the privacy tort of intrusion underscores the false dichotomy that is so tempting to embrace—that between simple privacy intrusion and actual harm (see also COURT & ATKINSON). As discussed elsewhere, the tort is complete on intrusion: intrusion is the injury, and subsequent harm is not a precondition for the injury of intrusion to have occurred. Additionally, while concepts of privacy as property or as another kind of tort are useful, they are not sufficient to exhaust the meaning or complexity of privacy in the practices of ordinary life.

## Concepts of Digital Privacy

Political reliance on the Fair Information Practices, with their emphasis on only government, on record information, on stand-alone information systems, and on single use of information, is necessary but not sufficient to address privacy in an increasingly networked society where private organizations hold, manipulate, and sell information related to everyone. On a similar note, we must move the polity beyond belief in the efficacy of the self-regulation of commercial enterprises. Simple posting of privacy policies on corporate Web sites, while a step forward, is not sufficient to protect individuals or groups from digital privacy intrusions. Posting also will not allay users' fears about privacy invasions, thereby further eroding the health of electronic commerce. Instead, clients must be given as many opportunities to opt in as possible, instead of relying on clients' ignorance about privacy, relying on corporate extortion to bully clients into revealing information about themselves, or relying on the much weaker form of privacy protection offered by opt out (but see BURKERT; GOLDMAN). We must move, as suggested by RAAB (1999), from balancing to steering.

Corporate use of digital information must also be limited in several important ways: except in compelling circumstances and with users' explicit permission, information use should be as limited as possible;

information use should not go beyond the initial corporate body that collected it even if that organization is part of some larger entity; and clients' information should be destroyed rather than sold as a corporate asset in case of corporate bankruptcy or going out of business.

A final recommendation is that we must encourage organizations of all kinds, large and small, private and public, to overcome their fanatical devotion to computerized risk assessment for identifying the eligibility of clients for services, especially since classification systems implemented in digital systems often propagate discriminatory and inequitable practices. The reliance of contemporary enterprises on risk assessment to support information entrepreneurialism often creates new problems and seduces us with a false sense of certainty about what is unknowable. Further, risk assessment, especially that facilitated by computing, relies on many unexamined epistemic and representational assumptions that often cannot withstand interrogation.

### The Politically Involved Scholar and Practitioner

Besides writing, speaking, teaching, and being politically active, one of the most essential contributions that information scholars and practitioners can make to the privacy conversation is to know the law: source law (e.g., the U.S. Constitution); statutory law (e.g., the privacy statutes of many nation states); case law (e.g., Judge Brandeis' dissent in *Olmstead*); and administrative or regulatory law (e.g., regulations issued by the Federal Trade Commission). Society relies on us to do so.

More importantly, however, we need to go beyond legalistic thinking (GLENDON). Law is only one perspective on privacy; there are many others with significant claims to expertise and much to contribute to privacy analysis. Among these are cultural practices, local and contingent behavior, and multiple disciplines, including women's/gender studies, public policy, philosophy, rhetoric, sociology, and psychology.

Besides contributing to the conceptual evolution and maturity described above, practitioners and scholars must perform a number of other tasks. First, we must inform society at large, policy makers, and large enterprises of all kinds of our concerns about privacy, the weaknesses of current practice, and our recommendations about privacy protections, whatever those recommendations might be. Second, we need to identify and help alleviate the asymmetry of relations between large private and governmental enterprises on the one hand and citizens on the other. We need to encourage organizations to collect less information about citizens and to demonstrate to enterprises both public and private how the use of strong encryption, pseudonyms, and similar means can achieve the goals of providing information while still protecting citizens' real identities (see also AGRE, 1997a; CHAUM).

While the Fair Information Practices have significant weaknesses when applied to networked technologies, they are still useful for many purposes. The reliance of FIPs on individuals' knowledge and consent are reminiscent of similar values in research ethics. In research situations, the powerless (especially children), the mentally challenged, prisoners, those in the armed services, and the socially marginalized are given special protections. Institutional Review Boards, while intended to protect everyone from unethical research, are especially enjoined to protect the powerless. The powerless in privacy situations, which means almost everyone when compared to powerful governmental and private enterprises, need organized representation and protection from predation. Just as research ethics and the boards to protect them resulted from public outrage as well as formal governmental action, so must protections from damaging digital intrusions. And as the power of research ethics also springs from the committed care of ethical researchers in their professional practice, so self-regulation and responsible organizational policies will also serve as necessary but not sufficient guarantees for digital privacy.

A number of important and provocative questions posed by analysts either stress organizational interests over privacy interests or deny the importance of privacy entirely. Posner says that: "Legislatures are increasingly creating rights to conceal information that is material to prospective creditors and employers, and at the same time forcing corporations and other organizations [including governmental agencies] to publicize information whose confidentiality is necessary to their legitimate operation" (POSNER, 1984, p. 344). The assumptions on which such a statement are based must be questioned. Just because information is material to operations of such organizations, recalling the terminology of "legitimate business interests," does not mean that such interest trumps concerns with privacy, although, according to Posner's and others' econometric analyses, it should. Further, the basic asymmetry between individuals and organizations goes unexamined. There is a fundamental but questionable assertion throughout Posner's (1984) work that people cannot and should not be trusted to represent themselves honestly. Posner also says that discussions of what he calls the privacy question have been characterized by "cant, sloganeering, emotion, and loose thinking" (p. 345). His critique is on target, requiring us to respond with close analysis and fundamentally sound arguments while confronting and questioning the assumptions upon which his argument is built and the conclusions that he reaches.

ETZIONI, a trenchant critic of most privacy initiatives, also poses an important question that must be addressed: "To be realistic, the probability of returning the genie to the bottle is nil. Therefore, the real question is: Will this capacity be available only for the profit makers or also for public protection and other social purposes?" (p. 131). Those who do not share his antiprivacy sentiments must acknowledge his question while being sufficiently creative to deconstruct his assumptions and his political values.

ORREN notes that: "Conceptual transformations . . . track social practices" (p. 217). We need to act differently so that we will think differently; as BRUNER and GEERTZ say, we live suspended in webs of significance that we have created through our language and conceptual frameworks. If we want to define and protect the privacy of digital information, then we need to integrate more complex understandings of digital privacy into everyday social practice and discursive behavior. Orren continues: "If history is any guide . . . practices will out" (p. 218). Despite whatever kinds of legal, philosophical, moral, and other so-called guarantees of privacy we believe we have, what matters is what we as members of society do to create digital privacy by speaking, thinking, and other practices of everyday life. The call to action is immediate, and we can afford neither blind optimism nor despair. What remains is the work of inventing what we want society and digital communication to be. Our most important obligation is to help create the kind of society to which we aspire to belong.

## BIBLIOGRAPHY

AGRE, PHILIP E. 1994a. Surveillance and Capture: Two Models of Privacy. The Information Society. 1994; 10(2): 101-127. ISSN: 0197-2243.

AGRE, PHILIP E. 1994b. Understanding the Digital Individual. The Information Society. 1994; 10(2): 73-76. ISSN: 0197-2243.

AGRE, PHILIP E. 1997a. Beyond the Mirror World: Privacy and the Representational Practices of Computing. In: Agre, Philip E.; Rotenberg, Marc, eds. Technology and Privacy: The New Landscape. Cambridge, MA: The MIT Press; 1997. 29-61. ISBN: 0-262-01162-X.

AGRE, PHILIP E. 1997b. Introduction. In: Agre, Philip E.; Rotenberg, Marc, eds. Technology and Privacy: The New Landscape. Cambridge, MA: The MIT Press; 1997. 1-28. ISBN: 0-262-01162-X.

AGRE, PHILIP E. 1999. The Architecture of Identity: Embedding Privacy in Market Institutions. Information, Communication and Society. 1999; 2(1): 1-25. ISSN: 1369-118X.

AGRE, PHILIP E.; ROTENBERG, MARC, eds. 1997. Technology and Privacy: The New Landscape. Cambridge, MA: The MIT Press; 1997. 325p. ISBN: 0-262-01162-X.

ALDERMAN, ELLEN; KENNEDY, CAROLINE. 1997. The Right to Privacy. New York, NY: Vintage Books; 1997. 413p. ISBN: 0-679-41986-1.

ALFINO, MARK. 1998. Information Ethics in the Workplace: Traditional vs. Information Management Theory. Journal of Information Ethics. 1998; 7(1): 5-9. ISSN: 1061-9321.

ALLEN, ANITA L. 1988. Uneasy Access: Privacy for Women in a Free Society. Totowa, NJ: Rowman & Littlefield; 1988. 226p. ISBN: 0-8476-7327-8.

ALLEN, DAVID S. 1995. The Supreme Court and the Creation of an (In)active Public Sphere. In: Allen, David S.; Jensen, Robert, eds. Freeing the First Amendment: Critical Perspectives on Freedom of Expression. New York, NY: New York University Press; 1995. 93-113. ISBN: 0-8147-0638-X.

ALLEN, JONATHAN P. 1994. Mutual Control in the Newly Integrated Work Environments. The Information Society. 1994; 10(2): 129-138. ISSN: 0197-2243.

AMERICAN CIVIL LIBERTIES UNION. 1999. Privacy in America: Electronic Monitoring. Available WWW: http://www.aclu.org/library/pbr2.html.

AMERICAN PSYCHOLOGICAL ASSOCIATION. 1994. Publication Manual of the American Psychological Association. 4th edition. Washington, DC: American Psychological Association; 1994. 368p. ISBN: 1-55798-241-4.

ANDERSEN, DAVID F.; DAWES, SHARON S. 1991. Government Information Management: A Primer and Casebook. Englewood Cliffs, NJ: Prentice-Hall; 1991. 227p. ISBN: 0-13-361866-8.

BAASE, SARA. 1997. A Gift of Fire: Social, Legal, and Ethical Issues in Computing. Upper Saddle River, NJ: Prentice Hall; 1997. 382p. ISBN: 0-13-458779-0.

BEARD, JOSEPH J. 1974. The Copyright Issue. In: Cuadra, Carlos A., ed. Annual Review of Information Science and Technology: Volume 9. Washington, DC: American Society for Information Science; 1974. 381-411. ISBN: 0-87715-209-8; CODEN: ARISBC.

BELLAH, ROBERT N.; MADSEN, RICHARD; SULLIVAN, WILLIAM M.; SWIDLER, ANN; TIPTON, STEVEN. 1996. Habits of the Heart: Individualism and Commitment in American Life. Updated edition. Berkeley, CA: University of California Press; 1996. 355p. ISBN: 0-520-20568-5.

BELOTTI, VICTORIA. 1997. Design for Privacy in Multimedia Computing and Communications Environments. In: Agre, Philip E.; Rotenberg, Marc, eds. Technology and Privacy: The New Landscape. Cambridge, MA: The MIT Press; 1997. 63-98. ISBN: 0-262-01162-X.

BENHABIB, SEYLA. 1992. Models of Public Space: Hannah Arendt, the Liberal Tradition, and Jürgen Habermas. In: Calhoun, Craig, ed. Habermas and the Public Sphere. Cambridge, MA: The MIT Press; 1992. 73-98. ISBN: 0-262-53114-3.

BENNETT, COLIN J. 1992. Regulating Privacy: Data Protection and Public Policy in Europe and the United States. Ithaca, NY: Cornell University Press; 1992. 263p. ISBN: 0-8014-2611-1.

BENNETT, COLIN J. 1995. The Political Economy of Privacy: A Review of the Literature. Prepared for the Center for Social and Legal Research, DOE Human Genome Project. Available WWW: http://web.uvic.ca/~polisci/bennett/research/gnom.htm.

BENNETT, COLIN J. 1997. Convergence Revisited: Toward a Global Policy for the Protection of Personal Data? In: Agre, Philip E.; Rotenberg, Marc, eds. Technology and Privacy: The New Landscape. Cambridge, MA: The MIT Press; 1997. 99-123. ISBN: 0-262-01162-X.

BENNETT, COLIN J. 1998. The EU Data Protection Directive: The North American Response. Presentation to the 11th Annual Conference "Privacy Laws and Business," St. John's College, Cambridge. Available WWW: http://web.uvic.ca/~polisci/bennett/research/plb98.htm.

BENNETT, COLIN; GRANT, REBECCA. 1999a. Introduction. In: Bennett, Colin; Grant, Rebecca, eds. Visions of Privacy: Policy Choices for the Digital Age. Toronto, Canada: University of Toronto Press; 1999. 4-16. ISBN: 0-8020-8050-2.

BENNETT, COLIN; GRANT, REBECCA, eds. 1999b. Visions of Privacy: Policy Choices for the Digital Age. Toronto, Canada: University of Toronto Press; 1999. 288p. ISBN: 0-8020-8050-2.

BERGER, PETER L.; LUCKMANN, THOMAS. 1989. The Social Construction of Reality: A Treatise in the Sociology of Knowledge. New York, NY: Anchor Books; 1989. 219p. ISBN: 0-385-05898-5.

BERK, GERALD. 1994. Alternative Tracks: The Constitution of American Industrial Order, 1865-1917. Baltimore, MD: The Johns Hopkins University Press; 1994. 243p. ISBN: 0-8018-4656-0.

BERNERS-LEE, TIM. 1999. Weaving the Web: The Original Design and Ultimate Destiny of the World Wide Web by its Inventor. With Mark Fischetti. New York, NY: HarperSanFrancisco; 1999. 226p. ISBN: 0-06-251586-1.

BERNSTEIN, PETER L. 1996. The New Religion of Risk Management. Harvard Business Review. 1996; 74(2): 47-51. ISSN: 0017-8012.

BEZANSON, RANDALL P. 1992. The Right to Privacy Revisited: Privacy, News, and Social Change, 1890-1990. California Law Review. 1992; 30(5): 1133-1175. ISSN: 0008-1221.

BIELEFIELD, ARLENE; CHEESEMAN, LAWRENCE. 1994. Maintaining the Privacy of Library Records: A Handbook and Guide. New York, NY: Neal-Schuman; 1994. 203p. ISBN: 1-55570-066-7.

BISHOP, ANN PETERSON; STAR, SUSAN LEIGH. 1996. Social Informatics of Digital Library Use and Infrastructure. In: Williams, Martha E., ed. Annual Review of Information Science and Technology: Volume 31. Medford, NJ: Information Today, Inc. for the American Society for Information Science; 1996. 301-401. ISSN: 0066-4200; ISBN: 1-57387-033-1; CODEN: ARISBC.

BLOUSTEIN, EDWARD J. 1984. Privacy as an Aspect of Human Dignity: An Answer to Dean Prosser. In: Schoeman, Ferdinand David, ed. Philosophical Dimensions of Privacy: An Anthology. Cambridge, UK: Cambridge University Press; 1984. 156-202. ISBN: 0-521-25555-4.

BOLING, PATRICIA. 1996. Privacy and the Politics of Intimate Life. Ithaca, NY: Cornell University Press; 1996. 192p. ISBN: 0-8014-8351-4.

BOYLE, JAMES. 1997. A Politics of Intellectual Property: Environmentalism for the Net? Duke Law Journal. 1997; 47(1): 87-116. ISSN: 0012-7086.

BRAMAN, SANDRA. 1995. Policy for the Net and the Internet. In: Williams, Martha E., ed. Annual Review of Information Science and Technology: Volume 30. Medford, NJ: Information Today, Inc. for the American Society for Information Science; 1995. 5-75. ISSN: 0066-4200; ISBN: 1-57387-019-6; CODEN: ARISBC.

BRANSCOMB, ANNE WELLS. 1994. Who Owns Information? From Privacy to Public Access. New York, NY: BasicBooks; 1994. 241p. ISBN: 0-465-09175-X.

BRIEN, ANDREW. 1998. Professional Ethics and the Culture of Trust. Journal of Business Ethics. 1998; 17(4): 391-409. ISSN: 0167-4544.

BRIN, DAVID. 1998. The Transparent Society: Will Technology Force Us to Choose Between Privacy and Freedom? Reading, MA: Perseus Books; 1998. 378p. ISBN: 0-7382-0144-8.

BRINKLEY, ALAN. 1997a. Liberty and Community. In: Brinkley, Alan; Polsby, Nelson W.; Sullivan, Kathleen M., eds. New Federalist Papers: Essays in Defense of the Constitution. New York, NY: W.W. Norton; 1997. 87-101. ISBN: 0-393-04619-2.

BRINKLEY, ALAN. 1997b. The Privatization of Public Discourse. In: Brinkley, Alan; Polsby, Nelson W.; Sullivan, Kathleen M., eds. New Federalist Papers: Essays in Defense of the Constitution. New York, NY: W.W. Norton; 1997. 139-150. ISBN: 0-393-04619-2.

BROWN, WENDY. 1995. States of Injury: Power and Freedom in Late Modernity. Princeton, NJ: Princeton University Press; 1995. 202p. ISBN: 0-691-02990-3 .

BRUNER, JEROME. 1990. Acts of Meaning. Cambridge, MA: Harvard University Press; 1990. 181p. ISBN: 0-674-00360-8.

BUCKOVICH, SUZY A.; RIPPEN, HELGA E.; ROZEN, MICHAEL J. 1999. Driving Toward Guiding Principles: A Goal for Privacy, Confidentiality, and Security of Health Information. Journal of the American Medical Informatics Association. 1999; 6(2): 122-133. ISSN: 1067-5027.

BURKERT, HERBERT. 1997. Privacy-Enhancing Technologies: Typology, Critique, Vision. In: Agre, Philip E.; Rotenberg, Marc, eds. Technology and Privacy: The New Landscape. Cambridge, MA: The MIT Press; 1997. 125-142. ISBN: 0-262-01162-X.

BYRNE, EDMUND F. 1998. Privacy. In: Encyclopedia of Applied Ethics: Volume 3. San Diego, CA: Academic Press; 1998. 649-659. ISBN: 0-12-227068-1.

CALHOUN, CRAIG, ed. 1992. Habermas and the Public Sphere. Cambridge, MA: The MIT Press; 1992. 498p. ISBN: 0-262-53114-3.

CALHOUN, CRAIG. 1998. Community without Propinquity Revisited: Communications Technology and the Transformation of the Urban Public Sphere. Sociological Inquiry. 1998; 68(3): 373-397. ISSN: 0038-0245.

CAMP, L. JEAN. 1999. Web Security and Privacy: An American Perspective. The Information Society. 1999; 15(4): 249-256. ISSN: 0197-2243.

CAMPBELL, KARLYN KOHRS. 1996. The Rhetorical Act. 2nd edition. Belmont, CA: Wadsworth Publishing; 1996. 398p. ISBN: 0-534-16752-7.

CAREY, JAMES W. 1988. Communication as Culture: Essays on Media and Society. Boston, MA: Unwin Hyman; 1988. 241p. ISBN: 0-04-445064-8.

CAREY v. POPULATION SERVICES INTERNATIONAL. 1977. 431 U.S. 678, 687.

CARLSON, WALTER M. 1977. Privacy. In: Williams, Martha E., ed. Annual Review of Information Science and Technology: Volume 12. White Plains,

NY: Knowledge Industry Publications, Inc. for the American Society for Information Science; 1977. 279-305. ISSN: 0066-4200; ISBN: 0-914236-11-3; CODEN: ARISBC.

CARMAN, DAWN MURTO. 1997. Balancing Patient Confidentiality and Release of Information. In: Flood, Barbara, ed. Personal Privacy: An Introduction to Some Issues and What to Do about Them. Bulletin of the American Society for Information Science. 1997; 23(3): 16-17. ISSN: 0095-4403.

CARPENTER v. UNITED STATES. 1987. 484 U.S. 19.

CARROLL, JOHN M. 1996. Computer Security. 3rd edition. Boston, MA: Butterworth-Heinemann; 1996. 648p. ISBN: 0-7506-9600-1.

CASTELLS, MANUEL. 1996. The Rise of the Network Society. Volume I, The Information Age: Economy, Society and Culture. Cambridge, MA: Blackwell; 1996. 556p. ISBN: 1-55786-617-1.

CASTELLS, MANUEL. 1998. End of Millennium. Volume III, The Information Age: Economy, Society and Culture. Malden, MA: Blackwell; 1998. 418p. ISBN: 1-55786-871-9.

CATE, FRED H. 1997. Privacy in the Information Age. Washington, DC: Brookings Institution Press; 1997. 248p. ISBN: 0-8157-1316-9.

CAVOUKIAN, ANN. 1999. The Promise of Privacy-Enhancing Technologies: Applications in Health Information Networks. In: Bennett, Colin; Grant, Rebecca, eds. Visions of Privacy: Policy Choices for the Digital Age. Toronto, Canada: University of Toronto Press; 1999. 116-145. ISBN: 0-8020-8050-2.

CAVOUKIAN, ANN; TAPSCOTT, DON. 1997. Who Knows: Safeguarding Your Privacy in a Networked World. New York, NY: McGraw-Hill; 1997. 221p. ISBN: 0-07-063320-7.

CENTER FOR PUBLIC INTEGRITY. 1998. Nothing Sacred: The Politics of Privacy. Washington, DC: The Center for Public Integrity; 1998. 73p. ISBN: 1-882583-12-4. Available WWW: http://www.publicintegrity.org/nothing_sacred.html.

CHAUM, DAVID. 1985. Security without Identification: Transaction Systems to Make Big Brother Obsolete. Communications of the ACM. 1985; 28(10): 1030-1044. ISSN: 0001-0782.

CLARKE, ROGER A. 1988. Information Technology and Dataveillance. Communications of the ACM. 1988; 31(5): 498-512. ISSN: 0001-0782.

CLARKE, ROGER A. 1994. The Digital Persona and Its Application to Data Surveillance. The Information Society. 1994; 10(2): 77-92. ISSN: 0197-2243.

CLEEK, MARGARET ANNE; LEONARD, SHERRY LYNN. 1998. Can Corporate Codes of Ethics Influence Behavior? Journal of Business Ethics. 1998; 17(5): 619-630. ISSN: 0167-4544.

CLOUD, MORGAN. 1996. The Fourth Amendment during the Lochner Era: Privacy, Property, and Liberty in Constitutional Theory. Stanford Law Review. 1996; 48: 555-631. ISSN: 0038-9765.

COLLINS, LOUISE. 1994. Gossip: A Feminist Defense. In: Goodman, Robert F.; Ben-Ze'ev, Aaron, eds. Good Gossip. Lawrence, KS: University Press of Kansas; 1994. 100-105. ISBN: 0-7006-0669-6.

COOMBS, MARY I. 1987. Shared Privacy and the Fourth Amendment, or the Rights of Relationships. California Law Review. 1987; 75(5): 1593-1664. ISSN: 0008-1221.

COURT, RANDOLPH H.; ATKINSON, ROBERT D. 1999. On-Line Privacy Standards: The Case for a Limited Federal Role in a Self-Regulatory Regime. A Report of the Technology & The New Economy Project of the Progressive Policy Institute. 1999 March 1. 8p. Available WWW: http://www.ppionline.org/ppi_ka.cfm?knlgAreaID=107.

CULNAN, MARY J. 1993. "How Did They Get My Name?": An Exploratory Investigation of Consumer Attitudes toward Secondary Information Use. MIS Quarterly. 1993; 17(3): 341-363. ISSN: 0276-7783.

CULNAN, MARY J. 1999a. Georgetown Internet Privacy Policy Survey: Report to the Federal Trade Commission. Available WWW: http://www.msb.edu/faculty/culnanm/gippshome.html.

CULNAN, MARY J. 1999b. Privacy and the Top 100 Web Sites: Report to the Federal Trade Commission. Prepared for the Online Privacy Alliance. Available WWW: http://www.msb.edu/faculty/culnanm/gippshome.html.

CULNAN, MARY J.; ARMSTRONG, PAMELA K. 1999. Information Privacy Concerns, Procedural Fairness and Impersonal Trust: An Empirical Investigation. Organization Science. 1999; 10(1): 104-115. ISSN: 1047-7039.

CULNAN, MARY J.; BIES, ROBERT J. 1999. Managing Privacy Concerns Strategically: The Implications of Fair Information Practices for Marketing in the Twenty-First Century. In: Bennett, Colin; Grant, Rebecca, eds. Visions of Privacy: Policy Choices for the Digital Age. Toronto, Canada: University of Toronto Press; 1999. 149-167. ISBN: 0-8020-8050-2.

CULNAN, MARY J.; MILBERG, SANDRA J. 1999. Consumer Privacy. Available WWW: http://www.msb.edu/faculty/culnanm/research/conspriv.pdf.

CULNAN, MARY J.; SMITH, H. JEFF. 1995. Lotus Marketplace: Households . . . Managing Information Privacy Concerns. In: Johnson, Deborah G.; Nissenbaum, Helen, eds. Computers, Ethics & Social Values. Englewood Cliffs, NJ: Prentice Hall; 1995. 269-278. ISBN: 0-13-103110-4.

DAHL, TOVE STANG; SNARE, ANNIKA. 1978. The Coercion of Privacy: A Feminist Perspective. In: Smart, Carol; Smart, Barry, eds. Women, Sexuality and Social Control. London, UK: Routledge & Kegan Paul; 1978. 8-26. ISBN: 0-7100-8723-3.

DAM, KENNETH W.; LIN, HERBERT S., eds. 1996. Cryptography's Role in Securing the Information Society. Committee to Study National Cryptography Policy, Computer Science and Telecommunications Board, Commission on Physical Sciences, Mathematics, and Applications, National Research Council. Washington, DC: National Academy Press; 1996. 688p. ISBN: 0-309-05475-3.

DARKO, KENDRA L. 1999. The Power of Opt-In. American Demographics. 1999; 43(10): 4043. ISSN: 0163-4089.

DAVIES, SIMON G. 1997. Re-Engineering the Right to Privacy: How Privacy Has Been Transformed from a Right to a Commodity. In: Agre, Philip E.;

Rotenberg, Marc, eds. Technology and Privacy: The New Landscape. Cambridge, MA: The MIT Press; 1997. 143-165. ISBN: 0-262-01162-X.

DAVIS, LUKE; DOMM, JENNIFER A.; KONIKOFF, MICHAEL R.; MILLER, RANDOLPH A. 1999. Attitudes of First-Year Medical Students toward the Confidentiality of Computerized Patient Records. Journal of the American Medical Informatics Association. 1999; 6(2): 53-60. ISSN: 1067-5027.

DE SOUSA, RONALD. 1994. In Praise of Gossip: Indiscretion as a Saintly Virtue. In: Goodman, Robert F.; Ben-Ze´ev, Aaron, eds. Good Gossip. Lawrence, KS: University Press of Kansas; 1994. 23-33. ISBN: 0-7006-0669-6.

DENNING, DOROTHY. 1991. The United States vs. Craig Neidorf. Communications of the ACM. 1991; 34(3): 24-32. ISSN: 0001-0782.

DERLEGA, VALERIAN J.; METTS, SANDRA; PETRONIO, SANDRA; MARGULIS, STEPHEN T. 1993. Self-Disclosure. Newbury Park, CA: Sage; 1993. 142p. ISBN: 0-8039-3954-X.

DIFFIE, WHITFIELD; LANDAU, SUSAN. 1998. Privacy on the Line: The Politics of Wiretapping and Encryption. Cambridge, MA: The MIT Press; 1998. 342p. ISBN: 0-262-04167-7.

DYSON, ESTHER. 1998. Privacy Protection: Time to Think and Act Locally and Globally. First Monday. 1998; 3(6). ISSN: 1396-0466. Available WWW: http://www.firstmonday.dk/issues/issue3_6/dyson/index.html.

EISENSTADT v. BAIRD. 1972. 405 U.S. 438, 453.

ELECTRONIC PRIVACY INFORMATION CENTER. 1997. Surfer Beware: Personal Privacy and the Internet. Available WWW: http://www.epic.org/reports/surfer-beware.html.

ELEY, GEOFF. 1992. Nations, Publics, and Political Cultures: Placing Habermas in the Nineteenth Century. In: Calhoun, Craig, ed. Habermas and the Public Sphere. Cambridge, MA: The MIT Press; 1992. 289-339. ISBN: 0-262-53114-3.

ETZIONI, AMITAI. 1999. The Limits of Privacy. New York, NY: Basic Books; 1999. 280p. ISBN: 0-465-04089-6.

EUROPEAN UNION. 1995. Common Position (EC) No /95. On the Protection of Individuals with Regard to the Processing of Personal Data and on the Free Movement of Such Data. Available WWW: http://europa.eu.int/ISPO/legal/en/dataprot/compenfr.html.

FARRELL, HELEN; FARRELL, BRIAN J. 1998. The Language of Business Codes of Ethics: Implications of Knowledge and Power. Journal of Business Ethics. 1998; 17(5): 587-601. ISSN: 0167-4544.

FEATHERMAN, JOHN. 1997. Moses Meets Big Brother: The Ten Commandments of Privacy. In: Flood, Barbara, ed. Personal Privacy: An Introduction to Some Issues and What to Do about Them. Bulletin of the American Society for Information Science. 1997; 23(3): 26-27. ISSN: 0095-4403.

FERRARO, ANTHONY. 1998. Electronic Commerce: The Issues and Challenges to Creating Trust and a Positive Image in Consumer Sales on the World Wide Web. First Monday. 1998; 3(6). ISSN: 1396-0466. Available WWW: http://www.firstmonday.dk/issues/issue3_6/ferraro/index.html.

FLAHERTY, DAVID H. 1989. Protecting Privacy in Surveillance Societies: The Federal Republic of Germany, Sweden, France, Canada, and the United States. Chapel Hill, NC: The University of North Carolina Press; 1989. 483p. ISBN: 0-8078-1871-2.

FLAHERTY, DAVID H. 1997. Controlling Surveillance: Can Privacy Protection Be Made Effective? In: Agre, Philip E.; Rotenberg, Marc, eds. Technology and Privacy: The New Landscape. Cambridge, MA: The MIT Press; 1997. 167-192. ISBN: 0-262-01162-X.

FLAHERTY, DAVID H. 1999. Visions of Privacy: Past, Present, and Future. In: Bennett, Colin; Grant, Rebecca, eds. Visions of Privacy: Policy Choices for the Digital Age. Toronto, Canada: University of Toronto Press; 1999. 19-38. ISBN: 0-8020-8050-2.

FLOOD, BARBARA. 1997a. The Emotionality of Privacy. In: Flood, Barbara A., ed. Personal Privacy: An Introduction to Some Issues and What to Do About Them. Bulletin of the American Society for Information Science. 1997; 23(3): 7-8. ISSN: 0095-4403.

FLOOD, BARBARA, ed. 1997b. Personal Privacy: An Introduction to Some Issues and What to Do about Them. Bulletin of the American Society for Information Science. 1997; 23(3): 4-27. ISSN: 0095-4403.

FLOOD, BARBARA; LUTZ, WILLIAM E. 1997. Creeping Problems: Database Development and Privacy Loss. In: Flood, Barbara, ed. Personal Privacy: An Introduction to Some Issues and What to Do about Them. Bulletin of the American Society for Information Science. 1997; 23(3): 5-6. ISSN: 0095-4403.

FORESTER, TOM; MORRISON, PERRY. 1994. Computer Ethics: Cautionary Tales and Ethical Dilemmas in Computing. 2nd edition. Cambridge, MA: The MIT Press; 1994. 347p. ISBN: 0-262-56073-9.

FOUCAULT, MICHEL. 1977. Discipline and Punish: The Birth of the Prison. Translated from the French by Alan Sheridan. New York, NY: Pantheon Books; 1977. 333p. ISBN: 0-394-49942-5.

FRASER, NANCY. 1992. Rethinking the Public Sphere: A Contribution to the Critique of Actually Existing Democracy. In: Calhoun, Craig, ed. Habermas and the Public Sphere. Cambridge, MA: The MIT Press; 1992. 109-142. ISBN: 0-262-53114-3.

FRAWLEY, KATHLEEN A. 1997. Testimony on Health Information Confidentiality. In: Flood, Barbara, ed. Personal Privacy: An Introduction to Some Issues and What to Do about Them. Bulletin of the American Society for Information Science. 1997; 23(3): 22-25. ISSN: 0095-4403.

FRAZER, ELIZABETH; LACEY, NICOLA. 1993. The Politics of Community: A Feminist Critique of the Liberal-Communitarian Debate. New York, NY: Harvester Wheatsheaf; 1993. 268p. ISBN: 0-7450-0861-5.

FREEDMAN, WARREN. 1987. The Right of Privacy in the Computer Age. New York, NY: Quorum Books; 1987. 163p. ISBN: 0-89930-187-8.

FROW, JOHN. 1997. Gift and Commodity. In: Frow, John. Time and Commodity Culture: Essays in Cultural Theory and Postmodernity. Oxford, UK: Clarendon Press; 1997. 102-217. ISBN: 0-19-815947-1.

GANDY, OSCAR H. 1993. The Panoptic Sort: A Political Economy of Personal Information. Boulder, CO: Westview Press; 1993. 283p. ISBN: 0-8133-1656-1.

GANDY, OSCAR H. 1995. It's Discrimination, Stupid! In: Brook, James; Boal, Iain A., eds. Resisting the Virtual Life: The Culture and Politics of Information. San Francisco, CA: City Lights; 1995. 35-47. ISBN: 0-87286-299-2.

GAUTHRONET, SERGE; NATHAN, FRÉDÉRIC. 1998. On-Line Services and Data Protection and the Protection of Privacy: Study for the Commission of the European Community (DG XV). Available WWW: http://europa.eu.int/comm/internal_market/en/dataprot/studies/servint.htm.

GAVISON, RUTH. 1995. Privacy and the Limits of Law. In: Johnson, Deborah G.; Nissenbaum, Helen, eds. Computers, Ethics & Social Values. Englewood Cliffs, NJ: Prentice Hall; 1995. 332-351. ISBN: 0-13-103110-4.

GEERTZ, CLIFFORD. 1973. The Interpretation of Cultures. New York, NY: Basic Books; 1973. 470p. ISBN: 0-465-03425-X.

GELLMAN, ROBERT. 1995. Public Records—Access, Privacy, and Public Policy: A Discussion Paper. Government Information Quarterly. 1995; 12(4): 391-425. ISSN: 0740-624X.

GELLMAN, ROBERT. 1996. Privacy. In: Hernon, Peter; McClure, Charles R.; Relyea, Harold C., eds. Federal Information Policies in the 1990s: Views and Perspectives. Norwood, NJ: Ablex; 1996. 137-163. ISBN: 1-56750-283-0.

GELLMAN, ROBERT. 1997a. Conflict and Overlap in Privacy Regulation: National, International, and Private. In: Kahin, Brian; Nesson, Charles, eds. Borders in Cyberspace: Information Policy and the Global Information Infrastructure. Cambridge, MA: The MIT Press; 1997. 255-282. ISBN: 0-262-11220-5.

GELLMAN, ROBERT. 1997b. Does Privacy Law Work? In: Agre, Philip E.; Rotenberg, Marc, eds. Technology and Privacy: The New Landscape. Cambridge, MA: The MIT Press; 1997. 193-218. ISBN: 0-262-01162-X.

GELLMAN, ROBERT. 1999. Personal, Legislative, and Technical Privacy Choices: The Case of Health Privacy Reform in the United States. In: Bennett, Colin; Grant, Rebecca, eds. Visions of Privacy: Policy Choices for the Digital Age. Toronto, Canada: University of Toronto Press; 1999. 129-145. ISBN: 0-8020-8050-2.

GILLIS, ROBERT PETER; RILEY, THOMAS B. 1997. Privacy in the Information Age: A Handbook for Government and Industry Professionals. Washington, DC: Government Technology Press; 1997. 286p. OCLC: 37433547.

GIVENS, BETH. 1997. The Privacy Rights Handbook: How to Take Control of Your Personal Information. With the Privacy Rights Clearinghouse and Dale Fetherling. New York, NY: Avon Books; 1997. 335p. ISBN: 0-380-78684-2.

GLENDON, MARY ANN. 1991. Rights Talk: The Impoverishment of Political Discourse. New York, NY: The Free Press; 1991. 218p. ISBN: 0-02-911825-5.

GLOBAL INTERNET LIBERTY CAMPAIGN. 1998. Privacy and Human Rights: An International Survey of Privacy Laws and Practice. Available WWW: http://www.gilc.org/privacy/survey/.

GOFFMAN, ERVING. 1990. The Presentation of Self in Everyday Life. New York, NY: Anchor Books; 1990. 259p. ISBN: 0-385-09402-7.

GOLDMAN, JANLORI. 1999. Privacy and Individual Empowerment in the Interactive Age. In: Bennett, Colin; Grant, Rebecca, eds. Visions of Privacy: Policy Choices for the Digital Age. Toronto, Canada: University of Toronto Press; 1999. 97-115. ISBN: 0-8020-8050-2.

GOODMAN, ROBERT F.; BEN-ZE'EV, AARON, eds. 1994. Good Gossip. Lawrence, KS: University Press of Kansas; 1994. 215p. ISBN: 0-7006-0669-6.

GRISWOLD v. CONNECTICUT. 1965. 381 U.S. 479.

HABERMAS, JÜRGEN. 1991. The Structural Transformation of the Public Sphere: An Inquiry into a Category of Bourgeois Society. Cambridge, MA: The MIT Press; 1991. (Translated by Thomas Burger and Frederick Lawrence). 301p. ISBN: 0-262-58108-6.

HAGEL, JOHN, III; RAYPORT, JEFFREY F. 1997. The Coming Battle for Customer Information. Harvard Business Review. 1997; 75(1): 64-76. ISSN: 0017-8012.

HALBERT, DEBORA J. 1999. Intellectual Property in the Information Age: The Politics of Expanding Ownership Rights. Westport, CT: Quorum; 1999. 186p. ISBN: 1-56720-254-3.

HALL, EDWARD T. 1959. The Silent Language. Greenwich, CT: Fawcett; 1959. 192p. OCLC: 172930.

HALL, EDWARD T. 1966. The Hidden Dimension. Garden City, NY: Doubleday; 1966. 201p. OCLC: 203769.

HARRIS v. MCRAE. 1980. 448 U.S. 297.

HATCH, DENISON. 1996. Privacy: How Much Data Do Direct Marketers Really Need. In: Kling, Rob, ed. Computerization and Controversy: Value Conflicts and Social Choices. 2nd edition. San Diego, CA: Academic Press; 1996. 669-678. ISBN: 0-12-415040-3.

HAYWOOD, TREVOR. 1998. Global Networks and the Myth of Equality: Trickle Down or Trickle Away? In: Loader, Brian, ed. Cyberspace Divide: Equality, Agency and Policy in the Information Society. London, UK: Routledge; 1998. 19-34. ISBN: 0-415-16969-0.

HELLING, BILL. 1998. Web-Site Sensitivity to Privacy Concerns: Collecting Personally Identifiable Information and Passing Persistent Cookies. First Monday. 1998; 3(2). ISSN: 1396-0466. Available WWW: http://www.firstmonday.dk/issues/issue3_2/helling/index.html.

HERNON, PETER; MCCLURE, CHARLES R. 1993. Electronic U.S. Government Information: Policy Issues and Directions. In: Williams, Martha E., ed. Annual Review of Information Science and Technology: Volume 28. Medford, NJ: Learned Information, Inc. for the American Society for Information Science; 1993. 45-110. ISSN: 0066-4200; ISBN: 0-938734-75-X; CODEN: ARISBC.

HERNON, PETER; RELYEA, HAROLD C. 1986. The U.S. Government as a Publisher. In: Williams, Martha E., ed. Annual Review of Information Science and Technology: Volume 23. Amsterdam, The Netherlands: Elsevier Science Publishers for the American Society for Information Science; 1986. 3-33. ISSN: 0066-4200; ISBN: 0-444-70543-0; CODEN: ARISBC.

HILL, WILLIAM C.; HOLLAN, JAMES D. 1994. History-Enriched Digital
    Objects: Prototypes and Policy Issues. The Information Society. 1994;
    10(2): 139-145. ISSN: 0197-2243.
HINE, CHRISTIE; EVE, JULIET. 1998. Privacy in the Marketplace. The
    Information Society. 1998; 14(4): 253-262. ISSN: 0197-2243.
HODSON, SARA S. 1991. Private Lives: Confidentiality in Manuscripts
    Collections. Cases from the Huntington Library; Presented to the Society
    of California Archivists. Rare Books & Manuscripts Librarianship. 1991;
    6(2): 108-118. ISSN: 0884-450X.
HOLDEN,VICTORIA SMITH. 1995. Effective Voice Rights in the Workplace.
    In: Allen, David S.; Jensen, Robert, eds. Freeing the First Amendment:
    Critical Perspectives on Freedom of Expression. New York, NY: New York
    University Press; 1995. 114-139. ISBN: 0-8147-0638-X.
HOWE, ADRIAN. 1991. The Problem of Privatized Injuries: Feminist Strate-
    gies for Litigation. In: Fineman, Martha Albertson; Thomadsen, Nancy
    Sweet, eds. At the Boundaries of Law: Feminism and Legal Theory. New
    York, NY: Routledge; 1991. 148-167. ISBN: 0-415-90306-8.
HUNTER, LAWRENCE. 1995. Public Image. In: Johnson, Deborah G.;
    Nissenbaum, Helen, eds. Computers, Ethics & Social Values. Englewood
    Cliffs, NJ: Prentice Hall; 1995. 293-299. ISBN: 0-13-103110-4.
INGLIS, FRED. 1993. Cultural Studies. Oxford, UK: Blackwell; 1993. 262p.
    ISBN: 0-631-18454-6.
IPPEL, PIETER; DE HEIJ, GUUS; CROUWERS, BART. 1995. Privacy Disputed.
    The Hague, The Netherlands: SDU; 1995. 140p. ISBN: 90-346-3196-6.
JOHNSON, DEBORAH G. 1994. Computer Ethics. 2nd edition. Englewood
    Cliffs, NJ: Prentice Hall; 1994. 181p. ISBN: 0-13-290339-3.
JOHNSON, DEBORAH G. 1997. Ethics Online. Communications of the ACM.
    1997; 40(1): 60-65. ISSN: 0001-0782.
JOHNSON, DEBORAH G.; NISSENBAUM, HELEN, eds. 1995. Computers,
    Ethics & Social Values. Englewood Cliffs, NJ: Prentice-Hall; 1995. 714p.
    ISBN: 0-13-103110-4.
KAHIN, BRIAN; NESSON, CHARLES, eds. 1997. Borders in Cyberspace:
    Information Policy and the Global Information Infrastructure. Cambridge,
    MA: The MIT Press; 1997. 374p. ISBN: 0-262-11220-5.
KAPLAN, ABRAHAM. 1979. The Conduct of Inquiry: Methodology for
    Behavioral Science. New York, NY: Harper & Row; 1979. 428p. ISBN: 0-
    352-11700-1.
KAPTEIN, MUEL; WEMPE, JOHAN. 1998. Twelve Gordian Knots When
    Developing an Organizational Code of Ethics. Journal of Business Ethics.
    1998; 17(8): 853-869. ISSN: 0167-4544.
KATSH, M. ETHAN. 1995. Shining Lights: Privacy. In: Katsh, M. Ethan. Law
    in a Digital World. New York, NY: Oxford University Press; 1995. 227-236.
    ISBN: 0-19-508017-3.
KATZ v. UNITED STATES. 1967. 389 U.S. 347, 351.
KENT, STEPHEN T. 1993. Internet Privacy Enhanced Mail. Communications
    of the ACM. 1993; 36(8): 48-60. ISSN: 0001-0782.
KEPLINGER, MICHAEL S. 1980. Copyright and Information Technology. In:
    Williams, Martha E., ed. Annual Review of Information Science and

Technology: Volume 15. White Plains, NY: Knowledge Industry Publications, Inc. for the American Society for Information Science; 1980. 3-33. ISSN: 0066-4200; ISBN: 0-914236-65-2; CODEN: ARISBC.

KILGER, MAX. 1994. The Digital Individual. The Information Society. 1994; 10(2): 93-99. ISSN: 0197-2243.

KLING, ROB, ed. 1996a. Computerization and Controversy: Value Conflicts and Social Choices. 2nd edition. San Diego, CA: Academic Press; 1996. 961p. ISBN: 0-12-415040-3.

KLING, ROB. 1996b. Information Technologies and the Shifting Balance between Privacy and Social Control. In: Kling, Rob, ed. Computerization and Controversy: Value Conflicts and Social Choices. 2nd edition. San Diego, CA: Academic Press; 1996. 614-636. ISBN: 0-12-415040-3.

KLING, ROB; ACKERMAN, MARK S.; ALLEN, JONATHAN P. 1996. Information Entrepreneurialism, Information Technologies, and the Continuing Vulnerability of Privacy. In: Kling, Rob, ed. Computerization and Controversy: Value Conflicts and Social Choices. 2nd edition. San Diego, CA: Academic Press; 1996. 727-743. ISBN: 0-12-415040-3.

LANDAU, SUSAN; KENT, STEPHEN; BROOKS, CLINT; CHARNEY, SCOTT; DENNING, DOROTHY; DIFFIE, WHITFIELD; LAUCK, ANTHONY; MILLER, DOUG; NEUMANN, PETER; SOBEL, DAVID. 1994. Codes, Keys and Conflicts: Issues in U.S. Crypto Policy. Report of a Special Panel of the ACM U.S. Public Policy Committee (USACM). 74p. Available WWW: http://Info.acm.org/reports/acm_crypto_study.html.

LANE, CAROLE A. 1997. Naked in Cyberspace: How to Find Personal Information Online. Burwell, Helen; Davies, Owen B., eds. Wilton, CT: Pemberton Press; 1997. 513p. ISBN: 0-910965-17-X.

LAPERRIÈRE, RENÉ. 1999. The "Quebec Model" of Data Protection: A Compromise between Laissez-Faire and Public Control in a Technological Era. In: Bennett, Colin; Grant, Rebecca, eds. Visions of Privacy: Policy Choices for the Digital Age. Toronto, Canada: University of Toronto Press; 1999. 182-196. ISBN: 0-8020-8050-2.

LAUDON, KENNETH C. 1995. Ethical Concepts and Information Technology. Communications of the ACM. 1995; 36(12): 33-39. ISSN: 0001-0782.

LAUDON, KENNETH C. 1996. Markets and Privacy. Communications of the ACM. 1996; 39(9): 92-104. ISSN: 0001-0782.

LAWSON, IAN; WOODS, DAVID. 1995. Privacy and the Information Highway: Regulatory Options for Canada. 1995. Available WWW: http://strategis.ic.gc.ca/SSG/ca00257e.html.

LESSIG, LAWRENCE. 1999. Code and Other Laws of Cyberspace. New York, NY: Basic Books; 1999. 297p. ISBN: 0-465-03912-X.

LIGHT, PAUL. 1995. The Presidential Policy Stream. In: Theodoulou, Stella Z.; Cahn, Matthew A., ed. Public Policy: The Essential Readings. Englewood Cliffs, NJ: Prentice Hall; 1995. 224-237. ISBN: 0-13-059255-2.

LINDBLOM, CHARLES E. 1959. The "Science" of Muddling Through. Public Administration Review. 1959; 15: 79-88. ISSN: 0033-3352.

LINDBLOM, CHARLES E. 1988. Still Muddling, Not Yet Through. In: Democracy and Market System. Oslo, Norway: Scandinavian Universities Press; 1988. 237-259. ISBN: 82-00-18435-8.

LINOWES, DAVID F. 1989. Privacy in America: Is Your Private Life in the Public Eye? Urbana, IL: University of Illinois Press; 1989. 191p. ISBN: 0-252-01604-1.

LIPINSKI, THOMAS A. 1998. Information Ownership and Control. In: Williams, Martha E., ed. Annual Review of Information Science and Technology: Volume 33. Medford, NJ: Information Today, Inc. for the American Society for Information Science; 1998. 3-38. ISSN: 0066-4200; ISBN: 1-57387-065-X; CODEN: ARISBC.

LOCH, KAREN D.; CONGER, SUE; OZ, EFFY. 1998. Ownership, Privacy and Monitoring in the Workplace: A Debate on Technology and Ethics. Journal of Business Ethics. 1998; 17(5): 653-663. ISSN: 0167-4544.

LOCHNER v. NEW YORK. 1905. 98 U.S. 45.

LUTZ, WILLIAM E. 1997. Monitoring Your Movements. In: Flood, Barbara, ed. Personal Privacy: An Introduction to Some Issues and What to Do about Them. Bulletin of the American Society for Information Science. 1997; 23(3): 8-10. ISSN: 0095-4403.

LYON, DAVID. 1994. The Electronic Eye: The Rise of Surveillance Society. Cambridge, UK: Polity Press; 1994. 270p. ISBN: 0-7456-0839-6.

MACKINNON, CATHARINE A. 1987a. Feminism Unmodified: Discourses on Life and Law. Cambridge, MA: Harvard University Press; 1987. 315p. ISBN: 0-674-29873-X.

MACKINNON, CATHARINE A. 1987b. Privacy and Equality: Beyond Roe v. Wade. In: MacKinnon, Catharine A. Feminism Unmodified: Discourses on Life and Law. Cambridge, MA: Harvard University Press; 1987. 93-102. (Speech originally given in 1983). ISBN: 0-674-29873-X.

MACNEIL, HEATHER. 1992. Without Consent: The Ethics of Disclosing Personal Information in Public Archives. Metuchen, NJ: The Scarecrow Press; 1992. 224p. ISBN: 0-8108-2581-3.

MAJONE, GIANDOMENICO; WILDAVSKY, AARON. 1995. Implementation as Evolution. In: Theodoulou, Stella Z.; Cahn, Matthew A., ed. Public Policy: The Essential Readings. Englewood Cliffs, NJ: Prentice Hall; 1995. 140-153. ISBN: 0-13-059255-2.

MANN, STEVE. 2000. Computer Architectures for Protection of Personal Information Property: Putting Pirates, Pigs, and Rapists in Perspective. First Monday. 2000 July; 5(7). ISSN: 1396-0466. Available WWW: http://www.firstmonday.dk/issues/issue5_7/mann/index.html.

MARGOLIS, DIANE ROTHBARD. 1998. The Fabric of Self: A Theory of Ethics and Emotions. New Haven, CT: Yale University Press; 1998. 207p. ISBN: 0-300-06990-1.

MARX, GARY T. 1985. I'll Be Watching You: Reflections on the New Surveillance. Dissent. 1985; 32(1): 26-34. ISSN: 0012-3846.

MARX, GARY T. 1990. The Case of the Omniscient Organization. Harvard Business Review. 1990; 90(2): 12-30. ISSN: 0017-8012.

MARX, GARY T. 1999. Ethics for the New Surveillance. In: Bennett, Colin; Grant, Rebecca, eds. Visions of Privacy: Policy Choices for the Digital Age. Toronto, Canada: University of Toronto Press; 1999. 39-67. ISBN: 0-8020-8050-2.

MASON, RICHARD O.; MASON, FLORENCE M.; CULNAN, MARY J. 1995. Ethics of Information Management. Thousand Oaks, CA: Sage; 1995. 327p. ISBN: 0-8039-5755-6.

MAYER-SCHÖNBERGER, VIKTOR. 1997a. Generational Development of Data Protection in Europe. In: Agre, Philip E.; Rotenberg, Marc, eds. Technology and Privacy: The New Landscape. Cambridge, MA: The MIT Press; 1997. 219-241. ISBN: 0-262-01162-X.

MAYER-SCHÖNBERGER, VIKTOR. 1997b. The Internet and Privacy Legislation: Cookies for a Treat? West Virginia Journal of Law & Technology. 1997; 1(1). Available WWW: http://www.wvu.edu/~wvjolt/Arch/Mayer/Mayer.htm.

MCCURLEY, KEVIN S. 1995. Protecting Privacy and Information Integrity of Computerized Medical Information. Available WWW: http://www.swcp.com/~mccurley/cs.sandia.gov/health/health.html.

MILBERG, SANDRA J.; BURKE, SANDRA J.; SMITH, H. JEFF; KALLMAN, ERNEST A. 1995. Values, Personal Information Privacy, and Regulatory Approaches. Communications of the ACM. 1995; 38(12): 65-74. ISSN: 0001-0782.

MILLER, ARTHUR R. 1971. The Assault on Privacy: Computers, Data Banks, and Dossiers. Ann Arbor, MI: University of Michigan Press; 1971. 333p. OCLC: 125649.

MILLER, SEUMAS. 1998. Privacy, Data Bases, and Computers. Journal of Information Ethics. 1998; 7(1): 42-48. ISSN: 1061-9321.

MINDLE, GRANT B. 1989. Liberalism, Privacy, and Autonomy. Journal of Politics. 1989; 51(3): 575-598. ISSN: 0022-3816.

MODELL, ARNOLD H. 1993. The Private Self. Cambridge, MA: Harvard University Press; 1993. 250p. ISBN: 0-674-70752-4.

MONTGOMERY, KATHRYN; PASNIK, SHELLEY. 1996. Web of Deception: Threats to Children from Online Marketing. Washington, DC: Center for Media Education; 1996. 1 volume. OCLC: 44166829.

MUNZER, STEPHEN R. 1990. A Theory of Property. Cambridge, UK: Cambridge University Press; 1990. 491p. ISBN: 0-521-37886-9.

NAGEL, THOMAS. 1995. Personal Rights and Public Space. Philosophy & Public Affairs. 1995; 24(2): 83-107. ISSN: 0048-3915.

NAGEL, THOMAS. 1998. Concealment and Exposure. Philosophy & Public Affairs. 1998; 27(1): 3-30. ISSN: 0048-3915.

NASRI, WILLIAM Z., ed 1987a. Legal Issues for Library and Information Managers. New York, NY: Haworth Press; 1987. 145p. ISBN: 0-86656-591-4.

NASRI, WILLIAM Z. 1987b. Professional Liability. In: Nasri, William Z., ed. Legal Issues for Library and Information Managers. New York, NY: Haworth Press; 1987. 141-145. ISBN: 0-86656-591-4.

NATIONAL RESEARCH COUNCIL. COMMISSION ON PHYSICAL SCIENCES, MATHEMATICS, AND APPLICATIONS. COMPUTER SCIENCE AND TELECOMMUNICATIONS BOARD. NII 2000 STEERING COMMITTEE. 1996. The Unpredictable Certainty: Information Infrastructure through 2000. Washington, DC: National Academy Press; 1996. 281p. ISBN: 0-309-05432-X.

NISSENBAUM, HELEN. 1997. Toward an Approach to Privacy in Public: Challenges of Information Technology. Ethics & Behavior. 1997; 7(3): 207-219. ISSN: 1050-8422.

NISSENBAUM, HELEN. 1998. Protecting Privacy in an Information Age: The Problem of Privacy in Public. Law and Philosophy. 1998; 17: 559-596. ISSN: 0167-5249.

OLMSTEAD v. UNITED STATES. 1928. 277 U.S. 438.

OPPENHEIM, CHARLES; EISENSCHITZ, TAMARA S. 1994. Legal Issues for Information Professionals. In: Encyclopedia of Library and Information Science: Volume 54. New York, NY: Marcel Dekker; 1994. 224-261. ISBN: 0-8247-2054-7.

ORGANISATION FOR ECONOMIC CO-OPERATION AND DEVELOPMENT (OECD). DIRECTORATE FOR SCIENCE, TECHNOLOGY AND INDUS-TRY. COMMITTEE FOR INFORMATION, COMPUTER AND COMMU-NICATIONS POLICY. GROUP OF EXPERTS ON INFORMATION SECU-RITY AND PRIVACY. 1998a. Implementing the OECD "Privacy Guide-lines" in the Electronic Environment: Focus on the Internet. (DSTI/ICCP/REG(97)6/FINAL). Available WWW: http://www.oecd.org/dsti/sti/it/secur/prod/reg97-6e.htm.

ORGANISATION FOR ECONOMIC CO-OPERATION AND DEVELOPMENT (OECD). DIRECTORATE FOR SCIENCE, TECHNOLOGY AND INDUS-TRY. COMMITTEE FOR INFORMATION, COMPUTER AND COMMU-NICATIONS POLICY. GROUP OF EXPERTS ON INFORMATION SECU-RITY AND PRIVACY. 1998b. Practices to Implement the OECD Privacy Guidelines on Global Networks. 1998 December 23. (DSTI/ICCP/REG(98)6/FINAL). Available WWW: http://appli1.oecd.org/olis/1998doc.nsf/linkto/dsti-iccp-reg(98)6-final.

ORGANISATION FOR ECONOMIC CO-OPERATION AND DEVELOPMENT (OECD). DIRECTORATE FOR SCIENCE, TECHNOLOGY AND INDUS-TRY. COMMITTEE FOR INFORMATION, COMPUTER AND COMMU-NICATIONS POLICY. GROUP OF EXPERTS ON INFORMATION SECU-RITY AND PRIVACY. 1998c. Privacy Protection in a Global Networked Society: An OECD International Workshop with the Support of the Busi-ness and Industry Advisory Committee (BIAC). (DSTI/ICCP/REG(98)5/FINAL). Available WWW: http://www.oecd.org/dsti/sti/it/secur/prod/reg98-5final.pdf.

ORGANISATION FOR ECONOMIC CO-OPERATION AND DEVELOPMENT (OECD). DIRECTORATE FOR SCIENCE, TECHNOLOGY AND INDUS-TRY. COMMITTEE FOR INFORMATION, COMPUTER AND COMMU-NICATIONS POLICY. WORKING PARTY ON INFORMATION SECU-RITY AND PRIVACY. 1998. Ministerial Declaration on the Protection of Privacy on Global Networks. (DSTI/ICCP/REG(98)10/FINAL). Avail-able WWW: http://appli1.oecd.org/olis/1998doc.nsf/linkto/dsti-iccp-reg(98)10-final.

ORREN, KAREN. 1991. Belated Feudalism: Labor, the Law, and Liberal Development in the United States. Cambridge, UK: Cambridge University Press; 1991. 238p. ISBN: 0-521-41039-8.

PALMER, R. R. 1997. Jean-Baptiste Say: An Economist in Troubled Times: Writings. Princeton, NJ: Princeton University Press; 1997. 167p. ISBN: 0-691-01170-2.

PHILLIPS, DAVID J. 1997. Cryptography, Secrets, and the Structuring of Trust. In: Agre, Philip E.; Rotenberg, Marc, eds. Technology and Privacy: The New Landscape. Cambridge, MA: The MIT Press; 1997. 243-276. ISBN: 0-262-01162-X.

POSCH, ROBERT J. 1993. Don't Take Lou Harris Too Seriously. Direct Marketing. 1993; 56(8): 44-48. ISSN: 0012-3188.

POSCH, ROBERT J. 1996. Direct Marketing Is Not a Significant Privacy Threat. In: Kling, Rob, ed. Computerization and Controversy: Value Conflicts and Social Choices. 2nd edition. San Diego, CA: Academic Press; 1996. 679-685. ISBN: 0-12-415040-3.

POSNER, RICHARD A. 1984. An Economic Theory of Privacy. In: Schoeman, Ferdinand David, ed. Philosophical Dimensions of Privacy: An Anthology. Cambridge, UK: Cambridge University Press; 1984. 332-345. ISBN: 0-521-25555-4.

POSNER, RICHARD A. 1995. Overcoming Law. Cambridge MA: Harvard University Press; 1995. 597p. ISBN: 0-674-64925-7.

POST, ROBERT C. 1989. The Social Foundations of Privacy: Community and Self in the Common Law Tort. California Law Review. 1989; 77(5): 957-1010. ISSN: 0008-1221.

POST, ROBERT C. 1994. The Legal Regulation of Gossip: Backyard Chatter and the Mass Media. In: Goodman, Robert F.; Ben-Ze'ev, Aaron, eds. Good Gossip. Lawrence, KS: University Press of Kansas; 1994. 65-71. ISBN: 0-7006-0669-6.

POSTER, MARK. 1990. The Mode of Information: Postmodernism and Social Context. Chicago: University of Chicago Press; 1990. 179p. ISBN: 0-226-67596-3.

PRIVACY RIGHTS CLEARINGHOUSE. 1994. Privacy Survival Guide. Fact Sheet No. 1. (Updated October 2000). Available WWW: http://www.privacyrights.org/FS/fs1-surv.htm.

PRIVACY RIGHTS CLEARINGHOUSE. 1995. Privacy in Cyberspace: Rules of the Road for the Information Superhighway. Fact Sheet No. 18. (Updated August 2000). Available WWW: http://www.privacyrights.org/FS/fs18-cyb.htm.

PRIVACY RIGHTS CLEARINGHOUSE. 1998. Children in Cyberspace: A Privacy Resource Guide for Parents. Fact Sheet No. 21. (Updated November 2000). Available WWW: http://www.privacyrights.org/FS/fs21-children.htm.

PROSSER, WILLIAM LLOYD. 1984. Privacy [A Legal Analysis]. In: Schoeman, Ferdinand David, ed. Philosophical Dimensions of Privacy: An Anthology. Cambridge, UK: Cambridge University Press; 1984. 104-156. ISBN: 0-521-25555-4.

PROSSER, WILLIAM LLOYD; KEETON, PAGE. 1984. Handbook of the Law of Torts. 5th ed. St. Paul, MN: West Publishing; 1984. 1286p. ISBN: 0-314-74880-6.

PUTNAM, ROBERT D. 1995. Bowling Alone: America's Declining Social Capital. Journal of Democracy. 1995; 6(1): 65-78. ISSN: 1045-5736.

RAAB, CHARLES D. 1997. Privacy, Democracy, Information. In: Loader, Brian D., ed. The Governance of Cyberspace. London, UK: Routledge; 1997. 155-174. ISBN: 0-415-14724-7.

RAAB, CHARLES D. 1999. From Balancing to Steering: New Directions for Data Protection. In: Bennett, Colin; Grant, Rebecca, eds. Visions of Privacy: Policy Choices for the Digital Age. Toronto, Canada: University of Toronto Press; 1999. 68-93. ISBN: 0-8020-8050-2.

RAAB, CHARLES D.; BENNETT, COLIN J. 1998. The Distribution of Privacy Risks: Who Needs Protection? The Information Society. 1998; 14(4): 263-274. ISSN: 0197-2243.

RAAB, CHARLES D.; BENNETT, COLIN J.; GELLMAN, ROBERT M.; WATERS, NIGEL. 1999. Application of a Methodology Designed to Assess the Adequacy of the Level of Protection of Individuals with Regard to Processing Personal Data: Test of the Method on Several Categories of Transfer. Final report. Luxembourg: Office for Official Publications of the European Communities; 1999. 212p. ISBN: 92-8285-638-0.

RACHELS, JAMES. 1985. Why Privacy Is Important. In: Johnson, Deborah G.; Snapper, John W., eds. Ethical Issues in the Use of Computers. Belmont, CA: Wadsworth Publishing; 1985. 194-201. ISBN: 0-534-04257-0.

RADIN, MARGARET J. 1993. Reinterpreting Property. Chicago, IL: University of Chicago Press; 1993. 265p. ISBN: 0-226-70227-8.

RADIN, MARGARET J. 1996a. Contested Commodities. Cambridge, MA: Harvard University Press; 1996. 279p. ISBN: 0-674-16697-3.

RADIN, MARGARET J. 1996b. Property Evolving in Cyberspace. Journal of Law and Commerce. 1996; 15: 509-547. ISSN: 0733-2491.

RAKOVE, JACK N. 1997. Original Meanings: Politics and the Ideas in the Making of the Constitution. New York, NY: Alfred A. Knopf; 1997. 439p. ISBN: 0-394-57858-9.

RATH, CHARLA M.; CLEMENT, JOHN R. B. 1988. Information Policy Issues in Science and Technology. In: Williams, Martha E., ed. Annual Review of Information Science and Technology: Volume 23. Amsterdam, The Netherlands: Elsevier Science Publishers for the American Society for Information Science; 1988. 35-57. ISSN: 0066-4200; ISBN: 0-444-70543-0; CODEN: ARISBC.

RAY, DON. 1998. Don Ray's 104 Privacy Tips. Available WWW: http://www.privacyrights.org/ar/donray.htm.

REGAN, PRISCILLA M. 1995. Legislating Privacy: Technology, Social Values, and Public Policy. Chapel Hill, NC: University of North Carolina Press; 1995. 310p. ISBN: 0-8078-2226-4.

REGAN, PRISCILLA M. 1999. American Business and the European Data Protection Directive: Lobbying Strategies and Tactics. In: Bennett, Colin; Grant, Rebecca, eds. Visions of Privacy: Policy Choices for the Digital Age. Toronto, Canada: University of Toronto Press; 1999. 199-216. ISBN: 0-8020-8050-2.

REIDENBERG, JOEL R. 1999. The Globalization of Privacy Solutions: The Movement towards Obligatory Standards for Fair Information Practices.

In: Bennett, Colin; Grant, Rebecca, eds. Visions of Privacy: Policy Choices for the Digital Age. Toronto, Canada: University of Toronto Press; 1999. 217-228. ISBN: 0-8020-8050-2.

ROE v. WADE. 1973. 410 U.S. 113.

ROSENBERG, VICTOR. 1982. National Information Policies. In: Williams, Martha E., ed. Annual Review of Information Science and Technology: Volume 17. White Plains, NY: Knowledge Industry Publications, Inc. for the American Society for Information Science; 1982. 3-32. ISSN: 0066-4200; ISBN: 0-86729-032-3; CODEN: ARISBC.

ROTENBERG, MARC. 1994. Privacy and Security for Medical Information Systems. Keynote Address: Seizing the Opportunity: The Power of Health Information. AHIMA National Convention; 1994 October; Las Vegas, NV. Available WWW: http://www.epic.org/privacy/medical/epic_review.html.

ROTENBERG, MARC. 1998. Testimony and Statement for the Record on H.R. 2281. The WIPO Copyright Treaties Implementation Act and Privacy Issues. Subcommittee on Telecommunications, Trade, and Consumer Protection, Committee on Commerce, U.S. House of Representatives. Available WWW: http://www.epic.org/privacy/copyright/epic-wipo-testimony-698.html.

RUBIN, RICHARD E.; FROEHLICH, THOMAS J. 1996. Ethical Aspects of Library and Information Science. In: Encyclopedia of Library and Information Science: Volume 58. New York, NY: Marcel Dekker; 1996. 33-52. ISBN: 0-8247-2058-X.

RULE, JAMES; HUNTER, LAWRENCE. 1999. Towards Property Rights in Personal Data. In: Bennett, Colin; Grant, Rebecca, eds. Visions of Privacy: Policy Choices for the Digital Age. Toronto, Canada: University of Toronto Press; 1999. 168-181. ISBN: 0-8020-8050-2.

RULE, JAMES B.; MCADAM, DOUGLAS; STEARNS, LINDA; UGLOW, DAVID. 1995. Preserving Individual Autonomy in an Information-Oriented Society. In: Johnson, Deborah G.; Nissenbaum, Helen, eds. Computers, Ethics & Social Values. Englewood Cliffs, NJ: Prentice Hall; 1995. 314-332. ISBN: 0-13-103110-4.

SACHS, ALBIE. 1978. The Myth of Male Protectiveness and the Legal Subordination of Women: An Historical Analysis. In: Smart, Carol; Smart, Barry, eds. Women, Sexuality and Social Control. London, UK: Routledge & Kegan Paul; 1978. 27-40. ISBN: 0-7100-8723-3.

SALVAGGIO, JERRY L. 1989. Is Privacy Possible in an Information Society? In: Salvaggio, Jerry L., ed. The Information Society: Economic, Social, and Structural Issues. Hillsdale, NJ: Lawrence Erlbaum Associates; 1989. 115-130. ISBN: 0-8058-0103-0.

SAMARAJIVA, ROHAN. 1997. Interactivity As Though Privacy Mattered. In: Agre, Philip E.; Rotenberg, Marc, eds. Technology and Privacy: The New Landscape. Cambridge, MA: The MIT Press; 1997. 277-309. ISBN: 0-262-01162-X.

SAMUELSON, PAMELA. 1991. Is Information Property? Communications of the ACM. 1991; 34(3): 15-18. ISSN: 0001-0782.

SANTA CLARA COUNTY v. SOUTHERN PACIFIC RAILROAD COMPANY. 1886. 118 U.S. 394.

SCHEMENT, JORGE REINA; CURTIS, TERRY. 1997. Tendencies and Tensions of the Information Age: The Production and Distribution of Information in the United States. New Brunswick, NJ: Transaction Publishers; 1997. 285p. ISBN: 1-56000-928-4.

SCHNEIDER, ELIZABETH M. 1991. The Dialectics of Rights and Politics: Perspectives from the Women's Movement. In: Fineman, Martha Albertson; Thomadsen, Nancy Sweet, eds. At the Boundaries of Law: Feminism and Legal Theory. New York, NY: Routledge; 1991. 301-319. ISBN: 0-415-90306-8.

SCHNEIER, BRUCE. 1996. Applied Cryptography: Protocols, Algorithms, and Source Code in C. 2nd edition. New York, NY: John Wiley & Sons; 1996. 758p. ISBN: 0-471-12845-7.

SCHOEMAN, FERDINAND DAVID. 1992. Privacy and Social Freedom. Cambridge, UK: Cambridge University Press; 1992. 225p. ISBN: 0-521-41564-0.

SCHOEMAN, FERDINAND DAVID. 1994. Gossip and Privacy. In: Goodman, Robert F.; Ben-Ze'ev, Aaron, eds. Good Gossip. Lawrence, KS: University Press of Kansas; 1994. 72-84. ISBN: 0-7006-0669-6.

SCHÖN, DONALD A. 1983. The Reflective Practitioner: How Professionals Think in Action. New York, NY: Basic Books; 1983. 374p. ISBN: 0-465-06874-X.

SCHÖN, DONALD A. 1993. Generative Metaphor: A Perspective on Problem-Setting in Social Policy. In: Ortony, Andrew, ed. Metaphor and Thought. 2nd edition. Cambridge, UK: Cambridge University Press; 1993. 137-163. ISBN: 0-465-06878-2.

SCHWARTZ, BERNARD. 1993. A History of the Supreme Court. New York, NY: Oxford University Press; 1993. 465p. ISBN: 0-19-509387-9.

SCOTT, JAMES C. 1998. Seeing Like a State: How Certain Schemes to Improve the Human Condition Have Failed. New Haven, CT: Yale University Press; 1998. 445p. ISBN: 0-300-07016-0.

SENNETT, RICHARD. 1977. The Fall of Public Man. New York, NY: Alfred A. Knopf; 1977. 373p. ISBN: 0-394-48715-X.

SEVERSON, RICHARD W. 1997. The Principles of Information Ethics. Armonk, NY: M.E. Sharpe; 1997. 161p. ISBN: 1-56324-958-8.

SHAPIRO, STUART. 1998. Places and Spaces: The Historical Interaction of Technology, Home, and Privacy. The Information Society. 1998; 14(4): 275-284. ISSN: 0197-2243.

SHEPARD, IRA MICHAEL; DUSTON, ROBERT L.; RUSSELL, KAREN S. 1989. Workplace Privacy: Employee Testing, Surveillance, Wrongful Discharge, and Other Areas of Vulnerability. 2nd edition. Washington, DC: The Bureau of National Affairs; 1989. 509p. ISBN: 1-55871-137-6.

SIMITIS, SPIROS. 1987. Reviewing Privacy. University of Pennsylvania Law Review. 1987; 135(3): 707-746. ISSN: 0041-9907.

SINGLETON, SOLVEIG. 1998. Privacy as Censorship: A Skeptical View of Proposals to Regulate Privacy in the Private Sector. 1998 January 22. 32p. (Cato Institute Policy Analysis No. 295). Available WWW: http://www.cato.org/pubs/pas/pa-295es.html.

SINGLETON, SOLVEIG. 1999. "Know Your Customer" as Incoherent Privacy Policy. Testimony before the U.S. House of Representatives Committee on the Judiciary, Subcommittee on Commercial and Administrative Law. 1999 March 4. Available WWW: http://www.cato.org/testimony/ct-ss030499.html.

SIPIOR, JANICE C.; WARD, BURKE T. 1995. The Ethical and Legal Quandary of E-Mail Privacy. Communications of the ACM. 1995 December; 38(12): 48-54. ISSN: 0001-0782.

SIPIOR, JANICE C.; WARD, BURKE T.; RAINONE, SEBASTIAN M. 1998. Ethical Management of Employee E-Mail Privacy. Information Systems Management. 1998; 15(1): 41-47. ISSN: 1058-0530.

SMART, CAROL; SMART, BARRY. 1978. Women and Social Control: An Introduction. In: Smart, Carol; Smart, Barry, eds. Women, Sexuality and Social Control. London, UK: Routledge & Kegan Paul; 1978. 1-7. ISBN: 0-7100-8723-3.

SMITH, H. JEFF. 1993. Privacy Policies and Practices: Inside the Organizational Maze. Communications of the ACM. 1993; 36(12): 105-122. ISSN: 0001-0782.

SMITH, H. JEFF; HASNAS, JOHN. 1999. Ethics and Information Systems: The Corporate Domain. MIS Quarterly. 1999; 23(1): 109-127. ISSN: 0276-7783.

SMITH, JANNA MALAMUD. 1997. Private Matters: In Defense of the Personal Life. Reading, MA: Addison-Wesley; 1997. 278p. ISBN: 0-201-40973-9.

SMITH, MARTHA MONTAGUE. 1997. Information Ethics. In: Williams, Martha E., ed. Annual Review of Information Science and Technology: Volume 32. Medford, NJ: Information Today, Inc. for the American Society for Information Science; 1997. 339-366. ISSN: 0066-4200; ISBN: 1-57387-047-1; CODEN: ARISBC.

SOWELL, THOMAS. 1972. Say's Law. An Historical Analysis. Princeton, NJ: Princeton University Press; 1972. 247p. ISBN: 0-691-04166-0.

SPINELLO, RICHARD A. 1997. Case Studies in Information and Computer Ethics. Upper Saddle River, NJ: Prentice Hall; 1997. 285p. ISBN: 0-13-533845-X.

STEFIK, MARK. 1999. The Internet Edge: Social, Technical, and Legal Challenges for a Networked World. Cambridge, MA: MIT Press; 1999. 320p. ISBN: 0-262-019418-X.

STETSON, DOUGLAS M. 1997. Achieving Effective Medical Information Security: Understanding the Culture. In: Flood, Barbara, ed. Personal Privacy: An Introduction to Some Issues and What to Do about Them. Bulletin of the American Society for Information Science. 1997; 23(3): 17-21. ISSN: 0095-4403.

STREETER, THOMAS. 1995. Some Thoughts on Free Speech, Language, and the Rule of Law. In: Allen, David S.; Jensen, Robert, eds. Freeing the First Amendment: Critical Perspectives on Freedom of Expression. New York, NY: New York University Press; 1995. 31-53. ISBN: 0-8147-0638-X.

SUSSMAN, GERALD. 1997. Communication, Technology, and Politics in the Information Age. Thousand Oaks, CA: Sage; 1997. 317p. ISBN: 0-8039-5140-X.

SWIRE, PETER P.; LITAN, ROBERT E. 1998. None of Your Business: World Data Flows, Electronic Commerce, and the European Privacy Directive. Washington, DC: Brookings Institution Press; 1998. 269p. ISBN: 0-8157-8240-3.

TANG, PUAY. 1998. How Electronic Publishers Are Protecting against Piracy: Doubts about Technical Systems of Protection. The Information Society. 1998; 14(1): 19-32. ISSN: 0197-2243.

TARROW, SIDNEY. 1996. Making Social Science Work across Space and Time: A Critical Reflection on Robert Putnam's Making Democracy Work. American Political Science Review. 1996; 90(2): 389-397. ISSN: 0003-0554.

TEDESCHI, JAMES T. 1986. Private and Public Experiences and the Self. In: Baumeister, Roy F., ed. Public Self and Private Self. New York, NY: Springer-Verlag; 1986. 1-20. ISBN: 0-387-96303-0.

THOMAS, LAURENCE. 1994. The Logic of Gossip. In: Goodman, Robert F.; Ben-Ze'ev, Aaron, eds. Good Gossip. Lawrence, KS: University Press of Kansas; 1994. 47-55. ISBN: 0-7006-0669-6.

THOMSON, JUDITH JARVIS. 1984. The Right to Privacy. In: Schoeman, Ferdinand David, ed. Philosophical Dimensions of Privacy: An Anthology. Cambridge, UK: Cambridge University Press; 1984. 272-289. ISBN: 0-521-25555-4.

THOMSON, JUDITH JARVIS. 1990. The Realm of Rights. Cambridge, MA: Harvard University Press; 1990. 383p. ISBN: 0-674-74948-0.

TURN, REIN. 1985. Privacy Protection. In: Williams, Martha E., ed. Annual Review of Information Science and Technology: Volume 20. White Plains, NY: Knowledge Industry Publications, Inc. for the American Society for Information Science; 1985. 27-50. ISSN: 0066-4200; ISBN: 0-86729-175-3; CODEN: ARISBC.

U.S. CONGRESS. OFFICE OF TECHNOLOGY ASSESSMENT. 1993. Making Government Work: Electronic Delivery of Federal Services. Washington, DC: U.S. Government Printing Office; 1993. 178p. (OTA-TCT-578). ISBN: 0-16-042080-6.

U.S. CONGRESS. OFFICE OF TECHNOLOGY ASSESSMENT. 1994. Information Security and Privacy in Network Environments. Washington, DC: U.S. Government Printing Office; 1994. 244p. (OTA-TCT-606). ISBN: 0-16-045188-4.

U.S. CONGRESS. OFFICE OF TECHNOLOGY ASSESSMENT. 1995. Electronic Surveillance in a Digital Age. Washington, DC: U.S. Government Printing Office; 1995. 74p. (OTA-BP-ITC-149). ISBN: 0-16-048121-X.

U.S. DEPARTMENT OF COMMERCE. FEDERAL TRADE COMMISSION. 1998. Privacy Online: A Report to Congress. 63p. Available WWW: http://www.ftc.gov/reports/privacy3/priv-23a.pdf.

U.S. GENERAL ACCOUNTING OFFICE. 1999. Medical Records Privacy: Access Needed for Health Research, But Oversight of Privacy Protections Is Limited. Washington, DC: Government Printing Office; 1999. 28p. (GAO/HEHS-99-55). OCLC: 40903148.

U.S. NATIONAL INFORMATION INFRASTRUCTURE TASK FORCE. 1995. Privacy and the National Information Infrastructure: Principles for Providing and Using Personal Information. Available WWW: http://www.iitf.nist.gov/documents/committee/infopol/niiprivprin_final.html.

U.S. NATIONAL INFORMATION INFRASTRUCTURE TASK FORCE. 1997. Options for Promoting Privacy on the National Information Infrastructure. Available WWW: http://www.iitf.nist.gov/ipc/privacy.htm.

U.S. PRIVACY PROTECTION STUDY COMMISSION. 1985. Introduction to Personal Privacy in an Information Society. In: Johnson, Deborah G.; Snapper, John W., eds. Ethical Issues in the Use of Computers. Belmont, CA: Wadsworth Publishing; 1985. 215-239. ISBN: 0-534-04257-0.

UNITED STATES v. MILLER. 1976. 425 U.S. 435.

WACKS, RAYMOND. 1989. Personal Information: Privacy and the Law. Oxford, UK: Clarendon Press; 1989. 327p. ISBN: 0-19-825611-6.

WACKS, RAYMOND. 1995. Privacy and Press Freedom. London, UK: Blackstone Press Limited; 1995. 181p. ISBN: 1-85431-454-8.

WARE, WILLIS H. 1993. The New Faces of Privacy. The Information Society. 1993; 9(3): 195-211. ISSN: 0197-2243.

WARREN, SAMUEL D.; BRANDEIS, LOUIS D. 1985. The Right to Privacy. In: Johnson, Deborah G.; Snapper, John W., eds. Ethical Issues in the Use of Computers. Belmont, CA: Wadsworth Publishing; 1985. 173-182. ISBN: 0-534-04257-0.

WARWICK, SHELLY. 1997. Privacy and Policy. In: Flood, Barbara A., ed. Personal Privacy: An Introduction to Some Issues and What to Do about Them. Bulletin of the American Society for Information Science. 1997; 23(3): 14-15. ISSN: 0095-4403.

WEBER, MAX. 1995. Bureaucracy. In: Theodoulou, Stella Z.; Cahn, Matthew A., eds. Public Policy: The Essential Readings. Englewood Cliffs, NJ: Prentice Hall; 1995. 259-265. ISBN: 0-13-059255-2.

WECKERT, JOHN; ADENEY, DOUGLAS. 1997. Computer and Information Ethics. Westport, CT: Greenwood Press; 1997. 175p. ISBN: 0-313-29362-7.

WEIL, BEN H. 1975. Copyright Developments. In: Cuadra, Carlos A., ed. Annual Review of Information Science and Technology: Volume 10. Washington, DC: American Society for Information Science; 1975. 359-381. ISBN: 0-87715-210-1; CODEN: ARISBC.

WEISBAND, SUZANNE P.; REINIG, BRUCE A. 1995. Managing User Perceptions of Email Privacy. Communications of the ACM. 1995; 38(12): 40-47. ISSN: 0001-0782.

WENGER, ÉTIENNE. 1998. Communities of Practice: Learning, Meaning, and Identity. Cambridge, UK: Cambridge University Press; 1998. 318p. ISBN: 0-521-66363-6.

WEST, ROBIN L. 1991. The Difference in Women's Hedonic Lives: A Phenomenological Critique of Feminist Legal Theory. In: Fineman, Martha Albertson; Thomadsen, Nancy Sweet, eds. At the Boundaries of Law: Feminism and Legal Theory. New York, NY: Routledge; 1991. 115-134. ISBN: 0-415-90306-8.

WESTIN, ALAN F. 1967. Privacy and Freedom. New York, NY: Atheneum; 1967. 487p. OCLC: 359695.

WESTIN, ALAN F. 1985. Privacy in the Modern Democratic State. In: Johnson, Deborah G.; Snapper, John W., eds. Ethical Issues in the Use of Computers. Belmont, CA: Wadsworth Publishing; 1985. 184-194. ISBN: 0-534-04257-0.

WHITAKER, REGINALD. 1999. The End of Privacy: How Total Surveillance Is Becoming a Reality. New York, NY: The New Press; 1999. 195p. ISBN: 1-56584-378-9.

WHITE, JAMES BOYD. 1987. Rhetoric and Law: The Arts of Cultural and Communal Life. In: Nelson, John S.; Megill, Allan; McCloskey, Donald N., eds. The Rhetoric of the Human Sciences: Language and Argument in Scholarship and Public Affairs. Madison, WI: University of Wisconsin Press; 1987. 298-318. ISBN: 0-299-11024-9.

WILLIAMS, RAYMOND. 1983. Keywords. Revised edition. New York, NY: Oxford University Press; 1983. 349p. ISBN: 0-19-520469-7.

WORLD WIDE WEB CONSORTIUM (W3C). 2000. Platform for Privacy Preferences (P3P) Project. Available WWW: http://www.w3.org/P3P/.

YOUNG, JOHN B., ed. 1978. Privacy. Chichester, UK: John Wiley & Sons; 1978. 350p. ISBN: 0-471-99590-8.

ZUBOFF, SHOSHANA. 1988. In the Age of the Smart Machine: The Future of Work and Power. New York, NY: Basic Books; 1988. 468p. ISBN: 0-465-03212-5.

ZWASS, VLADIMIR. 1996. Ethical Issues in Information Systems. In: Encyclopedia of Library and Information Science: Volume 57. New York, NY: Marcel Dekker; 1996. 175-195. ISBN: 0-8247-2057-1.

## USEFUL WEB SITES

Americans for Computer Privacy (ACP). Available WWW: http://www.computerprivacy.org/.

Anonymizer. Available WWW: http://www.anonymizer.com.

Better Business Bureau Online. Available WWW: http://www.bbbonline.org.

Bennett, Colin. Politics of Information. Available WWW: http://web.uvic.ca/~polisci/bennett/courses/456/index.htm.

Center for Democracy & Technology (CDT). Data Privacy. Available WWW: http://www.cdt.org/privacy/.

Computer Professionals for Social Responsibility (CPSR). Available WWW: http://www.cpsr.org.

Culnan, Mary. Teaching & Research Page. Available WWW: http://www.msb.georgetown.edu/faculty/culnanm/.

EDUCAUSE. Privacy in a Networked Environment. Available WWW: http://www.educause.edu/issues/privacy.html.

Electronic Frontier Foundation (EFF). Available WWW: http://www.eff.org/.

Electronic Privacy Information Center (EPIC). Available WWW: http://www.epic.org.

Federal Trade Commission. Available WWW: http://www.ftc.gov.

Global Internet Liberty Campaign (GILC). Available WWW: http://www.gilc.org/.

Marx, Gary T. Available WWW: http://web.mit.edu/gtmarx/www/garyhome.html.

National Telecommunications and Information Administration. Privacy Issues. Available WWW: http://www.ntia.doc.gov/ntiahome/privacy/.

Online Privacy Alliance. Available WWW: http://www.privacyalliance.org.

Organisation for Economic Co-Operation and Development (OECD). Available WWW: http://www.oecd.org/dsti/sti/it/secur/index.htm.

Princeton University. University Center for Human Values. Available WWW: http://www.princeton.edu/~uchv/.

Privacy Exchange. Available WWW: http://www.privacyexchange.org.

Privacy International (PI). Available WWW: http://www.privacy.org/pi/.

Privacy Rights Clearinghouse (PRC). Available WWW: http://www.privacyrights.org/.

Raab, Charles D. Available WWW: http://www.brunel.ac.uk/research/virtsoc/people/raab.htm.

Rotenberg, Marc. Law of Information Privacy. Available WWW: http://www.epic.org/misc/gulc/.

TRUSTe. Available WWW: http://www.truste.org.

# II

# Basic Techniques and Technologies

The three chapters in Section II are: "Subject Access Points in Electronic Retrieval" by Birger Hjørland of University College of Borås in Sweden and Lykke Kyllesbech Nielsen of the Royal School of Library and Information Science in Copenhagen, Denmark, "Methods of Generating and Evaluating Hypertext" by James Blustein of Dalhousie University, Canada, and Mark S. Staveley of the University of Toronto, Canada, and "Digital Preservation" by Elizabeth Yakel of the University of Michigan.

In the first half of their chapter Birger Hjørland and Lykke Kyllesbech Nielsen review the status of subject access points (SAPs) (search fields or document representations) for accessing electronically stored information and data. They briefly review the history of SAPs, whether they are terms, codes, contexts, relationships, etc. and provide a taxonomy or classification of SAPs. They classify access points as follows: verbal vs. nonverbal or symbolic; long form (e.g., abstracts) vs. short form (e.g., a single keyword or classification code); controlled (closed) vs. uncontrolled (open systems) forms; derived (e.g., titles) vs. assigned (e.g., identifiers) forms; forms based on checklist or facet analysis vs. forms based on free analysis; explicit vs. implicit; content-oriented (or descriptive) vs. question-oriented (or evaluative); pre-coordinated vs. post-coordinated indexing forms; syntactic indexing forms (e.g., links and role indicators) vs. forms without syntax ; and manually produced vs. computer-generated.

The balance of the chapter is devoted to research on specific subject access points including: document titles; abstracts; references/citations; full text; and descriptors, identifiers, classification codes, and other kinds of access data. Various Internet search engines and traditional online search systems provide search capability of different sets of access points depending on what is included in or is added to the documents to be searched. Hjørland and Nielsen review investigations of various data elements as access points both from the quantitative and qualitative points of view. Chain searching or the use of citation analysis adds another dimension to access points for searching. The authors of this chapter review investigations of these access points with respect to their utility for increasing precision or recall. Investigations of full text, descriptors, identifiers, classification codes, and other kinds of access data are similarly reviewed to determine their relative value as access points.

James Blustein and Mark S. Staveley have produced the first *ARIST* chapter devoted to hypertext. Their specific focus is on methods of generating and evaluating hypertext. The chapter starts with a brief presentation of historical landmarks—Vannevar Bush's Memex in 1945, Ted Nelson's coining the term hypertext in describing his proposed Xanadu system in 1965, and Doug Engelbart's demonstration of the first computerized hypertext system in 1968. Blustein and Staveley provide several researchers' definitions of hypertext and explain hypermedia, nonlinearity (non-sequentiality), as well as semantics/ syntactics, and literary hypertext as they apply to hypertext in specific cases. They then explain several models of hypertext—spatial, link-based, formal definition (mathematically based), and open hypertext.

There are several approaches to generating hypertext— manual construction approach, semiautomatic approaches, fully automatic, and interactive /dynamic approaches—and the authors explain the limitations of each. The fully automatic approaches include those based on syntactics, artificial intelligence (AI), and information retrieval (IR). The final sections of the chapter cover evaluation—mathematical models for hypertext evaluation (computing path lengths, coverage, and correlation) and human factors in hypertext evaluation (e.g., evaluation experiments and human-computer interaction).

Elizabeth Yakel has written the first *ARIST* chapter on digital preservation. In many ways maintaining and preserving paper-based documents is easier than preserving digital documents. Fortunately considerable efforts are addressing the problem throughout the world. Digital preservation is required for both born-digital documents and digitally recreated documents. Yakel's discussion of born-digital documents covers the first generation (machine-readable) and second generation of electronic records research; metadata and other standards; preservation of email; preserving Web-based documents; preservation of media for capturing moving images (video); and current research.

The balance of the chapter is appropriately devoted to administrative issues in the management of digital files, media stability studies, and the economics of digital preservation. "After almost a decade of digitization projects, major research libraries are beginning to address the long-term preservation issues associated with the maintenance of digital files and to recognize that the projects must become established programs if the digital files are to survive."

# 5 Subject Access Points in Electronic Retrieval*

**BIRGER HJØRLAND**
University College of Borås

**LYKKE KYLLESBECH NIELSEN**
Royal School of Library and Information
Science, Copenhagen

## INTRODUCTION

This is the first *ARIST* chapter devoted to subject access points (SAPs, also called search fields or document representations) in databases. The term is used here in a much wider sense than just headings. ROWLEY & FARROW use this narrower sense and find that "the concept of the access point belongs to manually searched indexes, and is arguably irrelevant to databases with search systems allowing keyword access" (p. 253). In our wider sense, SAPs are fundamental to any kind of document retrieval. This subject has earlier been scattered in many different chapters (especially those on document representation, which have not been reviewed in *ARIST* since 1974 by HARRIS). A systematic cumulating of findings related to each kind of subject access data has never been undertaken in *ARIST* or elsewhere, although texts such as that by LANCASTER cover much of the relevant findings. This review cannot cover all relevant studies but concentrates on the broader theoretical perspective.

## SUBJECT AND ACCESS DATA

Much more research has been done on searching and retrieving documents and information[1] and on users than on access points. Retrieval, however, is essential to the use of access data, and people

---

*We thank Raya Fidel, rector emeritus Tor Henriksen, and other reviewers for valuable feedback during the writing of this article.

[1] In this article the word "information" is used synonymously with data, which we believe is the ordinary sense of this word. In other papers we apply a more Shannon-inspired meaning of information. However, it is outside the scope of this article to discuss this concept further.

*Annual Review of Information Science and Technology (ARIST)*, Volume 35, 2001
Martha E. Williams, Editor
Published for the American Society for Information Science and Technology (ASIST)
By Information Today, Inc., Medford, NJ

cannot use something that is not there. Access points determine in a rather firm way the objective possibilities that are provided for the talented user (or for any formalized, algorithmic, or automatic procedure). Therefore, it is essential in information science (IS) to develop knowledge about what kinds of subject data exist as well as the strengths, weaknesses, and relative contributions of each kind. For example, what proportion of a given set of relevant documents is missed by using only one access point such as words from titles? How much can additional access points increase recall, and how do they affect precision? Only from such knowledge are we able to study how the users or algorithms utilize these possibilities, which form the subjective factors in retrieval. For example, if people (or algorithms) do not use references as access points (in citation databases) because they do not know about this possibility or they misjudge it, then an objective possibility in retrieval is not utilized.

Knowledge about SAPs is also crucial in relation to the design of information systems because it is related to the fundamental question of which possibilities should be provided. It is rather trivial to think that systems should provide as many retrieval possibilities as possible—to believe, for example, that databases providing access to searching abstracts are better than those that do not, other things being equal. Faster access to more information is an important demand from users, but this is primarily provided by better computer technology, especially storage technology, not by IS. The availability of many kinds of access points in databases demands much space, which is provided by developments in information technology (IT). There has therefore been an IT-driven growth in subject access data that is outlined below. This growth is mainly quantitative, while the qualitative ways in which the technological potential has been utilized is a central issue for research in IS.

Information science is concerned about how IT developments can best be used to represent and to retrieve documents and information. This is related more to qualitative characteristics of subject access points than to quantitative issues. IS should ask questions such as: Given certain constraints, what are the optimal ways to design a system? Theoretically we should have a comprehensive knowledge of the kinds of access data and their characteristics. Each existing retrieval system should then be seen as realizing more or fewer of these possibilities.

The term information retrieval (IR) was introduced by MOOERS in 1951. He also introduced the term "information retrieval languages" as the generic term for classification codes, keywords, free-text retrieval, and other search elements or SAPs. At the same time the empiricist, experimental approach to document retrieval (references, surrogates, or information) was founded as an important research tradition in IS.

This tradition is normally termed the information retrieval tradition in IS, and it has some distinctive characteristics that distinguish it from other research traditions within the field, such as the facet analytic tradition, the cognitive approach, and semiotic approaches. Analytically it is important to distinguish IR as a field of study from IR as a specific approach or research tradition because different traditions may provide useful contributions to this field. (The IR tradition may, like empiricism in general, have certain blind spots.)

The basic element in IR is the user's interaction with a database (or with electronic information environments such as the World Wide Web). The user has a query[2] that has to match, more or less exactly or directly,[3] some elements, which may be termed access points, search keys, retrieval keys, data elements, or document representations. There are many kinds of such access points, they have many different functions, and they have different informational values in different search situations. What are these subject access points?

Many texts in IS differentiate between subject access data and so-called descriptive data and other kinds of data such as call numbers. Metadata is the generic term for all such kinds of data. In major research libraries, librarians usually provide the descriptive data and subject specialists provide the subject data. Many people think that there is a clear and sharp functional division among subject data, descriptive data, and other kinds of metadata.[4] This was virtually true in the age of printed card catalogs, where the descriptive data allowed for searches for known items and subject data allowed for searches for known or unknown documents about a given subject. In the age of electronic retrieval, however, there is no clearcut functional division. All words in titles have become searchable, and titles are thus both descriptive elements and SAPs. Search profiles can include many kinds of data. Hypothetically, it may be relevant to limit a subject search according to the name of a publisher, a journal, or even a language code. Subject data are

---

[2] There have been attempts in IR to avoid queries, and systems that allow "navigating" seem to avoid this concept. We do not see this as a theoretical problem for our views on subjects; we do not discuss it here. We are also aware that advanced technologies, such as Latent Semantic Indexing (LSI), can retrieve relevant documents even when they do not share any words with the query. LSI uses statistically derived "concepts" to improve searching performance (see GORDON & DUMAIS). However, such "concepts" must be based on subject access points, so knowledge of these still is necessary.

[3] A direct match is obtained in systems based on Boolean logic. Such a match is between words (a lexical match), not between concepts (a semantic match). Implicit or latent semantic matches can be obtained by taking advantage of the implicit higher order structure in the association of terms with documents. Such structures represent important associative relationships that are not evident in individual documents (cf. BERRY ET AL.).

[4] Such a sharp dichotomy can be found in, for example, a Danish dictionary of information science, *Informationsordbogen*, published in 1996 by The Danish Standardization Organization (FRIIS-HANSEN ET AL.).

not strictly limited to specific kinds of data; under specific circumstances any kind of data may serve to identify documents about a
subject (cf. HJØRLAND, 1997, pp. 11-37). But what is that "something"
that subject data are meant to identify? What are subjects?

"Subject" is one of several related terms used in the literature. Terms
that are sometimes considered synonyms and sometimes used with
different meanings are shown below:

Subject (subject matter; subject-predicate)
Aboutness
Topic (topicality; topic/comment)
Theme (with "central theme" and the German "leitmotiv")[5]
Domain (cognitive domain, scientific domain)
Field (information field, field of knowledge, field of research)
Content
Information[6]
Other (including related terms such as "discipline" and "concept")

These concepts are considered very difficult both in IS and in linguistics, and when used in other fields such as semiotics, psychology, and
cognitive sciences. One proposal for differentiation of some of these
terms is given by BERNIER (p. 192). In his opinion, subject indexes are
different from, and can be contrasted with, indexes to concepts, topics,
and words. Subjects are what authors are working and reporting on.
Presentations can be organized into topics and use words and concepts.
A document can have the subject of Chromatography. Papers using
Chromatography as a research method or discussing it in a subsection
do not have Chromatography as subjects. Indexers can easily drift into
indexing concepts and words rather than subjects, but this is not good
indexing. Bernier does not, however, differentiate authors' subjects
from those of the information seeker. A user may want a document
about a subject that is different from the one intended by its author.
From the point of view of information systems, the subject of a document is related to the questions that the document can answer for the
user. Such a distinction between a content-oriented and a request-
oriented approach is emphasized by SOERGEL (1985). A request-ori-
ented approach implies that subject analysis should thus predict the
questions that the document will help to answer. Based on such analyses, HJØRLAND (1997) proposes that subjects are the epistemological
or informative potentials of documents, and he sees the job of the
indexer as that of predicting the most important future applications of

---

[5] Theme is opposed to rheme: what an author tells about a theme.
[6] "Information analysis" is, for example, used for subject analysis in the INSPEC database.

the document. This view corresponds to the functional theory about sources in history, which states that what counts as an information source is always relative to the question that it is supposed to answer.

In linguistics, the corresponding concept is mostly known as "topic" (which is contrasted by the notion of "comment," i.e., what is said about a given topic). A concise encyclopedic article on this topic with further references is provided by VAN KUPPEVELT. A 1975 conference was devoted to Subject and Topic at the University of California, Santa Barbara (LI). In one of the papers, CHAFE treats a range of phenomena related to subject: topic, point of view, givenness, contrastiveness, and definiteness. In her text, NORD (1991) addresses subject matter from the point of view of translation theory. In psychology, subject/predicate has been treated by HORNBY.

In recent years the terms "topic" and "topicality" have been popular in IS. Many writers (e.g., BOYCE and WANG & SOERGEL) agree that topicality is only one of many factors influencing relevance, but they have not succeeded in defining this concept in a clear way. GREEN (1995) and GREEN & BEAN found that there is not one kind, but rather many kinds of relationships between texts and questions that are perceived as being "on the same topic." They have not, however, considered how concepts such as aboutness, theme, or subject relate to topic. These are different concepts that people use when searching for unknown documents, but we do not know much about how such concepts differ or overlap in ordinary use, nor have we any theory that provides a well-defined meaning for these concepts. According to JANES (p. 167): "Over the last several decades, a number of other words have been used to not only describe what goes on in people's heads when they make judgments about documents, but also to ask them to tell us about it. Our results might lead one to believe that these several concepts and terms overlap . . . . But it may go further than this. Perhaps what we have called 'topicality,' 'utility,' 'satisfaction,' 'pertinence,' and a variety of other names are in fact dimensions of a larger, multidimensional, dynamic concept . . . " This problem is still unsolved, although some hints are given. For example, WANG & SOERGEL suggest that "field" is (or should be used as) a broader term than "topic," and BOYCE (p. 109) suggests that the use of references or citation indexes is a recall-oriented technique in which each iteration brings in more and more documents of questionable topicality. This last suggestion points to a difference between a field defined as a network of citing papers and a topic defined as a conceptual or terminological structure. What kind of theory is needed to clarify these concepts further? Because they are concepts about structures in knowledge, epistemology is the most relevant discipline. Different theories in epistemology imply, however, different views of knowledge structures. Classical rationalism imagines a highly ordered universe of knowledge, in which every concept has its well-defined place in relation to all other concepts. The modern view is much more pragmatic—viz., that knowledge serves cognitive systems and that the structures of knowledge reflect the needs and behavior of activity systems and discourse communities. This view implicates that the concepts we are talking about (e.g., topic) are concepts we use about units or parts relating to (human) communication and that their definition must be grounded in sociocognitive theories.

Different kinds of SAPs describe the subject of a given document in different ways, such as more or less exhaustive, more or less general or specific, in a more-or-less open or closed way, and so on. Most importantly, they may describe the subject of a document from different interpretations of the relevance of the given document to future questions put to the database. Because any document can in principle answer an unlimited number of questions, subject analysis prioritizes the most important questions that the document is supposed to answer in the future. The most valuable SAPs are those that make it possible for the user to identify the most highly relevant documents, that is, make the highly relevant documents the most visible in the database at the expense of less-relevant documents.

## Major Technology-Driven Stages in the Development of Subject Access Points (SAPs)

*Manual indexing and classification in libraries.* This first stage has deep roots in the history of libraries and comprises especially books and other physical units. A more formal research area was established about 1876 by Melvil Dewey and others. This stage concentrated mostly on the organization of specific physical collections of documents and enabling access either to known documents or to documents on specific subjects in these collections. Important developments in this stage were Charles A. Cutter's (1837-1903) rules for a dictionary catalog; Melvil Dewey's (1851-1931) Decimal Classification system, Henry E. Bliss's (1870-1955) Knowledge Organization, and principles developed by S. R. Ranganathan (1892-1972). This stage still influences some research traditions in library science. Classification research is built on theoretical traditions and assumptions other than the IR tradition. The most influential work in this tradition is Ranganathan's Colon Classification from 1933, and the most important kinds of SAPs in this stage are classification codes and subject headings. The main approach to subject access is a top-down division of "the universe of knowledge" according to some rational principles. A more empirical orientation was established by HULME (1911a) in the principle of bibliographical warrant or literary warrant, which states that a class or a subject heading must be established only if there exists literature to be classified by that group. In this way subject retrieval was not only built on top-down analyses of the universe of knowledge but was also somewhat influenced by the existing literature in a bottom-up manner. SAPs in this stage are produced and controlled by librarians and information specialists (including subject specialists) and constrained by their subject knowledge. Another major constraint in this stage/tradition is that the principles were developed for subject access to physical units (e.g., books), not documentary units (e.g., journal articles). This implies a level of subject description and concepts that are often much broader than those needed by researchers in specific investigations. A third major constraint in this stage/tradition is that because the available space (e.g., on printed catalog cards) was very limited, the SAPs tended to contain scanty information. Nevertheless, this stage/tradition developed important principles that many researchers find useful in a fully electronic environment (see, e.g., POLLITT ET AL.). What de Grolier wrote in 1965 is still regarded by many as true.[7]

> We feared some years ago that classification was becoming useless, that the treatment of natural language texts by machines . . . would replace classification. Classification and the classificationists would become something like the dinosaurs, killed by the progress of evolution. This has proved to be a complete fallacy. When you examine the new literature you find that more and more classification . . . is considered as something quite essential in information retrieval . . . It is quite evident that hierarchies, generally speaking, are something which can not be avoided in an information retrieval language which is to be useful for the reader. (DE GROLIER, p. 11)

*"Documentation" and scientific communication.*    "Documentation" is the name of a movement founded by Paul Otlet (1868-1944). The establishment of The International Institute of Bibliography in Brussels in 1895 (from 1937 called Fédération Internationale de Documentation (FID)) and of the Universal Decimal Classification (UDC) system in 1905 with the aim of universal bibliographical control, was a major achievement in this movement. The documentalists often regarded themselves as more service-minded, more technology-oriented, and more advanced than librarians. Where traditional librarians often had an orientation toward the humanities, the documentalists were mostly affiliated with science, technology, and business. They indexed single articles in journals and books and played a central role in establishing

---

[7] SALTON is an example of an explicit disagreement with this view.

international abstracting journals.[8] They were less interested in collection development and more concerned with providing better access to knowledge that is independent of specific collections. They were less interested in keeping books for their own sake or for broad cultural purposes and highly interested in establishing services that could stimulate the application of knowledge to specific purposes. The foundations of user studies (BERNAL) and bibliometrics (e.g., BRADFORD) are also part of this stage/tradition, which is primarily characterized by a more specific subject approach, a deeper level of indexing, and a more scientific attitude toward goals and problems.

*Information storage and retrieval by computers.* This stage has been developing mainly since 1950 and can be seen as a technological modernization of documentation (American Documentation Institute (ADI), founded in 1937, changed its name in 1968 to American Society for Information Science (ASIS), then ASIS in 2000 added "Technology" (ASIS&T)). The establishment of computer-based abstract services, such as Chemical Abstracts and MEDLINE, in the 1960s was important during this stage. The development of descriptor-based and free-text retrieval (mainly based on titles and abstracts), Boolean logic, field-specific subject access, as well as the measurements of recall and precision and other innovations were extremely important in document retrieval. Information retrieval (IR) as a research tradition started with the Cranfield experiments in the 1950s, and today's Text REtrieval Conference (TREC) full-text experiments continue this tradition (see NATIONAL INSTITUTE OF STANDARDS AND TECHNOLOGY).

This third stage improved information services and research efforts in IS in an important way. Computer technology made it possible to use many kinds of SAPs, both the traditional kinds produced by information specialists and the use of words from the documents themselves (e.g., titles and abstracts). It removed the monopoly of librarians and information specialists over subject access and established a direct competition between SAPs produced by different agencies.

An underlying premise in this stage has often been that the length of the searchable record itself was the most important parameter in retrieval (LANCASTER, pp. 6-8). SAPs were often seen merely as "semantic condensations" of the texts represented (implying that the ultimate goal was full-text representation and nothing more). Research was dominated by quantitative methodologies, and not much research on qualitative differences (semantics or meanings) among different kinds of SAPs was established. The premise was empiricist, first and foremost, in its attempt to measure the efficiency of subject retrieval

---

[8] The history of the abstract journal goes back, however, to 1665 (cf. MANZER).

points empirically (e.g., by measuring recall and precision). It was also empiricist in its avoidance of "metaphysical"-based classifications and in its favoring of "atomist" SAPs, such as the Uniterm system devised by Mortimer Taube in 1951 and similar systems that depended on specific words from the documents themselves.

One associated tendency in this stage was the attempt to formalize and to automate retrieval and to eliminate human interpretation and subject analysis. We must distinguish between the economic pressure to automate practical systems on one side and the scientific evaluation of the performance of various aspects of human-based and mechanized retrieval systems on the other side. It is legitimate and highly desirable to reduce costs and improve efficiency in information systems. Basic research, however, should illuminate basic strengths and drawbacks in different approaches and not be blinded by the pressure to use auto-mated or cheap solutions. Because of such tendencies, important ap-proaches related to interpretation were neglected, and the research did not yield as satisfactory a body of knowledge as desired.

*Citation-based retrieval (1963-).* Eugene Garfield's introduction of the Science Citation Index in 1963 marks the fourth important stage in the development of SAPs. The possibility of retrieving documents according to the citations they receive represents a real innovation in IR, and this technique is able to supplement all forms of term-based retrieval in very important and qualitative new ways. This innovation has also prompted research on motives to cite other documents, on sociological patterns in citing, on the relative role of terms and refer-ences as SAPs, and on the semantic relations between citing and cited papers.

In this way, citation-based retrieval has changed our understanding not only of subject relatedness but also of the concept of subject matter and of the fundamental aim of IR itself. Because it may be relevant to cite papers that have no words in common with the citing papers (or no simple semantic relation such as narrower terms, broader terms, and synonyms), naive conceptions of subject relatedness or subject matter can no longer persist. Semantic relations may be implicit or latent. Semantic relations in science are determined by theoretical advances, which may change the verbal description of the research phenomena completely; this is why statistical patterns in vocabulary may some-times be a less efficient measure of subject relatedness than patterns in citations.

Citation behavior is extremely important because the goal of IR is to provide the references that are useful in solving a specific problem. A scientific article is a documentation of how a specific research problem is solved. The problem is formulated in the article, and the problem has determined the kind of information needed[9] by the author to solve the problem. Based on need, information was sought and selected, and the documents actually used were finally cited in the article. Each of the thousands of articles produced weekly is a kind of case study in IR. Every article not only poses a definite IR problem, but the list of references provided by the author is also the key to how that particular person has solved the problem. Thus, it is possible to check theories of IR against how they match the actual documents cited. According to the traditional view in philosophy of science, science should be able to predict future events. In other words, theories and models of IR should be able to predict citations that will appear in particular papers. Most research on relevance and on IR seems to have overlooked this fact. From what we do know, it seems extremely unlikely that an algorithm would be able to select references from electronic databases and end up with exactly the same references that appear in a given article. From this point of view, theories of IR seem naive and unrealistic (and the goal of prediction seems to be wrong). A more detailed study of citation behavior can illuminate the real problem of IR, which is that cited documents are not simply a set of documents sharing a fixed set of attributes that are not represented in the nonselected items. Documents that are similar from the point of view of retrieval algorithms need not be co-cited, whereas documents that are not similar are often co-cited. Ordinary retrieval algorithms and citation practices seem simply to reflect different theories about subject relatedness.

Because authors may cite other papers in order to flatter or to impress, the prediction of which references a given author will finally select for a given paper cannot be used as a valid criterion in IR. The criteria for IR should not be based on social or psychological motives but on epistemological principles for the advancement of public knowledge. In this way, our insight from citation indexes has profoundly changed not only the methods of IR but also the concept of subject relatedness itself and the basic aim of retrieving information. We can no longer regard the prediction of individual use as the ideal criterion for IR, nor can we regard IR as a value-free technique. Instead, we have

---

[9] Information need is an important concept in IS. People may have many needs with complicated interrelations. A more precise need arises when a specific decision is made to write a paper. From that point and until the paper is printed, the author seeks information, selects information, and decides what to cite in the paper. The references in the paper represent only one stage in the development of the author's information need. However, they are the most tangible, public, and available expression of how the author has seen and resolved his or her needs. People who are used to reading and interpreting papers can evaluate authors' conceptual horizons, compare them with others, and study their development and how they are influenced. In this way scholars may have methods to determine information needs other than behavioral methods.

to face the fact that the goals of IR are deeply rooted in epistemological norms for what should be regarded as good science and good citation behavior.

*Full text, hypertext, Internet, and digital libraries.*   Full-text retrieval marks the fifth and final step in the development of SAPs. Until this point, space limits were a major constraint in the development of subject access systems because length of the record in itself is an important parameter in retrieval. At this stage, every single word and every possible combination of words in full-text documents are potential SAPs, as is every conceivable kind of value-added information provided by authors, readers, or intermediaries. Given full-text representations, the first important theoretical problem that arises is whether any kind of value-added information is necessary. Can the extra information provided by abstracting and indexing, at least in principle, increase recall and/or precision? If not, then we seem to have reached the end of the line in that no further contributions from research or practice in IS are needed. The answer to this question is closely linked to theoretical views on the concept of subject. POULSEN sees a subject as something that is expressed in the literature (in a transparent and self-evident way?). By defining subjects in this way it is impossible even to pose the problem of whether a given text always represents the optimal representation of itself. By defining subjects as informative or epistemological potentials, HJØRLAND (1992; 1997) established the possibility that documents may be implicit or even wrong about their own subject matter; hence, information professionals are still needed. To take an extreme example, a document about Jews written by a Nazi author should not only be indexed as being about Jews, but it is also important to make the Nazi view visible in the subject analysis (e.g., to index it as Nazi propaganda about Jews). Subjects are not objectively "given" but are influenced by broader views, which are important for the information seeker to know and should therefore be part of the subject analysis. Whether this is also practical, economic, and realistic is another question that must be explored by evaluating specific subject access systems.

## Toward a Taxonomy of Subject Access Points

Figure 1 outlines some important criteria for the classification of SAPs. In general, access points should be regarded as a system wherein each element contributes to the overall performance of the retrieval system. For example, in research libraries, it would be a waste of resources to provide subject access to articles in the library catalog if this access is redundant with the subject information that can be found in, for example, CD-ROM databases in the same library.

---

### Access Points Classified by Provider or Agent

---

Author-generated (e.g., document titles, abstracts, and keywords)
Value-added, including those provided by publisher or editor (e.g., journal name, publisher name, and cover information); indexer/abstractor/information specialist (e.g., classification codes, descriptors, identifiers, and abstracts); reviewers, readers, and other writers (e.g., reviews with links on Internet, best-seller statistics, citations, and citation indexing)

---

### Access Points Classified by Kind

---

Verbal vs. nonverbal (nonverbal is sometimes called symbolic)
Long forms vs. short forms (e.g., abstracts vs. single keywords or classification codes)
Controlled vs. uncontrolled forms (or closed vs. open systems)
Derived vs. assigned forms (e.g., titles vs. identifiers)
Forms based on checklist or facet analysis vs. forms based on free analysis
Explicit vs. implicit (e.g., descriptors vs. references, journal names, or publishers. Implicit SAPs are mostly made for purposes other than IR. Titles are explicit SAPs when the authors intend them to be used for IR)
Content-oriented (or descriptive) vs. question-oriented (or evaluative)
Precoordinated vs. postcoordinated indexing forms
Syntactic indexing forms vs. forms without syntax (syntactic devices are, e.g., roles and links; they are also applied in the PRECIS indexing system)
Manually produced vs. computer-generated (computer-generated access points are sometimes produced by retroconversions in databases)

---

Figure 1. Some taxonomic criteria for subject access points

It is evident that a comprehensive description of all potential kinds of access points generated by the authors of documents implies a comprehensive typology of kinds of documents and a description of the structure (architecture or composition) of each kind of document listing all types of SAPs. Because document structures develop in response to different demands, they are also influenced by epistemological positions or paradigms. Figure 2 shows the potential SAPs in a typical scientific article.

| Norms (of scientific method and philosophy of science external to the article) | Elements Contained in the Article | Value-Added Information (Subject access points, access, and evaluation information) |
| --- | --- | --- |
| Observation and description | Bibliographical identification | Bibliographical description |
| Problem statement | (Journal name, volume, pages) | Relationship to other editions |
| Hypothesis | | |
| Experiment | Title | Biographical information |
| Theory building (According to the basic view formulated in HJØRLAND (1997), there exist different epistemological views (and each implies different standards or ideals regarding the structure of documents. Thus a typical empiricist article reflects the development of the empiricist research tradition.) | Author(s) | |
| | Corporate affiliation and address | Institutional information |
| | Author abstract | Indexer abstracts |
| | Author keywords | Indexer descriptors and identifiers |
| | Introduction | Classification codes |
| | Apparatus and materials, method, results, discussion | Language codes |
| | | Document type codes |
| | Conclusion | Editorial comments |
| | Acknowledgements | Links to citing papers, reviews, and criticism |
| | References | Information about availability of document |
| | | Evaluations |
| | | Target group information |
| | | "Key word plus" and "research fronts" |
| | | Other kinds of links and semantic networks |

Figure 2. Structure and elements in a typical scientific article

In monographs, additional subject access points could be based on their composition—e.g., books/volumes, parts, chapters, sections, subsections, and bibliography and index. Internet documents form a third kind. The Internet search engine AltaVista provides the SAPs shown in Figure 3.

---

Searchable by Search Engine AltaVista

(Search codes in brackets)

- Words or phrases contained in the URL (Uniform Resource Locator) of the document [url:]
- Title [title: ]
- Links (URL to other documents to which there is a reference) [link:]
- Word from the clickable text to a link [anchor:]
- Words in filenames of pictures contained in documents [image:]
- Words and phrases in full text (except image tags, links and URLs) [text:]
- Java Applets [applet:]

(Also searchable are domain names, host names, and "similar URLs")

---

**Figure 3. Subject access points in Internet (HTML) documents (Based on ALTAVISTA: Advanced Search Cheat Sheet)**

Other kinds of documents, such as newspapers, popular magazines, patents, pictures, and sound recordings, present different structures and different kinds of potential access points and retrieval problems.

The information to be derived from a document depends on the information contained in that document. Some documents have, for example, author-generated titles, abstracts, and keywords while others do not; the need to add such elements is more evident, but not necessarily redundant, in the last case. A taxonomy of derived SAPs thus clearly must be based on a taxonomy of documents and document structures. Some research in this area has been done in such fields as composition studies (e.g., BAZERMAN, 1988) and genre analysis (e.g., MALMKJÆR). In this still new and relatively unexplored field, we lack a taxonomy of document types, their composition and elements, and consequently the relative contributions of such elements in IR. We know more about scientific research articles than about all other kinds of documents, including scholarly monographs. Thus, unless otherwise stated, this review considers only primary scientific articles.

In our view, the essential quality of SAPs is their ability to express that aspect of a given document that would be most useful in answering the questions put to the specific database from which the SAPs' performance is to be evaluated. Poor titles, bad indexing, and in general poor SAPs are those that express unimportant (or perhaps even false) information about a given document. All questions concerning the choice of formal aspects of retrieval language (e.g., standardization, pre- vs. postcoordination, length of representation) are subordinate.

If a need for value-added information is to be justified in future systems, it must be done by arguments about the ability of information specialists to interpret documents in relation to other documents and to the specific user group they are serving. Meaning, semantics, and epistemology become the most important theoretical perspectives that can be generalized from specific domains.

## RESEARCH ON SPECIFIC SUBJECT ACCESS POINTS

### Document Titles

A title is the name of a document given by the author and influenced by existing norms at the given time. According to BERNARD, there exists an entire discipline within literary history called titrology, which confines itself to the study of titles. For nearly 30 years it has generated an impressive number of publications (mostly in French). One survey of titrology is given by GENETTE, who defines the functions of titles in the following way: "The first function, the only mandatory one in literary practice and institution, is the function of designation or identification. It is the only one to be mandatory, but impossible to separate from the others, since under the semantic pressure of the environment, even a simple opus number can be invested with meaning. The second one is the descriptive function: thematic, rhematic,[10] mixed, or ambiguous . . . [the last] is the function called seductive" (GENETTE, pp. 718-719). Whereas most books and journal articles have titles, other kinds of documents (e.g., pictures, and nonprinted documents such as letters) may lack them. Names may characterize what they name, and their use in retrieval is based on this assumption, which, however, is not always true. The most common measure of title informativity has been the number of "substantive" words that it includes (e.g., by counting all words except trivial words, such as articles from a stop list). Because

---

[10] A rhematic title indicates the kind of document considered rather than what the document is about—e.g., the terms "novel," "letter," "dissertation" are examples of rhematic titles.

titles can express many different things, this method gives a very rough measure and can be misleading.

According to NORD (1995) titles can be intended to achieve six communicative functions, four of which (referentiality, expressivity, appellativity, and phatic function) can be universally assigned to all texts and text types. The other two (metatextuality and distinctive function) can be observed as specific functions of particular text types; the distinctive function is typical of names or labels, and the metatextual function is found in metatexts such as text commentaries, reviews, abstracts, and summaries. Therefore, titles are not just texts but typical texts presenting a complex hierarchy of communicative functions. In spite of their complex functionality, titles present simple syntactic–semantic structures. Nord found only four macrostructural types (simple titles, title–subtitle combinations, duplex titles with "or," and title series), six syntactic forms (nominal titles, verbal titles, sentence titles, adverbial titles, attributive titles, and interjection titles), and a limited number of microstructural patterns such as "NP & NP"= nominal phrase + connective + nominal phrase (as in *John Jakes: Heaven and Hell*). Therefore, title elements have to be polyfunctional if the title is to achieve its intended functions, which is also typical of other communicative signs.

The design or form of a title varies over time, culture, subject matter, and document type. BERNARD analyzed a representative sample of French monographs from 880 to 1991 and found that titles in the nineteenth and twentieth centuries are distinctly shorter than those of the seventeenth and eighteenth centuries, whereas titles from 880 to 1673 are as short as recent ones. Books republished in modern times often bear titles that are abbreviations of their original title. In modern terms, Renaissance titles served as both title, subtitle, signature, and fourth cover page. The development of carefully structured titles and subtitles legitimizes the use of the title without the subtitle. Another development is homonymic works. Sometimes there is an intentional repeat of a title, with, for example, parody or location within a tradition as the objective. In general, books from the Middle Ages and Renaissance did not, however, take the precaution of attaching to their works a unique label, which we consider so important today.

Titles are intended to indicate what the document is about (its subject). Authors usually choose a name that draws potential readers, indicating the document's content at a glimpse and thus contributing to its initial selection or rejection. We have little knowledge of how titles are actually used or should be interpreted in selection processes. Among the few studies on this subject are those by ATKINSON, BAZERMAN (1985), and NAHL-JAKOBOVITS & JAKOBOVITS. Studies such as the one by SARACEVIC on the comparative effects of titles, abstracts, and full texts on the relevance judgment of documents are pertinent. He found that of 207 answers judged relevant from full text, 131 were judged so from titles and 160 from abstracts.[11] He also found that it seems to be easier for users to recognize nonrelevant documents than to recognize relevant documents from the title.

A title normally constitutes the most concise statement of a document's content. It is often used as a surrogate for the document in bibliographies, databases, indexes, tables of contents, current-awareness services, and reference lists, and it is heavily used in IR. However, because the title is a name, it is the author's decision as to how informative it will be, and what kind of information is given priority. The great importance of informative titles is almost unanimously emphasized in the literature by many writers, journal editors, and authors of guidance books for scientific and professional authors (YITZHAKI, 1996).

When we are evaluating titles as SAPs, we have to consider the kind of skills, motives, and norms that may influence the author's choice of title and hence its subsequent possibilities and limitations in IR. For example, an author may want a title that "sounds good," perhaps poetic. Metaphorical language is one of the most common problems with titles in IR. A title such as "The Conflict between Egypt and Israel: A Nightmare in Modern Politics" is a problem for the psychologist who is seeking information about nightmares by looking in Social Sciences Citation Index using titles for subject access. Another problem with title words is the lack of control of synonyms and homonyms. In a given time period of the Social Sciences Citation Index, "AIDS" is a useful access point for the illness, but when it is used in the total time span of the database, other meanings such as "teaching aids" may cause a very low precision rate.

In composition studies, CROSBY suggests a high correlation between the quality of a written composition and its title. The shuttlecock process of finding an appropriate title stimulates creativity, unity, revision, and significance. He classified 300 titles according to their apparent purpose in order to infer certain lessons for writers. The classification includes:

- Titles announcing the general subject, such as "The Age of Adolescence" and "The Collective Corporation";
- Titles indicating a specific topic, including "The Decline of Courtesy" and "Toward a New Morality";
- Titles indicating the controlling question; some titles

---

[11] The ability to evaluate relevance from bibliographical records seems to be much better in the study reported by SARACEVIC than in the study by WELWERT, reported in English in HJØRLAND (1988).

indicate the question that the writer is answering, and they go a long way to help the writer stay focused: e.g., "Is Culture Worthwhile?" and "How Can We Recover Our Joy?";

- Titles announcing the thesis, such as "This Thing Called Love is Pathological" and "The Rip-Off Age is the Clue to Nation's Ills"; and
- Titles that bid for attention. Some methods of attracting attention include alliteration, deliberate ambiguity, intriguing word coupling, allusions from serious and pop culture, and the twist (something unexpected).

The length of a title is also important for retrieval. The longer the title, the more words it contains and the greater should be the probability that it will be retrieved by a given query. This is not always the case, however. KELLER found that masters theses with 1 to 12 words in the title had a greater chance of being retrieved than did titles with 13 to 18 words, showing that factors other than number of words are at work.

The difference between titles in professional scientific journals and in popular science journals is not just a question of length but also of emphasis (see Figure 4). It should be remembered that the title is always a choice among possible alternatives. What is considered the core subject by the author is not necessarily the same as the searcher's core interest. A paper may be relevant for a searcher from a point of view different from the one expressed in the title (or expressed explicitly at all). Titles often express more general claims than are covered by the paper; they may be seductive or inflated, and a given subculture may stimulate a kind of marketing of a paper that resembles commercial thinking more than scientific precision.

The hard sciences tend to have longer titles than the softer and popular sciences. An analysis by BUXTON & MEADOWS (1977) and YITZHAKI (1992; 1996; 1997) demonstrated a trend toward longer (and more informative) titles, which occurred over a wide range of subject fields and was apparent before KWIC indexes and computer-based searching of title words became common. Although this trend preceded the introduction of these tools, the tools undoubtedly contributed greatly to the growing awareness of the importance of title informativity. In the humanities a somewhat similar trend seems to have occurred but in a weaker way and at a slower pace. (These studies do not discuss alternative hypotheses such as the need for longer titles because of increasing specialization in research, creating a need for more words to express a given piece of research.)

VOORBIJ studied the relative roles of title keywords and subject descriptors of monographs in the humanities and social sciences held

| Articles for Professional Audiences | Articles for Popular Audiences |
| --- | --- |
| Insects as Selective Agents on Plant Vegetative Morphology: Egg Mimicry Reduces Egg Laying by Butterflies (K. Williams and L. Gilbert, *Science*, 1981) | Coevolution of a Butterfly and a Vine  (L. Gilbert, *Scientific American*, 1982) |
| Female Sex Pheromone in the Skin and Circulation of a Garter Snake  (W. Garstka and D. Crews, *Science*, 1981) | The Ecological Physiology of a Garter Snake (D. Crews and W. Garstka, *Scientific American*, 1982) |
| The Reproductive Behavior and the Nature of Sexual Selection in Scatophaga stercoraria L. (Diptera: Scatophagidae). IX. Spatial Distribution of Fertilization Rates and Evolution of Male Search Strategy within the Reproductive Area (G. Parker, *Evolution*, 1974) | Sex around the Cow-pats (G. Parker, *New Scientist*, 1979) |

**Figure 4. Comparison of professional and popular titles**
**(Based on MYERS, p. 275)**

by the online public access catalog (OPAC) of the National Library of the Netherlands. He found that 37% of the records were considerably enhanced by a subject descriptor and that 49% were slightly or considerably enhanced. In a second study he found that when subject librarians performed subject searching using title keywords and subject descriptors on the same topic, the relative recalls were 48% and 86%, respectively. Failure analysis revealed why so many records that were found by descriptors were not found by title words. First, the title of a publication does not always offer sufficient clues for retrieval. Second, and more important, is the wide diversity of expressing a topic in titles. Descriptors remove the burden of vocabulary control from the user. While the study clearly demonstrates the benefits of descriptors over title words, it does not consider the functions of those descriptors in relation to other kinds of subject access data that will probably soon be available from other sources (such as tables of contents and book descriptions as used, for example, by Amazon.com).

A study of COMPENDEX by BYRNE comparing titles and abstracts as subject access points found that titles retrieved 22% of citations, abstracts retrieved 61%, and titles and abstracts combined retrieved 75%. This study did not, however, report any percent for precision, but it indicates that titles alone perform very poorly compared with abstracts. COMPENDEX is dominated by articles, and we must expect that this problem is even greater with monographs. In another study, BARKER ET AL. examined chemical databases and found that summaries increased recall over titles by 68% but at the expense of a 23% drop in precision. Keywords increased recall by 35% with a 10% drop in precision.

HODGES tested the effectiveness of title keywords in retrieval and concluded that less than 50% of the relevant titles were retrieved by words in titles. Surprisingly, this study found that the social sciences had better retrieval from titles (48%) than the hard sciences (42%); arts and humanities retrieved 31%. This low rate of retrieval from titles was attributed to three sources: (1) titles themselves, (2) ignorance by the user and information specialist of the subject vocabulary in use, and (3) general language problems. Even the best efforts of users and specialists are not likely to improve this rate significantly. Hodges argues, however, that in many instances this recall is more than adequate for the user. Many students and faculty do not require the entire body of literature on a topic; they are just trying to determine the kinds and amount of material being written on a given topic, or they wish an introduction to a topic or an entry point into the literature. Also, because of their timeliness and economy, title-word indexes will, in her view, remain an important element of indexing.

When titles are used for retrieval, their words are merged with those from other titles in the same journal, other journals, other kinds of documents in the domain, and perhaps also words from titles in other domains. IR is always done in one or more specific collections, and the actual context determines the most rational search strategy. The principal disadvantages in having authors rather than professional indexers provide access points may be related to the fact that authors do not have the same overview of the total database (or total literature in the field). Hence, they may have difficulty in predicting the discriminative value of words and their combinations. Their selections can easily be either too specific or too general.

Because titles are different in their informational values, they have a different status in different databases. Some printed bibliographies (e.g., ERIC) use titles as document surrogates or document representations in the index (under each descriptor), while others (e.g., Psychological Abstracts), apply a value-added index phrase with a higher informational value. (This may of course reflect a decision that is not grounded in a difference in the informativeness of titles in educational and psychological research.)

PERITZ examined the frequency of noninformative titles in library and information science (LIS) and in sociology. Noninformative articles totaled 21% in LIS and 15% in sociology. For both fields the study showed that the noninformative articles were concentrated in a few journals.

*Conclusion.* Investigations of titles as access points tend to emphasize quantitative aspects, such as length, number of "substantive" words, and differences between domains and over time. Studies of qualitative aspects of titles are scarce and are found mostly in disciplines outside IS (e.g., linguistics and composition studies). If we assume that different theoretical views or paradigms have different views on a given paper and on what in that paper is of interest, then such different views should be able to express different criteria for the informativity of given titles. For example, we might expect positivist-oriented information seekers to value titles that express the kind of statistical methods used in a paper, and hermeneutical-oriented seekers to value titles that express the interpretative attitudes of the author. This implies that title informativity cannot be measured by an objective standard, for example, by number of words. Nor is such informativity simply a subjective or cognitive value in an individual, psychological way. The epistemological view implies that the informativity of titles is something to be inferred theoretically by views formulated in epistemology.

## Abstracts

According to ALTERMAN, text summarization is not a single phenomenon. There are many different kinds of summaries, such as abstracts, epitomes, overviews, abridgements, digests, and recapitulations. Alterman does not, however, describe the differences among them. We can add the following: annotations, briefs, cuts, extracts, part texts (e.g., half texts as opposed to full texts), précis, and Zentralblätter. However, in IS the two most common distinctions are indicative vs. informative abstracts—respectively, evaluative (or critical) vs. nonevaluative abstracts.

In the philosophy of science there is an important argument—viz., that one's observations are not independent of one's theoretical assumptions (cf. CHALMERS, chaps. 1 and 2). This principle is also valid concerning the observation/reading of documents and the interpretation of their essential or core information (or rather their informational potentials) and thus the summarization of them. As a consequence, even nonevaluative abstracts cannot just be regarded as objective descriptions of a document but are influenced by norms, interests, and epistemological positions.

Today most scientific journals publish authors' abstracts for all their articles. These abstracts may be used directly in bibliographical databases, or they may be edited, revised, or replaced by an abstract written by a professional abstractor, who usually then signs it. We call such value-added abstracts "indexer abstracts."

LANCASTER believes that the length of a given search field is the most important factor in information retrieval:

> For retrieval purposes, the longer the abstract the better. At least, the longer the abstract the more access points it provides, and the more access points the greater the potential for high recall in retrieval. At the same time, it must be recognized that precision is likely to deteriorate: the longer the abstract, the more "minor" aspects of the document that will be brought in and the greater the potential for false associations. (LANCASTER, p. 21)

> Because the brief abstract provides more access points than title or selective indexing, the item it represents will be more retrievable. Likewise, the exhaustive indexing may make this item more retrievable than it would be in a search on the brief abstract but less retrievable than it would be in a search on the expanded abstracts . . . . The longer the record, the greater the chance that spurious relationships will occur. Spurious relationships, of course, cause lower precision. (LANCASTER, pp. 227ff.)

From our point of view, however, this quantitative measure—that is, the length of the field—is less interesting than how well it will satisfy the needs of users in given situations. Because some subject analyses are simply better than others, the strategy of unlimited aliasing, which implies that as many different subject descriptions as possible be put into the document representations, is not a correct theory or strategy. This can be disproved both theoretically and empirically (cf. BROOKS). Therefore, we need a theory about what should be expressed in different SAPs (viewed as a system) and what is the abstract's role in this system. The ability to see what is important and to express it in a way that maximizes its visibility to the user must be the only factor that matters.

LANCASTER writes further:

> At the present time, authors and publishers have little incentive for "embroidering" abstracts to make the underlying

> work seem more attractive than it really is. Price . . . has
> argued that this could become a danger in a completely
> electronic environment . . . . Publishers would want to pro-
> mote use because they would probably be paid on this basis.
> Authors would want to promote use if this factor became, as
> it might, a criterion used in promotion and tenure decisions.
> The term "spoofing" has been used to refer to the embroi-
> dering of Web pages to increase their retrievability . . . .
> (LANCASTER, p. 116)

This quotation is the key to understanding the role of value-added information provided by information specialists. Their perspective is different from those of authors and publishers. Ideally they read on behalf of the user (or on behalf of science or some collective goals and values). Perhaps the commercial or self-promoting embroidering of abstracts is rare in the printed world, but a more "scientistic" "embroi-dering" of the whole text including name dropping, for example, may be the rule rather than the exception (and some embroidering may be unconscious and subtle). Abstractors can—at least ideally—have an overview of the system in which the single document is going to be organized. They have an implicit knowledge of the visibility and retrievability of different documents in the database, and they can improve the visibility of those aspects of a given document that will be most useful. Most importantly, because all documents are based on implicit assumptions, information professionals can make a difference in explicating such epistemological assumptions. Two specific examples of how this can make an important difference are given by HERRELL and by WINDSOR.

The work of abstractors can be guided by thesauri, classification systems, checklists, and facet analysis (FIDEL, 1986). In this way their specific subject analysis can be somewhat formalized. The most impor-tant factor is not the degree of formalization but the fact that the abstractor write on behalf of the users and from the perspective of a more-or-less specific collection or database with more-or-less well-de-fined functions in the information environment.

*Conclusion.* Abstracts are important in IR as access points and as indicators of the relevance of documents during a search. Abstracts increase recall and precision much better than titles and keywords. Their efficiency depends not only on their length but also on their content. With titles they share the problem of providing users with a relevant description of the document being represented. Such a de-scription is in principle not value free or neutral but always biased in one direction or another. In information systems, abstracts should ide-ally be written on behalf of the user and from the perspective and goals implicit in the specific system. This is why many information systems have their own abstractors and do not rely on author-created abstracts.

## References/Citations

Searches that use the references in documents as SAPs, directly or via citation indexes, are called chain searches.[12] They represent a qualitatively different method from term searching. How should we evaluate the relative strengths and weaknesses of term searching vis-a-vis citation or chain searching?

Chain searching is often quite valuable (e.g., see WELWERT, which is (reported in English in HJØRLAND (1988)). A search for the subject "reading comprehension vs. listening comprehension" resulted in 79 relevant references using database searching, 47 using manual sources, and 82 using chain searching in the references that were located. The last 82 references could, of course, not have been found without the previous bibliographic search, but this example indicates the significance of chain searching. It may also indicate the high degree of uncertainty of bibliographic searching in that so many references were not found by a thorough search of databases and printed bibliographies.

Chain searching vs. bibliographic searching can be further illustrated by field studies (PAO, 1993) and controlled studies (PAO & WORTHEN) in terms of literature references vs. terms as search criteria. These studies, which were performed in medicine and which built on a pool of common references in MEDLINE (a database that maintains a high level of indexing quality) and SCISEARCH (a science citation index), cannot be regarded as definitive, but they do indicate the following:

- The level of overlap is low (4-5%) when terms and references are used for searching.
- Given a high quality of indexing, term searching seems to be more efficient than reference searching (term searching in MEDLINE gave a mean recall of 77% and a precision level of 56%; reference searching in SCISEARCH gave a recall of 33% and a precision level of 60%).
- Compared with term searching alone, reference searching increased recall by a mean of 24%. Moreover, the overlap between the two search strategies had high precision.

---

[12] An advanced way to do chain searching is by using the Web of Science produced by Institute for Scientific Information.

Unfortunately, these studies lack a closer analysis of the nature of the terms and references that result in few or no results. These kinds of studies are typically quantitative rather than qualitative. If recall can be increased by 24% by including reference searching, it would be relevant to analyze what kinds of concepts typically should have been included in the bibliographic records, but were not. Might these kinds of experiences lead to new instructions for the indexers so that indexing practices could be improved? HARTER ET AL. also found that the subject similarity among pairs of cited and citing documents typically is very small, indicating that term searching and chain searching are complementary methods.

GREEN (2000) compared chain searching with the use of standard bibliographic tools in the humanities and found that less than 5% of the references were found by both types of searches. Precision of retrieval based on bibliographical references from "seed documents" appears to be high. Whereas bibliographical tools generally observe a well-defined boundary of coverage relative to subject, date, format, and language, the relevant literature may not respect the same boundaries, especially in the humanities. This is one reason chain searching is so important. Green also found (p. 224) that although most of the sample documents were covered in the bibliographic tools being used, only 10% were assigned index terms that matched the user's need in terms of both breadth and depth. She says, "Suffice it to say that there are no trivial or easy solutions to the overwhelming problem of assigning subject descriptors to documents that will consistently enable users to locate all, but only, the literature relevant to their needs" (p. 225).

The efficiency of bibliographic searching is, of course, determined by how much of the relevant literature has been recorded, analyzed by subject, and described in a way that allows searchers to locate it via bibliographies, databases, and reference literature. The bibliographic approach is characterized by formal rules that determine what is included in a bibliography or database and how it is described (e.g., by using descriptors). The document description is largely an expression of the competence that is tied to the administration of a set of rules. The efficiency of the result depends in particular on whether the formal rules are able to ensure the design of a product that meets the users' needs. The strength of the formal approach is that little material is excluded because of value-based criteria. The weakness is that because they are formal, these systems do not give priority to materials according to relevance. They may, for example, include all books longer than 49 pages or exclude book reviews or not index parts of a document. A lack of resources or of adequate rules to carry out the formal program might lie behind the random inclusion of both the highly relevant and the nonrelevant references. In real life, there is almost always a lack of resources, which means that highly relevant references are often absent. Such formal omissions should not be expected in references, which may, however, contain other kinds of omissions.

The efficiency of chain searching—assuming that one can identify relevant seed documents—is determined by how well the document identifies and cites relevant information in the reference list. The method presupposes that the scientific literature in the field is neither unrelated to other research in the field nor simply redundant. In other words, it assumes that researchers are extremely conscientious in their literature searching and their referencing to relevant sources and that the references are selected with a view to informing the reader of important literature. It also presupposes that the scientist does not cite on purely formal or presentational grounds, for example. Most importantly, it presupposes that authors are not biased in selecting information but give even consideration to papers that argue both for and against their own view. This last assumption seems to contradict the results of psychological research:

> As shown by a multitude of studies, such information-seek-ing processes often are not balanced: people prefer informa-tion that supports their favored or chosen decision alterna-tive compared to information that opposes it. . . . the prefer-ence for supporting (consonant) compared to conflicting (dis-sonant) information occurs if people have decided voluntar-ily and with a certain degree of commitment for a particular alternative . . .We will refer to this preference for supporting information as *confirmation bias.* . . . Therefore, it can be concluded that individuals carry out biased information seek-ing while making decisions, and that this happens from the moment they commit themselves to a particular alternative. (SCHULZ-HARDT ET AL., p. 655)

In citation studies MACROBERTS & MACROBERTS (1988; 1989) have considered authors' motives for not citing relevant documents, just as they represent—together with SEGLEN (and GARFIELD himself)—some of the most qualified and dedicated critics of the misuse of citation indexes. Psychological factors are important in studying why authors quote other documents. As GARFIELD (p. 85), points out, there are many kinds of citation motivations:

- Paying homage to pioneers;
- Giving credit for related work (homage to peers);
- Identifying methodology, equipment, and so on;

- Providing background reading;
- Correcting one's own work;
- Correcting the work of others;
- Criticizing previous work;
- Substantiating claims;
- Alerting to forthcoming work;
- Providing leads to poorly disseminated, poorly indexed, or uncited work;
- Authenticating data and classes of facts—physical constants, and so on;
- Identifying original publications in which an idea or concept was discussed;
- Identifying original publications or other work describing an eponymic concept or term;
- Disclaiming work or ideas of others (negative claims); and
- Disputing priority claims of others (negative homage).

SEGLEN (p. 29) also lists a range of problems concerning selection of references:

- References are selected because of their usefulness for the author, which is something different from their quality;
- Only a small fraction of all used material is cited;
- General knowledge is not cited;
- Knowledge is often cited from secondary sources;
- Documents supporting an author's arguments are cited more often than other documents;
- Flattering (citing editors, potential referees, and other authorities);
- Showing off (citing hot new "in" articles);
- Reference copying (references provided by other authors);
- Conventions (in biochemistry, for example, methods are cited but not reagents);
- Self citations; and
- Citing colleagues (often reflecting informal transfer of information)

Such research says something about the usefulness of references vs. descriptors in information seeking. To the degree that the conventions can be generalized and described, they are of immediate relevance. For example, with the knowledge given above, we can state that citation indexing should perform well on a search for biochemical methods but rather badly on a search for a reagent. There are many studies in this exciting area of citation behavior that directly or indirectly illuminate both the strengths and weaknesses of citations as SAPs, but space limitations prevent us from referring to more of them.

It should be clear that the evaluation of the possibilities of chain searching is connected with studies of cooperation and competition among scientists and subsequent citation behavior. Studies in the sociology of science and in epistemology are highly relevant. It is not difficult to see the importance of, for example, KUHN's well-known theory of scientific paradigms, which directly explains how groups of scientists develop different criteria for relevance and subsequent citation behavior.

*Conclusion.* A given subject access point (e.g., descriptors, references) cannot be expected to have a fixed information value regardless of conventions in the knowledge domain and the writing culture. This is a serious argument against positivistic approaches, which try to develop general algorithms and measures without regard for the contents and the context of the information. To the extent that the demands on "optimal citation behavior" are met, the reference list of every document represents a perfect, "selective" bibliography in the field or together with other articles is part of a network that represents a perfect bibliography. Inclusion in the bibliography that is formed by the reference list is characterized in particular by the fact that the bibliography expresses more limited disciplinary and paradigmatic priorities. The strength of chain searching is that, within a scholarly discipline, there is little risk of overlooking the most important documents. The weakness of this method is related to the fact that any given assumptions within a field can be reevaluated. The documents that become relevant after a reevaluation (e.g., a paradigm shift) typically will not be found by chain searching because references are selected according to paradigmatic norms. In addition, the motives of the scientists are not always pure; these authors may not inform the reader of important sources because they wish to reap the fruit of these at some later date.

Both bibliographic searching and chain searching depend on certain conditions that determine their efficiency. Neither method can a priori be said to be the more systematic, and to some degree they are prerequisites for each other. In areas where quality bibliographies exist, bibliographic searching will be strong. In areas where the scientific standard is very high, chain searching will be strong. In the end, scientific work might develop into an efficient bibliography and efficient bibliographies into products of scholarly quality. Under these conditions the subject bibliography will represent the best map of the research area, a sort of empirical map of the structure of a field, while the article or book and its reference list will be the most accurate answer to a well-defined question, a sort of microsounding in its structure. In other words, bibliographies are more metascientifically oriented. The two products will be able to use each other in this process.

## Full Text

There are today several prominent research projects and different research strategies concerned with the retrieval of full-text documents (or parts of these). Among the most important are the Text REtrieval Conference (TREC)[13] experiments, the Digital Libraries Initiative (DLI),[14] research on the Internet including studies on hypertext markup language (HTML), and programs devoted to the analysis of linguistic problems in natural-language processing (NLP). This chapter can present only a selective review of this research that focuses on our theoretical approach to SAPs. The reader should also consult other reviews, including the review of TREC by SPARCK JONES and various *ARIST* chapters on metadata, information retrieval, and full-text databases.

One of the key components of the success of the World Wide Web is HTML, which has been formalized according to the rules defined by the INTERNATIONAL ORGANIZATION FOR STANDARDIZATION (1986), which defines Standard Generalized Markup Language (SGML). Research and development on this issue has a strong bearing on SAPs and is illuminating for people interested in the underlying intellectual structure of texts rather than just the physical display of that text on paper or screen. BRYAN is an influential source, showing how markup languages operate with document type definitions (DTDs) as well as document analysis and information modeling. Bryan also describes the structures of different kinds of documents such as letters, textbooks, and scientific articles and provides explicit coding of all elements in each type of document, showing why they are important tools for improved subject access based on specified text elements.

---

[13] The First Text REtrieval Conference (TREC-1) was held in Gaithersburg, MD, November 4-6, 1992. The eighth Text REtrieval Conference (TREC-8) was held in Gaithersburg, MD, November 17-19, 1999. See also http://trec.nist.gov/.

[14] The Digital Libraries Initiative (DLI) Phase One (1994-1998) comprised six projects at six research universities under the joint initiative of the National Science Foundation (NSF), the Department of Defense Advanced Research Projects Agency (DARPA), and the National Aeronautics and Space Administration (NASA). The DLI's goal is to advance the means to collect, store, and organize information in digital forms and make it available for searching, retrieval, and processing via communication networks in user-friendly ways. The following sites contain conference information, DLI publications, DLI workshop series, and related projects and resources to the DLI. URL: http://dli.grainger.uiuc.edu/national.htm and http://www.dli2.nsf.gov/.

In IS, ELLIS ET AL. explore the retrieval effectiveness of creating hypertext links in full-text documents, while BATES (1998) discusses human and domain factors in indexing for digital libraries and the Internet. MALET ET AL. describe how medical document retrieval on the Internet can be enhanced utilizing medical core metadata, such as the National Library of Medicine's Medical Subject Headings (MeSH) vocabulary and MEDLINE-type content descriptions. TURNER & BRACKBILL found that the use of the keywords-attribute in a META tag substantially improves accessibility. They suggest that HTML document authors should consider using keywords attribute META tags and that more search engines should index the META tag to improve resource discovery.

One example of relevant research on SAPs using the natural-language processing approach (NLP) is the article by PIRKOLA & JÄRVELIN, who studied the effect of anaphor[15] and ellipsis[16] resolution on proximity searching in a newspaper article database. Their findings indicate a recall increase of 38.2% in sentence searches and 28.8% in paragraph searches when proper-name ellipses were resolved. The increase in recall was 17.6% in sentence searches and 10.8% in paragraph searches when proper-name anaphora were resolved. This result suggests that some simple and computationally justifiable resolution method might be developed for proper-name phrases to support keyword-based full-text IR. PEREZ-CARBALLO & STRZALKOWSKI describe "stream-architecture," a method they designed to combine evidence from different document representations by also applying NLP. DR-LINK, described by LIDDY & MYAENG and by MANNING & NAPIER INFORMATION SERVICES, is an advanced approach to NLP, in which it is possible to search for causes and consequences of events, for example.

With this brief introduction to current research, we now look at a few important studies. TENOPIR & RO report some experiments in full-text retrieval. In a study of *Harvard Business Review* online, they found that full-text searching retrieved 7.4 times more documents than did abstracts, 5.7 times more than controlled vocabulary, and 3.4 times more than the bibliographical union (abstracts, controlled vocabulary, and titles). They define relative recall as the proportion of relevant documents a searcher would retrieve if searching only with that one method.

---

[15] An anaphor is the repetition of a word or phrase in successive clauses as a literary device—e.g., "for them he worked, for them he went hungry, for them he was tempted to steal." (LEXICON PUBLICATIONS)

[16] An ellipsis is a construction that omits one or more words that must be understood for the grammatical completeness of a sentence, for example, in "it's a book I would d . . . d well like to read." The dots indicate that a word, words, or part of a word has been omitted, in this case "d . . . d" for damned." (LEXICON PUBLICATIONS)

On average almost three-fourths of all relevant documents could be retrieved by full-text searching without any value-added fields. Controlled vocabulary contributed on average 28%, abstracts 19.3%, and the bibliographical union 44.9%. These results indicate the value of full-text searching in this database. However, Tenopir and Ro also suggest the importance of value-added fields because in some queries certain documents would not be retrieved without them, and, as hypothesized, full-text searches have a lower precision ratio than do abstracts or controlled-vocabulary searches.

Whereas most studies (e.g., SARACEVIC; SIEVERT ET AL.; TENOPIR, 1985a) compare the overall performance of full-text retrieval with value-added fields, some studies try to illuminate the parts of a full-text document that contribute to its retrievability. VOOS & DAGAEV studied the placement of citations to four highly cited articles in the citing papers. Dividing the articles into four parts—introduction, methodology, discussion, and conclusion—they found that "on the average, the source articles, when highly cited, seem to occur more in the introduction than anywhere else in the article" (p. 20). They conclude that the value of a citation to a researcher depends not only on the number of times it is referenced but also on its placement in the citing article. In the same way we may assume that future full-text retrieval systems may consider the relative information value of terms from different parts of documents.

BISHOP describes DeLIver, a web-based testbed that is a part of the Digital Libraries Initiative at the University of Illinois. DeLIver contains the full text of recent articles from more than 50 science and engineering journals and has the capacity, through Standard Generalized Markup Language (SGML) and enhanced search features, to support retrieval of newly foregrounded document components. Information in individual parts can be disaggregated from the surrounding textual package and retrieved for use in a way not possible with traditional bibliographic retrieval systems. One can search for terms in particular components of documents (e.g., "spectrum" in a figure caption) to enhance the precision of the search. Users can either execute a search "anywhere in article" or limit the search to title, abstract, table text, figure caption, cited references, and more. (The body of the article itself is not distinguished according to introduction, methods, and conclusion). In DeLIver, one can also view certain components before retrieving the full text of the article (including full texts of documents referred to in references if they are included in DeLIver).

A central theme in Bishop's article is a discussion of the need to replace the traditional linear structures in documents with a free combination of "info-bricks." The traditional structure of documents is seen as an artifact of both the technology of printing and beliefs about the scientific method that prevailed in the seventeenth century. This raises the question of whether the unit to be retrieved in IR should be seen as a document or another kind of unit, such as an info-brick.

This question is important in the search process, and much valuable research has been done on passage or paragraph retrieval (PR). Studies such as those by AL-HAWAMDEH ET AL., AL-HAWAMDEH & WILLETT, and LALMAS & RUTHVEN can provide knowledge on the function of parts of texts as SAPs. Studies in PR divide documents in segments based on different principles. A motivated segment can be determined by the content (semantics) or explicit structure of the document (including SGML). An unmotivated segment (or "window") can be determined by number of words (e.g., 25 or 1,000 words). Strangely, experiments by CALLAN and others suggest that motivated segmentation of a given text does not always perform as well as windows. It is, however, too early to draw firm conclusions on this.

If searchers need only a part of a document, they will usually need the whole document as the reference (HJØRLAND, 2000). From our point of view, the most interesting point is not PR as an aim in itself but how the retrieval of whole documents can be improved by using SAPs in full text (in general or by using searches limited to parts of full texts, as for example, the use of conclusions to enhance precision[17]).

Because different kinds of texts have different structures with different consequences for retrieval, we first need a typology of documents. Newspaper articles, for example, usually are organized in a pyramid structure, with the most important information in the heading, then less important information in the first paragraph, and so on. This is done in order to keep the attention of the reader as long as possible. Information retrieval from full-text newspaper databases should take advantage of this structure, whereas IR in scientific articles could vary the retrieval strategy depending, for example, on whether methodological issues or conclusions are of most interest.

DIODATO offers a study on how title words appear in parts of research papers. Given the assumption that title words reflect article content, they propose some interesting ways in which more relevant search terms from the text itself could be identified. Despite a general similarity among the disciplines, they found some important differences. First, the absence of a significant change over time in the number of title words per article in history and philosophy indicates that IR systems would expect changes to occur more slowly in the vocabulary of these two fields than in the other fields. Second, the better matching

---

[17] In Boolean searches recall cannot be improved by PR. This is not the case if other retrieval methods such as vector-space models are used.

in history and philosophy than in chemistry of title words with first-paragraph words emphasizes that IR systems should be aware that history and philosophy articles often begin with long introductory paragraphs, while chemistry articles assign some of the important introductory material to abstracts. Extraction of terms from a chemical abstract may well be comparable to extraction of terms from the first paragraph of a history or philosophy article. Third, the better match in history, philosophy, and economics than in chemistry and mathematics between title words and last-paragraph words suggests the tendency of the former group of journals to use last paragraphs for recapitulation. The latter group often terminates articles when the final result has been demonstrated or the final theorem proved. An IR system that extracts data from only the last section of a chemistry or mathematics journal would get an incomplete picture. Fourth, the better match in chemistry, mathematics, and economics than in history and philosophy between citing and cited titles is partly due to many non-English language titles cited by the latter group. The use of the bibliography of an article for clues to its content would find this a more effective strategy in chemistry, mathematics, and economics than in history and philosophy.

BLAIR & MARON reported on the problems of language in full-text IR in the STAIRS experiment. How can one identify, for example, all documents about a certain train accident? The searcher will think of some obvious terms, and there is a good chance that these will retrieve some relevant documents. However, the searcher may not realize that many other relevant documents will not contain the terms "train" and "accident" or obvious synonyms. Blair and Maron write that this occurs because natural language can be used to discuss a subject using an unpredictably varied and creative combination of words and phrases. The size of such problems is illustrated by the results that recall was on average no better than 20% with a 79% mean precision level. According to the authors, these results were achieved in an environment that was unusually favorable for effective retrieval.

What Blair and Maron do not say—but what is implied in their example–is that relevant documents can describe events leading to the accident, which is not terminologically linked to documents about the accident itself. Then retrieval is not just a matter of the creative expressiveness of natural language, but it is also a matter of real knowledge of what is searched (e.g., the accident). In the process of retrieval, searchers must learn about the object about which they are seeking information, and this subject knowledge must then be fed into the retrieval process to expand the search criteria (iterative searching). For example, an accident can be caused by a failure in a certain kind of signal; thus, the name of the manufacturer of the signal could be a relevant search term. No linguistic theory can provide such knowledge. Searchers thus face the problem of predicting three interacting levels of problems:

- What is in reality (e.g., causes of train accidents)? This is substantive knowledge. At the most fundamental and general level this is ontological knowledge.
- What is known and described so that it can be retrieved and trusted (e.g., engineering studies of train accidents and newspaper reports on train accidents)? These are problems related to theory of knowledge, science studies, and theory of information sources.
- How is recorded knowledge described (e.g., engineering terminology, legal language, and ordinary language)? These require familiarity with document composition and discourse communication and thus particularly relate to terminological, linguistic, and library and information science knowledge.

Such knowledge is *not* the same as subject knowledge as ordinarily taught at universities, although people with subject knowledge often have implicit knowledge about methodological problems, publication patterns, and terminology. Normally, however, they are not experts in such issues. Theories of information seeking and retrieval should provide more explicit knowledge of such questions. Information scientists studying bibliometric patterns, terminological problems (e.g., thesauri), and the like have some advantages in relation to ordinary subject specialists in this respect (which is in accordance with the view expressed by BATES (1999)).

So far these problems have not been seriously addressed theoretically in IS, but mostly by common-sense approaches to ontology, epistemology, and text theory. Controlled systems for information selection and vocabularies normally reduce the searcher's load of predicting such knowledge. Retrieval of documents, for example, on train accidents, is very different in a dedicated journal or database about accident research and prevention than in a merged journal or database. The cognitive and social organization of knowledge in disciplines and literatures facilitates the retrieval of information by reducing the semantic distances between documents and searchers (and in the variance among the documents). A well-designed thesaurus could provide information about, for example, the manufacturer of signals.

*Conclusion.* Full-text databases form the ultimate challenge to information professionals and to information science. We have put forward empirical and theoretical evidence demonstrating that full-text databases without value-added information are not performing with 100%

effectiveness and that value can be added successfully. We have also tried to show that further investigation into the typology and architecture of the texts themselves has potential for the further advancement of full-text retrieval systems.

## Descriptors, Identifiers, Classification Codes, and Other Kinds of Access Data

Classification and indexing are big areas in library and information science with a lot of literature that cannot be reviewed here. We limit ourselves to a few principal aspects related to the overall perspective of this review.

When indexers assign keywords to a record, they are influenced by the title, the abstract, and other access points already given. (Often, for example, the subject headings given by the Library of Congress and printed on the colophon in books affect the way books are classified and indexed in other libraries.) This fact presents a problem in interpreting the relative role of such access points. In other words, the value-added services provided by classifiers, indexers, and abstractors are not always independent interpretations of a document's subjects. If they were (or to the degree that they are independent), their relative importance in retrieval could be determined in relation to those provided by the document itself (i.e., by the author). Certainly, empirical evidence tells us that descriptors and other indexer-assigned keywords do improve retrieval considerably (e.g., PAO, 1994). However, the nature of this improvement is not described well today, although FUGMANN (1993; 1994), among others, has contributed much to the theoretical clarification.

In the literature of information science it is often thought to be ideal if different indexers are mutually consistent. However, as COOPER demonstrated, indexing can be consistently bad, which is why consistency is not necessarily a good criterion of quality in indexing. One can even imagine that indexers who are careless or mechanical in their work are much more apt to use keywords very similar to words from the title, for example. If the title is misleading, the indexing will be misleading. However, indexers and different SAPs could appear consistent and in a way confirm each other in a wrong subject analysis (which again may make the users judge those bibliographical records as relevant on an erroneous basis).

If indexing does not add information to a record, it is unnecessary. However, the repetition of words from titles in indexes is not always redundant. It is only redundant if the repetition is based on mechanical, noninterpretative indexing. Titles often contain metaphorical expressions, so searchers should avoid using titles as access points. In those

cases repetition of words from nonmetaphorical words is often necessary, and the indexer has contributed value-added information by distinguishing titles that are useful from those that are not.

The primary contribution of indexers and abstractors is the determination of the subjects of the documents to be indexed (which may vary
according to different user groups, so that the indexing should be
tailored to the target group). The secondary contribution from indexers
is the formulation of the subjects in one or more languages, which
facilitates retrieval. There are important investigations of the relative
role of controlled vs. uncontrolled vocabularies in indexing (ROWLEY)
and of closed systems as classifications vs. open systems as kinds of
keywords. One of the most ambitious modern projects for establishing
controlled vocabularies is the Unified Medical Language System (UMLS)
of the NATIONAL LIBRARY OF MEDICINE.

*Conclusion.* Earlier IS research has been dominated by the search for
one perfect all-purpose IR language that would accommodate users
who prefer different languages, such as UDC, PRECIS, Bliss, descriptor-based systems, and citation indexes. Today the trend is to view
different IR languages as complementary elements in a system. In other
words, it seems important to define the relative strengths and weaknesses of different kinds of IR languages and to match them to special
needs in different kinds of documents, media, domains, and user groups.
The search for an ideal IR language seems to be related to the old
philosophical dream of building a perfect language (cf. ECO).[18]

## CONCLUSION

Studies have convincingly demonstrated that searchers who use
different SAPs produce different but more-or-less overlapping results.
PAO (1994) found that duplicate documents retrieved by the use of any
two search fields had much higher odds of being judged relevant than
those retrieved by only one of the fields. She concludes that the underlying principle of low overlap is still not well understood and that more
research is needed.

What she and others have showed convincingly is that the quality of
the subjective relevance evaluation increases dramatically when there
are more and different cues in the records. This is not surprising. The
quality of the judgment increases when its basis improves.

When researchers are attacking a problem—say, how to cure a dis-
ease—they are led by different hypotheses and assumptions about
what is relevant. In this process they are using parts of the scientific

---

[18] The same rationalistic dream seems to lie behind the search for one perfect search
algorithm in mainstream IR.

literature that are judged relevant on those premises. However, because this is a dynamic process, the relevance criteria are likely to be changing during the process itself (cf. HJØRLAND, 1997, pp. 165-166). The most tangible expression for what researchers find relevant are the references they include in the final document. However, some relevant documents may not be cited because they seem too general. Also, some nonrelevant documents may be cited for various reasons. Most importantly, if there appears to be a change in the theoretical approach in the field, the researchers may change their previous relevance criteria and reevaluate what they first considered relevant. When seeking new documents based on a changed concept of the problem, users will interpret every cue, which may indicate which documents will be relevant from the changed position. For example, a cue might be that the relevant papers cite other papers that demonstrate a similar conceptualization of the problem or that use a terminology developed to discriminate this conceptualization from others (or that is published in places or by journals devoted to such a conceptualization).

One problem is whether documents are judged relevant or are discarded given ideal conditions for studying them. Another problem is whether they are judged relevant or are discarded on the basis of certain cues (such as author, title, abstracts, recommendations). Even careful studies of single documents are often subjective and uncertain (as we know, for example, from book reviews and hermeneutic studies). Judgment of the relevance of single documents based on a quick examination of a few search fields increases this subjectivity and uncertainty in relevance evaluation dramatically. A given record may contain relevant words in the title or in the descriptors, it may cite well-known studies among its references, it may be published in a leading journal in the field, and so forth. Given the high degree of uncertainty in relevance assessment, it is not surprising that a given person is more likely to regard a document as being relevant if more than one cue indicates relevance. This finding is obvious. Overlap as a retrieval strategy can therefore be used to increase precision in searches, as PAO (1994) concludes. This occurs, however, at the expense of recall.

Because subjective relevance assessments are necessarily based on the available information, IS must focus more on the study of the objective informativeness of different SAPs, that is, on the given possibilities that searchers have, regardless of how they evaluate them and whether or not they understand how to use them. As BATES (1987) suggests, behavioral studies to date have not explained much of the variation in online search success; that is why a hard look at the information itself, especially its structure and organization, is likely to prove more fruitful. Although valuable behavioral research has since been carried out (e.g., FIDEL, 1991a, 1991b, 1991c; SARACEVIC & KANTOR), the study of texts and "information" is still underrepresented. The more we know about how authors use titles and terminology, how they compose their documents, how they cite other documents, and how they are affected by metatheoretical trends, as well as the more we know about the indexing and abstracting process, the more we know about objective search possibilities. From here we can go on to study how those possibilities are actually used (the subjective, behavioral, and computerized side of searching).

## BIBLIOGRAPHY

AL-HAWAMDEH, SULIMAN; DE VERE, RACHEL; SMITH, GEOFF; WILLETT, PETER. 1991. Using Nearest-Neighbour Searching Techniques to Access Full-Text Documents. Online Review. 1991 June/August; 15(3/4): 173-191. ISSN: 0309-314X.

AL-HAWAMDEH, SULIMAN; WILLETT, PETER. 1989. Comparison of Index Term Weighting Schemes for the Ranking of Paragraphs in Full-text Documents. International Journal of Information and Library Research. 1989; 1(2): 116-130. ISSN: 0953-556X.

ALTAVISTA. 2000. Advanced Search Cheat Sheet. Available WWW: http://help.altavista.com/adv_search/syntax.

ALTERMAN, RICHARD. 1991. Understanding and Summarization. Artificial Intelligence Review. 1991; 5(4): 239-254. ISSN: 0269-2821; CODEN: AIRVE6. Also available as: Text Summarization. In: Shapiro, Stuart C., ed. Encyclopedia of Artificial Intelligence. New York, NY: Wiley; 1992. 1579-1587. ISBN: 0-471-50307-X; LC: 91-37272.

ATKINSON, ROSS. 1984. The Citation as Intertext: Toward a Theory of the Selection Process. Library Resources & Technical Services. 1984 April/June; 28(2): 109-119. ISSN: 0024-2527.

BARKER, FRANCES H.; VEAL, DOUGLAS C.; WYATT, BARRY K. 1972. Comparative Efficiency of Searching Titles, Abstracts, and Index Terms in a Free-text Data Base. Journal of Documentation. 1972 March; 28(1): 22-36. ISSN: 0022-0418.

BATES, MARCIA J. 1987. Information: The Last Variable. In: Chen, Ching-chih, ed. ASIS '87: Proceedings of the American Society for Information Science (ASIS) 50th Annual Meeting; 1987 October 4-8; Boston, MA. Medford, NJ: Learned Information, Inc. for ASIS; 1987. 6-10. ISSN: 0044-7070; ISBN: 0-938734-19-9; CODEN: PAISDQ.

BATES, MARCIA J. 1998. Indexing and Access for Digital Libraries and the Internet: Human, Database, and Domain Factors. Journal of the American Society for Information Science. 1998 November; 49(13): 1185-1205. ISSN: 0002-8231; CODEN: AISJB6.

BATES, MARCIA J. 1999. The Invisible Substrate of Information Science. Journal of the American Society for Information Science. 1999 October; 50(12): 1043-1050. ISSN: 0002-8231; CODEN: AISJB6.

BAZERMAN, CHARLES. 1985. Physicists Reading Physics: Schema-Laden Purposes and Purpose-Laden Schema. Written Commmunication. 1985 January; 2(1): 3-23. ISSN: 0741-0883.

BAZERMAN, CHARLES. 1988. Shaping Written Knowledge: The Genre and Activity of the Experimental Article in Science. Madison, WI: The University of Wisconsin Press; 1988. 356p. ISBN: 0-299-11690-5; ISBN: 0-299-11694-8 (pbk.).

BERNAL, JOHN DESMOND. 1948. Preliminary Analysis of Pilot Questionnaire on the Use of Scientific Literature. In: Royal Society [Great Britain]. The Royal Society Scientific Information Conference: Report and Papers Submitted; 1948 June 21-July 2; London, UK. London, UK: Royal Society; 1948. 589-637. OCLC: 1820040.

BERNARD, M. 1995. À juste titre: A Lexicometric Approach to the Study of Titles. Literary & Linguistic Computing. 1995; 10(2): 135-141. ISSN: 0268-1145; CODEN: LLCOEI.

BERNIER, CHARLES L. 1980. Subject Indexes. In: Kent, Allen; Lancour, Harold; Daily, J.E., eds. Encyclopedia of Library and Information Science: Volume 29. New York, NY: Marcel Dekker; 1980. 191-205. ISBN: 0-8247-2027-X.

BERRY, MICHAEL W.; DUMAIS, SUSAN T.; O'BRIEN, GANIN W. 1995. Using Linear Algebra for Intelligent Information-Retrieval. SIAM Review. 1995 December; 37(4): 537-595. ISSN: 0036-1445; CODEN: SIREAD.

BISHOP, ANN PETERSON. 1999. Document Structure and Digital Libraries: How Researchers Mobilize Information in Journal Articles. Information Processing & Management. 1999; 35(3): 255-279. ISSN: 0306-4573; CODEN: IPMADK.

BLAIR, DAVID C. 1990. Language and Representation in Information Retrieval. Amsterdam, The Netherlands: Elsevier Science Publishers; 1990. 335p. ISBN: 0-444-88437-8; LC: 89-29881.]

BLAIR, DAVID C. 1996. Stairs Redux: Thoughts on the Stairs Evaluation, 10 Years After. Journal of the American Society for Information Science. 1996 January; 47(1): 4-22. ISSN: 0002-8231.

BLAIR, DAVID C.; MARON, M.E. 1990. Full-Text Information-Retrieval: Further Analysis and Clarification. Information Processing & Management. 1990; 26(3): 437-447. ISSN: 0306-4573; CODEN: IPMADK.

BORKO, HAROLD S.; CHATMAN, S. 1963. Criteria for Acceptable Abstracts: A Survey of Abstracters' Instructions. American Documentation. 1963 April; 14(2): 149-160. ISSN: 0096-946X.

BOYCE, BERT. 1982. Beyond Topicality: A Two Stage View of Relevance and the Retrieval Process. Information Processing & Management. 1982; 18(3): 105-109. ISSN: 0306-4573; CODEN: IPMADK.

BRADFORD, SAMUEL CLEMENT. 1948. Documentation. London, UK: C. Lockwood; 1948. 156p. LC: 49-12638; OCLC 1347246.

BROOKS, TERRENCE ALAN. 1993. All the Right Descriptors: A Test of the Strategy of Unlimited Aliasing. Journal of the American Society for Information Science. 1993 April; 44(3): 137-147. ISSN: 0002-8231; CODEN: AISJB6.

BRYAN, MARTIN. 1997. Web SGML and HTML 4.0 Explained. Available WWW: http://www.sgml.u-net.com/book/home.htm. Also published as: SGML and HTML Explained. 2nd edition. Harlow, UK: Addison Wesley Longman; 1997. 234p. ISBN: 0-201-40394-3.

BUCKLEY, CHRISTOPHER; MITRA, MANDAR; WALZ, JANET; CARDIE, CLAIRE. 2000. Using Clustering and SuperConcepts within SMART: TREC 6. Information Processing & Management. 2000 January; 36(1): 109-131. ISSN: 0306-4573; CODEN: IPMADK.

BUXTON, ANDREW B.; MEADOWS, A. J. 1977. The Variation in the Information Content of Titles of Research Papers with Time and Discipline. Journal of Documentation. 1977 March; 33(1): 46-52. ISSN: 0022-0418.

BUXTON, ANDREW B.; MEADOWS, A.J. 1978. Categorization of the Information in Experimental Papers and Their Author Abstracts. Journal of Research Communication Studies. 1978 August; 1(2): 161-182. ISSN: 0378-5939.

BYRNE, J.R. 1975. Relative Effectiveness of Titles, Abstracts, and Subject Headings for Machine Retrieval from the COMPENDEX Services. Journal of the American Society for Information Science. 1975 July/August; 26(4): 223-229. ISSN: 0002-8231; CODEN: AISJB6.

CALLAN, JAMES P. 1994. Passage-Level Evidence in Document Retrieval. In: Croft, W. Bruce; van Rijsbergen, C. J. eds. SIGIR '94: Proceedings of the Association for Computing Machinery Special Interest Group on Information Retrieval (ACM SIGIR) 17th Annual International Conference on Research and Development in Information Retrieval; 1994 July 3-6; Dublin, Ireland. Berlin, Germany: Springer Verlag; 1994. 302-310. ISBN: 3-540-19889-X.

CHAFE, W.L. 1976. Givenness, Contrastiveness, Definiteness, Subject, Topic, and Point of View. In: Li, Charles N., ed. Symposium on Subject and Topic; 1975 March; Santa Barbara, CA. New York, NY: Academic Press; 1976. 25-55. ISBN: 0-12-447350-4; LC: 75-43861.

CHALMERS, ALAN F. 1999. What Is This Thing Called Science? 3rd edition. Buckingham, UK: Open University Press; 1999. 266p. ISBN: 0-335-20109-1.

CHEN, HSINCHUN; HOUSTON, ANDREA L.; SEWELL, ROBIN R.; SCHATZ, BRUCE R. 1998. Internet Browsing and Searching: User Evaluations of Category Map and Concept Space Techniques. Journal of the American Society for Information Science. 1998 May; 49(7): 582-603. ISSN: 0002-8231.

COLLISON, ROBERT LEWIS. 1971. Abstracts and Abstracting Services. Santa Barbara, CA: ABC-Clio; 1971. 122p. ISBN: 0-87436-078-1; LC: 78-149635.

COOPER, WILLIAM S. 1969. Is Interindexer Consistency a Hobgoblin? American Documentation. 1969 July; 20(3): 268-278. ISSN: 0096-946X; CODEN: AMDOA7.

CORMACK, GORDON V.; CLARKE, CHARLES L. A.; PALMER, CHRISTOPHER R.; TO, SAMUEL S. L. 2000. Passage-Based Query Refinement. Information Processing & Management. 2000 January; 36(1): 133-153. ISSN: 0306-4573; CODEN: IPMADK.

CROSBY, HARRY H. 1976. Titles, A Treatise On. College Composition and Communication. 1976 December; 27(4): 387-391. ISSN: 0010-096X; CODEN: CCCOAM.

DE GROLIER, ERIC. 1965. Current Trends in Theory and Practice of Classification. In: Atherton, Pauline, ed. Classification Research: Proceedings of the

2nd International Study Conference; 1965 September 14-18; Elsinore, Denmark. Copenhagen, Denmark: Munksgaard; 1965. 9-14. (FID Publication no. 370). OCLC: 9499510.

DIODATO, VIRGIL. 1982. The Occurrence of Title Words in Parts of Research Papers: Variations among Disciplines. Journal of Documentation. 1982 September; 38(3): 192-206. ISSN: 0022-0418.

DONG, XIAOYING; SU, LOUISE T. 1997. Search Engines on the World Wide Web and Information Retrieval from the Internet: A Review and Evaluation. Online & CD-ROM Review. 1997 April; 21(2): 67-82. ISSN: 1353-2642.

ECO, UMBERTO. 1995. The Search for the Perfect Language. [Translated from Italian: Ricerca della lingua perfetta nella cultura europea]. Oxford, UK: Blackwell; 1995. 385p. ISBN: 0-631-17465-6; LC: 94-29141.

ELLIS, DAVID; FURNER, JONATHAN; WILLETT, PETER. 1996. On the Creation of Hypertext Links in Full-Text Documents: Measurement of Retrieval Effectiveness. Journal of the American Society for Information Science. 1996 April; 47(4): 287-300. ISSN: 0002-8231; CODEN: AISJB6

FEDOSYUK, M.YU. 1978. Linguistic Criteria for Differentiating Informative and Indicative Abstracts. Automatic Documentation and Mathematical Linguistics. 1978; 12(3): 98-110. ISSN: 0005-1055.

FIDEL, RAYA. 1986. Writing Abstracts for Free-Text Searching. Journal of Documentation. 1986 March; 42(1): 11-21. ISSN: 0022-0418.

FIDEL, RAYA. 1991a. Searchers' Selection of Search Keys, 1: The Selection Routine. Journal of the American Society for Information Science. 1991 August; 42(7): 490-500. ISSN: 0002-8231; CODEN: AISJB6.

FIDEL, RAYA. 1991b. Searchers' Selection of Search Keys, 2: Controlled Vocabulary or Free-Text Searching. Journal of the American Society for Information Science. 1991 August; 42(7): 501-514. ISSN: 0002-8231; CODEN: AISJB6.

FIDEL, RAYA. 1991c. Searchers' Selection of Search Keys, 3: Searching Styles. Journal of the American Society for Information Science. 1991 August; 42(7): 515-527. ISSN: 0002-8231; CODEN: AISJB6.

FIDEL, RAYA; EFTHIMIADIS, EFTHIMIS NIKOLAOS. 1995. Terminological Knowledge Structure for Intermediary Expert-Systems. Information Processing & Management. 1995 January/February; 31(1): 15-27. ISSN: 0306-4573; CODEN: IPMADK.

FLYNN, PETER. 1997. W[h]ither the Web?: The Extension or Replacement of HTML. Journal of the American Society for Information Science. 1997 July; 48(7): 614–621. ISSN: 0002-8231; CODEN: AISJB6.

FRAENKEL, AVIEZRI S.; KLEIN, SHMUEL T. 1999. Information Retrieval from Annotated Texts. Journal of the American Society for Information Science. 1999 August; 50(10): 845-854. ISSN: 0002-8231; CODEN: AISJB6.

FRIIS-HANSEN, JENS B.; STEEN LARSEN, POUL; HØST, TORBEN; SPANG-HANSSEN, HENNING. 1996. Informationsordbogen: Ordbog for informationshåndtering, bog og bibliotek, 2. udg. [Dictionary of Information Terms]. Charlottenlund, Denmark: Dansk Standard (DS); 1996. 196p. (DS-Håndbog 109). ISSN: 0903-0484; ISBN: 87-7310-186-9.

FUGMANN, ROBERT. 1993. Subject Analysis and Indexing: Theoretical Foundation and Practical Advice. Frankfurt am Main, Germany: Index Verlag; 1993. 250p. (Textbooks for Knowledge Organization, vol. 1). ISBN: 3-88672-500-6.

FUGMANN, ROBERT. 1994. Representational Predictability: Key to the Resolution of Several Pending Issues in Indexing and Information Supply. In: Albrechtsen, Hanne; Ørnager, Susanne, eds. Knowledge Organization and Quality Management: Proceedings of the 3rd International Conference of the International Society for Knowledge Organization (ISKO); 1994 June 20-24; Copenhagen, Denmark. Frankfurt am Main, Germany: Index Verlag; 1994. 414-422. (Advances in Knowledge Organization, vol. 4). ISBN: 3-88672-023-3.

GARFIELD, EUGENE. 1965. Can Citation Indexing Be Automated? In: Stevens, Mary E.; Giuliano, Vincent E.; Heilprin, Laurence B., eds. Statistical Association Methods for Mechanized Documentation, Symposium Proceedings; 1964; Washington, DC. Washington, DC: National Bureau of Standards; 1965. 189-192. (National Bureau of Standards Miscellaneous Publication, no. 269). Also published in: Essays of an Information Scientist: 1962-1973. Volume 1. Philadelphia, PA: ISI Press; 1973. 84-90. Also available WWW: http://www.garfield.library.upenn.edu/essays/V1p084y1962-73.pdf.

GENETTE, GÉRARD. 1988. Structure and Functions of the Title in Literature. Critical Inquiry. 1988; 14(4): 692-720. ISSN: 0093-1896.

GERICK, THOMAS. 1999. Content-based Information Retrieval auf Basis Semantischer Abfragenetze. NFD Information-Wissenschaft und Praxis. 1999 July; 50(4): 205-209. ISSN: 1434-4653: CODEN: NADOAW.

GILLASPIE, DEBORAH L. 1992. Why Online Legal Retrieval Misses Conceptually Relevant Documents. In: Shaw, Debora, ed. ASIS '92: Proceedings of the American Society for Information Science (ASIS) 55th Annual Meeting: Volume 29; 1992 October 26-29; Pittsburgh, PA. Medford, NJ: Learned Information, Inc. for ASIS; 1992. 256-259. ISSN: 0044-7870; ISBN: 0-938734-69-5; CODEN: PAISDQ.

GILLASPIE, DEBORAH L. 1995. The Role of Linguistic Phenomena in Retrieval Performance. In: Kinney, Tom, ed. ASIS '95: Proceedings of the American Society for Information Science (ASIS) 58th Annual Meeting: Volume 32; 1995 October 9-12; Chicago, IL. Medford, NJ: Information Today, Inc. for ASIS; 1995. 90-96. ISSN: 0044-7870; ISBN: 1-57387-017-X; CODEN: PAISDQ.

GORDON, MICHAEL D.; DUMAIS, SUSAN T. 1998. Using Latent Semantic Indexing for Literature Based Discovery. Journal of the American Society for Information Science. 1998 June; 49(8): 674-685. ISSN: 0002-8231; CODEN: AISJB6

GREEN, REBECCA. 1995. Topical Relevance Relationships 1: Why Topical Matching Fails. Journal of the American Society for Information Science. 1995 October; 46(9): 646-653. ISSN: 0002-8231.

GREEN, REBECCA. 2000. Locating Sources in Humanities Scholarship: The Efficacy of Following Bibliographic References. Library Quarterly. 2000 April; 70(2): 201-229. ISSN: 0024-2519.

GREEN, REBECCA; BEAN, CAROL A. 1995. Topical Relevance Relationships
2: An Exploratory Study and Preliminary Typology. Journal of the American Society for Information Science. 1995 October; 46(9): 654-662. ISSN:
0002-8231.

HARRIS, JESSICA L. 1974. Document Description and Representation. In:
Cuadra, Carlos A., ed. Annual Review of Information Science and Tech-
nology: Volume 9. Washington, DC: American Society for Information
Science; 1974. 81-117. ISSN: 0066-4200; ISBN: 0-87715-209-8.

HARTER, STEPHEN P.; HERT, CAROL A. 1997. Evaluation of Information
Retrieval Systems: Approaches, Issues, and Methods. In: Williams, Martha
E., ed. Annual Review of Information Science and Technology: Volume 32.
Medford, NJ: Information Today, Inc. for the American Society for Infor-
mation Science; 1997. 3-94. ISSN: 0066-4200; ISBN: 1-57387-047-1.

HARTER, STEPHEN P.; NISONGER, THOMAS E.; WENG, AIWEI. 1993.
Semantic Relationships between Cited and Citing Articles in Library and
Information Science Journals. Journal of the American Society for Infor-
mation Science. 1993 October; 44(9): 543-552. ISSN: 0002-8231; CODEN:
AISJB6.

HERRELL, JAMES M. 1979. Abstract Thinking in APA Journals. American
Psychologist. 1979 February; 34(2): 178-180. ISSN: 0003-066X.

HJØRLAND, BIRGER. 1988. Information Retrieval in Psychology. Behavioral
and Social Sciences Librarian. 1988 December; 6(3/4): 39-64. ISSN: 0163-
9269.

HJØRLAND, BIRGER. 1992. The Concept of "Subject" in Information Science.
Journal of Documentation. 1992 June; 48(2): 172-200. ISSN: 0022-0418;
CODEN: JDOCAS.

HJØRLAND, BIRGER. 1997. Information Seeking and Subject Representation:
An Activity-Theoretical Approach to Information Science. Westport, CT:
Greenwood Press; 1997. 213p. (New Directions in Information Manage-
ment ; 34). ISBN: 0-313-29893-9.

HJØRLAND, BIRGER. 1998. Information Retrieval, Text Composition, and
Semantics. Knowledge Organization. 1998; 25(1/2): 16-31. ISSN: 0943-
7444.

HJØRLAND, BIRGER. 2000. Documents, Memory Institutions, and Information Science. Journal of Documentation. 2000; 56(1): 27-41. ISSN: 0022-
0418.

HODGES, PAULINE R. 1983. Keyword in Title Indexes. Special Libraries.
1983 January; 74(1): 56-60. ISSN: 0038-6723.

HORNBY, PETER A. 1972. The Psychological Subject and Predicate. Cognitive
Psychology. 1972 October; 3(4): 632-642. ISSN: 0010-0285.

HULME, E. WYNDHAM. 1911a. Principles of Book Classification: Introduction. Library Association Record. 1911; 13: 354-358. ISSN: 0024-2195.

HULME, E. WYNDHAM. 1911b. Principles of Book Classification: Chapter II –
Principles of Division in Book Classification. Library Association Record.
1911; 13: 389-394. ISSN: 0024-2195.

HULME, E. WYNDHAM. 1911c. Principles of Book Classification: Chapter III
– On the Definition of Class Headings, and the Natural Limit to the

Extension of Book Classification. Library Association Record. 1911; 13: 444-449. ISSN: 0024-2195.

IIVONEN, MIRJA; SONNENWALD, DIANE H. 1998. From Translation to Navigation of Different Discourses: A Model of Search Term Selection during the Pre-Online Stage of the Search Process. Journal of the American Society for Information Science. 1998 April; 49(4): 312-326. ISSN: 0002-8231; CODEN: AISJB6.

INTERNATIONAL ORGANIZATION FOR STANDARDIZATION (ISO). 1976. Documentation: Abstracts for Publications and Documentation. 1st edition. 6p. (ISO 214:1976). Available from: International Organization for Standardization, http://www.iso.ch/.

INTERNATIONAL ORGANIZATION FOR STANDARDIZATION (ISO). 1986. Information Processing—Text and Office Systems—Standard Generalized Markup Language (SGML). 1st edition. 155p. (ISO 8879:1986). Available from: International Organization for Standardization, http://www.iso.ch/.

JANES, JOSEPH W. 1994. Other People's Judgments: A Comparison of Users' and Others' Judgments of Document Relevance, Topicality, and Utility. Journal of the American Society for Information Science. 1994 April; 45(3): 160-171. ISSN: 0002-8231; CODEN: AISJB6.

KEEN, E. MICHAEL. 1992. Some Aspects of Proximity Searching in Text Retrieval-Systems. Journal of Information Science. 1992; 18(2): 89-98. ISSN: 0165-5515; CODEN: JISCDI.

KELLER, BARBARA. 1992. Subject Content through Title: A Masters Theses Matching Study at Indiana State University. Cataloging & Classification Quarterly. 1992; 15(3): 69-80. ISSN: 0163-9374.

KUHN, THOMAS S. 1962. The Structure of Scientific Revolutions. Chicago, IL: University of Chicago Press; 1962. 172p. LC: 62-19621.

LALMAS, MOUNIA; RUTHVEN, IAN. 1998. Representing and Retrieving Structured Documents Using the Dempster-Shafer Theory of Evidence: Modelling and Evaluation. Journal of Documentation. 1998 December; 54(5): 529-565. ISSN: 0022-0418; CODEN: JDOCAS.

LANCASTER, FREDERICK WILFRID. 1998. Indexing and Abstracting in Theory and Practice. 2nd edition. London, UK: Library Association Publishing; 1998. 412p. ISBN: 1-85604-268-5.

LANGRIDGE, DEREK W. 1989. Subject Analysis: Principles and Procedures. London, UK: Bowker-Saur; 1989. 146p. ISBN: 0-408-03031-3.

LARSON, RAY R. 1991. The Decline of Subject Searching: Long-Term Trends and Patterns of Index Use in an Online Catalog. Journal of the American Society for Information Science. 1991 April; 42(3): 197-215. ISSN: 0002-8231; CODEN: AISJB6.

LEXICON PUBLICATIONS. 1990. The New Lexicon Webster's Dictionary of the English Language. New York, NY: Lexicon Publications; 1990. 2000p. ISBN: 0-7172-04546-2.

LI, CHARLES N., ed. 1976. Subject and Topic: Symposium on Subject and Topic; 1975 March; Santa Barbara, CA. New York, NY: Academic Press; 1976. 594p. ISBN: 0-12-447350-4; LC: 75-43861.

LIDDY, ELIZABETH D.; MYAENG, SUNG H. 1993. Linguistic-Conceptual Approach to Document Detection. In: Harman, D.K., ed. The 1st Text REtrieval Conference (TREC-1); 1992 November 4–6; Gaithersburg, MD. Washington, DC: U.S. Department of Commerce, National Institute of Standards and Technology; 1993. 113-129. NTIS: PB93-191641.

LIU, MENGXIONG. 1993. The Complexities of Citation Practices: A Review of Citation Studies. Journal of Documentation. 1993 December; 49(4): 370-408. ISSN: 0022-0418.

MACROBERTS, MICHAEL H.; MACROBERTS, BARBARA R. 1988. Author Motivation for Not Citing Influences: A Methodological Note. Journal of the American Society for Information Science. 1988 November; 39(6): 432-433. ISSN: 0002-8231; CODEN: AISJB6.

MACROBERTS, MICHAEL H.; MACROBERTS, BARBARA R. 1989. Problems of Citation Analysis: A Critical Review. Journal of the American Society for Information Science. 1989 September; 40(5): 342-349. ISSN: 0002-8231; CODEN: AISJB6.

MALET, GARY; MUNOZ, FELIX; APPLEYARD, RICHARD; HERSH, WILLIAM R. 1999. A Model for Enhancing Internet Medical Document Retrieval with "Medical Core Metadata". Journal of the American Medical Informatics Association. 1999 March/April; 6(2): 163-172. ISSN: 1067-5027.

MALMKJÆR, KIRSTEN. 1995. Genre Analysis. In: Malmkjær, Kirsten, ed. The Linguistics Encyclopedia. London, UK: Routledge; 1995. 170-181. ISBN: 0-415-12566-9.

MANNING & NAPIER INFORMATION SERVICES. 2000. DR-LINK: Document Retrieval Using LINguistic Knowledge. Available WWW: http://www.textwise.com/dr-link.html.

MANZER, BRUCE M. 1977. The Abstract Journal, 1790-1920: Origin, Development and Diffusion. Metuchen, NJ: Scarecrow Press; 1977. 312p. ISBN: 0-8108-1047-6; LC: 77-24143.

MOOERS, CALVIN NORTHRUP. 1951. Zatocoding Applied to Mechanical Organization of Knowledge. American Documentation. 1951 January; 2(1): 20-32. ISSN: 0096-946X.

MOOERS, CALVIN NORTHRUP. 1972. Descriptors. In: Kent, Allen; Lancour, Harold; Daily, J.E., eds. Encyclopedia of Library and Information Science: Volume 7. New York, NY: Marcel Dekker; 1972. 31-45. ISBN: 0-8247-2107-1.

MYERS, GREG. 1990. Writing Biology: Texts in the Social Construction of Scientific Knowledge. Madison, WI: University of Wisconsin Press; 1990. 304p. ISBN: 0-299-12230-1; LC: 89-40263.

NAHL-JAKOBOVITS, DIANE; JAKOBOVITS, LEON A. 1987. Teaching the Analysis of Titles: Dependent and Independent Variables in Research Articles. Research Strategies. 1987 Fall; 5(4): 164-171. ISSN: 0734-3310.

NATIONAL INSTITUTE OF STANDARDS AND TECHNOLOGY (NIST). 2000. Proceedings of the 8th Text REtrieval Conference (TREC-8); 1999 November 17-19; Gaithersburg, MD. (NIST Special Publication 500-246). Available WWW: http://trec.nist.gov/pubs/trec8/t8_proceedings.html.

NATIONAL LIBRARY OF MEDICINE. 2000. Unified Medical Language System (UMLS). Available WWW: http://www.nlm.nih.gov/research/umls/umlsmain.html.

NORD, CHRISTIANE. 1991. Text Analysis in Translation: Theory, Methodology, and Didactic Application of a Model for Translation-Oriented Text Analysis. Amsterdam, The Netherlands: Rodopi; 1991. 250p. (Amsterdamer Publikationen zur Sprache und Literatur; 94; Translated from the German by Christiane Nord and Penelope Sparrow). ISBN: 9-05183-311-3.

NORD, CHRISTIANE. 1995. Text-Functions in Translation: Titles and Headings as a Case in Point. Target. 1995; 7(2): 261-284. CODEN: TARGEC; OCLC: 20768955.

OLSEN, KAJ A.; SOCHATS, KENNETH M.; WILLIAMS, JAMES G. 1998. Full Text Searching and Information Overload. International Information & Library Review. 1998 June; 30(2): 105-122. ISSN: 1057-2317.

PAO, MIRANDA LEE. 1993. Term and Citation Retrieval: A Field Study. Information Processing & Management. 1993 January/February; 29(1): 95-112. ISSN: 0306-4573; CODEN: IPMADK.

PAO, MIRANDA LEE. 1994. Relevance Odds of Retrieval Overlaps from Seven Search Fields. Information Processing & Management. 1994 May/June; 30(3): 305-314. ISSN: 0306-4573; CODEN: IPMADK.

PAO, MIRANDA LEE; WORTHEN, DENNIS B. 1989. Retrieval Effectiveness by Semantic and Pragmatic Relevance. Journal of the American Society for Information Science. 1989 July; 40(4): 226-235. ISSN: 0002-8231; CODEN: AISJB6.

PEREZ-CARBALLO, JOSE; STRZALKOWSKI, TOMEK. 2000. Natural Language Information Retrieval: Progress Report. Information Processing & Management. 2000 January; 36(1): 155-178. ISSN: 0306-4573; CODEN: IPMADK.

PERITZ, BLUMA C. 1984. On the Informativeness of Titles. International Classification. 1984; 11(2): 87-89. ISSN: 0340-0050.

PINTO, MARÍA; GÁLVEZ, CARMEN. 1999. Paradigms for Abstracting Systems. Journal of Information Science. 1999; 25(5): 365-380. ISSN: 0165-5515; CODEN: JIOSED.

PIRKOLA, ARI; JÄRVELIN, KALERVO. 1996. The Effect of Anaphor and Ellipsis Resolution on Proximity in a Text Database. Information Processing & Management. 1996 March; 32(2): 199-216. ISSN: 0306-4573; CODEN: IPMADK.

POLLITT, A. S.; TINKER, AMANDA J.; BRAEKEVELT, PATRICK A.J. 1998. Improving Access to Online Information Using Dynamic Faceted Classification. In: McKenna, Brian; Graham, Catherine; Kerr, J., eds. Online Information 98: Proceedings of the 22nd International Online Information Meeting; 1998 December 8-10; London, UK. Oxford, UK: Learned Information Europe; 1998. 17-21. ISBN: 1-900871-31-9.

POULSEN, CLAUS. 1994. Informationens skygge og foran: informationskvalitet, informationseksplosion og online kataloger. Roskilde, Denmark: Institut for Datalogi, Kommunikation og Uddannelsesforskning, Roskilde Universitetscenter; 1994. 198p. (Papirer om faglig formidling; 36). ISBN: 87-7349-264-7.

PRICE, DOUGLAS S. 1983. Possible Impact of Electronic Publishing on Abstracting and Indexing. Journal of the American Society for Information Science. 1983 July; 34(4): 288. ISSN: 0002-8231; CODEN: AISJB6.

RAO, ASHWIN; LU, ALLAN; MEIER, ED; AHMED, SALAHUDDIN; PLISKE, DANIEL. 2000. Query Processing in TREC-6. Information Processing & Management. 2000 January; 36(1): 179-186. ISSN: 0306-4573; CODEN: IPMADK.

ROWLEY, JENNIFER. 1994. The Controlled Versus Natural Indexing Languages Revisited: A Perspective on Information Retrieval Practice and Research. Journal of Information Science. 1994; 20(2): 108-119. ISSN: 0165-5515.

ROWLEY, JENNIFER; FARROW, JOHN. 2000. Organizing Knowledge: An Introduction to Managing Access to Information. 3rd edition. Aldershot, Hampshire, UK: Gower; 2000. 404p. ISBN: 0-566-08047-8.

SALTON, GERARD. 1996. A New Horizon for Information Science. Journal of the American Society for Information Science. 1996 April; 47(4): 333. (Letter to the Editor). ISSN: 0002-8231; CODEN: AISJB6.

SARACEVIC, TEFKO. 1969. Comparative Effects of Titles, Abstracts and Full Texts on Relevance Judgments 1. In: North, J.B., ed. Proceedings of the American Society for Information Science (ASIS) 32nd Annual Meeting: Volume 6; 1969 October 1-4; San Francisco, CA. Westport, CT: Greenwood Publishing; 1969. 293-299. OCLC: 8416080.

SARACEVIC, TEFKO; KANTOR, PAUL. 1988. A Study of Information Seeking and Retrieving. III: Searchers, Searches, and Overlap. Journal of the American Society for Information Science. 1988 May; 39(3): 197-216. ISSN: 0002-8231; CODEN: AISJB6.

SCHULZ-HARDT, STEFAN; FREY, DIETER; LÜTHGENS, CARSTEN; MOSCOVICI, SERGE. 2000. Biased Information Search in Group Decision Making. Journal of Personality and Social Psychology. 2000; 78(4): 655-669. ISSN: 0022-3514.

SEGLEN, PER O. 1996. Bruk av siteringer og tidsskrift-impaktfaktor til forskningsevaluering. [The Use of Citations and Journal Impact Factors for Evaluation of Research]. Biblioteksarbejde. 1996; 48: 27-34. ISBN: 87-88524-55-8.

SIEVERT, MARYELLEN; MCKININ, EMMA JEAN. 1989. Why Full-Text Misses Some Relevant Documents: An Analysis of Documents Not Retrieved by CCML or MEDIS. In: Katzer, Jeffrey; Newby, Gregory B., eds. ASIS '89: Proceedings of the American Society for Information Science (ASIS) 52nd Annual Meeting: Volume 26; 1989 October 30-November 2; Washington, DC. Medford, NJ: Learned Information, Inc. for ASIS; 1989. 34-39. ISSN: 0044-7870; ISBN: 0-938734-40-7; CODEN: PAISDQ.

SIEVERT, MARYELLEN; MCKININ, EMMA JEAN; SLOUGH, MARLENE. 1988. A Comparison of Indexing and Full-Text for the Retrieval of Clinical Medical Literature. In: Borgman, Christine L.; Pai, Edward Y.H., eds. ASIS '88: Information & Technology: Planning for the Next Fifty Years: Proceedings of the American Society for Information Science (ASIS) 51st Annual Meeting: Volume 25; 1988 October 23-27; Atlanta, GA. Medford, NJ: Learned Information, Inc. for ASIS; 1988. 143-146. ISSN: 0044-7870; ISBN: 0-938734-29-6; CODEN: PAISDQ.

SILLINCE, JOHN A. A. 1992. Argumentation-Based Indexing for Information Retrieval from Learned Articles. Journal of Documentation. 1992 December; 48(4): 387-405. ISSN: 0022-0418; CODEN: JDOCAS.

SOERGEL, DAGOBERT. 1985. Organizing Information: Principles of Data Base and Retrieval Systems. Orlando, FL: Academic Press; 1985. 450p. ISBN: 0-12-654260-0; LC: 83-15741.

SOERGEL, DAGOBERT. 1994. Indexing and Retrieval Performance: The Logical Evidence. Journal of the American Society for Information Science. 1994 September; 45(8): 589-599. ISSN: 0002-8231; CODEN: AISJB6.

SPANG-HANSSEN, HENNING. 1974. Kunnskapsorganisasjon, informasjonsgjenfinning, automatisering og språk. [Knowledge Organization, Information Retrieval, Automatization and Language]. In: Kunnskapsorganisasjon og informasjonsgjenfinning: Seminar arrangert 3.-7.desember 1973 i samarbeid mellom Norsk hovedkomité for klassifikasjon, Statens Biblioteksskole og Norsk Dokumentasjonsgruppe. [Knowledge Organization and Information Retrieval: A seminar held December 3rd-7th 1973: A Cooperation between the Norwegian Commitee for Classification, The Norwegian School of Librarianship, and the Norwegian Documentation Group]. Oslo, Norway: Riksbibliotektjenesten; 1973. 11-61. (Skrifter fra Riksbibliotektjenesten, Nr. 2). ISBN: 82-7195-001-0.

SPARCK JONES, KAREN. 2000. Further Reflections on TREC. Information Processing & Management. 2000 January; 36(1): 37-85. ISSN: 0306-4573; CODEN: IPMADK.

SPARCK JONES, KAREN; WALKER, STEPHEN; ROBERTSON, STEPHEN E. 2000. A Probabilistic Model of Information Retrieval: Development and Comparative Experiments, Part 1. Information Processing & Management. 2000 November; 36(6): 779-808. ISSN: 0306-4573; CODEN: IPMADK.

SPARCK JONES, KAREN; WALKER, STEPHEN; ROBERTSON, STEPHEN E. 2000. A Probabilistic Model of Information Retrieval: Development and Comparative Experiments, Part 2. Information Processing & Management. 2000 November; 36(6): 809-840. ISSN: 0306-4573; CODEN: IPMADK.

SPINK, AMANDA. 1995. Term Relevance Feedback and Mediated Database Searching: Implications for Information Retrieval Practice and Systems Design. Information Processing & Management. 1995 March/April; 31(2): 161-171. ISSN: 0306-4573; CODEN: IPMADK.

SPINK, AMANDA; SARACEVIC, TEFKO. 1997. Interaction in Information Retrieval: Selection and Effectiveness of Search Terms. Journal of the American Society for Information Science. 1997 August; 48(8): 741-761. ISSN: 0002-8231; CODEN: AISJB6.

TAUCHERT, WOLFGANG; HOSPODARSKY, JÜRGEN; KRAUSE, JÜRGEN; SCHNEIDER, CHRISTINE; WOMSER-HACKER, CHRISTA. 1991. Effects of Linguistic Functions in Information Retrieval in a German-Language Full-Text Database: Comparison between Retrieval in Abstract and Full-Text. Online Review. 1991 April; 15(2): 77-86. ISSN: 0309-314X; CODEN: OLREDR.

TENOPIR, CAROL. 1984. Retrieval Performance in a Full Text Journal Article Database. Urbana-Champaign, IL: University of Illinois, Graduate School of Library and Information Science; 1984. 264p. Available from: UMI, Ann Arbor, MI. (UMI order no. 85-02315).

TENOPIR, CAROL. 1985a. Full Text Database Retrieval Performance. Online Review. 1985 April; 9(2): 149-164. ISSN: 0309-314X.
TENOPIR, CAROL. 1985b. Searching Harvard Business Review. Online. 1985 March; 9(2): 71-78. ISSN: 0146-5422.
TENOPIR, CAROL; RO, JUNG SOON. 1990. Full Text Databases. New York, NY: Greenwood Press; 1990. 252p. (New Directions in Information Management no. 21). ISBN: 0-313-26303-5; LC: 89-25683.
TIBBO, HELEN R. 1993. Abstracting, Information Retrieval and the Humanities: Providing Access to Historical Literature. Chicago, IL: American Library Association; 1993. 276p. ISBN: 0-8389-3430-7.
TURNER, THOMAS P.; BRACKBILL, LISE. 1998. Rising to the Top: Evaluating the Use of the HTML META Tag to Improve Retrieval of World Wide Web Documents through Internet Search Engines. Library Resources & Technical Services. 1998 October; 42(4): 258-271. ISSN: 0024-2527.
VAN KUPPEVELT, J. 1997. Topic and Comment. In: Lamarque, Peter V.; Asher, R.E., eds. Concise Encyclopedia of Philosophy of Language. Oxford, UK: Pergamon; 1997. 191-198. ISBN: 0-08-042991-2; LC: 97-28781.
VAN RIJSBERGEN, C. J. 1986. A New Theoretical Framework for Information Retrieval. In: Rabitti, Fausto, ed. SIGIR '86: Proceedings of the Association for Computing Machinery Special Interest Group on Information Retrieval (ACM SIGIR) 9th Annual International Conference on Research and Development in Information Retrieval; 1986 September 8-10; Pisa, Italy. New York, NY: ACM Press; 1986. 194-200. ISBN: 0-89791-187-3.
VOORBIJ, HENK J. 1998. Title Keywords and Subject Descriptors: A Comparison of Subject Search Entries of Books in the Humanities and Social Sciences. Journal of Documentation. 1998 September; 54(4): 466-476. ISSN: 0022-0418.
VOOS, HENRY; DAGAEV, KATHERINE S. 1976. Are All Citations Equal? Or, Did We Op. Cit. Your Idem? Journal of Academic Librarianship. 1976 January; 1(6): 19-21. ISSN: 0099-1333.
WANG, PEILING; SOERGEL, DAGOBERT. 1993. Beyond Topical Relevance: Document Selection Behavior of Real Users of IR Systems. In: Bonzi, Susan, ed. ASIS'93: Proceedings of the American Society for Information Science (ASIS) 56th Annual Meeting: Volume 30; 1993 October 24-28; Columbus, OH. Medford, NJ: Learned Information, Inc. for ASIS; 1993. 87-92. ISSN: 0044-7870; ISBN: 0-938734-78-4; CODEN: PAISDQ.
WELWERT, CLAES. 1984. Läsa eller lyssna?: redovisning av jämförande undersökningar gjorda åren 1890-1980 rörande inlärning vid auditiv och visuell presentation samt ett försök till utvärdering av resultaten. Malmö, Sweden: CWK Gleerup; 1984. 233p. (Studia psychologica et paedagogica. Series altera; LXX). ISBN: 91-40-05065-3.
WINDSOR, DONALD A. 1995. Abstract Concerns. Journal of the American Society for Information Science. 1995 October; 46(9): 717-718. ISSN: 0002-8231; CODEN: AISJB6.
WORMELL, IRENE. 1985. Subject Access Project—SAP: Improved Subject Retrieval for Monographic Publications. Lund, Sweden: Lund University; 1985. 174p. (Doctoral thesis at Department of Information and Computer Science, Lund University). OCLC: 19763326.

WRIGHT, LAWRENCE W.; NARDINI, HOLLY K. GROSSETTA; ARONSON, ALAN R; RINDFLESCH, THOMAS C. 1999. Hierarchical Concept Indexing of Full-Text Documents in the Unified Medical Language System[R] Information Sources Map. Journal of the American Society for Information Science. 1999 May; 50(6): 514-523. ISSN: 0002-8231; CODEN: AISJB6.

YITZHAKI, MOSHE. 1992. The Variation in Informativity of [Titles of] Research Papers with Time and Field. In: Neelameghan, A.; Gopinath, M. A.; Raghavan, K. S.; Sankaralingam, P., eds. Cognitive Paradigms in Knowledge Organisation: 2nd International ISKO Conference; 1992 August 26-28; Madras, India. Madras, India: Sarada Ranganathan Endowment for Library Science; 1992. 401-418. OCLC: 28511718.

YITZHAKI, MOSHE. 1996. Informativity of Journal Article Titles: The Ratio of "Significant" Words. In: Ingwersen, Peter; Pors, Niels Ole, eds. Proceedings of the 2nd International Conference on Conceptions of Library and Information Science (COLIS): Integration in Perspective; 1996 October 13-16; Copenhagen, Denmark. Copenhagen, Denmark: The Royal School of Librarianship; 1996. 447-458. ISBN: 87-7415-260-2.

YITZHAKI, MOSHE. 1997. Variation in Informativity of Titles of Research Papers in Selected Humanities Journals: A Comparative Study. Scientometrics. 1997 February; 38(2): 219-229. ISSN: 0138-9130.

ZOBEL, JUSTIN; MOFFAT, ALISTAIR; WILKINSON, ROSS; SACKS-DAVIS, RON. 1995. Efficient Retrieval of Partial Documents. Information Processing & Management. 1995 May/June; 31(3): 361-377. ISSN: 0306-4573; CODEN: IPMADK.

# 6    Methods of Generating and Evaluating Hypertext

**JAMES BLUSTEIN**
**Dalhousie University**

**MARK S. STAVELEY**
**University of Toronto**

## INTRODUCTION

This chapter focuses on methods of generating and evaluating hypertext. We begin with a definition of hypertext and a brief survey of some types of hypertext and their applications.

In discussing methods of generation and evaluation of hypertext we concentrate on work done in the past five years mostly with link-based hypertext and published in English. We are concerned with links added to discursive works written in traditional form. Our discussion of automatic linking necessarily excludes fictional literature, annotation, groupware, and automated outliners.

### Historical Landmarks

Vannevar BUSH is often cited as the visionary who described semi-automated hypertext in his Memex system in 1945. Today Memex would be considered a multimedia storage and retrieval system with full annotational and linking support. In 1965 Ted Nelson coined the term hypertext to describe his proposed system, Xanadu (cited again in NELSON). Douglas Engelbart demonstrated the first computerized hypertext system, called NLS/Augment, ca. 1968. An overview of the field by CONKLIN (1987; see also CONKLIN, 1991) summarized the state of the art and promoted the idea of using computerized linked-based hypertext to augment human efforts. Two of that paper's many contributions were the classifications of types of hypertext systems and a call for better maps to help navigate in hypertext. SIMPSON ET AL. provide summaries of some of the speeches and panels at a multidisciplinary symposium held to honor Bush's memory and vision.

*Annual Review of Information Science and Technology (ARIST)*, Volume 35, 2001
Martha E. Williams, Editor
Published for the American Society for Information Science and Technology (ASIST)
By Information Today, Inc., Medford, NJ

## Major Publications, Sources, and Overviews

As a follow-up to the Bush symposium, Rosemary Simpson created and maintains an indexed collection of documents pertaining to the recent history and development of hypertext at a World Wide Website titled "Memex and Beyond" (NATIONAL SCIENCE FOUNDATION GRAPHICS AND VISUALIZATION CENTER). The first hypertext conference was held in 1987 under the auspices of the Association for Computing Machinery (ACM). From 1988 to 1994 that conference alternated with ACM's European Conference on Hypertext, until they were unified under the title, ACM Conference on Hypertext and Hypermedia. CHEN & CARR have created author co-citation maps showing patterns of influence and citations in the accepted papers at that conference from 1988 to 1998. The maps are encoded using version 2.0 of the virtual reality markup language (VRML 2.0) and are available on the World Wide Web (WWW). They found five main branches of hypertext publication: (1) writing, (2) open hypertext, (3) design models, (4) user interfaces, and (5) visualization. All of these branches are connected by a small core of classic papers.

Three special issues of the *Communications of the ACM* have been devoted to hypertext (BIEBER & ISAKOWITZ; *COMMUNICATIONS OF THE ACM*; GRØNBÆK & TRIGG). NIELSEN (1990; 1995), a well-known researcher of hypertext and user interfaces, wrote two books surveying hypertext and included annotated bibliographies. A recent electronic symposium of *ACM COMPUTING SURVEYS* is devoted to hypertext.

Although hypertext research appears in many publications, two peer-reviewed journals currently concentrate on it: the electronic *JOURNAL OF DIGITAL INFORMATION* and *THE NEW REVIEW OF HYPERMEDIA AND MULTIMEDIA*.

## DEFINING HYPERTEXT

The meaning of the term hypertext is often taken for granted in discussion. Hypertext is sometimes viewed as merely part of a system. For instance, hypertext links in the World Wide Web are only a part of the interface to a network-based document access and delivery system. Some people view hypertext as an interface method or an information delivery technology.

We view hypertext as an enabling technology, that is, as an integral part of software. Hypertext can be applied as an interface method and used as a tool for information delivery. However, those are only some of the possible applications of hypertext. To reduce the chances of confusion we define hypertext and provide examples to clarify.

SIMPSON & WEINER define hypertext as "text which does not form a single sequence and which may be read in various orders; especially text and graphics (usually in machine-readable form) which are interconnected in such a way that a reader of the material (as displayed at a computer terminal, etc.) can discontinue reading one document at certain points in order to consult other related matter." The functionality of hypertext is sometimes confused with the mechanisms used to implement it and with its applications. Hypertext does not require the use of a computer, although that is its most common method of presentation. Some notable noncomputerized hypertexts are the traditional presentation of the Talmud, *Information Mapping* by HORN, Choose-Your-Own-Adventure books, and the 1989 NATO Advanced Research Workshop on Designing Hypertext/Hypermedia for Learning (JONASSEN & MANDL).

The Talmud is among other things a written form of much Jewish law with accompanying commentary. Since the late fifteenth century the main text has been printed in a wide column, the main commentary in a narrower column, with further commentaries and cross references (referring to commentaries and the main text) referring to those columns (GOLDENBERG). The book by HORN shows an elaborate hypertextual style. It includes icons and extensive cross references. Many of the pages have the appearance of high-resolution graphical computer interfaces. (The appearance of the pages suggests a "notecard mentality," the idea that hypertext should be composed of small chunks of text that are linked together and that the explicit structure imposed by the links is essential to the author's concept of hypertext.) The printed conference proceedings of the 1989 NATO Advanced Research Workshop on Designing Hypertext/Hypermedia for Learning (JONASSEN & MANDL) contains revised versions of papers presented at the conference, along with annotations by all the authors noting related passages in all the articles and brief indications of how the passages were related.

## Hypermedia

Although many hypertext systems include graphic components, much as traditional books often include illustrations, hypertext-like systems that include graphics and other nontext media (e.g., sound and animation) are most properly termed hypermedia. Because hypertext and hypermedia are often used together, and because many hypermedia documents include significant textual components, many authors use the term hypertext to refer to both. Hypertext-like documents without a textual component are most certainly hypermedia. The annual Association for Computing Machinery conference for hypertext and hypermedia is named Hypertext. It is clear that the term hypertext can refer to applications such as groupware, outliners, and annotation support systems. Further discussion of such applications is beyond the scope of this chapter.

## Nonlinearity

Nelson, who coined the terms hypertext and hypermedia, defines hypertext in part as "*non-sequential writing*—text that branches and allows choices to the reader, best read at an interactive screen" (NELSON, p. 0/2, author's emphasis). Hypertext is often described as nonlinear text; however, that term is somewhat confusing and inaccurate. As FLORIDI notes, there are at least four ways in which a document can be nonlinear. One may distinguish linearity, or nonlinearity, in both the sequence of appearance and in the serialization of transmission of signs. These signs can be the physical representation of the content (the signifiers) or the semantic content of the document (the signifieds).

Some examples may clarify these aspects of (non)linearity. This chapter is physically sequential in that the words that comprise it appear in order. A schedule is semantically linear because its signifieds constitute a one-dimensional progressive narrative (FLORIDI). Most books are syntactically linear, and many are semantically linear—that is, the words that comprise them can be read only sequentially, but the narrative meaning encoded by those words may form multidimensional structures. The signifiers of a scroll are presented/transmitted linearly; to reach one part of a scroll, you must see all of the parts before it as well, whereas there is no such restriction on the order of viewing the pages of a bound book.

Thus there can be a linear presentation in words with nonlinear semantics in a traditional story. Floridi uses the familiar example of Homer's epic narrative *The Odyssey*. It does not have the linear structure of a schedule, so it is not strictly semantically linear. Clearly a similar analysis can be applied to almost all written works. Most written works are syntactically linear but not semantically linear. Syntactic linearity is soften a convenience for transmission in book publishing but is not a necessary quality of a work. Some written works are semantically linear but many are not. The concept of nonlinearity does not help distinguish hypertext from other types of text.

## Literary Hypertext

We describe literary hypertext to clarify the limits of this chapter. Automated linking in such works is beyond the scope of this chapter.

Hypertext fiction and poetry are the most prevalent forms of literary hypertext. Hypertext fictions are "fiction[s] with many features uncharacteristic of print fiction: multiple paths through the same text; multiple endings (and beginnings); questions posed to the reader which, once answered, influence what the reader will read; audiovisual attachments; navigable maps; and so on" (SHUMATE).

Although the hypertextual qualities do not wholly define those literary works, the works could not exist without hypertextual qualities. Hypertext fictions often use rhetorical structures that are not available in traditional printed form. BERNSTEIN identified some of the structures. The cycle is an important example. Cycles, according to Bernstein, are patterns in which the reader follows links back to a node and then follows a previously unchosen link. The forced rereading and reinterpretation is essential to hypertext fiction. He identifies five subtypes of cycle. Another example of a pattern is montage, in which a number of different nodes are presented at once, often in overlapping windows. Very often the reader must choose to view or follow links from one node at a time. WALKER showed that the most famous computer-based hypertext fiction (*afternoon, a story* by JOYCE) can be fruitfully subjected to some of the same literary analyses as other works.

For more information, see the Hypertext Compendia at the Web page of EASTGATE SYSTEMS, the Web page of the ELECTRONIC LITERATURE ORGANIZATION, and the Hyperizons Web page (SHUMATE).

## Types and Models of Hypertext

Many types of hypertext have been proposed and implemented. We do not provide an exhaustive description of all types of hypertext. However, to demonstrate some of the diversity, we describe spatial hypertext, basic link-based hypertext, and open hypertext. All current models of open hypertext are link-based.

*Spatial hypertext.* One of the most intriguing types of hypertext that does not rely on links is spatial hypertext (MARSHALL & SHIPMAN; SHIPMAN ET AL.). Spatial hypertext systems such as VIKI (MARSHALL ET AL.) are intended for information analysis tasks (NÜRNBERG & ASHMAN) in densely packed information spaces. Spatial hypertext does not include links or other explicit relationships between nodes. It is based on maps of the "information space." Documents are typically represented by colored shapes on a screen. The size, color, and proximity of the shapes to each other can be used by readers and the system to organize and manipulate the documents. Hierarchies of documents can be represented in collections (i.e., through nodes that contain other documents or collections) (SHIPMAN ET AL.).

*Link-based hypertext.* Link-based hypertext is perhaps the easiest to imagine, and it is what most people think of when they encounter the term hypertext. Various formal models of hypertext have been created to ease the development and integration of various computer-based hypertext systems. For precision we give both formal and informal definitions of link-based hypertext.

Informally, link-based hypertext can be thought of as "a series of text chunks connected by links which offer the reader different" pathways of the chunks to read (NELSON, p. 0/2). The parts of a hypertext document that contain text are known as its nodes; each node is a part of the document.

Although the definition is often only necessary for software that implements the underlying hypertext functionality, many authors arrange their text so that each of its logical units is a node. In the World Wide Web hypertext system, for instance, a node is often a computer file containing text.

Links are connections between nodes. Continuing with the WWW example, the presence of a link in the text is indicated by special formatting of some text, often underlining. The text that indicates the presence of a link is known as anchor text. When the link is followed, the destination node or nodes are presented to the reader.

Many people assume that hypertext is merely a collection of text chunks and links. Such a definition leaves out some important properties of links, namely that they can (1) be many-ended, (2) have properties such as weights and types, and (3) need not constitute actions. An example of the third property might be a link that has only a type and no destination.

*Formal definition.* A formal definition not only clarifies what is meant by hypertext but also allows one to apply much mathematically-based reasoning about and manipulation of hypertext documents (e.g., PARK's proof that a link-based hypertext can be represented as a context-free grammar).

Link-based hypertext can be exactly represented as a directed hypergraph composed of chunks of text connected by links. A hypergraph may be thought of as a generalization of a graph. Formally, a graph $G = (N,E)$ is a tuple composed of two finite sets: a set of nodes, $N$, and a set of edges, $E$, connecting the nodes. The set of edges, $E$, is a subset of the Cartesian square of $N$. If some tuple of nodes $(u,v)$ is a member of $E$, then there is an edge from node $u$ to node $v$.

In directed graphs the presence of an edge from some node $u$ to some node $v$ does not mean that there must also be an edge from $v$ to $u$. If there is an edge, $e$, from some node $u$, then we say that edge $e$ leaves node $u$.

Edge weights in graphs can indicate the strength of a relationship between nodes. In a weighted graph, every edge has an associated weight, given by a function, $w$, mapping from $E$ to the set of real numbers. If there is an edge from some node $u$ to some node $v$, then $w(u,v)$ is the weight (or cost of traversing) from $u$ to $v$.

The essential difference between a graph and a hypergraph is that in a graph an edge can have only one endpoint, whereas in a hypergraph an edge may have more than one endpoint. In other words, in a hypergraph the set of edges is a proper subset of the Cartesian product of $N$ and the set of all nonempty subsets of $N$. That is, the edges connect one node to one or more nodes.

A path is a sequence of nodes connected by edges. The number of edges in the path is the path length. The shortest path between two nodes contains the minimum number of edges that must be traversed to go from one to the other. The out-degree of a node is the number of edges leaving it. One says that a hypergraph is connected if and only if every pair of its nodes is connected by a path. The term "path" refers to properties of a graph, whereas "trail" is the preferred term for hypertexts.

In general, there is not necessarily a path between every two nodes in a directed (hyper)graph. If there is no path between two chunks of text in a hypertext document, then there is no way to get from one of those chunks to the other solely by following links. (Many computer-based hypertext systems include the ability to search for strings of text; thus, they do not restrict the reader to following links to find chunks to read.)

The extensible markup language (XML) defined by BRAY ET AL. seems poised to be the basis for much hypertext development in the near future. The World Wide Web Consortium has re-specified HTML (the markup language used in the WWW) in XML, and XML support is being built into the most widely used WWW browsers. XLink (DEROSE ET AL.) is being created as a language for specifying links in XML documents and, although still a draft, we expect the final version to fully support the hypergraph model of hypertext (described above). Using that model, users will be able to attach annotation to both links and nodes. The model is expected to provide semantics for describing multi-ended links. XLink could also allow links to be made to parts of documents in a more open fashion, that is, without the author of the documents needing to change them.

*Open hypertext.* The goal of open hypertext system (OHS) research is to enable the presentation of documents with links in them regardless of the encoding used in the underlying computer files (WIIL). So an OHS could create links to and from, say, a file created in a word processor even though the author of the document, and indeed the original software, made no special accommodation for hypertext links. Because the source and destination of links do not need to be encoded as part of the document, the links could be updated without any need to change the original document. One advantage of an open hypertext system is that it can eliminate the problem of stale links—links that cannot be followed because the destination document is no longer at the location stored in the link.

The Open Hypermedia Systems Working Group is a collaborative effort by open hypertext researchers to form OHS standards. They use the term open hypermedia environment to describe the combination of a user interface and one or more software programs to present the links (OPEN HYPERMEDIA SYSTEMS WORKING GROUP; WIIL).

Open hypertext systems are typically implemented as middleware: software that is interposed between the user interface and some other software that accesses data. Open hypertext systems are intended to be what is known in the software engineering community as loosely coupled or, in other words, easily interchangeable (NÜRNBERG & ASHMAN). Such systems provide support for hypertext functionality to be made available through the user interface.

The pervasiveness of the WWW has greatly increased the practicality of network-based hypertext. BOUVIN provides an overview of the techniques and tools that have been and are being developed to provide services that are more open (in the sense of open hypertext) to the WWW. Nürnberg & Ashman also examine ways to bridge the divide between more open hypertext systems and the WWW. They examine the approaches of the two groups. They recognize differences in those approaches and judge the strengths of the various systems. We take from their study that, as with other hypertext systems, there is great opportunity for WWW developers to learn from earlier hypertext projects and that the open hypertext researchers can learn from the advantages of the WWW.

Their opinion is that the two groups differ in their interpretation of the term hypertext. World Wide Web researchers and developers think of hypertext as a type of user interaction, but the OHS researchers and developers think of hypertext as systems with structural awareness. According to this view, the main advantage of the WWW is that it is easy to provide a consistent interface. All but the most basic structural awareness is in the minds of WWW users. Structurally aware systems, however, allow for great openness in client implementation and the creation of multiple independent structures over the same data set. These systems provide a framework for implementing many things that are impractical otherwise, such as collaboration support, traversal computation, and versioning.

ØSTERBYE & WIIL (see also WIIL & ØSTERBYE) offer The Flag Taxonomy, a novel scheme to classify open hypertext systems depending on which subparts are open and extensible. The name of the scheme derives from its diagrammatic representation as a flag of the type known as a Scandinavian cross: four rectangles separated by the four arms of a cross. Each rectangle represents one of the four functional modules (storage manager, viewer or browser, data model manager, and network session manager). The terms used come from the Dexter

Hypertext Model (HALASZ & SCHWARTZ, 1990; 1994). The arms represent the protocols between the bordering modules.

The main intent of the taxonomy is to separate runtime and storage aspects, and contents and structural information. In practice these four areas may overlap, so we cannot say that the four parts are atomic units. For example, in the WWW model as of 1996, the flag diagram would consist of three parts: (1 )a rectangle for the combined storage and data manager modules (combined into WWW servers); (2) a rectangle for the combined browser and session manager; and (3) an arm for the hypertext transfer protocol (HTTP) protocol that they use to share data.

## WAYS OF GENERATING HYPERTEXT

Having completed our review of background definitions and milestones, we turn to a discussion about techniques for generating and evaluating hypertext.

Two decisions need to be made before a hypertext structure can be implemented. The first concerns the method of hypertext construction to be used. The second relates to how the links are to be identified to the user once they have been constructed. The process of creating hypertext can be done in many different ways. Some of the more common approaches are discussed below. Methods include: (1) links that are inserted manually into a document's text; (2) links that are inserted through a semi-automatic approach (i.e., making implicit use of a document's structure or some other property); (3) links that are inserted through the use of semantics, or artificial intelligence, or through the use of information retrieval methods; and (4) links that are inserted in an interactive nature.

### Manual Construction Approach

Manual construction occurs when hypertext links (within a document or collection of documents) are identified, crafted, and inserted by a human author. Many different people create these links. Sometimes it is the author of the original document text (e.g., the creator of a Web page); at other times, a system manager or librarian is left to insert the hypertext links (e.g., an editor of an online version of a newspaper). In any case, there are two problems with this method.

The first problem is that the methods may require a great deal of time to make the hypertext, and the hypertext they make must be useful to people. When dealing with multigigabyte collections—collections that contain at the very least tens of thousands of documents (e.g., the NEW ZEALAND DIGITAL LIBRARY)—it is too time consuming to read all documents and insert links manually. Time becomes even more of a concern if the electronic collection is being updated continually. Every time the collection is updated, new links need to be inserted and existing ones re-evaluated.

The second problem concerns the consistency of the links. There is evidence (ELLIS ET AL., 1994, 1996; GREEN, 1999), that human-constructed links within documents are inconsistent. This observation supports previous experimental results obtained by FURNAS ET AL., which showed that subjects agreed less than 20% of the time when choosing terms to describe objects. This kind of descriptive inconsistency makes it very difficult to evaluate and assess manually inserted links. Links that are of interest to one reader may to be inappropriate to another.

To benefit readers, the conversion of text to hypertext, such as in the case of the NATO Workshop, requires more than the insertion of new material. The risk of reader confusion (the "lost in hyperspace" problem) is a concern for people who create hypertexts.

People create hypertext through linking for many reasons. The purpose for which a hypertext is created is important in determining its form. From time to time claims are made that hypertext frees readers from the "tyranny of linear text." However, for any text to be useful, it must be intelligible. The convolutions of structure possible within hypertext can seriously dimish an author's attempt at communication. As FLORIDI notes, authoring hypertext refers to the combined processes of composing the words of a text and arranging their structure. BROCKMANN ET AL. and PARUNAK considered various structures for presenting information using link-based hypertext. They classified some of the various structures that can be built using links and made general suggestions as to which were most appropriate for certain tasks. The work of BOTAFOGO ET AL. in providing concrete measures for some of the properties of hypertext link structures is discussed below in the section on information retrieval measures of the success of automatically linked hypertext.

BROCKMANN ET AL. consider that there is a tradeoff between expressive power for the author of a hypertext and the risk of confusion for readers. A sequence of nodes, in which the only explicit links from a node are to the next and previous nodes (with no direct links between the first and last nodes), has the lowest expressive power but the least risk of reader confusion. A highly interconnected yet unstructured web in which any node could be linked to any other does not limit the expressive power of the author, but it provides little structure to help ground the reader. Between these two extremes Brockmann et al. place the grid—a multilevel structure of sequences with links between the corresponding nodes at each level—and a hierarchy much like a corporate structure chart. There are no direct links between nodes at the same level. Those nodes are connected only by their immediate parent node.

Brockmann et al. suggest that the grid is superior in both expressive power and predictability. Although they do not say so, it is apparent that the hierarchy does not help the reader as much as the grid does because it contains no part that is a sequence.

PARUNAK considered three specific subcases of the web classification of Brockmann et al. Two are of interest: directed acyclic graphs and clumped. Directed acyclic graphs (DAGs) contain no cycles, that is, if one follows only links and never returns to the start of a link, then one will never return to the same node. Such structures are similar to hierarchies, and their mathematical properties are well known, which may seem to be an advantage to someone who creates such a hypertext. It is not clear how helpful such a structure is to readers. Readers who follow links to the most similar other nodes may never see the extent of a hypertext. This potential problem might be reduced by the use of dynamic maps in hypertext, but there have been few careful studies of the use of such maps.

ALLEN generalized from experiments to conclude that features such as maps can lead to poorer performance if the users work (or reason) in a way that is incompatible with the map's representation. MCDONALD & STEVENSON found that spatial maps may reduce users' confusion and help navigation but lead to users learning less. The learning effect might be because the subset of users who do learn from hypertext learn because of the active process of making sense out of a hypertext presentation. The maps may alleviate some of the need for such active concentration. The literature is not clear, however, on how learning with hypertext should be measured (e.g., by concepts, facts, or recall of headings and keywords), although fill-in-the-blanks tests for recall have been ruled out (DILLON). It is no surprise that the literature also is not clear on what types of maps are appropriate for which types of users in which situations.

Clumped hypertext consists of knots of nodes that are highly interconnected but with few connections between the knots. A drawing of the resulting hypertext looks like beads connected by string. In such a hypertext, the knots of nodes are often closely related. PARUNAK suggests that the knots be considered as single nodes at a higher level of abstraction when one is reasoning about the overall hypertext structure. Such structures may correspond to clusters in information retrieval contexts.

## Semi-Automatic Approaches

Many different methods can be used to generate hypertext links semi-automatically, but many of them have one common idea—to use the structural or formatting information within a document's text to generate links. Such links are known as structural (BLUSTEIN ET AL.)

or vocative links (KAPPE). Some specific examples of where structural links can be inserted are: alternative versions or translations of text, footnotes, references, indexes, and tables of contents (CONRAD & UTT; FAHMY & BARNARD). Highly structured and carefully written texts, especially those with many cross references, are ideal candidates for hypertext links because much of the structure that links would make explicit has already been included in the document. Structural links created in this way have the advantage of being consistent with the original text and therefore unlikely to lead to user confusion. However, the issues surrounding the effort and the time required in order to convert the text into a structurally suitable state still remain. Often documents are not in a format that can be readily interpreted by linking software. Substantial time may be required to translate or reformat documents before links can be generated. An example of the kind of formatting that must be done can be seen in the Justus suite of programs (WILSON), which converts traditional legal documents into an integrated hypertext database. The hypertext links are inserted and structured based on a highly specified legal reference format. If the documents are not in that format initially, they must be converted before processing. In cases where the format of the text required by the link-generating system is quite specific, the formatting translations are done by hand.

Another type of structural property that can be exploited in documents is the use of markup or formatting tags. If one parses these markup tags (that are designed to interact with a typesetting or publishing system), then additional information about the text in question can be obtained and converted into links. An example of this kind of system is Management Environment for Structured Retrieval Online (MAESTRO) (BARNARD & MACLEOD). It uses the properties found in Standard Generalized Markup Language (SGML) markup tags to create a structural hierarchy of a document, which can then be used to insert and construct links. This method is a step toward a fully automated system that generates hypertext links because, generally speaking, the process of inserting formatting tags into plain text documents is automated. The interpretation of structural markup is an excellent way to make correct structural links (FURUTA ET AL.; RAYMOND ET AL.). With organizations such as the TEXT ENCODING INITIATIVE supporting the generation of highly marked-up text, projects to make hypertext links by interpreting structural and semantic markup (DRAKOS; FAHMY & BARNARD) are becoming more feasible.

Although semi-automatic approaches are an improvement over manual approaches in terms of link consistency and link construction times, they are still limited in that the documents need to be specifically formatted or possess specific characteristics. It is these characteristics that can require manual intervention and consequently introduce inefficiencies into link construction.

## Fully Automatic Approaches

Some of the earliest methods of generating hypertext-linking structures from document texts relied heavily on the fact that the documents were highly structured, such as REXX (NUNN ET AL.). The principles behind these systems were extended to include a more general structural property (i.e., markup tags). This method of hypertext generation is not without its own problems and inconsistencies. Some types of markup tags were designed specifically to represent the formatting of a document, not its underlying structure (e.g., different types of font tags, CyBib (CYBIB) tags, and BibIX (BIBIX) tags). Consequently, when these types of markup tags are used as a representation of a document's structure, they can be misleading and produce poor results. An alternate approach for generating hypertext links is to use a consistent fully automated method. In the following paragraphs a number of fully automated hypertext construction methods are presented and discussed.

*Syntactic approach.*   Various methods of generating hypertext take advantage of related parts within a document—e.g., the identification and use of predefined phrases or words to establish links. According to CONRAD & UTT, specific mechanisms can be used to detect quotations and associate them with corresponding references. The types of phrases that can be used to establish links are "see also," "as person $X$ states," and "according to person $X$." The basic principles behind this idea have been extended through the use of natural-language processing so that cross-referencing links and anchors can be detected automatically (LEHNERT).

This method has two main advantages. Because low-level syntactic processing is computationally cheap, links can be formed in a short time. Also, the links that are formed should, at least in theory, reflect the author's intent and so make the resulting documents easier to understand.

Extending the phrase-based link identification idea further leads to an automatic method of hypertext generation based on lexical chaining. A lexical chain can be defined as a sequence of semantically related words that are found within a document's text. As GREEN (1998) explains, if a text contains the words "apple" and "fruit," then they will appear in a lexical chain together, since apple is a kind of fruit.

Futher, the organization of these lexical chains can be used to represent the structure of the document (MORRIS & HIRST). Lexical chains are identified through a resource that relates words according to their meanings (e.g., a thesaurus). One of the common systems for identifying and establishing lexical chains is the WordNet database (BECKWITH ET AL.). WordNet divides words into synonym sets or synsets, groups of words that are synonyms of one another. These synsets are then connected using connectives such as "is-a" or "includes." A particular word may occur in several synsets, depending on how many senses the word has. The information obtained from the lexical chains is then used to generate hypertext links.

Unlike traditional document vectors that are used in information retrieval (IR) methods for generating hypertext, the lexical chains for each document are a more fluid representation of its ideas. The task of determining the similarity between documents using lexical chains is difficult because the meanings of words vary depending on their context. Parsing written language can be difficult for native speakers, and it is more difficult still for software that operates with only partial (albeit carefully distilled) information about the text. Lexical chaining methods typically require more time than traditional IR document processing tasks (e.g., key phrase extraction). For example, it takes five hours to locate and structure lexical chains within a database of 30,000 newspaper articles, whereas the same collection can be processed with a traditional IR system in 15 minutes. However, lexical chaining systems are not as prone to the problems relating to synonymy (many words referring to the same concept) and polysemy (many concepts having the same word) as traditional IR systems.

*Artificial intelligence approach.* A number of noteworthy artificial intelligence (AI) approaches have been adopted to create hypertext links automatically (CLITHEROW ET AL.; HAHN & REIMER; HAMMWOHNER & THIEL). AI methods of creating hypertext links use semantic parsers and knowledge bases to deal with texts. An example is the VISAR hypertext system (CLITHEROW ET AL.) used to maintain a database of journal citations. VISAR uses semantic parsers and knowledge bases to search for citations that satisfy certain relationships between concepts. These relations have previously been defined through training data provided to the VISAR system.

Other AI-based systems include TOPIC (HAHN & REIMER) and Answer Garden (ACKERMAN, 1993). TOPIC depends on explicit domain-specific knowledge bases. It uses a semantic parser, which allows the topical structure of the text to be represented by a hierarchical graph. The links within the graph are based on a semantic understanding of thematically connected sections of the text. As the system is queried, hypertext links between nodes in the graph are generated. Although AI systems offer another approach to the construction of hypertext, they are typically restricted by topic domains and training data. As the authors of TOPIC point out, the system was not designed to create links within collections of thematically varied texts.

The Answer Garden system, on the other hand, was designed to interact with users and create links based on a user's response to questions. Although Answer Garden can be tied in with the AI approach to constructing hypertext, it can also be related to interactive methods for creating hypertext. Thus, more detail about Answer Garden is given in the section on interactive approaches to hypertext construction.

In general, AI approaches have the advantages that come with the possibility of deeper analysis of text than the other automatic methods we survey. By combining a more thorough analysis of text with a knowledge base, developers of the AI-based software aim to produce more meaningful links and avoid problems of text ambiguity (polysemy and synonymy). An AI-based system is more likely to detect that an author who writes "variation in vocabulary" in one place and "choosing different words to express the same thoughts" in another is discussing the same idea in both places. Further, the AI-based approaches we discuss may be considered steps toward systems that will not only make links but also create summaries and customized précis from texts.

The automatic linking approaches based on AI that we survey may be subject to two classes of constraints that limit how well they function. First, the approaches all rely on training data. A person must evaluate each decision by the software (to link or not to link, if to link then what type of link and to where, etc.) to provide a sufficient base of patterns for the software to recognize later. The introduction of a human increases the chances of inconsistency. Furthermore these AI systems must be trained with texts from a specific domain. If the systems are presented with texts that they have not been trained for, then the results may be untrustworthy. The second problem relates to efficiency: a system may require a great deal of training time in order to deal with very specific domains.

*Information retrieval approach.* The information retrieval (IR) approach for generating and constructing hypertext links is considered to be a special case within general IR research. The basic theory behind most IR systems is that if two documents are related in some way, they will contain the same words or terms. There are many different types of terms, and they can range from a phrase that has been extracted from a document to any word that appears in a document. In the IR vector model, information about the terms associated with a document is stored in term vectors. These term vectors are then compared using some type of vector-based similarity measure, such as the dot product or cosine measure (WITTEN ET AL.). With such vector-based measures, the degree of similarity between two documents can be represented by a real number.

Further, links can then be established between documents based on their relative similarity scores. Using this approach, if two documents are about similar topics, then the documents will be connected by a link. According to MELUCCI, most automatic hypertext construction methods are based on the computation of the vector cosine to assess the similarity between document nodes. Such links may create the type of clumped hypertext we discuss above. How useful such links are depends largely on what tasks the hypertext users are trying to accomplish. If they are doing the equivalent of searching a shelf of library books for more information about a related topic, then links to similar documents may be very helpful. If they are following links in an attempt to form an overview of the structure of the information available in the hypertext, then links that lead only to similar materials are likely to give them a mistaken impression of the hypertext.

GREEN (1999) draws attention to a very serious problem with this approach. There are two significant linguistic factors that can affect this operation: synonymy (many words referring to the same concept) and polysemy (many concepts having the same word). Green goes on to explain how these linguistic factors directly influence results obtained by IR systems. The impact of synonymy is that documents that use words that are synonyms will not be considered related or at best will be considered to be less related than they actually are. Polysemy will have the opposite effect, causing documents that use the same word in different senses to be considered related when they should not be. Although IR-based systems suffer from the aforementioned linguistic problems, they are quite efficient (in terms of storage space and computational intensity) and consistent in link construction, unlike other automatic methods of hypertext generation.

ALLAN used the SMART IR system to find suitable links automatically among articles in an electronic version of an encyclopedia. The links were made in several steps. The first steps detected passages that used similar vocabulary. The next steps combined some links to simplify the structure. Finally, basic types were assigned to describe how the linked passages were related.

SALTON ET AL. applied other techniques based on vocabulary analysis, using SMART to a machine-readable version of the Funk and Wagnalls *Encyclopedia*. Their method finds and automatically ranks related articles. In the first step, their method finds related articles using global vocabulary similarity, and then makes finer distinctions and corrections through an analysis of the levels of vocabulary overlap in subarticle structures, such as paragraphs and sentences. Their method may be used to generate hypertext graphs of various types.

## Interactive/Dynamic Approach

Another issue relating to the automatic generation of hypertext links is whether to insert links that are static or dynamic. This approach can make a significant difference in IR-based systems. If the process of inserting and creating links can become more interactive and still maintain the same levels of efficiency and consistency, then the linguistic problems identified by GREEN (1999) can be dealt with. By allowing a user to formulate queries and select regions of related text, the sense and meaning of the terms used can be put into a proper context.

Consequently, interactive querying, browsing, and linking systems have been developed. Two systems of particular interest are Visualization of Information Retrieval (VOIR) (GOLOVCHINSKY) and Phrasier (JONES & STAVELEY). The VOIR system is a newspaper-based dynamic hypertext interface. Users can specify their search intent in various ways, such as querying, selecting visible text passages, and selecting hypertext links. In these ways important terms are identified and then can become hypertext link anchors. As these anchors are selected, they are combined with information about the context in which they appear, and queries are formed. The Phrasier system uses automatically extracted key phrases (FRANK ET AL.) rather than the single-term anchors used by VOIR. Phrasier also can give users previews of the target documents when link anchors are selected. It also allows the user to make selections across ranges of the document, thereby allowing for a more flexible definition of the context for link-based queries. Both VOIR and Phrasier show how links can be dynamically created and inserted. VOIR is considered dynamic because links are generated on the fly as user queries are processed. The hypertext links inserted by VOIR cannot be precomputed because part of the link construction relies on user interaction. Phrasier, on the other hand, can compute links within a known collection of documents ahead of time. In order to give the appearance that all of the links are dynamic, the links are not inserted until browse time. Should Phrasier be presented with a document that is not part of a known collection, the necessary links must then be computed on the fly.

With another system, Answer Garden (ACKERMAN, 1993; ACKERMAN & MALONE), users seek answers to common questions through a set of diagnostic questions or other IR mechanisms (ACKERMAN, 1998). Answer Garden possesses some key features that are very important when thinking about hypertext generation and construction. First it allows for the production of information on demand, and the system grows in relation to the information that is stored and the types of requests for information that it receives. Also, Answer Garden was designed to work with an information database that is constantly growing, so the system can deal with user feedback, link corrections, and changes in the indexing structure.

## How to Represent Hypertext

After identifying and creating a hypertext structure, it is then necessary to represent the information within the hypertext. Two types of representation are needed: (1) a storage method to preserve the information contained within a hypertext structure, and (2) some way to convey the information from the hypertext structure to a potential user.

*Data structures.* Once links have been constructed, a decision must be made about how to store the hypertext structure that is produced. Two methods of hypertext representation are an adjacency list and an adjacency matrix. A sample adjacency list is shown in Figure 1. It shows the documents that are connected by one link (being adjacent to each other in the hypertext structure). Figure 2 shows a sample adjacency matrix.

| >From | To |
|-------|-----|
| 1 | 1, 8 |
| 3 | 2, 9 |
| 4 | 5, 7 |
| 5 | 2, 9 |
| 6 | 3 |
| 7 | 1 |
| 8 | 4 |
| 9 | 6 |
| 10 | 3 |

**Figure 1. Sample adjacency list. The commas (,) mark the boundaries between document ID numbers.**

```
1 0 0 0 0 0 0 1 0 0
0 1 0 0 0 0 0 0 0 0
0 1 1 0 0 0 0 0 1 0
0 0 0 1 1 0 1 0 0 0
0 1 0 0 1 0 0 0 1 0
0 0 1 0 0 1 0 0 0 0
1 0 0 0 0 0 1 0 0 0
0 0 0 1 0 0 0 1 0 0
0 0 0 0 0 1 0 0 1 0
0 0 1 0 0 0 0 0 0 1
```

**Figure 2. Sample adjacency matrix**

The adjacency matrix above represents the same information contained in the adjacency list. In the adjacency matrix the links are represented as follows: if the documents are directly connected, their corresponding entry in the matrix is given the value of 1; and if there is no direct link between the documents, then the value is 0.

Each storage method has its advantages. If the hypertext structure that is produced is sparse (not many links), the more efficient option in terms of the space required is the adjacency list. However, if the hypertext structure is dense, then the adjacency matrix becomes the more efficient storage option.

*Visualizing hypertext information.*   There are many different ways of presenting information relating to a hypertext structure to a potential user. By using markup tags on a document, links corresponding to the structure of the hypertext can be inserted into document collections without predetermining how the links will be presented. Markup is the use of embedded codes, known as tags, to describe the structure of a document or to embed instructions (such as links to related documents) that can be used by layout processors or other document management tools (RAYMOND ET AL.)

## MATHEMATICAL MODELS FOR HYPERTEXT EVALUATION

We identify three types of approaches that can be used to evaluate hypertext. The first is a mathematical representation of what a user might want in a hypertext structure, such as coverage and quality. The second and third approaches, described in the next section on human factors, are recording users' "journeys" within the hypertext structures, and applying various  human-computer interaction (HCI) research methods.

In this section we discuss two mathematical models: coverage, which is a quantitative technique, and correlation, which is more of a qualitative technique. Applications of this type of hypertext evaluation approach (MCENEANEY 1999; 2000) suggest that it might yield useful insight into how people use hypertexts, which can lead to improvements through redesign. The first step in performing an evaluation using these two mathematical models is to determine the shortest path length between documents within the hypertext structure, as this information is needed to calculate coverage and correlation. When dealing with large hypertext structures it is important that the process of determining path lengths be as efficient as possible because time is an important consideration when maintaining and evaluating collections of documents.

### Computing Path Lengths

One common method for computing the path lengths within a hypertext structure is the Floyd-Warshall Shortest Path Algorithm

(CORMEN ET AL.). A disadvantage of the algorithm is that it has a tight asymptotic bound of the number of documents cubed. The algorithm is also more disposed towards the adjacency matrix representation.

Alternatively, there is a version of an algorithm for performing a breadth-first search for finding the shortest paths from a single source (CORMEN ET AL.) that is more efficient because it runs in a lower-bound of $n + E$ (where $E$ is the number of edges) for a single source, thus giving it a lower-bound of $n(n + E)$ or an upper-bound of $n^3$ in the worst case. With this algorithm the hypertext can be stored in either an adjacency matrix or adjacency list. The worst case for this method has the same performance as the Floyd-Warshall (Shortest Path) Algorithm.

When evaluating hypertext structures, it is necessary to compute the shortest path between all pairs of documents in the collection because this information is used to determine the coverage and correlation values.

## Computing Coverage

After all path lengths have been computed, the results are transformed into a matrix that represents the shortest path lengths (also referred to as a Converted Distance Matrix) between all documents in the collection. Wherever a row and a column meet, that value is the path length between the two documents. An example of this data structure is shown in Figure 3.

Figure 3 shows the shortest paths between documents within the collection. The column labels correspond to the source document IDs and the row labels to the destination document IDs. The value at the position where the two ID numbers intersect is the number of links

|     | 1 | 2 | 3 | 4 | 5 | 6 | 7 | 8 | 9 | 10 |
|-----|---|---|---|---|---|---|---|---|---|----|
| 1   | 0 | * | * | 2 | * | * | 1 | 3 | * | *  |
| 2   | 4 | 0 | 1 | 2 | 1 | 2 | 5 | 3 | 3 | 2  |
| 3   | 6 | * | 0 | 4 | 3 | 1 | 7 | 5 | 2 | 1  |
| 4   | 2 | * | * | 0 | * | * | 3 | 1 | * | *  |
| 5   | 3 | * | * | 1 | 0 | * | 4 | 2 | * | *  |
| 6   | 5 | * | 2 | 3 | 2 | 0 | 6 | 4 | 1 | 3  |
| 7   | 3 | * | * | 1 | * | * | 0 | 2 | * | *  |
| 8   | 1 | * | * | 3 | * | * | 2 | 0 | * | *  |
| 9   | 4 | * | 1 | 2 | 1 | 2 | 5 | 3 | 0 | 2  |
| 10  | * | * | * | * | * | * | * | * | * | 0  |

Figure 3. Sample of shortest path length matrix

between the source document and the destination. This shows that there is a distance of six links between document 1 and document 3. Additionally, it shows a distance of 1 between document 1 and document 8. Some entries do not contain a numerical value but rather an asterisk (*), indicating that there is no possible way of getting from the source document to the destination document—that the distance is infinite. Note that the graph is directed: there is a link between documents 1 and 3 but none going in the reverse direction.

It is helpful for the creator of a hypertext structure to know the relationship between the number of links and nodes. This information gives an indication of the connectedness and complexity of the hypertext. BOTAFOGO ET AL. developed a series of measures that can give an overall measure of how well organized a hypertext document is. The measures also suggest which nodes should be seen first to help make sense of the text. Their main measures are compactness, which is roughly equivalent to what others call coverage, and stratum, which indicates whether the hypertext is designed to be read in a particular order. Coverage is a measure of the proportion of node pairs that have paths between them. Their measures have been applied and validated (in somewhat modified form) by YAMADA ET AL.

Coverage is computed by taking the total number of entries that are not equal to zero and not equal to infinity and dividing this number by the total number of possible links (i.e., the total number of entries within the shortest path length matrix). This value is then converted into a percentage. For example, the coverage of the linking structure being represented in Figure 3 would be the number of actual links divided by the total number of links or entries in the adjacency matrix. By inserting corresponding values into the equation, one gets 49/(10*10), or 49%.

## Computing Correlation

Correlation complements the information obtained from coverage. Correlation can give an indication of the quality of links. The correlations are computed between a measure of the similarity between each pair of nodes and the minimum path length between them. A strong negative correlation indicates that the length of the path between all pairs of nodes corresponds to the similarity of those nodes. If one accepts the premise that similar nodes should be linked, then one should expect a high correlation.

Care must be taken when computing correlation values to make one small adjustment to the shortest-path-length matrix. Within hypertext linking structures, it is possible to have documents with no links between them; these are the links with distance "*" (Figure 3). A common

320 JAMES BLUSTEIN AND MARK S. STAVELEY

solution is to use a figure that is one number larger than the largest possible path length. Figure 4 illustrates the effect of this solution on the shortest-path-length matrix in Figure 3. The infinite lengths have been replaced with the number 11, one greater than the largest possible link distance for a collection of 10 documents.

| | | | | | | | | | |
|---|---|---|---|---|---|---|---|---|---|
| 00 | 11 | 11 | 02 | 11 | 11 | 01 | 03 | 11 | 11 |
| 04 | 00 | 01 | 02 | 01 | 02 | 05 | 03 | 03 | 02 |
| 06 | 11 | 00 | 04 | 03 | 01 | 07 | 05 | 02 | 01 |
| 02 | 11 | 11 | 00 | 11 | 11 | 03 | 01 | 11 | 11 |
| 03 | 11 | 11 | 01 | 00 | 11 | 04 | 02 | 11 | 11 |
| 05 | 11 | 02 | 03 | 02 | 00 | 06 | 04 | 01 | 03 |
| 03 | 11 | 11 | 01 | 11 | 11 | 00 | 02 | 11 | 11 |
| 01 | 11 | 11 | 03 | 11 | 11 | 02 | 00 | 11 | 11 |
| 04 | 11 | 01 | 02 | 01 | 02 | 05 | 03 | 00 | 02 |
| 11 | 11 | 11 | 11 | 11 | 11 | 11 | 11 | 11 | 00 |

**Figure 4. Sample of shortest-path-length matrix for a collection of 10 documents**

Once the structure of the hypertext links is represented in this fashion, it is possible to compute the correlation between the path lengths and the similarity scores that were used to generate the links. The degree of correlation between the path lengths and the real-valued similarity scores is determined by computing the Pearson coefficient of correlation ($r$). (A variation of this method is to use the Spearman rank order correlation coefficient.) By using both correlation and coverage it is possible to get an idea about the theoretical quality of the hypertext structure that has been created.

Numerical approaches to hypertext evaluation such as we describe are often intended to provide useful feedback to authors and designers (BOTAFOGO ET AL.), not to be complete measures of quality. Also of interest is a systematic inspection-based method for hypertext evaluation, SUE (GARZOTTO & MATERA), and an automated analysis tool for the WWW, SAT, which are described in the section on Evaluation Experiments below.

## HUMAN FACTORS IN HYPERTEXT EVALUATION

Ultimately a hypertext must be considered a document used by a person for a purpose. The success or failure of the document depends on how well it is suited to the goals within its context of use (DIX ET AL.). Studies based on properties of hypertexts such as link distances between nodes containing related information (BLUSTEIN ET AL.) and complexity of hypertext structures (BOTAFOGO ET AL.) relate only to certain properties of hypertexts and cannot account for all of their features or uses. When they are contrasted with user experiments they seem quite limited.

One step toward more user influence in evaluating hypertext is to record the "journeys" or paths that users follow as they make their way through a hypertext structure. This path is then evaluated using mathematical methods. An interesting example of this type of evaluation is presented by MCENEANEY (1999; 2000). He applied a method developed to analyze hypertext (BOTAFOGO ET AL.) to an approximation of the paths users followed when reading hypertexts. Their results confirm expectations that individual differences in the cognitive styles of hypertext readers affect their success with hypertext (CASTELLI ET AL.; DILLON & WATSON; NIELSEN, 1989).

It is widely believed that articles with hypertext links can be more useful than versions without links. Hypertext is not always a suitable application, however: people sometimes prefer hypertext even when they do more poorly with it (NIELSEN & LEVY). SMITH found little correlation between the success of users in actually finding information in a hypertext and their self-reported confidence in finding the information. Hypertext, therefore, should be evaluated with people performing realistic tasks in ways that the systems are expected to be used. Evaluation must measure users' performance, not merely their satisfaction.

Text comprehension is a complex process, and changes in the way text is presented change the way people think (CARLSON). Different types of text (e.g., poetry, narrative, and discourse) create different expectations in readers (CHARNEY). Readers who are unfamiliar with the topic of the text, in particular, become confused when a document's structure is inconsistent with their expectations of its contents (DEE-LUCAS, 1999). Because hypertext allows for unfamiliar types of text structuring, this problem can be considerably worse for hypertext readers than for readers of ordinary text. Of course, readers often expect the reading of hypertext to be different from the reading of traditional text. One common difficulty readers have with hypertexts is determining when they have read enough (e.g., SMITH).

The effects of the user interface (UI) cannot easily be separated from the effects of the structure. Hypertext documents may be missing many of the cues that readers are familiar with in ordinary text because following hypertext links (especially in WWW browsers) often removes the text near the starting point of the link from their view.

## Evaluation Experiments

Two main divisions of testing are recognized by the human factors research community (HIX & HARTSON): formative and summative. Formative evaluation is conducted during the development of software and is part of an iterative design development process to determine how close the product is to achieving the design goals. Because the entire software life-cycle model being used may be iterative, the design goals may change too. Summative evaluation is rarely used for usability testing, but rather to compare two products or two versions of a product. It is usually a thorough comparison applied to a complete or nearly complete product.

A famous case of formative evaluation was the development of the SuperBook hypertext reference manual software (EGAN ET AL.; LANDAUER ET AL.). The experimenters (who also designed and wrote the software) compared student performance at locating the answers to questions using an encoded textbook (presented with the software) with their performance of the same task using a traditional textbook. Three trials were run. After the first and second trials, the software was refined and retested. The speed of successful searching using the software improved until it was considerably better than searching with the textbook alone. However, part of the second and third trials involved changes in the goals of the experiment; since searching for words seemed to be an advantage for the software, changes were made to encourage users to search. Further, although a significant difference for success when searching for words in section headings was found, only the overall success rate was reported. Through formative testing and redesign SuperBook was improved, and some important observations about users' behavior with hypertext were noted. Unfortunately, it is not clear from the experiments how much of the performance gain was due to the software's being suitable for real-world tasks and how much the tasks were suited to the strengths of the system.

BLUSTEIN (2000) conducted a summative evaluation of hypertext using realistic tasks. He compared the performance of two IR systems for detecting locations for linking and users' preferences for different types of links in online survey articles.

Intradocument links were created between passages of long survey articles (as found in this volume). Three types of links were used: (1) structural links, such as tables of contents and cross references; (2) definition links, which connected the use of technical terms with their definitions within the article; and (3) semantic links, which connected passages that concerned the same subject but were physically separate. The semantic links were found automatically using methods based on the work of SALTON ET AL.

The experiment was conducted in two parts. First, users read an article to answer questions and summarize it. They were allowed up to 40 minutes before they were not permitted to read any more. They were, however, permitted to continue writing for as long as they wanted.

In the second part of the test the users rated a sample of links in the article. The passages for semantic links were determined by two IR systems: SMART and Latent Semantic Indexing (LSI). The users read three articles. All contained structural and definition links, but two of them also contained semantic links, which were made using one of the IR systems.

A strong difference between link types was found. Users did not feel that the intradocument semantic links were helpful, but there was a statistically insignificant preference for definition links over structural links. There was no difference for either users' satisfaction rating (their preference) or for the quality of their answers or summary on the basis of which IR system was used to make the semantic links (BLUSTEIN, 1999). This result is particularly interesting because in the annual Text REtrieval Conference (TREC) significant differences were reported for the performance of SMART and LSI for more routine IR tasks (TAGUE-SUTCLIFFE & BLUSTEIN). Few of the test subjects finished reading in the allotted 40 minutes, and a more realistic experiment may yet find differences between the methods. Blustein concluded that part of the reason interlinker consistency was so low is that linking is inherently idiosyncratic and that therefore semantic links within articles should not be made automatically.

Readers can more easily agree on where basic (structural) links should begin and end than semantic links. The utility of semantic links depends on the users' purpose in reading the text and state of mind (LAWLESS & KULIKOWICH; TAGUE-SUTCLIFFE). Blustein suggests that structural links can provide necessary scaffolding to reduce the cognitive load and allow individual readers to make semantic links (within and between) articles themselves.

Many usability issues can be detected using inspection methods, which are a useful adjunct to full-blown user testing. GARZOTTO & MATERA present a good example of a systematic inspection-based method for hypertext evaluation. It is a refinement of the more general Systematic Methodology for Evaluating Hypermedia Usability (SUE) that Matera developed for her Ph.D. dissertation. In this method, usability experts use design models to guide their evaluation. It differs from other types of user testing in that actual users are not observed using hypertext but rather expert evaluators systematically judge the hypertexts' conformance to various standard heuristic measures of suitability. Another approach to testing without users is demonstrated by a tool that was developed exclusively for use on the WWW. The static analyzer tool (SAT) in the U.S. National Institute of Standards and Technology (NIST) Web Metrics Tool Suite (LASKOWSKI ET AL.; SCHOLTZ ET AL.) performs automated checks against several published (but largely unvalidated) guidelines.

## Reviews of HCI-Based Evaluation

Much research on hypertext has been with specific systems of which hypertext has only been one part. Review papers are attempts to find aspects of hypertext that are common in all systems.

NIELSEN (1989) compared 92 published measurements of factors that were reported to have had an effect on performance with hypertext. Nothing is said about the validity of the measures. The factors are grouped in the following categories: 24 hardware characteristics, 6 basic software aspects of the user interface, 13 comparisons between hypertext software and other software, 20 comparisons between hypertext software and paper, 19 various hypertext facilities, 10 effects of task and individual user differences. The largest effects were found for spatial ability, age, experience with the software, knowledge of the domain, enthusiasm for the experiment, and possession of active reading skills.

CHEN & RADA conducted a meta-analysis of the results of 23 experimental studies of hypertext systems by others. They examined the reported effects of user type, tasks, tools (such as indices, tables of contents, graphical maps) on measures of effectiveness and efficiency. Effectiveness was defined as achievement scores on tasks and coverage, that is, the amount of the hypertext document that a reader had completed reading. Efficiency was essentially the speed of reading. They divided tasks into open and closed. Open tasks have general goals; closed tasks, specific goals. For example, writing a summary of a hypertext document is an open task. The experimental participants had to decompose the general goals into concrete subgoals in order to complete a task.

Chen & Rada found that participants who read hypertexts tended to perform tasks more efficiently and effectively than readers of traditional texts. The authors suspect that these results depend on additional underlying factors, for example, different substantive material in the hypertext documents. Complexity of task had the greatest effect on levels of the various effectiveness measures. The greatest effect on efficiency levels was from the spatial ability of readers, followed by the complexity of tasks. They cite NIELSEN (1989) as saying that age and motivation are major influences on hypertext readers.

DILLON & GABBARD reviewed 30 studies from the empirical literature on the use of hypertext and computer multimedia in education. They considered hypertext as a "form of information presentation" and, in their analysis, treated hypertext and multimedia as indistinct. They evaluated the following claims: (1) that hypertext can improve students' comprehension of lessons, (2) that varying levels of control over how the content of lessons is delivered will help students, and (3) that certain individual differences play a key role in determining which students will be successful with which types of hypertext presentations. There is considerable evidence to support their third claim (DEE-LUCAS, 1996; LAWLESS & KULIKOWICH ).

Dillon & Gabbard found that the task that students are asked to perform with the hypertext has a strong effect on the successful use of the technology. In particular, they note that there does not seem to be much study or knowledge of how best to author hypertext to exploit the cognitive capabilities of students to structure information. The possibility for additional control afforded by hypertext seems to have no effect except in the case of highly able learners, although the five studies they cite had different results. Learner style and ability seem to be the two major factors determining success. Users with high ability tend to do better with hypertext than others. Determining useful classifications of learner style is much more difficult, though.

Dillon & Gabbard conclude that hypertext is best suited for tasks requiring quick searching through substantial information sources and in situations in which data must be manipulated and compared. However, existing formats (e.g., books) are better for other tasks. Whether students benefit from increased control of access to information through hypertext depends on students', cognitive abilities and otherwise. Not unexpectedly, students with the lowest ability have the most trouble. It has long been recognized that hypertext places a greater cognitive load on the user than traditional forms of presentation (SELBER). Studies (DEE-LUCAS, 1999; DILLON & WATSON) indicate that, although individual differences between users can have negative effects on performance, appropriate interface design and user training can reduce these problems.

## REFLECTIONS

There is much enthusiastic support for hypertext as an expressive technology. With the popularity of the WWW people have access to much more link-based hypertext than ever before, and it sometimes seems that making information accessible in hypertext form is all that is necessary to benefit users. However, studies of hypertext use show that this is a misguided view. With rare exceptions, hypertext structure cannot be considered separately from its presentation medium. Individual differences between users and their information needs also play a large role in determining how successful any hypertext document will be.

Although hypertext can be a useful tool for expressing and communicating one's thoughts, it is not clear how it should best be used. There are important differences in the ways that people perceive and use information presented in hypertext that cannot be ignored. Current mathematical models of hypertext quality are clean and clear, but they lack the depth necessary to address the myriad user types and tasks for which hypertexts can be used. Several studies have found that individual differences in users can have a significant effect on success with hypertext systems. It may be that hypertext is more suitable for users (alone or in groups) to create documents for their own use than as an automatically generated interface to data. Radical examples of this approach can be seen in spatial hypertext systems.

As with any information system intended for human use, hypertext must be designed while keeping in mind from the beginning the people who will use it, what they will use it for, and the context in which they will use it. A sensible way to combine these goals is to employ rapid prototyping to develop simultaneous understandings of users, their needs, and how they work.

## BIBLIOGRAPHY

ACKERMAN, MARK S. 1993. Answer Garden: A Tool for Growing Organizational Memory. Cambridge, MA: Massachusetts Institute of Technology; 1993. 253p. (Ph.D. dissertation). OCLC: 30692313.

ACKERMAN, MARK S. 1998. Augmenting Organizational Memory: A Field Study of Answer Garden. ACM Transactions on Information Systems. 1998 July; 16(3): 203-224. ISSN: 1046-8188.

ACKERMAN, MARK S.; MALONE, THOMAS W. 1990. Answer Garden: A Tool for Growing Organizational Memory. SIGOIS Bulletin. 1990; 11(2/3): 31-39. ISSN: 0894-0819.

ACM COMPUTING SURVEYS. 1999. Hypertext and Hypermedia Electronic Symposium. ACM Computing Surveys. 1999 December; 31(4es). ISSN: 0360-0300. Available WWW: http://www.acm.org/pubs/contents/journals/surveys/1999-31/#4es.

ALLAN, JAMES. 1996. Automatic Hypertext Link Typing. In: Hypertext '96: Proceedings of the 7th ACM Conference on Hypertext; 1996 March 16-20; Washington, DC. New York, NY: Association for Computing Machinery; 1996. 42-52. ISBN: 0-89791-778-2.

ALLEN, BRYCE. 1998. Information Space Representation in Interactive Systems: Relationship to Spatial Abilities. In: Witten, Ian H.; Akscyn, Robert M.; Shipman, Frank M., III, eds. Proceedings of the 3rd ACM Conference on Digital Libraries; 1998 June 23-26; Pittsburgh, PA. New York, NY: Association for Computing Machinery; 1998. 1-10. ISBN: 0-89791-965-3.

BARNARD, DAVID T.; MACLEOD, IAN A. 1989. An Archive of Structured Texts. Kingston, Ontario: Queen's University, Department of Computing and Information Science; 1989. 10p. (Technical Report 89-262). OCLC: 21268340.

BECKWITH, RICHARD; FELLBAUM, CHRISTIANE; GROSS, DEREK; MILLER, GEORGE A. 1991. WordNet: A Lexical Database Organized on

Psycholinguistic Principles. In: Zernik, Uri, ed. Lexical Acquisition: Exploiting On-Line Resources to Build a Lexicon. Hillsdale, NJ: Lawrence Erlbaum Associates; 1991. 211-231. ISBN: 0-8058-0829-9.

BERNSTEIN, MARK. 1998. Patterns of Hypertext. In: Hypertext '98: Proceedings of the 9th ACM Conference on Hypertext and Hypermedia; 1998 June 20-24; Pittsburgh, PA. New York, NY: Association for Computing Machinery; 1998. 21-29. ISBN: 0-89791-972-6.

BIBIX. BibIX 2.1: Bibliographic Data Base & Text Formatting System. Available WWW: http://otl.berkeley.edu/BibIX.html.

BIEBER, MICHAEL; ISAKOWITZ, TOMÁS, eds. 1995. Designing Hypermedia Applications. Communications of the ACM. 1995 August; 38(8): 26-112. (Special issue). ISSN: 0001-0782.

BLUSTEIN, JAMES. 1999. Hypertext Versions of Journal Articles: Computer Aided Linking and Realistic Human-Based Evaluation. London, Ontario: University of Western Ontario; 1999. (Ph.D. dissertation).

BLUSTEIN, JAMES. 2000. Automatically Generated Hypertext Versions of Scholarly Articles and Their Evaluation. In: HT '00: Proceedings of the 11th ACM Conference on Hypertext and Hypermedia; 2000 May 30-June 3; San Antonio, TX. New York, NY: Association for Computing Machinery; 2000. 201-210. ISBN: 1-58113-227-1.

BLUSTEIN, JAMES; WEBBER, ROBERT E.; TAGUE-SUTCLIFFE, JEAN. 1997. Methods for Evaluating the Quality of Hypertext Links. Information Processing & Management. 1997; 33(2): 255-271. ISSN: 0306-4573.

BOTAFOGO, RODRIGO A.; RIVLIN, EHUD; SHNEIDERMAN, BEN. 1992. Structural Analysis of Hypertexts: Identifying Hierarchies and Useful Metrics. ACM Transactions on Information Systems. 1992 April; 10(2): 142-180. ISSN: 1046-8188.

BOUVIN, NIELS OLOF. 1999. Unifying Strategies for Web Augmentation. In: Hypertext '99: Proceedings of the 10th ACM Conference on Hypertext and Hypermedia; 1999 February 21-25; Darmstadt, Germany. New York, NY: Association for Computing Machinery; 1999. 91-100. ISBN: 1-58113-064-3.

BRAY, TIM; PAOLI, JEAN; SPERBERG-MCQUEEN, C. M.; MALER, EVE, eds. 2000. Extensible Markup Language (XML) 1.0 (Second Edition): A W3C Recommendation. 2000 October 6. Available WWW: http://www.w3.org/TR/REC-xml.html.

BROCKMANN, R. JOHN; HORTON, WILLIAM; BROCK, KEVIN. 1989. From Database to Hypertext via Electronic Publishing: An Information Odyssey. In: Barrett, Edward, ed. The Society of Text: Hypertext, Hypermedia and the Social Construction of Information. Cambridge, MA: MIT Press; 1989. 162-205. ISBN: 0-262-02291-5.

BUSH, VANNEVAR. 1945. As We May Think. Atlantic Monthly. 1945 July; 176(1): 101-108. Also available WWW: http://www.theatlantic.com/unbound/flashbks/computer/bushf.htm.

CARLSON, PATRICIA ANN. 1989. Hypertext and Intelligent Interfaces for Text Retrieval. In: Barrett, Edward, ed. The Society of Text: Hypertext, Hypermedia and the Social Construction of Information. Cambridge, MA: MIT Press; 1989. 59-76. ISBN: 0-262-02291-5.

CASTELLI, CARLO; COLAZZO, LUIGI; MOLINARI, ANDREA. 1998. Cognitive Variables and Patterns of Hypertext Performances: Lessons Learned for Educational Hypermedia Construction. Journal of Educational Multimedia and Hypermedia. 1998; 7(2/3): 177-206. ISSN: 1055-8896.

CHARNEY, DAVIDA. 1994. The Effect of Hypertext on Processes of Reading and Writing. In: Selfe, Cynthia L.; Hilligoss, Susan, eds. Literacy and Computers: The Complications of Teaching and Learning with Technology. New York, NY: Modern Language Association of America; 1994. 238-263. ISBN: 0-87352-580-9.

CHEN, CHAOMEI; CARR, LES. 1999. Trailblazing the Literature of Hypertext: Author Co-citation Analysis (1989-1998). In: Hypertext '99: Proceedings of the 10th ACM Conference on Hypertext and Hypermedia; 1999 February 21-25; Darmstadt, Germany. New York, NY: Association for Computing Machinery; 1999. 51-60. ISBN: 1-58113-064-3.

CHEN, CHAOMEI; RADA, ROY. 1996. Interacting with Hypertext: A Meta-Analysis of Experimental Studies. Human-Computer Interaction. 1996; 11(2): 125-156. ISSN: 0737-0024.

CLITHEROW, PETER; RIECKEN, DOUG; MULLER, MICHAEL. 1989. VISAR: A System for Inference and Navigation of Hypertext. In: Hypertext '89: Proceedings of the 2nd ACM Conference on Hypertext; 1989 November 5-8; Pittsburgh, PA. New York, NY: Association for Computing Machinery; 1989. 293-304. ISBN: 0-89791-339-6.

COMMUNICATIONS OF THE ACM. 1990. Hypertext. Communications of the ACM. 1990 March; 33(3): 296-321. (Section devoted to Hypertext). ISSN: 0001-0782.

CONKLIN, JEFF. 1987. Hypertext: An Introduction and Survey. Computer. 1987 September; 20(9): 17-41. ISSN: 0018-9162.

CONKLIN, JEFF. 1991. Hypertext. In: Encyclopedia of Microcomputers: Volume 8. New York, NY: Marcel Dekker, Inc.; 1991. 377-432. ISBN: 0-8247-2707-X.

CONRAD, JACK G.; UTT, MARY HUNTER. 1994. A System for Discovering Relationships by Feature Extraction from Text Databases. In: SIGIR '94: Proceedings of the Association for Computing Machinery Special Interest Group on Information Retrieval (ACM/SIGIR) 17th Annual International Conference on Research and Development in Information Retrieval; 1994 July 3-6; Dublin, Ireland. New York, NY: Springer-Verlag; 1994. 260-270. ISBN: 0-387-19887-X.

CORMEN, THOMAS H.; LEISERSON, CHARLES ERIC; RIVEST, RONALD L. 1990. Introduction to Algorithms. Cambridge, MA: MIT Press; 1990. 1028p. ISBN: 0-262-03141-8.

CYBIB. CyBib. Web site: http://www-cyanosite.bio.purdue.edu/cybib/cybibhome.html.

DEE-LUCAS, DIANA. 1996. Instructional Hypertext: Study Strategies for Different Types of Learning Tasks. In: Proceedings of the ED-MEDIA 96 World Conference on Educational Multimedia and Hypermedia; 1996 June 17-22; Boston, MA. Charlottesville, VA: Association for the Advancement of Computing in Education; 1996. 178-183. ISBN: 1-88009-421-5.

DEE-LUCAS, DIANA. 1999. Information Location in Instructional Hypertext: Effects of Content Domain Expertise. In: Proceedings of the ED-MEDIA 99 World Conference on Educational Multimedia, Hypermedia, and Tele-communications; 1999 June 19-24; Seattle, WA. Charlottesille, VA: Association for the Advancement of Computing in Education; 1999. 242-247. ISBN: 1-88009-435-5.

DEROSE, STEVE; MALER, EVE; ORCHARD, DAVID, eds. 2000. XML Linking Language (XLink) Version 1.0: A W3C Proposed Recommendation. 2000 December 20. Available: http://www.w3.org/TR/xlink.

DILLON, ANDREW. 1992. Reading from Paper Versus Screens: A Critical Review of the Empirical Literature. Ergonomics. 1992; 35(10): 1297-1326. ISSN: 0014-0139.

DILLON, ANDREW; GABBARD, RALPH. 1998. Hypermedia as an Educational Technology: A Review of the Quantitative Research Literature on Learner Comprehension, Control and Style. Review of Educational Research. 1998 Fall; 68(3): 322-349. ISSN: 0034-6543.

DILLON, ANDREW; WATSON, CHARLES. 1996. User Analysis in HCI: The Historical Lessons from Individual Differences Research. International Journal of Human-Computer Studies. 1996 December; 45(6): 619-637. ISSN: 1071-5819.

DIX, ALAN; FINLAY, JANET E.; ABOWD, GREGORY D.; BEALE, RUSSELL. 1998. Human-Computer Interaction. 2nd edition. London, UK: Prentice Hall Europe; 1998. 638p. ISBN: 0-13-239864-8.

DRAKOS, NIKOS. 1994. From Text to Hypertext: A Post-hoc Rationalisation of LaTeX2HTML. Computer Networks and ISDN Systems. 1994 November; 27(2): 215-224. ISSN: 0169-7552.

EASTGATE SYSTEMS. Web site: http://www.eastgate.com.

EGAN, DENNIS E.; REMDE, JOEL R.; GOMEZ, LOUIS M.; LANDAUER, THOMAS K.; EBERHARDT, JENNIFER; LOCHBAUM, CAROL C. 1989. Formative Design-Evaluation of SuperBook. ACM Transactions on Information Systems. 1989 January; 7(1): 30-57. ISSN: 0734-2047.

ELECTRONIC LITERATURE ORGANIZATION. Web site: http://www.eliterature.org.

ELLIS, DAVID; FURNER, JONATHAN; WILLETT, PETER. 1996. On the Creation of Hypertext Links in Full-Text Documents: Measurement of Retrieval Effectiveness. Journal of the American Society for Information Science. 1996 April; 47(4): 287-300. ISSN: 0002-8231.

ELLIS, DAVID; FURNER-HINES, JONATHAN; WILLETT, PETER. 1994. On the Creation of Hypertext Links in Full-Text Documents: Measurement of Inter-Linker Consistency. Journal of Documentation. 1994 June; 50(2): 67-98. ISSN: 0022-0418.

FAHMY, EANASS; BARNARD, DAVID T. 1990. Adding Hypertext Links to an Archive of Documents. The Canadian Journal of Information Science. 1990 September; 15(3): 25-41. ISSN: 0380-9218.

FLORIDI, LUCIANO. 1999. Philosophy and Computing: An Introduction. New York, NY: Routledge; 1999. 257p. ISBN: 0-415-18025-2.

FRANK, EIBE; PAYNTER, GORDON W.; WITTEN, IAN H.; GUTWIN, CARL; NEVILL-MANNING, CRAIG G. 1999. Domain-Specific Keyphrase Extraction. In: Dean, Thomas, ed. Proceedings of the 16th International Joint Conference on Artificial Intelligence (IJCAI 99): Volume 2; 1999 July 31-August 6; Stockholm, Sweden. San Mateo, CA: Morgan Kaufmann; 1999. 668-673. ISBN: 1-55860-613-0.

FURNAS, GEORGE W.; LANDAUER, THOMAS K.; GOMEZ, LOUIS M.; DUMAIS, SUSAN T. 1987. The Vocabulary Problem in Human-System Communication. Communications of the ACM. 1987 November; 30(11): 964-971. ISSN: 0001-0782.

FURUTA, RICHARD; PLAISANT, CATHERINE; SHNEIDERMAN, BEN. 1989. Automatically Transforming Regularly Structured Linear Documents into Hypertext. Electronic Publishing. 1989 December; 2(4): 211-229. ISSN: 0894-3982.

GARZOTTO, FRANCA; MATERA, MARISTELLA. 1997. A Systematic Method for Hypermedia Usability Evaluation. The New Review of Hypermedia and Multimedia. 1997; 3: 39-65. ISSN: 1361-4568.

GOLDENBERG, ROBERT. 1984. Talmud. In: Holtz, Barry W., ed. Back to the Sources: Reading the Classic Jewish Texts. New York, NY: Summit Books; 1984. 128-175. ISBN: 0-671-45467-6.

GOLOVCHINSKY, GENE. 1997. What the Query Told the Link: The Integration of Hypertext and Information Retrieval. In: Hypertext '97: Proceedings of the 8th ACM Conference on Hypertext; 1997 April 6-11; Southampton, UK. New York, NY: Association for Computing Machinery; 1997. 67-74. ISBN: 0-89791-866-5.

GREEN, STEPHEN J. 1998. Automated Link Generation: Can We Do Better Than Term Repetition? Available WWW: http://www7.scu.edu.au/programme/fullpapers/1834/com1834.htm.

GREEN, STEPHEN J. 1999. Building Hypertext Links by Computing Semantic Similarity. IEEE Transactions on Knowledge and Data Engineering. 1999 September/October; 11(5): 713-730. ISSN: 1041-4347.

GRØNBAEK, KAJ; TRIGG, RANDALL H., eds. 1994. Hypermedia. Communications of the ACM. 1994 February; 37(2): 26-96. (Special issue). ISSN: 0001-0782.

HAHN, UDO; REIMER, ULRICH. 1988. Automatic Generation of Hypertext Knowledge Bases. SIGOIS Bulletin. 1988 April/July; 9(2/3): 182-188. ISSN: 0894-0819.

HALASZ, FRANK; SCHWARTZ, MAYER. 1990. The Dexter Hypertext Reference Model. In: Moline, Judi; Benigni, Daniel R.; Baronas, Jean, eds. Proceedings of the Hypertext Standardization Workshop; 1990 January 16-18; Gaithersburg, MD. Gaithersburg, MD: National Institute of Standards and Technology; 1990. 95-133. (NIST Special Publication 500-178). OCLC: 26135808.

HALASZ, FRANK; SCHWARTZ, MAYER. 1994. The Dexter Hypertext Reference Model. Communications of the ACM. 1994 February; 37(2): 30-39. ISSN: 0001-0782.

HAMMWOHNER, RAINER; THIEL, ULRICH. 1987. Content Oriented Relations between Text Units: A Structural Model for Hypertexts. In: Hypertext '87 Proceedings; 1987 November 13-15; Chapel Hill, NC. New York, NY: Association for Computing Machinery; 1987. 155-174. ISBN: 0-89791-340-X.

HIX, DEBORAH; HARTSON, H. REX. 1993. Developing User Interfaces: Ensuring Usability Through Product & Process. New York, NY: John Wiley & Sons, Inc.; 1993. 381p. ISBN: 0-471-57813-4.

HORN, ROBERT E. 1976. Information Mapping. Lexington, MA: Information Resources; 1976. 440p. OCLC: 2635655.

HYPERMEDIA. 1989-1994. London, UK: Taylor Graham Publishing. (Continued as The New Review of Hypermedia and Multimedia). ISSN: 0955-8543.

JONASSEN, DAVID H.; MANDL, HEINZ. 1990. Designing Hypermedia for Learning. Updated Proceedings of the North Atlantic Treaty Organization (NATO) Advanced Research Workshop on Designing Hypertext/Hypermedia for Learning; 1989 July 3-8; Rottenburg am Neckar, Federal Republic of Germany. New York, NY: Springer-Verlag; 1990. 482p. (NATO ASI Series. Series F. Computer and Systems Sciences, Vol. 67). ISBN: 0-38752-958-6.

JONES, STEVE; STAVELEY, MARK S. 1999. Phrasier: A System for Interactive Document Retrieval Using Keyphrases. In: SIGIR'99: Proceedings of the Association for Computing Machinery Special Interest Group on Information Retrieval (ACM/SIGIR) 22nd Annual International Conference on Research and Development in Information Retrieval; 1999 August 15-19; Berkeley, CA. New York, NY: ACM; 1999. 160-167. ISBN: 1-58113-096-1.

JOURNAL OF DIGITAL INFORMATION. 1997-. McKnight, Cliff, ed. ISSN: 1368-7506. Available WWW: http://jodi.ecs.soton.ac.uk.

JOYCE, MICHAEL. 1987. afternoon, a story. Watertown, MA: Eastgate Systems; 1987. (Electronic fiction). ISBN: 1-884511-01-5.

KAPPE, FRANK. 1996. The Need for Second-Generation Hypermedia Systems. In: Maurer, Hermann, ed. Hyper-G Now Hyperwave: The Next Generation Web Solution. Harlow, UK: Addison-Wesley; 1996. 88-102. ISBN: 0-201-40346-3.

LANDAUER, THOMAS K.; EGAN, DENNIS E.; REMDE, JOEL R.; LESK, MICHAEL E.; LOCHBAUM, CAROL C.; KETCHUM, DANIEL. 1993. Enhancing the Usability of Text through Computer Delivery and Formative Evaluation: The SuperBook Project. In: McKnight, Cliff; Dillon, Andrew; Richardson, John, eds. Hypertext: A Psychological Perspective. New York, NY: Ellis Horwood; 1993. 71-136. ISBN: 0-13-441643-0.

LASKOWSKI, SHARON J.; SCHOLTZ, JEAN; SHEPPARD, CHARLES; HSIAO, PAUL; CUGINI, JOHN; DOWNEY, LAURA. 2000. WebMetrics Testbed. Available WWW: http://zing.ncsl.nist.gov/WebTools.

LAWLESS, KIMBERLY A.; KULIKOWICH, JONNA M. 1998. Domain Knowledge, Interest, and Hypertext Navigation: A Study of Individual Differences. Journal of Educational Multimedia and Hypermedia. 1998; 7(1): 51-69. ISSN: 1055-8896.

LEHNERT, WENDY G. 1992. Automating the Construction of a Hypertext System for Scientific Literature. In: Proceedings of the AAAI Workshop on Communicating Scientific and Technical Knowledge. Available from: AAAI, 445 Burgess Drive, Menlo Park, CA 94025.

MARSHALL, CATHERINE C.; SHIPMAN, FRANK M., III. 1995. Spatial Hypertext: Designing for Change. Communications of the ACM. 1995 August; 38(8): 88-97. ISSN: 0001-0782.

MARSHALL, CATHERINE C.; SHIPMAN, FRANK M., III; COOMBS, JAMES H. 1994. VIKI: Spatial Hypertext Supporting Emergent Structure. In: ECHT '94: Proceedings of the 1994 ACM European Conference on Hypermedia Technology; 1994 September 18-23; Edinburgh, Scotland. New York, NY: Association for Computing Machinery; 1994. 13-23. ISBN: 0-89791-640-9.

MCDONALD, SHARON; STEVENSON, ROSEMARY J. 1999. Spatial Versus Conceptual Maps as Learning Tools in Hypertext. Journal of Educational Multimedia and Hypermedia. 1999; 8(1): 43-64. ISSN: 1055-8896.

MCENEANEY, JOHN E. 1999. Visualizing and Assessing Navigation in Hypertext. In: Hypertext '99: Proceedings of the 10th ACM Conference on Hypertext and Hypermedia; 1999 February 21-25; Darmstadt, Germany. New York, NY: Association for Computing Machinery; 1999. 61-70. ISBN: 0-58113-064-3.

MCENEANEY, JOHN E. 2000. Navigational Correlates of Comprehension in Hypertext. In: Hypertext '00: Proceedings of the 11th ACM Conference on Hypertext and Hypermedia; 2000 May 30-June 3; San Antonio, TX. New York, NY: Association for Computing Machinery; 2000. 254-255. ISBN: 1-58113-227-1.

MELUCCI, MASSIMO. 1999. An Evaluation of Automatically Constructed Hypertexts for Information Retrieval. Information Retrieval. 1999; 1(1/2): 91-114. ISSN: 1386-4564.

MORRIS, JANE; HIRST, GRAEME. 1991. Lexical Cohesion Computed by Thesaural Relations as an Indicator of the Structure of Text. Computational Linguistics. 1991 March; 17(1): 21-48. ISSN: 0891-2017.

NATIONAL SCIENCE FOUNDATION GRAPHICS AND VISUALIZATION CENTER. 1996. Memex and Beyond. Available WWW: http://www.cs.brown.edu/memex.

NELSON, THEODOR HOLM. 1990. Literary Machines: The Report on, and of, Project Xanadu Concerning Word Processing, Electronic Publishing, Hypertext, Thinkertoys, Tomorrow's Intellectual Revolution, and Certain Other Topics Including Knowledge, Education and Freedom. Edition 90.1 Sausalito, CA: Mindful Press; 1990. 1 volume. OCLC: 25907500. Available from: Eastgate Systems, 134 Main Street, Watertown, MA 02472.

NEW ZEALAND DIGITAL LIBRARY. 2000. Department of Computer Science, University of Waikato, New Zealand. Web site: http://www.nzdl.org.

NIELSEN, JAKOB. 1989. The Matters That Really Matter for Hypertext Usability. In: Hypertext '89: Proceedings of the 2nd ACM Conference on

Hypertext; 1989 November 5-8; Pittsburgh, PA. New York, NY: Association for Computing Machinery; 1989. 239-248. ISBN: 0-89791-339-6.

NIELSEN, JAKOB. 1990. Hypertext and Hypermedia. San Diego CA: Academic Press; 1990. 263p. ISBN: 0-12-518410-7.

NIELSEN, JAKOB. 1995. Multimedia and Hypertext: The Internet and Beyond. Boston, MA: AP Professional; 1995. 480p. ISBN: 0-12-518408-5.

NIELSEN, JAKOB; LEVY, JONATHAN. 1994. Measuring Usability: Preference vs. Performance. Communications of the ACM. 1994 April; 37(4): 66-75. ISSN: 0001-0782.

NUNN, DEBBIE; LEGGETT, JOHN J.; BOYLE, CRAIG; HICKS, DAVID. 1988. The REXX Project: A Case Study of Automatic Hypertext Construction. College Station, TX: Department of Computer Science, Texas A&M University; 1988 April. 72p. (Technical Report TAMU 88-021). OCLC: 36502577.

NÜRNBERG, PETER J.; ASHMAN, HELEN. 1999. What Was the Question? Reconciling Open Hypermedia and World Wide Web Research. In: Hypertext '99: Proceedings of the 10th ACM Conference on Hypertext and Hypermedia; 1999 February 21-25; Darmstadt, Germany. New York, NY: Association for Computing Machinery; 1999. 83-90. ISBN: 1-58113-064-3.

OPEN HYPERMEDIA SYSTEMS WORKING GROUP. 1997. OHSWG Compendium. 1997 November 5. Available WWW: http://www.csdl.tamu.edu/ohs/ohswg.html.

ØSTERBYE, KASPER; WIIL, UFFE KOCK. 1996. The Flag Taxonomy of Open Hypermedia Systems. In: Hypertext '96: Proceedings of the 7th ACM Conference on Hypertext; 1996 March 16-20; Washington, DC. New York, NY: Association for Computing Machinery; 1996. 129-139. ISBN: 0-89791-778-2.

PARK, SEONGBIN. 1998. Structural Properties of Hypertext. In: Hypertext '98: Proceedings of the 9th ACM Conference on Hypertext and Hypermedia; 1998 June 20-24; Pittsburgh, PA. New York, NY: Association for Computing Machinery; 1998. 180-187. ISBN: 0-89791-972-6.

PARUNAK, H. VAN DYKE. 1991. Ordering the Information Graph. In: Berk, Emily; Devlin, Joseph, eds. Hypertext/Hypermedia Handbook. New York, NY: Intertext Publications; 1991. 299-325. ISBN: 0-07-016622-6.

RAYMOND, DARRELL R.; TOMPA, FRANK W.; WOOD, DERICK. 1993. Markup Reconsidered. London, Ontario: Department of Computer Science, University of Western Ontario; 1993 May. 15p. ISBN: 0-7714-1504-4.

SALTON, GERARD; ALLAN, JAMES; BUCKLEY, CHRIS. 1994. Automatic Structuring and Retrieval of Large Text Files. Communications of the ACM. 1994 February; 37(2): 97-108. ISSN: 0001-0782.

SCHOLTZ, JEAN; LASKOWSKI, SHARON; DOWNEY, LAURA. 1998. Developing Usability Tools and Techniques for Designing and Testing Web Sites. In: Proceedings of the 4th Conference on Human Factors and the Web; 1998 June 5; Basking Ridge, NJ. Available WWW: http://www.research.att.com/conf/hfweb/proceedings/scholtz.

SELBER, STUART A. 1995. Metaphorical Perspectives on Hypertext. IEEE Transactions on Professional Communication. 1995 July; 38(2): 59-67. ISSN: 0361-1431.

SHIPMAN, FRANK M., III; MARSHALL, CATHERINE C.; LEMERE, MARK. 1999. Beyond Location: Hypertext Workspaces and Non-Linear Views. In: Hypertext '99: Proceedings of the 10th ACM Conference on Hypertext and Hypermedia; 1999 February 21-25; Darmstadt, Germany. New York, NY: Association for Computing Machinery; 1999. 121-130. ISBN: 1-58113-064-3.

SHUMATE, MICHAEL. 1997. Hyperizons. 1997 July 22. Available WWW: http://www.duke.edu/~mshumate/hyperfic.html.

SIMPSON, JOHN A.; WEINER, EDMUND S.C., eds. 1993. Hypertext. In: Oxford English Dictionary Additions Series: Volume 2. Oxford, UK: Clarendon Press; 1993. 152. ISBN: 0-19-861299-0.

SIMPSON, ROSEMARY; RENEAR, ALLEN; MYLONAS, ELLI; VAN DAM, ANDRIES. 1996. 50 Years After "As We May Think": The Brown/MIT Vannevar Bush Symposium. interactions. 1996 March; 3(2): 47-67. ISSN: 1072-5220.

SMITH, PAULINE A. 1996. Towards a Practical Measure of Hypertext Usability. Interacting with Computers. 1996 December; 8(4): 365-381. ISSN: 0953-5438.

TAGUE-SUTCLIFFE, JEAN. 1995. Measuring Information: An Information Services Perspective. San Diego, CA: Academic Press; 1995. 206p. ISBN: 0-12-682660-9.

TAGUE-SUTCLIFFE, JEAN; BLUSTEIN, JAMES. 1995. A Statistical Analysis of the TREC-3 Data. In: Proceedings of the 3rd Text REtrieval Conference (TREC-3); 1994 November 2-4; Gaithersburg, MD. Gaithersburg, MD: National Institute for Standards and Technology; 1995. 385-392. (NIST Special Publication 500-226). NTIS: PB95-216883.

TEXT ENCODING INITIATIVE. Web site: http://www.tei-c.org.

THE NEW REVIEW OF HYPERMEDIA AND MULTIMEDIA. 1995-. Tudhope, Douglas, ed. London, UK: Taylor Graham Publishing. (Previously titled Hypermedia). ISSN: 1361-4568.

WALKER, JILL. 1999. Piecing Together and Tearing Apart: Finding the Story in afternoon. In: Hypertext '99: Proceedings of the 10th ACM Conference on Hypertext and Hypermedia; 1999 February 21-25; Darmstadt, Germany. New York, NY: Association for Computing Machinery; 1999. 111-117. ISBN: 1-58113-064-3.

WIIL, UFFE KOCK. 1997. Open Hypermedia: Systems, Interoperability and Standards. Journal of Digital Information. 1997 December; 1(2). ISSN: 1368-7506. Available WWW: http://jodi.ecs.soton.ac.uk.

WIIL, UFFE KOCK; ØSTERBYE, KASPER. 1998. Using the Flag Taxonomy to Study Hypermedia System Interoperability. In: Hypertext '98: Proceedings of the 9th ACM Conference on Hypertext and Hypermedia; 1998 June 20-24; Pittsburgh, PA. New York, NY: Association for Computing Machinery; 1998. 188-197. ISBN: 0-89791-972-6.

WILSON, E. 1990. Links and Structures in Hypertext Databases for Law. In: Streitz, Norbert; Rizk, Antoine; André, Jacques, eds. Hypertext: Concepts, Systems and Applications: Proceedings of the 1st European Conference on Hypertext; 1990 November 27-30; Versailles, France. Cambridge, UK: Cambridge University Press; 1990. 194-211. ISBN: 0-521-40517-3.

WITTEN, IAN H.; MOFFAT, ALISTAIR; BELL, TIMOTHY C. 1994. Managing Gigabytes: Compressing and Indexing Documents and Images. New York, NY: Van Nostrand Reinhold; 1994. 429p. ISBN: 0-442-01863-0.

YAMADA, SHOJI; HONG, JUNG-KOOK; SUGITA, SHIGEHARU. 1995. Development and Evaluation of Hypermedia for Museum Education: Validation of Metrics. ACM Transactions on Computer-Human Interaction. 1995 December; 2(4): 284-307. (See also correction to formula for downward compactness in 1996 September; 3(2): 285). ISSN: 1073-0516.

# 7 Digital Preservation

## ELIZABETH YAKEL
## University of Michigan

## INTRODUCTION

The term digital preservation is viewed by many as an oxymoron. ACKERMAN & FIELDING assert that the long-term maintenance of digital documents will pose significantly more difficult challenges than collection maintenance for paper-based materials. However, a great deal of research on digital preservation issues is currently being conducted around the world. The past several years have witnessed a significant increase in collaborative international efforts addressing a variety of questions on digital preservation (BERTHON & WEBB). These and similar efforts are working to make digital preservation a reality.

Digital preservation concerns both born-digital and digitally recreated documents. Born-digital materials are those that were initially created using some form of digital technology. Digital preservation of born-digital documents in electronic form is essential to maintain their authenticity, reliability, and functionality. Digitally recreated materials, or "born-again" digital materials, as LYMAN & KAHLE refer to them, have been transformed from analog to digital form through some means (e.g., rekeying the information or scanning the object to create a surrogate image). This process can also be referred to as preservation digitization and is highly controversial. A. SMITH and WEBER & DÖRR argue that digitization is primarily a means of enhancing access and at present is not a reliable means of preservation. In the end both types of digital documents face similar problems in relation to their long-term preservation.

Throughout this chapter, all types of digital materials are referred to as documents, whether they are textual, image-based, or multimedia.

*Annual Review of Information Science and Technology* (*ARIST*), Volume 35, 2001
Martha E. Williams, Editor
Published for the American Society for Information Science and Technology (ASIST)
By Information Today, Inc., Medford, NJ

However, digital preservation of textual and image-based documents, not digital-audio or moving-picture materials, is the focus. STEEN LARSEN asserts that it is important to designate digital objects as documents because this definition connotes their value as evidence. This sense of the term document aligns with other recent definitions that encourage information professionals to think about media less in terms of physical properties and more in terms of intellectual attributes. In fact, GRAHAM (1994) identified the greatest challenge in digital preservation as intellectual preservation, or preserving the authenticity and integrity of the original document through time and potentially across platforms. Much of the research addresses this challenge in some manner.

Numerous research agendas have been proposed in the area of digital preservation. In 1991, the NATIONAL HISTORICAL PUBLICA-TIONS AND RECORDS COMMISSION (NHPRC) solicited input from the archival community on the most pressing research issues regarding electronic records. The result was 10 research questions concerning systems design requirements, policy issues, and educational needs within the archival profession to address these issues. The significance of these questions in providing a framework for research into the preservation of electronic records continues today. HEDSTROM (1991) noted that research on electronic records should also focus on the social, political, and economic aspects of organizations that affect how institutions and individuals adopt and adapt technologies. WATERS & GARRETT described further research issues in the report from the Task Force on Archiving of Digital Information. The areas include systems design, the need to foster learning through critical case studies, standards development, and organizational and economic issues surrounding the long-term maintenance of authentic digital documents. In the Association of Research Libraries (ARL) conference proceedings on the preservation of digital information, GRAHAM (1997) grouped the research issues for digital preservation into two major areas: technical and organizational. It is important to acknowledge that structural, political, and economic factors in organizations affect digital preservation. The diversity of these issues also demonstrates the breadth of potential topics under the umbrella of digital preservation research.

This chapter recognizes the range of potential research questions on digital preservation and is divided primarily into two sections: born-digital documents, often referred to as electronic records, and digitally recreated or "born-again" digital documents. Topics concerning born-digital documents include how the major research initiatives approach digital preservation from the standpoint of ensuring authenticity and reliability, metadata and other standards, digital preservation initiatives focusing on three genres of born-digital documents (electronic mail, web-based materials, and digital moving-image records). Technical research into specific functionalities for preserving authenticity and reliability (e.g., date stamping, digital watermarks, encryption) are not covered. This section ends with an overview of current research initiatives.

The section on digitally recreated documents begins with a discussion of selection for digitization and then is divided primarily according to genre or format. Topics include the different criteria and concerns of digitizing books, image-based documents, and primary sources or archival materials. This section also examines research on the long-term management of digital files and the administration of digital initiatives.

Two final sections deal with research on media stability and economic issues related to digital preservation. The greatest challenge in digital preservation is not deterioration of the physical media, although research on media stability is discussed briefly at the end of this chapter. The main problem is technological obsolescence, so research that is aimed at this problem is the focus here. Even though digitization has been closely identified with access, this chapter does not cover research that examines reference services for electronic records; the evaluation of interfaces and applications that display, represent, or facilitate use of digital documents; and copyright issues.

The research literature on digital preservation is populated by case studies of digitization projects and the results of several large-scale and numerous small research projects on electronic records; the latter fall primarily into the category of applied research. The case studies provide in-depth information on digitization or digital preservation projects. Perhaps because the documents being digitized are unique, there are few overarching analyses or comparative research studies of these projects. The literature on electronic records research discusses research and demonstration projects aimed at developing sustainable models for the digital preservation of documents.

## BORN-DIGITAL DOCUMENTS

### The First Generation of Electronic Records Research

T. COOK has divided electronic records into two eras. The first era concerned the preservation of what was then referred to as machine-readable records. In terms of file format, these were flat or comma-delimited ASCII files, consisting primarily of large-scale social science data sets and business applications for such functions as accounting and inventory control. The classic works on preserving machine-readable records are by HEDSTROM (1984) and by NAUGLER. This problem was seen as solved by refreshing the data or periodically copying the data from one medium to another to avoid media decay. However, recent research shows that refreshing alone is not sufficient to ensure long-term preservation of social science data sets and that many older data sets are in danger of destruction. Two studies by the NATIONAL RESEARCH COUNCIL (NRC) (1995a; 1995b) provide cogent evidence of the extensive problems relating to scientific and technical data generated between 1960 and 1980 by the federal government. In a similar study GREEN ET AL. examined the challenge of maintaining large statistical data sets at Yale University. They outline the nine-step migration process they followed. Their findings revealed that the flat file or, as they refer to it, the column binary format, was robust and lent itself to many migration options. Still, the challenge of preserving the documentation or code books that carry critical metadata for deciphering the information in these data sets correctly over time remained. ZELENOCK & MARZ, who are active in building the data archives at the Interuniversity Consortium for Social and Political Research at the University of Michigan, further underline the importance of working with the creators of data in order to access clean data sets as well as comprehensive documentation of the research project.

## The Second Generation of Electronic Records Research

Relational and object-oriented databases and multimedia files characterize the second generation of electronic records. The meaning of these digital documents is embedded in the relationships among data elements and functionalities of the objects established by the software and perhaps also by the hardware and/or operating system. These software-dependent documents require a different approach to digital preservation from the flat-file data sets and pose more complex research issues. Maintaining the reliability and authenticity of records over time is a major thrust of the research. In this context, reliability refers to the ability of a system to maintain the accuracy of the information content. For example, migration from an older to a newer version of a software application may entail slight changes in formatting elements (italics, boldface) that affect the meaning of a document. Authenticity refers to the capability of a record-keeping system to ensure that the record has been created, changed, and maintained according to established authority or procedures (COUNCIL ON LIBRARY AND INFORMATION RESOURCES (CLIR); DURANTI). In order to interpret the authenticity of a document, a reader would need access to more than the informational content. The reader would need to examine the metadata, which would indicate when and if changes were made and whether these were authorized. Specific mechanisms for maintaining authenticity and reliability include authentication, version control, date stamping, digital signatures, and encryption.

Second-generation electronic records cannot be reduced to column binary format because critical relationships among elements are essential for reliability, and maintaining embedded objects, such as digital signatures, is critical for ensuring authenticity. In fact, the focus of digital preservation is on the record-keeping system rather than on individual documents. Preservation of born-digital documents and record-keeping systems is easier if systems are designed with long-term value and maintenance in mind. A significant amount of the research has focused on system design and implementation requirements to ensure that authenticity and reliability can be sustained over time.

HEDSTROM & BLOUIN have analyzed the electronic records research projects funded by NHPRC that address its 10 research questions noted above. They found that the NHPRC-sponsored research projects have had the greatest impact on policy, practices, and standards, particularly on systems design requirements. Most of the projects focused on how electronic records could maintain reliability and authenticity over time, and many examined various types of metadata schemes to ensure ongoing reliability and authenticity. Several projects discussed by Hedstrom and Blouin bear mention because of their continuing impact on the electronic records research community. These are the Pittsburgh Project, New York State's Building Partnerships project, and a project at the University of British Columbia.

The Pittsburgh Project addressed functional requirements for record keeping. It examined organizations and different professional communities to determine what constituted authentic and reliable evidence in each community (COX; DUFF, 1996). Based on these data, the Pittsburgh investigators developed record-keeping requirements to support records as evidence and production rules leading to metadata specifications for implementing the record-keeping requirements. The metadata specification for evidence-based records is referred to as the Reference Model for Business Acceptable Communications (BAC). In related research, DUFF (1998) tested the concept of warrant and what types of warrant were accepted as valid in different professional communities. Warrant is defined as oral or written legal, professional, or administrative statements leading to the determination of a record as authentic. This is directly related to what constitutes authentic records in a digital environment and holds lessons for the implementation of electronic record-keeping systems in different types of organizations or within various professional cultures.

A number of additional projects have sought to apply some of the functional requirements and metadata specifications derived from the research in the Pittsburgh Project. Two of these applied research projects were at Indiana University and the city of Philadelphia. BANTIN (1998; 1999) applied the Pittsburgh functional requirements and metadata specifications to two electronic systems: Financial Management Support and University Enrollment Services at Indiana University. The Indiana University project was able to refine the Pittsburgh metadata specifications and tested four methodologies (functional analysis, identification of transactions, review of existing records systems, and evaluation of systems) for meeting the functional requirements. In the end, the Indiana University project adopted many of the Pittsburgh metadata specifications, particularly concerning context and user history. In the context of business records, it was determined that metadata from the handle layer concerning self-describing metadata objects were redundant with contextual metadata elements. Of primary concern was the ability to maintain the relationship between records and metadata over time, which the project principals thought they accomplished. However, the investigators also found their methodologies to be costly and time consuming and pointed to the need to streamline methodologies in the future.

The focus of the Philadelphia project incorporated some of the Pittsburgh functional requirements for record keeping into two electronic transactional systems at different points in the records continuum. The two systems selected were a mid-sized human resources information system and a smaller adjudication tracking system. Records management functions were incorporated into the human resources application at the systems design/procurement stage. The adjudication tracking application involved a records management functionality retrofit. The project used a record-description record-encapsulation strategy to bind contextual information (records management functions, such as disposition as well as security data) to the content. The unique aspect of this approach was the gathering of metadata at the time of the original electronic transaction. The goal was to reuse the software code for this records-management oversight system for other systems in the future.

The New York State Archives and Records Administration (SARA) spearheaded the Building Partnerships project. Building Partnerships was a series of comparative case studies to identify and to analyze effective electronic records management and to understand better the organizational incentives for maintaining data in electronic form over time. New York State's information management policies and practices were also analyzed. As a result, SARA's Center for Electronic Records changed its focus to policy setting, guidance and assistance to agencies actually doing electronic records management, and training. SARA also developed a strong research ally in Albany, the Center for Technology in Government (CTG), a part of the State University of New York at Albany. SARA and CTG collaborated in the Models for Action project that was designed to develop duplicable models for dealing with electronic information resources and legacy systems. The New York State Adirondack Park Agency (APA) was selected as a testbed based on its business need to integrate data from a number of different applications. For example, APA's land-use permit process was a focus of the research because of the need to integrate information from such diverse sources as a geographic information system (GIS), a relational database, paper maps of various sizes, and legal documents (ANDERSON ET AL.; KELLY ET AL.). The Center for Technology in Government has conducted numerous other applied research projects focusing on electronic record-keeping systems and has aided the New York State government in assessing the long-term viability of its electronic record-keeping systems.

A third project with international impact was conducted at the University of British Columbia (UBC) and funded by the Social Sciences and Humanities Research Council of Canada (SSHRCC). This project, the Preservation of the Integrity of Electronic Records, addressed issues surrounding the creation and maintenance of authentic and reliable electronic records in their active, pre-archival state (DURANTI & MACNEIL). The project also developed eight templates or metadata schemes for ensuring that records had the necessary components to guarantee authenticity within a given record-keeping environment. One of the products that took advantage of this research was the U.S. Department of Defense's (DoD) 5015.2 Standard for Electronic Records Management Applications (DURANTI ET AL.). The INTERNATIONAL RESEARCH ON PERMANENT AUTHENTIC RECORDS IN ELECTRONIC SYSTEMS (InterPARES) project extends this research by addressing the problems of maintaining the authenticity of electronic records of enduring value. InterPARES is a multidisciplinary, international, collaborative archival research project that is developing a typology of requirements for maintaining the authenticity of records over time. It involves an analysis of appraisal and preservation processes in order to establish the extent to which they support the requirements. UBC's research differs in approach from the Pittsburgh and Building Partnership projects. The UBC approach envisions a more custodial role for the archives, whereas the former two projects see the role of the archives more as an auditor or advisor from the design of the system through its retirement.

## Metadata and Other Standards

Metadata models are another prime focus of digital preservation research. One principal metadata scheme is by the Consultative Committee for Space Data Systems (CCSDS), called the Reference Model for an Open Archival Information System (OAIS). OAIS is moving through the International Organization for Standardization (ISO) standards process. OAIS identifies the types of metadata to support digital resources. In this model, each digital document is packaged with metadata as a total information package, which combines content information, context information, provenance information, and fixity information and which uses descriptive, administrative, and structural metadata to provide for long-term digital information preservation and access (CONSULTATIVE COMMITTEE FOR SPACE DATA SYSTEMS).

The Cedars Consortium of University Research Libraries (CURL) project on exemplars in digital archives in the United Kingdom is built on the OAIS model (RUSSELL & SERGEANT). One of its goals is to develop metadata for effective long-term digital preservation. This metadata must support a wide range of archival functions, from access control to document integrity as well as preservation itself. Cedars has now developed an outline specification describing the complete set of metadata elements that attempts to reflect the multiple needs and functions that need to be addressed: acquisition, management, storage, searching, retrieval, access, delivery, and preservation (CEDARS PROJECT TEAM).

Several research projects concerning the use of metadata to support records as evidence have taken place in Australia. The NATIONAL ARCHIVES OF AUSTRALIA (1999) has published a record-keeping metadata standard for federal government agencies. Another example is the Strategic Partnerships with Industry–Research and Training (SPIRT) research project: Recordkeeping Metadata Standards for Managing and Assessing Information Resources in Networked Environments and Accessing Information Resources in Networked Environments Over Time for Government, Commerce, Social, and Cultural Purposes. The metadata model proposed by SPIRT attempts to specify the range of metadata elements required to manage digital information over time. It consists of these record-keeping elements: business (title, mandate, place, content label), agents, and records information. The SPIRT model has been widely adapted in Australia and is part of the Victoria Electronic Records Strategy (MCKEMMISH ET AL.).

As evident from the research discussed above, metadata elements that ensure authenticity as well as describe the digital documents and standards that facilitate migration and/or emulation are the major focus of research efforts. Australia has been a leader in applied electronic records research projects on both of these fronts. The vitality of its research is fostered by various mechanisms, including the federal government's collaborative grants scheme administered by the Australian Council of Research, the SPIRT scheme, and the federal government's sponsorship of national Cooperative Research Centres (CRCs). A typical CRC involves collaboration between university and industry partners, and several projects are underway in which universities, government agencies, and businesses are working together to ensure the preservation of digital documents (MCKEMMISH).

Among the other Australian contributions to the international community is the Australian Standard: Records Management (AS 4390) (STANDARDS AUSTRALIA) that is now under consideration by the ISO to become an international standard. AS 4390 has five main sections: records management, strategies, control, appraisal and disposal, and storage. Interestingly, AS 4390 minimizes the amount of metadata that must be collected. For example, the control section stipulates that only two metadata elements are required for document registration, a unique identifier and the date and time of registration; all others are optional.

The DoD standard for records-management applications, mentioned above, is even more limited than AS 4390. It addresses a minimum set of baseline functional requirements that apply to all records management applications regardless of organizational and site-specific implementations. Overall, interest in the functionalities of records management applications and their ability to maintain the authenticity of individual digital documents within these systems has risen. In fact, one industry analyst firm, DOCULABS, has published a report comparing records management applications.

In addition to standards aimed at ensuring the authenticity of digital documents, other types of standards form a necessary framework for successful digital preservation. LE CERF ET AL. describe various consortia that are involved in the development and promotion of standards for the interoperability of electronic record-keeping systems, both between repositories as well as through different hardware and software systems. Both the standardization of file formats and the designation of certain file formats as standards are essential for the migration of digital documents over time. The proprietary and continuously evolving nature of even commonly used file formats makes this interoperability difficult because any given document, even from common word-processing software, may also have legacy elements from older versions of the application embedded within it (BENNETT). The interdependence of digital document genre, format, media, and platform has also been documented by Bennett. This has implications for any potential long-term preservation approach. For example, if migration is selected, interdependence may make it difficult to detach metadata from the document in the record-keeping system, and thus these two elements will be migrated separately. Other types of metadata, such as a digital signature, may also need to be migrated with a digital object to ensure authenticity. If the metadata and the object must be migrated together, the process becomes more complex.

Closely related to the idea of standards is canonicalization, a concept forwarded by LYNCH as a means of preserving the authenticity and reliability of digital documents over time. Canonicalization is the process whereby one uses a canonical form that applies to all digital objects within a class or genre and uses underlying established algorithms to ensure authenticity, maintaining the integrity of referential links to a given digital object. The other advantage to a canonical form is that much is known about how reformatting impacts the integrity of the object and its metadata. Defining metadata elements is an underlying construct in many of these projects (DAY). Other research pertaining to born-digital documents concerns different genres of documents.

## Preservation of Electronic Mail

The preservation of electronic mail (email) became a political issue during the Iran Contra affair when hundreds of email messages deleted by Oliver North and John Poindexter were recovered and provided evidence of their involvement in the illegal sale of weapons and the arming of the Nicaraguan contras (BEARMAN, 1993; BLANTON). This led to a court battle over the preservation of email in the White House and litigation that sought to change the way in which the National Archives and Records Administration (NARA) directed federal agencies to manage all types of electronic records in the federal government (PLOCHER). LUKESH also identified the importance of preserving email for social history and the history of scholarly communication. Email presents a preservation problem not only because its functionalities are system-dependent but also because of the sheer volume of messages. Early research by NOWICKE examined various ways to pare down the volume to email messages even worthy of preservation. GILLILAND-SWETLAND developed an expert system to identify messages of enduring value. More recent research has led to the development of guidelines for email management that advocate early intervention and initial assessments of the enduring value of the messages through systems design, implementation, and policy decisions as well as through the creation of metadata (NATIONAL ARCHIVES OF AUSTRALIA, 1997; NEW YORK STATE ARCHIVES AND RECORDS ADMINISTRATION). It has long been recognized that the printing of email is insufficient to preserve its authenticity. Preservation of email entails maintaining the functionalities and relationships between messages established in the original record-keeping system (BEARMAN,

1994). In this way, email is similar to other types of born-digital documents embedded in any electronic record-keeping system.

## Preservation of Web-Based Documents

The growth in the World Wide Web has generated interest in preserving documents that were not only born-digital but also born-digital for publication on the Web. The most publicized project to capture Web-based information has been carried out by KAHLE, who developed the technology to take snapshots of the Web, thus creating the Internet Archive. He sees this project as complementing other research on ensuring the preservation of information on the Internet. In a less optimistic report, MCCLURE & SPREHE examined information published on the Web by the U.S. state and federal governments. They found a lack of long-term thinking about management of the digital information and also about which digital documents were important to preserve for evidence of government actions and accountability to citizens. A third piece of research on Web-based information concerns electronic journals. W. SMITH reports on the Preserving and Accessing Networked Documentary Resources of Australia (PANDORA) project sponsored by the National Library of Australia. PANDORA's goals are to develop and to implement procedures for the identification, capture, and long-term digital preservation of online Australian publications, such as serials, newspapers, books, scholarly papers, theses, and home pages. Preliminary conclusions are that the National Library cannot archive all Web-based documents and that, therefore, a collaborative effort is needed by universities, organizations, and state libraries to take responsibility for their own sites and some other types of materials. The article also advocates a proactive stance, foreshadowing the report by the NATIONAL RESEARCH COUNCIL (2000) (NRC) on the U.S. Library of Congress (LC) (discussed below).

Similar efforts to preserve electronic publications are occurring in Europe. VAN DER WERF-DAVELAAR reports on the Networked European Deposit Library (NEDLIB), a collaborative project of eight national libraries, one national archive, two organizations, and three publishers. Its goals are to create a common architectural framework and basic tools to build a deposit system for electronic publications and to address long-term preservation issues. Like the Cedars and PANDORA projects, NEDLIB tested the applicability of CCSDS's Open Archival Information System (OAIS) model as a framework for functional and information modeling of digital data for a depository digital library environment. In total, NEDLIB adopted five of the OAIS modules and added a dedicated and explicit preservation module that generates preservation metadata. This is added to the digital object to assist in verifying its authenticity and reliability.

The Nordic countries are host to two other Web-based preservation projects: (1) the Kulturarw³ Heritage Project, which focuses on the Long-Term Preservation of Published Electronic Documents in Sweden, and (2) EVA, The Acquisition and Archiving of Electronic Network Publications in Finland, which is collecting Web-based materials in that country.

The Royal Library, the NATIONAL LIBRARY OF SWEDEN, began Kulturarw³ (The Swedish Archiw³e) to collect Swedish electronic documents, including periodicals, electronic magazines and newspapers, static documents (e.g., texts in electronic text archives), and dynamic documents with links (e.g., HTML pages accessible online). The goal is to develop a system for long-term preservation of electronic documents. This project will test methods of collecting, preserving, and providing access to Web-based documents. Instead of selecting materials, such as in the PANDORA project, the Swedish National Library is researching the feasibility of large-scale capture of Web-based information through robotic technology to capture and index the materials, similar to that done by KAHLE. Once captured, the goal is to determine long-term forms of storage that will facilitate migration to future software and hardware environments. Simultaneous storage in several formats is one alternative that will be investigated and tested.

Preservation of the content vs. the functionality (e.g., links, moving images, and sound) is another problem being addressed. LOUNAMAA & SALONHARJU describe EVA as a collaborative activity among libraries (Helsinki University Library and the National Library), publishers, and expert organizations to test methods of capturing, registering, preserving, and providing access to the online documents published by Finnish publishers on the Finnish Internet. EVA uses the Dublin Core metadata template and converter, a Universal Resource Number (URN) generator, and an enhanced version of the harvesting and indexing application borrowed from the Nordic Web Index (NWI). The Finnish libraries are also examining the feasibility of identifying standard formats for deposit. They recognize that authenticity is important and that it depends somewhat on the ability to retain the original look and feel of the documents; thus they envision an extensive list of approved formats. Long-term preservation will be done through migration and perhaps emulation (see Current Research below).

## Preservation of Media for Capturing Moving Images

For the past decade, digital media have become increasingly common for capturing moving images. More than other digital media, moving images are plagued by a plethora of standards with little inter-changeability and few emerging industry standards. The most significant research being pursued in the area of moving-image preservation is the Universal Preservation Format (UPF) project (SHEPARD & MACCARN). It seeks to identify and to promote open standards for the exchange of digital moving-image media and proposes a container model for the long-term preservation of these documents; it would include the content created and compressed using some open standards and metadata wrapped or encapsulated as one digital object. The final report suggests that the practices it recommends would work for all types of electronic records. The Universal Preservation Format (UPF) is a data file mechanism that uses a container or wrapper structure. ROTHENBERG (1996) refers to this as encapsulation. Within the wrapper, descriptive metadata identify its contents while administrative and structural metadata keep the document accessible over time. UPF is designed to keep documents independent of the computer applications that created them, the operating system from which these applications originated, and the physical media on which that content was originally stored. Documents using UPF are "self-described" because their metadata include all the technical specifications required to build and to rebuild appropriate media browsers to access contained materials throughout time. Documents get a unique identifier that travels with the document through time. Any modification made to the content of the object must be reflected in its identifier. Shepard and MacCarn detail both user requirements and technical specification for UPF in their final project report.

## Current Research

HODGE & CARROLL provide a summary of recent research in terms of organizational models for maintaining digital information, life-cycle managers and their roles, best practices, and costs/resources. Their research focused on the administrative aspects of what they refer to as digital electronic archiving. Their findings indicated that the major concern was intellectual property and its attendant issues of security and authentication, and they predict that the most common organizational model for digital electronic archives will be loose networks of specialized archives with some degree of interoperability.

Other current research has focused on migration and emulation, two approaches that hold promise for preserving a sufficient percentage of a digital object intact in order to ensure reliability and authenticity. Migration, or the periodic transfer of digital documents from one hardware/software platform to a more current platform or subsequent generation, has been seen as the primary model for this second generation of electronic records. The newer approach to digital preservation is emulation. This is a strategy by which emulators of software, hardware, and operating systems would be embedded in the contents of digital documents so that they could be viewed in the future in their original format.

The best discussion of migration and the problems associated with it for digital preservation is by WATERS & GARRETT. They note that while migration is a solution for simple files, the best preservation method for complex and multimedia files has yet to be established. They argue that the authenticity of these complex digital objects cannot be maintained either by simply changing the media or by reducing the format to its lowest common denominator (e.g., ASCII files). Rather, standards must be incorporated and migration paths built in early in the development of the electronic record-keeping system. These strategies address the problems of software dependence and technological obsolescence. GRANGER notes, however, that migration is prone to data loss as well as to failure to sustain the "look and feel" of the document as represented in the original record-keeping system.

Interest in emulation has arisen because it has the potential to ensure authenticity, functionality, and the look and feel of the original. ROTHENBERG (1996; 1999) provides a good, albeit controversial, discussion of emulation and how metadata would be handled within this strategy for digital preservation. ROTHENBERG (1999) has engendered at least one heated response that disputes the ability of emulation to maintain authentic evidence over time (BEARMAN, 1999). Granger argues that some of the same problems that ROTHENBERG (1999) identified with migration, such as its expense, the labor-intensive nature of the work, and the time involved in setting it up, also apply to emulation. ROSS & GOW provide a detailed description of an attempted emulation, demonstrating the difficulty of developing emulators for legacy programs, at least retrospectively. They also point out that there is no consensus on what to emulate—the processor, the operating system, or the hardware. Further variations on the emulation strategy have been proposed by KRANCH, who combines emulation strategy with a self-contained reading and storage device he calls a digital tablet.

Funding agencies are also collaborating to support international research projects aimed at digital preservation. The U.S. National Science Foundation (NSF) and the Joint Information Systems Committee (JISC) in the United Kingdom have jointly funded several international digital library grants (CAMILEON PROJECT; WISEMAN ET AL.). Of particular note are two projects: Creative Archiving at Michigan & Leeds: Emulating the Old on the New (CAMiLEON) and Preservation, Reliability, Interoperability, Security, and Metadata (PRISM).

CAMiLEON investigators are researching the feasibility of using emulation as a preservation strategy to maintain the original functionalities and design of software-dependent born-digital documents (WISEMAN ET AL.). Cornell University is involved in PRISM which is examining policies and other approaches required for information integrity in a component-based digital library architecture (LAGOZE & KENNEY; RIEGER). PRISM focuses on born-again digital objects.

Another research effort that focuses on emulation is the Dutch Digital Repository project being conducted by the National Archives of the Netherlands (HOFMAN). This project has several goals, including that of testing different preservation strategies, particularly emulation. Data will be analyzed to determine how well the authenticity of digital documents can be maintained. Jeff Rothenberg and Tora Bikson of the Rand Corp. were involved in the early stages of this effort and have developed a model for a generic digital preservation process.

In Australia, one current initiative is a CRC-funded program supporting collaboration between the Distributed Systems Technology Centre (DSTC), the faculty at Monash University, agencies within the Australian government, and industry partners. This research, the Information Ecology project, has a significant record-keeping component. The overall objectives are to understand better the electronic information environments and the information needs of workers in those environments as well as to enhance information ecology through improved accessibility, reliability, authenticity, transparency, and accountability of their business activities and services and of the information about them (MCKEMMISH).

Another project funded by NSF and NHPRC is underway at the San Diego Supercomputer Center. This project is focusing on collection-based persistent archives and is examining the feasibility of extracting XML information models from collections of software-dependent data objects and developing software tools to preserve and to access those objects over time (MOORE; MOORE ET AL., 2000a, 2000b). Along with the InterPARES research previously described, these efforts should enhance our knowledge of electronic records in the next decade.

## DIGITALLY RECREATED DOCUMENTS

Digitization for preservation has two connotations. First, it can mean the creation of a surrogate for preservation. Preservation microfilm is seen as just such a surrogate, something that can authentically represent the original item. In terms of digitization, the goal of preservation digitization would be to create such a surrogate. Digitization for preservation also signifies the creation of a surrogate for access in order to retire the original document, thus preserving it by limiting its use. At a minimum, digitally born-again surrogates are images of the original. Search and retrieval depend on indexing or descriptive metadata associated with an image. In selected cases, such as with digitized printed books, optical character recognition (OCR) can be applied to the image, allowing full-text retrieval and recreating a functional digital document that can be manipulated and even changed.

As noted, much of the research on digitally recreated documents is reported as case studies. Within these case studies, however, is considerable testing of resolution requirements, technical issues, and use of varying standards and metadata frameworks. One exception is a 1999 survey sponsored by the International Federation of Library Associations (IFLA) and the United Nations Educational, Scientific, and Cultural Organization (UNESCO) (GOULD & EBDON). Gould and Ebdon surveyed national libraries to present a snapshot of digitization activities worldwide. They admit, however, that their survey is far from comprehensive given the large number of digitization projects organized by universities and other organizations. Their findings indicate that there was little consistency in the standards used for digitization and a lack of coordination and information sharing among institutions carrying out digitization projects. Gould and Ebdon also found that 36% of the libraries had no digital preservation policy, and 45% had no policy for migrating their digital documents to newer technological platforms. Their research and that by KENNEY and KENNEY & SHARPE demonstrate the difficulty in comparing digitization projects or determining whether standardized digitization processes exist across institutions and genres of documents. Much of the research on preservation digitization is linked to a specific genre or items made up of multiple genres (e.g., illustrated books) and media formats (e.g., books, photographs). One issue that does span different genres and formats is selection. Therefore, this section begins with a discussion of selection for digitization and then examines digitization decision making and research on different genres and media.

## Selection for Digitization

Selection for digitization is problematic. In the library world there has been a certain degree of consensus on selection criteria for preservation microfilming (CHILD; WILLIAMS & LUNDE). In the archival world, although there have been several attempts to develop selection standards (COMMISSION ON PRESERVATION AND ACCESS), there has been little consensus and no agreed-on selection standards. Given this situation, it might be expected that this would translate into the digital world. In terms of library materials, the initial printed book-digitization projects at Cornell (KENNEY) and Yale (CONWAY & WEAVER) were based on the selection criteria for preservation microfilming (e.g., the Conspectus project). However, since the early 1990s, selection criteria for the digitization of books have moved away from these roots. Digitizers of archival materials, with no guidelines to rely on, have either interpreted overall guidelines for selection for digitization or have digitized on an ad hoc basis or according to whatever a funding agency will provide monies to digitize.

Interest in selection criteria for digital projects has increased recently. One emerging model for selection for digitization was developed at Harvard University by HAZEN ET AL. They identify copyright as the overarching factor in digitization and note that copyright issues in the digital realm are still in flux. Other selection factors include the intellectual nature of the material, current and potential users, actual and anticipated nature of the use, the format and nature of the digital product, the ability to describe, deliver, and retain the digital product, and relationships to other digital efforts. These researchers present these criteria and then help an institution explore how those criteria apply to their materials through a series of questions. At the end of their volume, they provide a decision-making matrix. BRANCOLINI applied the Harvard matrix to the Hohenberger photographic collection at Indiana University. Although Brancolini pointed out several inconsistencies between the text and the decision-making matrix, she affirmed that the overall model was a good starting point. Still, she argued that local adaptation would be necessary with any model for digital selection.

What is significant in the criteria presented by Hazen et al. is the degree to which the criteria are dynamic and not static. Elements such as copyright status, the format and nature of the digital product, and relationships to other digital projects can change overnight as courts render decisions, as new technologies, standards, and applications emerge, and as other digital projects are initiated. Perhaps such dynamic and changeable selection elements are natural in the digital world, but they pose incredible challenges for digital preservation projects.

GERTZ emphasizes that selection criteria for digitization are not linear and must be considered in total. She also notes that although the same selection elements may be present for preservation decisions in the analog and digital worlds, the weighing of these criteria is different. Gertz states that "the fundamental difference is that the selection process often starts from a desire for better access rather than due to physical deterioration" (p. 98). User demand, intellectual property issues, and the technological potential for rendering the object are also more influential factors in digital preservation, she says.

Selection for digitization is critical. As demonstrated below and perhaps quite logically, greater research efforts have gone into establishing technical criteria than selection criteria. The development of the

Harvard model may signal that interest in selection is increasing. The Harvard matrix is a good beginning, but rigorous testing of other models and an investigation of the benefits and dangers of localization of selection criteria is needed. Further, as noted by DE STEFANO, different selection criteria may exist depending on whether the goal of a project is digitization for preservation or for access.

## Preservation Digitization and Books

In 1992 the Commission on Preservation and Access published the WILLIS report on a hybrid approach to preservation. It entails the creation of microfilm for preservation purposes and digital images for access. Willis carefully outlines options for creating film and digital files and identifies the advantages and disadvantages of each. He also discusses whether to film first and subsequently scan from the film or to scan first and create film from the digital files. Willis hypothesizes that the costs of each approach are comparable. He sees a hybrid systems approach as a viable preservation strategy for research institutions to pursue until they develop and implement digital preservation programs. The critical research question for Willis is determining the circumstances under which the film-first approach or the scan-first approach should be pursued. As a result, in 1994 the National Endowment for the Humanities (NEH) funded two research projects, one at Cornell and the other at Yale, designed to test and to evaluate the interrelationship between microfilm and digital imagery.

KENNEY addressed this research question and found that both the film-first and scan-first strategies are viable. Kenney and CONWAY (1996a) agree, however, that digital scanning from an original (if possible) invariably produces better quality results than scanning from microfilm. The determination of selecting one approach over the other still requires further research into such variables as the attributes of the originals, institutional priorities and capabilities, and the availability of appropriate imaging products and services. In addition to addressing Willis's research question, the Cornell and Yale projects generated other significant research findings.

Cornell conducted the Digital-To-Microfilm Conversion project, a two-and-a-half year applied research effort to test and to evaluate the use of high-resolution bitonal (1-bit, black and white) scanning to generate computer-output microfilm (COM) that could meet national preservation standards for quality and permanence (KENNEY). This project has had far-reaching effects. It resulted directly in the development of guidelines for capture (KENNEY & PERSONIUS), the establishment of benchmarking standards for digital images, quantitative means of assessing the quality of the digitization process (KENNEY & CHAPMAN,

1995), cost estimates, and recommendations for the creation and inspection of preservation-quality microfilm produced from digital imagery. As a consequence of their research, CHAPMAN & KENNEY argue that while there is always information loss, digitization projects should capture an image once at high quality if any digital preservation initiatives are envisioned because the costs and politics of rescanning later may be insurmountable. They refer to this process as the case for full capture that includes balancing legibility and fidelity. For Chapman and Kenney, legibility is the technical ability to capture a readable image; fidelity is the technical ability to capture all of the significant information on the image. Full capture is initially scanning at higher resolutions. It also increases functionality; for example, a higher-resolution scan of printed text increases the accuracy of OCR. At the same time, they note that scanning at the highest resolution is not always the best decision because after a certain point there is no appreciable gain in comprehension, detail, or functionality.

Many of Cornell's initial research findings were compiled in the book by KENNEY & CHAPMAN (1996), *Digital Imaging for Libraries and Archives*. Continued research at Cornell has led to a completely revised version of this book by KENNEY & RIEGER (2000). Kenney and Rieger take a more holistic approach that focuses less on the technical aspects of digitization and more on the administrative and decision-making elements that surround digitization decisions. As a result, they place digital projects within overall institutional goals and help others to match their own institution's objectives to digital applications.

Project Open Book at Yale University researched the feasibility of digital conversion of microfilmed library materials. Although this project was completed in 1996, it is still one of the most comprehensively documented digital conversion projects (CONWAY, 1996b; CONWAY & WEAVER; WATERS & WEAVER). Yale integrated components with the assistance of Xerox Corp. to create a networked multiworkstation conversion system to convert 2,000 previously microfilmed books to digital image files (representing 430,000 images). The reports on Project Open Book also highlight the evolution of the project and the technical, administrative, and financial challenges faced during each phase.

The continuing importance of hybrid approaches to digital preservation of digitally recreated documents is clear. However, researchers have come to different conclusions concerning the balance and implementation of such an approach. In 1997, WEBER & DÖRR reported on studies carried out at the German Research Association. Microfilming and digitization experiments were conducted with standardized test materials, and the results were evaluated. Minimum standards for the printout quality of microforms (material, image quality, and filming organization) leading to problem-free digitization were determined. The research also established requirements for high-quality digitization, relying on the Cornell quality index for the reproduction quality of manuscripts. Conclusions supported limited use of digitization in preservation projects and highly favored microfilm as a recording and storage medium because of its quality and stability over time. Somewhat different results emerged from a 1999 report. CHAPMAN ET AL. discuss subsequent research at Yale and Cornell. Their report presents a decision tree on when to scan or to film first, recommendations concerning the creation of microfilm, computer output microfiche (COM), and digital images in terms of costs, quality, and technology, and it discusses administrative and structural metadata elements that need to be associated with an image. The authors call for dialog among vendors, researchers examining digital preservation issues, and content holders.

Finally, improvements in OCR have enabled better preservation of the information even when preservation of the original or digital recreation of the original was a problem. CHAPMAN & KENNEY documented an increase in accuracy between scanning at 300 dpi and 600 dpi; error rates were cut in half. This finding argues for an initial full-information capture, and illustrates Chapman and Kenney's critical distinction between legibility (a document that is readable) and fidelity (full information capture). In more recent research, MCCLEAN compares various OCR software applications used in the EuroText Project. Rather than presenting quantitative findings, McClean discusses qualitative measures such as the functionality of each application, interoperability with other applications, interface design, and the types of materials with which a given application works best.

## Preservation Digitization and Image-Based Documents

Preservation digitization of visual documents offers many more advantages and perhaps more challenges than digitization of textual records. ESTER notes that although there are long-term preservation considerations with any digital document, digitizing an image so as to achieve full information capture is difficult. Still, he argues, there are unique benefits to digitizing images. First, visual materials are deteriorating physically and chemically more swiftly than most paper-based materials. Second, digitizing image-based materials creates a means of integrating the image with descriptive information Finally, if captured well, the digital media provide a means of reproducing the image with minimal information loss and identical reproduction quality from the digital master among any subsequent copies.

Significant research on digital preservation has also gone on at the Library of Congress (LC) and nowhere has LC's impact been as great as in the area of images. Through its in-house experimentation with digitization for preservation and through its Ameritech Digital Library Competitions, LC has developed and sought to publicize its knowledge in this area. Based on its own research, LC has developed several sets of guidelines concerning digital preservation (e.g., FLEISCHHAUER). It has also commissioned research reports on the digitization of images (KENNEY & SHARPE; PICTURE ELEMENTS, INCORPORATED; REILLY & FREY).

Reilly and Frey's 1996 report demonstrated how the rigorous image-quality control procedures using targets and visual inspection can be applied in both the analog and digital environments. This is the most comprehensive technical discussion of image attributes and how they are transformed through digitization. Reilly and Frey also detail the automatic techniques that exist or must be developed to ensure the long-term usefulness of digital files.

Building on Reilly and Frey's report, Picture Elements, Inc. developed guidelines for the electronic preservation of visual materials. Its report presents a comprehensive model of considerations at each step of the digitization process, from collection analysis and selection for digitization to outlining specifications for digitizing different genres of visual materials. The authors do not provide one set of recommended practices, technical specifications, or scanning settings. Instead, they have developed decision trees to aid readers in selecting appropriate choices for their unique collections. These recommendations are based on a series of scanning and compression experiments that are discussed in the report.

KENNEY & SHARPE extended their earlier work by researching how digitization could best be applied to illustrated books from the 19th and early 20th century. KENNEY & CHAPMAN (1995) had previously characterized illustrations based on essence, detail, and structure. Picture Elements, Inc. developed the LC guidelines for the digitization of visual materials. Building from this previous research, Kenney and Sharpe developed mappings of different physical content regions (representing instances of different illustration processes) to their electronic content types. These mappings were based on the genre of the illustration and on the need to preserve information at the levels of essence, detail, and structure. Experiments tested different genres of illustrations at various digitization settings (e.g., gray-scale, color, and resolution), and the surrogates were judged on their ability to retain evidence of the information at the structure or process level. A consensus was reached that 400 dpi, 8-bit capture would preserve the essence and detail in all the illustration types studied, regardless of the process used to generate the published originals, even though this specification did not provide complete information on the structure of the illustration. The authors reached this recommendation after a cost–benefit analysis of scanning at a higher resolution, particularly when scanning mass-produced books with both illustrations and text. Using a public-domain utility created for this research, Kenney and Sharpe also investigated automatic detection of illustration content regions and methods for automatically discriminating different illustration process types, encoding, and processing them, although these automatic methods for detection and processing proved to be less successful at 400 dpi.

CARTOLANO ET AL. and GERTZ ET AL. at Columbia extended other research (CONWAY, 1996a, 1996b; KENNEY) by applying a hybrid approach to the digitization of texts with color and oversized illustrations. In phase 1, Cartolano et al. investigated whether a film-first or scan-first methodology would work best with these oversized color images. Their findings indicate that scanning the microfiche produced digital files with a resolution equal to that of the scanned originals. They also tested whether the benchmarking resolution techniques developed at Cornell (KENNEY & CHAPMAN, 1995) were applicable to oversized color images. Findings indicated that the Cornell benchmarking techniques were effective for these images (CARTOLANO ET AL.). In phase II, the Columbia investigators sought to integrate the text and image files for the volumes being scanned, to create metadata to help administer and to use the files. While these aspects of the project were a success, the user evaluation revealed problems in using the maps and in maintaining the same levels of broad detail and granularity that characterized the originals (GERTZ ET AL.).

Much of the digitization of visual materials being conducted is primarily done for access. However, one case study by HOPKIN discusses the importance of clearly conceptualizing a digitization project and articulating its goals. He recounts the problems that ensued at the National Railway Museum when project objectives were too diffuse and did not meet the needs of the organization. This article is unique because few of the case studies openly discuss problems.

Another ongoing project of note is sponsored by the EUROPEAN COMMISSION ON PRESERVATION AND ACCESS (ECPA). ECPA is designing a model framework for its Safeguarding European Photographic Images for Access (SEPIA) project. SEPIA deals with historic photographic collections deemed to be an essential part of the European cultural heritage. The project's aim is to enhance awareness of the need to preserve photographic collections, to provide training for those involved in preservation and digitization of photographic collections, and to develop a model framework under which future projects in this area can be brought together.

## Digitization of Primary Sources

Numerous projects have sought to digitize archival materials. Many of these employ digitization primarily as a means of preserving the original by creating a surrogate that can be used first or that will satisfy a user's need. Several of these have been high-profile projects with international attention, and a few have been groundbreaking applied research to test the feasibility of some aspect of digital conversion. These projects include the Making of America project (MOA), Advanced Papyrological Information System (APIS), the Heinz Electronic Library Interactive Online System (HELIOS), and the Archivo General de Indias (AGI).

The Making of America II (MOA II) testbed project focused on primary sources. HURLEY ET AL. report on its object-oriented approach to digital library construction, the definition and collection of structural and administrative metadata elements, and the development of a Digital Library Service model to assist scholars. The identification of structural and administrative metadata elements as they relate to digitally recreated documents is particularly important. Hurley et al.'s findings outline the three layers of the project: services, tools, and digital library objects. The authors provide an in-depth discussion of implementing the service model. They also attempted to create classes or genres of archival materials and to understand their characteristics and use patterns better.

Digitization has greatly increased access to papyri. In fact, BAGNALL argues that digitization, as well as subsequent digital manipulation (e.g., enlargement, adding contrast), actually facilitates research. The role of the papyrological research community and its development of the Advanced Papyrological Information System (APIS) not only provides an important example for others interested in digital preservation but also in how different communities may have specific requirements for authenticity and evidence for working with a type of record. This community worked with technical staff and archivists to establish standards for digitization of papyri to create surrogates that met the test of intellectual preservation.

HELIOS is admittedly the one project with the smallest preservation component (GALLOWAY). The research question asked was whether a large archival collection (over one-half million images) could be digitized so as to provide access and to support various research needs. Galloway describes how a collaborative team of researchers, including computer scientists, archivists, and computational linguists, developed a system to digitize, index, and retrieve these materials. As proof of the concept that digital surrogates could be created for a large collection of modern records, HELIOS was a success. It is doubtful whether it will or should be replicated because the costs are prohibitive for most institutions and the need or desire to digitize entire 20th century collections is questionable.

A final digitization project concerning primary sources is Archivo General de Indias (AGI). A discussion of this project last is ironic because chronologically it is the earliest, beginning in 1986. It was a highly publicized project because the collection documents Spanish exploration in the Caribbean and Central and South America. AGI was announced just as plans for the 500th anniversary of Christopher Columbus's voyage to America were being finalized and its impact debated. These cultural and political events put the project and the desire for increased access to these documents in the spotlight. There are two reports on this project: an early external report (RÜTIMANN & LYNN) and a final internal report in 1998 (GONZÁLEZ). Not surprisingly, the early report is more critical of the project. The authors cite as problems the lack of open standards and a reliance on proprietary systems, the plan for only local access, and the need for a long-term preservation plan for the digital images. The second report, by González, focuses on the achievements. The project did not digitize nearly the number of documents originally planned, nor has the system become scalable. However, a viable system is currently in use at AGI. The timing of this project also contributed to its criticisms. As it began in 1986, there were few standards and no best practices for digitizing. In addition, technology was just being developed, and there were few integrated systems from which to select. As was the case even later with Project Open Book and Cornell, the AGI project was heavily tied to a vendor (IBM Corp.; at Yale and Cornell it was Xerox Corp.). The hope is that this digitization work will not be lost and can be migrated in some way to make it more widely accessible. Given the timing and constraints of AGI, however, its accomplishments should be noted.

Finally, in a report that bridges media stability, technological obsolescence studies, and the case studies on digital preservation strategy and techniques, KENNEY & RIEGER (1998) discuss the use of Kodak Photo CD technology for capturing and storing a wide variety of digitized materials. Their study indicated that this technology was appropriate for a limited number of document genres. Oversized documents that included fine detail, such as maps and architectural drawings, were unsuitable. Overall, participants cited the quality of resolution as a greater problem than color capture. Open questions are technological obsolescence and the ability of an institution to migrate as technology evolves.

## ADMINISTRATIVE ISSUES IN THE MANAGEMENT OF DIGITAL FILES

Developing a long-term preservation strategy for the management and maintenance of digital documents, whether they are born-digital or digitally recreated, is a key aspect of digital preservation programs. The long-term administrative implications of digital preservation receive little focus compared with other topics concerned with the creation of digital documents. Two research reports succeed in identifying high-level administrative and policy variables needed for the long-term maintenance of digital documents. To varying extents, they use a comparative case-study approach. One of these works, which summarizes the applied research on the management of electronic records and draws lessons from it, is a compilation of case studies by HEDSTROM (1993). BEAGRIE & GREENSTEIN also use case studies to illustrate a best-practice framework of policies that they developed to manage born-digital and digitally recreated collections better. These authors first developed a theoretical framework and then tested its premises during structured interviews with data managers, archivists, librarians, and others with experience in data management. Interviewees represented a cross section of media formats as well as different types of institutions, including archives, museums, university computer centers, and scientific data centers. Case studies were identified through these interviews and an extensive literature review. These case studies were designed to illustrate how best practices were implemented.

Since many of the digitization projects previously described are just that—projects—the institutionalization necessary to think about and commit to the long-term maintenance of digital documents has not occurred. In a study of research libraries, HEDSTROM & MONTGOMERY found that few libraries were planning for the digital preservation of their electronic files. The lack of a model for such preservation is cited by ALLEN as one barrier to the development of such programs. Lack of strategic and long-term thinking about this issue stretches to the Library of Congress. The NATIONAL RESEARCH COUNCIL (2000) report, *LC21: A Digital Strategy for the Library of Congress*, detailed a lack of strategic thinking and preservation planning in terms of both technological capacity and digital collection development on the part of LC. FLECKER presents a case study of Harvard University, detailing its development from a digital project-based environment to one focusing on digital programs. This case study is significant, and one hopes that the report will be the first in a series of articles by Harvard and other institutions detailing the specifics of this transformation.

The attitudes of potential stakeholders from institutions that might become responsible for the long-term maintenance of digital files was the topic of one research project in the United Kingdom. HAYNES ET AL. found that institutions were looking for a leader. Individuals from the focus groups and interviews cited the need for a large agency to set standards and produce guidelines. They were also looking for partners and grant funding to help address some of the long-term preservation issues.

Case studies can also be instructive in examining administrative issues. TANNER compares key issues for the implementation of digital document management in two case studies, one from a corporate setting in which he worked and one from a higher-education setting for which he served as a consultant. Tanner describes the benefits organizations are looking for as outcomes of implementing a digital document-management system as well as potential pitfalls faced by each organization. While cost and time are perceived as both a plus and a minus, other benefits, such as space savings and health and safety issues, must be carefully weighed against such potential pitfalls as the complexity of the systems and the inability to articulate clear goals for the document-management application.

Ongoing administrative support for the long-term preservation of born-again digital files is necessary. Of primary importance is the management of files in the face of rapidly changing software. LAWRENCE ET AL. report on an experiment at Cornell University to migrate two common file formats, TIFF 5.0 and Lotus 1-2-3.wk1. Although they were able to migrate digital documents in each format, they cite several difficulties, including the lack of readily available file specifications for different versions of these applications and the lack of off-the-shelf conversion software that met all the requirements they needed to migrate files and maintain authenticity. The authors also refer to problems they have had in migrating digital documents from less-common proprietary applications. To assist institutions in digitizing collections, LC has issued guidelines and best practices concerning file formats for different types of digitally recreated documents (FLEISCHHAUER). COLEMAN & WILLIS discuss the strength of SGML for structuring digital documents and for more effective retrieval of digital materials.

## MEDIA STABILITY STUDIES

LESK originally outlined the problems of media stability and technological obsolescence in his 1992 report. Since then, both topics have received attention. ROSS & GOW present an excellent summary of the research and science that comprise media stability studies. They also summarize several case studies on disaster recovery efforts on various digital media formats. While recovery is possible, particularly at sophisticated laboratories such as the U.S. National Media Laboratory (NML), it is costly and expensive, and such efforts are not likely to become routine in many organizations.

The classic studies of the stability of magnetic media are those by VAN BOGART (1994; 1995), a scientist at NML. His work and statistics from the NML are the most reliable estimates for the life span of physical media. Various vendors also provide information on their websites concerning the longevity of their products. Particularly in the area of digital preservation where new products abound and manufacturing processes for digital media change frequently, the manufacturers' technical information is often the only source of information on a product. A good example is Kodak's discussion of CD-ROMs (KODAK).

## ECONOMICS OF DIGITAL PRESERVATION

Beyond specific projects, the economics of digital preservation is an essential factor in the development and diffusion of full-scale digital preservation programs. For electronic records, WATERS & GARRETT initially attempted to model capture and storage costs. This work has been extended by HENDLEY. Although he shies away from suggesting many actual figures, Hendley's framework for assessing potential costs is comprehensive. He includes costs associated with systems design and development through long-term storage and preservation. Costs are also modeled for different options (e.g., migration vs. emulation). An overview of the costs associated with the long-term management of electronic files at NARA was reprinted by DOLLAR. These costs refer to recopying or reformatting flat files and not to the migration of relational or more complex digital documents.

Costs associated with recreating analog documents in digital form are harder to assess. A 1992 NEH grant to Cornell and another to Yale directed them to document the finances surrounding the generation of preservation-quality digital images. Both CONWAY (1996b) and KENNEY fulfilled this requirement. Kenney found that the scan-first approach cost less than the film-first approach. When extant film was available for scanning, such as in Project Open Book, then it was less expensive to scan from the extant film. If only digital images and no preservation microfilm are to be produced, the costs of scanning from paper vs. film are comparable.

CONWAY (1996b) carefully documented the costs of the production-conversion phase of Project Open Book. His comprehensive analysis covers equipment costs, process time and cost, and book and film characteristics. In the end, Conway reports that the unit costs for storage and access of digital documents are higher than in a traditional paper-based library. WATERS & GARRETT hypothesize, however, that over ten years, the costs of storing digital documents would decline while the costs of maintaining a paper-based library would rise. Kenney was able not only to compute costs associated with the Cornell project, but she also used Conway's findings for comparison. Kenney also analyzed the reasons for different rates of expenditure. For example, Yale did more detailed indexing, so preprocessing took more time. It should be noted that the cost figures in both the Conway and Kenney reports are from demonstration projects and not full-fledged production operations. Also, neither the Kenney nor Conway figures includes long-term maintenance for the digital files.

Since the 1996 reports by Conway and Kenney, few comparative cost analyses have been done. PUGLIA compared the cost of digital conversion projects funded by LC's National Digital Library/Ameritech Competition and those of NARA's Electronic Access project. Puglia's costs included selection, preparation, metadata creation, preservation/conservation of the original item, production of intermediates, digitization, quality control, technical infrastructure, and ongoing maintenance of images and metadata. Puglia compared costs according to stage in the digitization process, the nature of the materials, and the type of processing (rekeying vs. OCR). He then examined how different types of materials compared with average costs for digitizing, metadata creation, and other administrative processes and found that it cost less to digitize books than other types of materials, such as archival collections or photographs. TANNER & SMITH provide a similar approach to cost estimates. They developed a cost matrix that factors in types of materials and digitization procedures from selection and retrieval, through preparation and handling, digitization, indexing or metadata creation, post-processing and quality control activities, and operator skill, among other variables. The addition of handling and quality control costs in their matrix is an important contribution.

Puglia also discussed the cost of ongoing storage and maintenance. Previous studies by LOWRY & TROLL estimated that the costs of maintaining digital files would be 16 times greater than for their paper counterparts. Based on the Electronic Access project, Puglia cited NARA's estimate that the cost of maintaining the data during the initial 10 years would be $1.70 to $4.70 per image. He notes that NARA's estimate is low compared with those of other libraries, archives, and commercial service bureaus. He concluded that the great disparity in cost projections for maintaining digital images and their associated metadata means that projects should plan for 50% to 100% of initial cost per image for maintenance in the first 10 years. DOLLAR provides cost figures for NARA's Center for Electronic Records (CER). Although the figures are slightly dated, he provides cost estimates for annual accessioning and preservation as well as the 10-year estimates for one data set ($19.82) and the entire CER ($13,594,396.00). It should be noted that CER has very stringent requirements for the types of data sets it will accession (primarily ASCII), so these costs are deflated because it is not dealing with a large number of complex files. BESSER & YAMASHITA identified the substantial long-term costs of maintaining digital image files as a potential problem in continuing access to sites, such as the Museum Educational Site Licensing (MESL) project that was the subject of their study.

Conway (1996a) noted that the costs of treating each item individually are prohibitive, so in Project Open Book efforts were made to facilitate the efficient production of digital images. M. COOK discusses a project at the Chicago Historical Society to digitize 55,000 glass-plate negatives dating from 1900 to 1929 from the *Chicago Daily News* photo morgue. The goal was to streamline photo digitization and to digitize faster and more economically than other projects. Although Cook does not cite cost figures, he does outline the production process and notes that increasing intellectual control over the digitized collection will be a major investment and will be more costly than the actual digitization process.

The long-term archiving and maintenance cost of electronic journals is also an issue. BOYCE reports that the American Astronomical Society has factored archival maintenance into its subscription fees. Likewise, one goal of Journal Storage (JSTOR) is to create a sustainable economic model of continued access to scholarly journals by research institutions. It is testing the hypotheses that the long-term storage and subscription costs to journals can be reduced by creating digital archives of back issues. According to GUTHRIE, JSTOR's Archive Capital Fee is intended as a capital reserve dedicated to long-term software development work and hardware purchases required to keep the system current as technologies evolve.

The need to plan for the long term and to develop sustainable digital preservation models is also apparent in the report of LEE. Acting as a consultant, Lee analyzed Oxford University's digital conversion projects. His final report suggested the establishment of a service bureau to digitize materials centrally. It modeled start-up costs for staffing, overhead, capital setup; it also projected revenue targets and external support for five years and provided a detailed breakdown of expenditures in these areas. Lee demonstrated that revenue would not come close to the costs of establishing and maintaining this facility. This is the most detailed published financial analysis available for establishing a digitization facility.

## CONCLUSIONS

Research on digital preservation includes investigations into strategies for both born-digital and born-again digital materials. In terms of the former, a considerable amount of research has been done to establish record-keeping requirements for systems design and implementation. The immediate question is whether the industry will adopt these standards, strategies, and functional elements to create evidence-based record-keeping systems that ensure their authenticity and reliability. If the model of the DoD guidelines is any indication, some sectors of the vendor population will respond to record-keeping specifications if there is sufficient customer leverage. Record-keeping requirements rely on various metadata schemes and the viability of standards. However, a number of competing metadata schemes have been proposed. Research is needed to determine the viability of each as well as the specific conditions under which one scheme might be more beneficial than another. Likewise, standards are constantly changing, and vendor incorporation of standards of interest to the digital preservation community is not a given.

Legacy systems pose a different set of digital preservation problems. The current debate over migration and emulation demonstrates that the preservation of these systems will be costly, complex, and time consuming no matter what approach is selected. One of the key problems with legacy systems is to identify them while they can still be migrated or emulated. While some of the readings appear to present an either/or scenario in the migration/emulation debate, research into a hybrid approach is needed. Decision criteria on how and when migration and emulation best preserve authenticity and reliability are needed to understand better the pros and cons presented by these different approaches.

Continuing research is also needed on administrative and managerial issues. There are few analyses of policy and planning for preservation or economic studies of digital preservation of born-digital documents. Of particular concern is the lack of studies presenting reliable information on the actual long-term costs for the preservation of record-keeping systems.

The preservation of digitally recreated materials initially focused on the technical aspects of image capture. Given the new technologies, the focus on how best to use them was understandable. However, more recent studies are beginning to address some of the other issues attendant on capturing large numbers of digital images. These include selection for digitization; the long-term ability to administer digital collections; the evolution of software, operating systems and hardware; metadata and other standards; and the economics of digitization. Of these, selection for digitization has received the least systematic research and presents problems in the library and archival communities that are still unresolved even in the analog world. In spite of these problems, selection issues are beginning to differentiate themselves, and common criteria (copyright, use, the applicability of the technological application) are emerging. While the underlying focus of maintaining the authenticity and reliability of the data bridges the born-digital and the digitally born-again communities, the issues are evoked in different ways. After almost a decade of digitization projects, major research libraries are beginning to address the long-term preservation issues associated with the maintenance of digital files and to recognize that the projects must become established programs if the digital files are to survive. Further, these institutions are beginning to experience their first round of data migration and therefore are attuned to the difficulties of maintaining authentic and reliable digital images in various file formats, proprietary software, and multitudinous evolving standards. Finally, the economics of digitally recreated documents is becoming clearer as institutions realize all the variables involved and begin to institutionalize digitization production capabilities. Still, because many of the cost studies are based, at least in part, on estimates, more information is needed on actual expenditures. Another problem is the difficulty of comparing costs across institutions. Common methods of accounting would help institutions to understand how different decisions affect project finances.

A final note concerns research methods. As noted, research on digital preservation is populated by case studies. We need not only more critical case studies but also an increased variety of research methods and more rigorous methodologies that would lead to more robust quantitative and qualitative data for comparisons across institutions. In spite of these problems, the research for both born-digital and born-again-digital documents is vibrant and working toward the development of strategies, technologies, and methods that will enable digital preservation to become an established reality.

## BIBLIOGRAPHY

ACKERMAN, MARK S.; FIELDING, ROY T. 1995. Collection Maintenance in the Digital Library. In: Proceedings of Digital Libraries '95: The 2nd International Conference on the Theory and Practice of Digital Libraries; 1995 June 11-13; Austin, TX. 39-48. Available WWW: http://www.csdl.tamu.edu/DL95/papers/ackerman/ackerman.html.

ALLEN, BARBARA MCFADDEN. 1997. The CIC-EJC as a Model for Management of Internet-Accessible E-Journals. Library Hi Tech. 1997; 59-60: 45-49. ISSN: 0737-8831.

ANDERSON, DAVID; AVERY, PETER; BLONIARZ, PETER; DAWES, SHARON; HYDE, STEVEN; KELLY, KRISTINE; MILLER, ANNE; RICH,

ELIOT. 1995. Balancing Environmental Quality and Economic Vitality in the Adirondack Park. Albany, NY: Center for Technology in Government; 1995 December. 76p. (CTG Project Report 95-3). OCLC: 34271754.

BAGNALL, ROGER S. 1995. Digital Imaging of Papyri: A Report to the Commission on Preservation and Access. Washington, DC: Commission on Preservation and Access; 1995 September. 8p. ISBN: 1-887334-44-0.

BANTIN, PHILIP C. 1998. Developing a Strategy for Managing Electronic Records: The Findings of the Indiana University Electronic Records Project. American Archivist. 1998; 61(2): 328-364. ISSN: 0360-9081.

BANTIN, PHILIP C. 1999. The Indiana University Electronic Records Project Revisited. American Archivist. 1999; 62(1): 153-163. ISSN: 0360-9081.

BEAGRIE, NEIL; GREENSTEIN, DANIEL. 1998. A Strategic Policy Framework for Creating and Preserving Digital Collections. Version 4.0, Final Draft. 1998 July 14. Available WWW: http://www.ahds.ac.uk/managing.htm.

BEARMAN, DAVID. 1993. The Implications of *Armstrong v. the Executive Office of the President* for the Archival Management of Electronic Records. American Archivist. 1993 Fall; 56: 674-689. ISSN: 0360-9081.

BEARMAN, DAVID. 1994. Managing Electronic Mail. Archives & Manuscripts. 1994 May; 22(1): 28-50. ISSN: 0157-6895.

BEARMAN, DAVID. 1999. Reality and Chimeras in the Preservation of Electronic Records. D-Lib Magazine. 1999 April; 5(4). ISSN: 1082-9873. Available WWW: http://www.dlib.org/dlib/april99/bearman/04bearman.html.

BENNETT, JOHN C. 1997. A Framework of Data Types and Formats, and Issues Affecting the Long Term Preservation of Digital Material. London, UK: British Library Research and Innovation Centre; 1997. 39p. (British Library Research and Innovation Report, No. 50). ISBN: 0-7123-3312-6. Also available WWW: http://www.ukoln.ac.uk/services/elib/papers/supporting/#blric.

BERTHON, HILARY; WEBB, COLIN. 2000. The Moving Frontier: Archiving, Preservation, and Tomorrow's Digital Heritage. Canberra, Australia: National Library of Australia; 2000. Available WWW: http://www.nla.gov.au/nla/staffpaper/hberthon2.html.

BESSER, HOWARD; YAMASHITA, ROBERT. 1998. The Cost of Digital Image Distribution: The Social and Economic Implications of the Production, Distribution, and Usage of Image Data. Berkeley, CA: School of Information Management & Systems, University of California at Berkeley; 1998. Available WWW: http://sunsite.berkeley.edu/Imaging/Databases/1998mellon/.

BLANTON, THOMAS S., ed. 1995. White House E-mail: The Top Secret Computer Messages the Reagan/Bush White House Tried to Destroy. New York, NY: New Press; 1995. 254p. ISBN: 1-56584-276-6.

BOYCE, PETER B. 1996. Scholarly Publishing Exists on the Web: We Don't Need CD-ROMs. Available WWW: http://www.aas.org/~pboyce/epubs/jasp-r.html#Boyce.

BRANCOLINI, KRISTINE. 2000. Selecting Research Collections for Digitization: Applying the Harvard Model. Library Trends. 2000 Spring; 48(4): 783-798. ISSN: 0024-2594.

CAMILEON PROJECT. Creative Archiving at Michigan and Leeds: Emulating the Old on the New (CAMiLEON). Available WWW: http://www.si.umich.edu/CAMILEON/.

CARTOLANO, ROBERT; GERTZ, JANET; KLIMLEY, SUSAN. 1997. Oversized Color Images: Addressing Issues of Preservation and Access. Available WWW: http://www.columbia.edu/dlc/nysmb/reports/phase1.html.

CEDARS PROJECT TEAM. 2000. Metadata for Digital Preservation: The Cedars Project Outline Specification. Available WWW: http://www.leeds.ac.uk/cedars/OutlineSpec.htm.

CHAPMAN, STEPHEN; CONWAY, PAUL; KENNEY, ANNE R. 1999. Digital Imaging and Preservation Microfilm: The Future of the Hybrid Approach for the Preservation of Brittle Books. Washington, DC: Council on Library and Information Resources; 1999. Available WWW: http://www.clir.org/pubs/archives/hybridintro.html#full.

CHAPMAN, STEPHEN; KENNEY, ANNE R. 1996. Digital Conversion of Research Library Materials: A Case for Full Information Capture. D-Lib Magazine. 1996 October; 2(10). ISSN: 1082-9873. Available WWW: http://www.dlib.org/dlib/october96/cornell/10chapman.html.

CHILD, MARGARET S. 1992. Selection for Preservation. Advances in Preservation and Access. 1992; 1: 147-158. ISSN: 1063-2263.

COLEMAN, JAMES; WILLIS, DON. 1997. SGML as a Framework for Digital Preservation and Access. Washington, DC: Commission on Preservation and Access; 1997 July. 47p. ISBN: 1-887334-51-3.

COMMISSION ON PRESERVATION AND ACCESS. 1993. The Preservation of Archival Materials: Report of the Task Forces on Archival Selection. Washington, DC: Commission on Preservation and Access; 1993. 8p. ISBN: 1-887334-23-8. Available WWW: http://www.clir.org/pubs/reports/arcrept/arcrept.html.

CONSULTATIVE COMMITTEE FOR SPACE DATA SYSTEMS. 1999. Reference Model for an Open Archival Information System, Red Book, Issue 1 (CCSDS 650.0-R-1). Available WWW: http://wwwdev.ccsds.org/documents/pdf/CCSDS-650.0-R-1.pdf.

CONWAY, PAUL. 1996a. Conversion of Microfilm to Digital Imagery: A Demonstration Project: Performance Report on the Production Conversion Phase of Project Open Book. New Haven, CT: Yale University Library; 1996 August. 22p. OCLC: 35799316.

CONWAY, PAUL. 1996b. Yale University Library's Project Open Book: Preliminary Research Findings. D-Lib Magazine. 1996 February; 2(2). ISSN: 1082-9873. Available WWW: http://www.dlib.org/dlib/february96/yale/02conway.html.

CONWAY, PAUL; WEAVER, SHARI. 1994. The Setup Phase of Project Open Book: A Report to the Commission on Preservation and Access on the Status of an Effort to Convert Microfilm to Digital Imagery. Washington, DC: Commission on Preservation and Access; 1994 June. 24p. ISBN: 1-887334-34-3. Available WWW: http://www.clir.org/pubs/reports/conway/conway.html.

COOK, MATTHEW. 2000. Economies of Scale: Digitizing the Chicago Daily News. RLG Diginews. 2000 February 15; 4(1). ISSN: 1093-5371. Available WWW: http://www.rlg.org/preserv/diginews/diginews4-1.html.

COOK, TERRY. 1991/1992. Easy to Byte, Harder to Chew: The Second Genera-
tion of Electronic Records Archives. Archivaria. 1991/1992; 35: 202-216.
ISSN: 0318-6954.
COUNCIL ON LIBRARY AND INFORMATION RESOURCES. 2000. Authen-
ticity in a Digital Environment. Washington, DC: Council on Library and
Information Resources; 2000 May. 84p. ISBN: 1-887334-77-7. Available
WWW: http://www.clir.org/pubs/reports/pub92/contents.html.
COX, RICHARD J. 1996. The Record in the Information Age: A Progress
    Report on Research. Records and Retrieval Report. 1996; 12(1): 1-16.
ISSN: 8756-0089.
DAY, MICHAEL. 1999. Metadata for Digital Preservation: An Update. Ariadne.
1999 December; 22. ISSN: 1361-3200. Available WWW: http://
www.ariadne.ac.uk/issue22/metadata/intro.html.
DE STEFANO, PAULA. 2000. Selection for Digital Conversion. In: Kenney,
Anne R.; Rieger, Oya. Moving Theory into Practice: Digital Imaging for
Libraries and Archives. Mountain View, CA: Research Libraries Group;
2000. 11-23. ISBN: 0-970022-50-6.
DOCULABS. 1998. Special Report on Records Management Systems. First
Edition 1.1. Chicago, IL: Doculabs; 1998. 135p. OCLC: 40555439.
DOLLAR, CHARLES M. 1999. Authentic Electronic Records: Strategies for
Long-Term Access. Chicago, IL: Cohasset Associates; 1999. 248p. OCLC:
20000222.
DUFF, WENDY. 1996. Ensuring the Preservation of Reliable Evidence: A
Research Report Funded by NHPRC. Archivaria. 1996; 42: 28-45. ISSN:
0318-6954.
DUFF, WENDY. 1998. Harnessing the Power of Warrant. American Archivist.
1998; 61(1): 88-105. ISSN: 0360-9081.
DURANTI, LUCIANA. 1995. Reliability and Authenticity: The Concepts and
Their Implications. Archivaria. 1995; 39: 5-10. ISSN: 0318-6954.
DURANTI, LUCIANA; MACNEIL, HEATHER. 1996. The Protection of the
Integrity of Electronic Records: An Overview of the UBC-MAS Research
Project. Archivaria. 1996; 42: 46-67. ISSN: 0318-6954.
DURANTI, LUCIANA; MACNEIL, HEATHER; UNDERWOOD, WILLIAM E.
1996. Protecting Electronic Evidence: A Second Progress Report on a
Research Study and Its Methodology. Archivi & Computer. 1996; (1): 37-
69. ISSN: 1121-2462.
ESTER, MICHAEL. 1996. Digital Image Collections: Issues and Practice.
Washington, DC: Commission on Preservation and Access; 1996 Decem-
ber. 36p. ISBN: 1-887334-53-X.
EUROPEAN COMMISSION ON PRESERVATION AND ACCESS (ECPA).
2000. Safeguarding European Photographic Images for Access (SEPIA).
Available WWW: http://www.knaw.nl/ecpa/sepia.
FLECKER, DALE. 2000. Harvard's Library Digital Initiative: Building a First
Generation Digital Library Infrastructure. D-Lib Magazine. 2000 Novem-
ber; 6(11). ISSN: 1082-9873. Available WWW: http://www.dlib.org/
dlib/november00/flecker/11flecker.html.
FLEISCHHAUER, CARL. 1998. Digital Formats for Content Reproductions.
Washington, DC: Library of Congress; 1998 July 13. Available WWW:
http://memory.loc.gov/ammem/formats.html.

GALLOWAY, EDWARD. 1998. H. John Heinz III Archives at Carnegie Mellon University: Preservation, Access, Research. D-Lib Magazine. 1998 July/August; 4(7/8). ISSN: 1082-9873. Available WWW: http://www.dlib.org/dlib/july98/07clips.html#HEINZ.

GERTZ, JANET. 2000. Selection for Preservation in the Digital Age. Library Resources & Technical Services. 2000 April; 44(2): 97-104. ISSN: 0024-2527.

GERTZ, JANET; CARTOLANO, ROBERT; KLIMLEY, SUSAN. 1996. Oversize Color Images Project Phase II: Final Report to the Commission on Preservation and Access. 1996 November. Available WWW: http://www.columbia.edu/dlc/nysmb/reports/phase2.html.

GIGUERE, MARK D. 1997. Automating Electronic Records Management in a Transactional Environment: The Philadelphia Story. Bulletin of the American Society for Information Science. 1997 June/July; 23(5): 17-19. ISSN: 0095-4403.

GILLILAND-SWETLAND, ANNE J. 1995. Development of an Expert Assistant for Archival Appraisal of Electronic Communications: An Exploratory Study. Ann Arbor, MI: University of Michigan; 1995. 256p. (Ph.D. dissertation). Available from: UMI, Ann Arbor, MI. (UMI order no. 9542845).

GILLILAND-SWETLAND, ANNE J.; EPPARD, PHILIP B. 2000. Preserving the Authenticity of Contingent Digital Objects. D-Lib Magazine. 2000 July/August; 6(7/8). ISSN: 1082-9873. Available WWW: http://www.dlib.org/dlib/july00/eppard/07eppard.html.

GONZÁLEZ, PEDRO. 1998. Computerization of the Archivo General de Indias: Strategies and Results. Washington, DC: Council on Library and Information Resources; 1998 September. 57p. ISBN: 1-887334-61-0. Available WWW: http://www.clir.org/pubs/reports/gonzalez/contents.html.

GOULD, SARA; EBDON, RICHARD. 1999. IFLA/UNESCO Survey on Digitisation and Preservation. International Federation of Library Associations and Institutions, Core Programmes for Preservation and Conservation (PAC) and Universal Availability of Publications (UAP) and UNESCO Memory of the World Programme. Wetherby, West Yorkshire, UK: IFLA Offices for UAP and International Lending; 1999. 43p. (International Preservation Issues, Number 2). ISBN: 0-95-324395-8.

GRAHAM, PETER. 1994. Intellectual Preservation: Electronic Preservation of the Third Kind. Washington, DC: Commission on Preservation and Access; 1994 March. 8p. ISBN: 1-887334-32-7. Available WWW: http://www.clir.org/pubs/reports/graham/intpres.html.

GRAHAM, PETER. 1997. Building Research & Action Agendas for Digital Archiving. In: Preservation of Digital Information: Proceedings of the Association of Research Libraries 131st Annual Meeting; 1997 October 15-17; Washington, DC. Washington, DC: Association of Research Libraries; 1997. OCLC: 40497286. Available WWW: http://www.arl.org/arl/proceedings/131/graham.html.

GRANGER, STEWART. 2000. Emulation as a Digital Preservation Strategy. D-Lib Magazine. 2000 October; 6(10). ISSN: 1082-9873. Available WWW: http://www.dlib.org/dlib/october00/granger/10granger.htm.

GREEN, ANN; DIONNE, JOANN; DENNIS, MARTIN. 1999. Preserving the Whole: A Two-Track Approach to Rescuing Social Science Data and

Metadata. Washington, DC: Digital Library Federation and the Council on Library and Information Resources; 1999 June. 53p. ISBN: 1-887334-68-8. Available WWW: http://www.clir.org/pubs/reports/pub83/contents.html.

GUTHRIE, KEVIN M. 2000. Challenges and Opportunities Presented by Archiving in the Electronic Era. Paper presented at the JSTOR Participants' Meeting; 2000 January 16. Available WWW: http://www.jstor.org/about/archiving.html.

HAYNES, DAVID; STREATFIELD, DAVID; JOWETT, TANYA; BLAKE, MONICA. 1997. Responsibility for Digital Archiving and Long Term Access to Digital Data: A JISC/NPO Study on the Preservation of Electronic Materials. London, UK: British Library Research and Innovation Centre; 1997. 71p. (British Library Research and Innovation Report 67). ISBN: 0-7123-3325-8.

HAZEN, DAN; HORRELL, JEFFREY; MERRILL-OLDHAM, JAN. 1998. Selecting Research Collections for Digitization. Washington, DC: Council on Library and Information Resources; 1998 August. 27p. ISBN: 1-887334-60-2. Available WWW: http://www.clir.org/pubs/reports/hazen/pub74.html.

HEDSTROM, MARGARET. 1984. Archives & Manuscripts: Machine-Readable Records. Chicago, IL: Society of American Archivists; 1984. 75p. ISBN: 0-931828-60-0.

HEDSTROM, MARGARET. 1991. Understanding Electronic Incunabula: A Framework for Research on Electronic Records. American Archivist. 1991 Summer; 54(3): 334-354. ISSN: 0360-9081.

HEDSTROM, MARGARET. 1993. Electronic Records Management Program Strategies. Pittsburgh, PA: Archives and Museum Informatics; 1993. 156p. (Archives and Museum Informatics Technical Report No. 18). ISSN: 1042-1459.

HEDSTROM, MARGARET; BLOUIN, FRANCIS X. 1997. Electronic Records Research and Development: Final Report of the 1996 Conference Held at the University of Michigan, Ann Arbor; 1996 June 28-29. Available WWW: http://www.si.umich.edu/e-recs/Report/FR0.TOC.html.

HEDSTROM, MARGARET; MONTGOMERY, SHEON. 1999. Digital Preservation Needs and Requirements in RLG Member Institutions: A Study Commissioned by Research Libraries Group, December 1998. Mountain View, CA: Research Libraries Group; 1999. 37p. Available WWW: http://www.rlg.org/preserv/digpres.html.

HENDLEY, A. M. 1998. Comparison of Methods & Costs of Digital Preservation. London, UK: British Library Research and Innovation Centre; 1998. 118p. (British Library Research and Innovation Report 106). ISBN: 0-7123-9713-2.

HODGE, GAIL M.; CARROLL, BONNIE C. 1999. Digital Electronic Archiving: The State of the Art and the State of the Practice. A Report Sponsored by the International Council for Scientific and Technical Information, Information Policy Committee and CENDI. 1999 April 26. 79p. Available WWW: http://www.dtic.mil/cendi/proj_dig_elec_arch.html.

HOFMAN, HANS. 1999. Shooting at a Moving Target: The Development of a Repository for the Preservation of Digital Information (Records). Paper presented at the 2nd DLM-Forum; 1999 October 18-19; Brussels, Belgium. Available WWW: http://www.archief.nl/DigiDuur/03-thema/shooting.htm.

HOPKIN, DIETER. 1997. Shifting the Focus: Digital Imaging & Photographic Collections Management at the National Railway Museum. Microform and Imaging Review. 1997; 26: 67-72. ISSN: 0949-5770.

HURLEY, BERNARD J.; PRICE-WILKIN, JOHN; PROFFITT, MERRILEE; BESSER, HOWARD. 1999. The Making of America II Testbed Project: A Digital Library Service Model. Washington, DC: The Digital Library Federation and the Council on Library and Information Resources; 1999 December. 42p. ISBN: 1-887334-72-6. Available WWW: http://www.clir.org/pubs/reports/pub87/contents.html.

INTERNATIONAL RESEARCH ON PERMANENT AUTHENTIC RECORDS IN ELECTRONIC SYSTEMS. InterPARES Project. Available WWW: http://www.interpares.org.

KAHLE, BREWSTER. 1997. Preserving the Internet: An Archive of the Internet May Prove to be a Vital Record for Historians, Businesses and Governments. Scientific American. 1997 March. Available WWW: http://www.sciam.com/0397issue/0397kahle.html.

KELLY, KRISTINE; PARDO, THERESA; DAWES, SHARON; DI CATERINO, ANN; HÉRARD, WINSOME. 1995. Sharing the Costs, Sharing the Benefits: The NYS GIS Cooperative Project. Albany, NY: NYS Department of Environmental Conservation and Center for Technology in Government; 1995 December. 84p. (CTG Project Report 95-4). OCLC: 34280495.

KENNEY, ANNE R. 1996. Digital to Microfilm Conversion: A Demonstration Project 1994-1996: Final Report to the National Endowment for the Humanities PS-20781-94. Available WWW: http://www.library.cornell.edu/preservation/com/comfin.html.

KENNEY, ANNE R.; CHAPMAN, STEPHEN. 1995. Digital Resolution Requirements for Replacing Text-Based Material; Methods for Benchmarking Image Quality. Washington, DC: Commission on Preservation and Access; 1995 April. 22p. ISBN: 1-887334-38-6.

KENNEY, ANNE R.; CHAPMAN, STEPHEN. 1996. Digital Imaging for Libraries and Archives. Ithaca, NY: Department of Preservation and Conservation, Cornell University Library; 1996. 1 volume. ISBN: 0-916582-02-3.

KENNEY, ANNE R.; PERSONIUS, LYNNE K. 1992. The Cornell/Xerox/Commission on Preservation and Access Joint Study in Digital Preservation: Report: Phase I: Digital Capture, Paper Facsimiles, and Network Access, January 1990-December 1991. Washington, DC: Commission on Preservation and Access; 1992. 47p. ISBN: 1-887334-17-3. Available WWW: http://www.clir.org/pubs/reports/joint/index.html.

KENNEY, ANNE R.; RIEGER, OYA Y. 1998. Using Kodak Photo CD Technology for Preservation and Access: A Guide for Librarians, Archivists, and Curators. Ithaca, NY: Department of Preservation and Conservation, Cornell University Library; 1998 May. Available WWW: http://www.library.cornell.edu/preservation/kodak/cover.htm.

KENNEY, ANNE R.; RIEGER, OYA Y. 2000. Moving Theory into Practice: Digital Imaging for Libraries and Archives. Mountain View, CA: Research Libraries Group; 2000. 189p. ISBN: 0-970022-50-6.

KENNEY, ANNE R.; SHARPE, LOUIS H., II. 1999. Illustrated Book Study: Digital Conversion Requirements for Printed Illustrations. 1999 July. Available WWW: http://lcweb.loc.gov/preserv/rt/illbk/ibs.htm.

KODAK. 1994. Permanance, Care, and Handling of CDs. Available URL: http://www.kodak.com/cluster/global/en/professional/products/storage/pcd/techinfo/permanence.shtml.

KRANCH, DOUGLAS A. 1998. Beyond Migration: Preserving Electronic Documents with Digital Tablets. Information Technology and Libraries. 1998 September; 17(3): 138-148. ISSN: 0730-9295.

LAGOZE, CARL; KENNEY, ANNE. 2000. The Prism Project: Vision and Focus; 2000 January. Available WWW: http://prism.cornell.edu/Publications/WorkingPapers/Visions.htm.

LAWRENCE, GREGORY W.; KEHOE, WILLIAM R.; RIEGER, OYA Y.; WALTERS, WILLIAM H.; KENNEY, ANNE R. 2000. Risk Management of Digital Information: A File Format Investigation. Washington, DC: Council on Library and Information Resources; 2000 June. 82p. ISBN: 1-887334-78-5. Available WWW: http//www.clir.org/pubs/reports/pub93/contents.html.

LE CERF, P.; DE BREMME, L.; SCHOCKAERT, R. 1997. Standards for Electronic Document Management. In: Proceedings of the DLM-Forum on Electronic Records; 1996 December 18-20; Brussels, Belgium. Luxembourg: Office for Official Publications of the EC; 1997. 217-222. ISBN: 92-8280-111-X.

LEE, STUART D. 1999. Scoping the Future of the University of Oxford's Digital Library Collections. 1999 September. Available WWW: http://www.bodley.ox.ac.uk/scoping/report.html.

LESK, MICHAEL. 1992. Preservation of New Technology. A Report of the Technology Assessment Advisory Committee to the Commission on Preservation and Access; 1992 October. 19p. ISBN: 1-887334-19-X. Available WWW: http://www.clir.org/pubs/reports/lesk/lesk2.html.

LOUNAMAA, KIRSTI; SALONHARJU, INKERI. 1999. EVA—The Acquisition and Archiving of Electronic Network Publications in Finland. Tietolinja News. 1999; 1. Available WWW: http://www.lib.helsinki.fi/tietolinja/0199/evaart.html.

LOWRY, CHARLES B.; TROLL, DENISE A. 1996. Carnegie Mellon University and University Microfilms International Virtual Library Projects. Serials Librarian. 1996; 28(1/2): 143-169. ISSN: 0361-526X.

LUKESH, SUSAN S. 1999. E-mail and Potential Loss to Future Archives and Scholarship or The Dog That Didn't Bark. First Monday. 1999 September; 4(9). ISSN: 1396-0466. Available WWW: http://www.firstmonday.org/issues/issue4_9/lukesh/index.html.

LYMAN, PETER; KAHLE, BREWSTER. 1998. Archiving Digital Cultural Artifacts: Organizing an Agenda for Action. D-Lib Magazine. 1998 July/August; 4(7/8). ISSN: 1082-9873. Available WWW: http://www.dlib.org/dlib/july98/07lyman.html.

LYNCH, CLIFFORD A. 1999. Canonicalization: A Fundamental Tool to Facilitate Preservation and Management of Digital Information. D-Lib Magazine. 1999 September; 5(9). ISSN: 1082-9873. Available WWW: http://www.dlib.org/dlib/september99/09lynch.html.

MCCLEAN, CLARE M. 1998. Digitization of Full-Text Documents before Publishing on the Internet: A Case Study Reviewing the Latest Optical Character Recognition Technologies. Library Software Review. 1998 September; 17(3): 165-169. ISSN: 0742-5759.

MCCLURE, CHARLES R.; SPREHE, J. TIMOTHY. 1998. Guidelines for Electronic Records Management on State and Federal Agency Websites. Available WWW: http://istweb.syr.edu/~mcclure/guidelines.html.

MCKEMMISH, SUE. 2000. Collaborative Research Models: A Review of Australian Initiatives. American Archivist. 2000 Fall/Winter; 63(2): 353-367. ISSN: 0360-9081.

MCKEMMISH, SUE; ACLAND, GLENDA; REED, BARBARA. 1999. Towards a Framework for Standardizing Recordkeeping Metadata: The Australian Recordkeeping Metadata Schema. Records Management Journal. 1999 December; 9(3): 177-202. ISSN: 0956-5698.

MOORE, REAGAN W. 1999. Persistent Archives for Data Collections. San Diego Supercomputer Center Technical Report. Available WWW: http://www.sdsc.edu/TR/sdsc-tr-1999-2.pdf.

MOORE, REAGAN W.; BARU, CHAITAN; RAJASEKAR, ARCOT; LUDAESCHER, BERTRAM; MARCIANO, RICHARD; WAN, MICHAEL; SCHROEDER, WAYNE; GUPTA, AMARNATH. 2000a. Collection-Based Persistent Digital Archives—Part 1. D-Lib Magazine. 2000 March; 6(3). Available WWW: http://www.dlib.org/dlib/march00/moore/03moore-pt1.html.

MOORE, REAGAN W.; BARU, CHAITAN; RAJASEKAR, ARCOT; LUDAESCHER, BERTRAM; MARCIANO, RICHARD; WAN, MICHAEL; SCHROEDER, WAYNE; GUPTA, AMARNATH. 2000b. Collection-Based Persistent Digital Archives—Part 2. D-Lib Magazine. 2000 April; 6(4). Available WWW: http://www.dlib.org/dlib/april00/moore/04moore-pt2.html.

NATIONAL ARCHIVES OF AUSTRALIA. 1997. Managing Electronic Messages as Records. Canberra, Australia: National Archives of Australia; 1997. Available WWW: http://www.naa.gov.au/recordkeeping/er/elec_messages/contents.html.

NATIONAL ARCHIVES OF AUSTRALIA. 1999. Recordkeeping Metadata Standard for Commonwealth Agencies. Version 1.0. Canberra, Australia: National Archives of Australia; 1999 May. Available WWW: http://www.naa.gov.au/recordkeeping/control/rkms/summary.htm.

NATIONAL HISTORICAL PUBLICATIONS AND RECORDS COMMISSION. 1991. Research Issues in Electronic Records: Report of the Working Meeting. St. Paul, MN: Minnesota Historical Society; 1991. 37p. OCLC: 27794177.

NATIONAL LIBRARY OF SWEDEN. Kulturarw$^3$ Heritage Project: Long-Term Preservation of Published Electronic Documents. Available WWW: http://kulturarw3.kb.se/html/projectdescription.html.

NATIONAL RESEARCH COUNCIL. 1995a. Preserving Scientific Data on Our Physical Universe: A New Strategy for Archiving the Nation's Scientific Information Resources. Steering Committee for the Study on the Long-Term Retention of Selected Scientific and Technical Records of the Federal Government, Commission on Physical Sciences, Mathematics, and Applications, National Research Council. Washington, DC: National Academy Press; 1995. 67p. ISBN: 0-309-05186-X.

NATIONAL RESEARCH COUNCIL. 1995b. Study on the Long-Term Retention of Selected Scientific and Technical Records of the Federal Government: Working Papers. Commission on Physical Sciences, Mathematics, and Applications, National Research Council. Washington, DC: National Academy Press; 1995. 127p. OCLC: 32785021.

NATIONAL RESEARCH COUNCIL. 2000. LC 21: A Digital Strategy for the Library of Congress. Committee on an Information Technology Strategy for the Library of Congress, Computer Science and Telecommunications Board, Commission on Physical Sciences, Mathematics, and Applications. Washington, DC: National Academy Press; 2000. Available WWW: http://www.nap.edu/openbook/0309071445/html/R1.html.

NAUGLER, HAROLD. 1984. The Archival Appraisal of Machine-Readable Records: A RAMP Study with Guidelines. Paris, France: United Nations Educational, Scientific and Cultural Organization, General Information Programme and UNISIST; 1984. 161p. OCLC: 13497372.

NEW YORK STATE ARCHIVES AND RECORDS ADMINISTRATION. 1995. Managing Records in E-Mail Systems. Albany, NY: State Archives and Records Administration; 1995. 43p. Available WWW: http://www.archives.nysed.gov/pubs/lgrtip.htm.

NOWICKE, CAROLE ELIZABETH. 1988. Managing Tomorrow's Records Today: Experiment in Archival Preservation of Electronic Mail. The Midwestern Archivist. 1988; 13(2): 67-75. ISSN: 0363-888X.

PICTURE ELEMENTS, INCORPORATED. 1995. Guidelines for Electronic Preservation of Visual Materials. 1995 March 2. Available WWW: http://lcweb.loc.gov/preserv/guide.

PLOCHER, DAVID. 1999. The Digital Age: Challenges for Records Management. Government Information Quarterly. 1999; 16(1): 63-69. ISSN: 0740-624X.

PUGLIA, STEVEN. 1999. The Costs of Digital Imaging Projects. RLG Diginews. 1999 October 15; 3(5). ISSN: 1093-5371. Available WWW: http://www.rlg.org/preserv/diginews/diginews3-5.html.

REILLY, JAMES M.; FREY, FRANZISKA S. 1996. Recommendations for the Evaluation of Digital Images Produced from Photographic, Microphotographic, and Various Paper Formats: Report to the Library of Congress National Digital Library Project. Rochester, NY: Image Permanence Institute; 1996 May. Available WWW: http://lcweb2.loc.gov/ammem/ipirpt.html.

RIEGER, OYA Y. 2000. Policies to Programs: Developing a Digital Preservation Policy. In: Kenney, Anne R.; Rieger, Oya Y., eds. Moving Theory into Practice: Digital Imaging for Libraries and Archives. Mountain View, CA: Research Libraries Group; 2000. 135-152. ISBN: 0-970022-50-6.

ROBINSON, PETER. 1993. The Digitization of Primary Textual Sources. Oxford, UK: University of Oxford Office of Humanities Communication; 1993 August. 104p. ISBN: 1-897791-05-4.

ROSS, SEAMUS; GOW, ANN. 1999. Digital Archaeology: The Recovery of Digital Materials at Risk. London, UK: British Library Research and Innovation Centre. 1999. 1 volume. OCLC: 44678063.

ROTHENBERG, JEFF. 1996. Metadata to Support Data Quality and Longevity. Paper presented at the 1st IEEE Metadata Conference; 1996 April 16-18; Silver Spring, MD. Available WWW: http://www.computer.org/conferences/meta96/rothenberg_paper/ieee.data-quality.html.

ROTHENBERG, JEFF. 1999. Avoiding Technological Quicksand: Finding a Viable Technical Foundation for Digital Preservation. Washington, DC: Council on Library and Information Resources; 1999 January. 35p. ISBN: 1-887334-63-7. Available WWW: http://www.clir.org/pubs/reports/rothenberg/contents.html.

RUSSELL, KELLY. 2000. Metadata for Digital Preservation: The Cedars Project Outline Specification Draft Now Available for Comment. D-Lib Magazine. 2000 April; 6(4). ISSN: 1082-9873. Available WWW: http://www.dlib.org/dlib/april00/04inbrief.html#RUSSELL.

RUSSELL, KELLY; SERGEANT, DEREK. 1999. The Cedars Project: Implementing a Model for Distributed Digital Archives. RLG DigiNews. 1999 June 15; 3(3). ISSN: 1093-5371. Available WWW: http://www.rlg.org/preserv/diginews/diginews3-3.html#feature.

RÜTIMANN, HANS; LYNN, M. STUART. 1992. Computerization Project of the Archivo General De Indias, Seville, Spain: A Report to the Commission on Preservation and Access. Washington, DC: Commission on Preservation and Access; 1992 March. 20p. ISBN: 1-887334-13-0. Available WWW: http://www.clir.org/pubs/reports/archivo/archivo.

SHEPARD, THOM; MACCARN, DAVE. 1999. The Universal Preservation Format: A Recommended Practice for Archiving Media and Electronic Records. Available WWW: http://info.wgbh.org/upf/.

SMITH, ABBY. 1999. Why Digitize? Washington, DC: Council on Library and Information Resources; 1999 February. 13p. ISBN: 1-887334-65-3. Available WWW: http://www.clir.org/pubs/reports/pub80-smith/pub80.html.

SMITH, WENDY. 1997. PANDORA—Boxing for Survival: Archiving, Preservation and Access Issues Related to Australian Internet Based Publications. Available WWW: http://www.nla.gov.au/nla/staffpaper/wsmith3.html.

STANDARDS AUSTRALIA. 1996. Australian Standard: Records Management (AS 4390). Homebush, New South Wales, AU: Standards Australia; 1996. ISBN: 0-7337-0309-7.

STEEN LARSEN, POUL. 1999. Books and Bytes: Preserving Documents for Posterity. Journal of the American Society for Information Science. 1999 September; 50(11): 1020-1027. ISSN: 0002-8231.

TANNER, SIMON. 1999. Case Studies in Digital Document Management: Focus on Implementation: Paper for Managing a Digital Environment; 1999 April 16; Glasgow University. Available WWW: http://heds.herts.ac.uk/resources/papers/HEDSglasgow.pdf.

TANNER, SIMON; SMITH, JOANNE LOMAX. 1999. Digitisation: How Much Does it Really Cost? Paper Presented at the Digital Resources for the Humanities Conference; 1999 September 12-15; London, UK. Available WWW: http://heds.herts.ac.uk/resources/papers/drh99.pdf.

VAN BOGART, JOHN W. C. 1994. Archival Stability of Digital Storage Media. Section 11 in NML Storage Technology Assessment: Final Report. St. Paul, MN: National Media Laboratory; 1994. 189p. OCLC: 43552683.

VAN BOGART, JOHN W. C. 1995. Magnetic Tape Storage and Handling: A Guide for Libraries and Archives. Washington, DC: Commission on Preservation and Access and St. Paul, MN: National Media Laboratory; 1995 June. 34p. ISBN: 1-887334-40-8. Available WWW: http://www.clir.org/pubs/reports/pub54/index.html.

VAN DER WERF-DAVELAAR, TITIA. 1999. Long-Term Preservation of Electronic Publications: The NEDLIB Project. D-Lib Magazine. 1999 September; 5(9). ISSN: 1082-9873. Available WWW: http://www.dlib.org/dlib/september99/vanderwerf/09vanderwerf.html.

WATERS, DONALD; GARRETT, JOHN. 1996. Preserving Digital Information: Report of the Task Force on Archiving of Digital Information. Commissioned by the Commission on Preservation and Access and the Research Libraries Group, Inc. Washington DC: Commission on Preservation and Access and Research Libraries Group; 1996. 59p. ISBN: 1-887334-50-5. Available WWW: http://www.rlg.org/ArchTF/index.html.

WATERS, DON; WEAVER, SHARI L. 1992. The Organizational Phase of Project Open Book. Washington DC: Commission on Preservation and Access; 1992 September. 11p. ISBN: 1-887334-18-1. Available WWW: http://www.clir.org/pubs/reports/openbook/openbook.html.

WEBER, HARTMUT; DÖRR, MARIANNE. 1997. Digitization as a Method of Preservation? Final Report of a Working Group of the German Research Association. Translated by Andrew Medlicott. Amsterdam, The Netherlands: European Commission on Preservation and Access; 1997 October. 24p. ISBN: 1-887334-53-6. Available WWW: http://www.clir.org/pubs/reports/digpres/digpres.html.

WILLIAMS, SARA; LUNDE, DIANE. 1997. Preservation and Collection Development in Academic Libraries of the United States: Joint History and Future Prospects: A Review Article. Advances in Librarianship. 1997; 21: 73-89. ISSN: 0065-2830.

WILLIS, DON. 1992. A Hybrid Systems Approach to Preservation of Printed Materials. Washington, DC: Commission on Preservation and Access; 1992 November. 67p. ISBN: 1-887334-21-1. Available WWW: http://www.clir.org/pubs/reports/willis/index.html.

WISEMAN, NORMAN; RUSBRIDGE, CHRIS; GRIFFIN, STEPHEN M. 1999. The Joint NSF/JISC International Digital Libraries Initiative. D-Lib Magazine. 1999 June; 5(6). ISSN: 1082-9873. Available WWW: http://www.dlib.org/dlib/june99/06wiseman.html.

ZELENOCK, TOM; MARZ, KAYE. 1997. Archiving Social Science Data: A Collaborative Process. ICPSR Bulletin. 1997 May; 1-4. ISSN: 0198-6848.

# III

# Applications

Section III contains one chapter, "Knowledge Management: An Introduction" by Noreen Mac Morrow of the University of Technology, Sydney, Australia. Knowledge management (KM) has grown in popularity in recent years as businesses have become increasingly aware of the fact that information and knowledge are essential to the development of corporate strategies for gaining competitive advantage and improved performance. Also, governments in several countries expect that leading industries will be knowledge-based industries and this is influencing government policies. Mac Morrow acknowledges that there is no single definition of knowledge and that there are many types of knowledge depending on different authors. Among the types of knowledge are: private and public knowledge; tacit and explicit knowledge; know-what and know-how; one author distinguishes among embodied, embedded, embrained, encultured, and encoded knowledge.

Mac Morrow stresses the importance of understanding the knowledge economy in which ideas, information, and knowledge are the basis of economic growth rather than goods or services as in the recent past. Intellectual capital accounts for the difference between the book value and market value of a company; these intangible assets do not appear on the balance sheet. Being knowledgeable implies being able to learn. Competitive advantage is increasingly dependent on learning. Mac Morrow devotes entire sections to knowledge and learning organizations, knowledge-management strategies and processes, and knowledge management in practice. Within KM for practice she covers: strategies; organizational culture; the role of technology; measurement of knowledge; and reasons why KM projects fail. The final section deals with the role of the information professional in KM. KM "represents a way of managing and behaving, which...must be integrated and embedded in the organization, its strategy, people, processes, and culture."

# 8    Knowledge Management: An Introduction

## NOREEN MAC MORROW
### University of Technology, Sydney

## INTRODUCTION

In recent years, knowledge management has become part of the rhetoric of corporate strategy. But is knowledge management just a fad or management jargon? While undoubtedly skeptics exist who argue that knowledge management is just another way for consultancies to sell their (very) expensive services, many respected authors have argued that knowledge is the only sustainable way for organizations to create value and profitability in the longer term. The impetus for this arises from a growing recognition that business use of information and knowledge is a key factor in developing and implementing corporate strategies so as to achieve competitive advantage and enhanced performance. DRUCKER (1993), for example, claims that knowledge is the crucial resource as we enter the new millennium. T. H. DAVENPORT & PRUSAK (1998) believe that an organization's only source of sustainable advantage is what it knows, how it uses this, and how fast it can know something new. Further, the creation of an economy whereby knowledge-based industries are the leading industries is the goal of government policy in a number of countries (e.g., the UK, Singapore, U.S.A., Malaysia, Australia). "Smart government," especially in the provision of health care and education, is also espoused through the application of knowledge management in the public sector. The WORLD BANK claims that knowledge may be the critical factor in development and the means by which poverty and social exclusion can be eliminated. The underlying reason for this interest in knowledge management is the belief that knowledge and its application are the means by which creativity can be fostered (NONAKA & NISHIGUCHI; NONAKA & TAKEUCHI), innovation enabled (HARGADON; VON KROGH ET

*Annual Review of Information Science and Technology (ARIST)*, Volume 35, 2001
Martha E. Williams, Editor
Published for the American Society for Information Science and Technology (ASIST)
By Information Today, Inc., Medford, NJ

AL.), and competencies leveraged in such a way as to improve overall organizational performance whether in the public, private, or not-for-profit sectors (PITT & CLARKE).

While information scientists have long had an interest in aspects of knowledge, especially its organization and representation (see, for example, *ARIST* chapters by CRONIN & DAVENPORT; E. DAVENPORT & MCKIM; POULTER ET AL.; TRYBULA), the current vogue for knowledge management has not come from this profession. Business and management, in particular the global consultancy companies, are spearheading knowledge-management programs.

The term knowledge management is used loosely to refer to a broad collection of organizational practices and approaches related to generating, capturing, disseminating, and applying knowledge. Developing new knowledge, sharing knowledge, combining existing knowledge, and valuing knowledge are all part of what has been termed knowledge management, but emphases and interpretations differ, as the following definitions show.

> Knowledge management is about enhancing the use of organizational knowledge through sound practices of information management and organizational learning. The purpose is to deliver value to the business . . . . [knowledge management] rests on two foundations: utilizing and exploiting the organization's information (which needs to be managed for this to occur); and second, the application of peoples' competencies, skills, talents, thoughts, ideas, intuitions, commitments, motivations and imaginations. (BROADBENT, 1998, p. 24)

> Knowledge management caters to the critical issues of organizational adaption, survival, and competence in face of increasingly discontinuous environmental change . . . . Essentially it embodies organizational processes that seek synergistic combination of data and information-processing capacity of information technologies and the creative and innovative capacity of human beings. (MALHOTRA, p. 58)

> Knowledge management involves the identification and analysis of available and required knowledge assets and knowledge asset related processes, and the subsequent planning and control of actions to develop both the assets and the processes so as to fulfil organisational objectives. (UNIVERSITY OF EDINBURGH)

> [Knowledge management is] a discipline that promotes an integrated approach to identifying, managing and sharing

all of an enterprise's information assets. These information assets may include databases, documents, policies and procedures, as well as previously unarticulated expertise and experience resident in individual workers. (Gartner Group Inc. quoted in CORRALL, p. 2)

Two common themes emerge from these definitions. First, the belief that organizational knowledge (or at least the environment within which this is created, transformed, organized, stored, communicated, and shared), is something worth managing as it can significantly affect the achievement of organizational objectives. Second, that knowledge is a human attribute and people are both a critical source of knowledge and central to knowledge processes.

From these definitions it should be clear that knowledge management encompasses a range of both theoretical and practical issues. This chapter reviews some of the key issues. It begins by considering how different authors have conceptualized knowledge and what this implies for knowledge management. It then discusses the nature of the knowledge economy and why knowledge is seen not only as the key competitive weapon of the 21st century and the way in which to deal with the complexity of the business environment but also as a means of social development. The relationship between knowledge management and the concept of intellectual capital is then explored.

Knowledge management is a holistic concept integrating knowledge, people, processes, strategies, and technologies. Many authors emphasize its strategic nature and the necessity of developing strategies and processes which take cognizance of this complexity and recognize the centrality of people within knoóledge-management initiatives. Approaches to the development of knowledge-management strategies are discussed, and the relationship between knowledge management and learning organizations is explored.

The latter part of the chapter focuses on knowledge management in practice and discusses this in sections on strategies, organizational culture, technology, and measurement, with a final section discussing some of the common reasons knowledge management projects fail. The opportunities or threats that knowledge management poses for library and information science (LIS) professionals and the skill base that is required for knowledge management professionals are then discussed. Finally, some conclusions are drawn based on the literature reviewed.

Although *ARIST* chapters aim to be comprehensive in a rapidly developing field such as this, it has been impossible to be anywhere near exhaustive in terms of literature review. New titles in the knowledge-management field are being published daily, as a cursory glance at Amazon.com's website will confirm. These vary widely in terms of scope, depth, and expertise. Further, there is a wealth of online sources on knowledge management, including websites, discussion groups, and online journals. Interested readers are referred to CORTADA & WOODS for a comprehensive list of online knowledge-management resources and also reprints of many seminal articles that are not reviewed in this chapter. Another useful series of books dealing with many different aspects of knowledge management is the "Resources for the Knowledge-Based Economy Series" published by Butterworth-Heinemann, a number of which are referred to in this chapter. Each of the books contains both classic articles as well as newer perspectives on aspects of the field.

## TYPES OF KNOWLEDGE

Work on knowledge is not a new activity. (See WIIG (1999) for an informative article on the emergence of knowledge management as a discipline rooted in a long history). PEMBERTON makes this explicit by discussing the concepts of knowledge adopted by Greek philosophers such as Heraclitus, Plato, and Aristotle, arguing that they were much more articulate about the nature and types of knowledge than we are today. Further, he identifies and distinguishes between two basic directions in the study of knowledge: the subjectivist and the objectivist approach. In the former, knowledge is conceived as being limited to people's personal experience in that they cannot get beyond their own ideas and know a world independent of or beyond their own thoughts. The relevance of this approach to knowledge management today, Pemberton maintains, is that it highlights the fact that knowledge transfer cannot be presumed to take place when two individuals share their private visions. Sharing of knowledge is dependent on shared perspectives and mental models of the world. This approach emphasizes the importance of cognition to knowledge management, a theme to which we return below.

On the other hand, the objectivist approach proposes that people can know a world of material objects or conceptual ideas outside their limited experience. They can learn or derive knowledge from both of these and can represent this as an objective knowledge that can be shared among many. Such knowledge can be developed, stored in a variety of containers, and communicated and acquired by others through spoken and written messages. This mediated knowledge, or knowledge by description, can be "challenged, tested, repeated, transmitted over time, and verified by others" (PEMBERTON, p. 62). The objectivist approach is most familiar to information scientists and the Western world in general. Pemberton concludes that we need to understand more deeply the nature and forms of knowledge and not rely on container, medium, or computer software to address the complexities of knowledge. His sentiments are echoed by FAHEY & PRUSAK, who argue that one of the most common mistakes in knowledge management is not to have a working definition of knowledge.

In information science literature, knowledge is commonly perceived as part of a continuum that runs from data, to information, to knowledge, to wisdom. Knowledge is defined as deriving from the processing and refinement of information in such a way as to create a stock of high-value expertise, know-how, or intelligence. Just as data can be structured and refined to produce information, so too can knowledge be derived from similar processing of information. Yet there is one essential difference between the two processes, one that underlies the concept and philosophy of knowledge management: knowledge creation comes from a process of social interaction. Unlike information, knowledge is embedded in people: it is their interaction with and interpretation of information that may (or may not) lead to the creation of knowledge. Human cognitive processes are central to this activity. The transformation of information into knowledge is not automatic nor can it be automated. It requires individuals to take a central role and apply their insight, creativity, expertise, and experience.

This idea is not new in information science. A recent article by TODD discusses the relationship between information and knowledge in terms of the work of BROOKES and relates this to the cognitive perspective on information utilization. Brookes saw knowledge as a structured entity that evolves by the accretion and integration of many increments of information over different exposures to information at different times. It is a dynamic and ever-changing entity. He characterizes knowledge along two dimensions: internal, private, cognitive knowledge and external, public, social knowledge. Todd's article highlights the centrality of information science to the study of knowledge and its management. Further, it firmly emphasizes the importance of understanding the cognitive aspects of knowledge creation.

This distinction between private and public knowledge is echoed by other writers, notably by NONAKA & TAKEUCHI, whose book *The Knowledge-Creating Company* has become a seminal work in the field. It illuminates the central differences between what they describe as Western approaches to knowledge and those of the Japanese. The former tend to view knowledge only in its explicit sense as something formal and systematic, hence the emphasis on tangible forms of knowledge that can be expressed in words and numbers, in documents, computer code, chemical formulae, etc. Explicit knowledge can be easily processed, transmitted electronically, or stored in databases. The Japanese have a very different understanding, seeing explicit knowledge as being only the tip of the iceberg and tacit knowledge as far more valuable within organizations. Tacit knowledge is personal, subjective, hard to formalize, and thus difficult to communicate and share. It depends on one's mental model of the world, the model by which one perceives reality. Information is transformed into knowledge only if it can be assimilated into the receiver's mental model of the world in such a way as to lead to a transformation in that mental model—a reordering of reality. In making this distinction and amplifying it, Nonaka & Takeuchi draw on the work of POLANYI, who discusses tacit knowledge. Polanyi says that human beings acquire knowledge by actively creating and organizing their own experiences. Thus knowledge that can be expressed in words and numbers represents only a small portion of the entire body of knowledge.

The work of Nonaka & Takeuchi is important because of their emphasis on tacit knowledge and knowledge conversion processes. These are socialization (tacit to tacit), externalization (tacit to explicit), combination (explicit to explicit), and internalization (explicit to tacit). This has significant implications. First, it implies a view of the organization as a living organism rather than as a machine for information processing. In this context, a shared understanding of what the company stands for, what its objectives are, and how it seeks to achieve these is considered far more crucial than processing objective information. Ideals, values, emotions, insights, intuition, and hunches—all highly subjective—are viewed as an integral part of knowledge.

Second, it highlights the link between knowledge creation and innovation. Once the importance of such tacit knowledge is realized, then innovation can be conceptualized in a different way. Innovation is viewed as an individual process of personal and organizational self-renewal. As Nonaka & Takeuchi say: "new and proprietary knowledge cannot be created without an intensive outside-inside interaction. To create knowledge, the learning that takes place from others and the skills shared with others need to be internalized—that is, reformed, enriched, and translated to fit the company's self-image and identity" (p. 11).

The third implication is that managers need to pay more attention to the less formal and systematic side of knowledge by focusing on subjective insights, intuition, and hunches.

Many writers in the business and management literature now recognize the value of both explicit and tacit knowledge and the difficulties of managing both. T. H. DAVENPORT & PRUSAK (1998), for example, define knowledge as "a fluid mix of framed experience, values, contextual information and expert insight that provides a framework for evaluating and incorporating new experiences and information. It originates and is applied in the minds of knowers. In organizations, it often becomes embedded not only in documents or repositories but also in organizational routines, processes, practices, and norms" (p. 5).

The WORLD BANK states that human minds can deal with two types of knowledge: the rational and the intuitive. In the West, intuitive knowledge has often been devalued in favor of rational scientific knowledge, and the rise of science has even led to claims that intuitive knowledge is not really knowledge at all. Recognition of the difficulties in transferring knowledge from one person to another, however, has highlighted the importance of tacit knowledge. In the East, by contrast, the tradition has been to celebrate the importance of the intuitive in comparison with the rational. The important point is that cultural background and upbringing influence one's perspectives of what constitutes knowledge.

BOISOT says knowledge builds on information that is extracted from data, but acknowledges that in practice the three terms are often confused. To him the value of knowledge lies in its ability to economize on the use of physical resources. He characterizes knowledge along three dimensions: degree of codification, degree of abstraction, and rate of diffusion. Together these constitute what he terms the information space. Boisot identifies four types of knowledge, which differ in terms of each of these dimensions: personal knowledge, proprietary knowledge, public knowledge, and common sense. He says that the dynamic evolution of knowledge can be viewed as a social learning cycle that goes through a number of transformational phases from personal knowledge to common sense. Personal knowledge is uncodified and undiffused. It represents internal perceptions, insights, and the expertise used to carry out tasks. Over time it may, through successive structuring, become more abstract and codified. It can then be shared and used by others. Codified shared expertise, under the control of its creators, can become proprietary knowledge or the intellectual capital of the organization on an aggregate scale. One of the paradoxes of such intellectual capital is that, while sharing does not reduce utility for the original possessor, it does reduce its value. Because shared knowledge loses scarcity, organizations seek to protect their intellectual capital to stop leaks so that scarcity is maintained. In time, though, proprietary knowledge falls into the public domain and can be considered public knowledge. Such knowledge is highly codified and diffused and represents that which is found in journals, manuals, patents, textbooks, databases, etc.

Public knowledge, in turn, is used and applied in a variety of ways. It becomes internalized by individuals and integrated into a tacit form of knowledge: a person's common-sense view of the world. This fourth type of knowledge is that which everybody knows without saying and which is built up and reinforced through accumulated experience. This type of knowledge is highly diffused and represents shared contexts. But because individuals pass this type of knowledge through their own unique cognitive filters, a large amount of what is taken to be a shared common-sense view of the world may in fact be highly personal and idiosyncratic experiences that become personal knowledge.

Boisot's proposition is that knowledge diffuses naturally and rapidly in some circumstances, whereas in others it does not. Understanding when it flows of its own accord and when it does not is crucial to mastering knowledge as a potential source of wealth. Therefore his conceptualization of what constitutes knowledge and how it diffuses through the social learning cycle is fundamental to managing knowledge.

Another categorization of knowledge is that of: know-what, know-why, know-how, and know-who (BROWN & DUGUID, 1998; DREW, 1999; SKYRME, 1999).

Know-what refers to knowledge about facts. This type of knowledge is close to what is normally called information in that it can be broken down into bits. In some occupations, such as medicine and law, the amount of such knowledge which experts must hold is great. Know-why knowledge refers to scientific knowledge of principles and laws of motion in nature, in the human mind, and in society. Such knowledge is largely produced and reproduced through institutions such as universities and research institutes or research and development departments. Access to such knowledge can speed the rate of innovation. Both know-what and know-how types of knowledge are often mastered through the channels of codified knowledge—books, databases, etc.

Know-how refers to the skills or the capability to do many types of activity within the economic sphere, from production to marketing. Know-how generally relates to the type of knowledge developed and kept within the boundaries of the individual firm. Know-how typically is gained in the apprenticeship system through learning by doing and learning by interacting. Know-who refers to a mix of largely social skills that enable an individual to know who knows what, and how to access these experts, and then use their knowledge effectively. Such knowledge is learned through social practice, through communities of interest such as professional associations, and via day-to-day interactions with customers, suppliers, and independent institutes. It is argued that these latter two types of knowledge are becoming more important in the economic conditions within which workers operate. For further discussion of the nature of information and knowledge, readers are referred to HILL, chapter 2.

BLACKLER distinguishes five knowledge types. Embrained knowledge is knowledge dependent on conceptual skills and cognitive abilities. Embodied knowledge is action-oriented and is likely to be only partly explicit. Encultured knowledge refers to the process of achieving shared understandings. Embedded knowledge is knowledge which resides in systemic routines, and encoded knowledge is information conveyed by signs and symbols. Blackler notes, however, that "The close relationship between encoded knowledge and the other images of knowledge highlighted in this discussion illustrates the point that it is a mistake to assume that embodied, embedded, embrained, encultured and encoded knowledge can sensibly be conceived as separate from the other. Knowledge is multifaceted and complex, being both situated and abstract, implicit and explicit, distributed and individual, physical and mental, developing and static, verbal and encoded. Analysis of the relationships between different manifestations of knowledge identified in this paper is at least as important as any delineation of their differences" (p. 1032).

From the above discussion it is clear there is no one single definition or type of knowledge, but rather different approaches and categorizations on the part of different authors. From a perspective of managing knowledge, the importance lies not so much in what categorization is adopted, but rather in recognizing the many facets of knowledge that exist, and the processes by which knowledge is transformed from one kind to another. Human cognition is central to these processes and it must be recognized that the transformation of information into knowledge is idiosyncratic and personal. Communication and sharing of information does not necessarily translate into the communication and sharing of knowledge.

## THE KNOWLEDGE ECONOMY

To understand why knowledge management has grown in importance in recent years, it is necessary to look at the economic context within which it is developing. This involves consideration of the networked economy and the role of information and knowledge in economic performance.

In the 1940s, economist Joseph Schumpeter theorized that major inventions lead to periods, or outbursts, of intense technical innovation. These periods are followed by creative destruction of old industries as innovation diffuses through the marketplace and transforms products and consumer expectations. Many commentators today believe that the current era is characterized by rapid technological change that is altering both the economy and society. This new era has variously been characterized as the information age (T. H. DAVENPORT & PRUSAK, 1997), the third wave (TOFFLER), the digital economy (TAPSCOTT, 1996), the network economy (SHAPIRO & VARIAN), the knowledge-based economy (NEEF), and the era of knowledge-based organizations (CLARKE & CLEGG). These characterizations share common themes: (1) that developments in technology, especially information and communication technologies, are altering the economic bases of, at least, developed countries; (2) that the key industries in this new economy are knowledge-intensive and heavily dependent on knowledge workers; (3) as a consequence of globalization (itself facilitated by the rapid diffusion of technology), competitive advantage between nations rests on the extent to which they can develop their knowledge industries and knowledge workers; and (4) that the knowledge component of all industries is increasing and value added comes from the substitution of intangible for physical resources (important in terms of sustainability).

The idea that knowledge is central to economic development is not new. MACHLUP in 1984 explicitly considers the role of knowledge in the economy. MASUDA in 1990 presents a clear vision of the importance of knowledge industries and knowledge workers and provides a lucid explanation of the transformational process by which these emerge. Since the early 1990s, many nations around the globe have recognized the economic and social significance of information and knowledge and have actively instituted policies to accelerate the development of information infrastructures to take advantage of developments in information and communication technologies. Globally, the past twenty years have seen a major shift in developed economies from production- to service-based economies dependent on skilled professionals and sophisticated technologies (NEEF). (It should be noted that not all jobs in service-based economies are highly skilled nor highly rewarded. Call centers for example, which are considered by many to epitomize the new types of jobs being created in the knowledge economy, have been called the sweatshops of the 21st century).

A key aspect of knowledge-based economies as emphasized by writers in the 1990s such as T. H. DAVENPORT & PRUSAK (1998), TAPSCOTT (1996), and others is that production of ideas rather than goods is the source of economic growth. According to ROMER, ideas are the most significant economic goods produced and the area in which people excel as economic animals. Technology facilitates growth in that it allows ideas in the form of techniques, research results, protocols, etc. to be globally distributed. It has also allowed industries to globalize and relocate to take advantage of low-cost, low-skilled labor elsewhere while still coordinating and controlling operations from home base. Technology has further facilitated the development of a whole new range of industries based primarily on the production of information and knowledge—industries such as software development, multimedia information and entertainment products and services, and Internet service providers, to name a few. Further technological development and the emergence of the networked-based economy have called into question existing business models and practices, leading in some industries to the deconstruction of traditional value chains (EVANS & WURSTER). Open ebusiness process standards such as those being developed by RosettaNet for the information technology, electronic component, and semiconductor manufacturing industries, are enabling new business opportunities and new forms of trading partnerships to be created (ROSETTANET). The result is a business environment of increasing complexity. The development of the digital economy has accelerated the pace of innovation and the competitiveness of markets. Products and services have become more complex and their information or knowledge component is increasing (STEWART, 1998). *Knowledge Capitalism* by BURTON-JONES is a comprehensive overview of the changing role of knowledge and its role in the new economy.

Rapid technological change, globalization, new possibilities for organization and management (including ecommerce and virtual organizations), and waves of mergers and alliances based on changing network relationships with customers and suppliers have forced companies to look critically at their core competencies and capabilities. According to PRAHALAD & HAMEL, a core competence displays the following characteristics: (1) It delivers a clear and valued customer benefit. (2) It is largely tacit and difficult to imitate by competitors. (3) It is organization-wide and can be applied across an organization's product/service offering. (4) Unlike physical assets, it appreciates with use; it is the fruit of an organizational learning process. (5) It cannot be traded—competencies have to be grown in house; they cannot be bought in the market. The authors view core competencies as an organization-specific integration of technologies that yields a set of core products that is a physical or intangible configuration of value-adding attributes that forms the basis of a product/service range. Core competencies are a source of differentiation and uniqueness for a firm, giving it a distinct identity and capacity. A capability is the strategic skill in the application and integration of competencies.

Disillusionment with the returns from large expenditures on information technology (STRASSMANN) have turned the focus in business management away from information technology per se to consideration of the value of information and knowledge in the context of overall business strategy. It is recognized that technology alone is not the way in which organizations attain competitive advantage, rather it is the use of information itself, particularly its conversion into knowledge and the use of knowledge to leverage unique core competencies and capabilities that enable sustained superior performance. Organizations are therefore competing on the basis of knowledge. Organizations that possess or can create such knowledge, convert it into intellectual capital, and leverage that capital effectively are in a winning position (PITT & CLARKE; STEWART, 1997).

## INTELLECTUAL CAPITAL AND KNOWLEDGE MANAGEMENT

Intellectual capital represents the difference between the book value of the company and its market value. Such capital represents the intangible assets of a company, the assets that frequently do not appear on its balance sheet. According to the Society of Competitive Intelligence Professionals thirty years ago 80% of a corporation's value could be found in its books. Ten years ago this was reduced to 50%. The new economy has reversed this 80/20 ratio so that for many companies only 20% of valuation can be identified in a traditional audit.[1]

BROOKING says intellectual capital tends to fit into four categories: (1) assets that give the company power in the marketplace, such as trademarks, customer loyalty, repeat business; (2) assets representing property of the mind—intellectual property such as patents and copyright; (3) assets that give the corporation internal strength such as corporate culture, management and business processes, and strength derived from information technologies; and (4) assets derived from people who work in the organization, such as their knowledge, competencies, work related know-how, networking capability, and so on.

EDVINSSON, Director of Intellectual Capital at Skandia, describes intellectual capital as "the possession of knowledge, applied experience, organizational technology, customer relationships, and professional skills that provides Skandia AFS with a competitive edge in the market" (p. 368). Skandia's value scheme divides intellectual capital into human capital, which is rented, and structural capital, which is owned. The key role of leadership within the organization is the transformation of human capital into structural capital by rapidly integrating corporate knowledge into tangible assets and enabling the company to apply it with maximum competitive effect. Human capital comprises the competencies and capabilities of the employees. Structural capital consists of the results of intellectual activities in data and knowledge bases, documents, etc.—what remains "after the employees have left for the night." Structural capital encompasses customer relationships, that is, the value of an organization's relationships with the people with whom it does business, the value of processes, the value of trademarks, patents, and other intangible assets. In his view, intellec-

---

[1]Remarks made at a Competitive Technical Intelligence seminar, held by the Society of Competitive Intelligence Professionals in San Francisco, CA in June 2000 and quoted to the author by an attendee in private correspondence.

tual capital management is more than just knowledge management; it is about leveraging human and structural capital together: "The goal of knowledge management is to improve the company's value creation capability through the more effective use of knowledge. The goal of intellectual capital is to improve the company's value generating capabilities through identifying, capturing, leveraging, and recycling intellectual capital. This includes both value creation and value extraction" (p. 372).

RIVETTE & KLINE argue that "the knowledge economy has given rise to a new ecology of competition in which intellectual assets rather than physical assets are the principal wellsprings of shareholder wealth and competitive advantage" (p. 56). Using examples drawn from a range of industries, they demonstrate how the successful strategic management of patents as intellectual assets can establish proprietary market advantage, improve financial performance, and enhance overall competitiveness. However, they emphasize that "Tapping the financial and competitive rewards of patents will require top-level involvement and enterprisewide organizational muscle; that means building a structure in which patents and the information they contain are available throughout the organization and are managed by senior executives as strategic assets of potentially enormous value to the enterprise" (p. 66). In other words, it requires that both human and structural capital be leveraged together.

WIIG (1997) also distinguishes between intellectual capital management and knowledge management. The former builds and governs intellectual assets from strategic and enterprise governance perspectives with some focus on tactics. It renews and maximizes the value of an enterprise's intellectual capital because this defines the future capabilities of the enterprise. Knowledge management has tactical and operational perspectives, is more detailed, and focuses on facilitating and managing knowledge-related activities such as creation, capture, transformation, and use. Its function is to plan, implement, operate, and monitor all knowledge-related activities and programs required for effective intellectual capital management. While acknowledging that intellectual capital management and knowledge management have some overlap and need to be integrated, Wiig emphasizes the importance of understanding the differences between the two. They are complementary; "by managing intellectual assets and knowledge appropriately, the employees, and the enterprise as a whole, will be in a position to act intelligently—the basic requirements for sustained competitiveness, success, and viability" (p. 400). SAINT-ONGE maintains that tacit knowledge is the key to the strategic alignment of intellectual capital. He discusses the Canadian Imperial Bank of Commerce, an organization that, through understanding tacit knowledge, has found ways to build a dynamic cohesiveness to enhance future performance and the means by which to maintain strategic agility. Knowledge management therefore needs to be placed within the context of wider intellectual capital management programs.

## KNOWLEDGE AND LEARNING ORGANIZATIONS

The concept of learning organizations is relevant to knowledge and its management. Being knowledgeable implies knowing how to learn, yet as ARGYRIS points out, although competitive success increasingly depends on learning, most people don't know how to learn and those members of the organization whom many assume to be the best at learning—professionals/managers—are not very good at it. Therefore there is much interest in building learning organizations. SENGE (1990) defines a learning organization as one "where people continually expand their capacity to create the results they truly desire, where new and expansive patterns of thinking are nurtured, where collective aspiration is set free and where people are continually learning how to learn together" (p. 1). Senge identifies five practices that foster organizational learning and knowledge: personal mastery, systems thinking, team learning, shared vision, and surfacing mental models. GARVIN further highlights the link between learning and knowledge, suggesting that three critical issues must be addressed to become a learning organization: meaning, management, and measurement. He says that "a learning organization is an organization skilled at creating, acquiring, and transferring knowledge and at modifying its behavior to reflect new knowledge and insights" (GARVIN, p. 51). Such organizations are skilled at five main activities: systematic problem solving, experimentation with new approaches, learning from their own experience and past history, learning from the experiences and best practices of others, and transferring knowledge quickly and efficiently throughout the organization. In terms of measurement, he says that organizational learning can usually be traced through three overlapping stages and that a complete learning audit of all three is a must. The stages are (1) cognitive, where members of the organization are exposed to new ideas, expand their knowledge, and begin to think differently; (2) behavioral, where they begin to internalize new insights and alter their behavior; and (3) performance-related, where changes in behavior lead to measurable improvements in results: superior quality, better delivery, increased market share, or other tangible gains. Learning, to be effective, must be both single and double loop. Single-loop learning occurs when there is modification of organizational actions, as a response to outcomes, that is sufficient to correct the error without challenging organizational norms. Its goal is to increase organizational effectiveness within existing organizational norms. Double-loop learning requires an explicit recognition and reworking of organizational norms and their associated strategies and assumptions (ARGYRIS & SCHÖN). The goal of double-loop learning is to ensure organizational growth and survival.

Intelligent organizations, or knowing organizations (CHOO, 1996), effectively integrate three processes—sensemaking (DAFT & WEICK), knowledge creation, and decision making. Sensemaking is the interpretation of environmental information in such a way as to create a shared understanding of enacted reality which provides the context for organizational action. It is the means by which organizations interpret events and it guides the knowledge creation process. The key to effective knowledge creation is the unlocking of the personal tacit knowledge of the organization's members. As NONAKA & TAKEUCHI put it, "when organizations innovate, they do not simply process information, from the outside in, in order to solve existing problems and adapt to a changing environment. They actually create new information and knowledge, from the inside out, in order to redefine both problems and solutions and, in the process, to re-create their environment" (p. 56). Through knowledge conversion, that is, through taking the tacit knowledge residing in individuals' minds and sharing this knowledge, the organization becomes primed for action and thus can evaluate alternative courses of action and choose its course rationally according to its goals. In turn, its choice of action "changes the environment and produces new streams of experience for the organization to adapt to, thus beginning another cycle" (CHOO, p. 336). Choo's article is significant because it highlights the interactivity and complementarity between these three processes (which are frequently considered individually and in isolation). Further, he places these within the context of organizational information needs and uses and clearly links information management with knowledge management. To him, information is the intellectual latticework for knowledge management. The central roles of organizational learning and adaptive behavior in the development of "knowing organizations" is emphasized. In his words, the knowing organization is one whose "actions are based upon a shared and valid understanding of the organization's environments and needs, and are leveraged by the available knowledge resources and skill competencies of its members. The Knowing Organization possesses information and knowledge that confers special advantage, allowing it to manoeuvre with intelligence, creativity, and occasionally, cunning" (p. 339).

One important element in the development of learning organizations is the concept of organizational memory, which is defined by STEIN as "the means by which knowledge from the past is brought to bear on present activities, thus resulting in higher or lower levels of organizational effectiveness" (p. 22). His article identifies ways of thinking about both the contents and processes of organizational memories and provides recommendations by which information managers can assess and control the effects of organizational memories.

## KNOWLEDGE-MANAGEMENT STRATEGIES AND PROCESSES

From the discussion so far, it should be clear that knowledge management is a holistic concept that integrates knowledge, people, processes, strategies, and technologies. The key thrust of knowledge-management strategies is to understand and exploit the role of knowledge in the process of managing organizations so as to cope effectively with rapid environmental change, and to do so in a way that enables the attainment of some form of competitive advantage. Information management facilitates the process of creating and sharing knowledge. While technologies can provide part of the infrastructure within which knowledge can be exchanged, they do not create knowledge and its sharing per se. It is people who convert information into knowledge and knowledge into information in a continuous fashion. The challenge for organizations is how to make tacit knowledge explicit and turn individual experience into organizational learning. Thus knowledge management is as much about managing people as it is about managing explicit knowledge and technologies. It requires an organizational culture conducive to, and supportive of, knowledge creation and sharing. This emphasis on the key role of people is clear in much of the literature on knowledge-management strategies. In an influential article, WIIG (1997) identifies five basic knowledge-centered strategies:

- Knowledge strategy as business strategy, which emphasizes knowledge creation, capture, organization, renewal, sharing, and use in all organizational activities
- Intellectual asset management strategy, which comprises enterprise-level management of specific intellectual assets such as patents, customer relationships, and other organizational structural capital
- Personal knowledge strategy, which emphasizes each employee's personal responsibility for knowledge management
- Knowledge creation strategy, which emphasizes organizational learning, research (both basic and applied) and development, and motivation of employees to innovate,

learn from past experiences, and obtain new and better knowledge to enhance competitiveness
- Knowledge transfer strategies, which emphasize the systematic transfer of knowledge across the organization, including capture as in organizational memories or data warehouses, restructuring/repackaging knowledge, learning from best practices, and sharing knowledge.

Wiig suggests that organizations undertake specific programs and activities covering five main areas: (1) top-down monitoring and facilitation of knowledge-related activities; (2) creation and maintenance of a knowledge infrastructure; (3) creation, renewal, organization, and transformation of knowledge assets and leveraging of knowledge assets to realize their value through knowledge sharing and collaboration; (4) adoption of best practices; and (5) development of products/services with high knowledge content.

DREW (1999) emphasizes the need to build knowledge management into the process of business strategy formulation, from mission statements to environmental scanning to core competencies to scenario analysis. In his view, a portfolio model is particularly helpful in strategic thinking about knowledge content and awareness. He identifies four important types of business knowledge:

- What we know we know
- What we know we don't know
- What we don't know we know
- What we don't know we don't know.

He states that many knowledge-management programs are concerned with the first of these: what we know we know. They focus on the sharing and distribution of existing knowledge in organizations including benchmarking, identification of best practices, and creation of communities of practice. Other programs focus on knowledge seeking and creation by emphasizing intelligence gathering, research and development, and market research which address the second type of business knowledge: what we know we don't know. The use of tools such as knowledge audits, knowledge mapping, and development of networks can be important in addressing the question of how to uncover hidden or tacit knowledge within the organization: what we don't know we know. From a strategic perspective, it is the fourth type of business knowledge—what we don't know we don't know—that has the potential to pose both the greatest threats and opportunities for the organization. The emphasis here is on discovering key risks, exposures, and opportunities such as emergence of unexpected technologies or competitors. Drew relates this type of knowledge to where, in terms of complexity theory, the "butterfly effect"[2] is most likely to be found—in small events that have momentous consequences.

By managing all four areas and building a knowledge dimension into the use of strategy tools, he says organizations are taking the first step toward developing a knowledge-based strategy whereby unique knowledge-driven sources of competitive advantage can both provide superior value to customers and be hard for competitors to duplicate.

The notion of using knowledge for business impact permeates knowledge-management strategies. According to BROADBENT (1998), the aim is for businesses to become more competitive through the capacities of their people to be more flexible and innovative. The key to knowledge-management strategies is the transformation of knowledge— from tacit to tacit, explicit to explicit, tacit to explicit, and explicit to tacit, with emphasis on the last two processes as the key challenges of knowledge management. She outlines four steps in getting started in knowledge management: (1) making knowledge visible, (2) building knowledge intensity, (3) developing a knowledge culture, and (4) building a knowledge infrastructure.

Knowledge management is again linked closely with the concept of learning organizations and information management. Learning organizations are those that effectively excel in leadership, have a culture conducive to knowledge creation and sharing, manage people as assets, and support structures and processes that facilitate, rather than hinder, knowledge-management initiatives. The interrelationship between these factors, rather than each factor separately, is considered important, and knowledge management is seen as an integrative process requiring attention in all four areas.

Integration of processes and enablers for knowledge management are also emphasized in the Knowledge Management Assessment Tool developed by Arthur Andersen and the American Productivity and Quality Center (in ALLEE, 1997a). The model identifies four key organizational enablers that allow knowledge to flourish and grow: culture, technology, leadership, and measurement. It also identifies the key processes for knowledge management: adapting, collecting, identifying, creating, sharing, applying, and organizing.

---

[2]The butterfly effect was first identified by Edward Lorenz, a research meteorologist, in 1961. Effectively it means that small errors can have catastrophic consequences. Errors and uncertainties multiply, cascading upward through a chain of turbulent features, such that the whirring of a butterfly's wings in central China today may lead to storm systems the following month in New York. It acquired a technical name: sensitive dependence on initial conditions. In systems like weather, sensitive dependence on initial conditions was an inescapable consequence of the way small systems intertwined with large. (GLEICK)

ALLEE (1997a) identifies seven aspects of knowledge that go beyond the traditional continuum of data, information, and knowledge to include meaning, philosophy, wisdom, and union. She says each of the aspects of knowledge should be consciously managed. Because they are on a continuum of increasing complexity and integration, each aspect is associated with different learning, information processing, and creative dynamics, which imply different tools and techniques for management. She then outlines ways in which this framework can be applied to enhance organizational performance.

From the above examples of knowledge management strategies, a number of points can be made that are relevant to the later discussion on practice. Knowledge management requires a strategic perspective, and the importance of a leadership role and guiding knowledge vision are emphasized. Knowledge management needs to be seen in the wider context of intellectual capital management and to be incorporated in, and integral to, business strategy. The importance of knowledge management to competitiveness, while leveraging core competencies, is closely allied with the concept of learning organizations.

Organizational culture and human resource policies are seen as major factors in knowledge management, particularly in the area of knowledge sharing. Learning from past experience, especially from past mistakes, is contrary to traditional systems for promotion and reward, where success is lauded and failures decried. Any discussion of organizational culture must also recognize the prevalence of information politics.

Technology is seen as just one element in knowledge management, albeit an important one. This chapter deliberately leaves aside discussion of specific knowledge-management technologies, as these warrant a chapter in their own right. In the discussion of knowledge management in practice below, reference is made to a range of technologies that have been employed in various companies, but emphasis is primarily on the matching of knowledge processes with appropriate technologies.

Measurement, be it of knowledge itself, of a firm's intellectual assets, or of the success of knowledge management programs, is another area of concern in the literature. Knowledge mapping, knowledge measurement, and benchmarking are among the issues discussed in the following sections.

## KNOWLEDGE MANAGEMENT IN PRACTICE

### Strategies

Differences in orientation toward knowledge management as discussed above are confirmed by empirical studies. A study by HANSEN

ET AL. óf consulting firms revealed the different approaches that companies in this sector took to the management of their knowledge. A range of strategies was identified. At one end of a continuum, these focused on information technology and the codification of knowledge, creation of large databases, electronic document management systems for knowledge transfer, etc. Such strategies emphasized re-use of knowledge. At the other end of the continuum were personalization strategies, which focused on people and the development of networks to link people together in such a way that tacit knowledge could be shared. Organizations adopting this latter type of strategy were also characterized by a commitment to mentoring and an ethic of continuous learning. The researchers discovered that companies that used knowledge effectively pursued one strategy predominantly and used the second strategy to support the first in an 80/20 split. Failure to concentrate on one strategy was associated with serious problems, although an exclusive focus was also unwise. On the basis of their results, the authors stress that competitive strategy must drive knowledge-management strategy. Specifically, organizations need to be able to answer three questions: Why do customers buy a particular company's products/ services rather than those of competitors? What value do customers expect from the company? and How does knowledge that resides in the company add value for customers? Without clear answers to these questions, an organization should not attempt to choose a knowledge-management strategy.

RUGGLES discusses the results of a study conducted by the Ernst and Young Center for Business Innovation of 431 U.S. and European organizations. This study explored what firms did to manage their knowledge, what they thought they could/should do, and what they felt were the greatest barriers in this process. The study identified several major categories of knowledge-focused processes relevant here: (1) creating new knowledge; (2) accessing knowledge from outside the organization; (3) embedding knowledge in processes and products/ services; (4) facilitating knowledge growth through culture and incentives; and (5) representing knowledge in documents, products, and software.

Ruggles reports that the executives responding to the survey did not hold high opinions of their organizations' performance in any of these areas. He also found that firms did not usually manage these areas as distinct processes, but rather that they tended to introduce specific projects with the aim of improving performance in one or more areas. Four major project types were identified as the predominant knowledge-management initiatives underway and all related to the introduction of technology. The first project type was intranet creation, which among other functions, was seen to support knowledge access and exchange. A second category of projects clustered around the data warehousing/creation of knowledge repositories. These aimed to capture explicit codified information wrapped in varying levels of context. The third type of project was implementation of decision-support tools, which codify knowledge such as best practices into rules/guidelines that are then available to others in the organization. The fourth category of projects related to the implementation of groupware technologies, such as Lotus Notes, to support collaboration and the sharing of ideas.

Ruggles points out the significant emphasis placed on technology by the executives. Yet when asked whether their organization's ability to compete based on knowledge depended more on people, process, or technology issues, the aggregate response placed the emphasis firmly on people (50%) with the other two areas carrying equal secondary weight (25% each). When asked what they should do with regard to knowledge management, respondents emphasized people issues more than technology. These efforts encompassed mapping sources of internal expertise, creating networks of knowledge workers, and establishing new knowledge roles such as chief knowledge officer. Ruggles surmises that, although these executives understood that knowledge is highly people-based, they were stuck with an investment model primarily geared toward technology implementations, which accounts for the emphasis on technology-driven projects. Yet changing people's behavior was identified by 56% as being the biggest difficulty in managing knowledge and 54% said that culture was the biggest impediment to knowledge transfer in their organization. Ruggles stresses that the lesson to be learned from this study is the importance of getting the balance right between people, process, and technology (50/25/25) from the outset and that technology-only solutions are not likely. Further, in addition to seeking ways to transfer and share knowledge, organizations need also to concentrate on generating new knowledge, as this is the key to growth.

MCKINSEY QUARTERLY discusses five cases of successful knowledge-based strategies. These range from a strategy that concentrated on the development and transfer of best practices (at McDonald's) to one that focused on fostering and commercializing innovation (at Oticon). In an insightful article, SIELOFF discusses knowledge-management development at Hewlett-Packard and notes that it is only recently, with the disruptive technology of the Internet and the World Wide Web, that more explicit and deliberate strategies for knowledge management have been developed.

ZACK (1999b) adopts a view that competitive advantage comes through strategic use of resources and capabilities, of which knowledge is considered the most important. He characterizes knowledge strategy as a balancing of knowledge-based resources with the capabilities required for providing superior products and services. His knowledge strategy framework parallels the traditional strengths-weaknesses-opportunities-threats (SWOT) analysis and is described along two dimensions. The first addresses the degree to which an organization needs to increase its knowledge in a particular area versus the opportunity it may have to leverage existing but under-exploited knowledge resources; that is, the extent to which the firm is primarily a creator, as opposed to a user, of knowledge. The second dimension addresses whether the primary sources of knowledge are internal or external. Together these two dimensions help a firm to describe its current and desired knowledge strategy. With respect to the first dimension, firms act both in terms of knowledge exploration (creator or acquirer of knowledge) and knowledge exploitation. These processes are not mutually exclusive. Exploration provides the knowledge capital to propel the company into new niches, while exploitation provides the financial capital to fuel successive rounds of innovation and exploration. The two activities must be linked. Zack's approach to integrating knowledge strategy with business strategy is illustrated with cases drawn from a number of organizations including Dow Chemical, Buckman Laboratories, Big6, and Image Corp. Knowledge strategies are analyzed in terms of their focus on internal and external sources of knowledge, and are discussed in terms of their degree of conservatism or aggression, recognizing that the nature and context of particular industries influence the extent to which particular stances are appropriate. The examples vividly illustrate the effectiveness of different knowledge-management strategies in a range of contexts. PFEFFER & SUTTON (2000) discuss the "knowing-doing" gap. It highlights the fact that strategy is not enough, that knowing what to do does not necessarily translate into a change in management practices. The authors discuss the reasons organizations find it so difficult to translate knowledge into practice and provide some guidelines to address the source of this problem. One key area for concern is organizational culture, which is discussed below.

## Organizational Culture

T. H. DAVENPORT ET AL. (1998) studied thirty-one knowledge-management projects in twenty-four companies. Four main types of projects were identified: (1) the creation of knowledge repositories; (2) improvement of knowledge access; (3) enhancement of the knowledge environment (including efforts to change the organizational norms and values related to knowledge, creating cultural receptivity to knowledge, and changing behavior relating to knowledge); and (4) management of knowledge as an asset.

A knowledge-friendly culture was identified as one of the most important factors for a project's success and the most difficult to create if it does not already exist. Characteristics of such a culture include people having intellectual curiosity and a positive orientation to knowledge, and placing a high value on learning both on and off the job. In such cultures those people are not inhibited in sharing knowledge and do not fear it will cost them their jobs. Expertise and rapid innovation supersede hierarchy. The researchers found significant evidence that knowledge-friendly cultures were characteristic of successful knowledge-management projects, whereas a lack of such a culture was associated with unsuccessful projects.

T. H. Davenport et al. (1998) also found that clear purpose and terminology were another characteristic of successful knowledge management projects: "effective knowledge use implicitly means changing the way people think about knowledge, which almost always means changing the language they use" (p. 101). Change in motivational practice to enable the creation, sharing, and use of knowledge was found to be an intangible critical success factor for virtually all knowledge-management projects. Short-term incentives, such as frequent flier points for contributing to building knowledge repositories, were not found to foster ongoing activity. To be effective, motivational approaches had to be linked to general evaluation and compensation structures. A further factor identified with success was the development of multiple and mutually reinforcing channels for knowledge transfer. Senior management support for knowledge-management projects was also critical to their success, especially with respect to transformation-oriented knowledge projects.

T. H. Davenport et al. conclude that "in knowledge management initiatives, we observed that the complexity of human factors to be managed was much greater than for most data or information management projects. Unlike data, knowledge is created invisibly in the human brain, and only the right organizational climate can persuade people to create, reveal, share and use it. Because of the human element in knowledge, a flexible, evolving structure is desirable, and motivational factors for creating, sharing, and using knowledge are very important. Data and information are constantly transferred electronically but knowledge seems to travel most felicitously through a human network" (p. 105).

The findings of BROWN & DUGUID (1998) reinforce this point. They state that within firms there are communities of practice that are able to create and transfer localized knowledge among individuals with common interests, and that social rather than contractual relationships facilitate the transfer of know-how within these communities and across the organization as a whole. WENGER & SNYDER discuss communities of practice as a new type of organizational form that can enhance knowledge sharing, learning, and change. These communities can add value to organizations by helping to drive strategy, start new lines of business, solve problems quickly, transfer best practices, develop professional skills, and help companies to recruit and retain talent. They are self-perpetuating in that as they generate knowledge they reinforce and renew themselves. The authors note that it isn't easy to build or sustain such communities because their informal organic nature makes them resistant to supervision and interference. They identify three factors associated with the successful nurturing of communities of practice. (1) The right people to form a potential community of practice that will enhance the company's strategic capabilities should be identified. (2) Infrastructure that will support the community and enable its members to apply their expertise should be provided. (3) Nontraditional methods of assessing the value of the community should be employed. DAWSON discusses the professional services context and the development of knowledge-based client relationships as a means of creating value in the knowledge economy through cooperative knowledge generation and transfer. SARVARY analyzes the impact of knowledge management on the consulting industry and concludes that success of knowledge-management systems depends on implementation, which in turn depends on a firm's business model, corporate culture, and history. He states that the few knowledge-management systems that have acted as benchmarks within the industry evolved naturally from the firm's culture and processes. He concludes that the likelihood (or indeed desirability) of their being replicated by others is not clear.

Similar emphases on organizational culture and the need for appropriate motivational practices are found in GALAGAN, GREENGARD, HICKINS, MARTINY, MULLIN, and WAH (1999a; 1999b), all of whom draw on specific company cases to illustrate their points.

SKYRME & AMIDON identify seven critical success factors for knowledge-management projects. In discussion of the lessons learned from their case studies, they state that the most important element for these projects was the creation of an effective knowledge infrastructure. This they define as knowledge leadership, knowledge roles and skills, and creation of a culture of knowledge characterized by openness, innovation learning, inquiry, and dialogue.

A final issue concerning the importance of organizational culture to knowledge-management initiatives relates to the politics of information. T. H. Davenport and colleagues (T. H. DAVENPORT ET AL. 1992; T. H. DAVENPORT & PRUSAK, 1997) demonstrate how information politics are a reality of corporate life and one of the reasons organizations fail to become information-sharing entities. They discuss five different types of models of information politics in organizations. They see the federal model as being most conducive to effective information and knowledge management, though they acknowledge that it is not appropriate for all organizations. Further, federalism can be both messy and time-consuming. It requires astute political skills, especially influencing and negotiating skills, on the part of managers if information and knowledge are to be effectively shared and used within the organization. T. H. Davenport and colleagues are some of the few writers in this domain to give explicit consideration to the issue of information politics and information governance within organizations and to consider the tactics of information exchange, brokering, leakage, and selective dissemination as realities of day-to-day organizational life.

## The Role of Technology

Technology has been a significant factor in knowledge-management projects and typically the focus of many knowledge-management initiatives (HANSEN ET AL.; RUGGLES; SKYRME & AMIDON). There are three major areas where technology has been brought to bear (CORRALL): (1) creation of knowledge databases and repositories for explicit knowledge; (2) development of knowledge route maps and directories pointing to people, resources, and document collections; and (3) creation of knowledge networks and communication tools for the exchange of tacit knowledge. Intranets as a favored technology are also common (see, for example, COHEN; HILLS). More recently, process knowledge has been the focus of attention and technologies such as those developed by MIT Sloan School of Management and commercialized by Phios Corp. are enabling companies such as Dow Corning to document all its process designs and, by placing this process repository on its intranet, enable learning of the steps involved in a process, link to detailed process guidebooks, check process performance, and share ideas for improving process designs. This section does not consider specific technologies per se, but rather addresses some of the challenges technologies will have to meet if they are to be effectively deployed for knowledge management.

FRAPPAOLO provides a useful model for matching technologies against knowledge-management functions. His model proposes four basic functions: externalization, internalization, intermediation, and cognition. (1) Externalization requires capturing knowledge in an external repository and organizing it according to a classification framework or taxonomy. (2) Internalization filters or matches that explicit knowledge to a particular user's need. (3) Intermediation brokers tacit knowledge by matching the knowledge seeker with the best source of knowledge in that area, such as another expert. (4) Cognition refers to the application of knowledge that has been transferred through the preceding functions. Frappaolo says that in seeking to match technologies with these knowledge processes, the trick is to see how existing technologies might be creatively employed together with new technologies, bearing in mind that the technologies overall should be context- and user-sensitive, flexible, heuristic, and suggestive. He also stresses that deployment of technology is secondary to creation of an appropriate knowledge culture.

MCDERMOTT echoes this view in his article discussing how technology may have inspired organizations to seek new ways of sharing and creating knowledge. He says issues of knowledge creation and sharing are hard to address as these depend more on building communities than on information technology. Instead of identifying information needs and tools such as document-management systems, intranets, or electronic networks, he suggests that the starting point for knowledge management should be identification of the community that cares about a topic and consideration of ways to enhance its members' ability to think together, stay in touch, share ideas, and connect with other communities. He stresses the importance not only of sharing information but also of creating opportunities for thinking about such information and knowledge as a community. The key technical challenge is to develop human and technical information systems that enable provision of information as well as thought and reflection about it. Drawing on examples from a number of companies, he shows how in practice different information technologies have been utilized in different organizational communities to leverage knowledge.

The social context of technology and its role in supporting knowledge transfer both within and between communities of practice in organizations is the subject of an article by BROWN & DUGUID (1998). They claim that organizations that set out to identify useful knowledge often underestimate the challenge of making that knowledge useful elsewhere. In their view, it is socially embedded knowledge that sticks, and trying to move the know-what, without the know-how, can lead to failure, as it is within practice that people distinguish what is worthwhile and valid from that which is not. They also claim that technologies play an enormous role in transfer of knowledge between communities of practice but will only be successful if they respond to the social context. One important issue the authors identify is the differences in formality within, as opposed to between, communities of practice. Internally, communities tend to informality and shared language, and technology that demands formality can disrupt more productive information relations. Technologies with differing degrees of informality and trust are required. Their book *The Social Life of Information* (2000) is a series of essays that address the social context of information from a variety of perspectives. They argue that the gap between the hype of technology and the disillusionment of end users results from "tunnel design" whereby technologies create as many problems as they solve. The problems arise from neglecting resources that lie outside the tight focus of information. Society and social resources, practice, and institutions can, they argue, solve many of the problems of both information and technology.

## Measuring Knowledge

We have already noted the relationship of knowledge management to the wider concept of intellectual capital and the recognition that it is through successful management of intangible assets that competitive advantage may be achieved. The question of how to measure the value of intellectual capital (including organizational knowledge) has drawn attention from a number of scholars. Why measure knowledge? A number of reasons are put forward. First, existing accounting measures do not reflect intangibles such as research and development, brand identity, and employee talent (MARTIN). As the importance of these to company performance begins in some industries to exceed the importance of traditional assets, some measurement, however imprecise, is required not only to evaluate the existing strengths/weaknesses of a company, but also to serve as a guide to its future performance (DRAKE). Second, some form of measurement is necessary in order to judge how effectively such assets are being managed. How can knowledge-management initiatives be assessed in terms of their effectiveness if no reliable metrics exist?

SVEIBY is one of the best-known scholars in the field of knowledge measurement. His "intangible assets monitor" focuses on three core elements: (1) Individual competence relates to the skills, abilities, education, and experience of employees, and their ability to act upon such competencies. (2) Internal structure relates to elements such as information systems, company culture, business processes, and patents. (3) External structure focuses on relationships with customers and suppliers, brand/trademarks, reputation, and image. In each area the value of these intangibles is measured by reference to three indicators: growth and renewal, efficiency, and stability, with subindicators of measurement derived for each according to the category of intangible asset being measured.

Skandia has developed a set of metrics that combine both traditional financial indicators and nontraditional measures to systematically visualize and measure its intellectual capital (EDVINSSON; MARTIN;

SKYRME, 1998), which comprises both human and structural capital. By combining five perspectives—financial, customer, human, process, renewal and development—the metrics assess the value of intellectual capital and measures by which capital can be leveraged and augmented.

The research of ROOS & ROOS resulted in an intellectual capital model that could provide companies with a way of assessing their intellectual performance. Rather than taking a balance-sheet or a snapshot approach they developed a profit-and-loss approach by monitoring the flows among different types of intellectual capital and between intellectual and financial capital.

GLAZER considers the measurement of tacit knowledge or what he calls measuring the knower. His premise is that the interaction between the subject (the knower) and the object (the known) is critical because the meaning of a piece of knowledge to the person determines whether it is used and ultimately whether it has value. Glazer draws on three successful examples of the valuation of knowledge assets in practice that implicitly involve measurement of the knower. He demonstrates with these examples that it is feasible to introduce tacit or subjective factors, the attributes of knowers, into formal measurement and models.

Other cases of companies that have also derived measures of measuring and valuating knowledge assets are presented by CORTADA & WOODS. A comprehensive overview of different measurement models, along with discussion of the practicalities of developing measurement systems, is provided by SKYRME (1998), who also offers a detailed case study of Skandia AFS.

DRUCKER (1999a; 1999b) calls knowledge-worker productivity the greatest challenge for management in the 21st century. He says six major factors determine knowledge-worker productivity, including enabling individual knowledge workers/units to determine appropriate indicators of performance. These factors are evident in companies that have successfully implemented knowledge-management initiatives and measured and leveraged their intellectual capital. He argues that the measurement issues cannot be separated from issues of organizational culture and practice. Having reliable indicators to measure intellectual capital and knowledge will not of themselves improve their management, he warns.

TEECE notes "the key sources of wealth creation at the dawn of the new millennium will lie with new enterprise formation; the renewal of incumbents; the exploitation of technological know-how, intellectual property, and brands; and the successful development and commercialization of new products and services. The implications for manage-

ment are clearly quite considerable. New forms of business organization—and new management styles that enable intangibles to be developed and dynamic capabilities to be practiced—are clearly critical" (p.
76). But, like Drucker, he warns that defining, categorizing, and measuring these intangibles is a necessary, but not sufficient, condition for
success in their exploitation.

Benchmarking is one method by which organizations can, to some
extent, attempt to assess the effectiveness of their management of knowledge processes and compare performance against that of other organizations. One well-known benchmarking tool, called the Knowledge
Management Assessment Tool, was developed by Arthur Andersen
and the American Productivity and Quality Center (HIEBELER).
Hiebeler notes that while it is difficult to identify specific companies
that are managing their knowledge better than others, it is possible to
identify key practices that individual companies use for effective knowledge management. For example, with respect to leadership benchmark
practices, he says that while many companies demonstrated that they
understood the importance of knowledge to the achievement of business strategy, many had not developed knowledge-management strategies. However, a clear group of companies could be identified as leaders in championing the cause both inside and outside their organizations. These include Hewlett-Packard, Ford, Skandia AFS, and Buckman
Labs, each of which adopted different methods of promoting knowledge management for strategic advantage. Similarly, several companies, including Chaparral Steel and Pfizer, were leading the way in
rewarding employees for knowledge sharing, again adopting methods
specific to each company.

While external benchmarking can have a powerful impact on organizations in providing models of excellence and creating a climate for
change, O'DELL & GRAYSON argue that internal benchmarking is
equally important. External benchmarking overlooks the vast amount
of untapped knowledge and best practices already residing in organizations that can be tapped through internal benchmarking. They claim
internal benchmarking and transfer of best practices is one of the most
tangible manifestations of knowledge management. Drawing on lessons learned in a number of companies, including Chevron, Kodak,
AMP, and Texas Instruments, they discuss the process of benchmarking
and best-practice transfer through the use of approaches such as
benchmarking teams, best-practice teams, knowledge and practice networks, and internal assessment and audits. Again, the importance of
the knowledge-management enablers of leadership, culture, technology, and measurement are stressed in the context of adopting these
practices.

## Why Knowledge-Management Projects Fail

The preceding sections indicate a number of reasons knowledge-management programs and initiatives fail by highlighting the importance of strategy and leadership, attention to human elements of knowledge management, and the development of an appropriate organizational culture that supports sharing and learning. FAHEY & PRUSAK provide an excellent summary of the key errors found in knowledge management. Most are connected with the concept of knowledge itself, and how it is understood in an organizational setting. First, they suggest that managers should continually reflect on knowledge as an organizational phenomenon and reach a consensual or shared understanding about what is meant by knowledge before considering how to manage it. Second, they recommend that managers critically assess knowledge content and think about knowledge as a flow rather than as a fixed stock, recognizing that some aspects of knowledge content are tentative, temporary, and subject to change. Third, they highlight the importance of "detecting and correcting errors in [the] processes of knowing—the generating, moving, and leveraging of knowledge throughout the firm" (p. 275). Such critical reflection, they say, is essential if the organization is to learn from its experiences, including its errors.

LUCIER & TORSILIERI, reporting on their experiences over a five-year period in knowledge and learning organizations programs, identify four key problems that cause knowledge programs to fail: (1) "No specific business objective, but only general aspirations like 'share best practices' or stimulate collaboration"; (2) "Incomplete program architecture that applies some principles of effective learning but does not build on the linked natural dynamics of organization change and knowledge creation and use"; (3) "Insufficient focus upon one or two strategic priorities"; and (4) "Top management sponsorship without active, ongoing involvement" (p. 263).

They believe that these problems arise because senior managers are confused and uncertain about their role in creating learning organizations in which knowledge creation, sharing, understanding, and use take place. To this end, they recommend specific actions under each of the four areas by which managers adopt a proactive and dynamic role in the management of organizational knowledge.

## ROLE OF THE INFORMATION PROFESSIONAL

In a seminal article in 1993, "Blow Up the Corporate Library," T. H. DAVENPORT & PRUSAK state that the time is ripe for a new model for the corporate library and the librarian. They propose moving away from the warehouse concept of information management and recasting librarians as overseers of a multimedia network with a key role in establishing connections between those who have information and those who want it. Since then, library and information science (LIS) has seen an explosion of interest in knowledge management with emphasis on knowledge creation, sharing, and use. But are LIS professionals at the center of knowledge-management strategies as envisaged in that 1993 article? In most instances they are not, although there are well-publicized exceptions, such as within major consultancy organizations, law firms, and the pharmaceutical and high-tech sectors. In an analysis of the reasons for this situation, E. DAVENPORT & CRONIN argue that complacency within the LIS profession and LIS literature about the whole area of knowledge management is to blame. This derives in part from a perception that knowledge management is basically what LIS has always done, namely organize and manage exoteric stocks of knowledge and provide access to that knowledge via the professional intermediary. They state that "[this] position is articulated in a spectrum of publications which includes professional bulletins and academic articles. At their most simplistic [these] statements combine myopia with territoriality" (p. 1). They claim that much of what is important in knowledge management is ignored or overlooked by LIS professionals because it belongs to other disciplinary areas such as technology and business management. This has detrimental consequences when knowledge-management initiatives are undertaken within organizations.

KLOBAS makes the point that, while the LIS profession may have considerable skills relevant to knowledge management, it is business-school graduates, especially those with an information systems background, who have taken the lead in this domain within organizations, because they are both intellectually and politically well-placed to do so. PEREZ makes similar observations.

CORRALL states that "although LIS people are not always prominently involved at the outset of KM initiatives, many organisations have brought them in at a later stage when the ongoing management of content usually emerges as the major technical challenge . . . . Some corporate libraries are being reinvented as knowledge centres, often with bigger budgets . . . . Nevertheless, their future is by no means assured as there is no shortage of other people ready to take on these tasks; librarians' traditional reluctance to move beyond the information container towards analysis and interpretation of its contents has resulted in organisations overlooking their potential contribution, even in areas where their competence should be obvious. Information professionals are seen as service-oriented but not value-oriented" (p. 5).

BROADBENT (1997) also stresses value, stating that "librarians are generally driven by a desire to provide access to information sources

and [they] match this desire with values that assume information sharing is a good thing . . . . Both of these attributes are important for the
practice of knowledge management. But they are not sufficient. They
need to be harnessed in two directions: towards specific organisational
objectives that provide greater value to customers and clients; and,
second, in the way in which library and information services are themselves managed. Knowledge management is not owned by any one
group in an organization nor by any one profession or industry. But if
[librarians and information specialists] want to be [key] player[s] in the
emerging knowledge management phenomenon, [they] need to understand the multiple perspectives of the other players" (p. 21).

ABRAM adopts what he calls a "heretical" position that challenges
some of the sacred cows of the profession, specifically that special
librarians are not in the information business nor can they manage
knowledge. He argues that only the knowledge environment can be
managed and here librarians can play a very important role as a key
catalyst in the knowledge continuum, a role of "transformational
librarianship." This process has two elements: (1) moving information
into knowledge and back, and (2) creating and enhancing knowledge
environments to have a material impact on the decision-making behaviors and results of organizations and the individuals therein. He sees
knowledge management as an opportunity, not a threat, to the profession. Rather than fearing the incursion of data professionals and technology experts into information roles, he encourages LIS professionals
to apply their skills in alliance with information technology professionals in order to transform enterprises and enable informed intelligent
decision making.

In its briefing paper based on research conducted for the UK Library
and Information Commission, TFPL LIMITED notes that the overlap
between recognized management competencies and knowledge practitioner competencies is significant, including change- and project-man-
agement skills, negotiating and influencing skills, leadership, facilitation and team-building skills, mentoring, coaching and training skills,
and the catchall communication skills. Key knowledge-management
enabling skills include business process identification and analysis;
understanding of both the knowledge processes within the business
and the value, context, and dynamics of knowledge and information;
knowledge asset identification, creation, maintenance, and exploitation; knowledge mapping and flows; and the ability to leverage technologies to create knowledge management enablers.

In discussing the organizational knowledge-management environment, TFPL suggests exploiting the experience and capabilities of a
wide range of organizational people whose backgrounds and experience relate to different aspects of information/knowledge manage-

ment, from records managers to information technology professionals to marketing and research and development experts. Knowledge-management people are distinguished by their can-do attitude, the fact that they relate more to opportunities than to functions.

TFPL's research demonstrates that the LIS profession appears to have had little impact on knowledge management in organizations and that this relates largely to a perception among organizations that it is a profession that seldom engages directly with the business. To redress this, TFPL recommends that within the LIS profession, an understanding be developed of knowledge-management concepts and strategies, the skills and competencies needed for knowledge management, and the context within which they are applied.

Schools of library and information science have, over the past two decades, brought onstream courses in information and knowledge management that do adopt multiple perspectives on information and knowledge and that focus on understanding business processes and organizational contexts. Graduates from such courses are entering careers far removed from what might be termed traditional and may not identify themselves as members of a distinct LIS profession. These graduates have opportunities to develop careers in the emerging field of knowledge management, albeit in competition with graduates from many other disciplines and professions.

## CONCLUSIONS

Knowledge management is not a chimera. It is not a fad nor is it a prescribed solution. Rather, it represents a way of managing and behaving, which, to be successful, must be integrated and embedded in the organization, its strategy, people, processes, and culture. To ignore the evolution of knowledge management would be to ignore the significance of knowledge in the economic, social, and technological context of the 21st century. Knowledge is substituting for physical resources. Knowledge does enable a competitive edge. Knowledge has profound effects on organizations.

The rate of production of explicit knowledge has never been more accelerated, yet as has been seen in this article, this is only the tip of the iceberg. We have a great deal to discover about the nature of tacit knowledge and about the transformational knowledge processes of externalization, combination, socialization, and internalization. Knowledge is in the brain of the beholder. It is people who transform information into knowledge and more importantly apply this knowledge to productive ends. To adopt a technology-driven paradigm for knowledge management is to fundamentally misunderstand the nature of knowledge and its application. But understanding and knowledge of how to apply technology, as part of a wider strategy of leveraging intellectual capital, are crucial, especially in the context of ecommerce.

This review aims to show that knowledge management poses significant challenges for organizations and for individuals. It is strategic in nature and in order to be successful must become integral to organizational culture (a culture that values and fosters continuous learning), to organizational processes, and most important, to the way individuals behave in their work. Knowledge management is not therefore the preserve of senior management alone, though their support is vital; it is becoming a component of everyone's work activities and will require changes in thinking and behaving at all levels. Knowledge management does not belong to a single discipline or profession.

Technologies assist in knowledge management, but while computers and networks connect, ultimately it is people who communicate. The communication process is central to the transfer, creation, and sharing of knowledge within and between organizations and indeed countries. A key challenge will be to bring together diverse individuals with their multiple perspectives, views, and beliefs about knowledge and its management in a synergistic way so as to assist in the creation, sharing, application, and use of knowledge in productive ways.

## BIBLIOGRAPHY

ABRAM, STEPHEN.   1999.  Post Information Age Positioning for Special Librarians: Is Knowledge Management the Answer? In: Matarazzo, James M.; Connolly, Suzanne D., eds. Knowledge and Special Libraries. Boston, MA: Butterworth-Heinemann; 1999. 185-193. ISBN: 0-7506-7084-3.

ALLEE, VERNA. 1997a. The Knowledge Evolution: Expanding Organizational Intelligence. Boston, MA: Butterworth-Heinemann; 1997. 274p. ISBN: 0-7506-9842-X.

ALLEE, VERNA. 1997b. 12 Principles of Knowledge Management. Training & Development. 1997 November; 51(11): 71-74. ISSN: 1055-9760.

ARGYRIS, CHRIS. 1998. Teaching Smart People How to Learn. In: Harvard Business Review on Knowledge Management.   Boston, MA: Harvard Business School Press; 1998. 81-108. ISBN: 0-87584-881-8.

ARGYRIS, CHRIS; SCHÖN, DONALD A. 1978. Organizational Learning: A Theory of Action Perspective. Reading, MA: Addison-Wesley; 1978. 344p. ISBN: 0-201-00174-8.

BLACKLER, FRANK. 1995. Knowledge, Knowledge Work and Organizations: An Overview and Interpretation. Organization Studies. 1995; 16(6): 1021-1046. ISSN: 0170-8406.

BOISOT, MAX. 1998. Knowledge Assets: Securing Competitive Advantage in the Information Economy. New York, NY: Oxford University Press; 1998. 284p. ISBN: 0-19-829086-1.

BROADBENT, MARIANNE. 1997. The Emerging Phenomenon of Knowledge Management. The Australian Library Journal. 1997 February; 46(1): 6-23. ISSN: 0004-9670.

BROADBENT, MARIANNE. 1998. The Phenomenon of Knowledge Management: What Does It Mean to the Information Profession? Information Outlook. 1998 May; 2(5): 23-31. ISSN: 1091-0808.

BROOKES, BERTRAM. 1974. Robert Fairthorne and the Scope of Information Science. Journal of Documentation. 1974; 30(2): 139-152. ISSN: 0022-0418.

BROOKING, ANNIE. 1999. Corporate Memory: Strategies for Knowledge Management. New York, NY: International Thomson Business Press; 1999. 181p. ISBN: 1-86152-268-1.

BROWN, JOHN SEELY; DUGUID, PAUL. 1998. Organizing Knowledge. California Management Review. 1998 Spring; 40(3): 90-111. ISSN: 0008-1256.

BROWN, JOHN SEELY; DUGUID, PAUL. 2000. The Social Life of Information. Boston, MA: Harvard Business School Press; 2000. 320p. ISBN: 0-87584-762-5.

BURTON-JONES, ALAN. 1999. Knowledge Capitalism: Business, Work and Learning in the New Economy. New York, NY: Oxford University Press; 1999. 248p. ISBN: 0-19-829622-3.

CARR, NICHOLAS G. 1999. A New Way to Manage Process Knowledge. Harvard Business Review. 1999 September-October; 77(5): 24-25. ISSN: 0017-8012.

CHOO, CHUN WEI. 1995. Information Management for the Intelligent Organization: The Art of Scanning the Environment. Medford, NJ: Information Today, Inc. for the American Society for Information Science; 1995. 255p. ISBN: 1-57387-018-8.

CHOO, CHUN WEI. 1996. The Knowing Organization: How Organizations Use Information to Construct Meaning, Create Knowledge and Make Decisions. International Journal of Information Management. 1996 October; 16(5): 329-340. ISSN: 0268-4012.

CHOO, CHUN WEI. 1998. The Knowing Organization: How Organizations Use Information to Construct Meaning, Create Knowledge and Make Decisions. New York, NY: Oxford University Press; 1998. 298p. ISBN: 0-19-511011-0.

CLARKE, THOMAS; CLEGG, STEWART. 1998. Changing Paradigms: The Transformation of Management Knowledge for the 21st Century. London, England: HarperCollins Business; 1998. 502p. ISBN: 0-00257-015-7.

COHEN, SACHA. 1998. Knowledge Management's Killer App: Here's How an Intranet Can Wire Employees to Information and Knowledge without Fragmenting a Company's Culture. Training & Development. 1998 January; 52(1): 50-56. ISSN: 1055-9760.

CORRALL, SHEILA. 1998. Knowledge Management: Are We in the Knowledge Management Business? Ariadne. 1998 December; Issue 18. ISSN: 1361-3200. Available WWW: http://www.ariadne.ac.uk/issue18/knowledge-mgt.

CORTADA, JAMES W., ed. 1998. Rise of the Knowledge Worker. Boston, MA: Butterworth-Heinemann; 1998. 240p. ISBN: 0-7506-7058-4.

CORTADA, JAMES W.; WOODS, JOHN A., eds. 1999. The Knowledge Management Yearbook 1999-2000. Boston, MA: Butterworth-Heinemann; 1999. 521p. ISBN: 0-7506-7122-X.

CRONIN, BLAISE; DAVENPORT, ELISABETH. 1993. Social Intelligence. In: Williams, Martha E., ed. Annual Review of Information Science and Technology: Volume 28. Medford, NJ: Learned Information, Inc. for the American Society for Information Science; 1993. 3-44. ISSN: 0066-4200; ISBN: 0-93873-475-X.

DAFT, RICHARD L.; WEICK, KARL E. 1984. Toward a Model of Organizations as Interpretation Systems. Academy of Management Review. 1984 April; 9(2): 284-295. ISSN: 0363-7425.

DAVENPORT, ELISABETH; CRONIN, BLAISE. 2000. Knowledge Management: Semantic Drift or Conceptual Shift. Paper presented at the Association for Library and Information Science Education  Conference; 2000 January 11-14; San Antonio, TX. Available WWW: http://www.alise.org/nondiscuss/conf00_Davenport-Cronin_paper.htm.

DAVENPORT, ELISABETH; MCKIM, GEOFFREY. 1995. Groupware. In: Williams, Martha E., ed. Annual Review of Information Science and Technology: Volume 30. Medford, NJ: Information Today, Inc. for the American Society for Information Science; 1995. 115-159. ISSN: 0066-4200; ISBN: 1-57387-019-6.

DAVENPORT, THOMAS H.; DE LONG, DAVID W.; BEERS, MICHAEL C. 1999. Successful Knowledge Management Projects. In: Cortada, James W.; Woods, John A., eds. The Knowledge Management Yearbook 1999-2000. Boston, MA: Butterworth-Heinemann; 1999. 89-107. ISBN: 0-7506-7122-X.

DAVENPORT, THOMAS H.; ECCLES, ROBERT G.; PRUSAK, LAURENCE. 1992. Information Politics. Sloan Management Review. 1992 Fall; 34(1): 53-65. ISSN: 0019-848X.

DAVENPORT, THOMAS H.; JARVENPAA, SIRKKA L.; BEERS, MICHAEL C. 1996. Improving Knowledge Work Processes. Sloan Management Review. 1996 Summer; 37(4): 53-66. ISSN: 0019-848X.

DAVENPORT, THOMAS H.; PRUSAK, LAURENCE. 1993. Blow Up the Corporate Library. International Journal of Information Management. 1993 December; 13(6): 405-412. ISSN: 0268-4012.

DAVENPORT, THOMAS H.; PRUSAK, LAURENCE. 1997. Information Ecology: Mastering the Information and Knowledge Environment. New York, NY: Oxford University Press; 1997. 255p. ISBN: 0-19-511168-0.

DAVENPORT, THOMAS H.; PRUSAK, LAURENCE. 1998. Working Knowledge: How Organizations Manage What They Know. Boston, MA: Harvard Business School Press; 1998. 199p. ISBN: 0-87584-655-6.

DAWSON, ROSS. 2000. Developing Knowledge-Based Client Relationships. Boston, MA: Butterworth-Heinemann; 2000. 275p. ISBN: 0-7506-7185-8.

DEMAREST, MARC. 1997. Understanding Knowledge Management. Long Range Planning. 1997; 30(3): 374-384. ISSN: 0024-6301.

DRAKE, KEITH. 1998. Firms, Knowledge and Competitiveness. OECD Observer. 1998 April-May; 211: 24-26. ISSN: 0029-7054.

DREW, STEPHEN A. W. 1997. From Knowledge to Action: The Impact of Benchmarking on Organizational Performance. Long Range Planning. 1997; 30(3): 427-441. ISSN: 0024-6301.

DREW, STEPHEN A. W. 1999. Building Knowledge Management into Strategy: Making Sense of a New Perspective. Long Range Planning. 1999 January; 32(1): 130-136. ISSN: 0024-6301.

DRUCKER, PETER F. 1993. Post-Capitalist Society. 1st edition. New York, NY: Harper Business; 1993. 232p. ISBN: 0-88730-620-9.

DRUCKER, PETER F. 1999a. Knowledge-Worker Productivity: The Biggest Challenge. California Management Review. 1999 Winter; 41(2): 79-94. ISSN: 0008-1256.

DRUCKER, PETER F. 1999b. Management Challenges for the 21st Century. Oxford, England: Butterworth-Heinemann; 1999. 205p. ISBN: 0-7506-4456-7.

EDVINSSON, LEIF. 1997. Developing Intellectual Capital at Skandia. Long Range Planning. 1997; 30(3): 367-373. ISSN: 0024-6301.

EVANS, PHILIP; WURSTER,THOMAS S. 1999. Blown to Bits: How the New Economics of Information Transforms Strategy. Boston, MA: Harvard Business School Press; 1999. 261p. ISBN: 0-87584-877-X.

FAHEY, LIAM; PRUSAK, LAURENCE. 1998. The Eleven Deadliest Sins of Knowledge Management. California Management Review. 1998 Spring; 40(3): 265-276. ISSN: 0008-1256.

FRAPPAOLO, CARL. 1998. Defining Knowledge Management: Four Basic Functions. Computerworld. 1998 February 23; 32(8): 80. ISSN: 0010-4841.

FRAPPAOLO, CARL; CAPSHAW, STACIE. 1999. Knowledge Management Software: Capturing the Essence of Know-how and Innovation. Records Management Quarterly. 1999 July; 33(3): 44-48. ISSN: 1050-2343.

GALAGAN, PATRICIA A. 1997. Smart Companies. Training & Development. 1997 December; 51(12): 20-24. ISSN: 1055-9760.

GARVIN, DAVID A. 1998. Building a Learning Organization. In: Harvard Business Review on Knowledge Management. Boston, MA: Harvard Business School Press; 1998. 47-80. ISBN: 0-87584-881-8.

GLAZER, RASHI. 1998. Measuring the Knower: Towards a Theory of Knowledge Equity. California Management Review. 1998 Spring; 40(3): 175-194. ISSN: 0008-1256.

GLEICK, JAMES. 1987. Chaos: Making a New Science. New York, NY: Viking; 1987. 352p. ISBN: 0-670-81178-5.

GREENGARD, SAMUEL. 1998. Storing, Shaping and Sharing Collective Wisdom. Workforce. 1998 October; 77(10): 82-88. ISSN: 1092-8332.

HANSEN, MORTEN T.; NOHRIA, NITIN; TIERNEY, THOMAS. 1999. What's Your Strategy for Managing Knowledge? Harvard Business Review. 1999 March-April; 77(2): 106-118. ISSN: 0017-8012.

HARGADON, ANDREW B. 1998. Firms as Knowledge Brokers: Lessons in Pursuing Continuous Innovation. California Management Review. 1998 Spring; 40(3): 209-227. ISSN: 0008-1256.

HARVARD BUSINESS SCHOOL PRESS. 1998. Harvard Business Review on Knowledge Management. Boston, MA: Harvard Business School Press; 1998. 223p. ISBN: 0-87584-881-8.

HICKINS, MICHAEL. 1999. Xerox Shares Its Knowledge. Management Review. 1999 September; 88(8): 40-46. ISSN: 0025-1895.

HIEBELER, ROBERT J. 1996. Benchmarking: Knowledge Management. Strategy & Leadership. 1996 March-April; 24(2): 22-28. ISSN: 1087-8572.

HILL, MICHAEL W. 1999. The Impact of Information on Society. New Providence, NJ: Bowker-Saur; 1999. 292p. ISBN: 1-85739-124-1.

HILLS, MELLANIE. 1997. Intranet as Groupware. New York, NY: John Wiley & Sons; 1997. 308p. ISBN: 0-471-16373-2.

HORIBE, FRANCES. 1999. Managing Knowledge Workers: New Skills and Attitudes to Unlock the Intellectual Capital in Your Organization. Toronto, Canada: John Wiley & Sons Canada; 1999. 292p. ISBN: 0-471-64318-1.

KLEIN, DAVID A., ed. 1999. The Strategic Management of Intellectual Capital. Boston, MA: Butterworth-Heinemann; 1999. 246p. ISBN: 0-7506-9850-0.

KLOBAS, JANE E. 1997. Information Services for New Millennium Organizations: Librarians and Knowledge Management. In: Raitt, David I., ed. Libraries for the New Millennium: Implications for Managers. London, England: Library Association; 1997. 39-64. ISBN: 1-85604-257-X.

LIEBOWITZ, JAY, ed. 1999. Knowledge Management Handbook. Boca Raton, FL: CRC Press; 1999. 1 volume. ISBN: 0-8493-0238-2.

LIEBOWITZ, JAY. 2000. Building Organizational Intelligence: A Knowledge Management Primer. Boca Raton, FL: CRC Press; 2000. 141p. + Optical Disc. ISBN: 0-8493-2036-4.

LUCIER, CHARLES E.; TORSILIERI, JANET D. 1999. Why Knowledge Programs Fail: A CEO's Guide to Managing Learning. In: Cortada, James W.; Woods, John A., eds. The Knowledge Management Yearbook 1999-2000. Boston, MA: Butterworth-Heinemann; 1999. 262-279. ISBN: 0-7506-7122-X.

MACHLUP, FRITZ. 1984. The Economics of Information and Human Capital. Princeton, NJ: Princeton University Press; 1984. 644p. ISBN: 0-691-04233-0.

MADHAVAN, RAVINDRANATH; GROVER, RAJIV. 1998. From Embedded Knowledge to Embodied Knowledge: New Product Development as Knowledge Management. Journal of Marketing. 1998 October; 62(4): 1-12. ISSN: 0022-2429.

MALHOTRA, YOGESH. 1998. Tools @ Work: Deciphering the Knowledge Management Hype. Journal for Quality & Participation. 1998 July/August; 21(4): 58-60. ISSN: 1040-9602.

MARTIN, W. J. 2000. Approaches to the Measurement of the Impact of Knowledge Management Programmes. Journal of Information Science. 2000; 26(1): 21-27. ISSN: 0165-5515.

MARTINY, MARILYN. 1998. Knowledge Management at HP Consulting. Organizational Dynamics. 1998 Autumn; 27(2): 71-77. ISSN: 0090-2616.

MASUDA, YONEJI. 1990. Managing in the Information Society: Releasing Synergy Japanese Style. Oxford, England: Basil Blackwell; 1990. 168p. ISBN: 0-631-17575-X.

MATARAZZO, JAMES M.: CONNOLLY, SUZANNE D., eds. 1999. Knowledge and Special Libraries. Boston, MA: Butterworth-Heinemann; 1999. 265p. ISBN: 0-7506-7084-3.

MCDERMOTT, RICHARD. 1999. Why Information Technology Inspired But Cannot Deliver Knowledge Management. California Management Review. 1999 Summer; 41(4): 103-117. ISSN: 0008-1256.

MCKINSEY QUARTERLY. 1998. Best Practice and Beyond: Knowledge Strategies. McKinsey Quarterly. 1998 Winter; 1: 19-25. ISSN: 0047-5394.

MULLIN, RICK. 1996. Knowledge Management: A Cultural Evolution. Journal of Business Strategy. 1996 September-October; 17(5): 56-59. ISSN: 0275-6668.

NEEF, DALE, ed. 1998. The Knowledge Economy. Boston, MA: Butterworth-Heinemann; 1998. 278p. ISBN: 0-7506-9936-1.

NONAKA, IKUJIRO; NISHIGUCHI, TOSHIHIRO, eds. 2000. Knowledge Emergence: Social, Technical, and Evolutionary Dimensions of Knowledge Creation. New York, NY: Oxford University Press; 2000. ISBN: 0-19-513063-4.

NONAKA, IKUJIRO; TAKEUCHI, HIROTAKA. 1995. The Knowledge-Creating Company: How Japanese Companies Create the Dynamics of Innovation. New York, NY: Oxford University Press; 1995. 284p. ISBN: 0-19-509269-4.

O'DELL, CARLA; GRAYSON, C. JACKSON. 1999. Identifying and Transferring Internal Best Practices: An APQC White Paper. Houston, TX: American Productivity and Quality Center; 1999. Available WWW: http://www.apqc.org/free/whitepapers/dispWhitePaper.cfm?ProductID=665.

PEMBERTON, J. MICHAEL. 1998. Knowledge Management (KM) and the Epistemic Tradition. Records Management Quarterly. 1998 July; 32(3): 58-62. ISSN: 1050-2343.

PEREZ, ERNEST R. 1999. Knowledge Management in the Library—Not. Database. 1999 April; 22(1): 75-78. ISSN: 0162-4105.

PFEFFER, JEFFREY; SUTTON, ROBERT I. 1999. Knowing "What" to Do Is Not Enough: Turning Knowledge into Action. California Management Review. 1999 Fall; 42(1): 83-108. ISSN: 0008-1256.

PFEFFER, JEFFREY; SUTTON, ROBERT I. 2000. The Knowing-Doing Gap: How Smart Companies Turn Knowledge into Action. Boston, MA: Harvard Business School Press; 2000. 314p. ISBN: 1-57851-124-0.

PITT, MARTYN; CLARKE, KEN. 1999. Competing on Competence: A Knowledge Perspective on the Management of Strategic Innovation. Technology Analysis & Strategic Management. 1999 September; 11(3): 301-316. ISSN: 0953-7325.

POLANYI, MICHAEL. 1997. The Tacit Dimension. In: Prusak, Laurence, ed. Knowledge in Organizations. Boston, MA: Butterworth-Heinemann; 1997. 135-146. ISBN: 0-7506-9718-0.

POULTER, ALAN; MORRIS, ANNE; DOW, JULIE. 1994. LIS Professionals as Knowledge Engineers. In: Williams, Martha E., ed. Annual Review of Information Science and Technology: Volume 29. Medford, NJ: Information Today, Inc. for the American Society for Information Science; 1994. 305-350. ISSN: 0066-4200; ISBN: 0-93873-491-1.

PRAHALAD, C. K.; HAMEL, GARY. 1990. The Core Competence of the Corporation. Harvard Business Review. 1990; 68(3): 79-91. ISSN: 0017-8012.

PRUSAK, LAURENCE, ed. 1997. Knowledge in Organizations. Boston, MA: Butterworth-Heinemann; 1997. 261p. ISBN: 0-7506-9718-0.

RIVETTE, KEVIN G.; KLINE, DAVID. 2000. Discovering New Value in Intellectual Property. Harvard Business Review. 2000 January-February; 78(1): 54-66. ISSN: 0017-8012.

ROMER, PAUL. 1993. Ideas and Things: The Concept of Production Is Being Re-tooled. Economist. 1993 September 11; 328(7828): 86-90. ISSN: 0013-0613.

ROOS, GORAN; ROOS, JOHAN. 1997. Measuring Your Company's Intellectual Performance. Long Range Planning. 1997; 30(3): 413-425. ISSN: 0024-6301.

ROSETTANET. Available WWW: http://www.rosettanet.org.

RUGGLES, RUDY. 1998. The State of the Notion: Knowledge Management in Practice. California Management Review. 1998 Spring; 40(3): 80- 89. ISSN: 0008-1256.

SAINT-ONGE, HUBERT. 1996. Tacit Knowledge: The Key to the Strategic Alignment of Intellectual Capital. Planning Review. 1996; 24(2): 10-14. ISSN: 0094-064X.

SARVARY, MIKLOS. 1999. Knowledge Management and Competition in the Consulting Industry. California Management Review. 1999 Winter; 41(2): 95-107. ISSN: 0008-1256.

SENGE, PETER M. 1990. The Fifth Discipline: The Art and Practice of the Learning Organization. New York, NY: Doubleday; 1990. 424p. ISBN: 0-385-26094-6.

SENGE, PETER M. 1994. The Fifth Discipline Fieldbook. London, England: Nicholas Brearley; 1994. 593p. ISBN: 1-85788-060-9.

SHAPIRO, CARL; VARIAN, HAL R. 1999. Information Rules: A Strategic Guide to the Network Economy. Boston, MA: Harvard Business School Press; 1999. 352p. ISBN: 0-87584-863-X.

SIELOFF, CHARLES G. 1999. If Only HP Knew What HP Knows: The Roots of Knowledge Management at Hewlett-Packard. Journal of Knowledge Management. 1999; 3(1): 47-53. ISSN: 1367-3270.

SKYRME, DAVID J. 1998. Measuring the Value of Knowledge: Metrics for the Knowledge-Based Business. London, England: Business Intelligence Ltd.; 1998. 156p. ISBN: 1-89808-539-0.

SKYRME, DAVID J. 1999. Knowledge Networking: Creating the Collaborative Enterprise. Boston, MA: Butterworth-Heinemann; 1999. 311p. ISBN: 0-7506-3976-8.

SKYRME, DAVID J.; AMIDON, DEBRA M. 1999. The Knowledge Agenda. In: Cortada, James W.; Woods, John A., eds. The Knowledge Management Yearbook 1999-2000. Boston, MA: Butterworth-Heinemann; 1999. 109-126. ISBN: 0-7506-7122-X.

SRIKANTAIAH, KANTI; KOENIG, MICHAEL E. D., eds. 1999. Knowledge Management for the Information Professional. Medford, NJ: Information Today, Inc. for the American Society for Information Science; 1999. 598p. ISBN: 1-57387-079-X.

STEIN, ERIC W. 1995. Organizational Memory: Review of Concepts and Recommendations for Management. International Journal of Information Management. 1995 February; 15(1): 17-32. ISSN: 0268-4012.

STEWART, THOMAS A. 1997. Intellectual Capital: The New Wealth of Organizations. New York, NY: Doubleday; 1997. 261p. ISBN: 0-385-48228-0.

STEWART, THOMAS A. 1998. Packaging What You Know. Fortune. 1998 November 9; 138(9): 253-254. ISSN: 0015-8259.

STRASSMANN, PAUL A. 1997. The Squandered Computer. New Canaan, CT: The Information Economics Press; 1997. 426p. ISBN: 0-962041-31-9.

STREATFIELD, DAVID; WILSON, THOMAS D. 1999. Deconstructing Knowledge Management. Aslib Proceedings. 1999 March; 51(3): 67-71. ISSN: 0001-253X.

STRENG, DEANNA J. 1999. Knowledge Management: An Essential Framework for Corporate Library Leadership. Advances in Library Administration and Organization. 1999; 16: 1-30. ISBN: 0-7623-0408-1.

SVEIBY, KARL ERIK. 1997. The New Organizational Wealth: Managing and Measuring Knowledge-Based Assets. San Francisco, CA: Berrett-Koehler Publishers; 1997. 220p. ISBN: 1-57675-014-0.

TAKEUCHI, HIROTAKA. 1998. Beyond Knowledge Management: Lessons from Japan. 1998 June. Available WWW: http://www.sveiby.com.au/LessonsJapan.htm.

TAPSCOTT, DON. 1996. The Digital Economy. New York, NY: McGraw-Hill; 1996. 342p. ISBN: 0-07-062200-0.

TAPSCOTT, DON. 1998. Growing Up Digital: The Rise of the Net Generation. New York, NY: McGraw-Hill; 1998. 338p. ISBN: 0-07-063361-4.

TEECE, DAVID J. 1998. Capturing Value from Knowledge Assets: The New Economy, Markets for Know-How and Intangible Assets. California Management Review. 1998 Spring; 40(3): 55-79. ISSN: 0008-1256.

TEECE, DAVID J.; NONAKA, IKUJIRO, eds. 2000. Managing Industrial Knowledge. London, England: Sage; 2000. 288p. ISBN: 0-7619-5498-8.

TFPL LIMITED. 1999. Skills for Knowledge Management: Building a Knowledge Economy. London, England: TFPL Ltd.; 1999. 120p. ISBN: 1-87088-984-3.

TODD, ROSS J. 1999. Back to Our Beginnings: Information Utilization, Bertram Brookes and the Fundamental Equation of Information Science. Information Processing & Management. 1999 December; 35: 851-870. ISSN: 0306-4573.

TOFFLER, ALVIN. 1980. The Third Wave. New York, NY: Morrow; 1980. 544p. ISBN: 0-688-03597-3.

TRYBULA, WALTER J. 1997. Data Mining and Knowledge Discovery. In: Williams, Martha E., ed. Annual Review of Information Science and Technology: Volume 32. Medford, NJ: Information Today, Inc. for the American Society for Information Science; 1997. 197-229. ISSN: 0066-4200; ISBN: 1-57387-047-1.

UNIVERSITY OF EDINBURGH. ARTIFICIAL INTELLIGENCE APPLICATIONS INSTITUTE. 1999. Knowledge Management. Available WWW: http://www.aiai.ed.ac.uk/~alm/kamlnks.html.

VON KROGH, GEORGE; ICHIJO, KAZUO; NONAKA, IKUJIRO. 2000. Enabling Knowledge Creation: How to Unlock the Mystery of Tacit Knowledge and Release the Power of Innovation. New York, NY: Oxford University Press; 2000. 292p. ISBN: 0-19-512616-5.

WAH, LOUISA. 1999a. Behind the Buzz. Management Review. 1999 April; 88(4): 16-26. ISSN: 0025-1895.

WAH, LOUISA. 1999b. Making Knowledge Stick. Management Review. 1999 May; 88(5): 24-29. ISSN: 0025-1895.

WENGER, ETIENNE. 1998. Communities of Practice: Learning, Meaning, and Identity. Cambridge, UK: Cambridge University Press; 1998. 318p. ISBN: 0-521-43017-8.

WENGER, ETIENNE; SNYDER, WILLIAM M. 2000. Communities of Practice: The Organizational Frontier. Harvard Business Review. 2000 January-February; 78(1): 139-145. ISSN: 0017-8012.

WIIG, KARL M. 1997. Integrating Intellectual Capital and Knowledge Management. Long Range Planning. 1997; 30(3): 399-405. ISSN: 0024-6301.

WIIG, KARL M. 1999. Knowledge Management: An Emerging Discipline Rooted in a Long History. Draft of Chapter 1 in: Chauvel, Daniele; Despres, Charles, eds. Knowledge Management. Available WWW: http://www.krii.com/downloads/km_emerg_discipl.pdf.

WORLD BANK. 1998. Knowledge for Development. New York, NY: Oxford University Press; 1998. 251p. ISBN: 0-19-521119-7.

ZACK, MICHAEL H. 1999a. Developing a Knowledge Strategy. California Management Review. 1999 Spring; 41(3): 125-145. ISSN: 0008-1256.

ZACK, MICHAEL H., ed. 1999b. Knowledge and Strategy. Boston, MA: Butterworth-Heinemann; 1999. 312p. ISBN: 0-7506-7088-6.

# IV

# The Profession

Section IV contains one chapter, "Library and Information Science Education in the Nineties" by Elisabeth Logan of Florida State University and Ingrid Hsieh-Yee of The Catholic University of America. Logan and Hsieh-Yee look at major aspects of library and information science (LIS) education in the decade of the 1990s in which changes took place with respect to administration, the profession, programs, curriculum, and faculty. In examining all of these the authors observe that responses to technological innovation and the expansion of the information economy, as well as a growing awareness of global and multicultural issues are among the factors that have influenced LIS education.

The authors provide an historical view of the 1980s as a prelude to discussing the context of the 1990s in which major changes to LIS education took place. The 1980s saw closings of LIS programs; integration of information science and library science education; new master's programs, concentration areas, and undergraduate programs; development of core curricula; and quality assessment. The discussion of the context of the 1990s includes: the political climate (copyright, access, and privacy issues); the social climate (international awareness and globalization and multicultural and minority issues); the technological context (changes in technology and increased collaboration); the economic context (economics and electronic publishing and electronic journals). The two final sections are a detailed presentation on the decade of change and expectations for the future.

Logan and Hsieh-Yee conclude that the field is much stronger than it was at the end of the 1980s, with most schools incorporating technology into their curricula as well as recognizing that knowledge of information technology (IT) is essential for information professionals.

# 9

# Library and Information Science Education in the Nineties

**ELISABETH LOGAN**
**Florida State University**

**INGRID HSIEH-YEE**
**The Catholic University of America**

## INTRODUCTION

Major aspects of library and information science (LIS) education during the decade of the 1990s are viewed in light of the preceding decade and within the larger social, political, economic, and technological context of the 1990s. Changes in administration, the profession, programs, curriculum, and faculty are all examined in detail. Chief among the changes identified are responses to technological innovation and the enormous expansion of the information economy, continued awareness of global and multicultural issues, recognition of the importance of a broader LIS focus and a continued support for areas of specialization, adoption of new delivery formats, expansion of the types of degree programs available, and the formation of interdisciplinary partnerships within and outside the university. Although maintaining an identity may not be easy in a world where an increasing number of workers are employed in the information sector, there is enormous opportunity for increased and new visibility for the entire field. However, there are old issues that have not been entirely resolved and new issues that have emerged during the nineties. Resolution of the relative positions of specialized training and general competence, competition for scarce resources within the university community, identification of the field's role in the larger information economy, positions on the use of remote learning technologies, and changes in the roles of faculty are all serious issues that we still face. Nevertheless, there is no question that the field is much stronger now than at the end of the eighties and that it is has developed a better sense of its own direction and purpose. By and large LIS schools are poised to make this happen.

*Annual Review of Information Science and Technology (ARIST)*, Volume 35, 2001
Martha E. Williams, Editor
Published for the American Society for Information Science and Technology (ASIST)
By Information Today, Inc., Medford, NJ

## HISTORICAL CONTEXT: A VIEW OF THE EIGHTIES

### Closings of LIS Programs

LIS education of the eighties is probably most remembered for the closings of library schools. Ten American LIS programs accredited by the American Library Association (ALA) were closed between 1982 and 1987. By the end of the eighties, LIS education seemed to be in a state of crisis (STIEG). The programs at the University of Chicago and Columbia University were closed, the program at the University of California at Berkeley was under review, and a study found nearly half of all LIS faculty planning to leave teaching before retirement (FUTAS & ZIPKOWITZ). The concerns of the field can be seen in papers, conference reports, and editorials. "Crisis," "erosion," and "survival" were often used in discussions of LIS education. There was no shortage of speculation on why LIS programs were closed, including inability to obtain outside funding, lack of university support (e.g., DYER & O'CONNOR), lower market demand and competition (e.g., ESHELMAN; GARDNER), isolation, poor quality, small size, and female-dominated programs. Drawing on data from four schools, PARIS (1988) identifies factors that contributed to their closings: isolation, ineffective leadership, inability to convince administrators of the need to have a library school on campus, turf battles with departments such as business and computer science, and poor quality as assessed by internal evaluation.

Several writers lament the irony that in the information age those preparing information professionals should find their programs under siege (e.g., HEIM). Nevertheless, many urge the field to heed the lessons of the past and turn crises into opportunities (e.g., BERRY, 1991; COUNCIL ON LIBRARY RESOURCES; GARDNER; OSTLER ET AL.; STIEG). Citing changes in technologies, markets, and users' access to information, GARDNER urges educators to revise curricula to meet the educational needs of a variety of information professionals. HEIM recommends that LIS programs strengthen their power base by addressing issues such as centrality, program excellence, external funding, alliance with the field, university policy making, and participation in university governance. STIEG examines LIS education in terms of the nature of the field, the nature of information professionals' work, the balance between education and training, the knowledge base(s) of the profession(s), the relationship between library science and information science, the role of technology, the balance between general and specialized education, and quality assurance. Her work provides a helpful framework for educators to consider the direction of LIS education for the nineties.

## Integration of Information Science
## and Library Science Education

Another major development in the eighties was the integration of information science into library school education, a move advocated by many LIS educators (e.g., BORKO; COOPER & LUNIN; HAYES). GARDNER notes that more than 80% of LIS programs incorporated "information science" or "information" in their names to reflect their expanded coverage and to help position graduates for employment in the information sector. FOSDICK learned from reviewing program catalogs that many schools offered at least two information science courses. He also found that many schools considered information science and computing technology central to information professionals. The extent of information science's penetration into the curriculum varied by school. The University of Pittsburgh offered a master's degree in information science and Syracuse University adopted an interdisciplinary approach to teaching by drawing from the fields of communication, computer science, information science, and library science (SETTEL & MARCHAND), while other schools took a more conservative approach.

## New Master's Programs, Concentration Areas,
## and Undergraduate Programs

Most schools continued to offer only one master's degree in library and information science, but several schools were innovative in creating new markets. The University of Pittsburgh began offering master's degrees in library science, information science, and telecommunications. Drexel University, Rutgers University, and Syracuse University introduced programs or concentrations in new topic areas such as information resource management and communication and information studies. Many schools began offering joint master's programs in various subjects—with law, business, or history, for example. The joint-degree programs approach was thought to help avoid isolation and attract more students (DANIEL).

Undergraduate programs in the early 1980s were part of a preprofessional program in library science. By the mid-1980s new models were adopted and most of the undergraduate programs were in information science (DANIEL). Following the model of the University of Pittsburgh, Drexel University (WOODWARD), Rutgers University (J. D. ANDERSON ET AL.), and Syracuse University (SETTEL & MARCHAND) introduced full baccalaureate programs in information systems and management. GARRISON (1987) attributes Drexel's decision to establish an undergraduate program to financial concerns over the drop in graduate enrollment, professional pressures to meet the educational needs of new information professionals, faculty interest, and the need to have closer ties to other academic units. These factors are probably the driving force behind many undergraduate programs today.

## Core, Technology, and Quality Assessment

Discussion of what should constitute the core of the LIS curriculum became more urgent in the eighties when LIS programs expanded their repertoire to meet the need for a variety of new kinds of information professionals. Several educators urged the field to be less institution-bound and to focus more on information because libraries no longer dominated the market for information services (e.g., GARDNER; *LIBRARY JOURNAL*). GARRISON (1978) advocates a core "that deals with information in the broadest sense and is not institution bound," but by the end of the 1980s there was still no consensus on this matter. KOENIG (1983) found disagreement among information specialists and educators about the importance of certain courses and concludes that there is no "necessary core in the field." WHITE & PARIS found no consensus among practitioners in academic, public, and special libraries about the core curriculum. Educators did agree that students must be knowledgeable about information technologies. The 1980s found online education reaching a mature stage (HARTER & FENICHEL; TENOPIR), and new topics being introduced, such as artificial intelligence, expert systems, database management, and data administration (e.g., M.D. COOPER; HOWDEN; KOENIG & KOCHOFF).

The AMERICAN ASSOCIATION OF LAW LIBRARIES (AALL) and Special Libraries Association (SLA) (TEES, 1986) put forward their curricula preferences and the competencies employers expect from new graduates. The American Library Association (ALA) was, however, less prescriptive. In response to practitioners' concern over the accreditation process and professional organizations' interest in taking part in accreditation, ALA proposed a project to explore possibilities for involving other associations in the accreditation process in 1984. The Association for Library and Information Science Education (ALISE), with a grant from the H. W. Wilson Foundation, held a meeting in the same year for 17 organizations to discuss the accreditation process (HORROCKS). The ALA/USDE Accreditation Project was launched at this meeting and its major recommendations were published in *Accreditation: A Way Ahead* (AMERICAN LIBRARY ASSOCIATION, COMMITTEE ON ACCREDITATION). The publication includes reports from six task groups and statements on educational outcomes by the Medical Library Association (MLA), Special Libraries Association, The Society of American Archivists (SAA), and American Society for Information Science (ASIS). The project's major recommendations include the establishment of an Inter-Association Advisory Committee on Accreditation, a continuing focus on the first professional degree, the participation of professional associations in preparing policy statements about educational requirements, and a major review of the 1972 Standards for Accreditation (TEES, 1987). It was clear that the accreditation program would change, but the cost of implementing all of the recommendations was also noted and the benefits of such effort remained to be determined (COOPER & LUNIN; TEES, 1987). In 1988 ALA's Committee on Accreditation (COA) and eight professional societies began reviewing the 1972 Standards.

## THE CONTEXT OF THE NINETIES

Schools of library and information science operate within the context of a socio-political environment and are thus the products of human enterprise, and as such are inevitably subject to the influences that accompany any social processes. In most cases it is impossible, and probably misleading, to discuss these influences as separate entities; however, for the sake of organization, we identify political, social, economic, and technological categories representing the major areas of influence on LIS schools.

### The Political Climate

The political climate of the nineties was largely supportive of some major education initiatives despite conservative attempts to abolish the Department of Education in 1995 as well as other attempts to derail educational funding. The economy continued to grow and realized the longest period of continuous growth in U.S. history. Support for information and library research came from the federal government for large projects such as the Digital Library Initiative I in 1993 and the Digital Library Initiative II in 1998. Initially projects associated with departments of computer science received the larger portion of the funding, but by the end of the decade, information and library research were awarded significant grant money. The National Science Foundation and federal agencies supported these initiatives and a large number of related workshops and planning committees. The projects and their outcomes are reported in special issues of the *Journal of the American Society for Information Science* (*JASIS*) (CHEN, 2000a, 2000b), *Communications of the ACM* (E. A. FOX ET AL.), and *Information Processing & Management* (*IP&M*) (MARCHIONINI & FOX). A BORGMAN introductory article to the *IP&M* issue offers both summary and synthesis of the digital libraries projects. Articles by LEVY & MARSHALL and WIEDERHOLD address additional important aspects. The report of The Santa Fe Planning Workshop on Distributed Knowledge Work Environments (DUGUID & ATKINS) summarizes the outcomes of digital libraries and considers the next steps.

The Text REtrieval Conferences (TREC) co-sponsored by National Institute of Standards and Technology (NIST) and Defense Advanced Research Projects Agency (DARPA) beginning in 1992 to support the infrastructure for large-scale evaluation and comparison of text retrieval methods was another important federally supported project of the nineties. A summary overview of TREC workshops is offered by HARMAN of NIST, but the most recent reports from TREC–6 are reported in a special issue of *IP&M* (VOORHEES) that includes articles by SMEATON, SPARCK JONES, and VOORHEES & HARMAN.

The Clinton Administration's National Information Infrastructure (NII) legislation in 1994 represented a somewhat different type of political support which, although not specifically targeted to education or LIS schools, supported the growth of the Internet and the information economy and defined the crucial role of information in the latter half of the nineties. A GORE article provides an early view of the justification for a high-speed network, while a special topic issue of *JASIS* on the National Information Infrastructure (FLETCHER & BERTOT) gives a view from the decade's end as it outlines considerations for building and implementing the NII and discusses policy issues. PRESS offers a discussion of the historical role of the federal government in Internet development. For a more current view, history and news of INTERNET2 is available on the Web. The continued development and popularity of the Internet and World Wide Web browsers such as Mosaic in 1991 and Netscape in 1995 probably had the single greatest impact on most phases of U.S. life in the last 20 years. BERGHEL (1998) provides a short summary of the development of Web browsers.

## Copyright, Access, and Privacy

Among other aspects of the Internet's impact is the need for additional legislation addressing issues of copyright, access, and privacy associated with the proliferation of electronic information. SAMUELSON (1994; 1995; 1996; 1998) contributes a regular column, "Legally Speaking," to *Communications of the ACM* in which she explores many of these issues. BOYCE addresses copyright's application to scholarly work, and a series of short articles in two issues of the *Bulletin of the American Society for Information Science* (*BULLETIN OF THE AMERICAN SOCIETY FOR INFORMATION SCIENCE*; FLOOD), discuss and update the issue of privacy. BRANSCOMB discusses the evolution of common law applied to issues of the electronic frontier, and LAUDON makes a strong case for individual control of personal data. LOHR (1999) notes the conflict of privacy and law in some of the newer Internet technologies, and SHAPIRO & VARIAN analyze some of the marketing concerns associated with the Internet and copyright legislation.

## The Social Climate

*International awareness and globalization.* Increased international awareness and a globalization of information issues, made possible largely through technological advances in electronic information transfer, expanded the sphere within which society in general and LIS schools in particular operated in the nineties. A recent article in the *Chronicle of Higher Education* details the increased numbers of international members of U.S. scholarly societies (MCMURTRIE). Although international librarianship is nothing new, issues of international LIS education pervade the associated literature of the nineties. FID has been active since 1895 and IFLA continues to address multiple issues of library and information science education. The column "International Library Education" began in the *Journal of Education for Library and Information Science (JELIS)* in 1981 and continues to be a regular feature of this journal. In *JELIS*, articles with an international focus were published more often than any other single topic during 1990 to 1999 (17 times compared with the next most frequent at 14). Articles discussing LIS education in many countries appear during the decade and include Slovenia (MARINKO), Brazil (ANTONIO & BALBY), Nigeria (NWEKE), and Morocco (MOKHTARI), among many others.

International articles appear in a number of other journals as well and include Cuba (JOHNSON), Taiwan (LU), Wales (STOKER, 1996, 1997), Philippines (VALLEJO), and Scotland (HERRING). Many of these articles are descriptive only and detail LIS education in a certain country, but others address specific issues in an international context: recent developments in LIS education in the UK (WHITBECK); distance education in Asia and the Pacific Rim (SACCHANAND), Estonia (VIRKUS) and Australia (MILLS); continuing education in Canada (MORTON); professional development in the UK (HAMILTON); and internships for professional education in Australia (ALDERMAN & MILNE). Still others describe international aspects of a broader information education such as information technology security in Sweden (YNGSTROM); information systems teaching in Singapore (RAMAN & YAP); and groupware and the LIS process in Scotland (DAVENPORT).

In ASIS, one of the most active special-interest groups continues to be International Information Issues (SIG/III) and in the association journal, *JASIS*, international board members, authors, and issues are common. *IP&M*, with an editorial board made up of about half international authors, provides an even greater forum for international issues.

*Multicultural and minority issues.* Closely related to the increased importance of international issues in the nineties was an increased concern for multicultural and minority issues in the social arena. The U.S. population continued to become more international as people from many countries sought employment, asylum, or citizenship. Although this tended to be concentrated in some states, the impact was felt in LIS schools because society expected all educational programs to demonstrate efforts toward increasing multiculturalism and diversity, including recruitment of students from minority groups (KNOWLES & JOLIVET). Although largely a product of the 1970s and 1980s, multiculturalism concerns continue to be a major focus within the profession. The COA Standards for Accreditation of Master's Programs in Library and Information Studies, adopted in 1992 by the AMERICAN LIBRARY ASSOCIATION, includes multiculturalism and diversity standards in guidelines for Mission, Goals, and Objectives and for Curriculum. Articles in the literature attest to a growing concern for multicultural aspects of LIS education as well. *JELIS* in the 1990s published articles on the topic of multicultural concerns in library education from the efforts of an ALISE special-interest group for ethnic, multicultural, and humanities concerns (BELAY; FREIBAND). The *Journal of Multicultural Librarianship* is of course devoted to these specific issues (JOSEY, 1990, 1991). Cultural diversity is also observed in the types of programs and curricula offered by a number of the LIS schools as well as in student populations.

## The Technological Context

*Changes in technology.* Changes in technology meant new ways of doing business and of offering educational opportunities. The Internet, the Web, and other media technology such as interactive television (ITV) made it possible to offer classes and degrees in distance or distributed learning environments. Articles appearing recently in the *Chronicle of Higher Education* (CARNEVALE, 2000b; MCCOLLUM) attest to broad areas of support for education via new technology. The latest figures for information technology use in higher education can be found at the CAMPUS COMPUTING PROJECT Web site. In LIS education there were many instances of new formats promoting wider audiences (HEINRICH; WALLING) and new educational cooperation (CHEPESIUK, 1998; ROPER ET AL.). These choices broadened the appeal of LIS programs to a larger group of potential students with wider areas of interest, which in turn may have led to a redesign of courses and curricula. A recent National Research Council study by the COMMITTEE ON WORKFORCE NEEDS IN INFORMATION TECHNOLOGY addresses the serious problem of an underqualified workforce in information technology (IT).

Many LIS schools found it expedient to broaden their programs beyond the more traditional areas typically found in programs of the seventies and eighties for reasons including an increasing focus on information-related business, the iteration of concerns regarding an information society, and availability of money from both government agencies and the business community to support information-related development. Nevertheless, many questioned or opposed these changes. Among them are BAKER in his notorious article in The *New Yorker*, CRAWFORD, and CROWLEY (1999b). But for the most part, LIS schools broadened their programs, changed curricula, and introduced new degrees in order to supply the eager market for information workers, and it appeared that professionals in the workplace were recognizing the challenge as well. CHEPESIUK (1999) and MURPHY are only two of many who write on this topic. The Kellogg-ALISE Information Professions and Education Reform (KALIPER) Project, funded by the Kellogg Foundation, analyzed 33 LIS schools in 1998 and 1999. *The KALIPER Report* (KALIPER ADVISORY COMMITTEE) mentions the broadening of curricula and programs of LIS schools to address "broad-based information environments that go beyond traditional library settings" (p. 1).

*Connection and collaboration.* Social influences reflected changes in technology and emphasized new ways of connecting and collaborating; new virtual communities arose around the Internet and its chat rooms. Collaboration among research teams with little or no geography in common, and networking arrangements for leisure and work, led to a realization on the part of LIS schools that this is an important aspect of information studies. A special issue of *JASIS*, "Social Informatics in Information Science" (KLING ET AL.), contains articles on trends in information employment (MARTIN), collaborative information retrieval (KARAMUFTUOGLU), and information exchange in a networked organization (HAYTHORNTHWAITE & WELLMAN). LIS schools themselves responded with program initiatives and unique collaborative arrangements (DAVENPORT; LAVAGNINO ET AL.; ROPER ET AL.; SCEPANSKI & VON WAHLDE). Of course none of the challenges and few of the rewards from these issues would have existed without the overwhelming influences of information technology. The rapid rise of technological development in information areas was an integral part of the political, economic, and social environments of the nineties; it is almost impossible to divorce any description of the nineties educational environment from considerations of technology. H. BRODY (1996) notes that "email projects never sleep; scientists on one side of the world can send off their results so their collaborators on the other side can immediately work with the information" (p. 45).

The Internet and World Wide Web, made possible by faster, smaller, more powerful computers, and the climate of open environments for information access within which the Internet developed, played a major role in life in the nineties (C. ANDERSON; LYNCH; PETERS). The importance of information technology for all phases of society cannot be overemphasized. Estimates of Internet use throughout the nineties continued to leap over those of previous years. In 1996, the number of U.S. households with Internet access was said to be 14.7 million, with an estimated 35 million Internet users (R. FOX). In 1998 the estimate was 58 million online users with a prediction that by 2002 global use would grow to 142 million people (MEEKS). In February 2000, the estimate was that by 2004, U.S. households with Internet access would grow from 46.5 million to 90 million (CYBERATLAS).

Technology changed the face of information and its transfer and use. LAUREL and DAGGATT explore some of the more extreme views of the time. "Survey: Telecommunications" appears as an entire section in an issue of The Economist in 1995 (ECONOMIST) and serves as an apt example of the many articles flooding the popular literature. The growth of the economy's information sector and the concomitant need for information workers placed LIS schools in an enviable but difficult position. Many LIS schools debated the question of change in focus, size, content, and direction of their programs (CRAWFORD; CROWLEY, 1999a; VAN HOUSE). They questioned the extent to which familiar skills of information handling translate into newer skills for the new environment and, given limited resources, what is an appropriate balance between the old and the new.

## The Economic Context

*Economics.* The economic context of the nineties cannot be separated from the political, social, or technical contexts (A. HARMON). The interrelationships were intense and intertwined; developments in one context invariably affected the others. The extent to which the U.S. economy was affected by technology in the nineties was no longer an issue because in many arenas they were viewed as a single concept (KING). The popularity and adoption of Web-based interchange altered the face of both U.S. business (MERRILL LYNCH) and international business (RAI ET AL.). New Internet companies and extensions of existing companies in business to business, e-commerce, and Web advertising led to an information economy with a need for information workers at many levels (CONHAIM; QUINT). This in turn created new opportunities for LIS schools and their graduates, especially in some of the nontraditional areas, and raised the issue of how to maintain a professional identity as new terminology invaded the information field. Terms such as "knowledge management" and "metadata" became buzzwords in the late nineties.

The U.S. economy was booming, corporate and government money was available for education, and there was a new emphasis on business/education partnerships rather than the traditional reliance on state or federal assistance alone. This too provided opportunities for schools including those in LIS, but also meant an emphasis on research and development results that benefited contributing businesses (GWYNNE). This was certainly true to a greater extent in the basic sciences and medicine, but it had a potential effect on all higher education (BÉRUBÉ; HENDERSON). Pressures on colleges and universities to run more efficient operations filtered down to the individual units. In some LIS schools this meant larger classes, more reliance on adjunct professors, and more creative ways of using scarce resources (SHELDON). Distance and distributed learning, undergraduate courses and programs, summer seminars, certificate classes, and continuing education in various formats were ways in which LIS schools dealt with these issues (KALIPER ADVISORY COMMITTEE).

*Electronic publishing and electronic journals.* Another important economic/technological/political issue of the nineties was the impact of electronic publishing and electronic journals. New ways to publish and retrieve information continued to raise new issues concerning copyright protection and information privacy as well as questions of peer review for publication in electronic journals. HERKERT & CARTWRIGHT draw attention to social and ethical issues of information technology and cite several important Websites, journals, and conferences that deal with these issues. With the potential of Web publication, questions of copyright clearance are debated in traditional journals such as *JASIS, JELIS,* and *IP&M.* BAILEY maintains a Website devoted to scholarly electronic publication. For LIS school faculty, copyright issues translate into questions of faculty publication as well as questions of Web access and intellectual ownership (BENNION; BERGHEL, 1999; GRIMWADE; OLSEN, 1999; PEEK, 1997, 1998; STIX; WHITMAN ET AL.). Web access issues affect students as well, especially those who participate in distance learning. A special issue of *JASIS,* "Perspectives on Copyright and Fair-Use Guidelines for Education and Libraries" (CREWS & BUTTLER), contains many articles that specifically address educational aspects of these issues (DAY; FRAZIER; GASAWAY; LEVERING).

In summary, the nineties environment in which LIS schools operated was one of increasing technological sophistication with opportunities and challenges for all participants. The new technology im-
pacted and was affected by political issues of globalization and cultural diversity, and by regulations concerning information transfer
and privacy protection. Social and economic issues of an information
economy were many and complex. LIS schools responded to many of
these pressures by upgrading technology and curricula to keep pace
with changes, addressing issues related to new digital information
formats, finding and retaining a new professional identity in a competitive information economy (DALRYMPLE; KALIPER ADVISORY
COMMITTEE), responding to new funding structures, recognizing
global information issues and questions of diversity and
multiculturalism, and using new technology to broaden the appeal of
LIS programs while retaining a commitment to traditional professional
values (*AMERICAN LIBRARIES*).

## A DECADE OF CHANGE
### Administration

*The university climate.*   The decade of the nineties witnessed some
interesting changes in the university climate and the associated role of
LIS schools within the university (DUDERSTADT; GWYNNE). STIEG
paints a picture of LIS schools and other professional schools as being
out of sync with the intellectual goals of scholarship and standards of
the hard sciences that drive the values of most university administrations. Further, they often lack wealthy alumni or ties to affluent business connections that contribute significant dollars to the university
and the school. SHELDON quotes Ashworth, who says that fundamental changes are inevitable with competition for scarce university funds
and that higher education cannot hope to do well by relying on the
same strategies and arguments used in the past. She notes that funding
sources now expect specific goals with measurable outcomes and claims
that "less than 30% of support for public universities comes from state
legislatures" (pp. 65-66). Thus most schools must look to external funding for research grants and scholarship aid. Among other efforts, LIS
schools are often urged to take a more proactive position toward consolidation with other campus units in order to obtain a greater university presence and perhaps additional funding. By the early nineties,
according to Stieg, Rutgers, UCLA, Kentucky, Berkeley, and Western
Ontario all formed alliances with other university units. Since then, a
number of additional schools formed collaborative arrangements within
their universities. The Website of the ASSOCIATION FOR LIBRARY
AND INFORMATION SCIENCE EDUCATION currently lists Alabama,

Missouri, and North Carolina at Greensboro as allied with or part of an associated program.

*A new information economy.*    While the role of professional schools within the university context may still remain suspect in the eyes of university administrations, the changing climate of an information economy and the increasing opportunities for information profession-als in the nineties led to increased visibility for many LIS schools within the university and the economy. A theoretical look at the position of LIS schools caught in the tension between these two forces is found in "The Panda Syndrome" (VAN HOUSE & SUTTON) and "The Panda Syn-drome II" (S. A. SUTTON, 1999). In many cases, the schools responded by restructuring their programs, broadening their focus, creating cor-porate partnerships for funding and internships, and forming collabo-rative bonds with other units on campus. A number of authors advo-cate and document the kinds of changes thought to be important to meet new challenges to the profession. AULD (1990), AZAR, CHEPESIUK (1996), and MARCUM all speak of transforming the pro-fession and/or the professionals. Name changes, undergraduate pro-grams, and new or revised courses with broader appeal are all men-tioned as necessary components of change and as ways to present new professional skills for new information positions.

LIS education via distance or distributed modes of learning emerged as another way to expand the appeal of LIS schools in the information community. Not only did it open doors for potential students unable to travel to a local school site, but it also inevitably introduced a level of technology most students found both appealing  and useful. Many studies and articles describe and argue for and against the introduction of this type of learning, and students speak both for and against it (COLEMAN; LIEBSCHER & MCCAFFREY; MYSZKOWSKI; SNYDER & FOX; TURNER). A special issue of *JASIS* on distance education (BESSER & DONAHUE) contains articles by BARRON, BESSER, FAULHABER, S. A. SUTTON (1996b), among others.

Among findings mentioned in *The KALIPER Report* (PETTIGREW & DURRANCE) are schools that changed their marketing position to capture new and more highly paid information jobs. Some respon-dents spoke of the impact employers exerted on their program, specifi-cally the business, industry, and government employment areas. Oth-ers indicated strategic partnerships with other units that might open new doors, hiring of faculty who conducted research in nonlibrary settings, and recruitment of students with diverse academic, cultural, and work backgrounds who were interested in varied information environments. Some authors also address the question of recruitment of diverse student populations (CVELJO; KNOWLES & JOLIVET; C. WATKINS).

## The Profession

*Changing information environments.* Several forces affected the information professions in the 1990s. The move from print to electronic
media changed how people communicated, exchanged knowledge,
and accessed information. Resources were increasingly dynamic and
multimedia, collections and services were distributed and available
globally, formal and informal information sources were increasingly
integrated, users desired access to source objects instead of metadata,
and personalized consulting services became more important. These
changes influenced library services, information system development,
and information organization (KOENIG, 1993; MALINCONICO, 1993;
SPECIAL LIBRARIES ASSOCIATION ET AL.; S. A. SUTTON, 1996a;
YOUNG). Information technology also blurred the boundary between
LIS, communications, computer science, and other similar disciplines
(KOENIG, 1993; YOUNG). Academic libraries were affected by financial pressures that affected higher education institutions (F. E. BRODY),
and the corporate environment became more competitive and stressed
accountability.

In response to changes in society and technology, the library profession increased its expectations of graduates' competencies in information technology, and LIS programs expanded their scope to stimulate
growth. Many LIS programs not only offered instruction in different
formats to meet the needs of a more diverse student body, but also
added master's degrees in new subjects and new undergraduate degrees to capture new sectors of the information industry (KALIPER
ADVISORY COMMITTEE).

The field continued to struggle with the library focus; to ask whether
LIS programs should continue to focus on activities central to libraries
and what knowledge and skills information professionals should possess to function effectively in the digital age. The cultural and educational roles of libraries were recognized by educators and the public
(BENTON FOUNDATION; *LIBRARY JOURNAL*). While some believed
strongly that libraries are a valuable market that LIS programs ignore at
their peril (M. GORMAN; *LIBRARY JOURNAL*), others urged the inclusion of other information contexts (G. E. GORMAN; KOENIG, 1993).
Recognizing that libraries are no longer the dominant information service provider, some educators advocated curricula that are not institution bound (MCCLURE & HERT). STIEG observes that "librarians have
ceased to identify themselves with the building in which they labor" (p.
3). MALINCONICO (1993) urges educators to design curricula beyond
the library scenario, and GRIFFITHS & KING stress the need to articulate the purposes and value of the field to other academic units on
campus and to develop better appreciation for "the strategic significance of information at a campus, an institution, or in a society"

*(LIBRARY JOURNAL,* p. 61). G. E. GORMAN asserts that professional values will remain largely the same in the future, professional parameters such as information retrieval and bibliographic control will change at a faster pace, and information technology will bring about rapid changes, and he urges educators to revise LIS programs accordingly.

*The KALIPER Report* overview notes that the LIS programs investigated became responsive to market demands beyond those of libraries and that core course revisions indicate a shift in focus away from traditional library institutions. This included a shift to the organization and management of digital information. The researchers also found that employers, especially those in the business, industry, and government environments, influenced LIS programs. Some schools formed strategic partnerships with other academic units or government agencies, hired faculty whose research was not limited to library settings, and recruited students with diverse academic background and work experience (PETTIGREW & DURRANCE).

*Professional competencies and curriculum implications.* The competencies required of LIS graduates have received much attention from researchers. *New Directions in Library and Information Science Education* (GRIFFITHS & KING) was one of the major studies of competencies in the 1980s and presented competencies (defined as knowledge, skills, and attitudes) by work setting (type of library), functions performed (cataloger), and by professional experience (new or senior librarian). Competencies common to all work environments and those common to all types of librarians were also presented. The study was heavily criticized by educators for its methodology (WHITE) and researchers continued to investigate competencies from their chosen perspective. Several educators have advocated revision of curricula to ensure that important competencies are covered in LIS programs (BUTTLAR & DU MONT; WOODSWORTH & LESTER). The challenge in identifying competencies is that practitioners' perception of competencies varies by their type of library (BUTTLAR & DU MONT; WHITE & PARIS) and that information specialists, managers, and educators disagree about the relative importance of courses (KOENIG, 1983). As electronic communication and computing technologies become pervasive, however, the search for new competencies in the digital environment has intensified.

The issue of competencies can be examined from several perspectives—practitioners, employers, professional societies, recent graduates, educators, and any other stakeholders. Researchers have analyzed job announcements to identify competencies specified by potential employers (HILL; SCHLESSINGER ET AL.; XU; ZHOU, 1994). Employers in corporate environments specified the qualities and skills they expect from LIS graduates (BUTCHER; TCHOBANOFF & PRICE), alumni of one school were asked to rank a set of competencies (BUTTLAR & DU

MONT), and program catalogs were analyzed for core courses and their subject areas (SCHLESSINGER ET AL.). Some researchers focused on the competencies needed in selected functions, for instance, computer skills required of catalogers and reference librarians (XU). Others limited their analysis to a particular type of library: computer-related qualifications in academic libraries (ZHOU, 1996) or a set of competencies in a research library environment (WOODSWORTH & LESTER). Many studies produced lists of similar competencies, including interpersonal skills, management skills, knowledge of technology, knowledge of information sources, and communication skills.

Professional associations have also taken part in the discussion of competency requirements and curricula preferences. The SPECIAL LIBRARIES ASSOCIATION (SLA) (1991) published four papers on competencies required by different sizes of special libraries. The MEDICAL LIBRARY ASSOCIATION (MLA) issued an educational policy statement, *Platform for Change*, that stresses lifelong learning, describes strategies for information professionals in health-related environments to keep up with changes, and provides specific guidelines for graduate programs in health sciences librarianship. In 1997 the SPECIAL LIBRARIES ASSOCIATION presented a report on personal and professional competencies for special librarians, *Competencies for Special Librarians of the 21st Century*. The competencies cover five key areas: vision, service, networks, professional growth, and political acumen. These competencies reflect common purposes among information professionals (GREALY & GREENMAN).

To determine whether LIS education provided students the knowledge and skills necessary for the new century and to identify future educational needs of the profession that could be met by continuing education programs from professional associations, SLA, in collaboration with ALISE and MLA, surveyed deans and administrators of LIS programs around the world (SPECIAL LIBRARIES ASSOCIATION ET AL.). The study had a 75 percent response rate among ALA-accredited American programs and 22 percent among international schools, but only the ALA schools' responses were fully analyzed. It found that, when grouped by essential competency areas, courses in American LIS programs covered six areas: information resources (23%), information management (20%), information access (19%), information systems and technology (18%), research (10%), and information policy (10%). Further analysis found that 17% of courses were core courses, but more than 25% of the programs did not require courses in information systems and technology, research, or information policy.

The AMERICAN ASSOCIATION OF SCHOOL LIBRARIANS & ASSOCIATION FOR EDUCATIONAL COMMUNICATIONS AND TECHNOLOGY (AASL and AECT) published *Information Power* in

1988 to guide curriculum revision of school library media programs. AASL guidelines for preparing school library specialists were adopted by the National Council for Accreditation of Teacher Education (NCATE) and published as *Curriculum Folio Guidelines for the NCATE Review Process* (AMERICAN ASSOCIATION OF SCHOOL LIBRARANS). These guidelines are revised every five years. The publication includes 67 professional competency statements covering ten major areas such as professionalism, communication, instructional leadership, and access. In addition, states issued their own certification standards for school media specialists. PERRITT (1992; 1994) reports that states tended to pay more attention to media specialists' roles as teachers and instructional technologists and to specify requirements of technology-related skills and the application of technologies in school instructional programs.

The SOCIETY OF AMERICAN ARCHIVISTS (SAA) (1994) also issued *Guidelines for the Development of a Curriculum for a Master of Archival Studies Degree* that defines the body of knowledge a graduate archival education program should provide. Focusing on library school education in California, the CALIFORNIA LIBRARY ASSOCIATION (CLA) (1995) issued a report, *Future Directions for the Library Profession and Its Education*, that identifies core areas of library expertise and practice and predicts likely changes to the profession. In response to this report, the Library Education and Recruitment Committee of CLA developed a list of core competencies that specifies the requisite knowledge, skills, attitudes, and values for providing library and information services (CALIFORNIA LIBRARY ASSOCIATION, 1997).

The proliferation of lists of core competencies reflects a strong interest in identifying skills and knowledge essential to the field. But the validity and utility of such lists are not without question. Some researchers obtained data from a small number of practitioners in a particular environment or graduates from a particular school, some collected opinions from practitioners and educators, while others drew on the wisdom of committees. In addition, very few researchers sought input from non-librarians. As a result, the lists are of varying degrees of validity, and not all of them can be generalized to the entire library and information field. Furthermore, many researchers strove to be comprehensive and ended up with long lists of competencies that are difficult for LIS programs to teach. Nevertheless, lists from SLA and CLA provide useful frameworks for reviewing LIS education programs, and some guidelines such as those developed by AASL and SAA are specific and helpful.

Although the 1992 ALA standards were approved and implemented to improve the accreditation process, practitioners alarmed by some ALA-accredited schools' shift away from librarianship continued to voice concerns about the accreditation process and how LIS education was provided. The concerns were so serious that the ALA decided to hold a summit on library education in spring 1999. ALA President Ann K. Symons explained that the Congress on Professional Education in 1999 was the first of a longer series of discussions and would focus on "the initial preparation of librarians, i.e. ALA accredited programs, NCATE programs" and other related issues such as "the 'L' word, perceived omission of core competencies in the field of librarianship, perceived lack of preparation to serve particular groups" (AMERICAN LIBRARY ASSOCIATION, 2000). The Congress had working groups on higher education, library and information science education, and the profession. Each group invited papers in its area and posted the papers and related readings prior to the Congress. More than 100 national and international LIS educators and professionals convened in Washington, D.C. to seek consensus on the values and core competencies of the professional and to develop strategies to address various issues.

The final report and recommendations of the Congress are available online at the American Library Association Website. Recommendations identify six topic areas: (1) core values and competencies for the profession, (2) accreditation, (3) roles of educators and employers in continuing education and mentoring, (4) librarianship as a 21st-century profession, (5) dialogue between educators and practitioners, and (6) diversity. The Congress recommended providing sessions on the accreditation process at ALA chapter conferences to get more practitioners involved in the effort. Whether these recommendations are suitable for the broad spectrum of information professionals or not will probably continue to be debated for some time.

After the Congress, the AMERICAN LIBRARY ASSOCIATION, CORE VALUES TASK FORCE developed a concise statement on core values shared by all types of librarians and other information professionals to help orient students to the profession, guide professionals in carrying out their responsibilities, and help the media and the public understand the values and principles of the library-oriented profession. The fifth draft has eight parts: (1) the connection of people to ideas; (2) unfettered access to ideas; (3) learning in all of its contexts; (4) respect for the individual person; (5) freedom for all people to form, to hold, and to express their own beliefs; (6) preservation of the human record; (7) professionalism in service; and (8) partnerships to advance these values. These are important values for librarians, but it should be noted that many information professions exist and not all information professionals may share these core values.

In fall 2000, the AMERICAN LIBRARY ASSOCIATION (2000) held a second Congress, in Chicago, that focused on continuing education.

## Programs

*Some resolution of old conflicts.* Although many of the old controversies over LIS programs and their focus remain, at least a few seemed on the way toward resolution in the nineties. The perennial debates over theory versus practice continued, although the first ALA Congress on Profession Education (AMERICAN LIBRARY ASSOCIATION, 2000) drafted a set of goals for LIS education that made progress toward a unified statement. Likewise, the long-term discussion of the relative roles of information science and library science school programs that was so evident in the eighties seems to be somewhat resolved, although not without debate (M. GORMAN). Views and definitions of library science and information science and their places relative to each other are found in STIEG. She comments: "Much criticized in the 1960s and 1970s for their failure to integrate information science into their curricula, library schools have now done so. This integration has taken place at all levels" (p. 117).

SMITH (1998a) reports that from just a few information science courses available in some schools in the sixties, by the nineties, most LIS schools offered programs that integrated information science with library science within the master's degree. At the time of writing, Smith says that Indiana, Michigan, and Pittsburgh offered separate IS degrees and that some schools offered the option of a post-master's degree in information science. Still others had doctoral programs in information science or related degrees: Pittsburgh, SUNY Albany, University of North Texas (UNT), Syracuse, and Hawaii. By 1996 only one of the accredited LIS schools in the U.S. remained a school of library science: most were called "library and information studies" or "library and information science," and five omitted the word "library" altogether. In 2000, according to the ASSOCIATION FOR LIBRARY AND INFORMATION SCIENCE EDUCATION Website, Clarion remains the only School of Library Science out of 56 accredited schools. Ten schools have no mention of "library," and the remainder have various combinations of "information studies" or "information science" with "library."

*Broadened program scope.* Within the field, the trend for programs in the nineties continued to be toward a broader scope. The COA Standards for Accreditation of Master's Programs in Library and Information Studies, adopted in 1992 by the AMERICAN LIBRARY ASSOCIATION, defines the field as including "recordable information and knowledge and the services and technologies to facilitate their management and use" (p. 2), but omits any reference to where or how this is to take place. Early in the decade a number of authors were calling for change largely in terms of meeting new technology requirements, but also in terms of programs with a broader perspective (CEPPOS; FORGIONNE; LESTER; MALINCONICO, 1992; SCHLESSINGER ET AL.; SINEATH;

VON DRAN, 1990). Later in the decade authors continued to write of the need for change (BUCKLAND; GALVIN; LANCASTER; MARCUM; MILLER; OLSGAARD & ROPER; PEMBERTON & NUGENT; QUATTROCCHI). *The KALIPER Report* (KALIPER ADVISORY COMMITTEE) states that "LIS schools are . . . addressing broad-based information environments and information problems in addition to library-specific operations" (p. 1).

*Interdisciplinary initiatives.* The broadened scope of LIS programs is also apparent in the increased number of interdisciplinary initiatives. These mergers may be due in large part to pressures from the economy and the larger university setting as discussed above, but also reflect the changing market for graduates with information skills that extends well beyond traditional library or information settings. Schools with interdisciplinary programs and affiliations in 2000 include UCLA (education), Alabama (communication), SUNY Buffalo (communication), SUNY Albany (public administration), Rutgers (communication), and Western Ontario (journalism). Still others offer joint degrees with other campus units: UCLA (joint MLIS/MBA from School of Management), Catholic University (joint MS with Law, History, Musicology, etc.), Dalhousie (joint MLIS/LLB from Law and proposed joint programs with Business Administration and Public Administration), Drexel (joint MSSE with Engineering and Arts and Sciences), Pittsburgh (joint MS with Public and International Affairs), Michigan (joint MSI/MBA, MSI/MPP, MSI/JD), and Syracuse (Law). UNT and SUNY Albany have joint doctorates with other campus units and Pittsburgh has dual degrees with the Center for Biomedical Informatics and doctorates in partnership with computer science, communications, and business. It appears that warnings of BERRY (1987) and others have not gone unheeded. Authors exploring the importance of cross-disciplinary education in LIS include CROWLEY (1999b), ETTINGER, KATZER, PARIS (1990a), and PEMBERTON & PRENTICE.

*Extended degree programs.* As part of the trend toward broadening the appeal of LIS programs, schools extended the number and scope of degree programs. Undergraduate degrees and minors in related information fields currently are offered at several accredited LIS schools, with others considering their implementation. Some, such as the University of Pittsburgh, Syracuse, and Drexel have had undergraduate degree programs since the 1980s. For others, such as Florida State University, University of Wisconsin-Milwaukee, Long Island University, University of Washington, and SUNY Albany, undergraduate programs are a phenomenon of the 1990s. Most schools state clearly that these are not library degrees, preferring to support the graduate MLS as the entry-level professional degree. LARGE examines undergraduate programs in North America specifically in some specialized areas,

SHERRON and SHERRON & LANDRY describe the development of an undergraduate program created in response to a demand for workers with information skills, WAGNER surveys undergraduate LIS programs in Australia, MCGARRY takes a retrospective look at undergraduate education, CARROLL examines undergraduate education in LIS schools and anticipates a revitalization of undergraduate programs, and B. SUTTON describes an undergraduate course with a multidisciplinary approach for teaching scientific and technical knowledge dissemination.

Responding to the influences of the expanding market and the wider scope of the field itself, as well as economic or market pressures exerted on the university, LIS schools throughout the nineties continued to investigate undergraduate degrees as a viable means of attracting students into the field, building a larger presence within the university, and playing a more visible role in the information economy. Offering courses, and, in some cases, entire programs in alternate formats such as ITV and the Web is another means by which schools sought to build larger constituencies (ROWAN UNIVERSITY). Discussed in greater detail in the section on curriculum below, this trend may prove to have a substantial impact on many aspects of LIS education.

*Continuing education.* Continuing education programs for professionals and paraprofessionals remained important throughout the 1990s. Many of these programs focused on information technology as both delivery mechanism and content. The Winter 1998 issue of *Library Trends* is devoted to "The Roles of Professionals, Paraprofessionals, and Nonprofessionals: a View from the Academy" and contains articles by EASUN, FROEHLICH (1998), HOWARTH, and WILSON & HERMANSON, among others. Other articles discussing the relative role of paraprofessional education include CRONIN ET AL., DAVIDSON-ARNOTT & KAY, OBERG, RUSSELL, and WINTER. The discussions reflect an awareness of new roles for professional and paraprofessional alike, such as the importance of the paraprofessional's role as guide to electronic information sources. STIEG and WOODSWORTH ET AL. both consider this topic worthy of inclusion in their books. The continuing education column in *JELIS* provides current and topical discussions of many pertinent issues (KEVIL; LIEBI; OKEY ET AL.; VARLEJS; WEINGAND, 1990, 1996, 1998; WOOLLS). Others contribute comments on more specialized aspects of continuing education such as the important role played by newer alternate delivery mechanisms such as the Web: ABELS ET AL. propose an alternative educational model, SIEVERT ET AL. suggest information technology as a format, and PRYOR and WEINGAND (1995) discuss evaluation of continuing education programs.

## Curriculum

*Programs with wider appeal.*    Responding to expressions of public
sentiment of the nineties that libraries may not be institutions on the
cutting edge of information technology and not the place to find the
latest technology (BALES; BENTON FOUNDATION), and to expanding markets for graduates with broad information skills, LIS schools
have been moving toward programs with wider appeal and curricula
that reflect these changes (DALRYMPLE). Pleas for responding to changing information professional roles come from BILLINGTON, BROWN,
and MARFLEET & KELLY, among others. However, despite increased
opportunities for LIS graduates, there remains a spectre of sexism
within the larger workplace (CNUDDE ET AL.; HILDENBRAND, 1999;
LAPLANTE), and within the curriculum itself (CARMICHAEL &
SHONTZ; HANNIGAN). *The KALIPER Report* (KALIPER ADVISORY
COMMITTEE) identifies six major curriculum trends: (1) LIS curricula
are addressing broad-based information environments and information problems, (2) LIS curricula contain a unique core of courses that are
primarily user-centered, (3) LIS schools are increasing investments and
infusion of information technology into curricula, (4) LIS programs are
offering students greater flexibility in tailoring their programs, (5) LIS
schools are offering instruction in different formats, and (6) LIS schools
are expanding their programs by offering degrees at multiple levels.
Interpretations of these trends may vary, but it is clear that changes are
evident in the curricula of many schools. The report also notes new
curriculum designs that reflect a transfer of library-based skills to broader
applications. "Cataloging" became "representing, organizing, and storing information" at the University of Toronto, and "organization of
recorded knowledge" became "information structures" at the University of Maryland. Van House and Sutton write more broadly on many
of these changes in their two Panda Syndrome articles (S.A. SUTTON,
1999; VAN HOUSE & SUTTON).

Commentary on curriculum changes is by no means confined to the
late nineties. STIEG notes curricular changes that presage many of
those reported more recently. ROBBINS addresses curricular reform in
terms of the inevitable "marriage" between libraries and information
science. Many others contribute to this discussion as well (LANCASTER;
MARCUM; SCHLESSINGER ET AL.; SINEATH). In some instances the
expansion of the program meant a re-alignment of the core where
courses with a narrower focus were moved to elective status. *The
KALIPER Report* states that UCLA is only one example of where this
was done (PETTIGREW & DURRANCE). New courses were designed
to address information problems on a broader scale as well: licensing,
legal issues, information product marketing, entrepreneurship, information consulting, and systems design were added by schools in the

study group. Core competencies, however, remained an issue on several fronts (JENG; NICHOLS ET AL.; ROBBINS). Others write about curricular change in general terms (GROVER ET AL.; MCINNIS; OSTLER & DAHLIN; B. T. WATKINS) or in more specific terms (LUCKER; TAYLOR; TOTTEN & KEYS). It is important to note that these discussions continue into 2000 with no sign of closure.

*Increased interdisciplinarity.*   The increased interdisciplinarity observed in LIS programs in terms of departmental mergers, joint faculty appointments and hires from fields outside the traditional LIS fields had a major impact on the types of courses being offered and on the flavor of school curricula. *The KALIPER Report* lists a number of schools in which changes to curricula were being made, and various authors discuss these changes in both general and specific applications. CVELJO, ETTINGER, HOLLAND, NUNAMAKER ET AL., SINEATH, and VON DRAN (1997) all address more general areas of interdisciplinarity. Others speak to the importance of creating an interdisciplinary approach to specific information-related areas such as science and technology and medical information (BRAUDE; DETLEFSEN; MORAN, 1997; PAHRE; PALMER; SADLER; SMITH, 1996; VISHIK; WIGGINS). Note that here also, the importance of this topic appears to span the entire decade and in fact continues discussions from the 1980s (J. D. ANDERSON ET AL.).

*Prevalence of technology.*   The prevalence of technology and technical issues in LIS curricula is another trend reported by the Kaliper Project. *The KALIPER Report* notes that the investment in information technology infrastructure and infusion of technology into the curricula were more than a sign of the times; they were a response to research money available for technological research and development and to university administrations anxious to flaunt programs and schools that were technologically advanced. Basic computer applications courses were dropped in favor of more specialized alternatives—emphasizing networking, hardware and software design, electronic database systems, library systems, and information transfer media." However, despite clear indications of the impact of technology on LIS curricula, more traditional coursework remained, including reference, research, and management as well as interdisciplinary ventures with archives, history, journalism, and education (PETTIGREW & DURRANCE).

Nonetheless, there is ample documentation that technology propelled significant changes in both the content and delivery mechanisms of LIS courses. CONNELL & FRANKLIN, FROEHLICH (1994), and HUBER discuss the impact of technology on LIS curricula. STIEG states in her 1992 book that "over the last ten years, the largest single [curriculum] modification has been the addition of numerous new courses in technology and information science" (p. 112). She lists database management, artificial intelligence for information retrieval, marketing of information, and national information policy as examples. DOTY addresses many aspects of information technology, its role in society and within the profession, and its impact on information science education. For viewpoints from outside the field on the importance of educating students in information technology, BARNIDGE, BRANDT, LOHR (1997), and MOLNAR offer diverse points of view, but all attest to the importance schools should place on this aspect of curriculum.

*Specialization.*   Specialization within a curriculum is another issue raised in the literature of the nineties as well as in *The KALIPER Report.* However, there seems to be little agreement on the extent to which specialization is to be supported or implemented. STIEG states positions both for and against specialization. *The KALIPER Report* indicates that schools had active programs and even certification in traditional specializations of school media, health sciences, and law, and less traditional programs in resource management and information economics. Schools with specializations included Kentucky, Rhode Island, Syracuse, Michigan, and Pittsburgh. Other schools such as Berkeley, UCLA, and UT Austin offered a more generic curriculum with fewer concentrations (PETTIGREW & DURRANCE). Authors contributing viewpoints on the general topic include COX & RASMUSSEN, GIBBS, MCCLURE & HERT, WILLIAMS, and WINTER. Descriptions of specific subspecialties in LIS programs appear in DETLEFSEN, GASSERT ET AL., GOPINATH, HALLMARK, MORAN (1997), SMITH (1998b), and WIGGINS & MONNIER.

*Distance or distributed learning.*   Another important curricular presence in the 1990s was that of distance or distributed learning. Largely due to the potential of information technology to provide access to courses and materials in other than the traditional on-campus classrooms, distance/distributed learning emerged as a major focus on many campuses. Although schools had offered off-campus programs for many years, these were largely delivered by adjunct faculty at remote sites or as site visits by faculty from the center campus. Courses offered over ITV by schools such as South Carolina and Hawaii laid the groundwork for the increased number of courses and programs offered via the Web. Much was written on this topic, discussing both advantages and shortcomings of classes in this format, but LIS schools offering courses and programs in this format were on the increase. By 1999, several schools offered complete master's programs via the Web and more were in initial stages. *The KALIPER Report* lists the LEEP program at Illinois, along with San Jose, Drexel, and Florida State University (FSU) (PETTIGREW & DURRANCE). Currently Drexel, FSU, Illinois, Southern Connecticut, Syracuse, and UW–Milwaukee all offer Web-based LIS master's programs, with University of Tennessee-Knoxville and Valdosta State planning programs for 2000. Arizona and SUNY

Buffalo have Web-based degrees but require that 9 to 12 credits be taken on campus (ROWAN UNIVERSITY). Other schools offer some or many courses via the Web.

With this much activity among the LIS schools, an enormous amount is being written on the subject of remote versus on-campus learning. STIEG sees distance education as a solution to the unequal distribution of LIS programs throughout the U.S. G. HARMON writes that positioning LIS schools in the distance market will help attract students from related fields, but cautions that cost-effectiveness is an important consideration. GALVIN warns that the ability to attract additional tuition revenue from electronically delivered courses should not obscure the importance of maintaining a quality learning experience. MARSHALL discusses academic support for distance education. Others writing on the topic include BOEHM & HORTON, DRESANG & ROBBINS, ESTABROOK, LIEBSCHER & MCCAFFREY, MERKEL, SMALL, STANDFORD, S.A. SUTTON (1996b), VISHIK, VON DRAN ET AL., WALTHER, WOLFRAM, and WOLPERT. A special issue of *JASIS* includes articles by BARRON, DOUGLAS, and S.A. SUTTON (1996b). Accompanying these is an even greater amount of discussion from outside the field. CARNEVALE (2000a: 2000b), CARR, GUERNSEY, OLSEN (1999; 2000), STEELE, and TRAUB present some of the different points of view. As might be expected, there are a number of Websites at which one can find additional material related to distance education, including many specific university sites. One of the best sites is managed by HIRST.

The availability of courses and/or programs offered in distance or distributed learning formats has had an impact beyond considerations of curriculum. Adopted in large part in response to needs for wider visibility, broader appeal, and a wider audience for LIS graduates, it remains to be seen whether in the long run this proves to be a viable course of action.

## Faculty

*Faculty composition.*   In the 1990s the literature covered a range of topics related to LIS faculty. The retirement issue received much attention when FUTAS & ZIPKOWITZ reported nearly half the faculty said they expect to leave teaching before retirement. But the school average number for full-time LIS faculty actually remained stable from 10 members in 1986 to 11 members in 1996 (DALRYMPLE), and the proportion of female faculty members increased from 41.5% in 1976 to 49.3% in 1996 (HILDENBRAND, 1997). Many schools employed part-time adjunct faculty to strengthen their programs, and reliance on adjuncts increased 23% from 1986 to 1996 (DALRYMPLE).

More dramatic statistics are presented in another KALIPER-related report prepared by CALLISON & TILLEY. They analyzed ALISE membership information and found full-time faculty increased 12% from 1988 to 1998, while part-time faculty increased 60% in the same period. *The KALIPER Report* (PETTIGREW & DURRANCE) found Syracuse used adjuncts and teaching assistants to cover more than 50% of the credits they offered. From a review of faculty job announcements in *American Libraries* and *ASIS Jobline*, CALLISON & TILLEY identified a dramatic decrease in demand for expertise in reference and specialized literature, especially in science and technology literature, and an increased call for information science and technology faculty. In addition, they found that courses in reference and collection development were increasingly covered by part-time faculty, while more full-time faculty claimed expertise in courses related to specialized aspects of technology and information management.

Diversity issues were also subjects of research. MAACK & PASSET analyzed social processes and relationships that inspired academic women and the kinds of mentoring and peer-support systems that enabled women to succeed. GARLAND (1990) tested gender differences in scholarly publications among LIS faculty and found no significant differences. DALRYMPLE & VARLEJS analyzed faculty publications from 1978 to 1988 and found that more male faculty published, although proportionally, male and female faculty published about the same amount. Citing statistics that reveal inadequate representation of minorities in LIS faculty and students, JOSEY (1993) urges the field to establish a recruiting program and to provide a support system for students, and TOTTEN offers ways to improve existing recruitment programs.

Another topic concerns the hiring of new faculty. *The KALIPER Report* found that most new assistant professors in LIS programs from 1997 to 1999 had doctorates in LIS, but that LIS programs increased recruitment of faculty from outside the field to cover the expanded curriculum. While the infusion of knowledge from non-LIS disciplines stimulated faculty and students intellectually, faculty with an LIS background and new faculty members may have had different views on the importance of library science in LIS programs. Some believed it should be the heart of a program, while others felt it should be replaced by something more progressive and forward-looking.

Joint appointments were another method often employed to strengthen faculty. Schools such as Pittsburgh and Michigan increased their faculty through joint appointments, and the disciplines for such arrangements were usually business, communications, computer science, psychology, engineering, or other allied fields (MARSHALL ET AL). Joint appointments seemed to be on the increase and, because such arrangements can affect the curriculum and the future direction of a program (BUDD), it is critical that they be carefully analyzed for their impact. Some schools used attrition to increase program strengths. Pittsburgh and Syracuse, for example, replaced retired faculty with faculty who had expertise in different areas. To cover the expanded curricula, Syracuse deliberately sought out "boundary-spanners" who could work across specialties or disciplines (MARSHALL ET AL.). Even with such strategies, however, Pittsburgh, Syracuse, and Michigan all felt understaffed.

*Scholarly productivity.* In a study funded by the Council on Library Resources, BIGGS & BIGGS examined how LIS educators compare to scholars in seven social sciences and humanities disciplines and conclude that these educators were "equal or superior in professional activity, publishing volume, respect for their professional literature, computer sophistication, and job satisfaction" to scholars in other fields (p. 282). They also found LIS educators to be more sophisticated users of libraries. CAYNON surveyed LIS educators to determine how selected factors may have contributed to their job satisfaction. He reports that educators were very satisfied with coworkers but generally dissatisfied with opportunities for promotion, and that satisfaction with work contributed most to overall job satisfaction, while satisfaction with pay had the least influence. Differences in gender, age, years of experience, and rank did not contribute to overall job satisfaction.

To understand the nature of LIS educators' work, GARLAND (1991) analyzed five years of their publications. She identified contributions to journals as the main faculty publishing activity (76.9%). She also found that only 39.3% of the publications analyzed were scholarly in nature, and concludes that LIS faculty's research was less scholarly and lower in volume than that of other scholars. In the study by BIGGS & BIGGS, educators reported a volume of publishing similar to that of scholars in other fields, but the researchers caution that the quality of the publications was hard to assess. DALRYMPLE & VARLEJS report steady gains in faculty productivity from 1978 to 1988, and PETTIGREW & NICHOLLS report that schools with doctoral programs and Carnegie Research Universities I schools had higher productivity.

Funding for LIS research was difficult to obtain because of the small number of funding sources. O'CONNOR & MULVANEY, in fact, caution LIS educators not to compare LIS funded project with those in the sciences because such a move could cause the university to place the LIS program in the wrong academic culture. Nevertheless, according to *The KALIPER Report,* several schools attracted major funding from various sources, and the experiences at Michigan, Pittsburgh, and Syracuse suggested that "funding for research continues to be central to the success of the school. The research program impacts on faculty recruitment, student recruitment, and the curriculum" (HARRIS ET AL., p. 24).

A number of articles deal with the importance of teaching and how teaching should be taken into account in promotion and tenure (AULD, 1991; MORAN, 1991). CURRAN surveyed 61 superior LIS teachers to understand how they plan courses, teach, and deal with students and presented the findings with the views of six observers of LIS teaching.

## THE FUTURE

The curricular tends identified by the KALIPER Project reflected a field responsive to changes in society and market, proactive in incorporating technology, and aggressive in securing its place in the academe. Many new courses covering the latest developments in information management were offered, including topics such as metadata, multimedia, digital libraries, knowledge management, public policy, social informatics, and museum informatics. To support the expanded scope of their teaching and research, educators drew on the knowledge and expertise of other disciplines, such as business, law, psychology, computer science, and engineering, and hired new faculty from those areas (PETTIGREW & DURRANCE). Addressing market demands and drops in graduate enrollment, several schools launched undergraduate programs and started distance education offerings. Graduate enrollment reached the lowest point between 1988 and 1989 with a total of 3,797 master's degree awarded, but that figure increased to 5,271 between 1995 and 1996 (SUMMERS). Further, some schools looked to national and international students for growth and formed partnerships with foreign institutions. These developments indicate that many in the field learned the lessons of library school closings in the eighties.

The growth of programs and expansion of curricula, however, come with a set of issues that deserve attention. The field has long struggled with the problem of identity. As specializations or degrees are offered in new areas, the place of library science in the program can, and has (in some schools), become an issue. Some educators consider the library market a low-growth area and feel justified in paying more attention to other more lucrative sectors of the information industry, although in recent years both NSF and NIST have become interested in information and information technology questions. Others believe knowledge and skills related to library work can be transferred to other settings, and feel library science ought to be the main base for LIS programs. As more faculty members are recruited from outside the LIS field, the debate over the proper place and treatment of library science is likely to continue. Practitioners also have serious concerns over LIS programs' shift toward technology-oriented areas. The first ALA Congress on Professional Education (AMERICAN LIBRARY ASSOCIATION, 2000) reflects such concerns, and MANGAN's report on the reactions of educators, students, and practitioners to changes in LIS curricula and program names suggests that the debate will rage on.

A related issue is whether there is a knowledge core common to the variety of specializations and degrees being offered. Some schools offer one degree with multiple specializations or concentrations; others offer multiple degrees in various subject areas. While library and information science is inherently interdisciplinary, it seems critical for the various information professionals produced by LIS programs to have a common set of values and an understanding of the domain that defines the field and differentiates it from other disciplines. The main concern of the field is addressing the information needs of individuals and groups; LIS services and systems are designed to satisfy those needs. The KALIPER Report states that, despite an increase in multidisciplinary perspectives in many schools, a unique user-centered core took shape at some schools as well (KALIPER ADVISORY COMMITTEE). If there could be agreement within the field on a common knowledge core, serious fracturing might be avoided. But the length of master's degree programs and the tension between library science and other information-related subfields pose major challenges for educators and practitioners (CRONIN; MANGAN; WIEGAND).

Competition from within the field is another issue that needs attention. Master's degrees, undergraduate degrees, and specializations proliferated in the 1990s, and various forms of distance education became available. Competition for students is now keener than before, but might strengthen the field. However, educators need to consider whether there is a true market for their graduates. They need to ask whether an undergraduate program will supplant the MLS degree program, whether specializations are clearly defined so they will not compete against each other, and whether distance education offerings will replace onsite courses. They need to ponder the implications of distance education for the field as a whole and develop strategies to use it to their advantage.

Another challenge is competition for resources. LIS programs became more expensive to operate in the 1990s, while the university environment continued to be highly competitive. Investments in technology and communications were significant and continuous. It was also costly to hire personnel to instruct in the areas of technology, to support broad subject coverage, and to offer instruction in several formats. Large schools such as Syracuse increased the size of their faculty, and yet felt understaffed and constrained by limited resources (HARRIS ET AL.). These schools were able to do more with some support from their institution, but many smaller programs have continued to do more with less. The problem of financial and human resources, if not solved, will affect the quality of teaching and learning and undermine the future of programs. Many creative solutions are available: offering new programs, forming alliances with other academic units, working with professional organizations, merging programs, or establishing partnerships with businesses and libraries. New business models are emerging, but it will take leadership, vision, political skills, and entrepreneurial spirit for LIS programs to obtain needed resources and thrive in a competitive academic environment.

Use of adjunct faculty members is related to the issue of resources as well. Many programs have relied on part-time instructors or teaching assistants. While practitioners can benefit students with their knowledge of cutting-edge technology and work experience, heavy reliance on adjunct instructors creates more administrative work and entails greater effort from the dean and the faculty to ensure quality teaching. It is also challenging to find part-time faculty willing to commit to a program on a long-term basis. As programs expand, an obvious solution is to turn to adjuncts, but administrators and educators should keep in mind the limitations of this approach.

As a whole the field is much stronger now than at the end of the 1980s. Schools have incorporated technology into their curricula to different extents, but all have recognized that knowledge of information technology is essential to information professionals. Various new subjects and programs have been added to broaden the focus and create growth, new partnerships have been established, and creative measures have been taken to expand the markets for our expertise. Issues of curricular focus and format, core requirements, competition from within and outside the field, and attracting resources will continue to demand attention. Nevertheless, the field has developed a better sense of its direction and has made good progress in moving forward. At the beginning of the twenty-first century, LIS programs are poised for an exciting future.

## BIBLIOGRAPHY

ABELS, EILEEN G.; MARCHIONINI, GARY; WASSERMAN, PAUL. 1997. A Prospective Alternative Direction for Educational Practice: A Conceptual and Operational Model. Journal of Education for Library and Information Science. 1997 Summer; 38(3): 211-214. ISSN: 0748-5786.

ALDERMAN, B.; MILNE, P. L. 1995. Internships for Professional Education in Library and Information Studies: Report of "Partners in Learning" Developed for the Library and Information Studies Program at the University of Canberra. Education for Library and Information Services: Australia. 1995 November; 12(3): 23-32. OCLC: 28881951.

AMERICAN ASSOCIATION OF LAW LIBRARIES. EDUCATIONAL POLICY COMMITTEE. 1988. Guidelines for Graduate Programs in Law Librarianship. 1988 November 5. Available WWW: http://www.aallnet.org/about/graduate_guidelines.asp.

AMERICAN ASSOCIATION OF SCHOOL LIBRARIANS. 1993. Competencies for the Initial Preparation of School Library Specialists. Chicago, IL: American Library Association; 1993.

AMERICAN ASSOCIATION OF SCHOOL LIBRARIANS; ASSOCIATION FOR EDUCATIONAL COMMUNICATIONS AND TECHNOLOGY. 1988. Information Power: Guidelines for School Library Media Programs. Chicago, IL: American Library Association; 1988. 171p. ISBN: 0-8389-3352-1.

AMERICAN ASSOCIATION OF SCHOOL LIBRARIANS. 1994. Curriculum Folio Guidelines for the NCATE Review Process: School Library Media Specialist Basic Preparation. Chicago, IL: American Library Association: 1994. 47p. ISBN: 0-8389-7749-9.

AMERICAN LIBRARIES. 1999. Practitioners, Educators Seek Library's Place in Professional Education. American Libraries. 1999 June/July; 30(6): 12-15. ISSN: 0002-9769.

AMERICAN LIBRARY ASSOCIATION. 1992. Standards for Accreditation of Master's Programs in Library and Information Studies. Chicago, IL: American Library Association; 1992. Available WWW: http://www.ala.org/alaorg/oa/standard.html.

AMERICAN LIBRARY ASSOCIATION. 2000. Congress on Professional Education. Available WWW: http://www.ala.org/congress/.

AMERICAN LIBRARY ASSOCIATION. COMMITTEE ON ACCREDITATION. 1986. Accreditation: A Way Ahead. Chicago, IL: American Library Association, Committee on Accreditation; 1986. 93p. OCLC: 17736299.

AMERICAN LIBRARY ASSOCIATION. CORE VALUES TASK FORCE. 2000. Librarianship and Information Service: A Statement on Core Values. 5th Draft. 2000 April 28. Available WWW: http://www.ala.org/congress/corevalues/draft5.html.

ANDERSON, CHRISTOPHER. 1995. The Accidental Superhighway. The Economist. 1995 July 1; 336: 3-6. ISSN: 0013-0613.

ANDERSON, JAMES D.; BELKIN, NICHOLAS J.; LEDERMAN, LINDA C.; SARACEVIC, TEFKO. 1988. Information Science at Rutgers: Establishing New Interdisciplinary Connections. Journal of the American Society for Information Science. 1988 September; 39(5): 327-330. ISSN: 0002-8231.

ANTONIO, IRATI; BALBY, CLAUDIA NEGRAO. 1994. The State of Computer Training in Brazilian Library Schools. Journal of Education for Library and Information Science. 1994 Spring; 35(2): 109-123. ISSN: 0748-5786.

ASSOCIATION FOR LIBRARY AND INFORMATION SCIENCE EDUCATION. 2000. ALISE Institutional Members. 2000 November 30. Available WWW: http://www.alise.org/nondiscuss/schools.html.

AULD, LAWRENCE W. S. 1990. Seven Imperatives for Library Education. Library Journal. 1990 May 1; 115(8): 55-59. ISSN: 0363-0277.

AULD, LAWRENCE W. S. 1991. A Department with a View. Journal of Education for Library and Information Science. 1991; 32: 203-206. ISSN: 0748-5786.

AZAR, A. PAULA. 1996. Job Opportunities Glitter for Librarians Who Surf the Net. American Libraries. 1996 September; 27(8): 66-69. ISSN: 0002-9769.

BAILEY, CHARLES W. 1998. Scholarly Electronic Publishing Bibliography. Available WWW: http://info.lib.uh.edu/sepb/sepb.html.

BAKER, NICHOLSON. 1994. Discards. The New Yorker. 1994 April 4; 70: 64-86. ISSN: 0028-792X.

BALES, SUSAN NALL. 1998. Technology and Tradition: The Future's in the Balance. American Libraries. 1998 June/July; 29(6): 82-86. ISSN: 0002-9769.

BARNIDGE, NOELL. 1998. Computer Networking Degree a Hot Ticket. The New York Times. 1998 January 9. ISSN: 0362-4331.

BARRON, DANIEL D. 1996. Distance Education in North American Library and Information Science Education: Applications of Technology and Commitment. Journal of the American Society for Information Science. 1996 November; 47(11): 805-810. ISSN: 0002-8231.

BELAY, GETINET. 1992. Conceptual Strategies for Operationalizing Multicultural Curricula. Journal of Education for Library and Information Science. 1992 Fall; 33(4): 295-306. ISSN: 0748-5786.

BENNION, BRUCE C. 1994. Why the Science Journal Crisis? Bulletin of the American Society for Information Science. 1994 February/March; 20(3): 25-26. ISSN: 0095-4403.

BENTON FOUNDATION. 1996. Buildings, Books, and Bytes: Libraries and Communities in the Digital Age. Washington, DC: Benton Foundation; 1996. 46p. OCLC: 40523632.

BERGHEL, HAL. 1998. Who Won the Mosaic War? Communications of the ACM. 1998 October; 41(10): 13-16. ISSN: 0001-0782.

BERGHEL, HAL. 1999. Value-Added Publishing. Communications of the ACM. 1999 January; 42(1): 19-23. ISSN: 0001-0782.

BERRY, JOHN N., III. 1987. Protecting Our Turf. Library Journal. 1987 March 15; 112(5): 43-46. ISSN: 0363-0277.

BERRY, JOHN N., III. 1991. Will Library Education Survive? Library Journal. 1991 March 1; 116(4): 55-56. ISSN: 0363-0277.

BÉRUBÉ, MICHAEL. 2000. A Shakespeare Department and Other Business Ideas for Colleges Everywhere. Chronicle of Higher Education. 2000 January 28; 46(21): A64. ISSN: 0009-5982.

BESSER, HOWARD. 1996. Issues and Challenges for the Distance Independent Environment. Journal of the American Society for Information Science. 1996 November; 47(11): 817-820. ISSN: 0002-8231.

BESSER, HOWARD; DONAHUE, STACEY, eds. 1996. Perspectives on . . . Distance Independent Education. Journal of the American Society for Information Science. 1996 November; 47(11): 799-883. ISSN: 0002-8231.

BIGGS, MARY; BIGGS, VICTOR. 1993. Library and Information Science Faculty: Their Lives as Scholars. Library Quarterly. 1993; 63(3): 282-317. ISSN: 0024-2519.

BILLINGTON, JAMES H. 1996. A Technological Flood Requires Human Navigators. American Libraries. 1996 June-July; 27(6): 39-40. ISSN: 0002-9769.

BOEHM, ERIC H.; HORTON, FOREST W., JR. 1991. The ISIM Distance-Learning Methodology and the IRM Curriculum. Journal of Education for Library and Information Science. 1991 Summer-Fall; 32(1/2): 26-37. ISSN: 0748-5786.

BORGMAN, CHRISTINE L. 1999. What Are Digital Libraries? Competing Visions. Information Processing & Management. 1999; 35: 227-243. ISSN: 0306-4573.

BORKO, HAROLD. 1984. Trends in Library and Information Science Education. Journal of the American Society for Information Science. 1984; 35(3): 185-193. ISSN: 0002-8231.

BOYCE, BERT R. 1996. On My Mind: Copyright Could Be Wrong. American Libraries. 1996 February; 27(2): 27-28. ISSN: 0002-9769.

BRANDT, D. SCOTT. 1997. Constructivism: Teaching for Understanding of the Internet. Communications of the ACM. 1997 October; 40(10): 112-117. ISSN: 0001-0782.

BRANSCOMB, ANNE W. 1991. Common Law for the Electronic Frontier. Scientific American. 1991 September; 265(3): 154-158. ISSN: 0036-8733.

BRAUDE, ROBERT M. 1994. Medical Librarianship and Medical Informatics: A Call for the Disciplines to Join Hands to Train Tomorrow's Leaders. Journal of the American Medical Informatics Association. 1994 November-December; 1(6): 467-468. ISSN: 1067-5027.

BRODY, FERN E. 1998. Assessing Professional Competencies. 37p. ERIC: ED 422 009.

BRODY, HERB. 1996. Wired Science. Technology Review. 1996 October; 99(7): 42-51. ISSN: 0040-1692.

BROWN, CAROLYN M. 1993. What's New in High-Tech Careers? To Remain Competitive in the Global Marketplace, Companies Rely on the Innovations of Information Technology Professionals. Black Enterprise. 1993 February; 23(7): 159-163. ISSN: 0006-4165.

BUCKLAND, MICHAEL K. 1996. Documentation, Information Science and Library Science in the USA. Information Processing & Management. 1996; 32: 63-76. ISSN: 0306-4573.

BUDD, RICHARD W. 1992. A New Library School of Thought. Library Journal. 1992 May 1; 117: 44-47. ISSN: 0363-0277.

BULLETIN OF THE AMERICAN SOCIETY FOR INFORMATION SCIENCE. 1997. Consumer Privacy Legislative and Regulatory Initiatives. Bulletin of the American Society for Information Science. 1997 April/May; 23(4): 18-19. ISSN: 0095-4403.

BUTCHER, HELEN. 1989. Business Information Curricula: An Employer's List of Essential Skills and Knowledge. Education for Information. 1989; 7(4): 335-341. ISSN: 0167-8329.

BUTTLAR, LOIS; DU MONT, ROSEMARY. 1996. Library and Information Science Competencies Revisited. Journal of Education for Library and Information Science. 1996; 37(1): 44-62. ISSN: 0748-5786.

CALIFORNIA LIBRARY ASSOCIATION. 1995. Future Directions for the Library Profession and Its Education. Available WWW: http://cla-net.org/pubs/future.html.

CALIFORNIA LIBRARY ASSOCIATION. 1997. Competencies for California Librarians in the 21st Century. Available WWW: http://cla-net.org/pubs/Competencies.html.

CALLISON, DANIEL; TILLEY, CAROL L. 2001. Descriptive Impressions of the Library and Information Education Evolution 1988-1998 as Reflected in Job Announcements, ALISE Descriptors and New Course Titles. Journal of Education for Library and Information Science. 2001 Summer; 42(3): 181-199. ISSN: 0748-5786.

CAMPUS COMPUTING PROJECT. 2000. The Campus Computing Project. Available WWW: http://www.campuscomputing.net/.

CARMICHAEL, JAMES V., JR.; SHONTZ, MARILYN L. 1997. Perceptions of Curricular Content Relating to Gender and Social Issues among 1993 MLIS/MLS Graduates. Journal of Education for Library and Information Science. 1997 Spring; 38(2): 98-115. ISSN: 0748-5786.

CARNEVALE, DAN. 2000a. Assessing the Quality of Online Courses Remains a Challenge, Educators Agree. Chronicle of Higher Education. 2000 February 18; 46(24): A59. ISSN: 0009-5982.

CARNEVALE, DAN. 2000b. U.S. Backs the Development of Dozens of Internet-Based Courses. Chronicle of Higher Education. 2000 January 28; 46(21): A46. ISSN: 0009-5982.

CARR, SARAH. 2000. Distance-Education Company Woos Bastions of the Liberal Arts. Chronicle of Higher Education. 2000 January 28; 46(21): A43. ISSN: 0009-5982.

CARROLL, DEWEY E. 1992. Undergraduate Education for Library and Information Studies. Journal of Library Administration. 1992; 16(1-2): 19-28. ISSN: 0193-0826.

CAYNON, WILLIAM. 1991. Satisfaction among Faculties of ALA-Accredited Library Schools. Journal of Education for Library and Information Science. 1991; 31: 294-313. ISSN: 0748-5786.

CEPPOS, KAREN F. 1992. Innovation and Survival in Schools of Library and Information Science. Journal of Education for Library and Information Science. 1992 Fall; 33(4): 277-283. ISSN: 0748-5786.

CHEN, HSINCHUN, ed. 2000a. Digital Libraries: Part 1. Journal of the American Society for Information Science. 2000 February; 51(3): 213-310. ISSN: 0002-8231.

CHEN, HSINCHUN, ed. 2000b. Digital Libraries: Part 2. Journal of the American Society for Information Science. 2000 March 1; 51(4): 311-413. ISSN: 0002-8231.

CHEPESIUK, RON. 1996. Librarians as Cyberspace Guerrillas. American Libraries. 1996 September; 27(8): 49-51. ISSN: 0002-9769.

CHEPESIUK, RON. 1998. Learning without Walls. American Libraries. 1998 October; 29(9): 62-65. ISSN: 0002-9769.

CHEPESIUK, RON. 1999. Organizing the Internet: The "Core" of the Challenge. American Libraries. 1999 January; 30(1): 60-63. ISSN: 0002-9769.

CNUDDE, SUE; FARRIS, PATRICIA; FLYNN, LEISA. 1996. A Survey of Florida Librarians: Salary and Job Satisfaction. Florida Libraries. 1996 May-June; 39(4): 68-70. ISSN: 0046-4147.

COLEMAN, ANITA. 1996. Public Performances and Private Acts. Journal of Education for Library and Information Science. 1996 Fall; 37(4): 325-342. ISSN: 0748-5786.

COMMITTEE ON WORKFORCE NEEDS IN INFORMATION TECHNOLOGY. 2000. Building a Workforce for the Information Economy. Washington, DC: National Academy Press. 2000 October 24. Also available WWW: http://books.nap.edu/html/IT_workforce/.

CONHAIM, WALLYS W. 1999. The Internet. Link-Up. 1999 January/
February; 28: 5, 12. ISSN: 0739-988X.

CONNELL, TSCHERA HARKNESS; FRANKLIN, CARL. 1994. The Internet:
Educational Issues. Library Trends. 1994 Spring; 42(4): 608-625. ISSN:
0024-2594.

COOPER, MARIANNE; LUNIN, LOIS F. 1989. Education and Training of the
Information Professional. In: Williams, Martha E., ed. Annual Review of
Information Science and Technology: Volume 24. Amsterdam, The Netherlands: Elsevier Science Publishers for the American Society for Information Science; 1989. 295-341. ISBN: 0-444-87418-6.

COOPER, MICHAEL D. 1985. Teaching Database Management System Use in
a Library School Curriculum. Journal of the American Society for Information Science. 1985 September; 36(5): 330-338. ISSN: 0002-8231.

COUNCIL ON LIBRARY RESOURCES. 1991. Library Schools in Research
Universities. Bulletin of the American Society for Information Science.
1991; 17(3): 19-21. ISSN: 0095-4403.

COX, RICHARD J.; RASMUSSEN, EDIE. 1997. Reinventing the Information
Professions and the Argument for Specialization in LIS Education: Case
Studies in Archives and Information Technology. Journal of Education for
Library and Information Science. 1997 Fall; 38(4): 255-267. ISSN: 0748-
5786.

CRAWFORD, WALT. 1999. The Card Catalog and Other Digital Controversies: What's Obsolete and What's Not in the Age of Information. American
Libraries. 1999 January; 30(1): 53-58. ISSN: 0002-9769.

CREWS, KENNETH D.; BUTTLER, DWAYNE K., eds. 1999. Copyright and
Fair-Use Guidelines for Education and Libraries. Journal of the American
Society for Information Science. 1999 December; 50(14): 1303-1357. ISSN:
0002-8231.

CRONIN, BLAISE. 1995. Cutting the Gordian Knot. Information Processing &
Management. 1995; 31(6): 897-902. ISSN: 0306-4573.

CRONIN, BLAISE; STIFFLER, MICHAEL; DAY, DOROTHY. 1993. The Emergent Market for Information Professionals: Educational Opportunities and
Implications. Library Trends. 1993 Fall; 42(2): 257-276. ISSN: 0024-2594.

CROWLEY, BILL. 1999a. Building Useful Theory. Journal of Education for
Library and Information Science. 1999 Fall; 40(4): 282-295. ISSN: 0748-
5786.

CROWLEY, BILL. 1999b. The Control and Direction of Professional Education.
Journal of the American Society for Information Science. 1999; 50(12):
1127-1135. ISSN: 0002-8231.

CURRAN, CHARLES C. 1998. What Sixty-one Superior LIS Teachers Say
about Superior LIS Teaching, Plus Comments from Six Knowledgeable
Observers. Journal of Education for Library and Information Science.
1998; 39(3): 183-194. ISSN: 0748-5786.

CVELJO, KATHERINE. 1992. Foreign Students in American Library and
Information Science Schools: An Overview. Journal of Library Administration. 1992; 16(1/2): 67-79. ISSN: 0193-0826.

CYBERATLAS. 2000. The Web Marketer's Guide to Online Facts. 2000
February 16. Available WWW: http://cyberatlas.internet.com/
big_picture/demographics/.

DAGGATT, RUSSELL. 1995. Satellites for a Developing World. Scientific
    American. 1995 September; 273(3): 94. ISSN: 0036-8733.
DALRYMPLE, PRUDENCE W. 1997. The State of the Schools. American
    Libraries. 1997; 28(1): 31-34. ISSN: 0002-9769.
DALRYMPLE, PRUDENCE; VARLEJS, JANA. 1995. Trends in Publication
    Productivity of Library and Information Science Faculty, 1978-1988. Jour-
    nal of Education for Library and Information Science. 1995 Spring; 36(2):
    87-103. ISSN: 0748-5786.
DANIEL, EVELYN H. 1987. New Curriculum Areas. In: Gardner, Richard K.,
    ed. Education of Library and Information Professionals: Present and
    Future Prospects. Littleton, CO: Libraries Unlimited; 1987. 53-70. ISBN: 0-
    87287-564-4.
DAVENPORT, ELISABETH. 1995. Groupware and Improved Understanding
    of LIS Processes: Some Observations from Experience and Suggestions for
    Future Work. FID News Bulletin. 1995 December; 45(12): 373-377. ISSN:
    0014-5874.
DAVIDSON-ARNOTT, FRANCES; KAY, DEBORAH. 1998. Library Techni-
    cian Programs: Skills-Oriented Paraprofessional Education. Library Trends.
    1998 Winter; 46(3): 540-563. ISSN: 0024-2594.
DAY, COLIN. 1999. The Economics of Publishing: The Consequences of
    Library and Research Copying. Journal of the American Society for Infor-
    mation Science. 1999 December; 50(14): 1346-1349. ISSN: 0002-8231.
DETFLEFSEN, ELLEN GAY. 1993. Library and Information Science Education
    for the New Medical Environment and the Age of Integrated Information.
    Library Trends. 1993 Fall; 42(2): 342-364. ISSN: 0024-2594.
DOTY, PHILIP. 1998. Information Technology and Education for the Informa-
    tion Professions. In: Roy, Loriene; Sheldon, Brooke E., eds. Library and
    Information Studies Education in the United States. London, England:
    Mansell; 1998. 161-198. ISBN: 0-7201-2232-5.
DOUGLAS, GAYLE. 1996. MLIS Distance Education at the University of South
    Carolina: Report of a Case Study. Journal of the American Society for
    Information Science. 1996; 47(11): 875-879. ISSN: 0002-8231.
DRESANG, ELIZA T.; ROBBINS, JANE B. 1999. Preparing Students for Infor-
    mation Organizations in the Twenty-First Century: Web-Based Manage-
    ment and Practice of Field Experience. Journal of Education for Library
    and Information Science. 1999 Fall; 40(4): 218-231. ISSN: 0748-5786.
DUDERSTADT, JAMES J. 2000. A Choice of Transformations for the 21st-
    Century University. Chronicle of Higher Education. 2000 February 4;
    46(22): B6. ISSN: 0009-5982.
DUGUID, PAUL; ATKINS, DANIEL E. 1997. Report of the Santa Fe Planning
    Workshop on Distributed Knowledge Work Environments: Digital Librar-
    ies; 1997 March 9-11; Santa Fe, NM. Ann Arbor, MI: School of Information,
    University of Michigan; 1997. 27p. OCLC: 39231069.
DURRANCE, JOAN C.; PETTIGREW, KAREN E. 1999. KALIPER: A Look at
    Library and Information Science Education at the Turn of a New Century.
    In: The Bowker Annual Library and Book Trade Almanac. 44th ed. New
    Providence, NJ: R. R. Bowker; 1999. 266-281. ISBN: 0-8352-4222-6.
DYER, ESTHER; O'CONNOR, DANIEL. 1983. Crisis in Library Education.
    Wilson Library Bulletin. 1983; 57: 860-863. ISSN: 0043-5651.

EASUN, SUE. 1998. It's Not Who We Are But Where We Are: Skating the Periphery Versus Pushing the Envelope. Library Trends. 1998 Winter; 46(3): 581-593. ISSN: 0024-2594.

ECONOMIST. 1995. Survey: Telecommunications. The Economist. 1995 September 30; 336: 5-28. ISSN: 0013-0613.

ESHELMAN, WILLIAM R. 1983. The Erosion of Library Education. Library Journal. 1983; 108(6): 1309-1312. ISSN: 0363-0277.

ESTABROOK, LEIGH. 1997. LEEP3 at the University of Illinois. Journal of Education for Library and Information Science. 1997 Spring; 38(2): 157-160. ISSN: 0748-5786.

ETTINGER, LINDA F. 1991. The Applied Information Management Program: Multidisciplinary Continuing Higher Education. Education for Information. 1991 March; 9(1): 29-38. ISSN: 0167-8329.

FAULHABER, CHARLES B. 1996. Distance Learning and Digital Libraries: Two Sides of a Single Coin. Journal of the American Society for Information Science. 1996 November; 47(11): 854-856. ISSN: 0002-8231.

FLETCHER, PATRICIA DIAMOND; BERTOT, JOHN CARLO, eds. 1999. The National Information Infrastructure. Journal of the American Society for Information Science. 1999 April 1; 50(4): 293-357. ISSN: 0002-8231.

FLOOD, BARBARA, ed. 1997. Personal Privacy. Bulletin of the American Society for Information Science. 1997 February/March; 23(3): 4-27. ISSN: 0095-4403.

FORGIONNE, GIUSSEPPI A. 1991. The College of Information Science: A Mechanism to Consolidate Information Science Education. Education for Information. 1991; 9: 285-304. ISSN: 0167-8329.

FOSDICK, HOWARD. 1984. Trends in Information Science Education. Special Libraries. 1984 October; 75(4): 292-302. ISSN: 0038-6723.

FOX, EDWARD A.; AKSCYN, ROBERT M.; FURUTA, RICHARD K.; LEGGETT, JOHN J., eds. 1995. Digital Libraries. Communications of the ACM. 1995 April; 38(4): 22-96. ISSN: 0001-0782.

FOX, ROBERT. 1997. News Track. Communications of the ACM. 1997 March; 40(3): 9. ISSN: 0001-0782.

FRAZIER, KENNETH. 1999. What's Wrong with Fair-Use Guidelines for the Academic Community? Journal of the American Society for Information Science. 1999 December; 50(14): 1320-1323. ISSN: 0002-8231.

FREIBAND, SUSAN J. 1999. Multicultural Issues and Concerns in Library Education. Journal of Education for Library and Information Science. 1999 Fall; 33(4): 287-306. ISSN: 0748-5786.

FROEHLICH, THOMAS J. 1994. Dilemmas in the Integration of Information Technologies into the Curriculum. In: Williams, Martha E., ed. Proceedings of the 15th National Online Meeting; 1994 May 10-12; New York, NY. Medford, NJ: Learned Information, Inc.; 1994. 153-162. ISBN: 0-938734-84-9.

FROEHLICH, THOMAS J. 1998. Ethical Considerations Regarding Library Nonprofessionals: Competing Perspectives and Values. Library Trends, 1998 Winter; 46(3): 444-466. ISSN: 0024-2594.

FUTAS, ELIZABETH; ZIPKOWITZ, FAY. 1991. The Faculty Vanishes. Library Journal. 1991 September 1; 116(14): 148-152. ISSN: 0363-0277.

GALVIN, THOMAS J. 1998. Options, Choices and Consequences: Prognosis for the Future of Library and Information Science Education. In: Roy, Loriene; Sheldon, Brooke E., eds. Library and Information Studies Education in the United States. London, England: Mansell; 1998. 199-211. ISBN: 0-7201-2232-5.

GARDNER, RICHARD K. 1987. Library and Information Science Education: The Present State and Future Prospects. In: Gardner, Richard K., ed. Education of Library and Information Professionals: Present and Future Prospects. Littleton, CO: Libraries Unlimited; 1987. 32-52. ISBN: 0-87287-564-4.

GARLAND, KATHLEEN. 1990. Gender Differences in Scholarly Publication among Faculty in ALA Accredited Library Schools. Library and Information Science Research. 1990; 12: 155-166. ISSN: 0740-8188.

GARLAND, KATHLEEN. 1991. The Nature of Publications Authored by Library and Information Science Faculty. Library and Information Science Research. 1991; 13: 49-60. ISSN: 0740-8188.

GARRISON, GUY. 1978. Needed: A Core Curriculum for a Diversifying Profession. Journal of Education for Librarianship. 1978; 19(2): 179-183. ISSN: 0022-0604.

GARRISON, GUY. 1987. Developing an Undergraduate Degree Program in Information Systems: The Drexel Experience. In: Gardner, Richard K., ed. Education of Library and Information Professionals: Present and Future Prospects. Littleton, CO: Libraries Unlimited; 1987. 71-82. ISBN: 0-87287-564-4.

GARRISON, GUY. 1988. Education of the Information Professional: New Dimensions, New Directions. Part V: The Future. Journal of the American Society for Information Science. 1988; 39: 362-366. ISSN: 0002-8231.

GASAWAY, LAURA N. 1999. Guidelines for Distance Learning and Interlibrary Loan: Doomed and More Doomed. Journal of the American Society for Information Science. 1999 December; 50(14): 1337-1341. ISSN: 0002-8231.

GASSERT, C. A.; MILLS, M. E.; HELLER, B. R. 1992. Doctoral Specialization in Nursing Informatics. In: Assessing the Value of Medical Informatics: Proceedings of the 15th Annual Symposium on Computer Applications in Medical Care; 1991 November 17-20; Washington, DC. New York, NY: McGraw-Hill; 1992. 253-267. ISBN: 0-07-055020-4.

GIBBS, B. L. 1993. Subject Specialization in the Scientific Special Library. Special Libraries. 1993 Winter; 84(1): 1-8. ISSN: 0038-6723.

GOPINATH, M. A. 1991. Information Economics—As an Area of Specialization. Library Science with a Slant to Documentation and Information Studies. 1991 June; 28(2): 65-67. ISSN: 0254-2553.

GORE, AL. 1991. Infrastructure for the Global Village. Scientific American. 1991; 265(3): 150-153. ISSN: 0036-8733.

GORMAN, G. E. 1999. The Future for Library Science Education. Libri. 1999; 49: 1-10. ISSN: 0024-2667.

GORMAN, MICHAEL. 1990. A Bogus and Dismal Science or the Eggplant That Ate Library Schools. American Libraries. 1990; 21: 462-463. ISSN: 0002-9769.

GREALY, DEBORAH S.; GREENMAN, BARBARA A. 1998. Special Librarians Set New Standard for Academe. Information Outlook. 1998; 2(8): 17-20, 22. ISSN: 1091-0808.

GRIFFITHS, JOSÉ-MARIE; KING, DONALD W. 1986. New Directions in Library and Information Science Education. White Plains, NY: Knowledge Industry Publications; 1986. 465p. ISBN: 0-86729-159-1.

GRIMWADE, ALEXANDER M. 1999. Why Science Journals Are So Expensive. The Scientist. 1999 February 1; 13(3): 12. ISSN: 0890-3670.

GROVER, ROBERT; ACHLEITNER, HERBERT; THOMAS, NANCY; WYATT, ROGER; VOWELL, FAYE N. 1997. The Wind beneath Our Wings: Chaos Theory and the Butterfly Effect in Curriculum Design. Journal of Education for Library and Information Science. 1997 Fall; 38(4): 268-282. ISSN: 0748-5786.

GUERNSEY, LISA. 1999. Click Here for the Ivory Tower: A Start-up Enlists Elite Schools for On-line Learning and Raises Eyebrows. The New York Times. 1999 September 2; D1, D9. ISSN: 0362-4331.

GWYNNE, PETER. 1999. Corporate Collaborations: Scientists Can Face Publishing Constraints. The Scientist. 1999 May 24; 13(11): 1-6. ISSN: 0890-3670.

HALLMARK, JULIE. 1998. Education for the Successful Geoscience Information Specialist. Science & Technology Libraries. 1998; 17(2): 81-91. ISSN: 0194-262X.

HAMILTON, FEONA J. 1996. IT, Distance Learning and Professional Development. Information Management Report. 1996 October; 14-18. ISSN: 0961-7612.

HANNIGAN, JANE ANNE. 1994. A Feminist Standpoint for Library and Information Science Education. Journal of Education for Library and Information Science. 1994 Fall; 35(4): 297-318. ISSN: 0748-5786.

HARMAN, DONNA. 1998. The Text REtrieval Conferences (TRECs): Providing a Test-Bed for Information Retrieval Systems. Bulletin of the American Society for Information Science. 1998 April/May; 24(4): 11-13. ISSN: 0095-4403.

HARMON, AMY. 2000. How Blind Alleys Led Old Media to New. The New York Times. 2000 January 16; (Section 3): 1, 14. ISSN: 0362-4331.

HARMON, GLYNN. 1998. Toward Electronically-Based Education: Internet versus Televised Delivery. In: Roy, Loriene; Sheldon, Brooke E., eds. Library and Information Studies Education in the United States. London, England: Mansell; 1998. 141-160. ISBN: 0-7201-2232-5.

HARRIS, ROMA; LIPSCOMB, CAROLYN; MARSHALL, JOANNE GARD; MARSHALL, VICTORIA; WILSON, TOM. 2000. KALIPER Project, Team 5 Report. Available from: Roma Harris, Vice-Provost and Professor, School of Library and Information Science, University of Western Ontario, London, Ontario.

HARTER, STEPHEN P.; FENICHEL, CAROL H. 1982. Online Searching in Library Education. Journal of Education for Librarianship. 1982; 23(1): 3-22. ISSN: 0022-0604.

HAYES, ROBERT M. 1988. Education of the Information Professional: A Library School Perspective. Journal of the American Society for Information Science. 1988; 39(5): 312-317. ISSN: 0002-8231.

HAYTHORNTHWAITE, CAROLINE; WELLMAN, BARRY. 1998. Work, Friendship, and Media Use for Information Exchange in a Networked Organization. Journal of the American Society for Information Science. 1998 October; 49(12): 1101-1114. ISSN: 0002-8231.

HEIM, KATHLEEN M. 1991. Not with a Bang but a Whimper: The Erosion of Support for Library and Information Science Education. A background paper for a Kellogg Foundation Sponsored Symposium; 1991 November 13-15. Available from: Kathleen de la Peña McCook at kmccook@chuma.cas.usf.edu.

HEINRICH, VIRGINIA. 1998. The University of Wisconsin-Milwaukee's School of Library Science Distance Education Offerings. Library Mosaics. 1998 March/April; 30: 16-17. ISSN: 1054-9676.

HENDERSON, ALBERT. 1999. Information Science and Information Policy: The Use of Constant Dollars and Other Indicators to Manage Research Investments. Journal of the American Society for Information Science. 1999; 50(4): 366-379. ISSN: 0002-8231.

HERKERT, JOSEPH R.; CARTWRIGHT, G. PHILLIP. 1998. The Conscience of Computer Science. Change. 1998 January/February; 28: 61-63. ISSN: 0009-1383.

HERRING, JAMES E. 1994. Meeting the Future Needs of Information Professionals: BA (Hons) Information Management Course at Queen Margaret College, Scotland. Scottish Libraries. 1994 May-June; 30(45): 16-17. ISSN: 0024-2373.

HILDENBRAND, SUZANNE. 1997. Still Not Equal: Closing the Library Gender Gap. Library Journal. 1997; 122(4): 44-46. ISSN: 0363-0277.

HILDENBRAND, SUZANNE. 1999. The Information Age vs. Gender Equity. Library Journal. 1999 April 15; 123(7): 44-47. ISSN: 0363-0277.

HILL, JANET. 1992. The Qualifications Sought by Academic Library Employers: A Content Analysis of Job Advertisements. Chapel Hill, NC: University of North Carolina, Chapel Hill; 1992. 41p. (Unpublished Master's paper).

HIRST, KRISTIN. 2000. Distance Learning. Available WWW: http://distancelearn.about.com.

HOLLAND, MAURITA PETERSON. 1998. Practical Engagement Programs: The "PEP" at Michigan's School of Information. Library Hi Tech. 1998; 16(2): 49-54. ISSN: 0737-8831.

HORROCKS, NORMAN. 1984. Sharing Accreditation. Library Journal. 1984; 109(20): 2238-2241. ISSN: 0363-0277.

HOWARTH, LYNNE C. 1998. The Role of the Paraprofessional in Technical Services in Libraries. Library Trends. 1998 Winter; 46(3): 526-539. ISSN: 0024-2594.

HOWDEN, NORM. 1988. Advanced Preparation in Microcomputer Systems. Journal of Education for Library and Information Science. 1988; 29: 15-27. ISSN: 0748-5786.

HUBER, JEFFREY T. 1995. Library and Information Studies Education for the 21st Century Practitioner. Journal of Library Administration. 1995; 20(3-4): 119-130. ISSN: 0193-0826.

INTERNET2. 2000. Internet2. Available WWW: http://www.internet2.edu/.

JENG, LING HWEY. 1993. From Cataloging to Organization of Information: A Paradigm for the Core Curriculum. Journal of Education for Library and Information Science. 1993 Spring; 34(2): 113-126. ISSN: 0748-5786.

JOHNSON, I. M. 1997. Progress in Education for Librarianship and Information Management in Cuba. Focus on International and Comparative Librarianship. 1997 December; 28(3): 165-167. ISSN: 0305-8468.

JOSEY, E. J. 1990. Meeting the Challenge: Educating for Universal Library and Information Service. In: Tallman, Julie I.; Ojiambo, Joseph B., eds. Translating An International Education to a National Environment. Metuchen, NJ: Scarecrow; 1990. 1-11. ISBN: 0-8108-2072-2.

JOSEY, E. J. 1991. Education for Library Services to Cultural Minorities. Journal of Multicultural Librarianship. 1991; 5: 104-111. ISSN: 0950-1649.

JOSEY, E. J. 1993. The Challenges of Cultural Diversity in the Recruitment of Faculty and Students from Diverse Backgrounds. Journal of Education for Library and Information Science. 1993; 34(4): 302-311. ISSN: 0748-5786.

KALIPER ADVISORY COMMITTEE. 2000. Educating Library and Information Science Professionals for a New Century: The KALIPER Report. Executive Summary. Reston, VA: Association for Library and Information Science Education; 2000 May. 9p. Available WWW: http://www.alise.org/nondiscuss/kaliper_Main.htm.

KARAMUFTUOGLU, MURAT. 1998. Collaborative Information Retrieval: Toward a Social Informatics View of IR Interaction. Journal of the American Society for Information Science. 1998 October; 49(12): 1070-1080. ISSN: 0002-8231.

KATZER, JEFFREY. 1990. Developing and Maintaining Interdisciplinary Relationships. In: Pemberton, J. Michael; Prentice, Ann E., eds. Information Science: The Interdisciplinary Context. New York, NY: Neal-Schuman; 1990. 84-89. ISBN: 1-55570-048-9.

KEVIL, L. HUNTER. 1996. Continuing Education and the Reinvention of the Library School. Journal of Education for Library and Information Science. 1996 Spring; 37(2): 184-190. ISSN: 0748-5786.

KING, DONALD W. 1998. Some Economic Aspects of the Internet. Journal of the American Society for Information Science. 1998; 49(11): 990-1002. ISSN: 0002-8231.

KLING, ROB; ROSENBAUM, HOWARD; HERT, CAROL. 1998. Social Informatics in Information Science. Journal of the American Society for Information Science. 1998 October; 49(12): 1047-1141. ISSN: 0002-8231.

KNOWLES, EM CLAIRE; JOLIVET, LINDA. 1991. Recruiting the Underrepresented: Collaborative Efforts between Library Educators and Library Practitioners. Library Administration and Management. 1991 Fall; 5(4): 189-193. ISSN: 0888-4463.

KOENIG, MICHAEL E. D. 1983. Education for Special Librarianship. Special Libraries. 1983; 74(2): 182-196. ISSN: 0038-6723.

KOENIG, MICHAEL E. D. 1990. Buttering the Toast Evenly. American Libraries. 1990 September; 21(8): 723-724, 726. ISSN: 0002-9769.

KOENIG, MICHAEL E. D. 1993. Educational Requirements for a Library-Oriented Career in Information Management. Library Trends. 1993; 42(2): 277-289. ISSN: 0024-2594.

KOENIG, MICHAEL E. D.; KOCHOFF, STEPHEN T. 1983. The Education of Librarians for Data Administration. Education for Information. 1983; 1: 217-228. ISSN: 0167-8329.

LANCASTER, F. W. 1994. The Curriculum of Information Science in Developed and Developing Countries. Libri. 1994; 44(3): 201-205. ISSN: 0024-2667.

LAPLANTE, ALICE. 1992. Woman IS Professionals Battle Entrenched High-Tech Sexism. Infoworld. 1992 October 19; 60. ISSN: 0199-6649.

LARGE, A. 1997. Undergraduate Library and Information Studies Programs in North America. Education for Information. 1997 July; 15(2): 137-151. ISSN: 0167-8329.

LAUDON, KENNETH C. 1996. Markets and Privacy. Communications of the ACM. 1996 September; 39(9): 92-104. ISSN: 0001-0782.

LAUREL, BRENDA. 1995. Virtual Reality. Scientific American. 1995 September; 273(3): 90. ISSN: 0036-8733.

LAVAGNINO, MERRI BETH; BOWKER, GEOFFREY C.; HEIDORN, P. BRYAN; BASI, MINDY MIRON. 1998. Incorporating Social Informatics into the Curriculum for Library and Information Science Professionals. Libri. 1998; 48: 13-25. ISSN: 0024-2667.

LESTER, JUNE. 1993. Education in Response to Change. Journal of Library Administration. 1993; 18(3-4): 39-54. ISSN: 0193-0826.

LEVERING, MARY. 1999. What's Right about Fair-Use Guidelines for the Academic Community? Journal of the American Society for Information Science. 1999 December; 50(14): 1313-1319. ISSN: 0002-8231.

LEVY, DAVID M.; MARSHALL, CATHERINE. 1995. Going Digital: A Look at Assumptions Underlying Digital Libraries. Communications of the ACM. 1995 April; 38(4): 77-84. ISSN: 0001-0782.

LIBRARY JOURNAL. 1994. Dean's List: 10 School Heads Debate the Future of Library Education. Library Journal. 1994 April 1; 119(6): 60-64. ISSN: 0363-0277.

LIEBI, WILLIAM A. 1997. Employers, Employees, and Continuing Education. Journal of Education for Library and Information Science. 1997 Spring; 38(2): 165-168. ISSN: 0748-5786.

LIEBSCHER, PETER; MCCAFFREY, NANCY. 1996. Library Education at a Distance. Journal of Education for Library and Information Science. 1996 Fall; 37(4): 384-388. ISSN: 0748-5786.

LOHR, STEVE. 1997. Information Technology Field Is Rated Largest U.S. Industry. The New York Times. 1997 November 18; 147: C12. ISSN: 0362-4431.

LOHR, STEVE. 1999. Privacy on Internet Poses Legal Puzzle. The New York Times. 1999 April 19; C4. ISSN: 0362-4431.

LU, S. J. 1997. The Undergraduate Program of Library and Information Science Education in Taiwan, ROC, and Its Subject Specialization Requirement. Bulletin of Library and Information Science. 1997 November; (23): 1-8. (In Chinese). ISSN: 1023-2125.

LUCKER, JAY K. 1998. The Changing Nature of Scientific and Technical Librarianship: A Personal Perspective over 40 Years. Science & Technology Libraries. 1998; 17(2): 3-10. ISSN: 0194-262X.

LYNCH, CLIFFORD. 1998. The Evolving Internet: Applications and Network Service Infrastructure. Journal of the American Society for Information Science. 1998; 49(11): 961-972. ISSN: 0002-8231.

MAACK, MARY NILES; PASSET, JOANNE E. 1993. Unwritten Rules: Mentoring Women Faculty. Library and Information Science Research. 1993; 15: 117-141. ISSN: 0740-8188.

MALINCONICO, S. MICHAEL. 1992. What Librarians Need to Know to Survive in an Age of Technology. Journal of Education for Library and Information Science. 1992; 33: 226-240. ISSN: 0748-5786.

MALINCONICO, S. MICHAEL. 1993. The Implications for Curriculum Design in an Age of Technology. In: Rugaas, Bendik, ed. Library/Information Science Education for the 21st Century: The Tromsø Conference. New York, NY: Neal-Schuman; 1993. 15-38. ISBN: 1-55570-148-5.

MANGAN, KATHERINE. 2000. In Revamped Library Schools, Information Trumps Books: Institutions' New Curricula and New Names Reflect Student Interests and the Job Market. Chronicle of Higher Education. 2000 April 7; 46(31): A43-A44. ISSN: 0009-5982.

MARCHIONINI, GARY; FOX, EDWARD A., eds. 1999. Progress toward Digital Libraries. Information Processing & Management. 1999; 35(3): 219-420. ISSN: 0306-4573.

MARCHIONNI, GARY; MAURER, HERMANN. 1995. The Roles of Digital Libraries in Teaching and Learning. Communications of the ACM. 1995 April; 38(4): 67-75. ISSN: 0001-0782.

MARCUM, DEANNA B. 1997. Transforming the Curriculum; Transforming the Profession. American Libraries. 1997 January; 28(1): 35-38. ISSN: 0002-9769.

MARFLEET, J.; KELLY, C. 1999. Leading the Field: The Role of the Information Professional in the Next Century. Electronic Library. 1999 December; 17(6): 359-364. ISSN: 0264-0473.

MARINKO, IRENA. 1999. Introduction to Library and Information Science Education in Slovenia. Journal of Education for Library and Information Science. 1999 Fall; 40(4): 299-305. ISSN: 0748-5786.

MARSHALL, JERILYN. 1997. Libraries and Other Academic Support Services for Distance Learning. Reference & User Services Quarterly. 1997 Winter; 37(2): 237-238. ISSN: 1094-9054.

MARSHALL, VICTORIA; WILSON, TOM; MARSHALL, JOANNE GARD; HARRIS, ROMA. 2001. Plus Ça Change, Plus C'est Differént: A Report from the KALIPER Project on Six Case Studies in LIS Education. Journal of Education for Library and Information Science. 2001 Summer; 42(3): 206-219. ISSN; 0748-5786.

MARTIN, STANA B. 1998. Information Technology, Employment, and the Information Sector: Trends in Information Employment 1970-1995. Journal of the American Society for Information Science. 1998 October; 49(12): 1053-1069. ISSN: 0002-8231.

MCCLURE, CHARLES R.; HERT, CAROL A. 1991. Specialization in Library/Information Science Education: Issues, Scenarios, and the Need for Action. Paper presented at the Conference on Specialization in Library/Information Science Education; 1991 November 6-8; Ann Arbor, MI. 23p. ERIC: ED 352 032.

MCCOLLUM, KELLY. 2000. Under New Federal Rules, Satellite Broadcaster Offers University Programming. Chronicle of Higher Education. 2000 January 28; 46(21): A46. ISSN: 0009-5982.

MCGARRY, K. J. 1997. Undergraduate Degrees in Information and Library Studies: A Retrospect and Revaluation. Education for Information. 1997 July; 15(2): 105-123. ISSN: 0167-8329.

MCINNIS, RAYMOND G. 1995. Why Library Schools Need to Change Their Curriculum. In: Russian-American Seminar on Critical Thinking and the Library. Champaign, IL: Graduate School of Library and Information Science; 1995. 127-150. (Occasional Paper no. 200/201). ISSN: 0276-1769.

MCMURTRIE, BETH. 2000. America's Scholarly Societies Raise Their Flags Abroad. Chronicle of Higher Education. 2000 January 28; 46(21): A53-A54. ISSN: 0009-5982.

MEDICAL LIBRARY ASSOCIATION. 1991. Platform for Change. Chicago, IL: Medical Library Association; 1991. 30p. Also available WWW: http://www.mlanet.org/education/platform.html.

MEEKS, BROCK N. 1998. Web Demographics Changing. 1998 April 30. Available WWW: http://www.zdnet.com/zdnn/content/msnb/0430/311653.html.

MERKEL, CECELIA. 1999. Folkloristics of Educational Spaces: Material Lore in Classrooms with and without Walls. Library Trends. 1999 Winter; 47(3): 417-438. ISSN: 0024-2594.

MERRILL LYNCH. 1999. The Internet without the .com: Investing for the Long-Term. Investment Insights. 1999 March 3; RC#41206204.

MILLER, MARILYN. 1996. What to Expect from Library School Graduates. Information Technology and Libraries. 1996 March; 15: 45-47. ISSN: 0730-9295.

MILLS, J. J. 1989. Teaching Reference Work by the Distance Education Mode: Reality or False Hope. Reference Librarian. 1989; 25/26: 601-615. ISSN: 0276-3877.

MOKHTARI, MIMOUN. 1994. Library and Information Science Education in Morocco: Curriculum Development and Adaptation to Change. Journal of Education for Library and Information Science. 1994 Spring; 35(2): 159-166. ISSN: 0748-5786.

MOLNAR, ANDREW R. 1997. Computers in Education: A Brief History. T.H.E. Journal. 1997 June; 24(11): 63-68. ISSN: 0192-592X.

MORAN, BARBARA B. 1991. Evaluation of Faculty in Schools of Library and Information Science: An Element in Educational Excellence. Journal of Education for Library and Information Science. 1991; 32: 207-215. ISSN: 0748-5786.

MORAN, BARBARA B. 1997. Preparing Tomorrow's Health Sciences Librarians: Feasibility and Marketing Studies: Final Report. Chapel Hill, NC: School of Information and Library Sciences, University of North Carolina; 1997 September. 186p. OCLC: 40228068.

MORTON, ELIZABETH. 1996. Canada's Library Schools: The View in 1996. Feliciter. 1996 October; 42: 14-18. ISSN: 0014-9802.

MURPHY, KATE. 1997. Moving from the Card Catalogue to the Internet. The New York Times. 1997 January 6; 146: C5. ISSN: 0028-7822.

MYSZKOWSKI, PETE. 1998. Education through Interactive Television. Library Mosaics. 1998 March/April; 9(2): 11. ISSN: 1054-9676.

NICHOLS, MARGARET T.; SIKES, JEANETTE; ISSELMANN, MARGARET M.; AYERS, RITA SEELIG. 1995/1996. Survival in Transition or Implementing Information Science Core Competencies. Bulletin of the American Society for Information Science. 1995 December/1996 January; 22(2): 11-15. ISSN: 0095-4403.

NUNAMAKER, J. F., JR.; BURGEON, J.; GLYNN, M. S.; WALSH, K. R. 1997. A Vision for a New Discipline [Information Technology]. Proceedings of the 30th Hawaii International Conference on System Sciences: Volume 2; 1997 January 7-10; Wailea, HI. Los Alamitos, CA: IEEE Computer Society Press; 1997. 3-11. ISBN: 0-8186-7743-0.

NWEKE, K. M. C. 1995. Education for Information in Nigerian Library Schools: An Overview of the Joint Admission and Matriculation Board (JAMB) Requirements for Admission to First Degree Programs. Journal of Education for Library and Information Science. 1995 Summer; 36(3): 265-271. ISSN: 0748-5786.

O'CONNOR, DANIEL O.; MULVANEY, JOHN PHILIP. 1996. LIS Faculty Research and Expectations of the Academic Culture Versus the Needs of the Practitioner. Journal of Education for Library and Information Science. 1996; 37: 306-316. ISSN: 0748-5786.

OBERG, LARRY R. 1992. The Emergence of the Paraprofessional in Academic Libraries: Perceptions and Realities. College and Research Libraries. 1992; 53(2): 99-112. ISSN: 0010-0870.

OKEY, ANDREW; WOOD, FRANCES; LAWES, ANNE. 1992. Surveying the Effectiveness of Short Course-Provision in the Professional Development of Library and Information Specialists. Journal of Education for Library and Information Science. 1992 Summer; 33(3): 249-253. ISSN: 0748-5786.

OLIVEIRA, SILAS MARQUES DE. 1990. Foreign Students in American LIS Schools: A Historical and Statistical Survey. Journal of Education for Library and Information Science. 1990; 31: 33-47. ISSN: 0748-5786.

OLSEN, FLORENCE. 1999. Colleges Weigh Legal Action against Web Sites That Publish Lecture Notes. Chronicle of Higher Education. 1999 November 26; 46(14): A69. ISSN: 0009-5982.

OLSEN, FLORENCE. 2000. California State U. Learns to Rely on Online Remedial-Math Courses. Chronicle of Higher Education. 2000 February 18; 46(24): A57. ISSN: 0009-5982.

OLSGAARD, JOHN N.; ROPER, FRED W. 1994. Future Directions for Programs of Library and Information Science Education. In: Williams, Delmus E.; Budd, John M.; Martin, Robert E.; Moran, Barbara; Roper, Fred, eds. For the Good of the Order: Essays in Honor of Edward G. Holley. Greenwich, CT: JAI Press; 1994. 297-304. ISBN: 1-55938-752-1.

OSTLER, LARRY J.; DAHLIN, THERRIN C. 1995. Library Education: Setting or Rising Sun? American Libraries. 1995 July-August; 26(7): 683-684. ISSN: 0002-9769.

OSTLER, LARRY J.; DAHLIN, THERRIN C.; WILLARDSON, J. D. 1995. The Closing of American Library Schools: Problems and Opportunities. Westport, CT: Greenwood Press; 1995. 158p. ISBN: 0-313-28461-X.

PAHRE, ROBERT. 1996. Patterns of Knowledge Communities in the Social Sciences. Library Trends. 1996 Fall; 44(2): 204-225. ISSN: 0024-2594.

PALMER, CAROLE L. 1996. Information Work at the Boundaries of Science Linking Library Services to Research Practices. Library Trends. 1996 Fall; 44(2): 165-191. ISSN: 0024-2594.

PARIS, MARION. 1988. Library School Closings: Four Case Studies. Metuchen, NJ: Scarecrow; 1988. 168p. ISBN: 0-8108-2130-3.

PARIS, MARION. 1990a. Interdisciplinary and Turf Battles. In: Pemberton, J. Michael; Prentice, Ann E., eds. Information Science: The Interdisciplinary Context. New York, NY: Neal-Schuman; 1990. 98-100. ISBN: 1-55570-048-9.

PARIS, MARION. 1990b. Why Library Schools Fail. Library Journal. 1990 October 1; 115: 38-40. ISSN: 0363-0277.

PEEK, ROBIN. 1997. Where Are Electronic Journals Going? Information Today. 1997 November; 16(10): 44-46. ISSN: 8755-6286.

PEEK, ROBIN. 1998. What to Do about the Other Generation? Information Today. 1998 June; 15(6): 56. ISSN: 8755-6286.

PEMBERTON, J. MICHAEL; NUGENT, CHRISTINE R. 1995. Information Studies: Emergent Field, Convergent Curriculum. Journal of Education for Library and Information Science. 1995; 36(2): 126-138. ISSN: 0748-5786.

PEMBERTON, J. MICHAEL; PRENTICE, ANN E., eds. 1990. Information Science: The Interdisciplinary Context. New York, NY: Neal-Schuman; 1990. 189p. ISBN: 1-55570-048-9.

PERRITT, PATSY H. 1992. School Library Media Certification Requirements 1992 Update. School Library Journal. 1992; 38(6): 30-49. ISSN: 0362-8930.

PERRITT, PATSY H. 1994. School Library Media Certification Requirements 1994 Update. School Library Journal. 1994 June; 40: 32-51. ISSN: 0362-8930.

PETERS, PAUL EVAN. 1993. Product and Service Development Strategies in the Rapidly Developing Marketplace for Internet Information. In: Three Views of the Internet. Philadelphia, PA: National Federation of Abstracting and Information Services, 1993. 21-31. ISBN: 0-942308-42-5.

PETTIGREW, KAREN E.; DURRANCE, JOAN C. 2000. KALIPER Study Identifies Trends in Library and Information Science Education. In: The Bowker Annual Library and Book Trade Almanac. 45th ed. New Providence, NJ: R. R. Bowker; 2000. 208-218. ISBN: 0-8352-4324-9.

PETTIGREW, KAREN E.; NICHOLLS, PAUL. 1994. Publication Patterns of LIS Faculty from 1982-1992: Effects of Doctoral Programs. Library and Information Science Research. 1994 Spring; 16(2): 139-156. ISSN: 0740-8188.

PRESS, LARRY. 1996. Seeding Networks: The Federal Role. Communications of the ACM. 1996 October; 39(10): 11-18. ISSN: 0001-0782.

PRESS, LARRY; BURKHART, GREY; FOSTER, WILL; GOODMAN, SY; WOLCOTT, PETER; WOODARD, JON. 1998. An Internet Diffusion Framework. Communications of the ACM. 1998 October; 41(10): 21-26. ISSN: 0001-0782.

PRYOR, BRANDT W. 1999. Three Longitudinal Impact Evaluations of Continuing Library Education: Participant Satisfaction, Program Effects, and

Future Participation. Journal of Education for Library and Information Science. 1999 January; 40(1): 10-26. ISSN: 0748-5786.

QUATTROCCHI, ED. 1999. An Outsider's Thoughts on the Education of Librarians. American Libraries. 1999 April; 30(4): 82-85. ISSN: 0002-9769.

QUINT, BARBARA. 1999. E-commerce and Traditional Online. Information Today. 1999 February; 16(2): 10-11, 58. ISSN: 8755-6286.

RAI, ARUN; RAVICHANDRAN, T.; SAMADDAR, SUBHASHISH. 1998. How to Anticipate the Internet's Global Diffusion. Communications of the ACM. 1998 October; 41(10): 97-106. ISSN: 0001-0782.

RAMAN, K. S.; YAP, C. S. 1991. Information Systems Teaching and Research at the National University of Singapore. In: Proceedings of the 25th Hawaii International Conference on System Sciences: Volume 3; 1992 January 7-10; Kanai, HI. Los Alamitos, CA: IEEE Computer Society Press; 1991. 630-641. ISBN: 0-8186-2420-5.

ROBBINS, JANE B. 1998. Curriculum Reform in Library and Information Science Education. In: Roy, Loriene; Sheldon, Brooke E., eds. Library and Information Studies Education in the United States. London, England: Mansell; 1998. 17-31. ISBN: 0-7201-2232-5.

ROBBINS, JANE B.; DRESANG, ELIZA T. 1999. Preparing Students for Information Organizations in the Twenty-First Century. Journal of Education for Library and Information Science. 1999 Fall; 40(4): 218-231. ISSN: 0748-5786.

ROPER, FRED W.; BARRON, DANIEL D.; FUNK, CARLA J. 1996. Collaboration in a Continuum of Learning: Developing the Next Generation of Leadership. Bulletin of the Medical Library Association. 1996 October; 84(4): 549-552. ISSN: 0025-7338.

ROWAN UNIVERSITY. 2000. Distance Education for Library and Information Science. Available WWW: http://www.rowan.edu/soe/librarianship/disted.htm.

ROY, LORIENE; SHELDON, BROOKE E., eds. 1998. Library and Information Studies Education in the United States. London, England: Mansell; 1998. 260p. ISBN: 0-7201-2232-5.

RUSSELL, PAULA VIVEIROS. 1992. Training of Library Technical Assistants: An Analysis of the Current Status of Programs (Associate Degree). Denton, TX: Texas Women's University; 1992. 186p. (Ph.D. dissertation). Available from: UMI, Ann Arbor, MI. (UMI order no. AAD93-00185).

SACCHANAND, CHUTIMA. 1999. Distance Education in Library and Information Science in Asia and the Pacific Region. IFLA Journal. 1999; 25(2): 97-100. ISSN: 0340-0352.

SADLER, LEWIS. 1991. A Paradigm for the Next Millennium: Health Information Science. Journal of Biocommunication. 1991; 18(2): 6-13. ISSN: 0094-2499.

SAMUELSON, PAMELA. 1994. Copyright's Fair Use Doctrine and Digital Data. Communications of the ACM. 1994 January; 37(1): 21-27. ISSN: 0001-0782.

SAMUELSON, PAMELA. 1995. Copyright and Digital Libraries. Communications of the ACM. 1995 April; 38(3): 15-21, 110. ISSN: 0001-0782.

SAMUELSON, PAMELA. 1996. Regulation of Technologies to Protect Copyrighted Works. Communications of the ACM. 1996 July; 39(7): 17-22. ISSN: 0001-0782.

SAMUELSON, PAMELA. 1998. Does Information Really Have to Be Licensed? Communications of the ACM. 1998 September; 41(9): 15-20. ISSN: 0001-0782.

SCEPANSKI, JORDAN M.; VON WAHLDE, BARBARA. 1998. Megasystem Collaboration: Cross-Continent Consortial Cooperation. Information Technology and Libraries. 1998 March; 17(1): 30-35. ISSN: 0730-9295.

SCHLESSINGER, BERNARD S.; SCHLESSINGER, JUNE H.; KARP, RASHELLE SCHLESSINGER. 1991. Information Science/Library Science Education Programs in the 1990s: A Not-So-Modest Proposal. Library Administration and Management. 1991 Winter; 5(1): 16-19. ISSN: 0888-4463.

SETTEL, BARBARA; MARCHAND, DONALD A. 1988. Syracuse University School of Information Studies: A Tradition of Innovation. Journal of the American Society for Information Science. 1988 September; 39: 331-333. ISSN: 0002-8231.

SHAPIRO, CARL; VARIAN, HAL R. 1998. Information Rules: A Strategic Guide to the Network Economy. Boston, MA: Harvard Business School Press; 1998. 352p. ISBN: 0-87584-863-X.

SHELDON, BROOKE E. 1998. Administration and Leadership in Library and Information Science Education. In: Roy, Loriene; Sheldon, Brooke E., eds. Library and Information Studies Education in the United States. London, England: Mansell; 1998. 65-79. ISBN: 0-7201-2232-5.

SHERRON, GENE T. 1997. A New Approach to Information Education. Education for Information. 1997 July; 15(2): 153-169. ISSN: 0167-8329.

SHERRON, GENE T.; LANDRY, MARIE B. 1999. Reinventing the Bachelor's Degree: Call It "Information Studies!" Journal of Education for Library and Information Science. 1999 Winter; 40(1): 48-56. ISSN: 0748-5186.

SIEVERT, MARYELLEN C.; JOHNSON, DIANE TOBIN; HARTMAN, TERESA; PATRICK, TIMOTHY B. 1997. New Educational Strategies for Training Information Professionals: Building Awareness, Concepts, and Skills through Learning Technologies. Journal of Education for Library and Information Science. 1997 Fall; 38(4): 303-313. ISSN: 0748-5786.

SINEATH, TIMOTHY W. 1992. Information Science in the Curriculum. Journal of Library Administration. 1992; 16(1/2): 55-65. ISSN: 0193-0826.

SMALL, RUTH V. 1999. A Comparison of the Resident and Distance Learning Experience in Library and Information Science Graduate Education. Journal of Education for Library and Information Science. 1999 Winter; 40(1): 27-47. ISSN: 0748-5786.

SMEATON, ALAN F. 2000. TREC-6: Personal Highlights. Information Processing & Management. 2000; 36(1): 87-94. ISSN: 0306-4573.

SMITH, LINDA C. 1996. Interdisciplinary Multi-Institutional Alliances in Support of Educational Programs for Health Sciences Librarians. Bulletin of the Medical Library Association. 1996 October; 84(4): 560-568. ISSN: 0025-7338.

SMITH, LINDA C. 1998a. Defining the Role of Information Science. In: Roy, Loriene; Sheldon, Brooke E., eds. Library and Information Studies Education in the United States. London, England: Mansell; 1998. 119-139. ISBN: 0-7201-2232-5.

SMITH, LINDA C. 1998b. Education for Health Sciences Librarianship. Science & Technology Libraries. 1998; 17(2): 59-80. ISSN: 0194-262X.

SNYDER, CAROLYN A.; FOX, JAMES W., eds. 1997. Libraries and Other Academic Support Services for Distance Learning. Greenwich, CT: JAI Press; 1997. 334p. ISBN: 0-7623-0229-1.

SOCIETY OF AMERICAN ARCHIVISTS. 1994. Guidelines for the Development of a Curriculum for a Master of Archival Studies Degree. Available WWW: http://www.archivists.org/prof-education/masguide.html.

SPARCK JONES, KAREN. 2000. Further Reflections on TREC. Information Processing & Management. 2000; 36(1): 37-85. ISSN: 0306-4573.

SPECIAL LIBRARIES ASSOCIATION. 1991. Future Competencies of the Information Professional. Washington, DC: Special Libraries Association; 1991. 24p. ISBN: 0-87111-377-5.

SPECIAL LIBRARIES ASSOCIATION. 1997. Competencies for Special Librarians of the 21st Century. Washington, DC: Special Libraries Association; 1997. 36p. ISBN: 0-87111-469-0. Also available WWW: http://www.sla.org/content/sla/professional/meaning/comp.cfm.

SPECIAL LIBRARIES ASSOCIATION; ASSOCIATION FOR LIBRARY AND INFORMATION SCIENCE EDUCATION; MEDICAL LIBRARY ASSOCIATION. 1998. Library and Information Studies Programs Survey, Final Report. Available WWW: http://www.sla.org/research/competency/computer.pdf.

STANDFORD, SERENA W. 1997. Evaluating ATM Technology for Distance Education in Library and Information Science. Journal of Education for Library and Information Science. 1997 Summer; 38(3): 180-190. ISSN: 0748-5186.

STEELE, RAY. 2000. A Distance-Education Advocate Calls for Better Financing for Such Programs. Chronicle of Higher Education. 2000 February 4; 46(22): A50. ISSN: 0009-5982.

STIEG, MARGARET F. 1992. Change and Challenge in Library and Information Science Education. Chicago, IL: American Library Association; 1992. 206p. ISBN: 0-8389-0576-5.

STIX, GARY. 1994. The Speed of Write. Scientific American. 1994 December; 271(6): 106-111. ISSN: 0036-8733.

STOKER, DAVID. 1996. A Quarter Century of Progress in Library and Information Education. Journal of Librarianship and Information Science. 1996 December; 28(4): 187-190. ISSN: 0961-0006.

STOKER, DAVID. 1997. Undergraduate Library and Information Science Education at Aberystwyth. Education for Information. 1997 July; 15(2): 125-135. ISSN: 0167-8329.

SUMMERS, F. WILLIAM. 1998. Accreditation and the American Library Association: A Background Paper Prepared for the Executive Board of the American Library Association. 1998 April. Available WWW: http://www.ala.org/congress/summers.html.

SUTTON, BRETT. 1996. Understanding Scientific Knowledge and Communication: Library and Information Science in the Undergraduate Curriculum. Journal of Education for Library and Information Science. 1996 Winter; 37(1): 11-29. ISSN: 0748-5186.

SUTTON, STUART A. 1996a. Future Service Models and the Convergence of Functions: The Reference Librarian as Technician, Author and Consultant. Reference Librarian. 1996; 54: 125-143. ISSN: 0276-3877.

SUTTON, STUART A. 1996b. Planning for the Twenty-First Century: The California State University. Journal of the American Society for Information Science. 1996 November; 47(11): 821-825. ISSN: 0002-8231.

SUTTON, STUART A. 1999. The Panda Syndrome II: Innovation, Discontinuous Change, and LIS Education. Journal of Education for Library and Information Science. 1999 Fall; 40(4): 247-262. ISSN: 0748-5786.

TAYLOR, ROBERT S. 1992. Chance, Change and the Future in the Information Profession. Bulletin of the American Society for Information Science. 1992 December; 19(2): 16-18. ISSN: 0095-4403.

TCHOBANOFF, JAMES B.; PRICE, JACK A. 1993. Industrial Information Service Managers: Expectations of, and Support of, the Education Process. Library Trends. 1993 Fall; 42(2): 249-256. ISSN: 0024-2594.

TEDESCHI, BOB. 1998. How Much Time Do Web Users Waste Waiting for Pages to Load? NetRatings Puts a Number on the World-Wide-Wait. The New York Times. 1998 August 8; C5. ISSN: 0362-4331.

TEDESCHI, BOB. 1999. E-commerce Report. The New York Times. 1999 April 19; C4. ISSN: 0362-4331.

TEES, MIRIAM. 1986. Graduate Education for Special Librarians: What Special Librarians Are Looking for in Graduates. Special Libraries. 1986; 77(4): 190-197. ISSN: 0038-6723.

TEES, MIRIAM. 1987. Accreditation and Certification. In: Gardner, Richard K., ed. Education of Library and Information Professionals: Present and Future Prospects. Littleton, CO: Libraries Unlimited; 1987. 108-120. ISBN: 0-87287-564-4.

TENOPIR, CAROL. 1989. Education for Database Intermediaries: How Library Schools Have Changed (And How They Haven't). Online. 1989 November; 13: 55-63. ISSN: 0146-5422.

TOTTEN, HERMAN L. 1992. Perspectives on Minority Recruitment of Faculty for Schools of Library and Information Science. Journal of Education for Library and Information Science. 1992; 33: 46-54. ISSN: 0748-5786.

TOTTEN, HERMAN L.; KEYS, RONALD L. 1994. The Road to Success. Library Trends. 1994 Summer; 43(1): 34-46. ISSN: 0024-2594.

TRAUB, JAMES. 1997. Drive-Thru U.: Higher Education for People Who Mean Business. The New Yorker. 1997 October; 73: 114-123. ISSN: 0028-792X.

TURNER, PHILIP M. 1996. Library and Information Studies Education in the Age of Connectivity. Texas Library Journal. 1996 Winter; 72: 172-174. ISSN: 0040-4446.

VALLEJO, R. M. 1991. Library and Information Science Education in the Philippines. Personnel Training and Education. 1991; 9(2): 44-52. ISSN: 0960-1619.

VAN HOUSE, NANCY A. 1985. The Return on the Investment in Library Education. Library and Information Science Research. 1985; 7: 31-52. ISSN: 0740-8188.

VAN HOUSE, NANCY A.; SUTTON, STUART A. 1996. The Panda Syndrome: An Ecology of LIS Education. Journal of Education for Library and Information Science. 1996 Spring; 37(2): 131-147. ISSN: 0748-5786.

VARLEJS, JANA. 1999. Continuing Education by the Numbers. Journal of Education for Library and Information Science. 1999 Fall; 40(4): 296-298. ISSN: 0748-5786.

VEATCH, JAMES R. 1999. Insourcing the Web. American Libraries. 1999 January; 30(1): 64-67. ISSN: 0002-9769.

VIRKUS, SIRJE. 1997. Distance Learning in a Networked Environment. FID News Bulletin. 1997; 47(1): 37-43. ISSN: 0014-5874.

VISHIK, CLAIRE. 1999. Intermediation and Quality Uncertainty in the Internet Environment: New Opportunities for LIS. Journal of Education for Library and Information Science. 1999 Fall; 40(4): 263-281. ISSN: 0748-5786.

VOGES, MICKIE A. 1995/1996. Beyond the Trees. Bulletin of the American Society for Information Science. 1995 December/1996 January; 22(2): 16-20. ISSN: 0095-4403.

VON DRAN, RAYMOND F. 1990. Rethinking Library Education in the Information Age. Journal of Library Administration. 1990; 11(3/4): 27-44. ISSN: 0193-0826.

VON DRAN, RAYMOND F. 1997. Organization for Information Education: Contrasts in Curriculum Structure and Administrative Locus of Control. In: Proceedings of the 30th Hawaii International Conference on System Sciences: Volume 2; 1997 January 7-10; Waile, HI. Los Alamitos, CA: IEEE Computer Society Press; 1997. 23-28. ISBN: 0-8186-7743-0.

VON DRAN, RAYMOND F.; SMALL, RUTH V.; SUTTON, STUART A. 1997. A Comparison of Graduate Student Perceptual Responses to Three Distance Delivery Models. In: Proceedings of the 1997 Information Resources Management Association International Conference; 1997; Vancouver, BC. Hershey, PA: Idea Group; 1997. 545-546. ISBN: 1-87828-945-4.

VOORHEES, ELLEN M., ed. 2000. The Sixth Text REtrieval Conference (TREC-6). Information Processing & Management. 2000 January; 36(1): 1-204. ISSN: 0306-4573.

VOORHEES, ELLEN M.; HARMAN, DONNA. 2000. Overview of the Sixth Text REtreival Conference (TREC-6). Information Processing & Management. 2000; 36(1): 3-35. ISSN: 0306-4573.

WAGNER, GÜLTEN S. 1997. Undergraduate Information Programmes in Australia: A Brief Survey. Education for Information. 1997 July; 15(2): 171-177. ISSN: 0167-8329.

WALLING, LINDA LUCAS. 1996. Going the Distance: Equal Education, Off Campus or On. Library Journal. 1996 December; 121(20): 59-62. ISSN: 0363-0277.

WALTHER, JAMES H. 1996. Students Sound Off on the Internet. American Libraries. 1996 February; 27(2): 45-51. ISSN: 0002-9769.

WATKINS, BEVERLY T. 1994. New Era for Library Schools. Chronicle of Higher Education. 1994 May 18; 40(37): A19-A20. ISSN: 0009-5982.

WATKINS, CHRISTINE. 1999. Can Librarians Play Basketball? American Libraries. 1999 March; 30(3): 58-61. ISSN: 0002-9769.

WEINGAND, DARLENE E. 1990. The Communication Imperative: A Challenge for Continuing Education. Journal of Education for Library and Information Science. 1990 Spring; 30: 340-342. ISSN: 0748-5786.

WEINGAND, DARLENE E. 1995. Accountability and Continuing Education. Journal of Education for Library and Information Science. 1995; 36(4): 351-352. ISSN: 0748-5786.

WEINGAND, DARLENE E. 1996. Do We Need a New Paradigm? Journal of Education for Library and Information Science. 1996 Summer; 37(3): 294-296. ISSN: 0748-5786.

WEINGAND, DARLENE E. 1998. Continuing Professional Education: Luxury or Necessity? Journal of Education for Library and Information Science. 1998 Fall; 39(4): 332-333. ISSN: 0748-5786.

WHITBECK, GEORGE W. 1990. Recent Developments in Library and Information Science Education in the United Kingdom. Journal of Education for Library and Information Science. 1990 Winter; 30: 238-241. ISSN: 0748-5786.

WHITE, HERBERT S. 1987. New Directions in Library and Information Science Education. Journal of Academic Librarianship. 1987; 12: 373-374. ISSN: 0099-1333.

WHITE, HERBERT S.; PARIS, MARION. 1985. Employer Preferences and the Library Education Curriculum. Library Quarterly. 1985; 55(1): 1-33. ISSN: 0024-2519.

WHITMAN, MICHAEL E.; TOWNSEND, ANTHONY M.; AALBERTS, ROBERT J. 1999. The Communications Decency Act Is Not as Dead as You Think. Communications of the ACM. 1999 January; 42(1): 15-17. ISSN: 0001-0782.

WIEDERHOLD, GIO. 1995. Digital Libraries, Value, and Productivity. Communications of the ACM. 1995 April; 38(4): 85-96. ISSN: 0001-0782.

WIEGAND, WAYNE A. 1999. Core Curriculum: A White Paper. 1999 March 29. Available WWW: http://www.ala.org/congress/wiegand.html.

WIGGINS, GARY. 1998. New Directions in the Education of Chemistry Librarians and Information Specialists. Science & Technology Libraries. 1998; 17(2): 45-58. ISSN: 0194-262X.

WIGGINS, GARY; MONNIER, CYNTHIA. 1994. Assessment of a Library Science Program Specializing in Chemical Information. Special Libraries. 1994; 85(3): 130-138. ISSN: 0038-6723.

WILLIAMS, ROBERT V. 1990. Specialization in the Education of Information Professionals. In: Encyclopedia of Library and Information Science: Volume 45 (Supplement 10). New York, NY: Marcel Dekker; 1990. 339-359. ISBN: 0-8247-2045-8.

WILSON, ANTHONY M.; HERMANSON, ROBERT. 1998. Educating and Training Library Practitioners: A Comparative History with Trends and Recommendations. Library Trends. 1998 Winter; 46(3): 467-504. ISSN: 0024-2594.

WINTER, MICHAEL F. 1996. Specialization, Territoriality, and Jurisdiction: Librarianship and the Political Economy of Knowledge. Library Trends. 1996 Fall; 44(2): 343-363. ISSN: 0024-2594.

WOLFRAM, DIETMAR. 1994. Audio Graphics for Distance Education: A Case Study in Student Attitudes and Perceptions. Journal of Education for Library and Information Science. 1994 Summer; 35(3): 179-186. ISSN: 0748-5786.

WOLPERT, ANN. 1998. Services to Remote Users: Marketing the Library's Role. Library Trends. 1998 Summer; 47(1): 21-41. ISSN: 0024-2594.

WOODSWORTH, ANNE; LESTER, JUNE. 1991. Educational Imperatives of the Future Research Library: A Symposium. Journal of Academic Librarianship. 1991; 17(4): 204-215. ISSN: 0099-1333.

WOODSWORTH, ANNE; PACKARD, RACE; SABIA, JILL. 1994. The Future of Education for Librarianship: Looking Forward from the Past. Washington, DC: Council on Library Resources; 1994 April. 95p. OCLC: 30319629.

WOODWARD, DIANA. 1988. Drexel University College of Information Studies: Evolving Programs, New Connections. Journal of the American Society for Information Science. 1988; 39(5): 334-336. ISSN: 0002-8231.

WOOLLS, E. BLANCHE. 1999. The Need for Change: The Information Professions and Continuing Education. Journal of Education for Library and Information Science. 1999 Fall; 40(4): 14. ISSN: 0748-5786.

XU, HONG. 1996. The Impact of Automation on Job Requirements and Qualifications for Catalogers and Reference Librarians in Academic Libraries. Library Resources and Technical Services. 1996; 40(1): 9-31. ISSN: 0024-2527.

YNGSTROM, L. 1994. Education in IT Security at Bachelor and Master Levels Using a Systemic-Holistic Approach. IFIP Transactions A: Computer Science and Technology. 1994; A-43: 161-181. ISSN: 0926-5473.

YOUNG, PETER R. 1996. Librarianship: A Changing Profession. Daedalus. 1996; 145(4): 103-145. ISSN: 0011-5266.

ZHOU, YUAN. 1994. Analysis of Trends in Demand for Computer Literacy for Librarians in Academic and Public Libraries from 1974 to 1989. Urbana, IL: University of Illinois at Urbana-Champaign; 1994. 284p. (Ph.D. dissertation). Available from: UMI, Ann Arbor, MI. (UMI order no. AADAA-I9512610).

ZHOU, YUAN. 1996. Analysis of Trends in Demand for Computer-Related Skills for Academic Librarians from 1974 to 1994. College and Research Libraries. 1996; 57(3): 259-272. ISSN: 0010-0870.

# Introduction to the Index

Index entries have been made for names of individuals, corporate bodies, subjects, geographic locations, and author names included in the text pages and for author and conference names from the bibliography pages. The page numbers referring to the bibliography pages are set in italics, and are listed after the page numbers relating to the text pages. This format allows one to distinguish references to bibliographic materials from references to text.

Acronyms are listed either under the acronym or under the fully spelled-out form, depending on which form is more commonly used and known. In either case a cross reference from the alternative form is provided. Postings associated with PRECIS, for example, would be listed under PRECIS as readers are generally less familiar with the full name "Preserved Context Index System." In a few cases, such as names of programs, systems, and programming languages, there is no spelled-out form either because there is none or because the meaning has been changed or is no longer used.

The Index is arranged on a word-by-word basis. The sort sequence places special characters first, followed by alpha characters, then numbers. Thus, O'Neill would precede Oakman and 3M Company would file after the Zs. Government organizations are generally listed under country name, with *see* references provided from names of departments, agencies, and other subdivisions. While index entries do correspond precisely in spelling and format, they do not follow the typographical conventions used in the text. Author names, which are all upper case in the text, and both programming languages and software packages (such as expert system shells), which are in small caps in the text, are in upper and lower case or normal upper case in the Index.

Subject indexing is by concepts rather than by words. When authors have used different words or different forms of the same word to express the same or overlapping concepts, the terminology has been standardized. An effort has been made to use the form of index entries for concepts that appear in previous *ARIST* Indexes and in the 1998 *ASIS Thesaurus of Information Science and Librarianship*.* *See also* references are used for overlapping or related (but not synonymous) concepts; *see* references are used to send the reader to the accepted form of a term used in the Index.

---

* Milstead, Jessica L., ed. 1998. *ASIS Thesaurus of Information Science and Librarianship,* 2nd ed. Medford, NJ: Information Today, Inc., for the American Society for Information Science; 1998. 169p. ISBN: 1-57387-050-1.

The Index was prepared by Debora Shaw, using the MACREX Plus Indexing Program, version 5.10 developed by Hilary and Drusilla Calvert and distributed in the United States by Bayside Indexing. The overall direction and coordination of the Index were provided by Martha E. Williams. Comments and suggestions should be addressed to the Editor.

# Index*

*Italicized page numbers refer to Bibliography pages.

# Introduction to the Cumulative Keyword and Author Index of *ARIST* Titles: Volumes 1-35

The following section is a Cumulative Keyword and Author Index (both single word and multiword terms have been used) to *ARIST* chapters for Volumes 1 through 35. Terms are largely based on the titles of *ARIST* chapters, with editing for consistency. It has been produced to assist users in locating specific topics and author names (in bold when at the entry position) for all *ARIST* volumes to date. The index terms are sorted alphabetically. Multiple forms (e.g., adjective, verb, and noun forms) of the same word have been combined, and *see* and *see also* references are provided. The sort word is followed by the author(s) name(s) and the *ARIST* citation. This Cumulative Keyword and Author Index was totally reworked in Volume 30 and the new indexing procedures have been employed in succeeding volumes.

# Cumulative Keyword and Author Index of *ARIST* Titles: Volumes 1-35

Abstracting and Indexing Services *see* Secondary Information Systems and Services

Access

    Hjørland, Birger and Lykke Kyllesbech Nielsen. Subject Access Points in Electronic Retrieval. **35**, p249

Acquisition and Use of Information

    Choo, Chun Wei and Ethel Auster. Environmental Scanning: Acquisition and Use of Information by Managers. **28**, p279

**Adams, Peter D.** Lerner, Rita G., Ted Metaxas, John T. Scott, Peter D. Adams and Peggy Judd. Primary Publication Systems and Scientific Text Processing. **18**, p127

**Adams, Scott** and Judith A. Werdel. Cooperation in Information Activities through International Organizations. **10**, p303

ADI (American Documentation Institute)

    Cuadra, Carlos A. Introduction to the ADI Annual Review. **1**, p1

**Adkinson, Burton W.** Berninger, Douglas E. and Burton W. Adkinson. Interaction between the Public and Private Sectors in National Information Programs. **13**, p3

Agriculture

    Frank, Robyn C. Agricultural Information Systems and Services. **22**, p293

**Aines, Andrew A.** and Melvin S. Day. National Planning of Information Services. **10**, p3

**Allen, Bryce L.** Cognitive Research in Information Science: Implications for Design. **26**, p3; Kinnucan, Mark T., Michael J. Nelson and Bryce L. Allen. Statistical Methods in Information Science Research. **22**, p147

**Allen, Thomas J.** Information Needs and Uses. **4**, p3

**Alper, Bruce H.** Library Automation. **10**, p199

**Alsberg, Peter A.** Bunch, Steve R. and Peter A. Alsberg. Computer Communication Networks. **12**, p183

**American Institute of Physics Staff.** Techniques for Publication and Distribution of Information. **2**, p339

**Amsler, Robert A.** Machine-Readable Dictionaries. **19**, p161

Analysis Methods

    Sugar, William. User-Centered Perspective of Information Retrieval Research and Analysis Methods. **30**, p77

Annual Review

    Cuadra, Carlos A. Introduction to the ADI Annual Review. **1**, p1

**Annual Review Staff.** New Hardware Developments. **1**, p191

Weiss, Stanley D.  Management Information Systems. **5**, p299
Managers
> Choo, Chun Wei and Ethel Auster.  Environmental Scanning:  Acquisition and Use of Information by Managers. **28**, p279;
> Katzer, Jeffrey and Patricia T. Fletcher.  The Information Environment of Managers. **27**, p227

**Marchionini, Gary** and Anita Komlodi. Design of Interfaces for Information Seeking. **33**, p89
Marketing
> Arnold, Stephen E.  Marketing Electronic Information:  Theory, Practice, and Challenges, 1980-1990. **25**, p87;
> Freeman, James E. and Ruth M. Katz.  Information Marketing. **13**, p37;
> Tucci, Valerie K.  Information Marketing for Libraries. **23**, p59;
> Webber, Sheila Anne Elizabeth. Pricing and Marketing Online Information Services. **33**, p39

**Markey, Karen**.  Visual Arts Resources and Computers. **19**, p271
**Markuson, Barbara Evans**.  Automation in Libraries and Information Centers. **2**, p255
**Marron, Beatrice** and Dennis Fife.  Online Systems—Techniques and Services. **11**, p163
**Martin, Susan K**.  Library Automation. **7**, p243
**Martin, Thomas H**. The User Interface in Interactive Systems. **8**, p203; Martin, Thomas H.  Office Automation. **23**, p217
**Martyn, John**.  Information Needs and Uses. **9**, p3
**Maskewitz, Betty F**. Carroll, Bonnie (Talmi) and Betty F. Maskewitz.  Information Analysis Centers. **15**, p147
**McCain, Katherine W**.  White, Howard D.  and Katherine W. McCain. Bibliometrics. **24**, p119; White, Howard D. and Katherine W. McCain. Visualization of Literatures. **32**, p99
**McCarn, Davis B**.  Online Systems—Techniques and Services. **13**, p85
**McClure, Charles R**. Hernon, Peter and Charles R. McClure.  Electronic U.S. Government Information:  Policy Issues and Directions. **28**, p45
**McCrank, Lawrence J**. History, Archives, and Information Science. **30**, p281
**McDonald, Dennis D**.  Public Sector/Private Sector Interaction in Information Services. **17**, p83
**McFarland, Anne S**. Shera, Jesse H. and Anne S. McFarland.  Professional Aspects of Information Science and Technology. **4**, p439
**McGill, Michael J**. and Jennifer Huitfeldt.  Experimental Techniques of Information Retrieval. **14**, p93
**McKim, Geoffrey** Davenport, Elisabeth and Geoffrey McKim.  Groupware. **30**, p115
**McLane, Alexander.**  Music as Information. **31**, p225
**Meadow, Charles T**. and Harriet R. Meadow.  Organization, Maintenance and Search of Machine Files. **5**, p169
**Meadow, Harriet R**. Meadow, Charles T. and Harriet R. Meadow.  Organization, Maintenance and Search of Machine Files. **5**, p169
Measurement
> Molyneux, Robert E. and Robert V.  Williams. Measuring the Internet. **34**, p287;

Evans, Glyn T.  Library Networks.  **16**, p211;

Lynch, Clifford A. and Cecilia M. Preston.  Internet Access to Information Resources.  **25**, p263;

Miller, Ronald F. and Ruth L. Tighe.  Library and Information Networks.  **9**, p173;

Olson, Edwin E., Russell Shank and Harold A. Olsen.  Library and Information Networks.  **7**, p279;

Overhage, Carl F. J.  Information Networks.  **4**, p339;

Palmour, Vernon E. and Nancy K. Roderer.  Library Resource Sharing through Networks.  **13**, p147;

Samuelson, Kjell.  International Information Transfer and Network Communication.  **6**, p277;

Segal, Jo An S.  Networking and Decentralization.  **20**, p203;

Shaw, Ward and Patricia B. Culkin.  Systems that Inform: Emerging Trends in Library Automation and Network Development.  **22**, p265

**Neufeld, M. Lynne** and Martha Cornog.  Secondary Information Systems and Services.  **18**, p151

**Newby, Gregory B**.  Virtual Reality.  **28**, p187

**Nichols, David M.** Twidale, Michael B. and David M. Nichols.  Computer Supported Cooperative Work in Information Search and Retrieval. **33**, p259

**Nielsen, Lykke Kyllesbech** Hjørland, Birger and Lykke Kyllesbech Nielsen.  Subject Access Points in Electronic Retrieval. **35**, p249

**Nilan, Michael** Dervin, Brenda and Michael Nilan.  Information Needs and Uses.  **21**, p3

**Nirenburg, Sergei** Tucker, Allen B., Jr. and Sergei Nirenburg.  Machine Translation: A Contemporary View.  **19**, p129

Numeric Databases

Luedke, James A., Jr., Gabor J. Kovacs, and John B. Fried.  Numeric Data Bases and Systems.  **12**, p119

**O'Brien, Ann**.  Online Catalogs: Enhancements and Developments.  **29**, p219

**O'Hare, Sheila**.  Erdelez, Sanda and Sheila O'Hare.  Legal Informatics: Application of Information Technology in Law.  **32**, p367

**O'Neill, Edward T**. and Diane Vizine-Goetz.  Quality Control in Online Databases.  **23**, p125

**Oard, Douglas W**. and Anne R. Diekema.  Cross-Language Information Retrieval. **33**, p223

Office Automation

Martin, Thomas H.  Office Automation.  **23**, p217

**Ojala, Marydee** and Ellen Bates.  Business Databases.  **21**, p87

**Olsen, Harold A**.  Olson, Edwin E., Russell Shank and Harold A. Olsen.  Library and Information Networks.  **7**, p279

**Olsen, Wallace C**.  Becker, Joseph and Wallace C. Olsen.  Information Networks.  **3**, p289

**Olson, Edwin E.**, Russell Shank and Harold A. Olsen.  Library and Information Networks.  **7**, p279

# About the Editor. . .

Professor Martha E. Williams assumed the Editorship of the *ANNUAL REVIEW OF INFORMATION SCIENCE AND TECHNOLOGY* with Volume 11 and has produced a series of books that provide unparalleled insights into, and overviews of, the multifaceted discipline of information science. Professor Williams held the positions of Director of the Information Retrieval Research Laboratory and Professor of Information Science in the Coordinated Science Laboratory (CSL), Professor of Information Science in the Graduate School of Library and Information Science, and affiliate of the Computer Science Department at the University of Illinois, Urbana-Champaign, Illinois from 1972-2000. As a chemist and information scientist Professor Williams brought to *ARIST* a breadth of knowledge and experience in information science and technology.

She has served as a Director and Chairman of the Board of Engineering Information, Inc.; founding editor of *Computer-Readable Databases: A Directory and Data Sourcebook*; editor of *Online & CDROM Review* (now *Online Information Review*); and Program Chairman for the National Online Meetings, 1980-2001. She was appointed by the Secretary of Health, Education and Welfare, Joseph Califano, to be a member of the Board of Regents of the National Library of Medicine (NLM) in 1978 and has served as Chairman of the NLM Board. She has been a member of the Numerical Data Advisory Board of the National Research Council (NRC), National Academy of Sciences (NAS). She was a member of the Science Information Activities task force of the National Science Foundation (NSF), chairman of the Large Database subcommittee of the NAS/NRC Committee on Chemical Information, and chairman of the Gordon Research Conference on Scientific Information Problems in Research in 1980.

Professor Williams is a Fellow of the American Association for the Advancement of Science, Honorary Fellow of the Institute of Information Scientists in England, Honorary Fellow of the National Federation of Abstracting and Information Services (NFAIS), recipient of the 1984 Award of Merit of the American Society for Information Science (ASIS), and recipient of the 1995 Watson Davis Award of ASIS. She is a member of, has held offices in, and/or is actively involved in various committees of the American Association for the Advancement of Science (AAAS), the American Chemical Society (ACS), and the Association for Computing Machinery (ACM) and served as president of the American Society for Information Science (ASIS). She has published over 250 books and papers, has maintained worldwide statistics on databases for over 25 years, and serves on the editorial boards of several journals. She is the founder and President of Information Market Indicators, Inc., and consults for many governmental and commercial organizations.

# More ASIST titles from Information Today, Inc.

## ARIST 36: Annual Review of Information Science and Technology
*Edited by Blaise Cronin*

Contents of Volume 36:
- ◆ *Scholarly Communication and Bibliometrics*, by Christine Borgman and Jonathan Furner
- ◆ *Collaboratories*, by Thomas A. Finholt
- ◆ *Computer Mediated Communication on the Internet*, by Susan C. Herring
- ◆ *Organizational Knowledge and Communities of Practice*, by E. Davenport and H. Hall
- ◆ *Discovering Information in Context*, by Paul Solomon
- ◆ *Data Mining*, by Gerald Benoît
- ◆ *Intelligence, Information Technology, and Information Warfare*, by Philip H. J. Davies
- ◆ *Competitive Intelligence*, by Pierrette Bergeron and Christine A. Hiller
- ◆ *Theorizing Information for Information Science*, by Ian Cornelius
- ◆ *Social Informatics* by Steve Sawyer and Kristin Eschenfelder
- ◆ *Intellectual Capital*, by Herbert W. Snyder and Jennifer Buerk Pierce
- ◆ *Digital Libraries*, by Edward A. Fox and Shalini R. Urs
- ◆ *Health Informatics*, by Marie Russell and J. Michael Brittain

**Hardbound • ISBN 1-57387-131-1**
**ASIST Members $79.95 • Non-Members $99.95**

## The Web of Knowledge: A Festchrift in Honor of Eugene Garfield
*Edited by Blaise Cronin and Helen Barsky Atkins*

Dr. Eugene Garfield, the founder of the Institute for Scientific Information (ISI), has devoted his life to the creation and development of the multidisciplinary Science Citation Index. The index, a unique resource for scientists, scholars, and researchers in virtually every field of intellectual endeavor, has been the foundation for a multidisciplinary research community. This ASIS monograph is the first to comprehensively address the history, theory, and practical applications of the Science Citation Index and to examine its impact on scholarly and scientific research 40 years after its inception. In bringing together the analyses, insights, and reflections of more than 35 leading lights, editors Cronin and Atkins have produced both a comprehensive survey of citation indexing and analysis and a beautifully realized tribute to Eugene Garfield and his vision.

**Hardbound • ISBN 1-57387-099-4**
**ASIST Members $39.60 • Non-Members $49.50**

## Evaluating Networked Information Services
## Techniques, Policy and Issues
*By Charles R. McClure and John Carlo Bertot*

As information services and resources are made available in the global networked environment, there is a critical need to evaluate their usefulness, impact, cost, and effectiveness. This new book brings together an introduction and overview of evaluation techniques and methods, information policy issues and initiatives, and other critical issues related to the evaluation of networked information services.

**Hardbound • ISBN 1-57387-118-4**
**ASIST Members $35.60 • Non-Members $44.50**

# Advances in Classification Research, Volume 10
*Edited by Hanne Albrechtsen and Jens-Erik Mai*

*Advances in Classification Research, Volume 10* is a compilation of papers prepared for the 10th ASIS SIG/CR Workshop of Classification Research. Contents include:
♦ *Wittgenstein and Indexing Theory*
♦ *Implicit Orders: Documentary Genres and Organizational Practice*
♦ *A Universal Classification System Going Through Changes*
♦ *Non Traditional Indexing Structures for the Management of Electronic Resources*
♦ *Combining Machine Learning and Hierarchical Indexing Structures*
♦ *Local Practice and the Growth of Knowledge: Decisions in Subject Access to Digitized Images*

**Softbound • ISBN 1-57387-105-2**
**ASIST Members $31.60 • Non-Members $39.50**

# Intelligent Technologies in Library and Information Service Applications
*By F. W. Lancaster and Amy Warner*

Librarians and library school faculty have been experimenting with artificial intelligence (AI) and expert systems for 30 years, but there has been no comprehensive survey of the results available until now. Here, authors Lancaster and Warner report on the applications of AI technologies in library and information services, assessing their effectiveness, reviewing the relevant literature, and offering a clear-eyed forecast of future use and impact.

**Hardbound • ISBN 1-57387-103-6**
**ASIST Members $31.60 • Non-Members $39.50**

# Statistical Methods for the Information Professional
*By Liwen Vaughan*

In this unique and useful book, Liwen Vaughan clearly explains the statistical methods used in information science research, focusing on basic logic rather than mathematical intimacies. Her emphasis is on the meaning of statistics, when and how to apply them, and how to interpret the results of statistical analysis. Through the use of real-world examples, she shows how statistics can be used to improve services, make better decisions, and conduct more effective research. Includes more than 80 helpful figures and tables, 7 appendices, bibliography, and index.

**Hardbound • ISBN 1-57387-110-9**
**ASIST Members $31.60 • Non-Members $39.50**

# Editorial Peer Review: Its Strengths and Weaknesses
*By Ann C. Weller*

This book is the first to provide an in-depth analysis of the peer review process in scholarly publishing. Author Weller offers a systematic review of published studies of editorial peer review in the following broad categories: general studies of rejection rates, studies of editors, studies of authors, and studies of reviewers. The book concludes with an examination of new models of editorial peer review intended to enhance the scientific communication process as it moves from a print to an electronic environment.

**Hardbound • ISBN 1-57387-100-1**
**ASIST Members $35.60 • Non-Members $44.50**

---

To order directly from the publisher include $3.95 postage and handling for the first book ordered and $3.25 for each additional book. Catalogs also available upon request.
**Information Today, Inc.**
143 Old Marlton Pike • Medford, NJ 08055 • (609) 654-6266
www.infotoday.com